THE CLASSICAL PAPERS
OF A. E. HOUSMAN

VOLUME I

THE CLASSICAL PAPERS
OF A. E. HOUSMAN

VOLUME I

A. E. H. at the age of 67

THE
CLASSICAL PAPERS
OF
A. E. HOUSMAN

COLLECTED AND EDITED BY

J. DIGGLE & F. R. D. GOODYEAR

Volume I 1882–1897

CAMBRIDGE
AT THE UNIVERSITY PRESS
1972

Published by the Syndics of the Cambridge University Press
Bentley House, 200 Euston Road, London NW1 2DB
American Branch: 32 East 57th Street, New York, N.Y. 10022

This collection and edition
© Cambridge University Press 1972

Library of Congress Catalogue Card Number: 74-158552

ISBNS:

0 521 08243 9 Vol. I
0 521 08511 X Vol. II
0 521 08479 2 Vol. III

Printed in Great Britain
at the University Printing House, Cambridge
(Brooke Crutchley, University Printer)

CONTENTS

[v]

PREFACE

'When a scholar of A. E. Housman's eminence has disposed of much of his work in periodicals, the convenience of scholars no less than respect for his memory commonly demands the publication of his Collected Papers.' These are the opening words of A. S. F. Gow's biographical sketch, published in 1936, the year of Housman's death. The reason why the re-publication of Housman's papers has been delayed for over thirty-five years is to be found in a clause of his will:

> 'I expressly desire and wish my desire to be made as widely known as possible that none of my writings which have appeared in periodical publications shall be collected and reprinted in any shape or form.'

For undertaking the publication of these papers in defiance of Housman's express wish we offer no apology, but we offer our reasons, and we offer them with all brevity. It is proper that Housman's friends and scholars nearer to him in time should have bound themselves by this prohibition; but posterity cannot be bound for ever. Housman's reputation is secure; and if he feared that the re-publication of earlier judgements later recanted might impair that reputation, or that the absence of an explicit recantation might be interpreted as a continued endorsement, then his fears were unfounded. And even if such fears had been well founded, *littera scripta manet, nescit uox missa reuerti*. In fifteen years the original copyright of Housman's papers expires, and it could not be expected that their re-publication would be delayed much beyond that time. It would be sad indeed to see them published in a hasty and slipshod manner, or otherwise than in their entirety. Our edition has, we hope, precluded this danger.

We have included all the papers and reviews on classical subjects published by Housman in learned journals; and we have placed in an Appendix the reports of papers read to the Cambridge Philological Society, when these were not published elsewhere in full, and contributions to the papers and books of other scholars when these were expressed in Housman's own words and offered a substantial statement of opinion, and several miscellaneous items which were unsuited to inclusion in the body of the work. We have decided to publish nothing which Housman did not publish or countenance the publication of in his lifetime. We have therefore made no attempt to include the 1911 Cambridge Inaugural Lecture or such other unauthorised pieces as have been printed or mentioned in print from time to time. That the London Inaugural Lecture of 1892 falls outside our scope may perhaps be disputed; but it can conveniently be read elsewhere. Apart from items later published in a fuller form, we have knowingly omitted only one item which may properly be described as a 'classical paper': the transcription of readings from three manuscripts of Ovid which Housman appended to a paper by J. P. Postgate in the *Journal of Philology* 22 (1894), 154–6. Without the bibliography compiled by Mr Gow, and the supplement to it published by Professor G. B. A. Fletcher in the *Durham University Journal* 38 (1946), 85–93, our task would have been more difficult and the result less complete. We have been able to add only one item to those which they have recorded, and we cannot be certain that there are not other items which we might have included.

We have tried to present what Housman wrote with the least possible obtrusion of editorial comment. The papers are presented in chronological sequence by years; within each year they are presented according to the alphabetical sequence of the titles of the periodicals in which they appeared. We have checked every reference. Those which we have found to be wrong (they are not few) we have silently corrected. Where Housman has cited the numeration of an edition which is no longer in general use, we have added in double square-brackets a reference to the numeration, if it differs, of the edition which may now be considered standard. The editions which we have used are listed on pp. xi–xiii. Misprints we have silently corrected, and we have reduced to a standard form certain insubstantial typographical details over which Housman probably had no control or perhaps had no concern. We have followed the practice of the Cambridge University Press in the elision of numerals (e.g. 107–11 instead of 107–111, and 117–18 instead of 117–8 or 117–118), but in all other respects we have maintained the style of reference used in each paper. There are many remaining inconsistencies in presentation which we have thought it unwise or unnecessary to remove. Whatever else we have added, such as the references to the places of original publication, or the cross-references in later papers to the page-numbers in this edition of earlier passages to which Housman has alluded, we have enclosed in brackets. Two vertical strokes in the text indicate the division between pages in the original publication; the original page-numbers are added in brackets at the top of the page. The footnotes have been numbered serially by the pages of this edition. To have retained the original numbers would have been cumbersome and confusing, and the reader can work them out for himself, if he wishes, without undue effort.

In the Indexes we have included all passages to whose interpretation or emendation Housman has made some contribution, and all words and topics which are discussed by him. It has often been difficult to adjudge entitlement to inclusion: we have preferred to be liberal rather than parsimonious in our decisions. Where we have added to the text a newer reference in brackets, the Index of Passages incorporates this and not the older reference.

We could not have completed this work had we not received at the outset the encouragement and help of various friends, in particular Mr E. J. Kenney, and the consent of Housman's great-nephew, Mr R. E. Symons. Our gratitude is also due

to the Librarian of the University of Cambridge for allowing his staff to undertake
the laborious task of producing two xerox prints of every page of the original
papers, to the Syndics of the Cambridge University Press for undertaking the
publication of this work, and to the staff of their Printing House and Editorial
Office for the patience, skill, and expert knowledge which they have brought
to its production. We have appealed to Dr J. B. Hall many times for advice
over editorial problems; and from him, as from Professor H. D. Jocelyn, we
have received generous and welcome help in the correction of the proofs.

A friend who has given his encouragement to this work from the beginning,
and to whom for many kindnesses we are both indebted, is also the holder of
Housman's chair at Cambridge. If we had felt free to prefix a dedication to this
edition of Housman's papers, we should have dedicated it to Professor C. O.
Brink.

Queens' College, Cambridge   J. D.
Bedford College, London   F. R. D. G.
30.9.1971

LIST OF EDITIONS CONSULTED[1]

Aeschylus	G. Murray	Oxford (OCT) 1955
fragmenta	A. Nauck	Leipzig 1889
	H. J. Mette	Berlin 1959
Anthologia lyrica Graeca[2]	E. Diehl	Leipzig (Teubner) 1936
Arcadius	A. Lentz, *Herodiani technici reliquiae vol.* i	Leipzig 1867
Bacchylides	B. Snell	Leipzig (Teubner) 1961
Callimachus	R. Pfeiffer	Oxford 1949–53
Comicorum Atticorum fragmenta	T. Kock	Leipzig 1880–8
Erotian	E. Nachmanson	Göteborg 1918
Euripides	G. Murray	Oxford (OCT) 1902–9
fragmenta	A. Nauck	Leipzig 1889
	H. von Arnim, *Suppl. Eurip.*	Bonn 1913
	D. L. Page, *Greek lit. pap. vol.* i	London (Loeb) 1942
Herodotus	C. Hude	Oxford (OCT) 1927
Hesiod	F. Solmsen	Oxford (OCT) 1970
fragmenta	R. Merkelbach and M. L. West	Oxford 1967
Hesychius	K. Latte	Copenhagen 1953–
Hippocrates	E. Littré	Paris 1839–61
Libanius	R. Foerster	Leipzig (Teubner) 1903–23
Menander	A. Koerte and A. Thierfelder	Leipzig (Teubner) 1955–8
Nonnus	R. Keydell	Berlin 1959
Orphica	E. Abel	Leipzig & Prague 1885
Paulus Alexandrinus	E. Boer	Leipzig (Teubner) 1958
Pindar	B. Snell	Leipzig (Teubner) 1959–64

[1] This list comprises editions of those texts in which sometimes or always we have found it necessary to supply in double square-brackets references additional to those given by Housman. For the numerous texts of which no edition is mentioned here it may be assumed that we have checked Housman's references against the latest edition (OCT or Teubner or other) commonly in use and that we have found no discrepancy.

[2] From this edition we cite only those poets who are not included by Page in *Poetae melici Graeci*.

Poetae melici Graeci	D. L. Page	Oxford 1962
Proclus, *chrest.*	T. W. Allen, *Homeri opera vol.* v	Oxford (OCT) 1912
Ptolemy, *tetr.*	F. E. Robbins	London (Loeb) 1940
Sophocles	A. C. Pearson	Oxford (OCT) 1924
fragmenta	A. Nauck	Leipzig 1889
	A. C. Pearson	Cambridge 1917
Stobaeus	C. Wachsmuth and O. Hense	Berlin 1884–1912
Strabo	A. Meineke	Leipzig (Teubner) 1852–3
Suidas	A. Adler	Leipzig 1928–38
Theon Smyrnaeus	E. Hiller	Leipzig (Teubner) 1878

LATIN

Aetna	F. R. D. Goodyear	Cambridge 1965
Asconius	A. C. Clark	Oxford (OCT) 1907
Ausonius	R. Peiper	Leipzig (Teubner) 1886
Catullus	R. A. B. Mynors	Oxford (OCT) 1958
Charisius	K. Barwick	Leipzig (Teubner) 1925
Cicero, *Q.fr.*	W. S. Watt	Oxford (OCT) 1958
Cyprianus Gallus, *hept.*	R. Peiper	Vienna (CSEL) 1891
Ennius, *ann.*	J. Vahlen	Leipzig 1903
trag.	H. D. Jocelyn	Cambridge 1967
Festus	W. M. Lindsay	Leipzig (Teubner) 1913
Filastrius	F. Marx	Vienna (CSEL) 1898
Firmicus Maternus	W. Kroll, F. Skutsch and K. Ziegler	Stuttgart (Teubner) 1968
Fronto	M. P. J. van den Hout	Leyden 1954
Grammatici Latini	H. Keil	Leipzig 1855–80
Hyginus, *fab.*	H. J. Rose	Leyden 1934
Lactantius, *inst. epit.*	P. Brandt	Vienna (CSEL) 1890
Lucretius	C. Bailey	Oxford (OCT) 1922
Manilius	A. E. Housman	Cambridge 1937
Martial	W. M. Lindsay	Oxford (OCT) 1929
Minucius, *Oct.*	J. P. Waltzing	Leipzig (Teubner) 1931
Nonius	W. M. Lindsay	Leipzig (Teubner) 1903
Oratorum Romanorum fragmenta	H. Malcovati	Turin 1967

Ovid, *her.*[1]	R. Ehwald	Leipzig (Teubner) 1916
Ibis	A. La Penna	Florence 1957
met.	R. Ehwald	Leipzig (Teubner) 1915
trist. and *ex P.*	S. G. Owen	Oxford (OCT) 1915
Petronius	K. Müller	Munich 1961
Phaedrus	J. P. Postgate	Oxford (OCT) 1919
Poetarum Latinorum fragmenta	W. Morel	Leipzig (Teubner) 1927
Poetarum scaenicorum fragmenta[2]	O. Ribbeck	Leipzig (Teubner) 1897–8
Probus, *in Verg. buc. et georg.*	G. Thilo and H. Hagen, *Seruii in Verg. comm.*	Leipzig 1880–1902
Propertius	E. A. Barber	Oxford (OCT) 1953
Scholia in Ouidi Ibin	A. La Penna	Florence 1959
Seneca maior	H. J. Müller	Vienna 1887
Seneca, *apoc.*	F. Buecheler and W. Heraeus	Berlin 1922
nat.	A. Gercke	Leipzig (Teubner) 1907
Solinus	T. Mommsen	Berlin 1864
Statius, *Ach.*	H. W. Garrod	Oxford (OCT) 1906
silu.	J. S. Phillimore	Oxford (OCT) 1918
Suetonius, *Caes.*	M. Ihm	Leipzig (Teubner) 1908
gramm.	G. Brugnoli	Leipzig (Teubner) 1960
Tacitus	E. Koestermann	Leipzig (Teubner) 1960–2
Tibullus	J. P. Postgate	Oxford (OCT) 1914
Valerius Flaccus	E. Courtney	Leipzig (Teubner) 1970

[1] In our references to Ehwald's edition of the *heroides* we have ignored the re-numbering of 15–21 which he adopts, although we continue to give his line numbers in the individual poems.

[2] Except the fragments of Ennius' tragedies, for which we refer instead to Jocelyn.

ABBREVIATIONS

AJPh	*American Journal of Philology*
BPhW	*Berliner Philologische Wochenschrift*
CPh	*Classical Philology*
CQ	*Classical Quarterly*
CR	*Classical Review*
CSEL	*Corpus Scriptorum Ecclesiasticorum Latinorum*
GLK	*Grammatici Latini*, ed. Keil
GLP	*Greek Literary Papyri*
JPh	*Journal of Philology*
OCT	*Oxford Classical Text*
ORF	*Oratorum Romanorum Fragmenta*
PCA	*Proceedings of the Classical Association*
PCPhS	*Proceedings of the Cambridge Philological Society*
PhW	*Philologische Wochenschrift*
PLF	*Poetarum Latinorum Fragmenta*
TCPhS	*Transactions of the Cambridge Philological Society*

1

HORATIANA [I]*

Carm. II 2 1–4

Nullus argento color est auaris
abdito terris, inimice lamnae
Crispe Sallusti, nisi temperato
splendeat usu.

Alike Lambinus' 'abditae' and Bentley's the only rational elucidation of the MS reading compel the words 'auaris terris' to mean the miser's coffers: now when Horace says carm. III 3 49 sqq. 'aurum *inrepertum* et sic melius situm, *Cum terra celat*, spernere fortior Quam cogere humanos in *usus*' he is to be sure taking the other side as a poet may, but the parallel does seem to show that 'auaris terris' here must have its natural sense of the mine, 'in her own loins She hutcht the all-worshipt ore' as Comus says. And is not 'inimice lamnae, nisi temperato splendeat usu' or 'auaris abditae terris inimice lamnae' a most dark and helpless way of saying 'open-handed Sallust'? And then how 'inimice' and its train of dependants encumber and overbalance the sentence. If then as seems likely it is in 'inimice' the corruption lies, this is what I would suggest:

nullus argento color est auaris
abdito terris, *minimusque* lamnae,
Crispe Sallusti, nisi temperato
splendeat usu.

'Silver in the mine has no lustre at all, nay even when coined it has next to none, without it is burnished by changing hands.' This at least does away with the obscurity and redresses the || balance of the sentence. It is chiefly I suppose because Horace was at no period unread that the corruptions in his MSS seldom lie on the surface, they present a resemblance at least superficial to sense and metre: if 'minimusque' by two common errors became 'inimusce' the further change to 'inimice' was all but inevitable.

Carm. III 5 31–40

Si pugnat extricata densis
cerua plagis, erit ille fortis

* [[*JPh* 10 (1882), 187–96]]

> qui perfidis se credidit hostibus,
> et Marte Poenos proteret altero
>   qui lora restrictis lacertis
>   sensit iners timuitque mortem.
> hic unde uitam sumeret inscius
> pacem duello miscuit. o pudor!
>   o magna Carthago probrosis
>   altior Italiae ruinis.

In this the reading of most MSS and well-nigh all editions Bentley justly finds fault with the lame climax 'timuitque mortem', and 'hic' used where the poet should and might have used 'ille': he might too have added, what sort of writer is Horace if 'mortem' and 'uitam' here have nothing to do with one another? But there is this deeper fault in the reading, that it makes Regulus lose the thread of his argument; for what is he debating? not what is done and cannot be undone, the surrender of the army, but its ransom, the matter in hand: his aim is to fence off the pernicies ueniens in aeuum, the flagitio additum damnum, the probrosae Italiae ruinae, and down to v. 36 he is speaking straight to the point; but here with a full stop at 'mortem' he loses his way and drifts off into mere exclamation about what is past mending and will remain the same whether he gains his cause or loses it.

But several good MSS, that of Queen's College Oxford among them, have 'aptius' for 'inscius', and very many more give it for a varia lectio: Bentley then, accepting this, proposed 'timuitque mortem Hinc, unde uitam sumeret aptius, Pacem *et* ‖ duello miscuit', comparing carm. III 11 38 'ne longus tibi somnus *unde* Non *times* detur'. This removes at once the faults of the passage and saves Horace's credit as a rhetorician: 'hinc' for 'hic' is the slightest of changes, carm. I 17 14 and 21 13 the MSS have 'hinc' where 'hic' must be right: but his insertion of 'et' has not much likelihood, as he himself tacitly acknowledges on IV 4 18.

But can 'pacem duello miscuit' in Horace mean 'confounded war with peace'? Horace who five times elsewhere uses 'duellum' uses it with a marked restriction, always of some single war, never of war in the abstract: the word's fancied connexion with 'duo' was maybe at the bottom of this: war as opposed to peace is 'bellum' carm. II 19 28 'idem *Pacis* eras mediusque *belli*' serm. II 2 111 'in *pace*, ut sapiens, aptarit idonea *bello*' 3 268 'in amore haec sunt mala, *bellum, Pax* rursum': if he wants to use 'duellum' thus he must use the plural epist. II 1 254 'tuisque Auspiciis totum confecta *duella* per orbem, Claustraque custodem *pacis* cohibentia Ianum'. I will suggest then that Horace here too was true to his custom and wrote 'pacem*que bello* miscuit': 'u' and 'b' are in his MSS as in others much confused, carm. III 23 19 'mollibit' for 'molliuit',

I 20 10 where Munro emends 'uides' for 'bides' or 'bibes', 25 20 Aldus' 'Euro' for 'Hebro' is probably right: 'be' then might well fall out after 'ue', and the senseless 'pacemquello' would be readily altered by the change of one letter to 'pacem duello'.

Carm. III 11 15–20

Cessit immanis tibi blandienti
 ianitor aulae
Cerberus, quamuis furiale centum
 muniant angues caput eius atque
spiritus taeter saniesque manet
 ore trilingui.

Perhaps neither 'eius' alone nor 'spiritus manet' alone would be intolerable, but surely the pair of them is more than man can stand: so at least thought Bentley Meineke and || Haupt. Haupt and Meineke however betake themselves to the coward's remedy of declaring the stanza spurious: Bentley perceiving that the alteration of 'eius atque' into a verb for 'spiritus' rids us at one stroke of both inconveniences proposes 'exeatque': he cites instances of 'spiritus exit' but candidly adds 'verum hic notandum est, quod in his locis *spiritus exit* de iis duntaxat dicatur, qui moribundi animam expirant. Quare ad evitandum Ambiguum, utinam Noster scripsisset potius *exeatque halitus teter*'. I propose then 'effluatque' a word which can well be applied to 'spiritus' or the like, Ovid met. VI 233 'ne qua leuis *effluat aura*', Cic. n.d. II 39 [[101]] '*aer effluens* huc et illuc uentos efficit'. Of all errors 'i' for 'l' is perhaps the most frequent, 's' for 'f' by no means unusual, and if a copyist read or wrote 'essiu atque' then 'eius atque' was not far off.

Carm. III 26 1–8

Vixi puellis nuper idoneus
et militaui non sine gloria:
 nunc arma defunctumque bello
  barbiton hic paries habebit,
laeuum marinae qui Veneris latus
custodit. hic hic ponite lucida
 funalia et uectes et arcus
  oppositis foribus minaces.

Of all weapons the one which doors and doorkeepers can best afford to laugh at is an 'arcus' in any known sense of the word: Bentley's 'securesque' however is not likely, no more is Keller's 'et ascias': indeed it surely is plain enough there is no keeping 'et': you can almost count up the available substantives on your fingers and see that none of them will do. But is it a substantive that is wanted?

Theocritus cited by Bentley has πελέκεις καὶ λαμπάδες, and that Horace had this in his head is likely enough; but why then when Theocritus mentions only two sorts of 'arma' should he mention three? Surely hatchets alone or crowbars alone are all that is wanted in addition to the torches, and his 'uectes' do duty for Theocritus' ‖ πελέκεις. Then as to the symmetry of the sentence: 'funalia' has an epithet to itself, and that 'uectes' should tally with it is at any rate as likely as not. What I am trying to make out is that here we have a corruption such as Bentley detected in 'eius atque', that 'et arcus' represents a single word, probably then an imperative co-ordinate with 'ponite': can it be 'et uectes sacrate Oppositis foribus minaces'? 'sacrate' with the change of one letter is 'et arcus' written backwards: to be sure I know of no quite parallel corruption, but in Propertius (Baehrens) III 5 24 DV give 'integras' for 'et nigras' precisely reversing the first four letters.

Carm. IV 4 65–8

Merses profundo, pulchrior euenit;
luctere, multa proruet integrum
   cum laude uictorem, geretque
      proelia coniugibus loquenda.

Many seem to have felt the strangeness of 'merses, euenit' followed by 'luctere, proruet geretque', yet 'exiet' is quite out of the question, and 'proruit' and 'geritque' are not very taking. And then the unexampled use of 'euenire'? The MSS vary between 'merses' 'mersus' and 'mersae': 'mersus' which has most authority is of course impossible and is attributed by Keller to the Mavortian recension: among those which have 'mersae' is Keller's liber archetypus F (= φψ), one of the MSS which preserve for instance the genuine reading 'rumpit' carm. III 27 5. I think it then not unlikely Horace wrote 'mersae profundo pulchri*us* euenit', like 'male istis eueniat' etc.: a copyist misunderstanding the construction might readily write 'pulchrior', compare the corruption of 'ad uentum' to 'aduentus' carm. I 23 6. This at all events does away with both difficulties at once.

Carm. IV 12 5–8

Nidum ponit Ityn flebiliter gemens
infelix auis et Cecropiae domus
   aeternum obprobrium, quod male barbaras
      regum est ulta libidines. ‖

Bentley says 'ideo aeternum opprobrium *quod* sive *quia* male ulta est mariti libidines', that is he makes 'obprobrium' nominative, 'quod' = 'quia' and refers 'ulta est' to 'auis': all commentators seem to follow him in the main. You can hardly have demonstration on a point like this; but does not 'auis et obprobrium ponit nidum' make a strange hendiadys? one would rather expect 'obprobrium' to be placed in apposition. I should be inclined to take 'obpro-brium' like 'Ityn' as governed by 'gemens', 'quod' = 'namely that', and refer 'ulta est' to Cecropia domus: 'Cecropiae domus' will then be the 'auis' and her sister: 'lamenting Itys, lamenting too her sister's infamy and her own, their dreadful revenge on Tereus'.

Epod. 1 7–14

Vtrumne iussi persequemur otium
    non dulce, ni tecum simul,
an hunc laborem mente laturi, decet
    qua ferre non molles uiros?
feremus et te uel per Alpium iuga
    inhospitalem et Caucasum
uel occidentis usque ad ultimum sinum
    forti sequemur pectore.

The great awkwardness of 'laturi' here = 'laturi sumus' has led Nauck to put a comma after 'laborem' and govern it by 'persequemur': this however only makes matters worse, as 'persequemur otium' means 'Shall I pursue my present stay-at-home life': now it is absurd to make Horace say 'Shall I con-tinue to stay at home or continue to go to the wars'. Another objection, though perhaps not a serious one, I will mention, which applies alike to both interpreta-tions: they make Horace ask a question of Maecenas to whom throughout this poem he is speaking, and then take the words out of Maecenas' mouth and give the answer in his own person. The punctuation I propose then is this,

utrumne iussi persequemur otium
    non dulce, ni tecum simul, ||
an hunc laborem mente laturi, decet
    qua ferre non molles uiros,
feremus, et te uel per Alpium iuga
    inhospitalem et Caucasum
uel occidentis usque ad ultimum sinum
    forti sequemur pectore?

He then makes Maecenas answer this question by a counter-question, 'roges, tuum labore quid iuuem meo Imbellis ac firmus parum', and everything runs smoothly. Perhaps it is not worth much that Porphyrion's lemma consists of these words thus written, 'an hunc laborem mente laturi decet qua ferre non molles uiros feremus'.

Epod. ix

Quando repostum Caecubum ad festas dapes
    uictore laetus Caesare
tecum sub alta (sic Ioui gratum) domo,
    beate Maecenas, bibam
5 sonante mixtum tibiis carmen lyra,
    hac Dorium, illis barbarum,
ut nuper, actus cum freto Neptunius
    dux fugit ustis nauibus,
minatus urbi uincla quae detraxerat
10   seruis amicus perfidis?
Romanus eheu (posteri negabitis)
    emancipatus feminae
fert uallum et arma miles et spadonibus
    seruire rugosis potest,
15 interque signa turpe militaria
    sol aspicit conopium.
ad hunc frementes uerterunt bis mille equos
    Galli canentes Caesarem,
hostiliumque nauium portu latent
20   puppes sinistrorsum citae.
io Triumphe, tu moraris aureos
    currus et intactas boues?
io Triumphe, nec Iugurthino parem ||
    bello reportasti ducem,
25 neque, Africani cui super Carthaginem
    uirtus sepulcrum condidit.
terra marique uictus hostis punico
    lugubre mutauit sagum.
aut ille centum nobilem Cretam urbibus
30   uentis iturus non suis
exercitatas aut petit Syrtes noto
    aut fertur incerto mari.
capaciores affer huc, puer, scyphos
    et Chia uina aut Lesbia,
35 uel quod fluentem nauseam coerceat
    metire nobis Caecubum.
curam metumque Caesaris rerum iuuat
    dulci Lyaeo soluere.

I am constrained to cite this poem in full, though it now has but one critical difficulty, because I think I can contribute something to its elucidation as a whole. It takes some nerve to say it, but I am much deceived if all the commentators I have read are not strangely out in supposing it written after, not before the battle of Actium: I really think this only wants pointing out to be self-evident. Let us see: vv. 1–6 will square equally well with either view: they are generally taken to mean 'when shall we have a chance of carousing together over this victory of Caesar's': they may just as well mean 'when will Caesar win his victory and set us carousing'. On vv. 7–10 I will only say it seems to me unlikely he would care to say so much about Sex. Pompeius in the full blaze of Actium, but I lay no great stress on this. Vv. 11–16 the tense is generally taken to be historical, if I am right it will be present. Vv. 17–20 are important: the critical hitch in v. 17 need not delay us for the present: vv. 17–18 seemingly refer to the defection of Amyntas and Deiotarus with their Galatians some time before the battle; what do vv. 19–20 refer to? The older commentators say to Cleopatra's flight to Alexandria: if that is so, my theory of course crumbles away, and with it Horace's reputation for a decent style: to announce the defection of ‖ 2000 men out of 100,000, and then in the same breath, as an afterthought, that the world is lost and won! The lines refer then to some naval defection or mishap or mismanagement matching the desertion of the Galli on land: what 'sinistrorsum citae' means perhaps no one will ever know: Bentley suggests it may be some nautical technicality, and if so we need not be astonished at our ignorance, seeing that Cicero did not know the meaning of 'inhibere remis'. What sort of poet now is this who with the thunder of Actium in his ears can dwell on the desertion of a handful of barbarians, and mention the 'hostilium nauium puppes' without saying they are burnt to the water's edge? To proceed: I suppose it is vv. 21–32 that have thrown the commentators off the scent: I shall be surprised if any one familiar with the locutions of poetry finds a difficulty here, but if he does I will cite a parallel: 'The mother of Sisera looked out at a window, and cried through the lattice, Why is his chariot so long in coming? why tarry the wheels of his chariots?' Set that now against 'io Triumphe, tu moraris' cet., and with 'terra marique uictus' cet. compare 'Her wise ladies answered her, yea she returned answer to herself, Have they not sped? have they not divided the prey; to every man a damsel or two; to Sisera a prey of divers colours?' this interrogation being of course in Hebrew poetry tantamount to the strongest affirmation. Horace too returns answer to himself, and the answer is not correct in its details: if these lines are meant as a rejoicing over Actium, then what is the meaning of 'terra uictus'? there was no land-fighting at all, except a cavalry skirmish some days before the battle: a week or so after the battle Antonius' main army laid down its arms without a blow disgusted at the desertion of Canidius. Is that then what Horace means? but if so this poem must have been written a full fortnight after the battle, and that is incompatible with the ignorance vv. 29–32 about Antonius' flight. Truth to tell the poet is trying like the mother of Sisera to cheer himself with glowing anticipations, and finding this unavailing is driven to 'capaciores scyphos'. The last lines vv. 33–8 are generally supposed to inaugurate a carouse over the victory, though Horace takes pains to say that ‖ they do nothing of the kind: 'curam metumque'! why, what anxiety, what fear could Horace have for the conqueror with the world at his feet? that Octavianus' difficulties were not over with Actium may be true as a matter of history, but was Horace the man to say so or this the time for saying it? 'Fluentem nauseam' alone should be enough to show that the poem was written in the breathless hush before the battle, when Italy and the world were in agonies of suspense, 'in dubioque fuere utrorum ad regna cadendum Omnibus humanis esset terraque marique'.

I now come to the well-known crux in v. 17: 'ad hunc' has by far the most MS authority: perhaps an easy and satisfactory correction would be 'at nunc', which Horace as Munro has pointed out probably wrote 'ad nunc'. 'Frementes' must surely belong to 'equos' not 'Galli', see carm. IV 14 23 'frementem mittere equum': it is almost an epitheton sollemne. If there is anything in what I have been saying above, 'nunc' will seem quite necessary to mark the change from dark to the first streak of light.

2

IBIS 539*

Conditor ut tardae laesus cognomine Myrrhae
orbis in innumeris inueniare locis.

Except that the codices vary between 'conditor' and 'cognitor', 'tardae' and
'tardus', this is the MS reading: modern editors however, Merkel Riese and
Ellis, adopt the conjecture of Leopardus 'conditor ut tardae, Blaesus cognomine,
Cyrae', that is, may you be a wanderer on the face of the earth as Battus the
stammerer was in the years before he founded Cyrene. Such a curse strikes me as
strangely tame amidst the wounds mutilation and violent death which the context imprecates; and I feel too another objection: the meaning of the pentameter
is surely fixed by trist. III 9 28 'atque ita diuellit diuulsaque membra per agros
Dissipat in multis inuenienda locis', and thus our passage must refer to some one
who perished by being torn in pieces.

I propose then to interpret the text above given as follows: may you be torn
in pieces like the author of the Zmyrna that was nine years in writing, brought
to grief by his cognomen of Cinna. True, Virgil's words ecl. IX 35 suffice to
show that C. Heluius Cinna the poet of the Zmyrna or Myrrha 'nonam post
denique messem Quam coepta est nonamque edita post hiemem' some years
outlived his namesake the tribune murdered in 709/44 by mistake for the con-
spirator L. Cornelius Cinna. Still I think the plain sense of the words is that
which I give them. Whether Ovid dreamt that the tribune and the poet were one,
or whether he was humouring a popular fancy, or whether these lines are not
Ovid's, let others say.

* [*JPh* 12 (1883), 167]

3

ON SOPH. *ELECTR.* 564, AND EUR. *I.T.*
15 AND 35*

In the second ἐπεισόδιον of Sophocles' *Electra* Clytaemnestra has arraigned Agamemnon in a set speech for the sacrifice of Iphigenia and has challenged Electra to justify his deed: δίδαξον δή με τοῦ χάριν τίνων ἔθυσεν αὐτήν. Electra in her reply meets this challenge with a counter-question, vv. 563 sq.

> ἐροῦ δὲ τὴν κυναγὸν Ἄρτεμιν τίνος
> ποινὰς τὰ πολλὰ πνεύματ' ἔσχ' ἐν Αὐλίδι.

These lines are explained by Hermann to mean 'ask Artemis why she restrained the frequent winds at Aulis': and indeed I do not see what other meaning can be wrung from the Greek: Mr Jebb has rightly abandoned his former interpretation by which ὁ πατήρ, that is Agamemnon, was imported from so far away as the πατέρα of v. 558 to oust the intervening Ἄρτεμις as the subject of ἔσχε. But Hermann's explanation, inexorably demanded by the words, is disastrous to the sense. Artemis did not restrain the winds at Aulis: had she done so, Agamemnon might have laughed her to scorn and Iphigenia would never have been sacrificed. To the ships of the heroic age and the age of Sophocles alike, a calm was no hindrance: they were equipped with oars. What it was that kept the fleet at Aulis we know very well from Aesch. *Ag.* 202 ⟦192⟧ sqq. and fifty other sources; we know that it was not a calm, but contrary winds. I am aware that Ovid in *met.* XIII 183 has blundered into the phrase '*nulla aut* contraria classi flamina erant', but that is in an opus mediis incudibus ablatum: emendaturus, si licuisset, erat. The question to ask of Artemis will then, I think, be this:

> τίνος
> ποινὰς τὰ πλοῖα πνεύματ' ἔσχ' ἐν Αὐλίδι

why gales detained the fleet at Aulis. Had we before us the series of MSS by which the text was handed down, we should probably find that the inversion of two consecutive letters, a most frequent error, first changed πλοῖα to πολιά; this once done, the difference between λι and λλ is so evanescent that the further corruption πολλά scarcely merits the name of a change.

Misled by this passage, Hermann and others have endeavoured to introduce

* ⟦*CR* I (1887), 240–1⟧

by conjecture a reference to this imaginary calm into Eur. *I.T.* 15. These conjectures I do not propose to discuss, as they seem to be put out of court by the considerations already adduced; but the verse is a celebrated crux and will perhaps repay examination. The passage vv. 10–16 runs thus:

> ἐνταῦθα γὰρ δὴ χιλίων ναῶν στόλον   10
> Ἑλληνικὸν συνήγαγ' Ἀγαμέμνων ἄναξ
> τὸν καλλίνικον στέφανον Ἰλίου θέλων
> λαβεῖν Ἀχαιοῖς, τούς θ' ὑβρισθέντας γάμους
> Ἑλένης μετελθεῖν, Μενέλεῳ χάριν φέρων.
> δεινῆς τ' ἀπλοίας πνευμάτων τ' οὐ τυγχάνων   15
> εἰς ἔμπυρ' ἦλθε, καὶ λέγει Κάλχας τάδε·

There is only one way of construing v. 15 so as to make sense: δεινῆς ἀπλοίας must be genitive absolute: 'as there was a dreadful impossibility of sailing and as he found the wind unfavourable'. But it is first of all apparent that δέ, not τε, is the conjunction demanded at the beginning of the verse; so Barnes, followed almost universally, alters τ' to δ'. Next, the ambiguity of the language is found unpardonable: the reader is inevitably led to construe ἀπλοίας, like πνευμάτων, with οὐ τυγχάνων; a construction which he then discovers to make nonsense of the passage. Hence the verse has been assailed by a host of conjectures, for the most part very unscientific; indeed the only one which seems to deserve mention is Madvig's. He proposes simply δεινῇ δ' ἀπλοίᾳ: the co-ordination of the causal dative with the causal participle is of course quite correct and natural. But the assumed error is not easily explicable: although δέ and τε are often enough confused, and although you might find here and there an instance of dative and genitive inflexions exchanged through sheer carelessness, still we can hardly postulate with prudence the occurrence of both mistakes together. And what is worse, we still have not rid the line of a third flaw pointed out by Badham: the flatness of the epithet δεινή might be tolerated by an indulgent schoolmaster in the verses of a beginner, but in this prince of rhetoricians it is surprising. The line is not emended till all three faults, of connexion, of construction, and of diction, are extirpated; and the sagacity of Badham told us years ago to look for the root of the evil in the letters δεινῆς τ'. And there, sure enough, we find it. The letters δ-ει-νηστ are the letters νηστ-ει-δ; and here, I fancy, is the hand of Euripides:

> νήστει δ' ἀπλοίᾳ πνευμάτων τ' οὐ τυγχάνων
> εἰς ἔμπυρ' ἦλθε.

The attraction of ἀπλοίᾳ into the case of δεινῆς is an error which has abundant examples and may almost be called inevitable. We know that famine was, as might be expected, the chief suffering of the weather-bound fleet; and in fact

Euripides is here giving a verbal reproduction of the account in Aesch. *Ag.* 198 sqq. ⟦188 sqq.⟧ εὖτ' ἀπλοίᾳ κεναγγεῖ βαρύνοντ' Ἀχαιϊκὸς λεὼς...πνοαὶ δ' ἀπὸ Cτρυμόνος μολοῦσαι, κακόσχολοι, νήστιδες, δύσορμοι...κατέξαινον ἄνθος Ἀργείων.

Transpositions of letters and syllables such as I have here assumed are naturally regarded by many as *a priori* improbable. The fact that they are frequent is well known to the alert and diligent student of Greek and Latin MSS; and the confusion of mind or eye which begets them has survived the introduction of printing: on p. 156 of vol. I of *The Classical Review* will be found such corrigenda to Holder's Herodotus as ταῦτα for τταῦα, ἐστρατεύετο for ατἐσρτεύετο, the latter a curiously apt parallel. It is impossible here to illustrate this subject as it might be illustrated and as I hope some day to illustrate it; but there occurs in this same πρόλογος a crux perhaps yet more notorious than v. 15, where ‖ I seem to detect a similar cause at work. Iphigenia relates how Artemis bore her away from Aulis to the land of the Tauri –

ναοῖσι δ' ἐν τοῖσδ' ἱερίαν τίθησί με,

35 ὅθεν νόμοισι, τοῖσιν ἥδεται θεὰ

"Αρτεμις, ἑορτῆς, τοὔνομ' ἧς καλὸν μόνον·

τὰ δ' ἄλλα σιγῶ τὴν θεὸν φοβουμένη.

θύω γάρ, ὄντος τοῦ νόμου καὶ πρὶν πόλει,

ὃς ἂν κατέλθῃ τήνδε γῆν Ἕλλην ἀνήρ.

So reads the best MS. Now we have here beginning with v. 35 a sentence which gets no further than the three words ὅθεν νόμοισιν ἑορτῆς: there is a relative clause subjoined to νόμοισι by τοῖσιν; there is another relative clause subjoined to ἑορτῆς by ἧς: at the end of this clause we come to a full stop, and begin an entirely new sentence introduced by an inferential particle. The heroes who undertake the defence of the text say that we have here an aposiopesis. Aposiopesis is a comforting word; but the sphere of the figure so named is limited by conditions which here preclude it. In cases of aposiopesis it is requisite that we should be able to form a notion how the speaker was about to complete the sentence which he breaks off: this is obviously necessary to the understanding of the situation, because it is the thought of the suppressed words which causes to arise in his mind the emotion which restrains him from uttering them. But here the spoken part of the sentence consists only of three words, and we cannot tell the meaning of the first or the construction of the second: we cannot tell whether ὅθεν means *since which time* or *for which reason*; we cannot tell whether the inflexion of νόμοισι means *with* or *by* or *in* or *for* or *to* or *because of*: much less then can we guess how the sentence would proceed. Hence this reading is now defended, I think, by no scholar of repute: a few have tried to mend matters by eliciting τοισίδ' from the τοῖσιδ' of the second-best MS in v. 35. We do indeed thus get a sentence, with ἥδεται for its principal verb; but sense is as far off as ever. The sacrifices, as the words ὄντος τοῦ νόμου καὶ πρὶν πόλει inform us, were instituted, not upon the arrival of Iphigenia, but long before; and there is no imaginable way in which Artemis' delight in them can have been caused by anything recounted in the narrative which has preceded. Therefore other conjectures have been proposed, of which I mention Weil's as the most ingenious and plausible. He retains τοῖσιν, strikes out Ἄρτεμις as a gloss on θεά, and replaces it by χρώμεσθ'. This, to be sure, is good sense; yet the hypothesis is precarious. The officiousness of the scribe is surely excessive and not complimentary to our intelligence: what goddess but Artemis could we dream of? Again how often θεά and ἡ θεός recur in this play for Artemis I do not waste time in counting, but it is very often indeed; yet nowhere else has the scribe importuned us with the explanation. I prefer then to look for light to the ductus litterarum; and I will suggest that if there once stood in the text the letters NOMOICINOΘNEIOICIN it required only the inversion of the two consecutive letters NE, and the infinitesimally slight change of T for I, to produce NOMOI-CIN OΘEN TOICIN; and that the only way to make metre of this was to arrange the words as they now stand in the MS, ὅθεν νόμοισι τοῖσιν. But the sentence

νόμοις ἵν' ὀθνείοισιν ἥδεται θεά
Ἄρτεμις ἑορτῆς

where Artemis delights in strange rites is surely just what is wanted; and it is curious to note how closely van Herwerden has approached to this sense with his conjecture ὅπου νόμοις ὠμοῖσιν.

4

ON CERTAIN CORRUPTIONS IN THE *PERSAE* OF AESCHYLUS*

145-9 ⟦142-6⟧
φροντίδα κεδνὴν καὶ βαθύβουλον
θώμεθα, χρεία δὲ προσήκει,
πῶς ἄρα πράσσει Ξέρξης βασιλεὺς
Δαρειογενής, τὸ πατρωνύμιον
γένος ἡμέτερον.

When the words γένος ἡμέτερον are applied to a single person, as they are applied to Xerxes here, they can signify only *our offspring*. They cannot signify, as the scholiast and most commentators would have them, συγγενὴς ἡμῖν, *our kinsman* or *our compatriot*: γένος has no such meaning. But the offspring of the elders who recite these lines Xerxes was not; and γένος ἡμέτερον, accordingly, they cannot call him. Further exception might be taken, were it not superfluous, to the epithet πατρωνύμιον, a natural title indeed for the whole people which drew from its forefather Perseus the name of Persian, but devoid of special application to the king and conveying, in his regard, nothing not already conveyed by Δαρειογενής. In Mr Paley's translation 'one of our race *which* bears the name of *its* ancestor Perseus' there is involved, even if we condone the rendering of γένος, a further fallacy which a glance at my italics will detect. As for Hermann's 'genus a Perseo ductum, unde nos nomen habemus, ideoque nobis cognatum', it has really little relation to the Greek.

What has happened seems clear. The dipodia τὸ πατρωνύμιον stands one line higher than it was meant to stand, and errs in one letter. The chorus should rightly enquire:

πῶς ἄρα πράσσει Ξέρξης βασιλεὺς
Δαρειογενὴς
γένος ἡμέτερόν τε πατρωνύμιον·

how it fares with Xerxes the king and with our Persian folk. Their care is not for Xerxes alone, but also for the men of whom he has emptied Persia: it is, as they say in vv. 8 sq., ἀμφὶ νόστῳ τῷ βασιλείῳ καὶ πολυχρύσου στρατιᾶς. ‖

* ⟦*AJPh* 9 (1888), 317–25⟧

162–7 [159–64]

ταῦτα δὴ λιποῦσ᾽ ἱκάνω χρυσεοστόλμους δόμους
καὶ τὸ Δαρείου τε κἀμὸν κοινὸν εὐνατήριον.
καί με καρδίαν ἀμύσσει φροντίς· ἐς δ᾽ ὑμᾶς ἐρῶ
μῦθον, οὐδαμῶς ἐμαυτῆς οὖσ᾽ ἀδείμαντος, φίλοι,   165 [162]
μὴ μέγας πλοῦτος κονίσας οὖδας ἀντρέψῃ ποδὶ
ὄλβον, ὃν Δαρεῖος ἦρεν οὐκ ἄνευ θεῶν τινός.

I have briefly signified elsewhere my view of v. 165 [162]. ἐμαυτῆς, which is
supposed to mean περὶ ἐμαυτῆς, is in the MS text destructive of sense: we learn
as Atossa proceeds that her fear is not for herself, but for her absent son and the
fortune of Persia. A corruption is recognized by all recent editors, and Weil,
with the approval of Kirchhoff and Wecklein, has conjectured μῦθον οὐδαμῶς
ἐμαυτῆς οὐδ᾽ ἀδείμαντον, referring to Soph. Aiax 481 οὐδεὶς ἐρεῖ ποθ᾽ ὡς ὑπό-
βλητον λόγον, | Αἴας, ἔλεξας, ἀλλὰ τῆς σαυτοῦ φρενός. This gives no suitable
meaning, for Atossa's speech is assuredly not ὑπόβλητος, nor, so far as I can
discern, in any sense οὐχ ἑαυτῆς; but that so unsatisfactory a conjecture should
have been made and approved is all the more striking a testimony to the strength
of feeling against the MS text. I have proposed to write:

ἐς δ᾽ ὑμᾶς ἐρῶ [sc. τὴν φροντίδα],
θυμὸν οὐδαμῶς ἐμαυτῆς οὖσ᾽ ἀδείμαντος κτλ.

ἐμαυτῆς then depending on θυμόν. To cite only the most apposite examples of
a widespread error, the Medicean MS gives μυθοῦσθαι for θυμοῦσθαι in Ag. 1367
[1368] and θυμῷ for μύθῳ in Soph. Ant. 718.

But my purpose in reverting to the passage is to champion a neglected emendation of Rauchenstein's in v. 166 [163]. πλοῦτος cannot κονίσαι nor can it
ἀντρέψαι ποδί, and is now generally given up for corrupt. The correction which
to me appears uniquely apt is Rauchenstein's στρατός. The change is really
a slight one: στ and π are much confused in cursives and minuscules, ρ and λ in
all MSS of all ages, α and ου with especial frequency in the text of Aeschylus.
Only by reading στρατός will you elicit any just sense from κονίσας οὖδας:
Atossa fears lest the flight of the great army covering the face of the earth with
dust should overthrow the fortune which Darius, God helping him, built up.
Homer in Ζ 145, speaking of an army, uses εὐρὺ κονίσουσιν πεδίον as an ornamental equivalent for φεύξονται, and has κονίοντες πεδίοιο, of horses and chariots,
more than once; Aeschylus in Sept. 60, the only other || place where he employs
the verb, has στρατὸς χωρεῖ, κονίει, and delights in the association of κόνις and
στρατός: Suppl. 186 [180] ὁρῶ κόνιν, ἄναυδον ἄγγελον στρατοῦ, Sept. 79
μεθεῖται στρατὸς στρατόπεδον λιπών... αἰθερία κόνις με πείθει φανεῖσα, probably
Ag. 500 [495]. Let it not be thought that this reading would require ποσίν for

ποδί: the singular πόδα is similarly used of a multitude in Suppl. 31. It is quite possible that Aeschylus wrote ἀντρέψῃ πέδοι, but I only mention this lest any one else should make the same guess and fall in love with it.

271–80 ⟦268–77⟧

str.		XO. ὀτοτοτοῖ, μάταν
		τὰ πολέα βέλεα παμμιγῆ
		γᾶς ἀπ' 'Ασίδος ἦλθ' ἐπ' αἶαν
		δᾴαν, 'Ελλάδα χώραν.
275 ⟦272⟧		ΑΓ. πλήθουσι νεκρῶν δυσπότμως ἐφθαρμένων
		Cαλαμῖνος ἀκταὶ πᾶς τε πρόσχωρος τόπος.
ant.		XO. ὀτοτοτοῖ, φίλων
		ἁλίδονα μέλεα παμβαφῆ
		κατθανόντα λέγεις φέρεσθαι
280 ⟦277⟧		πλαγκτοῖς ἐν διπλάκεσσιν.

All that I here propose to myself is to finish the correction of two errors already emended in the main. In vv. 273 sq. ⟦270 sq.⟧ the apposition αἶαν, χώραν is, to be sure, Greek, but not the Greek of a good writer. The function of apposition is to add something to the sense, and we therefore do not place in apposition two words which, like αἶα and χώρα, are synonyms. Weil has restored the diction of Aeschylus by what will be found on examination an easy change, τᾶσδ' ἀπ' 'Ασίδος ἦλθεν αἴας δᾴαν 'Ελλάδα χώραν, and this is approved by Oberdick and Wecklein. But the illustrious critic and his followers have over-looked the fact that αἶα is not employed by the tragic writers except in places where the metre refuses γαῖα, and that therefore tragedy may be ransacked in vain for such a phenomenon as αἴας preceded by an ephelcystic ν. No: just as Aeschylus writes Pers. 390 ⟦387⟧ κατέσχε γαῖαν not κατέσχεν αἶαν, 502 ⟦499⟧ λιταῖσι γαῖαν not λιταῖσιν αἶαν, Suppl. 272 ⟦266⟧ ἀνῆκε γαῖα not ἀνῆκεν αἶα, 1039 ⟦1028⟧ χεύμασι γαίας not χεύμασιν αἴας, so he must here have written not ἦλθεν αἴας but ἦλθε γαίας. And this will perhaps be even nearer to the MS, for the resemblance between Γ and Π in capitals and uncials often amounts almost to identity.

In v. 280 ⟦277⟧ we are at once arrested by the question: why πλαγκτοῖς instead of πλαγκταῖς? There is here no such metrical excuse as ‖ may be pleaded for πλαγκτὸς οὖσα in Ag. 598 ⟦593⟧. Further, it is felt on all hands that *in vagrant cloaks* is an absurd expression, and indeed that in this rapid summary of disaster such a detail as διπλάκεσσιν is itself somewhat trivial and beside the mark. Hence the rash invent unheard-of meanings for δίπλαξ; the prudent have recourse to conjecture. Hartung proposes σπιλάδεσσιν, which I think right and hope to establish; but plainly the passage is not emended yet. πλαγκτοῖς is now less defensible than ever; to get rid of it, Hartung ruins the metre by writing πλάγκτ', and is thus driven to more violence in the strophe; Weil suggests πλαγκτῶν, an improbable alteration; Wecklein πλαγκτούς, an improbable construction. And not only is further change thus involved, but it is also far from clear how σπιλάδεσσιν became διπλάκεσσιν.

If however Aeschylus wrote πλάγκτ' ἐνὶ σπιλάδεσσιν all is explained as the result of πλαγκτενκπιλαδεσσιν. By a frequent error κ was written for ισ; the correction, added above the line or in the margin, was mistaken, through the perpetual confusion of ι with οι, for a correction of πλάγκτ' to πλαγκτοῖς; and out of the monstrous κπιλάδεσσιν the Greek word διπλάκεσσιν inevitably emerged, for κπιλαδ and διπλακ are different arrangements of the same six letters. It says nothing against this correction that a trochee in the antistrophe thus answers a spondee in the strophe, since Aeschylus habitually admits such correspondence in glyconic bases: those scholars who retain δῖαν in v. 274 ⟦271⟧ may even prefer a trochee in v. 280 [277], but I myself find δᾳαν a necessary alteration. Let me add, in favour of ἐνί, that the epic form has a peculiar fitness as recalling the ποτὶ σπιλάδεσσιν of Homer; and, in favour of the entire emendation, that the words μέλεα λέγεις φέρεσθαι ἐνὶ σπιλάδεσσιν truthfully represent the πλήθουσι νεκρῶν ἀκταί of the messenger, while the MS reading puts into his mouth what he never said.

293–5 ⟦290–2⟧

σιγῶ πάλαι δύστηνος ἐκπεπληγμένη
κακοῖς· ὑπερβάλλει γὰρ ἥδε συμφορά,
τὸ μήτε λέξαι μήτ' ἐρωτῆσαι πάθη.

It appears impossible that v. 295 [292] should mean τὸ μήτε σε λέξαι πάθη μήτε ἐμὲ ἐρωτῆσαι αὐτά: besides, grant it possible, the statement is untrue: the messenger has already given, between the ejaculations of the chorus, a terse and comprehensive summary of the πάθη in question. It remains then to take λέξαι apart from πάθη, ‖ with Atossa for its subject, in the sense of φθέγξασθαι. But this again is impossible, for λέγω is not so used: μηδὲν λέξαι would be required. The difficulty seems to have been first apprehended by Wecklein, who proposes φωνεῖν: this word may have been expelled by a superscript gloss λέγειν, and λέγειν may then have been altered for metre's sake to λέξαι. There is a far simpler way: nothing more, I believe, is needed to restore the passage than the addition of a single letter:

τὸ μήτ' ἐλέγξαι μήτ' ἐρωτῆσαι πάθη.

ἐλέγξαι and ἐρωτῆσαι are almost synonyms; but this virtual tautology is of a kind rather sought after than shunned by the tragic style: closely parallel is Soph. O. T. 1305 πόλλ' ἀνερέσθαι, πολλὰ πυθέσθαι.

453–6 ⟦450–3⟧

ἐνταῦθα πέμπει τούσδ', ὅπως, ὅτ' ἐκ νεῶν
φθαρέντες ἐχθροὶ νῆσον ἐκσῳζοίατο,
κτείνοιεν εὐχείρωτον Ἑλλήνων στρατόν,
φίλους δ' ὑπεκσῴζοιεν ἐναλίων πόρων.

In this, the vulgate text, the word ἐκσῳζοίατο might not itself arouse suspicion. But suspicion is aroused when only two lines below we come to ὑπεκσῴζοιεν; aroused not by the mere repetition, for the Greeks are less careful than the Romans and the moderns to avoid this fault, but by the following considerations. When ἐκσῴζω and ὑπεκσῴζω occur with this brief interval, the element -σῴζω ought to mean the same thing in each verb, and the elements ὑπεκ- ought to mean something more than the element ἐκ-. But the reverse is the fact. There is no tangible difference, as there ought to be, between ἐκ- in v. 454 ⟦451⟧ and ὑπεκ- in v. 456 ⟦453⟧: there is a tangible difference, as there ought not to be, between σῴζω in v. 454 ⟦451⟧, which signifies merely *bring to land* (to meet death), and σῴζω in v. 456 ⟦453⟧, which signifies *save alive*. And suspicion mounts to something like certainty when we turn to the apparatus criticus and find that the MS reading is not ἐκσῳζοίατο but ἐξσωζοίατο, with κ written overhead as a correction. The question then is not whether we will stick to the MS or desert it; no one dreams of sticking to it: the question is whether we will take the conjecture of a Byzantine scribe, which imports some difficulty, or the conjecture of a modern critic with the resources of science at his disposal. M. Stahl has proposed ‖ ἐξοισοίατο, an amendment suggested, I presume, by Herod. VIII 76 ὡς, ἐπεὰν γένηται ναυμαχίη, ἐνθαῦτα μάλιστα ἐξοισομένων τῶν τε ἀνδρῶν καὶ τῶν ναυηγίων. But the future optative appears to be inexcusable; there is here no oratio obliqua. We shall approach the MS even more closely if we restore the word which the lexicons will show to be the most natural of all words for the occasion: ἐξωθοίατο.

668–71 ⟦664–6⟧

ὅπως καινά τε κλύῃς
νέα τ' ἄχη
δέσποτα δεσπότου
φάνηθι.

Dindorf's δεσποτᾶν for δεσπότου in v. 670 ⟦666⟧ seems to me probably right; but my present concern is with v. 668 ⟦664⟧. The answering verse in the strophe is βαλήν, ἀρχαῖος βαλήν: when we compare the two it appears that the scansion must be ∪–––∪–∪–. To shorten the penultimate αι of ἀρχαῖος, as of πετραῖος, παλαιός, γεραιός, δίκαιος and δείλαιος in tragedy, ἔμπαιος in Homer and ληθαῖος in Anacreon, is quite permissible. But it is not equally legitimate to lengthen τε before κλ in v. 668 [664]; and a long syllable is therefore required in its stead. This should seemingly be restored by the almost imperceptible change καινά γᾷ for καινά τε. The confusion of γᾶι and τε needs no explaining; but I will adduce another example of the same error, which I detect in Eum. 803 [800]. The MS there gives

> ὑμεῖς δέ τε τῇδε γῇ βαρὺν κότον
> σκήψητε.

The verse has no metre, and its meaning is precisely the opposite of the meaning demanded. I suppose that Aeschylus wrote

> ὑμεῖς δὲ γαίᾳ τῇδε μὴ βαρὺν κότον
> σκήψητε.

γαίαι, by the omission of one αι, became γᾶι; this surprising Doricism naturally evoked a marginal correction γῆ, which however missed its mark and was substituted not for γᾷ but for μή; then γᾷ was further corrupted, as in Pers. 668 [664], to τε.

815–17 [813–15]

τοιγὰρ κακῶς δράσαντες οὐκ ἐλάσσονα
πάσχουσι, τὰ δὲ μέλλουσι, κοὐδέπω κακῶν
κρηπὶς ὕπεστιν, ἀλλ᾽ ἔτ᾽ ἐκπιδύεται. ||

I take for a starting point Schuetz's ἐκπιδύεται, believing it to be the first stride, and that a great one, towards the restoration of the passage. True, it is to insult Aeschylus to suppose him the author of such a sentence as results from this correction, if correction here stops short. But every impeachment which can be brought against ἐκπιδύεται is equally an impeachment of the MS reading ἐκπαιδεύεται, which apparently therefore is recommended to its defenders merely by its intrinsic absurdity: neither κακὰ ἐκπαιδεύεται nor κρηπὶς ἐκπαιδεύεται has any vestige of a meaning. Against the emended line there lie two objections of great though unequal gravity. To take the lighter first, the clash of metaphor in κρηπίς and ἐκπιδύεται is hardly credible: the laying of a foundation and the welling forth of a spring are two images which refuse to be made one. Still, the Greeks were less sensitive to such incongruity than we are, and though I think no real parallel can be adduced, it might yet be possible to find examples only less harsh than this.

But there remains a far heavier, a fatal objection. It is entirely permissible to say, with impressive exaggeration, οὐδέπω κακῶν κρηπὶς ὕπεστιν, that is, *calamity is as yet not even begun*. Precisely thus does Prometheus say in P. V. 767 [741] οὓς γὰρ νῦν ἀκήκοας λόγους | εἶναι δόκει σοι μηδέπω 'ν προοιμίοις. But, having said so much, there you must stop: you cannot proceed to say ἀλλ᾽ ἔτ᾽ ἐκπιδύεται, *but it is still going on*. Begin by saying that a thing is not yet *finished*, then you may proceed to say, with such pleonasm as poets love, that it is still going on: οὐδέπω κακῶν | ἔπεστι θριγκός, ἀλλ' ἔτ' ἐκπιδύεται, for instance, would be the writing, not indeed of a decent stylist, but still the writing of a sane man. But to say that a thing *is not yet begun but is still going on* is such nonsense as not one of us can conceive himself uttering in the loosest negligence of conversation; only when centuries of transcription by barbarians have imputed it to an incomparable poet, then we accept it as a matter of course.

I will ask the reader not to take fright at what may strike the first glance as a violent change; it is not really such.

κοὐδέπω κακῶν

κρηνὶς ἀπέσβηκ', ἀλλ' ἔτ' ἐκπιδύεται.

ν and π are commonly confused in uncials, and even if they were not, two words like κρηνίς and κρηπίς, which coincide in five of their letters and differ only in one, are always easily interchanged. Why, in the verb σβέννυμι, β should tend to become τ, I cannot || tell; but the fact is so: thus in Eur. Med. 1218 ἀπέσβη has been corrupted to ἀπέστη, in Aesch. Ag. 879 [888] κατεσβήκασιν to καθεστήκασιν. But now ἀπέσβηκ' and ὕπεστιν are palaeographically almost the same thing: ἀπ- and ὑπ- are confused 'dici non potest quotiens', says Bast; η and ι were for ages identical in sound; κ and ν in uncial MSS nearly identical in shape. For the metaphor see v. 745 [743] κακῶν ἔοικε πηγὴ πᾶσιν ηὑρῆσθαι φίλοις.

847–53 [845–51]

ὦ δαῖμον, ὡς με πόλλ' ἐσέρχεται κακὰ
ἄλγη, μάλιστα δ' ἥδε συμφορὰ δάκνει
ἀτιμίαν γε παιδὸς ἀμφὶ σώματι

850 [848]   ἐσθημάτων κλύουσαν, ἥ νιν ἀμπέχει.

ἀλλ' εἶμι, καὶ λαβοῦσα κόσμον ἐκ δόμων
ὑπαντιάζειν ἐμῷ παιδὶ πειράσομαι·
οὐ γὰρ τὰ φίλτατ' ἐν κακοῖς προδώσομεν.

The earliest attempt to mend the metre of v. 852 [850] is the transposition παῖδ' ἐμῷ in the inferior MSS. This elision was of course impossible to Aeschylus, and the assumed corruption is inexplicable: few scribes would find παῖδ' ἐμῷ a difficulty, no scribe would find ἐμῷ παιδί an improvement. The same objection holds against Burges' παιδί μου and Lobeck's παῖδ' ἐμόν, which depart yet further from the MS: Lobeck's conjecture is moreover discountenanced by the ὑπαντίαζε παιδί of v. 836 [834]. Other proposals are even less plausible.

It seems to have been generally assumed that the words ἐμῷ παιδί, though themselves corrupt, nevertheless represent correctly the sense of the lost words or word. But there is no reason to think so, for παιδί is readily supplied from what precedes: the dative is in like manner omitted after this verb in v. 410 ⟦407⟧ Περσίδος γλώσσης ῥόθος ὑπηντίαзε. Disembarrassed of this preconception I think we shall restore the verse without much ado:

ὑπαντιάзειν ἐμποδών πειράσομαι

I will essay to meet him on his way. The descent from ἐμποδών through ἐμπέδωι to ἐμπαίδωι consisted of the easiest stages: thence the shortest way to Greek was the transposition of one letter, ἐμῶ παιδί, which may well have stood in some ancestor of our MS, for one school of copyists writes ἐμῶ where another writes ἐμῶι and where we write ἐμῷ. ‖

It will illustrate one stage in this corruption if I here emend Eur. I. T. 755–8:

ἐξαίρετόν μοι δὸς τόδ', ἤν τι ναῦς πάθῃ
χἠ δέλτος ἐν κλύδωνι χρημάτων μέτα
ἀφανὴς γένηται, σῶμα δ' ἐκσώσω μόνον,
τὸν ὅρκον εἶναι τόνδε μηκέτ' ἔμπεδον.

Pylades and Iphigenia have interchanged oaths, she that she will send him safely away, he that he will carry her letter to her brother. But then it strikes him that he may lose the letter through shipwreck and be therefore unable to fulfil his oath; so he desires to make the exception that in those circumstances it shall no longer be binding. But this is not the meaning of the words τὸν ὅρκον εἶναι τόνδε μηκέτ' ἔμπεδον. What ἔμπεδος ὅρκος means we perfectly well know from v. 790 τὸν δ' ὅρκον ὃν κατώμοσ' ἐμπεδώσομεν, *we will perform the oath which I sware*, and from many another passage where the phrase recurs: ἔμπεδος ὅρκος means an oath which is performed. Now Pylades cannot without absurdity beg of Iphigenia that if the letter is lost his oath shall not be *performed*: that is ex hypothesi certain. What he must ask is that his oath shall not be *considered incumbent on him to perform*, that he shall be held guiltless though he does not perform it. And this in Greek will be:

τὸν ὅρκον εἶναι τόνδε μηκέτ' ἐμποδών.

See Aesch. P. V. 13 σφῷν μὲν ἐντολὴ Διὸς | ἔχει τέλος δὴ κοὐδὲν ἐμποδών ἔτι.

5

ISOCR. *PANEG.* §40*

πρώτη γὰρ (ἡ πόλις ἡ ἡμετέρα) καὶ νόμους ἔθετο καὶ πολιτείαν κατεστήσατο. δῆλον δ᾽ ἐκεῖθεν· οἱ γὰρ ἐν ἀρχῇ περὶ τῶν φονικῶν ἐγκαλέσαντες, καὶ βουληθέντες μετὰ λόγου καὶ μὴ μετὰ βίας διαλύσασθαι τὰ πρὸς ἀλλήλους, ἐν τοῖς νόμοις τοῖς ἡμετέροις τὰς κρίσεις ἐποιήσαντο περὶ αὐτῶν.

Non intellego writes Dobree against the words οἱ γὰρ ἐν ἀρχῇ κτλ.; and indeed the vagueness of the expression is extraordinary. It is incredible that Isocrates should not mention, when mentioning would be so much to his purpose, the august character of the first litigants at Athens. The Athenian boast was that the court of the Areopagus dated back to no less an event than the trial of Ares for the slaying of Halirrothius son of Poseidon: it is to this divine origin that Isocrates, if he knows his business, must refer; but the words in the text contain no proper designation of it. It should seem then that ΟΙ is merely a mistake for ΘΙ as is suggested by the parallel of Dem. *Aristocr.* §66 ἐν μόνῳ τούτῳ τῷ δικαστηρίῳ δίκας φόνου θεοὶ καὶ δοῦναι καὶ λαβεῖν ἠξίωσαν καὶ δικασταὶ γενέσθαι διενεχθεῖσιν ἀλλήλοις. But the strongest confirmation of θεοὶ γὰρ ἐν ἀρχῇ I find in Eur. *El.* 1258 sq. ἔστιν δ᾽ ῎Αρεώς τις ὄχθος, οὗ πρῶτον θεοὶ | ἕζοντ᾽ ἐπὶ ψήφοισιν αἵματος πέρι.

* [[*CR* 2 (1888), 42]]

6

SCHOL. ON AESCH. *P.V.* 488 ⟦472⟧*

μεσολαβοῦσι δὲ αἱ τοῦ χοροῦ τὴν ἔκθεσιν τῶν κατορθωμάτων, διαναπαύουσαι τὸν ὑποκριτὴν Αἰσχύλου.

Not so: Aeschylus is not one of the *dramatis personae* in his own *Prometheus Vinctus*, and the actor whom the chorus here interrupts is the impersonator not of Aeschylus but of Prometheus; so that Oberdick actually proposes to read Προμηθέως for Αἰσχύλου, and Wecklein records the conjecture with approval. The true correction is much simpler. There is a well known error which perpetually introduces proper names into MSS where they were never written and obliterates them where they were. Σοφοκλῆς for σοφός, Δημοσθένης for δῆμος, and the like, are frequent blunders because the words are represented by identical abbreviations; and here is another example. The sentence ends with ὑποκριτήν: Αἰσχύλου is nothing but a misinterpretation of the compendium which really stood for αἰσχρόν, a gloss on the αἰκές of v. 488 ⟦472⟧ πέπονθας αἰκὲς πῆμα.

* ⟦*CR* 2 (1888), 42⟧

7

ΣΩΦΡΟΝΗ*

In our salvage from the wreck of Greek literature the word δυσφρόνη = δυσφροσύνη is found at one place, Hes. *Theog.* 102 δυσφρονέων, and a certain emendation of W. Dindorf's restores it at one more, Pind. *Ol.* II. 95 [52 Snell] δυσφρονᾶν. The MS variants in the latter ‖ passage, δυσφρόνων, δυσφροσύναν, δυσφροσύνας, δυσφορᾶν, δυσφόραν, δυσφορῶν, present a lively picture of the dangers encompassing a word so rare as this, and prove that if the Greeks also used εὐφρόνη = εὐφροσύνη, ἀφρόνη = ἀφροσύνη, and σωφρόνη = σωφροσύνη, it yet need not follow that any trace of the use should now survive in Greek literature. From Greek literature, accordingly, our lexicons cite no such trace: they cite only εὐφρόνη· νὺξ καὶ εὐφροσύνη from Hesychius, ἀφρόνη· ἡ ἀφροσύνη from Bekker's *Anecdota*, and the proper name Σωφρόνη from Arcadius, Aphthonius, Aristaenetus, and the Etymologicum Magnum. Yet that the words were really used might be suggested not by δυσφρόνη only, but by καλλονή beside καλλοσύνη and πημονή beside πημοσύνη, without reckoning the ἡδοσύνη = ἡδονή of Hesychius; and I here essay to shew at any rate the existence in Attic tragedy of σωφρόνη = σωφροσύνη.

Eur. *Hipp.* 1032–5

> εἰ δ᾽ ἥδε δειμαίνουσ᾽ ἀπώλεσεν βίον
> οὐκ οἶδ᾽· ἐμοὶ γὰρ οὐ πέρα θέμις λέγειν.
> ἐσωφρόνησεν οὐκ ἔχουσα σωφρονεῖν,
> ἡμεῖς δ᾽ ἔχοντες οὐ καλῶς ἐχρώμεθα.

Verse 1034 is interpreted *she was virtuous though she had not virtue*; and this no doubt is the sense required. Phaedra was virtuous in her conduct, acted virtuously γνώμῃ νικᾶν τὴν Κύπριν πειρωμένη and preferring death to shame, although, as the victim of incestuous passion, she had not virtue. When commentators demand this sense they do well, but they do ill when they thrust it on the Greek. No scholar, once challenged, will deliberately maintain that ἔχω σωφρονεῖν can mean ἔχω τὸ σωφρονεῖν *I have virtue*. It means *I am able to be virtuous*; and the line *she was virtuous though unable to be so* is a contradiction in terms. The assailant of an accepted text should be prepared for anything, and should therefore be prepared to hear that this is an oxymoron; to which one can

* [*CR* 2 (1888), 242–5]

only reply, with Cobet on a like occasion, 'τὸ μὲν μῶρον uideo, τὸ δ' ὀξύ non uideo.' No better sense is the next verse, *while I, though able to be virtuous, made no good use of it*: use of what? whence can an αὐτῷ be supplied? Had Euripides written τὸ σωφρονεῖν or σωφροσύνην, all except metre would have been right: what he wrote is surely ἐσωφρόνησεν οὐκ ἔχουσα σωφρόνην: the two words were pronounced alike, so the scribe altered the unknown word to the well-known.

Eur. *Tro.* 1055–7

> ἐλθοῦσα δ' Ἄργος ὥσπερ ἀξία κακῶς
> κακὴ θανεῖται, καὶ γυναιξὶ σωφρονεῖν
> πάσαισι θήσει.

This is the only instance in tragedy of the construction τίθημί τινι ποιεῖν τι : the tragedians say τινά. Of the accusative there are nine clear examples: Aesch. *Ag.* 1036 ἐπεί σ' ἔθηκε Ζεὺς ἀμηνίτως δόμοις | κοινωνὸν εἶναι χερνίβων, ib. 1174 καί τίς σε κακοφρονῶν τίθησι δαίμων...μελίζειν πάθη, Eur. *Hec.* 357 πρῶτα μέν με τοὔνομα | θανεῖν ἐρᾶν τίθησιν, *Heracl.* 990 Ἥρα με κάμνειν τήνδ' ἔθηκε τὴν νόσον, *Med.* 718 παίδων γονὰς | σπεῖραί σε θήσω, *Ion* 75 Ἴωνα δ' αὐτὸν... ὄνομα κεκλῆσθαι θήσεται καθ' Ἑλλάδα, *frag.* 63 Dind. [adesp. 414 Nauck] ἄκραντα γάρ μ' ἔθηκε θεσπίζειν θεός, *Rhes.* 918 ἔρις | τεκεῖν μ' ἔθηκε τόνδε δύστηνον γόνον, Stob. *flor.* 108 23 [vol. iii p. 971 Hense = Eur. fr. 1076 Nauck] τῶν δ' ἀμηχάνων ἔρως | πολλοὺς ἔθηκε τοῦ παρόντος ἀμπλακεῖν. These nine examples leave us in no doubt how to construe a tenth, Eur. *Herc. Fur.* 221 Θήβαις ἔθηκεν ὄμμ' ἐλεύθερον βλέπειν; the construction is ἔθηκεν ὄμμα, and βλέπειν is epexegetic. *Heracl.* 163 I leave out of count: θείς did not come from Euripides, and would not affect the question if it had. A tragic poet then had the choice of two constructions, τίθημι γυναῖκας σωφρονεῖν and τίθημι γυναιξὶ σωφροσύνην: here metre required γυναιξὶ σωφρόνην | πάσαισι θήσει.

Aesch. *Pers.* 829–30

> πρὸς ταῦτ' ἐκεῖνον σωφρονεῖν κεχρημένοι
> πινύσκετ' εὐλόγοισι νουθετήμασιν.

From σωφρονεῖν κεχρημένοι it is no longer attempted to extract sense: the old interpretations suited the context ill, and it was none too clear how the Greek could bear them. The reading now in vogue is κεχρημένον, which is proposed by a late scholiast and rendered χρείαν ἔχοντα σωφρονεῖν. It is not perhaps inconceivable that σωφρονεῖν κεχρημένον could mean κεχρημένον σωφροσύνης or τοῦ σωφρονεῖν; but I should like an example: why did not Aeschylus write, as has been conjectured, τοῦ φρονεῖν? As close as possible to the MS (for ν final is merely a superscript line) and thoroughly satisfactory in sense and construction alike will be σωφρόνῃ κεχρημένοι, *since ye are wise*, an equivalent of Homer's φρεσὶ γὰρ κέχρητ' ἀγαθῇσιν. And it is most encouraging to find that this is the conjecture, where proposed and how supported I do not know, of Meineke.

Aesch. *Ag.* 179–83

στάζει δ' ἔν θ' ὕπνῳ πρὸ καρδίας
μνησιπήμων πόνος
καὶ παρ' ἄκοντας ἦλθε σωφρονεῖν.
δαιμόνων δὲ ποῦ χάρις
βεβαίως σέλμα σεμνὸν ἡμένων.

στάζει πόνος is a phrase which could here convey to Greek ears no meaning whatever; but it is not easy to say which of the two ‖ words is corrupt. Wecklein's στηρίζει δ' ὕπνῳ is excellent sense and may be right, though it is plainly too far from the MS to convince. But my concern is with v. 181. It ought to mean *and wisdom comes to men without their wish*; but it cannot. The infinitive sans article, though it can be the subject of certain verbs, such as ἐστίν, γίγνεται and ξυμβαίνει, cannot be the subject of a verb outside this well defined class: ἦλθε σωφρονεῖν cannot be said for ἦλθε τὸ σωφρονεῖν. Of course MSS will furnish instances of this solecism, as of any other; but we rightly judge these instances too rare and too easily corrected to break down the rule. Thus in Eur. *Ion* 964 σοὶ δ' ἐς τί δόξης ἦλθεν ἐκβαλεῖν τέκνον it can hardly be doubted that we are to read δόξ' εἰσῆλθεν with Hermann. Again, corruption is generally recognised in Aesch. *Ag.* 584 ἀεὶ γὰρ ἡβᾷ τοῖς γέρουσιν εὖ μαθεῖν. The proposed corrections are various: I myself believe firmly in Mr Margoliouth's ἥβη; but perhaps the further alteration ἥβη καὶ γέρουσιν will give a more forcible verse, and will really better explain the error of the MS. Just as in *Suppl.* 79 ἢ καί has become ηβαι, so might ἥβη καί here become ηβηβαι, which the loss of one ηβ would reduce to the ἡβᾷι of the codex Florentinus: τοῖς, a natural supplement to the metre, is quite superfluous to the sense, and καί seems to point the antithesis: compare too *frag.* 278 Dind. [396 Nauck, 674 Mette] καλὸν δὲ καὶ γέροντα μανθάνειν σοφά. The solecism of v. 181 can be removed with the usual ease by the substitution of σώφρονα: how often α is confused with the compendium for ει need scarcely be said.

The evidence for σωφρόνη would be strengthened if we could discover in the tragic texts any vestige of ἀφρόνη or of εὐφρόνη = εὐφροσύνη. Now it will perhaps surprise the reader to hear that εὐφρόνη = εὐφροσύνη stares us in the face from all the MSS and editions of no meaner author than Sophocles. In *El.* 17–19 we read

ὡς ἡμὶν ἤδη λαμπρὸν ἡλίου σέλας
ἑῷα κινεῖ φθέγματ' ὀρνίθων σαφῆ,
μέλαινά τ' ἄστρων ἐκλέλοιπεν εὐφρόνη·

and we are direly troubled to find a construction for ἄστρων. ἐκλέλοιπεν does not take a genitive, and, even if it did, that would not help us. Nor, because χιόνος πτέρυγι can be rendered in English *a snowy wing*, does it follow that εὐφρόνη (νὺξ) ἄστρων can mean νὺξ ἀστερόεσσα, *the starry night*. To speak of a white wing as a wing of snow, that is, made of snow, is comprehensible and poetical; but night is not made of stars. Wunder in vain seeks to shew that *astrorum nigra nox* tallies with λαμπρὸν ἡλίου σέλας: it would tally with λαμπρὰ ἡλίου ἡμέρα, could such a phrase be found; but who will find it? Now all this trouble springs from the presumption that εὐφρόνη means νύξ. It means εὐφροσύνη: ἄστρων εὐφρόνη *the festal gathering of the stars* is an expression like the ἄστρων ὁμήγυρις of Aesch. *Ag.* 4. The conception of the stars as a choir of revellers was familiar to the ancients: it recurs for instance in Soph. *Ant.* 1147 χοράγ᾽ ἄστρων, Eur. *Ion* 1079 Διὸς ἀστερωπὸς ἀνεχόρευσεν αἰθήρ, χορεύει δὲ σελάνα, *El.* 467 ἄστρων αἰθέριοι χοροί, and *frag.* 593 Dind. ⟦593 Nauck⟧ ἄστρων ὄχλος ἐνδελεχῶς ἀμφιχο-ρεύει. Indeed almost a translation of μέλαιν᾽ ἄστρων εὐφρόνη is given by Tibullus in II. 1, 88 *lasciuo sidera fulua choro*. What is the true derivation of εὐφρόνη = νύξ I do not know, nor did Sophocles; but what Sophocles, and probably his contemporaries too, supposed to be its derivation, this passage appears to shew.

It is to the misconception which obscured its meaning that εὐφρόνη here owes its preservation. Had it not occurred in a context where it seemed susceptible of the meaning νύξ, we may be pretty certain that the scribes would have altered it as they altered δυσφρονᾶν in Pindar. Accordingly we shall not expect to find it uncorrupted in Aesch. *Cho.* 779–82 ⟦783–6⟧, if Aeschylus wrote it there, which I admit to be uncertain.

> νῦν παραιτουμένᾳ μοι, πάτερ
> Ζεῦ θεῶν Ὀλυμπίων,
> δὸς τύχας τυχεῖν δέ μου κυρίως
> τὰ σωφροσυνευ μαιομένοις ἰδεῖν.

The last two verses, which are obviously and perhaps hopelessly corrupt, should, to judge from the antistrophe, be reduced to these metres:

$$—\cup——\cup——\cup—$$
$$\overline{\cup}—\cup——\cup\cup—\cup—\,.$$

The former verse may reasonably be written δὸς τύχας εὖ τυχεῖν κυρίοις: δέ μου, which means nothing, seems to be rightly regarded by Bothe as a corruption of δόμου, and δόμου would be accounted for as an explanatory supplement if κυρίοις stood in the text: εὖ τυχεῖν is plausibly inferred by Hermann from the scholion εὐτυχίαν εὐτυχῆσαι. In the next verse Hermann writes σώφρον᾽ εὖ, which is believed to mean 'who desire to see virtue in the ascendancy'. The meaning, if possible, is surely poor, and dearly bought at the cost of assuming that so simple a word as σώφρονα would be changed to anything so monstrous as σωφροσυν. I see here no place for σώφρων or σωφροσύνη or σωφρόνη, and I propose ‖ the following as obtaining a better sense by more legitimate expedients:

δὸς τύχας εὖ τυχεῖν κυρίοις
τοῖς εὐφρόναν μαιομένοις ἰδεῖν·

grant that good luck befall my lords who yearn to see joy and gladness. I suppose
that just as Pindar's scribes wrote δυσφροσύναν in *Ol.* II. 95 [52] so the scribes of
Aeschylus here wrote εὐφροσύναν; that the likeness of οι to α, and a wrong division of letters, produced τὰ σευφροσύναν, instantly altered to σωφροσύναν;
and that a subsequent correction ευ was accidentally substituted, not, as was
intended, for ω, but for αν, whence σωφροσυνευ. But, as I said, the lines may
be past mending.

I have found no further trace of εὐφρόνη. The change of εὔφροσιν to εὐφρόναις
in Aesch. *Eum.* 635 [632] would render that passage translatable, but would not
remove all its faults; and there is more likelihood about Schuetz's hypothesis of
a lost verse, containing a finite verb and a substantive for εὔφροσιν to agree
with. On ἀφρόνη I may add one remark. In the first volume of the *Journal of
Hellenic Studies* Mr Verrall shewed that the tragedians, in their parsimonious
employment of words in -οσύνη, seldom or never lose sight of certain associa-
tions which these immigrants brought with them from Ionia. Now the text of
Euripides contains three examples of ἀφροσύνη where cause for its use is not
readily to be descried: *Tro.* 990 τὰ μῶρα γὰρ πάντ' ἐστὶν Ἀφροδίτη βροτοῖς | καὶ
τοὔνομ' ὀρθῶς ἀφροσύνης ἄρχει θεᾶς, *Bacch.* 1302 [1301] Πενθεῖ δὲ τί μέρος
ἀφροσύνης προσῆκ' ἐμῆς; *I.A.* 1431 [1430] οὔκουν ἐάσω σ' ἀφροσύνῃ τῇ σῇ
θανεῖν. It is quite possible then, I would not go so far as to call it probable, that
in these instances the form ἀφρόνη, which the metre equally permits, should be
restored. I say the metre equally permits it, for Euripides' reluctance to lengthen
a short vowel before a mute followed by ρ did not prevent him from writing
ἄφρονα with the first syllable long in *Alc.* 728.

8

EMENDATIONES PROPERTIANAE*

I see no hope of completing a presentable commentary on Propertius within the next ten years; but in the mean time I trust that the following list of corrections may be found of service to scholars. For my own sake too I have some desire to put my conjectures on record, as I am for ever seeing them forestalled by other students: Mr Konrad Rossberg in vol. 127 of Fleckeisen's annual has bereft me of no less than nine. True, it is agreeable enough to have one's results confirmed by a scholar who stands next to Mr Baehrens and Mr Palmer at the head of living Propertian critics; but I should like to retain something of my own. As many readers are apt to fancy that the textual critic proposes alterations out of pure gaiety of heart and not because the vulgate wants altering, I have added an examination in detail of the first elegy; 'ne mea dona tibi studio disposta fideli, Intellecta prius quam sint, contempta relinquas'. I employ Mr Baehrens' MSS and notation.

I i. Between 11 and 12 are lost two such verses as these: 'multaque desertis fleuerat arboribus, | et modo submissa casses ceruice ferebat'. ||

I i 23 tunc ego crediderim *uobis et sidera et amnes* | posse Cytinaeis ducere carminibus] *et manes et sidera uobis.*

I i 33 *in me* nostra Venus noctes exercet amaras] *me non.*

I ii 9 aspice quos summittat humus *formosa* colores] *morosa.*

I ii 13 litora natiuis *persuadent picta* lapillis] *superant depicta.*

I ii 23 non illis studium *uulgo conquirere* amantes DVN, *aquirere* AF] *fulgore anquirere.*

I iii. Between 6 and 7 should be inserted II ii 9–12 as follows: 'qualis et Ischomachi Lapithae genus heroine, | Centauris medio grata rapina mero, | *marcori Ossaeis* fertur Boebeidos undis | uirgineum primo composuisse latus, | talis' eqs. *Mercurio satis* FN, *Mercurioque satis* DV, *Ossaeis* Burmann.

I iii 37 *namque* ubi longa meae consumpsti tempora noctis] *nempe.* The interrogation at the end of 38 should be removed.

I iv 19 nec tibi *me* post haec committet Cynthia] *se.*

I iv 24 et quicumque sacer *qualis* ubique lapis] *quaeret.*

I iv 26 quam sibi cum rapto cessat amore *deus*] *decus.*

* [*JPh* 16 (1888), 1–35]

I v 9 quod si forte tuis non est contraria *nostris*] *uerbis*.

I vi 26 *hanc* animam *extremae* reddere nequitiae] *huic . . . extremam*.

I vii 16 quod nolim nostros *euiolasse* deos] *eualuisse*.

I vii 23 and 24 should be placed between 10 and 11: Mr Baehrens has seen that they are now out of place.

I viii 13 atque ego non uideam *tales* subsidere uentos] *laetos*: 13 and 14 should be placed after 16 with Scaliger.

I viii 22. Read 'de te | quin ego, uita, tuo limine, *nostra*, querar'. *uerba* MSS.

I ix 32 nedum *tu possis* spiritus iste leuis] *tutus erit*.

I xi 6 ecquis in extremo restat *amore locus*] *amor iecore*.

I xi 15 and 16 should be placed between 8 and 9.

I xi 22 *aut* sine te uitae cura sit ulla meae AFN, *an* DV] Perhaps *haut* or *hau*.

I xiii 12 nec noua quaerendo semper *amicus* eris] *iniquus* Guietus rightly, except that Propertius wrote *inicus*.

I xv 25 and 26 should seemingly be placed before 33, where *tam tibi* should be read with Mr Palmer after Madvig. ||

I xv 29 *multa* prius uasto labentur flumina ponto] Perhaps *aucta*.

I xvi 9 nec possum infamis dominae defendere *noctes*] *uoces*: thus no transposition is required.

I xvi 23 me mediae *noctes*, me sidera prona iacentem | frigidaque Eoo me dolet aura gelu] *noctis*.

I xvii 3 nec mihi *Casiopae solito uisura* carinam DV and nearly so AFN] *Castoreast stella inuisura*.

I xvii 28 mansuetis socio parcite *litoribus* ADVN, *thoribus* F] *pectoribus*.

I xviii 15 tua *flendo* | lumina deiectis turpia sint lacrimis] *flentis*.

I xviii 23 and 24 should be placed between 6 and 7 with *an tua quod* altered to *a tua quot* as in the interpolated MSS.

I xviii 27 *diuini fontes* et frigida rupes] *dumeti sentes*.

I xix 13 illic *formosae* ueniant chorus heroinae] *formosus*.

I xix 16 *et* Tellus hoc ita iusta sinat] *ut*.

I xx 3 and 4 should be written thus: 'saepe inprudenti fortuna occurrit amanti | crudelis: Minuis *trux erat* Ascanius.' *dixerat* O, *dixerit* N.

I xx 24 *raram* sepositi quaerere fontis aquam] Perhaps *sacram*.

I xx 30 et uolucres *ramo* submouet insidias] *armo*.

I xx 52 formosum *Nymphis credere uisus* Hylam ON, *rursus* Vm.2] *ni uis perdere rursus* Mr Palmer rightly, except that *rusus* should be read.

I xxii.   Between 8 and 9 should be inserted II xxx 21 and 22; after 10 should be placed IV i 65 and 66: 'si Perusina tibi patriae sunt nota sepulcra, | Italiae duris funera temporibus, | cum Romana suos egit discordia ciues | (sic, mihi praecipue puluis Etrusca dolor, | tu proiecta mei perpessa es membra propinqui, | tu nullo miseri contegis ossa solo) | spargereque alterna communes caede penates | et ferre ad patrios *proelia* dira lares, | proxima subposito contingens Vmbria campo | me genuit terris fertilis uberibus. | scandentes quisquis cernet de uallibus arces, | ingenio muros aestimet ille meo.' *praemia* MSS.

II i 5 siue *illam* Cois fulgentem incedere coccis] *iuuat*: thus no transposition is required. ||

II i 11 and 12 should be placed after 14, and *cum* in 11 should be changed to *tum*.

II i.　　After 38 should be inserted III ix 33 and 34: 'Theseus infernis, superis testatur Achilles, | hic Ixioniden, ille Menoetiaden; | Caesaris et famae uestigia iuncta tenebis: | Maecenatis erunt uera tropaea fides.'

II i.　　After 56 should perhaps be placed xv 31–6 which have no business in their present situation.

II ii 9–12 belong, as I have said, to I iii; their present place, between 8 and 13, must have been originally occupied by two such verses as these: 'aut patrio qualis ponit uestigia ponto | mille Venus teneris cincta Cupidinibus'.

II iii should be joined to ii; but iii 1–8, between 4 and 5 of which should be inserted with Scaliger ii 1 and 2, are a fragment which has no business here.

II iii 11 and 12 should be placed between 16 and 17, and the whole passage written thus: 'nec me tam facies, quamuis sit candida, cepit | (lilia non domina sunt magis alba mea), | nec de more comae per leuia colla fluentes, | non oculi, geminae, sidera nostra, faces, | nec siqua Arabio lucet bombyce puella | (non sum de nihilo blandus amator ego), | ut Maeotica nix minio si certat Hibero | utque rosae puro lacte natant folia | quantum quom posito formose saltat Iaccho' eqs.

II iii 45 and 46 (Hertzberg Haupt Palmer = iv 1 and 2 Mueller Baehrens) have no business where they now are; no more have iv 5 and 6 (H. H. P. = 15 and 16 M. B.).

II vi is a patchwork of these fragments: 1–8; 9–14; 15–26 after which we should seemingly with Mr Heydenreich place 35 and 36; 27–34 (so Lachmann); 37–40 (the same); finally 41 and 42 should be placed with Mr Baehrens after vii 12.

II vii 16 non mihi sat *magnus* Castoris iret equus] *nauus*.

II viii 3 and 4 are out of place; so are 11 and 12.

II viii 21–4 have no business here and should perhaps be placed after xxviii 40.

II viii 30 cessare in *tectis* pertulit arma sua] *Teucris*.

II ix 7 *uisura* et quamuis numquam speraret Vlixem] Perhaps *uisurum* [*uisuram*: see this edition, p. 91]. ||

II ix 12 et dominum lauit maerens captiua cruentum | appositum flauis in *Simoenta* uadis] *Simoente*.

II ix 15 *cum tibi* nec Peleus aderat nec caerula mater FN, *quom tibi* DV] *cui tum* or *quoi tum*.

II ix 18 *tunc etiam* felix inter et arma pudor] *otia tunc*.

II ix 29 and 30 should be placed between 20 and 21.

II ix 44 nunc quoque *eris*, quamuis sis inimica mihi] *era's*.

II x 2 *et campum Haemonio* iam dare tempus equo] *campum et Maeonio*.

II xii 6 fecit et *humano* corde uolare deum] *haut uano*.

II xiii 1 non tot Achaemeniis *armantur Etrusca* sagittis O, *armatur* N] *armatus Eruthra* or *Erythra*.

II xiii 38 *quam fuerant* Phthii busta cruenta uiri] *funere quam*.

II xiii 39 and 40 should be written thus: 'tu quoque si quando uenies *adfata* (memento) | hoc iter, ad lapides, cara, ueni memores.' *ad fata* MSS.

II xiii 45 nam quo tam dubiae seruetur spiritus *horae*] Perhaps *aurae*.

II xiii 48 cui si tam longae minuisset fata senectae | *Gallicus* Iliacis miles in aggeribus] *caelicus*.

II xiii 55 illic formosum *iacuisse paludibus*, illuc | diceris effusa tu, Venus, isse coma DVN, *plaudibus* F] *ciuisse a planctibus*: *ciuisse* Mr Baehrens.

II xiv 5 *saluum cum* aspexit Orestem FN, *suum saluum* DV] *cum saluum*.

II xiv 7 and 8 should be written thus: 'nec sic, *cum* incolumem Minois Thesea uidit, | Daedalium lino *cui* duce rexit iter.' The MSS omit *cum* in 7 and have *cum* for *cui* in 8.

II xiv 29 and 30 should be written thus: 'nunc *a te*, mea lux, *pendet*, mea litore nauis | *soluat an in* mediis sidat honusta uadis.' *ad te* and *ueniet* MSS; *seruata an* FN, *seruata in* DV.

II xv.　The verses of this elegy should be arranged as follows: 1–8, 37–40, 9–24, 49 and 50, 29 and 30, 27 and 28, 25 and 26, 51–4. 25 and 26 have already been placed after 28 by Mr Palmer. 41–8 should be placed after xxx 18; 31–6 perhaps after i 56.

II xv 1 should be written thus: '*io* me felicem, *io* nox mihi ‖ candida, *io* tu | lectule'. *o...o...o* F, *o...o...et o* N, *ah...o...et o* DV.

II xv 37 quod mihi si *tecum* tales concedere noctes | illa uelit] *interdum*.

II xvi 13 and 14 should be placed after 28; 17 and 18 after 12; 29 and 30 after 46; 41 and 42 after III xi 38.

II xvii 13 and 14 should be placed after 2; after 4 should be placed xxii 43–50. The verses 5–12 and 15–18 are a fragment of another poem.

II xviii 5 quid si iam canis aetas *mea caneret* annis] Perhaps *marceret ab*.

II xviii 9 illum saepe *suis* decedens fouit in ulnis | quam *prius adiunctos* sedula lauit equos] *prius...stadiis functos*: no transposition of verses should be made.

II xviii 23 *nunc* etiam infectos demens imitare Britannos | *ludis* et externo tincta nitore caput] *tune...uadis*.

II xviii 29 and 30 should be placed after 24, and in 29 *deme: mihi* should be written with Perreius.

II xviii 33 and 34 have no business here.

II xviii 37 and 38 should be placed at the end of xix, which see.

II xix 5 *nulla* neque ante tuas orietur rixa fenestras] *ulla*.

II xix 17–24 are no part of this poem.

II xix 18 me sacra Dianae | suscipere et *Veneri* ponere uota iuuat] Perhaps *Veneris*.

II xix 27 and 28 should be placed after 32; after 28 should be placed xviii 37 and 38.

II xix 31 quin ego in assidua mutem tua nomina lingua] The sense required is 'quin ego tua crimina metuam uelut in assidua turba'. In 29 *sic* should be changed to *set* with Munro.

II xx 8 nec tantum Niobae bis sex ad busta superbae | sollicito lacrimans defluit *a* Sipylo] *os*.

II xx 35 *hoc* mihi perpetuo *ius* est] *haec...laus*.

II xxi 12 *eiecta est tenuis* namque Creusa domo] *eiecit Aesonia*.

II xxii 43–50 should be placed after xvii 4, as I have said.

II xxiii 1 cui *fuit indocti fugienda et* semita uulgi FN, *et* omitted by DV] cui *fugienda fuit indocti* semita uulgi. ||

II xxiii 4 ut *promissa* suae uerba ferat dominae] *praemissa*.

II xxiii 23 and 24 should be placed after xxiv 4.

II xxiv 4 *aut* pudor ingenuus *aut reticendus* amor] *a* pudor, ingenuus *reiciendus* amor.

II xxiv 8 urerer et quamuis, *nomine* uerba darem] urerer et quamuis *non bene*, uerba darem.

II xxiv 51 *hi* tibi nos erimus] *hic*.

II xxv 35 at si saecla forent *antiquis grata* puellis] *gratis antiqua*.

II xxv 41 uidistis *pleno* teneram candore puellam, | uidistis fusco] Perhaps *niueo*.

II xxv 43 uidistis *quandam Argiua* prodente figura, | uidistis nostras O, *quadam* N] *patriam Argiuas*.

II xxv 45 *illaque* plebeio uel sit sandicis amictu] *aeque*.

II xxv.   Before 47 at least two verses have been lost: the passage may have run thus: '*quin tu uulgares, demens, compescis amores* | *in poenamque uagus desinis esse tuam,* | cum satis una tuis insomnia portet ocellis | una sit et cuiuis femina multa mala.'

II xxvi 23 non si *Cambysae (cambise)* redeant et flumina Croesi] *tam inuisi*.

II xxvi 31 and 32 should be placed before 29: after 28 two verses have been lost: the passage ran thus: '*siue iter in terris dominae sit carpere cura* | *terrestrem carpet me comitante uiam;* | unum litus erit *positis torus* unaque tecto | arbor, et ex una saepe bibemus aqua. | seu mare per longum' eqs. *sopitis* MSS, omitting *torus*.

II xxvi 54 nec umquam | alternante *uorans* uasta Charybdis aqua] *uacans* Ayrmann rightly, except that Propertius wrote *uocans*, a form preserved by F in IV ii 19 'mendax fama *uoces*'.

II xxvii 7 rursus et obiectum *flemus* caput esse tumultu O, *fletus* N] *fles tu.*

II xxviii.   After 2 should be placed 33–8: 33 and 34 were so placed by Passerat.

II xxviii 9–32 are no part of this poem.

II xxviii 40. After this verse should perhaps be placed viii 21–4, as I have said.

II xxviii 51 uobiscum *est iope*] If Mr Rossberg's *Creta* for ‖ *troia* in 53 and Jacob's *Beli* for *phebi* in 54 are correct, I propose *Hesione.*

II xxviii 57 and 58 should be placed before III xviii 25.

II xxviii 61 and 62 should be punctuated thus: 'redde etiam excubias diuae nunc ante iuuencae | uotiuas, noctes et mihi solue decem'.

II xxix 27 ibat et *hinc* castae narratum somnia Vestae] Perhaps *in.*

II xxix 36 signa *uoluptatis non iacuisse* duos. *uoluntatis* FN, *uolutantis* F man. 2, *nec* N] *uolutantis concaluisse.*

II xxx. Here are three elegies or fragments of elegies: the first 19 and 20, 1 and 2, 7–10, 3–6, 11 and 12; the second 13–18 (here insert xv 41–8), 37–40; the third 23–30, 33–6, 31 and 32. 21 and 22 should be placed after I xxii 8, as I have said. 13 eqs. have already been separated by Mr Heimreich and 23 eqs. by Lachmann from the verses which precede them in the MSS: 31 and 32 have been placed after 36 by Mr Rossberg.

II xxx 35 si tamen Oeagri quaedam compressa *figura* | Bistoniis olim rupibus accubuit] *figurae.*

II xxxii.   Before 1 should be placed 7 and 8.

II xxxii 5 *cur uatem* Herculeum deportant esseda Tibur O, *curua te* N] *curnam te.*

II xxxii 15 and 16 should be written thus: 'et leuiter lymphis *lato* crepitantibus orbe | quam subito Triton ore recondit aquam' or 'aqua'. *tota. . .urbe cum* MSS, *toto. . .orbe* Heinsius.

II xxxii 25 and 26 should be placed after 30.

II xxxii 32 et *sine* decreto uiua reducta domum est] *de.*

II xxxii 37 *hoc* et Hamadryadum spectauit turba sororum DVN, *non* F] *uos.*

II xxxii 41 and 42 have no business here and should perhaps be placed after III xiii 12.

II xxxii 43 and 44 should be placed after 46.

II xxxii 61 should be written 'quod si tu Graias *uinces* imitata Latina'. *tuque es* FN, *siue es* DV: I fancy O had *iuue es.*

II xxxiii 6 *quaecumque* illa fuit, semper amara fuit] Perhaps *quodcumque.* ‖

II xxxiv 12 *posses in* tanto uiuere flagitio N, *posset et in* F, *posses et in* DV] *posses tun.*

II xxxiv 31–54 should be thus arranged: 51–4, 41 and 42 (so Munro), 39 and 40 (Munro), 31 and 32 (Munro), 43 and 44, 33–8, 45–50. There should be a comma, not a full stop, at the end of 38.

II xxxiv 40 Amphiaraeae prosint tibi fata quadrigae | aut Capanei *magno* grata ruina Ioui? N, *magno* omitted by O] *irato*.

II xxxiv 59 *me iuuet* hesternis *positum* languere corollis] *mi lubet... posito*: retain *Vergilio* in 61. With 59 begins a new elegy.

II xxxiv 83 nec minor *his* animis, *aut sim* minor ore, canorus | anseris indocto carmine cessit olor] *hic...ut sit*.

III ii 24 annorum aut *ictu pondere* uicta ruent N, *ictu pondera* F, *ictus pondere* DV] *ictus pondera*.

III iii 41 nil tibi sit rauco *praeconia* classica cornu | flare N, *praeconica* O] Perhaps *Phoenicia*.

III iv 4 should be written ' *Thybris*, et Euphrates sub tua iura *fluet*'. *Tygris* N, *Tigris* O: *fluent* NO.

III iv 18 et subter *captos* arma sedere duces] *cautos*: 17 and 18 should be placed before 15 with Mr Keil.

III v 9 corpora disponens mentem non uidit in *arte*] *arto*.

III v 11 nunc maris in tantum *uento* iactamur] *ponto*.

III v 15 uictor cum uictis pariter *miscebitur* umbris] *miscetur in*.

III v 40 and 42 should exchange places.

III vi 3 and 4 should be placed after 8.

III vi 28 et lecta *exectis* anguibus ossa trahunt DVN, *exactis* F] *exuctis*.

III vi 40 me quoque consimili inpositum torquerier igni | iurabo bis sex integer *esse* dies] *ipse*.

III vii.   The verses of this elegy should be arranged thus: 1–10, 43–66, 17 and 18, 11–16, 67–70, 25–32, 37 and 38, 35 and 36, 19 and 20, 33 and 34, 21–4, 39–42, 71 and 72. 17 and 18 were placed after 66, 67–70 after 16, 25–8 after 70, 35 and 36 after 38, 39–42 after 24 by Scaliger; 43–66 after 10, 11 and 12 after 18 by Mr Baehrens. Further, 51 and 53 should exchange places as Mr W. Fischer bids them. ||

III vii 60 attulimus *longas* in freta uestra manus] *nocuas*: the sentence is interrogative.

III viii 12 *et* Veneris magnae uoluitur ante pedes] *haec*: a full stop should be placed at the end of the verse: 13–18 have no business here.

III viii 35 and 36 are out of place.

III ix 9 gloria Lysippo est animosa *effingere* signa N, *fingere* O] *ecfingere*.

III ix 16 Praxitelem propria *uindicat* urbe lapis] *uendit at: uenditat* Hertzberg.

III ix 25 Medorum *pugnaces ire per hostes*] Perhaps *pugna rescindere postes*.

III ix 33 and 34 should be placed after II i 38, as I have said.

III ix 49 and 51 should exchange places.

III x 23 tibia *nocturnis* succumbat rauca choreis] *continuis*.

III xi 13–16 should be placed after 20.

III xi 17 *Omphale* in tantum formae processit honorem] Perhaps *Maeonis*.

III xi 36 and 40 should exchange places as Lachmann bids them; then after 38 should be inserted II xvi 41 and 42: the passage should run thus: 'haec tibi, Pompei, detraxit harena triumphos: | *nulla Philippeost agmine* adusta nota. | issent Phlegraeo melius tibi funera campo; | *nec tua sic* socero colla daturus eras: | Caesaris haec uirtus et gloria Caesaris haec est, | illa, qua uicit, condidit arma manu.' *una Philippeo sanguine* and *uel tua si* MSS.

III xi 47–68 should be arranged thus: 51–8, 65–8, 59 and 60, 47–50. 67 and 68 were placed before 59 by Passerat.

III xi 55 and 56 should be written thus: '"non hoc, Roma, fui tanto tibi ciue uerenda" | *dixerat* assiduo lingua sepulta mero.' *dixit et* MSS.

III xi 70 *tantum* operis *belli* sustulit una dies] *tanti...bellum.*

III xii 25 castra decem annorum et Ciconum *mons* Ismara *calpe*] *mersa...clade* or *caede: domita...clade* Eldick.

III xiii 9 haec etiam *clausas* expugnant arma pudicas] *Euhadnas.*

III xiii 12. After this verse should perhaps be placed II xxxii 41 and 42, as I have said. ||

III xiii 19 and 20 should be written thus: 'et certamen habent, *letum* quae uiua sequatur | *coniugii*'. *leti...coniugium* MSS: editors put the comma after *leti.*

III xiii 35 hinulei pellis *totos* operibat amantes] Perhaps *lentos*: in 37 *laetas* should be read with F.

III xiii 39 corniger atque *dei* uacuam pastoris in aulam | dux aries saturas ipse reduxit oues] *die.*

III xiii 43–6 I fear have no business here.

III xiv 15 and 16 should be placed before 11; Scaliger placed them before 13.

III xvi 20 sanguine tam paruo quis enim spargatur amantis | improbus? *exclusis* fit comes ipsa Venus] *exsuctis.*

III xvi 21 quod si certa meos sequerentur funera *casus*] *cursus.*

III xvii 12 spesque timorque *animo* uersat utroque modo] *animae.*

III xvii 24 Pentheos in triplices funera *grata* greges] Perhaps *carpta.*

III xviii 10 errat et *in uestro* spiritus ille lacu] *inferno.*

III xviii 19 and 20 Attalicas supera uestes atque *omnia magnis* | gemmea sint *ludis*] ostra *ʒmaragdis...Indis.*

III xviii 21 sed *tamen* hoc omnes, huc primus et ultimus *ordo*] *manet...imus.*

III xviii 25. Before this verse should be placed II xxviii 57 and 58, as I have said.

III xviii 29 and 30 should be placed after IV vi 34.

III xviii 31–4 should be written thus: 'at tibi nauta, pias hominum qui traicit umbras, | *hac* animae portet corpus inane *uia*, | qua Siculae uictor telluris Claudius et qua | Caesar ab humana cessit in astra uice.' *huc...tuae* MSS.

III xix 25 and 26 should be placed after 28: thus *tamen* in 27 can be retained.

III xx 19–24 should be placed before 15: Lachmann placed 19 and 20 there.

III xx 25 qui *pactas in* foedera ruperit *aras*] Perhaps *tacta sic. . . ara.*

III xxii 3 Dindymis et sacra fabricata *iuuenta* Cybelle O, *inuenta* N] *in caute.* ||

III xxii 15 and 16 should be placed before 7 and written thus: '*siqua et olorigeri uisenda est ora Caystri | et quae* septenas temperat unda uias'. *et siqua* NF man. 2, *at siqua* O. *qua* NO.

III xxii 25 Albanus lacus et *socii* Nemorensis *ab unda* N, *sotii* F, *sotiis* DV] *foliis* Nemorensis *abundans.*

III xxii 41 hic tibi ad *eloquium* ciues] Perhaps *adloquium.*

III xxiii 14 an tu | non bona de nobis *crimina* ficta iacis] *carmina.*

III xxiii 17 and 18 should be punctuated thus: 'et quaecumque uolens reperit non stulta puella | garrula, cum blandis dicitur hora dolis'.

III xxiv 9 and 10 should be placed after 12 thus: 'haec ego non ferro, non igne coactus, et ipsa | naufragus Aegaea uerba fatebor aqua. | quod mihi non patrii poterant auertere amici | eluere aut uasto Thessala saga mari, | correptus saeuo Veneris torrebar aeno' eqs.

III xxiv 19 Mens Bona, siqua *deo* es, tua me in sacraria dono] *adeo.*

IV i 7 *Tarpeius. Tarpetius* N] *Tarpeiius.* So iv 1 1 should write *Tarpeiiae* for the *tarpeiie* of F, and iv 15 *Tarpeiia* for the *carpella* of the same MS.

IV i 19 annuaque accenso *celebrare* Palilia faeno FNV, *celebrate* D] *celebrante.*

IV i 28. After this verse should be inserted x 21 and 22; after 29 should be placed in reverse order x 19 and 20: the passage will run thus: 'nec rudis infestis miles radiabat in armis: | miscebant usta proelia nuda sude. | picta neque inducto fulgebat parma pyropo: | praebebant caesi baltea lenta boues. | prima galeritus posuit praetoria Lycmon, | *nec* galea hirsuta compta lupina iuba. | idem *equos* et frenis, idem fuit aptus aratris, | magnaque pars Tatio rerum erat inter oues.' *et* and *eques* MSS.

IV i 31–56. Out of these verses, 33–6 should be placed after x 26; the rest should be arranged thus: 37 and 38, 55 and 56 (so L. Lange), 31 and 32, 45 (write *hinc* with Heinsius) and 46, 39 and 40 (write *huc* with Messrs Baehrens and Palmer), 47–52, 41 (write *illos* with Schrader)–4, 53 and 54. ||

IV i 31 hinc Tities Ramnesque uiri Luceresque *coloni* O, *soloni* N] *seueri.*

IV i 50 *dixit Auentino rura pianda* Remo] Perhaps *dixerat a uentis non rapienda.*

IV i 57–70, when 65 and 66 have been removed and placed after I xxii 10, compose a prooemium to i (1–56), ii, iv, vi, ix, x, and should be arranged thus: 61–4, 57–60, 67–70.

IV i 81 eqs. should be written thus: 'nunc pretium fecere deos et *fallimus* auro | (Iuppiter!) obliquae signa iterata rotae | felicesque Iouis stellas' eqs. *fallitur* MSS.

IV i 85 and 86 should be placed after 108: 83–6 were placed there by Scaliger.

IV i 87 and 88 should with Scaliger be placed before 71: 88 should be written 'et maris et terrae *regna superba* canam'. *longa sepulcra* MSS.

IV i 120 incipe *tu lacrimis* aequs adesse nouis] *miraclis*.

IV i 124 et lacus aestiuis *intepet* Vmber aquis] *non tepet*.

IV i 143 and 144 should be placed before 141.

IV ii 2 accipe Vertumni *signa* paterna dei] *regna*.

IV ii 4. After this verse should be placed 49–56 in the following order: 51–4, 49–50, 55 and 56. There should be a comma at the end of 4, a full stop at the end of 52.

IV ii 12 Vertumni rursus *credidit* esse sacrum] *credis id*.

IV ii 35 *est etiam* aurigae species Vertumnus et eius eqs.] Perhaps *mentiar*.

IV ii 39 *pastorem ad baculum* possum *curare*] *da baculum, pastor me* possum *ornare. pastor me* Ayrmann.

IV iii 7–10 te modo *uiderunt iteratos* Bactra per *ortus*, | te modo munito Sericus hostis equo, | hibernique Getae pictoque *Britannia* curru, | *ustus* et Eoa decolor Indus aqua] *Ituraeos uiderunt. . .arcus. . .Hyrcania. . .tusus.*

IV iii 11 should be written thus: 'haecne marita fides *et [primae] praemia* noctis'. *hae sunt pactae mihi* DV, *et pacate mihi* F, [*et pactae mihi* O I fancy], *et parce auia* N, [*et prae mia* the archetype I fancy].

IV iii 29–62 should be arranged thus: 43–50 (so Mr Luetjohann), 29–32, 55 and 56, 33 and 34, 51 and 52, 35–42, 53 and 54, 59–62, 57 and 58. ||

IV iii 48 cum pater altas | *Africus* in glaciem frigore nectit aquas] *caelicus*.

IV iii 62 succinctique calent ad noua *lucra* popae] *lustra*.

IV iii 63 ne precor *ascensis* tanti sit gloria Bactris] *accensis*.

IV iv 17 and 18 should be placed after 86: Broukhusius placed them after 92.

IV iv 47 cras, ut rumor ait, tota *pugnabitur* urbe] *pigrabitur*.

IV iv 71 and 72 should be placed after viii 52.

IV iv 82 pacta ligat, *pactis* ipsa futura comes] *coeptis*.

IV iv 87 prodiderat portaeque fidem *patriam*que iacentem] Perhaps *patrem*.

IV v 19 and 20 should be written thus: '*exercebat* opus, uerbis *heu* blanda, *perinde* | saxosam *atque forat* sedula gutta uiam.' *exorabat. . .ceu. . .perure* MSS, *feratque* V, *que ferat* DFN, *forat* Messrs Rossberg and Palmer.

IV v 21 si te Eoa *derorantum* iuuat aurea ripa O, *doroʒantum* N] *topaʒorum*.

IV v 29–62 should seemingly be arranged thus: 59–62 (so Mr Luetjohann), 41–4, 47–58, 45 and 46, 31 and 32, 29 and 30, 33–6, 39 and 40, 37 and 38.

IV vi 26 armorum *et radiis picta* tremebat aqua ON, *que* for *et* V man. 2] *radiisque icta. icta* Heinsius.

IV vi 34. After this verse should be placed III xviii 19 and 20, as follows: 'non ille attulerat crines in colla solutos | aut testudineae carmen inerme lyrae, | sed quali aspexit Pelopeum Agamemnona uultu | egessitque auidis Dorica castra rogis | (hic olim ignaros luctus populauit Achiuos | Atridae magno cum stetit alter amor), | aut quali flexos soluit Pythona per orbes' eqs.

IV vi 45 and 46 should be placed after 52.

IV vi 49 *quod*que uehunt prorae Centaurica saxa minantis] Perhaps *quot*.

IV vi 81 siue *aliquis* pharetris Augustus parcet Eois] Perhaps *aequus*.

IV vii 4 *murmur ad extremae* nuper humata *uiae*] He should have written *Tibure ad extremam...uiam*.

IV vii 23 at mihi non oculos quisquam inclamauit *euntis*] *eunti*. ‖

IV vii 55–8 should be written thus: 'nam gemina est sedes turpem sortita*que ueram*, | *cumba*que diuersa remigat omnis aqua: | una Clytaemestrae stuprum uel adultera Cressam | portat mentitam lignea monstra bouis.' *per amnem turba* MSS.

IV vii 64 narrant historias, pectora *nota*, suas] *sancta*.

IV viii 1 disce quid Esquilias *hac nocte fugarit* aquosas] *nocte hac furiarit*.

IV viii 4 hic tibi tam *rarae* non perit hora morae] Perhaps *gratae*.

IV viii 9 and 10 should be placed after 12.

IV viii 39 should be written thus: '*unguentum*, tibicen erat, crotalistria, *phimus*'. *Nile tuus...phillis* MSS.

IV viii 52. After this verse should be placed iv 71 and 72 as follows: 'nec mora, cum totas resupinat Cynthia ualuas. | non operosa comis sed furibunda decens | illa ruit, qualis celerem prope Thermodonta | Strymonis abscisso pectus aperta sinu.'

IV ix 21 dixerat; *et* sicco torquet sitis ora palato] *at*.

IV ix 29 populus et *longis* ornabat frondibus aedem] *glaucis*.

IV ix 31 huc *ruit in siccam* congesta puluere *barbam*] Perhaps *in sicca ruit... labra*.

IV ix 60. Write 'haec lympha puellis, | auia secreti limitis *unda*, fluit'. *una* MSS.

IV ix 70 Hercule exterminium nescit inulta sitis] I had conjectured 'Herculea (extremum) nec sit inulta sitis'; but perhaps 'Herclei exterminium nec sit' is right.

IV x 19 and 20 should be placed after i 29, and 21 and 22 after i 28, as I have said.

IV x 23 and 24 should be placed as Passerat bids before 27; after 26 should be placed i 33–6 with Mr Lucian Mueller's transposition of 34 and 36: the passage should run thus: 'necdum ultra Tiberim belli sonus: ultima praeda | Nomentum et captae iugera terna Corae. | quippe suburbanae parua minus urbe Bouillae | ac tibi Fidenas longa erat ire uia; | et stetit Alba potens, albae suis omine nata, | et, qui nunc nulli, maxima turba Gabi. | Cossus at insequitur' eqs.

IV x 37 *di Latias* iuuere manus. *Romuleas* F, and D in marg.] *di Remulas*. ‖

IV xi.   The verses of this elegy should be arranged thus: 1–18, 47–54 (in 49 write *umbra* with Eldick), 19 (retain *aut*)–32, 43 and 44, 33–6, 45 and 46, 37–42, 55–62, 97 and 98, 65 and 66, 99 and 100, 69 and 70, 73 and 74, 63 (retain *te...te*) and 64, 75–96, 67 and 68, 71 and 72 (write *torum* with Schrader), 101 and 102. Mr Baehrens has placed 71 and 72 after 68.

IV xi 15 damnatae *noctes* et uos uada lenta paludes | et quaecumque meos implicat unda pedes] *testes.*

IV xi 40 quique tuas *proauo* fregit Achille domos O, *proauus* V man. 2] 'quique tuas proauus fregit, Auerne, domos' Munro: write *proauos.*

IV xi 50 turpior *assensu* non erit ulla meo] *accensu.*

IV xi 87 coniugium, pueri, *laudate* et ferte paternum] *durate.*

I hope I have managed to keep my neighbour's goods out of this catalogue, but I dare hardly expect it: at the very last moment I have cancelled an amendment of II xxxii 23 which I find was made forty years ago by Schneidewin and has been neglected by everyone since. To anyone who will enable me to restore misappropriated discoveries to their rightful owner I shall be honestly indebted. I now go on as I promised to comment on the text of the first elegy.

> Cynthia prima suis miserum me cepit ocellis
>   contactum nullis ante cupidinibus.
> tum mihi constantis deiecit lumina fastus
>   et caput inpositis pressit Amor pedibus,
> 5   donec me docuit castas odisse puellas
>   improbus et nullo uiuere consilio.
> et mihi iam toto furor hic non deficit anno,
>   cum tamen aduersos cogor habere deos.
> Milanion nullos fugiendo, Tulle, labores
> 10   saeuitiam durae contudit Iasidos.
> nam modo Partheniis amens errabat in antris
>   ibat et hirsutas ille uidere feras;
> ille etiam psilli percussus uulnere rami
>   saucius Arcadiis rupibus ingemuit. ||
> 15   ergo uelocem potuit domuisse puellam:
>   tantum in amore preces et bene facta ualent.
> in me tardus Amor non ullas cogitat artes
>   nec meminit notas, ut prius, ire uias.
> at uos, deductae quibus est fallacia lunae
> 20   et labor in magicis sacra piare focis,
> en age dum dominae mentem conuertite nostrae
>   et facite illa meo palleat ore magis.
> tunc ego crediderim uobis et sidera et amnes
>   posse cytalinis ducere carminibus.
> 25   et uos, qui sero lapsum reuocatis, amici,
>   quaerite non sani pectoris auxilia.
> fortiter et ferrum saeuos patiemur et ignes,
>   sit modo libertas, quae uelit ira, loqui.

> ferte per extremas gentes et ferte per undas,
>   qua non ulla meum femina norit iter.   30
> uos remanete, quibus facili deus annuit aure,
>   sitis et in tuto semper amore pares:
> in me nostra Venus noctes exercet amaras
>   et nullo uacuus tempore defit Amor.
> hoc, moneo, uitate malum: sua quemque moretur   35
>   cura neque assueto mutet amore locum.
> quod si quis monitis tardas aduerterit aures
>   heu referet quanto uerba dolore mea.

3. Among all the four thousand verses of the poet there is not a sounder or simpler than this. Not only are such locutions as 'deiecit lumina' for 'effecit ut lumina deicerem' frequent in both tongues – see for example Hor. epist. 1 5 22 'ne sordida mappa conruget naris' and Eur. Hel. 1122 πολλοὶ δ' Ἀχαιῶν... Ἄιδαν μέλεον ἔχουσιν, τάλαιναν ὧν ἀλόχων κείραντες ἔθειραν – but the very words of Propertius are closely imitated in Ouid. her. xi 35 'erubui gremioque pudor deiecit ocellos'. Again, inasmuch as 'lumina fastus' is not Latin, the genitive here is of course the genetiuus qualitatis cum epitheto: 'constantis lumina fastus' = 'constanter fastosa' just as Hor. carm. iii 7 4 'constantis iuuenem fide' = 'constanter fidelem'. Why then Fonteine should write in his margin 'tum me constantis deiecit ‖ culmine fastus', why Burmann should propose 'tum mihi constanti deiecit lumina fastu', why Mr Paley should say 'the expression is a remarkable one', why both he and Mr Palmer should repeat Burmann's conjecture a hundred years later, why Hertzberg should be driven to Tartara leti and Mr Postgate to Roby 1304, I am unable to discern.

5. Fonteine does not himself say why he desires 'cunctas' for 'castas', but Mr Baehrens prolegg. p. xlvii gives his own reasons for adopting the conjecture: these I will examine. In ii 3 1 an imaginary censor is made to address Propertius thus: 'qui nullam tibi dicebas iam posse nocere, | haesisti: cecidit spiritus ille tuus': these words, says Mr Baehrens, evidently refer to some passage in book i. But where in book i can this boast be found? nowhere: it must therefore be imported. This Mr Baehrens thinks he can do by writing here 'me docuit cunctas odisse puellas'. He states his reason, of which more anon, for deeming 'castas' corrupt, and proceeds 'immo omnes omnino feminas propter unius duritiem Propertium tum odisse innuere uidetur u. 30 (ferte per extremas gentes et ferte per undas, *qua non ulla meum femina norit iter*).' Now the phrase 'cunctas odisse puellas' can mean either of two things: it can mean either to dislike women because you are indifferent to them, or to dread them because you are too susceptible: either of these two things, I say, it can mean, but it cannot mean both at once. In the latter of the two senses it will be appropriate enough to this elegy

into which Mr Baehrens wants to bring it; but of course it will then be of no
service whatever to Mr Baehrens as an equivalent for the 'nulla mihi iam potest
nocere' of II 3 I. In the former of the two senses it will tally precisely with
'nulla mihi iam potest nocere'; but then it can by no possibility have a place in
this elegy. This elegy is written by a man desperately in love: first he invokes
magicians to turn his mistress's heart and colour her face paler *than his own*;
failing that, he invokes his friends to cure him of his slavish attachment by
surgery and cautery: 'nullo uacuus tempore defit Amor' he says; and we are
asked to believe that he said in the same poem 'nulla mihi iam potest nocere'!
That very verse 30 to which Mr ‖ Baehrens appeals is his confutation: why must
the poet be fleeing to the ends of the earth 'qua non ulla meum femina norit
iter'? quia omnes feminae nocent. I may add that the Pompeian inscription
C. I. L. IV 1520 'candida me docuit nigras odisse puellas' affords an indication, slight indeed, but still an indication, that the adjective here was at any rate
not 'cunctas' but a descriptive epithet such as both 'nigras' and 'castas' are.

It remains to consider whether Mr Baehrens' objection to 'castas' is better
supported than his advocacy of 'cunctas'. He writes 'uulgares meretrices qui
sectabatur, is sine iusta causa querebatur de tristi Venere noctes in se exercente
amaras (u. 33)'. Lachmann will answer him better than I: praef. p. XXIV 'tu ne
dubita quin poeta se, Cynthia et castis puellis relictis (hoc erat illud: *peccaram
semel et totum sum pulsus in annum*), iam per totum annum uiles quaerere et sine
consilio queratur uiuere, aduersa tamen Venere et Cynthiae desertae memoria
animum assidue subeunte. hunc uerum sensum esse certius fit ex his eiusdem
carminis uersibus: *hoc, moneo, uitate malum. sua quemque moretur cura, neque
assueto mutet amore locum.*' A very little consideration would have been enough
to convince a scholar of Mr Baehrens' acumen that 'castas' was unimpeachably
right and 'cunctas' the idlest of guesses.

11. But if critics have shewn morbid alertness above, they are cast into a deep
sleep when they come to this verse. If a poet in the year 26 B.C. or thereabouts
writes 'Milanion was *lately* roaming in the dells of Arcadia', he writes nonsense;
yet no other meaning does the Latin tongue permit these words to bear. For if
modo is to mean ἐνίοτε μέν it must be answered by an ἐνίοτε δέ in the shape of
a second *modo* or of some other competent adverb such as *nunc, rursus, interdum,
saepe, aliquando, non numquam*; and of course *etiam* in 13 is not a competent
adverb. If rules like this, built up by wide and orderly induction, are to be over-
thrown at the bidding of fourteenth century MSS, goodnight to grammatical
science. The MSS of Propertius exhibit the solecism four times in all, dutifully
followed in every instance by all modern editors but ‖ Mr Baehrens, and by
Mr Baehrens in two instances. The verses II 24 9 sqq. run thus: 'quare ne tibi
sit mirum me quaerere uiles: | parcius infamant: num tibi causa leuis? | et *modo*
pauonis caudae flabella superbae | et manibus dura frigus habere pila | et cupit

iratum talos me poscere eburnos | quaeque nitent Sacra uilia dona Via. | a peream si me ista mouent dispendia' eqs. Here, setting grammar aside, it is manifest and was remarked by Scaliger that 11 sqq. have not the remotest connexion in theme with the preceding verses: 11–16 are a fragment truncated of its head and inserted in a wrong place. Mr Baehrens therefore rightly marks a lacuna: his fellows print the lines as if they were coherent and grammatical. Mr Baehrens again is the only modern editor whose text of 1 11 1–5 is Latin or sense: this is the vulgate: 'ecquid te mediis cessantem, Cynthia, Bais, | qua iacet Herculeis semita litoribus, | et *modo* Thesproti mirantem subdita regno | proxima Misenis aequora nobilibus, | nostri cura subit memores a ducere noctes?' This was corrected long ago by the Italians of the renascence and again by Scaliger: Propertius wrote in 4 'et modo Misenis aequora nobilibus': 'proxima' is the interpolation of a scribe who not perceiving that 'subdita' was to be repeated from the hexameter imagined 'Misenis' to be without construction. Mr Baehrens most justly points out that the corruption has robbed 'mediis Bais' (= mediis inter aequora Thesproti regno subdita et aequora Misenis subdita) of its meaning, and, he adds, 'effecit ut plane singulariter ei quod legitur u. 3 *et modo* desit cui respondeat'; but alas, we have already seen that the phenomenon is not unique even in Mr Baehrens' text. In III 14 9 sqq. the MSS order the verses thus: 'nunc ligat ad caestum gaudentia bracchia loris, | missile nunc disci pondus in orbe rotat; | gyrum pulsat equis, niueum latus ense reuincit | uirgineumque cauo protegit aere caput, | qualis Amazonidum nudatis bellica mammis | Thermodontiacis turba lauantur aquis, | et *modo* Taygeti, crines aspersa pruina, | sectatur patrios per iuga longa canes; | qualis et Eurotae Pollux et Castor harenis.' That 15 and 16 'et modo...canes' are out of their place is evident from the manifest continuity of 17 and 18 with 13 and 14; hence Scaliger followed by ‖ Mr Baehrens places 15 and 16 after 12. But there too they separate lines which unmistakeably cohere (latus ense reuincit protegitque aere caput qualis Amazonidum turba, quae in Thermodonte lauatur);[1] and *modo* remains solecistic. The right place for 15 and 16 is after 10: 'missile *nunc* disci pondus in orbe rotat, | et *modo* Taygeti' eqs.

To return to our starting point: not only does syntax unveil a fraud, but I find too an external token that the MSS are cheating us. The verses 9–16 are closely imitated by Ovid, ars am. II 185–92.

> quid fuit asperius Nonacrina Atalanta?   185
> subcubuit meritis trux tamen illa uiri.
> saepe suos casus nec mitia facta puellae
> flesse sub arboribus Milaniona ferunt.

---

[1] So, for example, Hor. epist. 1 16 12 'fons etiam riuo dare nomen idoneus, ut nec frigidior Thracam nec purior ambiat Hebrus' = 'ut nec frigidior nec purior sit Hebrus, qui Thracam ambit'.

saepe tulit iusso fallacia retia collo,
190   saepe fera toruos cuspide fixit apros.
sensit et Hylaei contentum saucius arcum;
sed tamen hoc arcu notior alter erat.

Now here 187–90 cover the same ground as 11 and 12 in Propertius: 11 in Propertius has the same theme as 187 and 188 in Ovid, the disconsolate wandering of the ill-used lover (see too ars am. 1 731 'pallidus in Dirces siluis errabat Orion'); 12 in Propertius has the same theme as 189 and 190 in Ovid, the hard work of the chase at Atalanta's side. But in Ovid the two things are duly discriminated as happening one at one time, the other at another: to read Propertius you would fancy both happened at once. To be brief, with Ovid and Latin grammar for guides I infer that two verses have been lost between 11 and 12; lost through the recurrence of 'modo' in the same part of each hexameter. I have manufactured these stopgaps:

nam modo Partheniis amens errabat in antris
multaque desertis fleuerat arboribus, ||
et modo submissa casses ceruice ferebat
ibat et hirsutas eqs.

12. The task of essaying to shew that 'uidere feras' has any meaning suitable to this place is undertaken by Markland and Lachmann: truly 'si Pergama dextris defendi possent, etiam his defensa fuissent'. They cite many passages and might have cited more to prove that 'uidere' can be used in the sense of 'adire' or 'experiri': yes, so it can, but with this marked limitation, that the substantive which is its object must signify either a *place* or a *condition.* Thus on the one hand you have *uidere turbatum nemus, Tartara, uasto sub antro Scyllam, ignota flumina, alium Phasin, insanum forum*; on the other *uidere mortem, casus marinos, tanta mala, nihil infesti, alios menses, alium annum, altricemque niuem festinaque taedia uitae*: thus Propertius might have said *lustra uidere ferarum* had he so chosen, but say *uidere feras* for *encounter wild beasts* he could not. To this conviction Heinsius, Burmann and Mr Baehrens have borne witness by their conjectures; and in the fulness of time the verse has been most acutely corrected by Mr Palmer:

ibat et hirsutas *comminus* ille feras.

This phrase is copied word for word by Ovid fast. v 176 'in apros | audet et hirsutas comminus ire feras', and its sound he again echoes ex Pont. 1 5 74 'aspicit hirsutos comminus Vrsa Getas'; Propertius repeats the construction II 19 22 'aut celer agrestes comminus ire sues' though III 1 26 he writes 'fluminaque Haemonio comminus isse uiro'. But how got 'comminus ille' changed to 'ille uidere'? In this way. But for the position of the single letter s there is virtually no difference between *comminus* and *conuisum*: now this transportation of a letter to some distance is a common freak in MSS much older and better than ours: Verg. Aen. IV 564 uario*s* MP *s*uario F, georg. IV 71 a*e*ris M *a*ries P; and in ours too: 1 6 34 accepti par*s* ON accepti*s* par Prop., II 3 18 A*d*riana ON Aria*d*na Prop., 29 36 uolu*n*tatis FN uolu*t*antis Prop., III 13 31 uetu*s*tas F ue*s*titas DVN, IV 11 53 cui*u*s rasos O cui s̅r̅a su*o*s (sacra) Prop. The scribe then who found himself confronted ‖ with the unmetrical verse 'ibat et hirsutas conuisum ille feras' preserved the sense, such as it was, of 'ibat conuisum feras' and mended the metre by writing 'ille uidere'.

13. Volscus amended 'psilli' to 'Hylaei' by the light of Ovid's imitation quoted above 'sensit et Hylaei contentum saucius arcum'; Aelian too and Apollodorus agree that Atalanta was assaulted by Hylaeus. Some have been dissatisfied with this as straying too far from the MSS, and Hertzberg has proposed 'ille et Phyllei'; but *Phyllei rami* might be the club of a shepherd, a satyr, a river god or Pan himself as well as a centaur, with nothing in the context to point the allusion. I explain the corruption as follows: *Hylaei*, written *ilei*, was changed to *illi*: now the confusion of *ille* with *ipse* is perpetual, as II 4 17 (27) *ille* NV *ipse* DF, III 21 6 *ille* DV *ipse* FN, II 28 26 *illa* ON where *ipsa* must in my opinion be read (ipsa sepultura facta beata tua): I imagine then that *illi* stood here in some ancestor of our MSS, that a reader emended it from another MS thus *illi̇*̇ (*ps* written above), and that the next copyist misunderstanding the correction inserted the letters *ps* in a wrong place and gave us *psilli*.

VN uulnere, AF arbore. Lachmann has shewn that 'percussus uulnere rami' is irreproachable Latin; but that is not enough: the 'arbore' of half the MSS has to be accounted for: till that is done, nothing is done. This end is admirably achieved by Mr Baehrens' correction 'uerbere', which would be corrupted with about equal ease into 'arbore' and into 'uolnere': in Ouid. met. IV 727 the MSS vary between 'uulnerat' and 'uerberat'. The phrase 'percussus uerbere' will be illustrated by Ouid. met. XIV 300 '*percutimurque* caput conuersae *uerbere* uirgae' and Iuuen. XV 21 'tenui *percussum uerbere* Circes'.

16. *Such is the efficacy in love of prayers and service rendered.* Prayers! where has he said a word about prayers? They are not in the received text, there is no room for them in the lacuna which I have detected, there is no trace of them in Ovid's paraphrase. Those who to defend the credit of a scribe will impute any imbecility to a poet are, I suppose, capable of maintaining that Propertius here forgot what he had just said and imagined he had said something else. But even this loophole ‖ is blocked by the careful and orderly planning of the entire passage: Propertius says (9–10) that Milanion won Atalanta *nullos fugiendo labores*; then in 11 with the explanatory *nam* he proceeds to say what these *labores* were, namely (11) patient endurance of her cruelty, assistance (12) in

the hunting field, hard knocks (13–14) encountered in her defence; *therefore* (15) he won her; *such* (16) is the efficacy of... and deeds of merit. If the poet put *preces* in that gap, well might he cry to his friends 'quaerite non sani pectoris auxilia': the *ergo* of 15, the *tantum* of 16 pointedly invite attention to what has preceded, and there has preceded not a word, not a hint of *preces*. And yet this flagrant discrepancy has run the gauntlet of Scaliger, Heinsius, Hemsterhuys, Markland, Schrader and Lachmann, half a dozen of the greatest names in criticism, and has only been detected by the vigilance of Fonteine. Fonteine's conjectures are now first given to the world in Mr Baehrens' edition: many of them of course are the mere guesses which we all jot down in our margins simply to help us take up the thread of thought to-morrow where we drop it to-day, and although Mr Baehrens does well to print them entire, still most of them are necessarily worthless; but the residue betoken one of the most acute intellects that have ever been bent on the study of Propertius. Fonteine then proposed instead of 'preces' to read 'fides', a word most appropriate in itself and strongly confirmed by II 26 27 'multum in amore *fides*, multum constantia prodest: | qui durare potest multa, et amare potest', where the pentameter too recalls the 'nullos fugiendo labores' of our elegy. But, it may be said, the change is violent. No, that is not so: the same confusion recurs in Tibull. [Lygd.] III 4 64 'tu modo cum multa bracchia tende *prece*' G '*fide*' AV, 6 46 'aut fallat blanda subdola lingua *prece*' G excerpt. Paris. '*fide*' AV. Then turn to Hor. ars poet. 395 'dictus et Amphion, Thebanae conditor urbis, | saxa mouere sono testudinis et *prece* blanda | ducere quo uellet': even if you do not feel that 'prece' is a trifle ludicrous, still you will confess it is unique: neither Amphion nor Orpheus is elsewhere depicted as beseeching stocks and stones to follow him: the dead things are brought by the mere charm of song. Having regard then to carm. I 12 11 '*blandum* et || auritas *fidibus* canoris | ducere quercus' and 24 13 'quid si Threicio *blandius* Orpheo | auditam moderere arboribus *fidem*' I follow Peerlkamp when he reads '*fide* blanda'.

19. I conceive that so far as Latinity is concerned the words 'deductae fallacia lunae' may bear any one of three meanings. First, they may mean *false pretence of bringing down the moon*: a sense peremptorily forbidden by the context. Mr Lucian Mueller points out that Propertius cannot look for help to those whom he holds and asserts to be impostors, and that this argument is clinched by the 'tunc ego crediderim' of 23: Propertius now doubts whether the power of magic be real or no, but turn Cynthia's heart and he will believe. Secondly then, 'deductae fallacia lunae' may legitimately mean *deceiving men by bringing down the moon* on the analogy of Ouid. met. XIII 164 'deceperat omnes, | in quibus Aiacem, *sumptae fallacia uestis*'. But plainly this sense is no better than nonsense: if magicians bring down the moon as men believe them to do, then men are not deceived. Equally absurd is the third possible sense of the words

deceiving the moon and bringing her down. I know that 'Pan deus Arcadiae captam te, Luna, fefellit in nemora alta uocans', but in what sense do magicians *fallere lunam?* what conceivable *deceit* can they employ? manufacture a 'cerea effigies' of Endymion I suppose and lay it out on mountain-tops. The truth is that those who read and fancy they understand this passage translate 'deductae quibus est fallacia lunae' as Mr Postgate does, 'who *bewitch* the moon into coming down'. But the words cannot bear that meaning. Bewitchment comprises several departments, and of these departments *fallacia* is one: Prop. IV 5 14 'sua nocturno *fallere* terga lupo', Ouid. met. III 1 'iamque deus posita *fallacis* imagine tauri | se confessus erat', Verg. Aen. I 683 'tu faciem illius noctem non amplius unam | *falle* dolo et notos pueri puer indue uoltus', georg. IV 441 'omnia transformat sese in miracula rerum, | ignemque horribilemque feram fluuiumque liquentem. | uerum ubi nulla fugam reperit *fallacia*, uictus | in sese redit': there you have bewitchment which is *fallacia*. But it does not follow that you can use *fallacia* in season and out of season as an equivalent for bewitchment. To lure the moon from heaven, ghosts from the || grave, the standing corn from a neighbour's field, is not *fallacia* but, as L. Fruterius and J. M. Palmerius 300 years ago perceived, *pellacia*. Seruius on Verg. buc. VIII 99 quotes from the twelve tables 'neue alienam segetem *pellexeris*', Pliny hist. nat. XVIII 6 8 §41 has 'ceu fruges alienas *pelliceret* ueneficiis'. Now to shew the facility of the corruption: Verg. Aen. II 90 *pellacis* M, Velius Longus, Donatus, Seruius, *fallacis* P, Charisius; georg. IV 443 *fallacia* PRV, *phallacia* M, *pellacia b* (cod. Bern. saec. IX), '*fallacia*, legitur et *pellacia*' Philargyrus. Munro on Lucr. II 559 'placidi pellacia ponti' says 'Virgil has the adj. *pellax*: these two appear to be the only good writers who use the words': yes, but it is appearance only: if the MSS of Horace were as trusty in such matters, or the MSS of Propertius in any matters, as the MSS of Virgil and Lucretius, it would be another story. Horace in carm. III 7 professes to tell Asterie news of her absent Gyges: he lies awake all night weeping for her; and yet his hostess Chloe is in love with him and her minister tempts him by recounting her sighs, tells him what peril Bellerophon and Peleus incurred through continence, 'et (19) peccare docentis | *fallax* historias monet'. Now *fallere* can indeed signify seduction followed by desertion, but it is of course always the woman who in this sense *fallitur*, not the man: the reverse is absolutely meaningless in Greece, Rome or England. In these lines of Horace *fallax* can have but one meaning: it must mean that the 'nuntius' intends 'mentiri noctem, promissis ducere amantem', thus flatly disobeying the 'sollicita hospita' who sent him on his errand, and giving Gyges no chance to put his 'constans fides' to the proof: the whole poem is stultified. Write *pellax* with Bentley and all is straightforward. Finally in Prop. IV 1 135 we read 'at tu finge elegos, *fallax* opus, haec tua castra, | scribat ut exemplo cetera turba tuo': well, it is true that 'docere qua nuptae possint fallere ab arte uiros' is part of the office of elegy, but who could catch the allusion here with nothing to point it? the phrase would more naturally mean 'a slippery task'; a sense which is most inappropriate. The pentameter speaks loud for Heinsius' *pellax*, 'a fascinating, alluring task'; and it seems to me that Ovid with his 'imbelles elegi, genialis musa' imitates 'elegos, pellax opus'. To return then to the || first elegy, I can feel not the slightest doubt that 'deductae pellacia lunae' is what Propertius wrote. The construction of the sentence, I should add, is rightly explained by Mr F. Leo in vol. 35 of the *Rheinisches Museum* as 'uos quibus labor est deductae fallacia [pellacia] lunae et alter labor sacra piare'.

But what is 'sacra piare'? Hemsterhuys tells us '*sacra piare* usu uetusto nihil aliud quam sacra pie sollemnique ritu facere'. But Mr Lucian Mueller and others have rightly observed that 'sacra piare' in this sense is no peculiar office of magicians but common to all sacerdotes and indeed to the head of every Roman household. The mention is demanded of some magic portent answering the 'pellacia lunae' of the preceding verse. What this portent should be we shall be better able to judge when we have discussed verses 23 and 24.

Sidera et amnes ducere carminibus. Scores of times, when the ancients tell us of the wonders wrought by magic or by music, do they employ the verb *ducere*, its compounds and its synonyms; scores of times do they employ the substantive *amnes* and the other substantives which mean streams and rivers: never, save in this single place, do they employ the phrase *amnes ducere*. Here are the dealings of magic with rivers: Verg. Aen. IV 489 'haec se carminibus promittit. . . sistere aquam fluuiis', Tibull. I 2 46 'fluminis haec rapidi carmine uertit iter', Ouid. am. I 8 5 'illa magas artes Aeaeaque carmina nouit | inque caput liquidas arte recuruat aquas', II 1 25 'carmine dissiliunt abruptis faucibus angues | inque suos fontes uersa recurrit aqua', her. VI 87 'illa refrenat aquas obliquaque flumina sistit', met. VII 153 'uerbaque ter dixit. . . quae concita flumina sistunt', 198 'adeste | quorum ope, cum uolui, ripis mirantibus amnes | in fontes rediere suos', remed. amor. 257 (he disclaims magic) 'ut solet, aequoreas ibit Tiberinus in undas', Petron. 134 ⟦12⟧ 'his ego callens | artibus Idaeos frutices in gurgite sistam | et rursus fluuios in summo uertice ponam', Sen. Med. 760 'cantu meo. . . uiolenta Phasis uertit in fontem uada | et Hister in tot ora diuisus truces | compressit undas omnibus ripis piger', Luc. Phars. VI 472 'de rupe pependit | abscissa fixus torrens, amnisque cucurrit | non qua pronus erat', Sil. Punic. VIII 500 'Aeetae prolem. . . stridoribus amnes | || frenantem', Val. Fl. Arg. VI 443 'mutat agros fluuiumque uias', Claud. in Rufin. I 159 'uersaque non prono curuaui flumina lapsu | in fontes reditura suos', Appul. met. I 3 'magico susurramine amnes agiles reuerti', 8 'saga, inquit, et diuina, potens. . . fontes durare, montes diluere', Apoll. Rhod. Arg. III 532 καὶ ποταμοὺς ἵστησιν ἄφαρ κελαδεινὰ ῥέοντας. Here are the dealings of music with rivers: Verg. buc. VIII 4 'quorum stupefactae carmine lynces | et mutata suos requierunt flumina cursus', Hor.

carm. I 12 9 'arte materna rapidos morantem | fluminum lapsus', Prop. III 2 3
'Orphea delenisse feras et concita dicunt | flumina Threicia sustinuisse lyra',
Ouid. fast. II 84 'quae nescit Ariona tellus? | carmine currentes ille tenebat
aquas', met. XIV 339 'et mulcere feras et flumina longa morari | ore suo uolu-
cresque uagas retinere solebat', Calpurn. II 15 'affuerunt sicco Dryades pede,
Naides udo, | et tenuere suos properantia flumina cursus.' Thus *amnes sistere*,
amnes uertere, come over and over again: *amnes ducere* never. Now this cannot
be accident, for *lunam ducere, sidera, segetes, umbras, saxa, quercus ducere*, are for
ever recurring: what then is the reason? The reason is the simplest in the world.
Music and magic work miracles, invert the order of nature: thus Lucan Phars.
VI 437 'Haemonidum. . . quarum, *quidquid non creditur*, ars est': this he proceeds
to illustrate, 'calido producunt nubila Phoebo | et tonat ignaro caelum Ioue',
'uentis cessantibus aequor | intumuit: rursus uetitum sentire procellas | conticuit
turbante noto, puppimque ferentes | in uentum tumuere sinus', 'Nilum non
extulit aestas, | Maeander derexit aquas, Rhodanumque morantem | praecipitauit
Arar. submisso uertice montes | explicuere iugum: nubes suspexit Olympus. |
solibus et nullis Scythicae, cum bruma rigeret, | dimaduere niues'; so Appuleius
l. l. ascribes to his witch the power 'caelum deponere, terram suspendere,
fontes durare, montes diluere, manes sublimare, deos infimare, sidera extinguere,
Tartarum ipsum illuminare'. Such miracles, such inversions of nature, *amnes
sistere* and *amnes uertere* are; but *amnes ducere* is nothing of the sort: it is one of
the commonest operations of Italian agriculture: Virgil's graceful picture of the
process is familiar to everyone. A man would no more dream of invoking
incantations to *amnes ‖ ducere* than to shave his chin or cook his dinner; and when
this every-day work of the farmer is coupled with the 'sidera ducere' of the
magician, the absurdity is doubled. There are those who, if we had 'amnes et
sidera ducere', would take sanctuary at the shrine of Zeugma and pretend that
'sistere' or 'uertere' might be mentally supplied to 'amnes'; but as ill luck will
have it the order of the words is 'sidera et amnes ducere' and retreat in that
direction is cut off. Propertius then did not write what the MSS give: what did
he write? No feat of magic is more renowned than the evocation of departed
spirits: Lucan in Phars. VI, Statius in Theb. IV, Silius in Punic. XIII raise the
dead to life till they tire the reader to death, and Valerius Flaccus has a brief
episode of the sort at the end of Arg. I: pages might be filled with allusions
scattered throughout the poets, but I here content myself with passages where
the power of magic over the dead is coupled with its power over the heavenly
bodies. Such are Verg. Aen. IV 489 'haec se carminibus promittit. . . uertere
sidera retro, | nocturnosque mouet *manis*', Hor. epod. 17 78 'polo | deripere
lunam uocibus possim meis, | possim crematos excitare *mortuos*', Tibull. I 2 45
'hanc ego de caelo ducentem *sidera* uidi, | fluminis haec rapidi carmine uertit
iter, | haec cantu finditque solum *manes*que sepulcris | elicit et tepido deuocat

ossa rogo. | iam tenet *infernas* magico stridore *cateruas*, | iam iubet aspersas lacte referre pedem', Ouid. am. 1 8 11 'sanguine, siqua fides, stillantia *sidera* uidi, | purpureus *lunae* sanguine uultus erat. . .17 euocat antiquis *proauos atauosque* sepulchris | et solidam longo carmine findit humum', met. VII 205 'iubeoque tremescere montes | et mugire solum *manes*que exire sepulcris; | te quoque, *Luna,* traho', remed. amor. 253 'me duce non tumulo prodire iubebitur *umbra,* | non anus infami carmine rumpet humum, | non seges ex aliis alios transibit in agros | nec subito *Phoebi* pallidus orbis erit. | ut solet, aequoreas ibit Tiberinus in undas, | ut solet, in niueis *luna* uehetur equis', Sen. Herc. Oet. 460 'mea iussi prece | *manes* loquuntur. . .468 carmine in terras mago | descendat astris *luna* desertis licet', Val. Fl. Arg. VI 447 'quamuis Atracio *lunam* spumare ueneno | sciret et Haemoniis agitari cantibus *umbras*', Claud. in Rufin. 1 146 'noui, quo || Thessala cantu | eripiat *lunare iubar.* . .154 saepius horrendos *manes* sacrisque citaui | nocturnis Hecaten, et condita *funera* traxi | carminibus uictura meis.' To these passages I should add

> tunc ego crediderim et manes et sidera uobis
> posse Cytinaeis ducere carminibus.

Verg. Aen. IV 34 *manis* GMPR *amnis* F, 490 *manis* MP *amnis* F, II 296 *manibus* FMP *amnibus* V: in our MSS too this inversion of two consecutive letters is frequent: 1 3 27 *duxit* ON for *duxti*, 14 24 *alcioni* D for *Alcinoi*, II 6 6 *Phyrne* DVN for *Phryne*, 8 39 *marte* ON for *matre*, 13 55 *paludibus* DVN *plaudibus* F, 28 29 *herodias* DV for *heroidas*, III 5 35 *palustra* F for *plaustra*, 7 61 *alcinoum* F *alcionum* DV, 13 24 *ipa* F for *pia*, 55 *et* ON for *te*, 15 41 *parta* for *prata*, IV 5 74 *caltra* for *clatra*. When the unmetrical 'crediderim et amnes et sidera uobis' was thus produced, there was nothing for it but to arrange the words as they stand in the MSS to-day: similar transpositions for metre's sake will be found at II 9 18, 10 2, 13 38, 23 1, IV 2 39, 3 7, 8 1.

In 24 the good MSS have *Cytalinis, Citalinis, Cythalinis, Cithalinis,* which all come to the same thing and have all alike no meaning; the bad MSS have the impossible forms *Cytaeinis* or *Cytainis*: scholars have conjectured *Cytaei tuis, Cytaeaeis, Cytaines, Cytaiacis.* But the correction which is at once nearest to the MSS and most appropriate in sense is Hertzberg's *Cytinaeis.* Hertzberg, whose confidence in his own conjectures usually bears an inverse proportion to their value, did not place it in his text; and it seems thus to have escaped subsequent editors, until Mr Postgate, who again at 1 16 13 has recalled an excellent but neglected emendation of Scaliger's, has most properly accepted it. I say 'CytIN-AEis' is nearer to 'CytAL-INis' than are any of the other conjectures, because this permutation of syllables is one of the commonest phenomena: the first instances which occur to me are Verg. Aen. XI 711 *rapu* M for *pura* and Hor. carm. 1 36 17 *trespu* δ for *putres*: so in Prop. 1 2 13 I write *su-per-a-nt-de-picta* for *per-su-a-de-nt-picta*: but I will now cite only examples where this change is accompanied by the change of one letter, as here of E into L: II 32 17 ‖ fall*er*is ON for fall*i*s *et*, 34 53 resta*bit* er*ū*pnas F resta*uerit* undas DV, III 5 24 spars*it et* F spars*erit* DV, 23 21 retul*it et* F rettul*erit* DVN, IV I 106 umbra*que ne* O for umbra*ue quae*. As to the word, Hertzberg cites Lycophr. 1389 Λακμώνιοί τε καὶ Κυτιναῖοι, Κόδροι and Steph. Byz. Κύτινα· πόλις Θεσσαλίας, ὡς Θέων ἐν ὑπομνήμασι Λυκόφρονος· ὁ πολίτης Κυτιναῖος: now in the palinode to this elegy III 24 9 and 10 you have 'quod mihi non patrii poterant auertere amici | eluere aut uasto *Thessala* saga mari'. And this emendation will at once confirm my correction of the hexameter and derive confirmation thence. Necromancy, above all other forms of magic, was Thessalian: see Stat. Theb. III 141 'Thessalis... cui *gentile nefas* hominem reuocare canendo' and 559 where '*Thessalicum nefas*' stands κατ' ἐξοχήν for necromancy.

So we have settled the reading of 23 and 24: now we are better equipped for discussing 'sacra piare' in 20. Just as 'deductae pellacia lunae' tallies with 'sidera ducere' so we shall expect 'sacra piare' to tally with 'manes ducere'. This expectation will be strengthened if we observe how frequently *piare* is used with *manes* or the like: IV 7 34 'fracto busta piare cado', Verg. Aen. VI 379 'ossa piabunt', Ouid. fast. V 426 'compositique nepos busta piabat aui', met. VI 569 'piacula manibus infert', XIII 515 'hostilia busta piasti', Cic. in Pison. 16 'a me quidem etiam poenas expetistis, quibus coniuratorum manes mortuorum expiaretis': in Petron. 137 [[6]] Burmann perhaps rightly reads 'expiare manes pretio licet' for 'manus'. That *manes piare* would be a natural accompaniment of *manes ducere* is shewn by Cic. in Vatin. 14 'cum *inferorum animas elicere*, cum puerorum extis *deos manes mactare* soleas'. Now turn to III I I 'Callimachi *manes* et Coi *sacra* Philetae, | in uestrum, quaeso, me sinite ire nemus.' You cannot ask the *sacred rites* of Philetas for permission to do this or that, least of all when in the same breath you address the same request to the *spirit* of Callimachus. I hold it to be as certain as aught in these matters can be that in I I 20 and III I I either 'sacra' means 'manes' or else it is the corruption of another word which means 'manes'. That 'sacra' stood for 'manes' was maintained by Dousa in the former place and by Broukhusius ‖ in the latter; but this contention they entirely failed to establish by examples, and indeed it seems inconceivable that 'sacra' could come to have any such signification. So I infer that 'sacra' is in both places a corruption of the same word; and that word I think has been restored by Fonteine in the one place and by Mr Baehrens in the other: 'fata'. No two words I suppose are more commonly confused than *fata* and *facta*: see II 28 26, IV I 71, II 70: and how easily *facta* would become 'sacra' may be seen from the following blunders all culled within the compass of seven lines: 29 ferre A for fer*t*e, 30 *s*emina A for *f*emina, 31 remane*r*e A for remane*t*e, 34 de*s*it AN for de*f*it, 34 uita*r*e F for uita*t*e. Forcellini cites Mela for *fatum* = *umbra*, but

I think we can find better authority than Mela. In Hor. carm. I 24 15 sqq. we read 'num uanae redeat sanguis imagini, | quam uirga semel horrida | non lenis precibus fata recludere | nigro compulerit Mercurius gregi?' and it is usual to explain 'fata recludere' with Lambinus as 'fati nexus et necessitatem resoluere ac rescindere'. But there is no semblance of authority for such a use of 'recludere': if 'fata' here means destiny, then the words 'fata recludere' can only mean what 'pandere fata' means in Luc. Phars. VI 590, namely 'aperire futura'; and this meaning is totally foreign to the context. I believe then that 'fata recludere' = 'Orcum recludere': the lexicons will shew that the use of 'recludere' and its synonyms in regard of the infernal regions is very frequent. Again in Luc. Phars. VI 652 'nam quamuis Thessala uates | uim faciat *fatis*, dubium est, quod traxerit illuc, | aspiciat Stygias, an quod descenderit, umbras' the context seems to indicate that *fatis* = *manibus*. I think then that Propertius enjoys his own again when Fonteine writes 'in magicis fata piare focis'.

25. Hemsterhuys' correction 'aut' for 'et' is adopted by Lachmann, Hertzberg, Haupt, Mr L. Mueller and Mr Baehrens: three English editors, Mr Paley, Mr Palmer and Mr Postgate, all retain 'et' and do not seem to have the faintest suspicion of its entire absurdity. 'I am surprised' Mr Paley gravely says 'that Lachmann, Hertzberg, Müller, and Kuinoel should have admitted, and Jacob approved, *aut uos*, the conjecture of Hemsterhuis'; Mr Postgate acquiesces: '*et*, as Paley rightly with || the MSS for *aut* edd.'; Mr Palmer reads 'et' in silence. These three scholars award the poetry of Propertius commendation which I think too high; yet they impute to him without scruple the stupidity of praying that Cynthia may begin to love him *and* that he may cease to love Cynthia. If the impossibility of the MS reading is not made plain by this naked statement of its sense, pages of argument will be in vain; nor can I hope that those who are deaf to Hemsterhuys will listen to me.

33. I agree with Mr Baehrens that 34 means *Cupid is never idle, never absent*: if you take 'uacuus amor' to be ungratified passion you get the wonderful circumlocution *absence of fruition is never absent*. If then Amor in the pentameter is the god, Venus in the hexameter is the goddess. But 'nostra' has thus no meaning, and is altered accordingly by Francius to 'dura' and by Mr Baehrens to 'maesta': the latter appositely quotes I 14 15 'nam quis diuitiis *aduerso* gaudet *Amore*? | nulla mihi *tristi* praemia sint *Venere*.' There is however another difficulty unremoved: it must I think be conceded to Mr Postgate that 'in me noctes exercet' is harsh and quite unexampled. I propose to abolish both difficulties at once by this very slight alteration:

me non nostra Venus noctes exercet amaras

'noctes amaras' being then acc. of duration like Horace's 'longas pereunte noctes'. The use of *meus tuus suus noster uester* = *secundus* is well known: in

III 13 56 Mr Baehrens rightly reads with O 'te scelus accepto Thracis Poly-
mestoris auro | nutrit in hospitio non, Polydore, *tuo*' against the '*pio*' of N; and
this makes it all the stranger that he should miss the same use in II 25 31. There
we find 'tu tamen interea, quamuis te diligat illa, | in tacito cohibe gaudia
clausa sinu; | namque in amore *suo* semper sua maxima cuique | nescio quo pacto
uerba nocere solent. | quamuis te persaepe uocet, sepelire memento'; and Mr
Baehrens to my surprise says 'malim *nouo*': *suo* = *secundo*, see 27 'mendaces
ludunt flatus in amore secundi'. Thus then 'non nostra Venus' is 'aduersa
Venus'. The change of *non*, abbreviated *n̄*, to *in* is easy: in IV 5 9 F has *inducere*
for *non ducere*, and in IV 1 124 I think all our MSS have the same error: || 'qua
nebulosa cauo rorat Meuania campo | et lacus aestiuis intepet Vmber aquis'.
Since 'intepet' is not a Latin word Mr Lucian Mueller writes 'si tepet', Mr
Baehrens 'ut tepet': better than either, if I am not mistaken, will be 'non tepet'.
Their chill in the heat of summer is the natural praise of streams and lakes: 'te
flagrantis atrox hora Caniculae nescit tangere, tu frigus amabile fessis uomere
tauris praebes'; and Pliny epist. VIII 8 describing the source of the Clitumnus,
perhaps this very *lacus Vmber*, says 'rigor aquae certauerit niuibus, nec color
cedit.' The alteration of 'me in nostra Venus' to 'in me' would be demanded
by grammar and metre alike, and would perhaps be helped by the occurrence of
'in me' at the beginning of verse 17.

Of Mr Postgate's conjecture 'in me nostra Venus uoces exercet amaras'
'against me my darling plies her bitter speech' I am at a loss to know what to
say. There is some justice in Mr Baehrens' contention that the estranged and
obdurate Cynthia can hardly be called by the endearing name 'nostra Venus';
but that is nothing: the alteration makes nonsense of the whole elegy from
beginning to end. Mr Postgate tells his readers on p. XXII of his Introduction
that Lachmann's explanation of the circumstances of this poem seems to him
unquestionably correct: he holds, that is, and in my opinion rightly holds, that
this poem was written when Propertius had been banished from Cynthia's
presence for a year; and yet he makes her 'ply her bitter speech against' Propertius, from whom she was as many miles asunder as Hypanis is from Eridanus
of the Veneti! If this is the attention to context with which conjectural emendation is practised, no wonder that many students of the classics regard it as a game
played merely for the amusement of the conjectural emendator. The corruption
is not even new: 'uoces' is the reading of the codex Hamburgensis, where
everyone hitherto has left it lying justly contemned among a hundred other
blunders almost equally worthless. But I imagine that these considerations
will have occurred ere now to Mr Postgate himself, or will have been pointed
out to him by his friends.

36. So far as I am aware no one has even attempted to prove by examples that
mutare locum can have the metaphorical || sense *to be inconstant* which is here

required; nor do I believe there are examples to prove it. And even were such a sense established, still Propertius durst not employ it here. A reader fresh from 'ferte per extremas gentes et ferte per undas' and 'uos remanete' must necessarily at first sight be tempted to take 'mutet locum' literally; indeed in some commentaries it is actually so explained, despite the hopeless shipwreck of sense which such an interpretation causes. Markland with his usual acumen first detected the fault; but his alteration of 'locum' to 'nouum' is a violent remedy. Mr A. Otto in the *Philologische Wochenschrift* for 1884 has proposed 'torum' comparing IV 8 28 '*mutato* uolui castra mouere *toro*', and five or six years ago I noted down the same conjecture and the same parallel: this I mention not as wishing to wrangle with Mr Otto for ownership but merely because some weight is justly given to such coincidences. The confusion of *t* and *l* I need not exemplify; for *r* and *c* see II 6 21 *capere* F for *rapere*, 25 45 *sandyris* V for *sandicis*, 34 33 *rursus* ON for *cursus*, III 6 36 *cursu* DV for *rursus*, IV 1 83 *capacis* F for *rapacis*, 89 *Arria* FN *Accia* DV, 4 12 *foco* ON for *foro*, 72 *fertur* for *pectus*, 8 53 *recidere* D for *cecidere*. In Sen. Herc. Fur. 21 'escendat licet | meumque uictrix teneat Alcmene *locum*' I think 'escendat' shews Bentley's '*torum*' to be right. Then in Ouid. met. XI 471 sqq. 'ut nec uela uidet, uacuum petit anxia *lectum* | seque *toro* ponit. renouat *lectus*que *locus*que | Alcyonae lacrimas et, quae pars, admonet, absit' will any student of Ovid's style deny that the parallelism requires '*lectus*que *torus*que'? if he does, let him mark the next verse and ask himself whether *pars loci* or *pars tori* is the better sense.

9

THE *AGAMEMNON* OF AESCHYLUS*

Thanks to Wecklein it is at length possible to study Aeschylus in comfort. Next to an accurate collation of the cardinal MSS, a complete register of the conjectures of critics is the student's prime requisite. Nothing short of a complete register will serve: no man can be trusted to sift good from bad: some editors do not know a correction when they see one, others through childish jealousy of this scholar or that ignore his discoveries, the most candid and the soundest judgment is human and errs. The time lost, the tissues wasted, in doing anew the brainwork done before by others, and all for lack of a book like Wecklein's *Appendix*, are in our brief irreparable life disheartening to think of.

In the ensuing pages I have not set down all or nearly all the corrections which I imagine myself to have made in the *Agamemnon*: I know how easily one is satisfied with one's own conjectures. I have arraigned the MSS only where their delinquencies can be made as clear as daylight, and I have proposed only corrections which I think may possibly convince others as well as myself. For instance, however confident I may feel that in v. 17 Aeschylus wrote not ὕπνου but πόνου, still I have to own that the former can by hook or by crook be defended, and that the indications which suggest the latter are not decisive; so I leave the reader in peace. I need hardly say that I have not broached conjectures on a tithe of the passages I think corrupt: diagnosis is one thing and healing another: let us keep the precept ἢ λέγε τι σιγῆς κρεῖσσον ἢ σιγὴν ἔχε.

The numeration is Wecklein's, which for this play tallies with Dindorf's. ‖

4-7

ἄστρων κάτοιδα νυκτέρων ὁμήγυριν
καὶ τοὺς φέροντας χεῖμα καὶ θέρος βροτοῖς
λαμπροὺς δυνάστας ἐμπρέποντας αἰθέρι,
ἀστέρας, ὅταν φθίνωσιν, ἀντολάς τε τῶν.

I know the stars and the rulers of the seasons, the stars to wit. This of course is one of those sentences which a poet does not write; so most editors with Pauw and Valckenaer bracket v. 7 for spurious. It is a good riddance, that I see, but I do not see on what principles of criticism it can be justified: the Aeschylean archaism τῶν never came from the workshop of an interpolator. Fault has of

* [*JPh* 16 (1888), 244-90]

course been found, ὥστε σύγγονον βροτοῖσι τὸν πεσόντα λακτίσαι πλέον, with the initial dactyl, and when the faultfinders have got rid of *Cho.* 215 [216] καὶ τίνα σύνοισθά μοι καλουμένη βροτῶν; 984 [986] of the same play ἥλιος ἄναγνα μητρὸς ἔργα τῆς ἐμῆς, *Sept.* 640 [653] ὦ θεομανές τε καὶ θεῶν μέγα στύγος[1] and *fr.* 290, 4, Dind. [300 4 Nauck, 193 5 Mette] ἥλιος ἐν ᾗ πυρωπὸς ἐκλάμψας χθονί, then they may be heard: not before. But Hermann and others, who suppose themselves to have rescued the verse by trifling with the punctuation, ascribe to commas a cabalistic virtue which did not reside in the seal of Solomon. Mr Margoliouth writes 5–7 as follows: καὶ τοὺς φέροντας χεῖμα καὶ θέρος βροτοῖς | λαμπροὺς δυνάστας, ἐμπρέποντας αἰθέρι | ἀστέρας ὅταν φθίνωσιν, ἀντολαῖς τε τῶν: the λαμπροὶ δυνάσται, he says, are the Pleiades. If a year of sleepless nights has taught the watchman so little astronomy that he singles out this nebulous cluster from the host of heaven to call it λαμπρός, he is a signal confutation of his creator's favourite doctrine, παθήματα μαθήματα. Nay Mr Margoliouth's own witnesses turn round and testify against him: ὀλίγαι καὶ ἀφεγγέες, ἐπισκέψασθαι ἀφαυραί, 'ignis uix tenui longe face fit spectabilis' say Aratus and Auienus; and to set against this damaging evidence Mr Margoliouth can find nothing better than the following citation: 'Cic. Progn. 356 *fugiet cum* lucida *uisus Pleias.*' Now the employment of *lucida*, by Cicero or by || any one else, as an epitheton ornans for *Pleias* in a context which does not pit these stars against their fellows, concerns these verses of Aeschylus not a jot; but what is 'Cic. Progn. 356'? If Mr Margoliouth has access to 356 verses of Cicero's *Prognostica*, he is more fortunate than the rest of the world who know only 27. Truth to tell, however, the words which he ascribes to Cicero were written in the seventeenth century after Christ by Hugo Grotius. If Mr Margoliouth cares for Cicero's account of the Pleiades, here it is: *Phaen.* 27 'omnis *parte* locatas | *parua* Vergilias *tenui cum luce* uidebis', 37 'hae *tenues paruo* labentes *lumine* lucent'. And let the Pleiades be as brilliant as you will, masculine they will never be: even Cic. Progn. 356 does not present us with *lucidus Pleias.*

The passage is I believe to be righted, not by the change of a single letter, but by a simpler remedy; the simplest which can be applied to the text of any poet Greek or Roman. We should have heard no evil of the initial dactyl if the MS gave the verses thus:

ἄστρων κάτοιδα νυκτέρων ὁμήγυριν,
6 λαμπροὺς δυνάστας ἐμπρέποντας αἰθέρι,
5 καὶ τοὺς φέροντας χεῖμα καὶ θέρος βροτοῖς
ἀστέρας, ὅταν φθίνωσιν, ἀντολάς τε τῶν.

The watcher is grown acquainted with the stars, which he likens to a congregation of princes, and chiefly with the down-setting and the uprising of those

---

[1] *Pers.* 287 [284] and Soph. *Aiax* 1331 seem to answer Mr Verrall's objections to this verse.

which bring men winter and summer, the stars of the zodiac. These, by which
he reckons the passage of his year's vigil, are singled out from the other stars by
καί, as in *Pers.* 751 [749] the god of the sea is singled out from the other gods
whom Xerxes fought against when he bound the Hellespont: θεῶν δὲ πάντων
ᾤετ', οὐκ εὐβουλίᾳ, | καὶ Ποσειδῶνος κρατήσειν. It should be said that the
transposition must have taken place before the time of Achilles Tatius, who
quotes vv. 4–6 in the traditional order.

49–59

τρόπον αἰγυπιῶν, οἵτ' ἐκπάγλοις
ἄλγεσι παίδων ὕπατοι λεχέων ‖   50
στροφοδινοῦνται,
πτερύγων ἐρετμοῖσιν ἐρεσσόμενοι,
δεμνιοτήρη
πόνον ὀρταλίχων ὀλέσαντες·
ὕπατος δ' ἀΐων ἤ τις Ἀπόλλων   55
ἢ Πὰν ἢ Ζεὺς οἰωνόθροον
γόον ὀξυβόαν
τῶνδε μετοίκων ὑστερόποινον
πέμπει παραβᾶσιν Ἐρινύν.

The learner of Greek, in quest of probable or even plausible reasons for
believing that ὕπατοι λεχέων *summi cubilium* means ὑπὲρ λεχέων *super cubilia*, is
dismissed by Mr Paley to these references: 'ἐσχάτῃ χθονὸς Prom. 865 [846],
ὑστάτου νεὼς Suppl. 697 [717], ὕπατος χώρας Ζεὺς inf. 492 [509]'. The first two
of these passages, πόλις ἐσχάτη χθονός and οἴακος ὑστάτου νεώς, prove to him
what he could well believe without proof, that such a phrase as θριγκὸς ὕπατος
τείχους *a coping which is the highest part of a wall* is Greek; but since vultures on
the wing are not the highest part of their eyries the information does not help
him. Had he been referred, say, to a passage where a fish following a ship is
called ὕστατος νεώς, then he would have been helped; but Greek literature
contains no such passage: such a fish is ὕστερος νεώς. To the third reference he
turns with keen interest, because it is manifest that Mr Paley's translation of
ὕπατος χώρας must differ widely from the usual rendering. But no: Mr Paley
translates like everyone else 'supreme over the country'; and the learner of
Greek returns with a touch of resentment from his fool's errand.

I propose παίδων ἀπάτῃ λεχαίων, *because their brood is stolen away*. The
phrase παίδων λεχαίων finds an exact parallel in *Sept.* 278 [291] δράκοντας ὥς
τις τέκνων ὑπερδέδοικεν λεχαίων δυσευνάτορας πάντρομος πελειάς, the phrase
παίδων ἀπάτῃ in Soph. *Ant.* 630 ἀπάτας λεχέων ὑπεραλγῶν, *wroth that he is*

cheated of his bride. My reading is rather an interpretation than an alteration of the MS text: confusions of ἀπ- and ὑπ- are to be counted not by scores but by hundreds; and for century on century οι was identical with η in pronunciation, ‖ and ε with αι. In the passage which I have cited from the *Septem*, λεχαίων had to be restored by Lachmann: the MS there as here gives λεχέων. As for the scansion of λεχαίων as an anapaest, the penultimate αι of πετραῖος is shortened by Sophocles in lyrics, *Ant*. 827, of παλαιός and δίκαιος by Euripides in senarii, *El*. 497 and *Cycl*. 274, of γεραιός by Sophocles in lyrics, *O. C*. 200, and by Euripides in anapaests more than once, of δείλαιος by Sophocles in lyrics, *El*. 849, and by Aristophanes in senarii over and over again. In Soph. *Ant*. 1240 the MS gives τὰ νυμφικὰ | τέλη λαχὼν δείλαιος ἐν Ἅιδου δόμοις: the conjecture εἰν is not to be dreamt of: Sophocles seems to have written λαχὼν ἐν Ἅιδου δείλαιος δόμοις τέλη or δόμοις ἐν Ἅιδου δείλαιος τέλη λαχών. Finally in the *Agamemnon* itself, v. 723 ⟦722⟧, is found εὐφιλόπαιδα καὶ γεραροῖς ἐπίχαρτον: which now is the more prudent, to confer on γεραροῖς an alien and unexampled meaning, unexampled, for *Supp*. 675 ⟦667⟧ proves nothing at all, or to suppose that here, as in the same word in Eur. *Supp*. 43 (γεραιῶν Markland, γεραρῶν MSS), a scribe confused two letters which in old uncials can hardly be distinguished, I and P? I take the second alternative: uiris doctis aliter uisum.

But another check awaits us in v. 58. The dissension about the meaning of τῶνδε μετοίκων is of long standing. The scholiast refers the words to the nestlings, and renders ὑπὲρ τῶν μετοικισθέντων νεοσσῶν, a version which of course is peremptorily forbidden by τῶνδε. Another explanation is given in the scholion on Soph. *O. C*. 934 and reappears, somewhat curtailed, in Suidas: Αἰσχύλος...ἐν Ἀγαμέμνονι...μετοίκους...εἶπε τῶν ὑψηλῶν τόπων τοὺς οἰωνοὺς ...ἀντὶ τῶν ἐνοίκων. But obviously a poet who writes thus, a poet ὅς χ' ἕτερον μὲν κεύθῃ ἐνὶ φρεσὶν ἄλλο δὲ εἴπῃ, cannot hope that his audience will understand him: he might as well call the birds πελειάδας ἀντὶ αἰγυπιῶν. Mr Paley says that the parent vultures are called μέτοικοι to contrast them with the μέτοικοι of Athens who could obtain redress at law only through προστάται; an allusion frigid in itself, and so carefully obscured that even after Mr Paley has told us it is there one scans the Greek for it in vain. ‖

It will be conceded that a copyist who found in his exemplar the letters τωνδειμετοκων would be likely to make Greek of them by transposing the single letter ι to the place it holds in the text to-day. Such transpositions, intentional or unintentional, are common enough: in one play I notice these three: *Supp*. 22 ἱεροστέπτοισι for ἐριοστέπτοισι, 278 ⟦272⟧ λέγοι πρόσως for λέγοις πρόσω, 961 ⟦950⟧ ἴσθι μέν through σθιμεν for ἔοιγμεν. But if my hypothetical copyist had been so faithful or so dull as to write what he read, criticism would before now have restored, letter for letter, a phrase which seems to me the most appropriate in the world, τῶν αἰνοτόκων. The substitutions δ for α, ει for ι, μ for ν and ε for ο are so common, not in Aeschylus merely, but all of them in most Greek MSS and some of them in all, that I will not fill with illustrations the pages which might be filled; but take two instances where the αι of αἰνός by changing to δει has wrought further mischief: in Soph. *O. C.* 212 τόδ'; αἰνά is restored by Wunder for τόδε; δεινά, and in Eur. *Med.* 640 προσβάλοι μ' αἰνά by Verrall for προσβάλοιμι δεινά.[1] The terms αἰνοτόκος, αἰνοτόκεια, αἰνὰ τεκοῦσα are especially applied to parents rendered wretched by the calamities of their children: *Il.* A 414 ὤμοι τέκνον ἐμόν, τί νύ σ' ἔτρεφον αἰνὰ τεκοῦσα; says Thetis to Achilles; Oppian. *Hal.* v 526 μητρὶ παρ' αἰνοτόκῳ, the mother dolphin whose young one the fishermen harpoon; Nonn. *Dion.* II 160 [162 Keydell] αἰνοτόκοιο θεημάχον οὔνομα νύμφης, and XLVIII 428 Τανταλὶς αἰνοτόκεια, Niobe in both places. But let me ask especial attention to the employment of αἰνοτόκεια in Mosch. IV 27 where Megara relates the death of her children at the hands of Heracles: ὡς δ' ὄρνις δύρηται ἐπὶ σφετέροισι νεοσσοῖς | ὀλλυμένοις, οὖστ' αἰνὸς ὄφις ἔτι νηπιάχοντας | θάμνοις ἐν πυκινοῖσι κατεσθίῃ· ἡ δὲ κατ' αὐτοὺς | πωτᾶται κλάζουσα μάλα λιγὺ πότνια μήτηρ | …ὡς ἐγὼ αἰνοτόκεια φίλον γόνον αἰάζουσα | μαινομένοισι πόδεσσι δόμον κάτα πολλὸν ἐφοίτων. The poet who wrote this was imitating first and foremost *Iliad* B 308 sqq., but he would naturally remember also Aesch. *Sept.* 278 [291] and this passage of the *Agamemnon*: that he did remember this last, I find another indication besides αἰνοτόκεια. In v. 2 of the poem you have ‖ ἐκπάγλως ἀχέουσα, in v. 72 ἐκπάγλως ὀλοφύρομαι, in v. 93 δειμαίνω… ἐκπάγλως: in v. 2 is a variant ἀχέεσσι: if ἐκπάγλοις ἀχέεσσι is to be read, it is neither more nor less than a reproduction of the phrase which Blomfield has in *Ag.* 49 restored to Aeschylus, ἐκπάγλοις ἄλγεσι. The MS reading ἐκπατίοις is undoubtedly a word which might have existed, though in face of the resemblance between γλ and τι there is nothing approaching proof that exist it did; but in this passage it gives a totally inadequate sense, and ἐκπάγλοις as well as αἰνοτόκων seems to gain support from Moschus.

97–103

τούτων λήξασ' ὅ τι καὶ δυνατὸν
καὶ θέμις αἴνει
παιών τε γενοῦ τῆσδε μερίμνης,
ἢ νῦν τοτὲ μὲν κακόφρων τελέθει,　　　　　　100
τοτὲ δ' ἐκ θυσιῶν ἀγανὴ φανθεῖσ'
ἐλπὶς ἀμύνει φροντίδ' ἄπληστον
τὴν θυμοφθόρον λύπης φρένα.

Fortunately I need not demonstrate that v. 103 is corrupt. For my own part, if I could believe ὕπατοι λεχέων to be Greek or τῶνδε μετοίκων to be sense,

---

[1] See too *Cho.* 841 [842] δειματοσταγές for αἱματοσταγές.

I could believe τὴν θυμοφθόρον λύπης φρένα to be a paroemiac; but some scholars seem to find it the harder feat. Wecklein records over a score of conjectures, not one of which affords a plausible explanation of the phenomena presented by the MS. Those phenomena, as well as the scholion, are explained if Aeschylus wrote this:

> ἐλπὶς ἀμύνει φροντίδ' ἄπληστον
> θυμοῦ, λυπησίφρον' ἄτην.

θυμοῦ is of course to be construed with ἀμύνει. But the scholiast construed ἄπληστον θυμοῦ, and therefore paraphrased the words ἄπληστον θυμοῦ λυπησίφρονα by ἥτις ἐστὶ θυμοβόρος λύπη τῆς φρενός, rendering the adjective λυπησίφρονα by the phrase ἥτις ἐστὶ λύπη τῆς φρενός, the phrase ἄπληστον θυμοῦ by the adjective θυμοβόρος. Some reader of Aeschylus, under the same misapprehension, wrote θυμοφθόρον in the margin of his copy: that θυμοφθόρος and θυμοβόρος were to Byzantine ‖ ears identical in meaning is shown by Hesychius θυμοβόροιο· ψυχοφθόρου, and Photius θυμοβόρος· ἡ τὴν ψυχὴν διαφθείρουσα. A subsequent copyist took this marginal θυμοφθόρον to be a correction of θυμοῦ, and corrected accordingly. Hardly more than a wrong division of the letters was needed to convert the unfamiliar λυπησιφρονατην into λύπης φρένα τήν; and since τήν could not stand at the end of the line it was transplanted to the beginning, where it flourishes to-day. Hesiod *Op.* 795 ⟦797⟧ πεφύλαξο δὲ θυμῷ | τετράδ' ἀλεύασθαι φθίνοντός θ' ἱσταμένου τε | ἄλγεα θυμοβορεῖν, and Theognis 1323 σκέδασον δὲ μερίμνας | θυμοβόρους, were perhaps the passages which suggested to Aeschylus his ἀμύνει θυμοῦ and his φροντίδ' ἄπληστον, and to the scholiast his θυμοβόρος.

I learn from Wecklein that λυπησίφρονα was detected three centuries ago by Scaliger: how he completed the verse I do not know. Similar compounds with similar force are θελξίφρων Eur. *Bacch.* 404 and ῥηξίφρων Hesych.

131–5 ⟦126–30⟧

χρόνῳ μὲν ἀγρεῖ
Πριάμου πόλιν ἅδε κέλευθος
πάντα δὲ πύργων
κτήνη προσθετὰ δημιοπληθῆ
μοῖρ' ἀλαπάξει πρὸς τὸ βίαιον.

135 ⟦130⟧

Most editors adopt in v. 134 ⟦129⟧ the conjecture πρόσθε τὰ which appears in the Florentine apograph; but how to translate it they cannot agree. Half take πρόσθε in a temporal sense, which makes Calchas a lying prophet: if the wealth of Troy was exhausted before its fall, how comes it that Cassandra was πολλῶν χρημάτων ἐξαίρετον ἄνθος? Half, giving κτήνη its usual meaning of *cattle*, construe πρόσθε πύργων *in front of the walls*, which leaves the lines no point whatever: the Iliad shows that after nine years' siege neither Trojans nor Greeks were lacking in flocks and herds, whether those flocks and herds were or were not πρόσθε πύργων. So if πρόσθε is local the lines are trivial, if it is temporal they are not true. But against both renderings lies the further and fatal objection that they refer the sentence to circumstances of the leaguer ‖ when it must of necessity be referred to the taking of the town. It was the fall, not the siege, of Troy which depended on averting an ἄγα θεόθεν.

For these or for other reasons Pauw and Hermann prefer to write πρόσθετα, which indeed is virtually the reading of the MS, as many scribes preserve in compounds of θετός the accentuation of the simple adjective. But Weil justly observes that πρόσθετα cannot, as Hermann would have it, mean *congesta*, which is by no means the same thing as *additicia*. If then there were no other meaning of πρόσθετα the MS must be abandoned. But there is another and a most appropriate meaning. Over and over again in this play the Trojan war is likened to a lawsuit in which the Greeks prosecute the Trojans: 41 Πριάμου μέγας ἀντίδικος Μενέλαος, 458 [451] προδίκοις Ἀτρείδαις, 539 [534] ὀφλὼν γὰρ ἁρπαγῆς τε καὶ κλοπῆς δίκην | τοῦ ῥυσίου θ' ἥμαρτε κτλ., 804 [813] δίκας γὰρ οὐκ ἀπὸ γλώσσης θεοὶ | κλύοντες ἀνδροκνῆτας [-κμῆτας or -θνῆτας] Ἰλίου φθορᾶς | ἐς αἱματηρὸν τεῦχος οὐ διχορρόπως | ψήφους ἔθεντο· τῷ δ' ἐναντίῳ κύτει | ἐλπὶς προσείει χεῖρας οὐ πληρουμένῳ: in 537 [532] too συντελής seems to mean *paying joint penalty*. Now πρόσθετος, as the lexicons will show, has the technical meaning *addictus*, surrendered to a creditor. It is noticeable that the scholiast explains κτήνη by κτήματα, and that this very phrase κτήματα πρόσθετά τινι ποιεῖν occurs in Boeckh's *Corp. Inscr.* 2691. I think then that πρόσθετα is not only sound but exceedingly apt.

But πύργων κτήνη is a strange phrase. The wealth of the Trojans, the wealth of Troy, I could understand: the wealth of the fortifications, no. And this is not the only difficulty. The strophic verses answering 131-5 [126-30] are 110-14 [108-13]:

> ὅπως Ἀχαιῶν
> δίθρονον κράτος, Ἑλλάδος ἥβας
> ξύμφρονα τὰν γᾶν,
> πέμπει ξὺν δορὶ καὶ χερὶ πράκτορι
> θούριος ὄρνις Τευκρίδ' ἐπ' αἶαν.

How are we to amend τὰν γᾶν? Blomfield writes ταγόν, Hermann τάγαν: I am bound to suppose that these scholars attached some meaning to the phrase *a unanimous captain*, but ‖ what that meaning may have been I cannot divine. Neither is it possible, in Greece or anywhere else, for two persons to compose one ταγός or one τάγης: in v. 41 ἀντίδικος is of course Μενέλαος, not Μενέλαος ἠδ' Ἀγαμέμνων. If with Dindorf we write ξύμφρονε ταγώ we get a meaning, but we stray some distance to get it. The correction which is instantly suggested by the requirements of the sense is as old as the earliest apographs of the Medicean: ταγάν. Hesychius has ταγαῖς· ἀρχαῖς, ἡγεμονίαις, which is precisely the meaning wanted: the two Atridae compose one ταγή as they compose one κράτος. Dactyls are often varied with tribrachs by Pindar in Doric melodies, just as lyric anapaests are so varied in passages like Eur. *I. T.* 130, where see Monk and Dindorf. In the notation of J. H. H. Schmidt, which is familiar to Englishmen, the verse ξύμφρονα ταγάν will be – : ∪∪ <|–, see his *Leitfaden* § 12. But of course ταγάν in the strophe and πύργων in the antistrophe cannot live together: which shall be the victim? The inappropriate, not the appropriate word.

> πάντα δὲ Φρυγῶν
> κτήνη πρόσθετα δημιοπληθῆ
> μοῖρ' ἀλαπάξει πρὸς τὸ βίαιον.

The confusion of an aspirate with its tenuis is among the commonest of those errors of the ear to which copyists are subject: an apposite and undisputed instance of π for φ is *Cho.* 417 ⟦418⟧ πάντες for φάντες. Another of their favourite tricks is to reverse the order of two consecutive letters: disregarding such perpetual confusions as θράσος and θάρσος, κραδία and καρδία, I take the following examples from Aeschylus alone: *P. V.* 934 ⟦903⟧ προσδάρκοι for προσδράκοι, *Pers.* 689 ⟦687⟧ ῥοθιάζοντες for ὀρθιάζοντες, *Supp.* 372 ⟦367⟧ ἐκπνοεῖν for ἐκπονεῖν, 703 ⟦695⟧ θεαί τ' for θείατ', *Ag.* 117 ⟦115⟧ ἀργίας for ἀργᾶς, 797 ⟦806⟧ πόνος for πνόος, 1204 ⟦1205⟧ βαρύνεται for ἀβρύνεται, *Cho.* 270 ⟦271⟧ κᾆ ξοθριάζων for κᾆξορθιάζων, *Eum.* 260 χερῶν for χρεῶν. It is interesting to note that Mr Margoliouth has conjectured Τευκρῶν, as it counts for something that two minds should independently require the same meaning.

The adjective δημιοπληθῆ is one of those many poetical compounds in which the second element is purely ornamental: ‖ just as ἀρσενοπληθῆ in *Supp.* 29 means simply ἄρσενα, so δημιοπληθῆ here means simply δήμια; it would be wrong I think to say that it means even δήμια πολλά. But be that as it may, Mr Margoliouth by defending ἀβροτίμων προκαλυμμάτων is estopped from impugning κτήνη δημιοπληθῆ.

413–44 ⟦403–36⟧

str.

    λιποῦσα δ' ἀστοῖσιν ἀσπίστορας
    κλόνους τε καὶ λογχίμους ναυβάτας θ' ὁπλισμοὺς

415 ⟦406⟧   ἄγουσά τ' ἀντίφερνον Ἰλίῳ φθορὰν
    βέβακεν ῥίμφα διὰ πυλᾶν
    ἄτλητα τλᾶσα· πουλὺ δ' ἄνστενον
    τάδ' ἐννέποντες δόμων προφῆται·
    'ἰὼ ἰὼ δῶμα δῶμα καὶ πρόμοι,

420 ⟦411⟧   ἰὼ λέχος καὶ στίβοι φιλάνορες.

πάρεστι κοίτας ἀτίμας ἀλοίδορος,
ἄπιστος ἐμφανῶν ἰδεῖν.
πόθῳ δ᾽ ὑπερποντίας
φάσμα δόξει δόμων ἀνάσσειν.
εὐμόρφων δὲ κολοσσῶν   425 [416]
ἔχθεται χάρις ἀνδρί,
ὀμμάτων δ᾽ ἐν ἀχηνίαις
ἔρρει πᾶσ᾽ Ἀφροδίτα.
ὀνειρόφαντοι δὲ πειθήμονες   ant.
πάρεισι δόξαι φέρουσαι χάριν ματαίαν.   430 [421]
μάταν γάρ, εὖτ᾽ ἂν ἐς θιγὰς δοκᾶν ὁρᾷ,
παραλλάξασα διὰ χερῶν
βέβακεν ὄψις οὐ μεθύστερον
πτεροῖς ὀπαδοῖς ὕπνου κελεύθοις.᾽
τὰ μὲν κατ᾽ οἴκους ἐφεστίους ἄχη   435 [427]
τάδ᾽ ἐστὶ καὶ τῶνδ᾽ ὑπερβατώτερα·
τοπᾶν δ᾽, ἀφ᾽ Ἕλλανος αἴας ξυνορμένοις,
ποθεινὰ τλησικαρδίοις
δόμων ἑκάς που πρέπει.
πολλὰ γοῦν θιγγάνει πρὸς ἧπαρ·   440 [432]
οἵους μὲν γὰρ ἔπεμψαν
οὐδέν, ἀντὶ δὲ φωτῶν ||
τεύχη καὶ σποδὸς εἰς ἑκά-
στου δόμους ἀφικνεῖται.

414 [404] κλ. τε καὶ λ. ναυβάτας θ᾽ H. L. Ahrens, κλ. λ. τε καὶ ναυβάτας Flor. 417 [408] πουλὺ Arnaldus, πολὺ Flor. ἄνστενον scripsi, ἀνέστενον Flor. 418 [409] τάδ᾽ Auratus, τόδ᾽ Flor. 421 [412] κοίτας ἀτίμας scripsi, σιγᾶς ἄτιμος Flor. 422 [413] ἄπιστος ἐμφανῶν Margoliouth, ἅδιστος ἀφεμένων Flor. 429 [420] πειθήμονες scripsi, πενθήμονες Flor. 431 [423] ἐς θιγὰς δοκᾶν scripsi, ἐσθλά τις δοκῶν Flor. ὁρᾷ Scholefield, ὁρᾶν Flor. 435 [427] ἐφεστίους Vossius, ἐφ᾽ ἑστίας Flor. 437 [429] τοπᾶν scripsi, τὸ πᾶν Flor. Ἕλλανος Bamberger, Ἑλλάδος Flor. 438 [430] ποθεινὰ τλησικαρδίοις scripsi, πένθεια τλησικάρδιος Flor. 439 [431] ἑκάς που H. L. Ahrens, ἑκάστου Flor. 441 [433] οἵους G. C. W. Schneider, οὓς Flor. ἔπεμψαν scripsi, ἔπεμψεν Flor. 442 [434] οὐδέν scripsi, οἶδεν Flor.

To save space I have written down this passage at once in the form to which I propose to bring it: I will now render account of the changes made.

417 [408]. I think every edition reads here πολλὰ δ᾽ ἔστενον from Triclinius' conjecture; but how then arose the reading of the uninterpolated MS? I restore the metre simply by restoring the epic forms which the copyist translated into the common dialect. The form πουλύ should not be denied to Aeschylus: he has

πολεῖ and πολέα, both Sophocles and Euripides have πολλός, and πουλύπους is the regular Attic form: for ἄνστενον see v. 1552 [1553] κάππεσε, κάτθανε. I will not quarrel with anyone who prefers πολλά, but ἄνστενον must I think be read.

418 [409]. It seems that δόμων προφῆται is taken to mean the seers belonging to the household; but the verses 419–34 [410–26] needed no seer to utter them, for not one word of prophecy do they contain: they contain merely, as Mr Paley says, speculations on Menelaus' state of mind. And what is more, I altogether deny that προφήτης in tragedy can mean μάντις. If I may trust the lexicons, προφήτης and προφῆτις occur in tragedy eleven times. In eight of these instances the meaning *interpres* is beyond all doubt, the gen. of the person or thing interpreted being expressed or implied: Aesch. *Eum.* 19 Διὸς προφήτης, Eur. *Or.* 364 Νηρέως προφήτης, *Bacch.* 211 προφήτης λόγων, ‖ 551 Διόνυσε, σοὺς προφήτας, *Rhes.* 972 Βάκχου προφήτης, *Ion* 321 and 1322 Φοίβου προφῆτις, 42 κυρεῖ. . .προφῆτις ἐσβαίνουσα μαντεῖον θεοῦ, where, even if θεοῦ is not to be taken ἀπὸ κοινοῦ with προφῆτις and μαντεῖον, the word is correctly employed as the title of Apollo's interpreter, the Delphic priestess. There remain, besides the present passage, two others where προφήτης is construed *seer*: these I will now examine. In Aesch. *Ag.* 1083 sq. [1098 sq.] we read: ἦμεν κλέος σου μαντικὸν πεπυσμένοι, | ἦμεν προφήτας δ᾽ οὔτινας ματεύομεν: of course ἠμέν has been foisted in from the line above. The second verse is rendered by Mr Paley and almost all other commentators *we are not on the look-out for prophets*: a version which not only imputes to the coryphaeus highly uncivil and rather impious language, but is entirely uncalled-for. The words are explained with perfect correctness by the scholiast, though no one but Blomfield has listened to him: τοὺς λέξοντας ἡμῖν περὶ σοῦ· αὐτοὶ γὰρ αὐτόπται γινόμεθα. Cassandra has just scented in the palace the banquet of Thyestes; and the coryphaeus exclaims: We had been *told* of your divining power before, but now we seek for none to *tell* us of it: we witness it at first hand. Aeschylus probably wrote ἤδη προφήτας δ᾽ οὔτινας ματεύομεν: but that is by the way. Finally I come to *Sept.* 596 sqq. [609 sqq.]: οὕτως δ᾽ ὁ μάντις, υἱὸν Οἰκλέους λέγω, | σώφρων δίκαιος ἀγαθὸς εὐσεβὴς ἀνήρ, | μέγας προφήτης, ἀνοσίοισι συμμιγεὶς | θρασυστόμοισιν ἀνδράσιν . . .Διὸς θέλοντος ξυγκαθελκυσθήσεται. Here the rendering *seer* is necessary if the text is sound. But the fact that this is a solitary exception, for in *Ag.* 418 [409] as I said at the outset this meaning even if permissible would be inappropriate, is of itself some presumption against the soundness of the text; and it is not the only presumption. The words εὐσεβὴς ἀνήρ occur at the end of v. 589 [602] only eight lines above; and the nearness of that verse not only makes the repetition in v. 597 [610] unpleasant, but also, if Aeschylus wrote σώφρων, δίκαιος, ἀγαθός, εὐσεβής, θεοῦ (or θεῶν or Διὸς) μέγας προφήτης, explains the corruption by the wandering of the scribe's eye from the latter εὐσεβής to the former. I therefore, to return to my starting point, give to προφῆται in *Ag.* 418 [409] precisely the

sense it has in v. 1084 ⟦1099⟧: δόμων προφῆται are οἱ λέγοντες ἡμῖν περὶ δόμων, purveyors of ‖ gossip about the royal family: of course οἶκος αὐτός, εἰ φθογγὴν λάβοι, σαφέστατ᾽ ἂν λέξειεν, but in default of that the Argive people had to get their news through προφῆται, retailers at second hand.

421 ⟦412⟧. Here, first of all, the metrical dissension between strophe and antistrophe has to be removed. If the scansion of the two lines as handed down be compared

str. ∪–∪––∪–∪∪–∪– 421 ⟦412⟧

ant. ∪–∪–∪∪––∪–∪– 437 ⟦429⟧

it will be seen that the simplest and most rhythmical cure will be to alter the quantity of the 8th syllable in the strophic and of the 5th in the antistrophic verse. The latter change is merely the change of a letter, Ἕλλανος for Ἑλλάδος, and this easy and graceful emendation of Bamberger's has naturally found much favour. Lighted by this and by Mr Margoliouth's beautiful restoration of v. 422 ⟦413⟧ I have corrected the strophic passage thus: *there he stands, reviling not his dishonoured bed, believing not what is plain to see.* Menelaus does not upbraid his wife's unfaithfulness, nay he refuses to believe her unfaithful. πάρεστι sc. ὁ ἀνὴρ τῷ λέχει, as is readily understood from λέχος and φιλάνορες in the preceding verse. For the form ἀτίμας compare in the first place ὑπερποντίας only two lines below, and also *Sept.* 105 ⟦107⟧ εὐφιλήταν, 761 ⟦776⟧ ἁρπαξάνδραν, *Pers.* 600 ⟦596⟧ περικλύστα, *Ag.* 1104 ⟦1116⟧ ξυναιτία, *Cho.* 68 ⟦69⟧ πανάρκετας, 99 ⟦100⟧ μεταίτιαι, 617 ⟦619⟧ ἀθανάτας, *Eum.* 268 μητροφόνας, 792 ⟦789⟧ δύσοιστα; perhaps the ἀτίτα of the MS means ἀτίτη not ἀτίται in *Ag.* 72, and θελκτηρία is to be read in *Cho.* 666 ⟦670⟧; in *Supp.* 63 ⟦62⟧ Hermann with high probability writes κιρκηλάτας; in *Ag.* 796 ⟦805⟧ I should be disposed to read νῦν δ᾽ οὐκ ἀπ᾽ ἄκρας φρενὸς οὐδ᾽ ἀφίλης | εὔφρων πνόος εὖ τελέσασιν, as ἀφίλως εὔφρων is a phrase which conveys no meaning to me. The transmutation of ΚΟΙΤΑC into ΙCCΙΓΑC and the consequent loss of the letters ΙC in the sequence ΠΑΡΕCΤΙΙCCΙΓΑC are errors of the easiest sort: the confusion of Ο with C and of Τ with Γ Ι need not illustrate; but a word on the confusion in Aeschylus of Κ with ΙC. In *Cho.* 896 ⟦897⟧ is found ὠκύ for ὦι σύ (Robortellus), in *Sept.* 927 ⟦945⟧ κακός for ἴσος (Weil) through κος, in *Eum.* 178 ⟦177⟧ ἐκείνου for εἴσιν οὖ (Kirchhoff), ‖ in 864 ⟦862⟧ ἱδρύσηι κάρη for ἱδρύσῃς Ἄρη (Stephanus); an especially noticeable instance is *Cho.* 160 ⟦161⟧ where, for Σκυθικά, the MS has
ησ
σκυθιτά: that is, the scribe wrote τ in error and added κ above as a correction, and this κ was corrupted by successive copyists first to ισ, then to ησ. In *Ag.* 106 ⟦105⟧ I think Mr Margoliouth tries to extract the right sense from the corrupt ἐκτελέων, but his conjecture is unsatisfactory: Aeschylus seems to have written ἀνδρῶν εἷς τελέων, though the context is so obscure that we cannot speak with

certainty.[1] There is less doubt however about a scholion on the same passage explaining θεόθεν πειθώ by τὴν εἰς θεοὺς πειθώ: not even a scholiast could suppose that θεόθεν meant εἰς θεούς: he wrote ἐκ θεοῦ. As to v. 422 [[413]], Mr Margoliouth's alterations are very slight: for the confusion of Π and Δ see *Sept.* 654 [[667]] προσεῖπε for προσεῖδε: such transpositions of letters as αφεμ for εμφα are common enough, whether accompanied, as here, by the addition of a letter, or by the subtraction of a letter as in μακιστῆρα for μαστικτῆρα *Supp.* 475 [[466]], or by the change of a letter as in ἐκμετρούμενος for τεκμαρούμενος Soph. *O. T.* 795.

424 [[415]]. Those commentators whose opinion I can ascertain take φάσμα to be nom.: I think it is acc., the subject of δόξει being the same as the subject of πάρεστι, Menelaus. The tense is what may be called the conjectural future, = οἶμαι δοκεῖ, *methinks he sees in fancy a wraith queen of the palace,* just as in v. 349 [[337]] ἀφύλακτον εὐδήσουσι πᾶσαν εὐφρόνην = οἶμαι εὕδουσι, for the night is passing away as Clytaemestra speaks. We have the same idiom in English: *he will be crossing the Channel by now*; and it is Latin too: Iuu. I 126 *quiescet.*

429 [[420]]. I suppose we are all in the habit of thinking πενθήμονες a very poetical epithet and are ready to resent its expulsion ‖ as the act of a Vandal. Let us see: the word must mean one of two things. It may mean *of sorrowful aspect*: this is so thoroughly aimless that I suppose I may dismiss it at once: there is no assignable reason why the visions of Helen should always or ever wear a sorrowful look. It may mean, and it is commonly taken to mean, *causing sorrow.* This is not pointless like the other rendering; but it is something worse. That the visions cause sorrow is true; but how do they cause it? Not by their arrival – that causes joy – but by their departure. To call them πενθήμονες at the outset is to anticipate and utterly to ruin the exquisite turn of ματαίαν following hard on χάριν and echoed by μάταν, the key-note of the mournful cadence ensuing. If I had my own taste only to trust to, I would hold my peace; but hear Euripides. He in *Alc.* 348–56 is imitating this passage: the κολοσσῶν of Aeschylus suggests to him σοφῇ δὲ χειρὶ τεκτόνων δέμας τὸ σὸν | εἰκασθὲν ἐν λέκτροισιν ἐκταθήσεται | ᾧ προσπεσοῦμαι κτλ.; and then he goes on ἐν δ' ὀνείρασιν | φοιτῶσά μ' εὐφραίνοις ἄν · ἡδὺ γὰρ φίλους | κἀν νυκτὶ λεύσσειν, ὅντιν' ἂν παρῇ χρόνον. That is just what I said above: the visions themselves give joy, while they stay: what gives sorrow is their evanescence. I think then that whatever Euripides found in the text of Aeschylus he did not find πενθήμονες: the word that was in the text I will try to recover from another imitator. Propertius was familiar with this stasimon of the *Agamemnon*: one famous passage suggested to him III 12 13 'neue aliquid de te

[1] I would now read κύριός εἰμι θροεῖν ὅδιον κῦρος αἴσιον, ἀνδρῶν εἰς τελέων: κῦρος *hapax* is to κύρμα as πρᾶγος to πρᾶγμα: the scholiast explains τὸ συμβὰν αὐτοῖς σημεῖον ἐξιοῦσιν. For the confusion with κράτος see *Ag.* 10 (Margoliouth) and Soph. *O.T.* 1196 [[1197]] (Heimsoeth): that the MSS of Aeschylus and Aristophanes should agree in error is a strange accident due to the extreme rarity of the word.

flendum referatur in urna: | sic redeunt, illis qui cecidere locis': and in writing the poem whose mangled remains they call the Queen of Elegies he naturally resorted to this locus classicus for the griefs of the widower. There the dead Cornelia speaks thus, 81 sqq. 'sat tibi sint noctes, quas de me, Paule, fatiges, | somniaque in faciem credita saepe meam; | atque, ubi secreto nostra ad simulacra loqueris, | ut responsurae singula uerba iace'. In these lines *simulacra* comes from Aeschylus' κολοσσῶν; and *somnia in faciem credita meam*, Latin of an audacious sort which no Roman durst permit himself except he were translating or mistranslating Greek, reads to me like a rendering of ὀνειρόφαντοι πειθή-μονες δόξαι, visions which || persuade him that they are Helen.[1] Let me add that Euripides' ἐν ὀνείρασι φοιτῶσα awakes in me more than a suspicion that he read in his Aeschylus not ὀνειρόφαντοι but ὀνειρόφοιτοι. For this confusion see *P. V.* 684 [657] where the Medicean has νυκτίφαντα and other MSS νυκτίφοιτα, and *Ag.* 82 where it is impossible to say whether we ought to read ἡμερόφαντον with Triclinius or ἡμερόφοιτον with H. L. Ahrens for the corrupt ἡμερόφατον. But ὀνειρόφαντοι is faultless in itself, so I keep it: πενθήμονες is not faultless.

431 [423]. As this line runs in the MS it has no construction, and the usual remedy is Scholefield's ὁρᾷ. But if this mends the grammar it does little indeed to make sense. To begin with: I thought we were talking about Menelaus; but who is this τις to whom we are now introduced? To drift off into a generalisation is murder to the noble verses; and I trust there is no man so void of discrimination as to adduce the usage in Soph. *El.* 1406 βοᾷ τις ἔνδον, or Ar. *Ran.* 664 ἤλγησέν τις. Secondly, ἐσθλά is *good things*, a term which may indeed include, wretchedly inadequate though it be, the apparition of an absent wife, but which includes a thousand things besides, to all of which the sequel must perforce apply and cannot apply without extreme absurdity. Extremely absurd I call it to say that whenever a man sees good things in sleep they slip through his hands: suppose he sees the council of the elders, or the temples of the gods, or the gods themselves, is it through his hands that they slip when they vanish away? Thirdly, the words διὰ χερῶν demand that some mention of an attempt to *grasp* the apparitions shall have preceded. Keck's conjecture εἴτ' ἂν...ὁρᾶν is designed to meet this last difficulty, but leaves the others untouched. The reading given above, I hope, removes them all: *when he looks to touch the phantoms*. For ὁρῶ ἔς τι see Eur. *frag.* 161 Dind. [162 Nauck] ἀνδρὸς δ' ὁρῶντος εἰς Κύπριν νεανίου | ἀφύλακτος ἡ τήρησις, *I. A.* 1624 στρατὸς πρὸς πλοῦν ὁρᾷ. For δοκή = δόκησις see Hermann's note on the preceding || verse: he there proposes to substitute δοκαί for δόξαι, but Ahrens' transposition in the strophe seems the more rhythmical amendment. I cannot doubt that Karsten rightly introduces this

---

[1] πειθήμονες is supported also by Meleager *Anth. Gr.* v 166 ἆρα μένει στοργῆς ἐμὰ λείψανα καὶ τὸ φίλημα | μνημόσυνον ψυχρᾷ θάλπετ' ἐν εἰκασίᾳ; | ἆρά γ' ἔχει σύγκοιτα τὰ δάκρυα κἀμὸν ὄνειρον | ψυχαπάτην στέρνοις ἀμφιβαλοῦσα φιλεῖ;

word in v. 970 ⟦980⟧ δοκᾶν δυσκρίτων ὀνειράτων for the unintelligible δίκαν of the MS: Euripides seems to imitate the phrase in the δόκημα ὀνείρων of *H. F.* 111. For θιγή do not see the lexicons: it is not there. Aeschylus however had no foreknowledge of this circumstance, nor would such foreknowledge have deterred him from the use or coinage of a word which was his by indefeasible birthright to use or coin. Scholars who dispute either of these propositions are free to tell us that we must not introduce new words: scholars who do not dispute them are not free to tell us so. It is of course necessary that the would-be emender of Aeschylus should be grounded in the elementary laws of the Greek language; but so much being granted, the addition of new ἅπαξ εἰρημένα to the scores already registered is not merely safe but imperatively necessary. It is manifest that the more unfamiliar a word is to a copyist the more likely is he to corrupt it; and thus no word runs such risk of corruption as a word which occurs but once. Now for the history of the error here. The incessant confusion of Γ and T produced εσθιτας; this by the inversion of three letters became εσθα τις; the scribe then hastened to make Greek of the no-word εσθα, if indeed the Λ be not a mere iteration of the A. This inversion of three letters is a corruption with examples of which MSS, Greek and Latin, abound; but I confine myself to the Medicean MS. Here then I find Aesch. *P. V.* 55 λαβών for βαλών, *Ag.* 762 ⟦767⟧ κότον for τόκου, 1367 ⟦1368⟧ μυθοῦσθαι for θυμοῦσθαι, *Eum.* 500 ⟦497⟧ προσμένει for προσνεμεῖ, 719 ⟦716⟧ μένων for νέμων, 730 ⟦727⟧ δαίμονας for διανομάς, Soph. *Ai.* 1307 λέγων for γελῶν, *Ant.* 718 θυμῷ for μύθῳ, 965 ἠρέθιζε for ἠθέριζε, *El.* 567 ἐξεκίνησεν for ἐξενίκησεν, *Phil.* 680 ⟦678⟧ ἔλαβ᾽ ὁ for ἔβαλεν, 1429 ἐκβαλών for ἐκλαβών, *O. C.* 475 βαλών for λαβών. In Aesch. *Pers.* 164 sq. ⟦161 sq.⟧ we read καί με καρδίαν ἀμύσσει φροντίς· ἐς δ᾽ ὑμᾶς ἐρῶ | μῦθον, οὐδαμῶς ἐμαυτῆς οὖσ᾽ ἀδείμαντος, φίλοι, | μὴ κτλ., where ἐμαυτῆς has no meaning; neither in Weil's conjecture μῦθον οὐδαμῶς ἐμαυτῆς οὐδ᾽ ἀδείμαντον can I get any satisfactory sense from the words || οὐδαμῶς ἐμαυτῆς: I propose ἐς δ᾽ ὑμᾶς ἐρῶ, | θυμὸν οὐδαμῶς ἐμαυτῆς οὖσ᾽ ἀδείμαντος. Often too, as in our case of ATI for ΙΓΑ, this inversion is united with the change of one letter into another letter of like shape or sound: Aesch. *P. V.* 397 ⟦381⟧ προθυμεῖσθαι and προμηθεῖσθαι, 448 ⟦432⟧ βαθύς for βυθός, *Ag.* 1605 ἐπὶ δέκ᾽ ἀθλίῳ for ἔλιπε κάθλίῳ, 1621 γῆρας for ῥῖγος, *Cho.* 470 ⟦472⟧ ἑκάς for ἄκος, Soph. *O. T.* 48 προθυμίας and προμηθίας, *O. C.* 550 ἀπεστάλη for ἐφ᾽ ἀστάλη. The alteration of δοκᾶν to δοκῶν is no marvel: a Doric gen. of this declension may count itself lucky if the scribe neither translates it to the common form nor transmutes it to an acc. sing. With the adscript iota ὁρᾶι is in our MSS barely distinguishable from ὁρᾶν. And now turn to Milton's sonnet on his late espoused saint and see how, though the dust of centuries lay thick upon the page of Aeschylus, one great poet unwittingly repeated the very phrase of another: 'But lo, *as to embrace me she inclined,* I waked, she fled, and day brought back my night.'

434 [426]. πτεροῖς and κελεύθοις cannot both have been written by Aeschylus; but I hardly know which of the rival conjectures to accept: perhaps Karsten's κελεύθων is the simplest.

436 [428]. ὑπερβατώτερα is just defensible, only just; though the numerous editors who retain it do not seem to be aware that it needs defence. The word ὑπερβατός nowhere else means *passing* or anything like it; and if it did, you would expect τῶνδ' ὑπερβατά *passing these*, not τῶνδ' ὑπερβατώτερα *more passing than these*. Still ὑπερβατός undeniably might have an active sense, and might possibly, by the same inaccuracy which gives us *more transcendent* in English, have a comparative and superlative. But that Aeschylus wrote this when by writing ὑπερκοπώτερα he might have written what was more forcible, more like himself, and in our MSS most easily corrupted to ὑπερβατώτερα, I doubt.

437–9 [429–31]. If τὸ πᾶν ξυνορμένοις could mean πᾶσι τοῖς ξυνορμένοις, if ξυνορμένοις πρέπει could mean πρέπει, τὸ τῶν ξυνορμένων μέρος, if πένθεια could mean πένθος, if τλησικάρδιος could mean καρδιόδηκτος, if δόμων could mean ἐν δόμοις, if these five impossibilities were possible, then the sense, if sense it can be called, which commentators elicit from these ‖ three lines, would be elicited legitimately. But as things are it is elicited by casting down the foundations of Greek. In particular, the verse πένθεια τλησικάρδιος is perhaps the most appalling sight which the MSS of Aeschylus have to shew. When σέβεια, πάθεια, θυμία, πραξία and the like are words, then πένθεια will be a word: till then it is a mere collocation of letters. δυσπένθεια is a word: it is found in no Greek author, but it is a word: πένθεια would remain no word were it found in fifty Greek authors. Scholars who tamely accept from a scribe such monstrosities as this, or as εὔπραξις in v. 267 [255], are not entitled to laugh when Prof. Newman presents them with ὁσιογέννημα. But admit for an instant the inadmissible, admit that πένθεια can mean πένθος: to a substantive of that meaning the adjective τλησικάρδιος can by no possibility be applied, neither can τλησίφρων, ταλακάρδιος, ταλάφρων, ταλαίφρων, ταλασίφρων, τλήθυμος or φρεσὶν τλήμων: both their two significations forbid it. As to the interpretation of the passage as a whole, all commentators, I believe, supply Ἀχαιοῖς with ξυνορμένοις. The antithesis between κατ' οἴκους ἐφεστίους and ἀφ' Ἕλλανος αἴας pointed by μέν in v. 435 [427] and δέ in v. 437 [429] should have taught them to supply not Ἀχαιοῖς but Ἀτρείδαις. With this for a clue, vv. 437–9 [429–31] can be mended by the slightest of changes: *These are the sorrows of the hearth, ay and worse than these; but, I guess, since quitting Hellas, these sorrows look like joy in their eyes, amid their sufferings far from home.* Great as was the misery of the Atridae in their deserted palace, yet their misery at Troy, to see their followers dying around them and to hear the threatening murmurs of the survivors, is so much greater that they wish the former sorrow back: it seems desirable by contrast. So

Sophocles says *O. C.* 1697 πόθος τοι καὶ κακῶν ἄρ' ἦν τις: Euripides puts the same thought in still stronger language, *Tro.* 431 sqq., δύστηνος οὐκ οἶδ' οἷά νιν μένει παθεῖν · | ὡς χρυσὸς αὐτῷ τἀμὰ καὶ Φρυγῶν κακὰ | δόξει ποτ' εἶναι. It is of course to Mr Verrall's paper in vol. ıx of this Journal that I owe τοπᾶν, a lost verb which has the meaning of the cognate τοπάζειν. For the infin. of a like verb used in like manner (τοπᾶν = ὡς τοπᾶν) see Soph. *O. T.* 82 ἀλλ', εἰκάσαι μέν, ἡδύς: so very often ‖ δοκεῖν ἐμοί. If any one is afraid of the word I counsel him to take Karsten's τόπων, which also makes good sense. Since o and ε are hardly to be known from one another, the only difference between ποθεινά and πένθεια is the position of ν: of this corruption I spoke in my note on v. 58. As for the correction ἑκάς που, in which I find myself forestalled by Ahrens, π becomes τ if the ink of the two downstrokes runs together: see Wecklein's *app. crit.* on v. 1416 'εὐτόκοις, forte ut videtur ex εὐπόκοις factum, g.'

440 [432]. Those who render θιγγάνει as if it were χωρεῖ should favour us with a parallel. If the words are sound, as I think they are, we must understand αὐτῶν with Blomfield. I would not alter θιγγάνει, nor would I propose πόλλ' ἀγοῖν.

441 sq. [433 sq.]. The sum total of the changes which I have made here is no greater departure from the MS than Porson's insertion of τις after γάρ, and the sense I surely improve: in the vulgate you must strain οἶδεν to make it mean μέμνηται and then your imagination must furnish ἄγνωτα with τεύχη καὶ σποδός, to extort your antithesis. The construction of my text will be τοιοῦτον μὲν γὰρ οὐδέν, οἵους ἔπεμψαν ἑκάστου δόμοι, εἰς αὐτοὺς ἀφικνεῖται, τεύχη δὲ καὶ σποδὸς ἀντὶ φωτῶν: *for unto each one's home there returns nought in the semblance of those whom it sent forth, but arms only and ashes in lieu of men.* The frequent confusion of ı and υ accounts for the corruption of οἵους and οὐδέν both, and the inflexion of ἔπεμψαν was accommodated to that of οἶδεν, since metre forbade the converse error.

498–504 [493–9]

κήρυκ' ἀπ' ἀκτῆς τόνδ' ὁρῶ κατάσκιον
κλάδοις ἐλαίας · μαρτυρεῖ δέ μοι κάσις
πηλοῦ ξύνουρος διψία κόνις τάδε,
ὡς οὔτ' ἄναυδος οὔτε σοι δαίων φλόγα
ὕλης ὀρείας σημανεῖ καπνῷ πυρός
ἀλλ' ἢ τὸ χαίρειν μᾶλλον ἐκβάξει λέγων –
τὸν ἀντίον δὲ τοῖσδ' ἀποστέργω λόγον.

500 [495]

The coryphaeus catching sight of the herald sees also in the distance a cloud of dust which he supposes to be raised by the returning army; and the return of the army means something ‖ decisive, either victory or defeat. The crew of Agamemnon's ship, if Aeschylus followed Homer, would be 120 men; and these, together with an ἁμαξήρης θρόνος for Agamemnon and Cassandra, would raise in clear dry southern air a cloud of dust to be seen a great way off. No doubt to us the allusion seems obscurely worded; but I fancy the Attic audience recognised an old friend. Of the plays of Aeschylus only a tithe has come down to us, but in that tithe we find *Supp.* 186 〚180〛 ὁρῶ κόνιν, ἄναυδον ἄγγελον στρατοῦ, and *Sept.* 79 sqq. μεθεῖται στρατὸς στρατόπεδον λιπών. | ῥεῖ πολὺς ὅδε λεὼς πρόδρομος ἱππότας. | αἰθερία κόνις με πείθει φανεῖσ᾽ | ἄναυδος σαφὴς ἔτυμος ἄγγελος. How many repetitions of the phrase lie foundered in the wreck of antiquity we cannot tell; but it may be guessed that by the time the poet wrote this play – three years before his death – he had so familiarised his hearers with the conception of κόνις as an ἄγγελος στρατοῦ that he could dispense with an explicit reminder. The addition κάσις πηλοῦ ξύνουρος is mere ornament like the αἰόλην πυρὸς κάσιν of *Sept.* 481 〚494〛. What coherent sense those scholars who take κόνις to be the stains of travel on the herald's dress suppose themselves to extract from the passage, I have vainly tried to ascertain.

My business however is with the σοι of v. 501 〚496〛. Mr Margoliouth observes 'σοι *tibi*, Clytemnestrae'. That σοι means *tibi* is very true, and it is equally indisputable that only Clytaemestra can here be signified. But that is the very reason why σοι cannot be right; for it is as certain as anything about Greek plays can be certain that Clytaemestra is not now on the stage. The conjectures του, μοι, τοι and γ᾽ αὖ bear witness to a due appreciation of the difficulty; and if the reader is satisfied with any one of them he will not trouble himself about me when I propose ὡς οὐκ ἄναυδος οὗτος ἀνδαίων φλόγα | ὕλης ὀρείας σημανεῖ κτλ. The phrase ἀνδαίων φλόγα is chosen to recall the phrase in the ἀγγαρήιον at v. 317 〚305〛 πέμπουσι δ᾽ ἀνδαίοντες ἀφθόνῳ μένει | φλογὸς μέγαν πώγωνα. In the MSS of Aeschylus the wrongful omission or insertion of ν after a vowel is exceedingly common: it would seem indeed that the practice of denoting ν merely by a superscript line, usually confined to final syllables, must in some ancestral codex have prevailed in ‖ all parts of words alike. The confusion of α with the diphthong οι, which is simply α resolved into its constituent elements, is of course a very frequent error. The facility with which αν might so pass through α to οι is illustrated by the confusions of -φαντος and -φοιτος which I adduced on v. 429 〚420〛. Thus οὗτος ἀνδαίων is scarcely distinguishable from οὔτε σοι δαίων, and οὔτε of course demanded the change of οὐκ to οὔτ᾽: in fact οὐκ, οὔτ᾽ and οὐδ᾽ are for ever interchanged even when such excuse is absent.

550–2 〚545–7〛

ΚΗ. ποθεῖν ποθοῦντα τήνδε γῆν στρατὸν λέγεις.
ΧΟ. ὡς πόλλ᾽ ἀμαυρᾶς ἐκ φρενός μ᾽ ἀναστένειν.
ΚΗ. πόθεν τὸ δύσφρον τοῦτ᾽ ἐπῆν στύγος στρατῷ;

The last word is of course precisely the reverse of what we want: we want πόλει or the like. The only conjecture which merits consideration is Heimsoeth's λεώ (he writes it λεῷ), on which word he supposes στρατῷ was a mistaken gloss. My objection to this is that if Aeschylus wrote λεώ he was gravely in fault for using so ambiguous a word: λαός in the *Iliad* is the regular name for the army at Troy. I should therefore much prefer to read πάτρᾳ. The close likeness of one form of π to στ is notorious, the confusion of α and ω common enough, and such transposition as has here been suffered by ρ I have already illustrated: πατρᾳ, στατρᾳ, στρατᾳ, στρατῷ is the facilis descensus.

560–3 ⟦555–8⟧

μόχθους γὰρ εἰ λέγοιμι καὶ δυσαυλίας,
σπαρνὰς παρήξεις καὶ κακοστρώτους – τί δ' οὐ
στένοντες οὐ λαχόντες ἤματος μέρος;
τὰ δ' αὖτε χέρσῳ καὶ προσῆν πλέον στύγος.

'In a word, what was there we had not to complain about, or that we did not get for our daily share?' This is Mr Paley's translation of τί δ' οὐ στένοντες κτλ. How ἤματος μέρος *part of a day* comes to mean *daily share* he makes no attempt to explain, nor does he say a word about the difference in tense of ‖ στένοντες and λαχόντες; but these are trifles, I pass them by. What rivets my attention is the absurdity of the question thus put in the herald's mouth. *What was there that we did not get for our daily share?* Why, the things that they did not get for their daily share were like the sands of the sea for multitude. Their grievance was precisely this, that they got for their daily share no good thing whatever. But, to quit the translation for the text, of course one fatal objection which disposes at once of the MS reading and of half the conjectural essays is that the pendent nominative participles contravene not merely grammar, that is nothing, but the elementary rules of writing. An irregularity in grammar like *Cho.* 518 ⟦520⟧ τὰ πάντα γάρ τις ἐκχέας ἀνθ' αἵματος | ἑνός, μάτην ὁ μόχθος is not only legitimate but may be used with fine effect; but the man who thinks that because a nominative absolute can replace a genitive absolute therefore a participle can replace the principal verb of a sentence, is not destined to succeed in criticism. The most plausible of the conjectures which address themselves to the cure of this evil is perhaps Mr Margoliouth's στένοντας, ἀσχάλλοντας. This however though not very far from the MS is yet not very near: the change of the inflexions, in particular, is hard to explain: that I do not like the nature of the aposiopesis may be due merely to the fact that I have my own nostrum, which I will now prescribe. When I glance below at vv. 568–72 ⟦563–7⟧ χειμῶνα δ' εἰ λέγοι τις...ἢ θάλπος... – τί ταῦτα πενθεῖν δεῖ; παροίχεται πόνος I cannot stifle the suspicion that in v. 561 ⟦556⟧ the words τί δ' οὐ are simply the corruption, the very easy corruption, of τί δεῖ, breaking off the conditional sentence in a manner exactly parallel; and on this hint a touch or two will correct the lines.

– τί δεῖ
στένοντος εὖ λαχόντας ἥπατος μέρος;

what do men of right temper want with a mourner? The construction is the familiar one of αὐτὸν γάρ σε δεῖ προμηθέως: for τί δεῖ στένοντος compare *Eum.* 94 καθευδουσῶν τί δεῖ; for εὖ λαχόντας = τοὺς εὖ λαχόντας see v. 39 μαθοῦσιν αὐδῶ κοὐ μαθοῦσι λήθομαι and a dozen more passages in Aeschylus. The phrase εὖ λαχόντας ἥπατος μέρος finds a counterpart in v. 391 [380] ‖ εὖ πραπίδων λαχόντα: the poet might have written εὖ πραπίδων λαχόντα μέρος in that place or εὖ λαχόντας ἥπατος in this without a whit of difference to the sense. λαχεῖν τινος without μέρος is the more common, but you have Theogn. 453 εἰ γνώμης ἔλαχες μέρος and Soph. *Ant.* 918 οὔτε του γάμου | μέρος λαχοῦσαν: μεταλαχεῖν τινος but also Eur. *Supp.* 1078 μετέλαχες τύχας Οἰδιπόδα, γέρον, μέρος: μετέχειν τινός but also *Ag.* 512 [507] μεθέξειν φιλτάτου τάφου μέρος: μέτεστί τινος but also Eur. *I. T.* 1299 μέτεστι χὐμῖν τῶν πεπραγμένων μέρος, wrongfully suspected by Nauck and Wecklein. Throughout tragedy the ἧπαρ is the part of the mind or soul which feels regret and remorse: ὁ εὖ ἥπατος λαχών then is the man whose ἧπαρ is proof against the excess of these emotions, the man who is not the victim of self-tormenting regrets for the irremediable past, of the ἄλγος παλίγκοτον disapproved in v. 576 [571] if we there accept the correction of H. L. Ahrens as those must who are not prepared to invent a new meaning for παλίγκοτος. The herald therefore, as I understand him, checks himself in the midst of his recital with the reflexion that men of a right and happy temper of soul, like those to whom he speaks, do not want to hear unavailing lamentation over the past. But then at v. 563 [558] other hardships recur to his mind and spring to his lips: then he checks himself again at v. 572 [567] with a similar reflexion.

It will be seen that the incessant confusion of ε and ο is responsible for the change of δεῖ στένοντος εὖ into δ' οὐ στένοντες οὐ: the change of inflexion in λαχόντας was due of course to the στένοντες thus produced. The confusion of Π with that form of M in which one slightly curved line replaces the two diagonal strokes is chargeable with the errors ὅπως for ὅμως in v. 980 [990], βλέπει for βρέμει in v. 1015 [1030] and δυσπαθῆ for δυσμαθῆ in v. 1254 [1255]: besides the ἥματος for ἥπατος of our passage I think I detect another instance in the play. In v. 1432 sqq. [1431 sqq.] καὶ τήνδ' ἀκούεις ὁρκίων ἐμῶν θέμιν · | μὰ τὴν τέλειον τῆς ἐμῆς παιδὸς Δίκην κτλ. the use of ὁρκίων for ὅρκων is improper, and though ὅρκων θέμις might perhaps stand for ὅρκος θεμιστός *lawful oath* yet it is quite without point to call the oath which follows either lawful or unlawful: Clytaemestra ‖ simply swears that she is not afraid. When I contemplate this verse there rings in my ear another, *Cho.* 498 [500]: καὶ τῆσδ' ἄκουσον λοισθίου βοῆς, πάτερ. Should we not write καὶ τῶνδ' ἀκούοις ὁρκίων ἐπῶν, Θέμι? The restorations are all easy, ω for η, οι for ει, π for μ, ι for ῑ. Mr Margoliouth reads καὶ τήνδ' ἀκούειν ὁρκίαν φήμην θέμις: this meaning might be obtained at less expense by καὶ τῶνδ' ἀκούειν σ' ὁρκίων ἐπῶν θέμις, but I should still prefer the reading given above.

886–94 ⟦895–903⟧

νῦν, ταῦτα πάντα τλᾶσ', ἀπενθήτῳ φρενὶ
λέγοιμ' ἂν ἄνδρα τόνδ' ἐγὼ σταθμῶν κύνα,
σωτῆρα ναὸς πρότονον, ὑψηλῆς στέγης
στῦλον ποδήρη, μονογενὲς τέκνον πατρί,
καὶ γῆν φανεῖσαν ναυτίλοις παρ' ἐλπίδα,
κάλλιστον ἦμαρ εἰσιδεῖν ἐκ χείματος,
ὁδοιπόρῳ διψῶντι πηγαῖον ῥέος.
τερπνὸν δὲ τἀναγκαῖον ἐκφυγεῖν ἅπαν.
τοιοῖσδέ τοί νιν ἀξιῶ προσφθέγμασιν.

890 ⟦899⟧

In these lines as they stand three serious faults have been pointed out. Firstly, it is plain that when you call a man by seven προσφθέγματα you do not, if you have regard to style, connect the fourth and the fifth by καί leaving the rest ἀσύνδετα. To mend this fault Blomfield proposes γαῖαν for καὶ γῆν in v. 890 ⟦899⟧, a conjecture which gets some support from *Eum.* 758 ⟦755⟧ where Dindorf's γαίας for καὶ γῆς seems a probable emendation. Secondly, that Aeschylus did not put v. 893 ⟦902⟧ where it now stands, severing v. 894 ⟦903⟧ from the προσφθέγματα to which it refers, is evident to every one who understands, I do not say the art of poetry, but I say the art of writing respectable verse. To mend this fault Enger inserts v. 893 ⟦902⟧ as a parenthesis between 886 ⟦895⟧ and 887 ⟦896⟧. Thirdly, I cannot help feeling, with Hermann and Meineke, that the superlative κάλλιστον in v. 891 ⟦900⟧ as an epithet to ἦμαρ gravely impairs the force of the phrase. To mend this fault the conjectures γαληνόν and γανυστόν have been proposed, but of course are only valuable as testifying a perception of the difficulty. ‖

I have hit on a device, which seems at least as simple as Blomfield's and Enger's, to mend all three faults at once. I propose to remove the four verses 890–3 ⟦899–902⟧ from their present seat, so that μονογενὲς τέκνον πατρί shall be followed by τοιοῖσδέ τοί νιν ἀξιῶ προσφθέγμασιν, and to insert them nine lines lower down, with one slight change, in the following order:

εὐθὺς γενέσθω πορφυρόστρωτος πόρος
ἐς δῶμ' ἄελπτον ὡς ἂν ἡγῆται δίκη.
κάλλιστον ἦμαρ εἰσιδεῖν ἐκ χείματος,
ὁδοιπόρῳ διψῶντι πηγαῖον ῥέος
καὶ γῆ φανεῖσα ναυτίλοις παρ' ἐλπίδα·
τερπνὸν δὲ τἀναγκαῖον ἐκφυγεῖν ἅπαν.

902 ⟦911⟧
891 ⟦900⟧
892 ⟦901⟧
890 ⟦899⟧
893 ⟦902⟧

When the word ἄελπτον has passed Clytaemestra's lips, its ring of menace is so clear to her guilty ear that she hastens to obscure its real significance by resort to the familiar saw that unexpected pleasure is sweetest. Sweetest, she says, is sunshine after storm, water to a traveller athirst, land ahead when the mariner least expects it; and indeed there is pleasure in all escape from stress of fortune: therefore, she implies, Agamemnon's home-returning, in which both elements of pleasure, τἀναγκαῖον ἐκφυγεῖν and τὸ ἄελπτον, are combined, is sweetest of all. It is noticeable that her speech at the end of this episode is closed with a similar digression on a word, vv. 963-5 [972-4]: she has said ἀνδρὸς τελείου, and she bursts out Ζεῦ Ζεῦ τέλειε, τὰς ἐμὰς εὐχὰς τέλει. In v. 891 [900] κάλλιστον, transformed from attribute to predicate, is now without offence: the corruption in v. 890 [899] arose from the adhesion to φανεῖσα of the initial ν of ναυτίλοις, whence the further change, by assimilation, of γῆ to γῆν.

I seem to myself to find external confirmation of this arrangement in two passages imitated, I think, from this. One is the distich, ascribed to the name Asclepiades, which Blomfield cites: ἡδὺ θέρους διψῶντι χιὼν ποτόν, ἡδὺ δὲ ναύταις | ἐκ χειμῶνος ἰδεῖν εἰαρινὸν στέφανον [AP 5 169], almost a paraphrase of the verses as I write them. The second is Eur. fr. 552 Dind. [550 Nauck] ἐκ τῶν ἀέλπτων ἡ χάρις μείζων βροτοῖς | φανεῖσα μᾶλλον ἢ τὸ προσδοκώμενον. || 'Vs. 2 aut spurius aut corruptus' says Nauck: 'corrupt, surely not spurious' says Munro: neither spurious nor corrupt, I must take heart to say. Construe φανεῖσα with ἐκ τῶν ἀέλπτων, and for the pleonasm μείζων μᾶλλον see Hec. 377 θανὼν δ' ἂν εἴη μᾶλλον εὐτυχέστερος | ἢ ζῶν.

990-1009 [1001-24]

μάλα βροτοῖσι τᾶς πολλᾶς ὑγιέας	str.
ἀκόρεστον τέρμα. νόσος γὰρ
γείτων ὁμότοιχος ἐρείδει ·
καὶ πότμος εὐθυπορῶν
ἀνδρὸς ἔπαισεν ⟨ἄφνω
δυστυχίας⟩ ἄφαντον ἕρμα.
καὶ τὸ μὲν πρὸ χρημάτων	995 [1007]
κτησίων ὄκνος βαλὼν
σφενδόνας ἀπ' εὐμέτρου
οὐκ ἔδυ πρόπας δόμος
πημονᾶς γέμων ἄγαν
οὐδ' ἐπόντισε σκάφος ·	1000 [1013]
πολλά τοι δόσις ἐκ Διὸς ἀμφιλαφής τε καὶ
ἐξ ἀλόκων ἐπετειᾶν
νῆστιν ἤλασεν νόσον.
τὸ δ' ἐπὶ γᾶν ἅπαξ πεσὸν θανασίμου	ant.

1005 [1019]
πρόπαρ ἀνδρὸς τίς μέλαν αἷμ' ἂν
πάλιν ἀγκαλέσαιτ' ἐπαείδων;
τοῦδε τὸν ὀρθοδαῆ
τῶν φθιμένων ἀνάγειν
Ζεὺς ἀπέπαυσ' ἐπ' εὐλαβείᾳ.

Vv. 990–4 [1001–6] and 1004–9 [1017–24] I have restored provisionally to show the drift of the whole passage, but without firm faith that I am giving the precise words of Aeschylus. The metres of strophe and antistrophe now correspond, except twice in anacrusis, where correspondence is not required; though perhaps γείτων in v. 992 [1004] is a gloss on πελάτας. How much of the change is my own and how much borrowed I leave the curious reader to seek from Wecklein. But on vv. 995–1000 [1007–13] I hope I have something definite to say. ‖

With the pendent nominative ὄκνος βαλών I do not quarrel: harsh it may be, but it has ample warrant. But anyone who will consult the lexicons will see that of all the Greek words which we render in English by *fear*, ὄκνος is in this place the least appropriate: ὄκνος connotes shrinking and sluggishness, not the alertness and presence of mind which saves the ship by casting away the cargo. Further I should like to know what sense editors attach to σφενδόνας ἀπ' εὐμέτρου *from a sling of just proportions*. Mr Paley renders 'by a well-calculated throw'; on which I have to remark, first, that no engines of torture will wring that meaning from the Greek, and secondly that any such meaning is entirely irrelevant to the context. If you want to hit a mark, then you require a well-calculated (εὔστοχος) throw: but it is news to me that you need precision of aim to pitch your goods overboard. And setting aside these details I wish to point out that the general sense yielded by vv. 995–7 [1007–10], or perhaps I should rather say extorted from them, is not the sense which the context demands.

So far as I can discover the general opinion about the connexion of vv. 995–1009 [1007–24], that opinion is demonstrably wrong. All editors, I believe, put a full stop where I have put a colon after σκάφος in v. 1000 [1013], and all, I presume, summarise with Mr Sidgwick thus: 'a labouring boat may be saved (995–1000), a famine averted (1001–3), but blood once shed is irrevocable (1004–9).' It will not be denied, when it is once asserted, that this would require a connecting particle in v. 1001 [1014]. When Mr Paley translates 'doubtless *too* a good supply...puts an end to famine', and when Dr Kennedy translates '*And* truly gifts abundant...have brought...famine to an end', those scholars forge this necessary link on the anvil of their imagination: in the Greek they do not find it. Mr Sidgwick says 'the connexion is abrupt: perhaps τοι is corrupt'. But a right account of the connexion will show that τοι is quite sound. The chorus in vv. 990–4 [1001–6] lay down the doctrine, recurring in fifty passages of Greek verse and prose, that over-great prosperity brings ruin, strikes in mid career on a reef. Yet (995–1000 ⟦1007–13⟧: καί = atque) if a man then sacrifice his substance he may avert utter destruction from his house: God (1001–3 ⟦1014–16⟧) can ‖ restore him *substance* enough for his wants. But (1004–9 ⟦1017–24⟧) if that which is sacrificed be not man's substance but man's *life*, that none can restore. This seems clear and coherent sense, and the only sense which the form of the passage permits: vv. 1001–3 ⟦1014–16⟧ then have reference to 995–7 ⟦1007–10⟧. Now let me ask attention to the words νῆστιν νόσον in v. 1003 ⟦1016⟧: what brings this mention of *famine?* Does famine come from throwing overboard *a part* (τὸ μέν) of your cargo? No: from throwing overboard *the whole.*

> καὶ γόμον πρὸ χρημάτων
> κτησίων κενὸς βαλὼν
> σφενδόνας ἀπ᾽ εὐμέτρου
> οὐκ ἔδυ πρόπας δόμος.

Yet if the house cast overboard, till nought be left, its freight of possessions from a capacious sling (in English metaphor *with unstinting hand*), *it sinks not utterly.* The epithet εὐμέτρου now has its proper force *of just proportions*, that is, large enough to hold the entire freight. It is usually said that πρό and βαλών are in tmesi: I should prefer to call πρό the adverb. The change of ΓΟΜΟΝ to ΤΟ ΜΕΝ I need not explain; but perhaps I should say a word on the corruption of κενός. In my note on v. 133 ⟦128⟧ I gave instances of two consecutive letters reversed: here we have this error combined with alteration of one out of the two letters. This mistake is rendered the easier by the custom of writing one letter over another for brevity's sake. The rule requires that the superscript letter should be read as the latter of the two, but it often happens that an ignorant or inattentive scribe will misinterpret the abbreviation when copying it out at length. This is of course the more likely to occur if one of the two letters has been corrupted: when the correct order no longer gives a Greek word the copyist tries to obtain one by inversion. Similar errors to ὄκνος for κενός are *Ag.* 980 ⟦991⟧ ὑμνῳδεῖ contra metrum for μονῳδεῖ, *Cho.* 661 ⟦665⟧ λεχθεῖσιν for λέσχαισιν, 700 ⟦704⟧ δυσσεβείας for δ᾽ εὐσεβείας, *Supp.* 230 ⟦224⟧ κρέκω for κίρκων, *Sept.* 452 ⟦465⟧ εἰσημάτιστα for ἐσχημάτισται, 682 ⟦695⟧ αἰσχρά for ἐχθρά, a mistake which recurs in Soph. *Phil.* 1284, ἔχθιστος for αἴσχιστος. ‖

But we are not out of the wood yet. The phrase πημονᾶς γέμων is, in its proper place, which is not here, good sense: the phrase πημονᾶς γέμων ἄγαν is, and I am glad to see Weil thinks so too, ridiculous: as if there were such a thing as πημονᾶς γέμειν μετρίως! But further: whether my reading of vv. 995–7 ⟦1007–10⟧ be accepted or no, it is equally certain that the ship is there represented as laden not with πημονή but with χρήματα κτήσια. Therefore we have to say that the χρήματα themselves are here called πημονή as leading to disaster by their too great abundance. Now perhaps there are places where wealth can be called πημονή, but this is a place where it cannot: it cannot be called πημονή when it has just been called ὑγίεια. And the word ἄγαν survives to make nonsense of the present text and to tell us that just as Aeschylus began with the danger of ἡ πολλὴ ὑγίεια, so he here described the sinking ship as γέμων ἄγαν not πημονᾶς but ὄλβου or the like, γέμων τοῦ πολλοῦ ὄλβου. If the reader will turn to the parallel passage *Sept.* 753 sqq. [767 sqq.] he will find, I think, strong confirmation both of the correction I have made in vv. 995 [1007] and 996 [1008] and of the correction I am about to make in v. 999 [1012]. The passage is this: τὰ δ᾽ ὁλοὰ πενομένους παρέρχεται, | πρόπρυμνα δ᾽ ἐκβολὰν φέρει | ἀνδρῶν ἀλφηστᾶν | ὄλβος ἄγαν παχυνθείς. Here πρόπρυμνα (or πρόπρεμνα) ἐκβολάν, rendered by the scholiast ὅλου τοῦ φόρτου ἐκβολήν, is precisely my γόμον πρὸ κενὸς βαλών; and ὄλβος ἄγαν παχυνθείς is δόμος παμονᾶς γέμων ἄγαν.

The word παμονή, which the lexicons do not contain, is to πᾶμα as πημονή to πῆμα, χαρμονή to χάρμα and πλησμονή to πλῆσμα. Against the entire family of words akin to πέπαμαι the copyists πνέουσιν ἄσπονδον Ἄρη. The verb itself, which is common enough, usually escapes with no worse injury than the misspellings πέπαμμαι and ἐπασσάμην, but even the verb sometimes perishes. Thus in Soph. *O. C.* 528 Nauck has to restore δυσώνυμα λέκτρ᾽ ἐπάσω for ἐπλήσω, and Wecklein Ἄιδα μόνον φεῦξιν οὐ πεπάσεται for οὐκ ἐπάξεται in *Ant.* 362. The word πάτωρ has escaped death – Ἄιδα φεῦξιν πέπαται – only in Photius who has πάτορες· κτήτορες: elsewhere πατήρ has swallowed it: Hesych. πάτορες [W. Dindorf, πατέρες MS]· ‖ πλούσιοι, Eur. *fr.* 654 Dind. [659 Nauck] χρημάτων | πολλῶν κεκλῆσθαι βούλεται πάτωρ [W. Dindorf, πατὴρ MSS] δόμοις, *Phoen.* 473 ἐγὼ δὲ πάτωρ [Munro, πατρὸς MSS] δωμάτων προὐσκεψάμην | τοὐμόν τε καὶ τοῦδ᾽. The word πολυπάμων has escaped in *Iliad* Δ 433 and in Hesych. πολυπάμονος· πολλὴν κτῆσιν ἔχοντος, and πολυπάμων · πλούσιος, πολλὰ κεκτημένος, πολυχρήμων, πάματα γὰρ τὰ χρήματα; but it has perished in Soph. *El.* 515 οὔτι πω | ἔλιπεν ἐκ τοῦδ᾽ οἴκους | πολύπονος αἰκία, where the scholion τοὺς πολυκτήμονας δόμους points as Schneidewin has seen to the reading οἴκους πολυπάμονας. The word βουπάμων had to be restored for βουπαλίων by Valckenaer in an epigram of Leonidas Tarentinus (51 tom. 1, p. 167 Anth. Gr. Jacobs [*AP* 6 263]). Hesychius offers other corruptions: ἐπιπαματίδα [Maussacus, ἐπιματίδα MS]· τὴν ἐπίκληρον; ἐμπάμονι [Hemsterhuys, ἐμπαγμῷ MS]· πατρούχῳ; αὐτοπάμονα [Hemsterhuys, αὐτόπομα MS]· ἐπίκληρον. The word πᾶσις survives only in Hesych. πᾶσις· κτῆσις, but I propose to restore it once at least to Euripides. In *Andr.* 192 sqq. the heroine thus ridicules the jealousy of Hermione: εἴπ᾽, ὦ νεᾶνι, τῷ σ᾽ ἐχεγγύῳ λόγῳ | πεισθεῖσ᾽ ἀπωθῶ γνησίων νυμφευμάτων; | ὡς τῆς Λακαίνης ἡ Φρυγῶν μείζων πόλις | τύχῃ θ᾽ ὑπερθεῖ, κἄμ᾽ ἐλευθέραν ὁρᾷς; | ἢ τῷ νέῳ τε καὶ σφριγῶντι σώματι | πόλεως τε μεγέθει καὶ φίλοις ἐπηρμένη | οἶκον κατασχεῖν τὸν σὸν ἀντὶ σοῦ θέλω; It is plain that in v. 197 the words πόλεως τε μεγέθει cannot be right: the disparity between the one πόλις and the other has already been dealt with in v. 194; so Brunck amends the sense by writing πλούτου. A far slighter change suffices: ΠΟΛΕШC stands merely for ΠCAEШC, which is ΠΑCEШC with one letter misplaced. In Soph. *El.* 837 sqq. is this sentence: οἶδα γὰρ ἄνακτ' Ἀμφιάρεων χρυσοδέτοις ἕρκεσι κρυφθέντα γυναικῶν· καὶ νῦν ὑπὸ γαίας πάμψυχος ἀνάσσει. The two last words are diversely interpreted to mean πασῶν ψυχῶν ἀνάσσει or ἀθάνατος ἀνάσσει or παντὶ σθένει ἀνάσσει. The advocates of each rendering are so triumphantly successful in the easy task of exploding the other two that I can pass the question by to say that I should change one letter and write παμοῦχος ἀνάσσει *he is lord and king*: see Hesych. παμῶχος· ὁ κύριος, the Doric form. ἐπίπαμα is preserved, wrongly spelt, ‖ in the Theocritean scholia, but not in Eur. *I. T.* 414. The chorus there enquire concerning Orestes and Pylades *are they merchants who sail the sea* φιλόπλουτον ἄμιλλαν | αὔξοντες μελάθροισιν; | φίλα γὰρ ἐλπὶς γένετ' ἐπὶ πήμασιν βροτῶν | ἄπληστος ἀνθρώποις, | ὄλβου βάρος οἳ φέρονται | πλάνητες ἐπ' οἶδμα πόλεις τε βαρβάρους περῶντες. The greater part of this antistrophe corresponds very accurately with the strophe; but the verse φίλα γὰρ ἐλπὶς κτλ. differs greatly from the strophic verse 399 τίνες ποτ' ἄρα τὸν εὔυδρον δονακόχλοον, and moreover makes no sense. I would restore meaning and correspondence thus: φίλα γὰρ ἐγένετ' ἐλπὶς ἕν τ' ἐπιπάμασιν | ἄπληστος ἀνθρώποις, where ἐπιπάμασιν is my own conjecture, the other alterations borrowed: *dear unto men is hope, and insatiable in acquisition.* Finally, the word πᾶμα, outside lexicographers and scholiasts, seems to be found only twice in Greek literature: Theocr. *Fistul.* 12 and Dosiad. *Anth. Pal.* 15. 25. 5, pointed out by Valckenaer *Animadv. ad Ammon.* lib. 3, cap. 7. But either I am thoroughly mistaken, or two more instances are to be disinterred from the text of Aeschylus. In *Sept.* 926 sqq. 〚944 sqq.〛 the chorus lament over Eteocles and Polynices who have ended by mutual slaughter their contention for sovereignty: πικρὸς δὲ χρημάτων | ἴσος δατητὰς Ἄρης, ἀρὰν | πατρῴαν τιθεὶς ἀλαθῆ. | ἔχουσι μοῖραν λαχόντες, ὦ μέλεοι, | διοσδότων ἀχέων· | ὑπὸ δὲ σώματι γᾶς | πλοῦτος ἄβυσσος ἔσται. The verse διοσδότων ἀχέων should answer metrically to διατομαῖς οὐ φίλαις in the strophe. Meineke's διαδότων *parted between them* appears to be the first step towards emendation: for α and οσ confused see Porson on Eur. *Hec.* 782 〚794〛. But now are we to write ἀφίλοις with H. Voss in the strophe, or alter ἀχέων in the antistrophe? Assuredly the latter; for ἀχέων, quite apart from metre, does not give a right sense. The ἀρὰ πατρῴα whose fulfilment these lines describe was (773 sqq. 〚788 sqq.〛) σιδαρονόμῳ διὰ χερί ποτε λαχεῖν κτήματα, not ἄχη. Aeschylus seems to have written διαδότων παμάτων: some perversely ingenious reader chose to regard this as Doric for πημάτων, and signified his opinion by writing ἀχέων above it: then the gloss, as usual, expelled the genuine word. With the μοῖραν λαχόντες παμάτων thus restored compare vv. 890 sq. 〚906 sq.〛

ἐμοιράσαντο δ' ὀξυκάρδιοι κτήμαθ' ὥστ' ‖ ἴσον λαχεῖν. Last of all comes an instance of πᾶμα from the *Agamemnon* itself. Look at vv. 1567 sqq. [1568 sqq.]

ἐγὼ δ' οὖν
ἐθέλω δαίμονι τῷ Πλεισθενιδῶν
ὅρκους θεμένη τάδε μὲν στέργειν

1570 [1571] δύστλητά περ ὄνθ' · ὁ δὲ λοιπὸν ἰὼν
ἐκ τῶνδε δόμων ἄλλην γενεὰν
τρίβοι θανάτοις αὐθένταισιν.
κτεάνων τε μέρος
βαιὸν ἐχούσῃ πᾶν ἀπόχρη μοι

1575 [1576] μανίας μελάθρων
ἀλληλοφόνους ἀφελούσῃ.

The τε of v. 1573 [1574] is plainly insufferable. Auratus' δέ is sufferable but still an encumbrance: the connecting particle should be γάρ or there should be no connecting particle. Nor is this the only objection I feel: πᾶν ἀπόχρη μοι *anything suffices me* I could understand, and I could understand μέρος βαιὸν ἐχούσῃ ἀπόχρη μοι *it suffices me to have a small portion*; but μέρος βαιὸν ἐχούσῃ πᾶν ἀπόχρη μοι is a string of words which I am unable to construe, for πᾶν is not the same thing as παράπαν. Mr Paley translates 'I am content to keep even a small part out of *all* my possessions': that is to say, he renders πᾶν as a gen. plur. agreeing with κτεάνων. He does not translate τε, but ignores it. And now for the remedy. It must be observed that we have clear evidence of dislocation in this passage: the generally accepted μανίας μελάθρων ἀλληλοφόνους is Erfurdt's correction for δ' ἀλληλοφόνους μανίας μελάθρων, in which the meaningless δ' is an insertion to cure the hiatus caused by the displacement. I propose a similar transposition and the change of one letter:

βαιὸν ἐχούσῃ
πᾶμ' ἀπόχρη μοι κτεάνων τε μέρος.

The likeness of μ to ν, and the fact that a Byzantine copyist, if he knew the word at all, knew it only in the form πάμμα, make the alteration as easy as an alteration can well be. ‖

1205 [1206]

ἀλλ' ἦν παλαιστὴς κάρτ' ἐμοὶ πνέων χάριν.

'παλαιστής *a suitor*, lit. *a wrestler*; one of Aesch.'s picturesque and bold words' writes Mr Sidgwick, representing, I suppose, the general opinion. That it is bold to say *wrestler* when you mean *suitor* I cordially agree; but in what way it is picturesque, what picture it should present, I cannot guess. The term would be perfectly right and apt on the lips of Marpessa: to her Apollo really and truly ἦν παλαιστὴς κάρτα πνέων χάριν, when he contended with Idas for her hand. But story knows no rival of Apollo's in the suit of Cassandra; and the only picture which παλαιστής could present to an audience not specially informed beforehand is the picture of one beating the air. I should like then to substitute for a word which cannot here mean suitor a word which can: πελαστής. This is of course a legitimate formation from πελάζω, and is preserved by Ammonius: the cognate πελάτης is employed in the required sense of *temptator* by Sophocles *Phil.* 677 τὸν πελάταν λέκτρων ποτὲ τῶν Διὸς 'Ιξίονα. Having regard to the constant interchange of ε and αι the reader will see that this is an instance of that inversion of three consecutive letters which I illustrated on v. 431 [[423]]. The very same confusion occurs in Eur. *I. T.* 881, where one of the two MSS which contain the play gives πρὶν ἐπὶ ξίφος αἵματι σῷ πελάσαι, the other παλαῖσαι.

1321–5 [[1322–6]]

ἅπαξ ἔτ' εἰπεῖν ῥῆσιν ἢ θρῆνον θέλω
ἐμὸν τὸν αὑτῆς. ἡλίῳ δ' ἐπεύχομαι
πρὸς ὕστατον φῶς, τοῖς ἐμοῖς τιμαόροις
ἐχθροῖς φονεῦσι τοῖς ἐμοῖς τίνειν ὁμοῦ
δούλης θανούσης εὐμαροῦς χειρώματος.　　1325 [[1326]]

Once more I fain would speak my own harangue or dirge is a deplorable specimen of style. But bad as it is there is something worse, Hermann's οὐ for ἤ; an alteration which not only fails to remove the totally inappropriate ῥῆσιν but even introduces a fresh defect: it is, as Weil says, most certain that if Aeschylus had written οὐ θρῆνον he could not have added ἐμὸν ‖ τὸν αὑτῆς. In justice to Hermann it should be said that he himself put forward the conjecture with little confidence: he would marvel at its present vogue. Nor do I find among the other guesses enumerated by Wecklein a single proposal which repairs the passage with any critical probability.

I seem to find here the traces of a strange hallucination in the scribe, incredible to those who have not studied MSS and unnoticed by many of those who have, but not rare in Latin and not unknown in Greek: I mean the wholesale permutation of the letters which constitute a word. The letters ρησινηθ are the letters which in their proper order constitute the word ἠριθνής. The word, I say, for νεοθνής and ἡμιθνής on the one hand, and ἠριγέρων and ἠριγένεια (Aesch. *fr.* 346 Dind. [[426 Nauck, 660 Mette]]) on the other, will vouch for ἠριθνής *dying rathe*, though the lexicons know it not. This correction I think will add force to ἅπαξ ἔτι: since she must perish, and perish before her time, the double bitterness of her fate cries for a second dirge; so she enters the palace to chant it and there at last κύκνου δίκην ‖ τὸν ὕστατον μέλψασα θανάσιμον γόον ‖ κεῖται.

Were I to illustrate this error of permutation as fully as I might, and as I hope to do some other day, I should have to stray far from the *Agamemnon*, so I content myself with one more instance which the text of the play will furnish: vv. 1537 sq. ⟦1535 sq.⟧

Δίκα δ' ἐπ' ἄλλο πρᾶγμα θηγάνει βλάβας
πρὸς ἄλλαις θηγάναις μοῖρα.

I have written down these lines with Hermann's θηγάνει for the unmetrical θήγει which has come from λήγει in the line above, and with the necessary correction of βλάβης to the Doric form. In addition to these changes it is usual to read for metre's sake θηγάναισι, and Δίκαν for the sake of a construction. The sense thus elicited is given by Mr Paley as follows: 'Fate is whetting (the sword of) Justice upon another whetstone, for a new business of harm.' *Justice* I find in the Greek, but as for her sword, προχαλκεύει Mr Paley φασγανουργός: the words mean, as Dr Kennedy renders, 'Fate is sharpening Justice'; and the picture of this august divinity whetted on a hone ‖ like some article of cutlery must be to any mind a ridiculous image and to the mind of Aeschylus an impious one. Beyond comparison the best conjecture ventured is Musgrave's Δίκα...θηγάναις μάχαιραν, which gives precisely the sense required; but we can come even nearer to the MSS:

Δίκα δ' ἐπ' ἄλλο πρᾶγμα θηγάνει βλάβας
πρὸς ἄλλαις θηγάναισιν ἄορ.

Allow for the confusion of ν with μ, and the letters of ιναορ and of μοιρα are the same.

I return to vv. 1321–5 ⟦1322–6⟧. In 1322 ⟦1323⟧ Jacob's ἡλίου is necessary and now generally accepted. Than the ensuing sentence there is, it will be confessed, no sentence in tragedy more indisputably corrupt. But in my opinion there is also no sentence in tragedy more simply and certainly corrigible. The corrections which I am about to propose occurred to me the very first time I read the passage with attention. I am therefore not surprised to find from Wecklein that the main points of the emendation were anticipated years before: surprised I am that these obvious corrections are suffered to lie 'Orci tradita thesauro', while scholar on scholar pours forth conjectures which rival one another in rashness and lack of meaning. In particular, the number of distinguished critics, from Musgrave onwards, who have mistaken τίνειν for τίνεσθαι, is confounding.

First we must have a subject for τίνειν: this, since τίνειν after all is not τίνεσθαι, will be ἐχθροὺς...τοὺς ἐμούς. Next we must have an object for τίνειν which shall also furnish the gen. δούλης with a construction: this we shall seek in the otiose and misplaced φονεῦσι; and there it is, φόνευσιν. Thirdly, ὁμοῦ would tell us, if common sense did not, that Cassandra's prayer is not the absurd one that her own avengers may avenge her, but that certain destined avengers of some one else may in avenging him avenge her also: therefore ἐμοῖς in 1323 〚1324〛 is corrupt and shall be replaced by νέοις.

> ἡλίου δ' ἐπεύχομαι
> πρὸς ὕστατον φῶς, τοῖς νέοις τιμαόροις
> ἐχθροὺς φόνευσιν τοὺς ἐμοὺς τίνειν ὁμοῦ
> δούλης θανούσης εὐμαροῦς χειρώματος. ‖

The rare φόνευσιν – it is not in our lexicons though φόνευμα is – was mistaken for the familiar φονεῦσιν, and the adjacent accusatives were thus attracted into the dative, a change rendered the easier by the likeness of υ to ι. The corruption of νέοις into ἐμοῖς is an example of the error which gave us ὄκνος for κενός in v. 996 〚1009〛 and the other blunders cited in my note there: precisely the same alteration is found in Eur. *Med.* 1388 σὺ δ', ὥσπερ εἰκός, κατθανεῖ κακὸς κακῶς | πικρὰς τελευτὰς τῶν νέων γάμων ἰδών, where νέων is Weil's necessary correction of ἐμῶν. Of these changes, ἐχθροὺς . . . τοὺς ἐμούς belongs to Pearson, φόνευσιν to Bothe, νέοις only to me.

1456–8 〚1455–7〛

> ἰὼ παρανόμους Ἑλένα,
> μία τὰς πολλάς, τὰς πάνυ πολλὰς
> ψυχὰς ὀλέσασ' ὑπὸ Τροίᾳ.

The metre of v. 1456 〚1455〛 is usually mended by iterating ἰώ with Blomfield and writing παράνους with Hermann. This conjecture is so generally accepted that παράνους is received into the lexicons solely on the strength of it. Yet I neither understand how παράνους produced the portentous παρανόμους, nor do I find much point or even much sense in the epithet. I am willing to take Hermann's word that Helen was crazy; but this was not the place for saying so: her distraction of mind is one thing, her destruction of life another. Let us try to find something a trifle more appropriate. Everyone remembers the play on the name Ἑλένη in v. 693 〚689〛, ἑλέναυς, ἕλανδρος, ἑλέπτολις. Now there is another ἔτυμον of the name which Aeschylus could hardly overlook and which exactly suits the context here. If we write

> ἰὼ παρὰ πῦρ ὄνομ' οὖσ' Ἑλένα,

we shall write what the loss of πυρο after παρα would transform to παρανόμους. The facility of this loss is shown by the error παραφόροιο for πυροφόροιο in an epigram in the Medicean Life of Aeschylus. The construction παρά c. acc. is the technical phrase by which grammarians indicate the derivation of one word from another. The derivation of Ἑλένη from ἑλάνη a ‖ *firebrand* must, as I said, have been specially tempting and is here specially appropriate with reference to ὀλέσασα: fire, as our newspaper writers are aware, is the devouring element.

I think I find the same etymology in Euripides. In *Tro.* 891 sqq. Hecuba is warning Menelaus against the charm of Helen: ὁρᾶν δὲ τήνδε φεῦγε, μή σ᾽ ἕλῃ πόθῳ · | αἱρεῖ γάρ ἀνδρῶν ὄμματ᾽, ἐξαιρεῖ πόλεις – so far the ἔτυμον is ἑλεῖν; but then she goes on – πίμπρησι δ᾽ οἴκους: surely that is a glance at Ἑλάνη.

1476–85 ⟦1475–84⟧

ΚΛ. νῦν δ᾽ ὤρθωσας στόματος γνώμην
τὸν τριπάχυντον
δαίμονα γέννης τῆσδε κικλήσκων.
ἐκ τοῦ γὰρ ἔρως αἱματολοιχὸς

1480 ⟦1479⟧ νείρει τρέφεται, πρὶν καταλῆξαι
τὸ παλαιὸν ἄχος, νέος ἰχώρ.

ΧΟ. ἦ μέγαν οἴκοις τοῖσδε
δαίμονα καὶ βαρύμηνιν αἰνεῖς,
φεῦ φεῦ, κακὸν αἶνον ἀτη-

1485 ⟦1484⟧ ρᾶς τύχας ἀκορέστου.

'Before the old woe ceases, the new blood flows' is Mr Sidgwick's rendering of vv. 1480–1 ⟦1479–80⟧; and the verb *flows* is indisputably necessary to the sense but indisputably absent from the Greek. Therefore, and because νείρει, when altered into νείρᾳ, is quite superfluous, it seems to me that we should transpose that corrupt word; should read ἐκ τοῦ γὰρ ἔρως αἱματολοιχὸς | τρέφεται, and endeavour to get the verb *flows* from νείρει, πρὶν καταλῆξαι | τὸ παλαιὸν ἄχος, νέος ἰχώρ.

I think νείρει is simply νᾷ: ῥεῖ is the common gloss on the rarer νᾷ. Hesych. νάει · ῥέει; νάουσι · ῥέουσι; νῶντα · ῥέοντα; ναέτωρ · ῥέων; ναρᾶς · ῥευστικῆς; νᾶμα · ῥεῦμα; νάνας · τὰς ῥυτάς; νασμούς · ῥεύσεις; νασμῶν · ῥευμάτων. As the copula is desirable and would readily perish in the sequence -ται καὶ νᾷ, I suppose Aeschylus to have written ‖

ἐκ τοῦ γὰρ ἔρως αἱματολοιχὸς
τρέφεται, καὶ νᾷ, πρὶν καταλῆξαι
τὸ παλαιὸν ἄχος, νέος ἰχώρ.

The antistrophic verses answering vv. 1482–5 ⟦1481–4⟧ are these, vv. 1506–9 ⟦1505–8⟧,

ὡς μὲν ἀναίτιος εἶ
τοῦδε φόνου τίς ὁ μαρτυρήσων;
πῶ πῶ; πατρόθεν δὲ συλλή-
πτωρ γένοιτ᾽ ἂν ἀλάστωρ.

To reconcile the metres of 1506 and 1482 is a problem which has caused much torment: the many conjectures recorded by Wecklein are all violent or ineffectual. But the first step towards emendation has I think been taken by Schuetz, who reads in the antistrophe ὡς μὲν ἀναίτιος εἶ σύ: the pronoun, if not absolutely necessary in poetry as it would be in prose, is at any rate an improvement; and the metre now approximates to that of the strophe. The likeness of ΕΙ to CY makes the loss of the latter easy to understand: the same loss has happened in *Supp.* 950 [939] where everyone now accepts Bothe's εἴσει σύ τ' αὐτός for εἰσθιγαυτος: that means, CY was absorbed by ΕΙ which afterwards became ΘΙ. The strophe I propose to amend thus:

> ἦ μέγαν εἰκόσι τᾶῖσδε
> δαίμονα καὶ βαρύμηνιν αἰνεῖς

verily a great and vengeful demon is he of whom thou speakest in these parables, that is, in the metaphorical language of vv. 1479–81 [1478–80]: εἰκών *a metaphor* occurs in Aristophanes and Plato. Virtually εἰκόσι and οἴκοις differ only in the order of their two final letters: when the inversion (see on v. 133 [128]) had taken place, the good scribe justly proud of knowing the gender of οἶκος completed the corruption by writing τοῖσδε.

1531 [1529]

τείσας ἅπερ ἦρξεν.

μεταβολὴ πάντων γλυκύ: let us play the conservative for once. Wecklein has recalled attention to Spanheim's very attractive conjecture ἔρξεν, certainly a more just and pointed ‖ opposition to τείσας. But I think it well to sound the warning that ἦρξεν would seem to have been read here by Euripides. See Eur. *fr.* 825 Dind. [adesp. 490 Nauck] τιμωρίαν ἔτεισεν ὧν ἦρξεν κακῶν and *H. F.* 1169 τίνων δ' ἀμοιβὰς ὧν ὑπῆρξεν Ἡρακλῆς.

1590–7

> ξένια δὲ τοῦδε δύσθεος πατὴρ			1590
> Ἀτρεύς, προθύμως μᾶλλον ἢ φίλως, πατρὶ
> τὠμῷ, κρεουργὸν ἦμαρ εὐθύμως ἄγειν
> δοκῶν, παρέσχε δαῖτα παιδείων κρεῶν.
> τὰ μὲν ποδήρη καὶ χερῶν ἄκρους κτένας
> ἄσημ'· ὁ δ' αὐτῶν αὐτίκ' ἀγνοίᾳ λαβὼν			1595
> ἔσθει βορὰν ἄσωτον ὡς ὁρᾷς γένει.

In v. 1591 προθύμως is condemned not merely by its own absurdity but by the presence of εὐθύμως in the next verse: I should write without hesitation προσηνῶς. This seems to give just the sense required, and of course the difference between σην and θυμ is palaeographically nothing.

Vv. 1594–7 I have written down just as they are in the MSS, with one exception: I have of course accepted Dindorf's ἄσημ'· ὁ δ' for ἄσημα δ'. Unless this change be made, the subject of ἔσθει will of necessity be Atreus: when Mr Paley writes 'and Thyestes' and when Dr Kennedy writes 'so my sire', they are translating the ὁ δέ which they exclude from their texts, not the MS reading which they print. Mr Paley, Dr Kennedy, Mr Sidgwick, Mr Margoliouth, retain the solecism ἀνδρακὰς καθήμενος *uiritim sedens*. Casaubon's ἀνδρακὰς καθημένοις and Wecklein's ἀνδρακὰς δατούμενος are Greek: they are most obscure, and so far as they do yield a meaning that meaning would seem to be that Atreus gave the murdered children for meat not to Thyestes only but to the rest of the company as well; but still they are Greek. But in no tongue save the tongue of Soli can one person καθῆσθαι ἀνδρακάς, any more than he can form himself in square to receive cavalry. Because Suidas, quite correctly, renders ἀνδρακάς by χωρίς, we should not therefore jump to the conclusion that whenever we mean χωρίς we can say ἀνδρακάς. ||

Whatever else in this passage may be sound, I think ἀνδρακάς must be corrupt. That word necessarily imports an allusion to the other guests at the banquet. Now if that allusion were introduced at all, which was not needful, it should at least have been made more intelligible. The mention of the guests starts our curiosity to know how Atreus contrived to set the children's flesh before Thyestes alone among their number; and our curiosity is not gratified. What I propose then is this:

τὰ μὲν ποδήρη καὶ χερῶν ἄκρους κτένας
ἔθρυπτ' ἄνωθεν ἄνθρακος καθημμένου
ἄσημ'.

Once let θ become δ, as in v. 988 ⟦999⟧ ψύδη for ψύθη, nothing but ἀνδρακάς could ensue; then καθημμένου bereft of its substantive must change its inflexion: the remaining error μ for μμ recalls the converse blunder in v. 1418 λημμάτων for ἀημάτων. θρύπτειν is a technical term in cookery, see lexx. sub vocc. ἔνθρυπτα and θρύμματα: it means properly to mince a solid, usually bread, into a liquid, thus forming a pulp. It would appear from v. 1082 ⟦1097⟧ ὀπτάς τε σάρκας πρὸς πατρὸς βεβρωμένας that such parts of the bodies as were not plainly recognisable for human were roast: the tell-tale hands and feet were, I presume, boiled in a λέβης. The lines thus emended seem to have been imitated by Euripides in his account of another ἀνθρωπομάγειρος. In *Cycl.* 244 sqq., σφαγέντες αὐτίκα | πλήσουσι νηδὺν τὴν ἐμὴν ἀπ' ἄνθρακος | θερμὴν ἑλόντος δαῖτ' ἄτερ κρεανόμου, | τὰ δ' ἐκ λέβητος ἐφθὰ καὶ τετηκότα, you have ἄνθρακος as here, αὐτίκα...ἑλόντος to recall Aeschylus' αὐτίκα...λαβών, and τετηκότα to recall ἔθρυπτ'...ἄσημα. It is true that ἄνθραξ is there in opposition to λέβης, as ἀνθρακιά is in opposition both to boiling and to roasting in v. 358 ἑφθὰ καὶ ὀπτὰ καὶ ἀνθρακιᾶς ἄπο (broiled) χναύειν...μέλη ξένων. But ἄνθραξ is used of boiling in vv. 373 sq. ἑφθά τε δαινύμενος μυσαροῖσιν ὀδοῦσιν | ἀνθρώπων θέρμ' ἀπ' ἀνθράκων κρέα. The compound καθάπτειν does not seem to occur elsewhere in the sense I give it here; but that is nothing: ἅπτειν *kindle* is warrant for καθ-άπτειν *kindle thoroughly*. The tragedians prefix with great freedom the intensive ἐξ and κατά: thus καταυχῶ for ‖ αὐχῶ is used once by Aeschylus, never by anyone else; and here he prefers to say ἄνθρακος καθημμένου while Thucydides IV 100 is content with ἄνθρακας ἡμμένους. ἄνωθεν c. gen. is found fifteen lines above, in a passage to which I will devote a word for its own sake, vv. 1578 sq.

> φαίην ἂν ἤδη νῦν βροτῶν τιμαόρους
> θεοὺς ἄνωθεν γῆς ἐποπτεύειν ἄχη.

Mr Paley and many others construe γῆς ἄχη: Auratus' instinct told him that this phrase was unsuitable, and he therefore conjectured ἄγη, which many accept. But anyone who will turn to Eur. *fr.* 959 Dind. ⟦991 Nauck⟧ ἔστι, κεἴ τις ἐγγελᾷ λόγῳ, | Ζεύς, καὶ θεοὶ βρότεια λεύσσοντες πάθη will see that Euripides found ἄχη in his Aeschylus and construed it with βροτῶν. γῆς therefore depends on ἄνωθεν.

In Wecklein's list of conjectures I find these: ἔκρυπτ' ἄνωθεν ἄνθρακας καθειμένος Tyrwhitt, ἔθρυπτ' ἄνω θεὶς ἄνθρακας καθημμένους Abresch, ἄνθρακος 'anonymus' with what context I know not. I cannot extract much sense from any of these readings; but it is right that I should mention conjectures which verbally resemble mine so nearly.

1654–65

KΛ. μηδαμῶς, ὦ φίλτατ' ἀνδρῶν, ἄλλα δράσωμεν κακά.
ἀλλὰ καὶ τάδ' ἐξαμῆσαι πολλά, δύστηνον θέρος.   1655
πημονῆς ἅλις δ' ὑπάρχει · μηδὲν αἱματώμεθα.
στείχετε δ' οἱ γέροντες πρὸς δόμους πεπρωμένους τούσδε,
πρὶν παθεῖν { ἔρξαντα / ἔρξαντες } καιρόν · χρῆν τάδ' ὡς ἐπράξαμεν.
εἰ δέ τοι μόχθων γένοιτο τῶνδ' ἅλις γ' ἐχοίμεθ' ἄν,
δαίμονος χηλῇ βαρείᾳ δυστυχῶς πεπληγμένοι.   1660
ὧδ' ἔχει λόγος γυναικός, εἴ τις ἀξιοῖ μαθεῖν.
AI. ἀλλὰ τούσδ' ἐμοὶ ματαίαν γλῶσσαν ὧδ' ἀπανθίσαι
κἀκβαλεῖν ἔπη τοιαῦτα δαίμονος πειρωμένους,
σώφρονος γνώμης δ' ἁμαρτῆτον κρατοῦντα.
XO. οὐκ ἂν Ἀργείων τόδ' εἴη, φῶτα προσσαίνειν κακόν.   1665

In considering the well-known difficulties of vv. 1657–9 I will begin with the hypermetrical τούσδε of 1657. To discard ‖ this with Auratus does not explain how it got into the text; to insert it in the next verse with Weil demands the extrusion of some other word. Now it is to be observed that just as we have two syllables too many at the end of v. 1657, so have we three too few at the end of v. 1664. Not only this, but I notice that while the verse to which τούσδε is tacked ends with πεπρωμένους, v. 1663, the next-door neighbour to the defective verse, ends with a word of almost identical appearance, πειρωμένους. I guess then that τούσδε is the missing end of v. 1664, and that either the end or the beginning has been misplaced through the homoeoteleuton of vv. 1657 and 1663. And indeed Hermann and others have already seen that v. 1664, supplement it how you will, is misplaced. Take vv. 1662–4 in Mr Paley's translation: 'But to think that these men should thus gather the flowers of their vain tongue against me, and have uttered such words, challenging their fate, *and so fail in sound judgment*' (ἁμαρτεῖν Casaubon) etc. Was ever such an impotent sequel as these words form to the two foregoing verses? Two enemies are in the heat of an envenomed altercation, insults and menaces flying to and fro: a friend exhorts them to be calm; and one of them bursts out '*But that this man should fail in sound judgment*'! No: it is not thus that mankind talk. Take this v. 1664 away, and 1665 follows appropriately on 1663: now let us see what can be done in the neighbourhood of τούσδε. Of the two MSS which are here our authorities the Florentine alone gives δ' ἁμαρτῆτον: the Venetian omits it, leaving a blank space. This indicates that in the common parent of both the MSS these letters were barely decipherable; so it will not be rash to alter one letter more than was altered by Casaubon. I should place v. 1664 between 1656 and 1657; and in the corrupt tradition

σώφρονος γνώμης δ' ἁμαρτῆτον κρατοῦντα τούσδε

I suggest that ἁμαρτῆ stands for ὁμαρτεῖ and τούσδε for τοῖς λε:

σώφρονος γνώμης δ' ὁμαρτεῖν τὸν κρατοῦντα τοῖς λεώς.

With σώφρ. γν. supply ἐστίν: to ὁμαρτεῖν I give the sense which προσχωρεῖν has in Eur. *Med.* 222 χρὴ δὲ ξένον μὲν κάρτα προσχωρεῖν πόλει. In the *Antigone* of Euripides, where the ‖ position of the τύραννος was canvassed, occurred the line, *fr.* 172 Dind. [171 Nauck], δεῖ τοῖσι πολλοῖς τὸν τύραννον ἀνδάνειν, which looks to me like a paraphrase of the verse I give to Aeschylus.

I am sorry to deal in this guesswork, but it was necessary to handle the matter in order to justify my rejection of τούσδε from v. 1657, to the correction of which I now proceed. Madvig and others have seen that δόμους πεπρωμένους *destined home* has no meaning which suits the context: 'πεπρωμένοι cur domus appellentur causa iure quaeritur nec reperitur': it could signify nothing but Ἅιδου δόμους. True, you can invest it with some sort of sense by accepting Franz's conjecture στεῖχε καὶ σὺ χοῖ γέροντες; but how a scribe could mistake καισυχ for τεδ, and how without gross superstition we can believe that scribes who made mistakes like this have preserved uncorrupted a single word that Aeschylus wrote, I do not know. Science here furnishes a correction so obvious, and so appropriate to the lips of Clytaemestra in her part of peacemaker, that far from being surprised to find it anticipated by Ahrens, I am surprised not to find it anticipated by Auratus. The scribe who corrupted στεῖχετ᾽, αἰδοῖοι γέροντες into the present reading of the MSS merely, for the hundredth time, substituted ε for αι, and wrote οι once when he should have written it twice. For the rest of the line the most plausible conjecture by far is Madvig's: πρὸς δόμους, πεπρωμέ-νοις, | πρὶν παθεῖν, εἴξαντες. This, though I do not like parting with the familiar juxtaposition of παθεῖν and ἔρξαι, is excellent sense so far as it goes; but now what are we to make of the sequel καιρὸν χρῆν τάδ᾽ ὡς ἐπράξαμεν? Of course καιρόν must be altered into an infinitive, but what infinitive? Heath's αἰνεῖν, which Madvig would like, is very wide of the MSS: Hermann's ἀρκεῖν, which Madvig accepts, is near to the MSS but very wide of a satisfactory meaning. I have seen no suitable and probable word suggested, and can suggest none myself. It seems to me that each of the vv. 1657 and 1658 is a complete sentence. The former is this:

στείχετ᾽, αἰδοῖοι γέροντες, πρὸς δρόμους πεπρωμένους.

See Eur. *Med.* 1245 ἕρπε πρὸς βαλβῖδα λυπηρὰν βίου. Clytaemestra ‖ counsels the elders to betake themselves to the new course of life to which it has pleased God to call them, submission to the rule of Aegisthus and herself. The wrongful omission or insertion of ρ after a mute is very common; commonest after β and τ, but common after all mutes: for δρόμος and δόμος confused see *fr.* 374 Dind. [388 Nauck, 742 Mette], where the MSS of Theocritus' scholia vary between πρόδρομος and πρόδομος, and Eur. *Andr.* 1099, where both δρόμοις and δόμοις are found.

In v. 1658 I suppose πρίν to be the adverb (= πρότερον), not the conjunction. When ἔρξαντες is found in the Florentine MS and ἔρξαντα in the Venetian, I think it is the most rational inference that ἔρξαντας was in the Medicean: καιρόν must in any case be altered for metre's sake, as the singular ἔρξαντα is indefensible. But already we have restored sense to the verse, and metre may be restored thus:

καιρόν
πρὶν παθεῖν ἔρξαντας ὥραν χρῆν, τάδ᾽ ὡς ἐπράξαμεν.

Hesych. ὥρα · καιρός; ὥραι · καιροί; ὥρη · τῷ καιρῷ; καθ᾽ ὥραν · κατὰ καιρόν. The adverbial use of τὴν ὥρην = *iusto tempore* occurs in Herod. II. 2: καιρόν itself is used in that sense in Soph. *Ai.* 34, 1316 and Eur. *Hel.* 479, but καιρόν is perhaps thus employed only with ἥκω or verbs of that meaning. Of course I cannot promise that ὥραν was the very word on which καιρόν is a gloss; but that καιρόν is a gloss, luckily detected by metre, I have no doubt. I render *you should have exchanged blows earlier, in season, when we did this deed.* Strictly I suppose πρίν belongs to παθεῖν, ὥραν to ἔρξαντας. In the same meaning which I here give to παθεῖν ἔρξαντας (smite and be smitten) Euripides *Phoen.* 480 uses κακόν τι δρᾶσαι καὶ παθεῖν.

In v. 1659 almost all editors now accept Martin's δεχοίμεθ᾽ ἄν. But manifestly this of itself is not enough to amend the line. To say εἰ μόχθων γένοιτο ἅλις the moment after you have said πημονῆς ἅλις ὑπάρχει is so obviously inconsistent that there is a general consent against the genuineness of ἅλις. Donaldson proposes and Paley approves ἄκος, which makes good sense. But the verse is to be corrected with much less change than ἄκος, δεχοίμεθ᾽ ἄν. The reading which I propose is really almost identical with that of the MSS: ‖

εἰ δέ τοι μόχθων γένοιτο τῶνδ᾽ ἄλη, στεγοίμεθ᾽ ἄν,

η for ι, Τ for Γ, γ for χ. *Should there be any way to ward off these ills* (civil war), *ward them off we should.* We moderns know only ἄλη *error*; but the Greeks knew also ἄλη *tritura* akin to ἀλέω *tero* and ἄλη *defensio* akin to ἀλέω *defendo*. The existence of the verbs might support this surmise, even were there no other proof; but it happens that both these lost substantives occur in the *Agamemnon*, though obscured in one place by the corruption of the copyists and in the other by the mistranslation of the commentators. In v. 204 ⟦194⟧ the winds that blew at Aulis are called βροτῶν ἄλαι, which is supposed to mean *causes of wandering to men*: a less happy name for winds which *prevented* the Greeks from sailing and kept their fleet on the shore it would need some ingenuity to devise. The true rendering is suggested by v. 207 ⟦197⟧ ἄνθος κατέξαινον Ἀργείων τρίβῳ (so I should arrange the words, making no change in the antistrophe but ῥείθροις for ῥεέθροις): βροτῶν ἄλαι are *grindings* or *tribulations of men*, winds *that wear men away* ἀπλοίᾳ κεναγγεῖ. In v. 1659 ἄλη is akin to ἀλέω *defendo*, a verb preserved, I think, only in Hesych. ἄλεε · φύλασσε: I imagine that ἀλέομαι *uito* is originally part of the same verb: compare too ἀλέη, ἀλεωρή, ἀλεύω, ἀλέξω. The verse means then εἰ μόχθων γένοιτο τῶνδε φυλακή, φυλασσοίμεθ᾽ ἄν, but Aeschylus chooses poet-like to vary his words.

Here therefore are the verses as I would write them:

στείχετ᾽, αἰδοῖοι γέροντες, πρὸς δρόμους πεπρωμένους.
πρὶν παθεῖν, ἔρξαντας ⟨ὥραν⟩, χρῆν, τάδ᾽ ὡς ἐπράξαμεν.
εἰ δέ τοι μόχθων γένοιτο τῶνδ᾽ ἄλη, στεγοίμεθ᾽ ἄν,
δαίμονος χηλῇ βαρείᾳ δυστυχῶς πεπληγμένοι.

10

NOTE ON EMENDATIONS
OF PROPERTIUS*

I said on p. 16 of this vol. of the *Journal of Philology* [this edition p. 40] that I feared some of the corrections there proposed had been forestalled by others. I am to blame that this is true of a larger number than one could wish, mainly through trusting to my memory of Burmann's notes instead of giving them a fresh perusal. I now make restitution: I xx 24 *sacram* Rutgersius, II ix 7 *uisuram* (*uisurum* is an error) Paley, xxviii 62 punctuated so by Postgate, xxxiv 12 *posses tun* and 40 *irato* Heinsius, III viii 12 *haec* Liuineius, xvi 21 *cursus* Markland, xvii 24 *carpta* Heinsius, xviii 21 *manet* Palmer, xxii 15 *siqua et* Heinsius, IV ii 12 *credis id* Postgate, vii 23 *eunti* Reland. The three living scholars will, I hope, accept my apologies.

Further, the following proposals have more or less in common with my own, and ought to be mentioned: I iii 37 *nempe ibi* Burmann, II viii 30 *Teucros* Passeratius, ix 12 *apposito. . . Simoente* Guietus, x 2 *campum Maeonio* and xxi 12 *excepta Aesonia est* Heinsius, III vi 28 *exsuccis unguibus* Burmann.

Let me here subjoin a few conjectures accidentally omitted from the paper of which I speak: II i 53 *an in me* for *siue*, II xxxii 9 *quid iubet* for *cum uidet*, III i 32 *terra* for *Troia*, III xix 17 *more parentis* for *tempore matris*, IV iv 83 *ascensum monstrat dubio* for *mons erat ascensu dubius*, IV viii 13 *fuerunt* for *fuerint*.

* [*JPh* 16 (1888), 291]

11

HORATIANA [II]*

Carm. 1 6

That vv. 13–16 of this ode should be among the hundreds of lines which Peerlkamp reckons spurious is in itself a matter to disquiet no one. But that Meineke Haupt and Mueller should expel them at his bidding is a sign of more than usual cogency in his objections; and indeed the case against the verses as they stand is to my mind invincible. Horace says to Agrippa: 'Varius will record your victories, for he is a swan of Homer's strain: I could as soon write an Iliad, an Odyssey, an Oresteia: conscious weakness forbids me to mar your deeds and Caesar's in the telling.' So far speaks a sane man; but now what Tisiphone impels him to subvert his own position by the following ejaculation? *Who is worthy to record the deeds of Mars Meriones and Diomed?* To a question cast in this form the only answer is *No one*: 'quis digne scripserit' in fact is simply the rhetorical equivalent for 'nemo digne scripserit'. But he said a moment ago that Varius was 'Maeonii carminis ales': well then, if Maeonides was worthy to record the deeds of Mars Meriones and Diomed, as he unquestionably was, so is Varius. In a poem designed to prove all living men unfit to sing Agrippa's praises this interrogation would have its place: in this poem which asserts Varius' fitness for that task and the unfitness merely of Horace it turns everything upside down. A blot of these dimensions dwarfs what would else be a noticeable fault, that having in vv. 5–8 declared himself unable to imitate the Iliad or the Odyssey he now harks back to say that the fifth book of the Iliad is inimitable.

If then the verses are cast out the ode is rid of grievous blemishes; but what did the supposed interpolator think he was ‖ doing? My difficulty is not so much that Horace should have inserted the stanza as that anyone should have inserted it. We do little to explain such absurdity by shifting it from the shoulders of a poet whose name we know to those of a poet whose name is lost. For the four verses apart from their connexion are quite worthy of Horace, nay they are Horatian. Mr Lucian Mueller, while rejecting them, candidly points out that if Horace did not write them they were written by one almost his contemporary, for the rhythm 'digne scripserit aut' though common enough in his Asclepiads no longer finds entrance in Seneca's. And to my ear 'ope

* [JPh 17 (1888), 303–20]

92   [303–4

Palladis Tydiden superis parem' is at least a very happy imitation of Horace's manner.

This is one place among many where amputation has been hastily prescribed for an ailment which demands another remedy. Here surely is an ode foursquare and faultless:

<blockquote>

scriberis Vario fortis et hostium
uictor Maeonii carminis alite,
    qua rem cumque ferox nauibus aut equis
        miles te duce gesserit,
qui Martem tunica tectum adamantina   13
digne scripserit aut puluere Troico
nigrum Merionen aut ope Palladis
        Tydiden superis parem.
nos, Agrippa, neque haec dicere nec grauem   5
Pelidae stomachum cedere nescii
nec cursus duplicis per mare Vlixei
        nec saeuam Pelopis domum
conamur tenues grandia, dum pudor
inbellisque lyrae Musa potens uetat   10
laudes egregii Caesaris et tuas
        culpa deterere ingeni.
nos conuiuia, nos proelia uirginum   17
sectis in iuuenes unguibus acrium
cantamus uacui, siuc quid urimur,
        non praeter solitum leues.

</blockquote>

'Varius will record your deeds, worthy as he is to record the || deeds of Mars Meriones or Diomed: I cannot sing such themes, the wrath of Achilles, the voyage of Ulysses, the tale of Pelops' line: too weak am I and will not tarnish your name: light songs for me.' I point with some confidence to the way in which the 'scriberis' of v. 1 now responds to the 'scripserit' of v. 14, and the 'nos' of v. 5 to the 'nos' of v. 17. How the transposition happened is clear. When the copyist had written 'parem' v. 16, the next word to write was 'nos'; but his eye glanced from v. 5 to the same word in v. 17 and he proceeded to copy out vv. 17–20, so that vv. 5–12 were omitted: then on observing his error he added those eight verses at the end, marking them as out of order; but when in due time they came to be inserted they were inserted wrongly, not before v. 17 but before v. 13. The confusion of 'qui' and 'quis' is frequent, whether the next word begins with *s* or not: it occurs for instance without excuse in serm. 1 6 30 and 79. It may be objected to an emendation, though it would not be noticed in a MS reading, that the relative ought to signify the nearer 'miles' not the remoter 'Vario'. This negligence however is quite common both in prose and verse: the lexicons under 'qui' cite flagrant examples from Cicero: from a poet take a passage whose argument is the argument of this ode: Prop. II 34 59 sqq. 'mi lubet hesternis posito languere corollis | quem tetigit iactu certus ad ossa deus; | Actia *Vergilio* custodis litora Phoebi | *Caesaris* et fortes dicere posse rates, | *qui* nunc Aeneae Troiani suscitat arma', i.e. Vergilius, not Caesar. Priscian, I ought perhaps to mention, found 'quis' in his Horace; but then he found also 'sterilisque diu palŭs aptaque remis' in ars 65.

Carm. I 12 33–40

Romulum post hos prius an quietum
Pompili regnum memorem an superbos
Tarquini fasces dubito an Catonis
    nobile letum.
Regulum et Scauros animaeque magnae
prodigum Paulum superante Poeno
gratus insigni referam camena
    Fabriciumque. ||

35

40

No one requires of Horace that he should stick to the precise order of date, or cavils because Fabricius follows Paulus; but that Cato, in a muster-roll which else preserves chronological sequence in the main, should stand with the kings, apart from the republicans and before them, is a caprice not easy to defend against the strictures of Bentley. Further, even if Horace at years of discretion retained much admiration for the honest pedant who committed suicide at Vtica rather than live beneath any but an oligarchical government, still this is a poet of little prudence and less taste who under the rule and patronage of Augustus inscribes on his list of Roman worthies the man whose memory so angered Augustus himself and the dictator before him that each turned pamphleteer to blacken it. There is not only common reason to tell us so; there are Horace's own words, perfect for justice and fitness, carm. II 1 23 'cuncta terrarum subacta praeter atrocem animum Catonis', giving Cato the praise he gives Cleopatra, no more; there is the eloquent silence of all Augustan poetry beside. I say its silence, for no one would dream of finding the younger Cato in epist. I 19 14 or Verg. Aen. VIII 670 except for the words now on their trial. And what of Cato's does Horace here celebrate? his simple life? his honest purpose? no: his 'nobile letum', his preference of suicide to the rule of Caesar.[1]

It is sought to save the text by contending that the presence of Tarquinius Superbus in this roll of worthies is as strange as Cato's. But this is not so: after Romulus the founder of the city Horace places side by side Numa foremost

---

[1] Mr Keller quotes Sil. Punic. XII 585 sq. 'iam uos exemplo proauorum ad *nobile letum* | expectant de more senes': he might add with equal pertinence Luc. Phars. VII 595 'nondum...meruit fatis tam *nobile letum*'.

among its kings in the works of peace and Tarquin foremost in the works of
war: 'uir iniustus, fortis ad arma tamen; ceperat hic alias, alias euerterat urbes.'
By the precise balance grammatical and metrical of 'quietum | Pompili regnum'
against 'superbos | Tarquini fasces' he tells his readers plain that they are to see
in Tarquin not the tyrant but the victorious captain with his *fasces laureati* at the
head of a people 'late regem *bello*que *superbum*'. Besides, if the contention that
Tarquin has no || business here is just, the natural inference will be that 'Tar-
quini' is corrupt, not that 'Catonis' is sound.

But I find yet another difficulty, which is not solved by Bentley's violent
alteration 'anne Curti'. Horace doubts whether to tell of Romulus Numa Tarquin or another: then in the twinkling of an eye these worthies and his doubts
are forgotten together and he is all at once resolved to celebrate Regulus the
Scauri Paulus and Fabricius. If this strange abruptness is to be removed there
is only one way: the two stanzas must be so united that 'referam' may be pres.
subj. in dependence on 'dubito an'. The following correction, half of which is
anticipated I find by Hamacher, cannot fairly be called a change of more than
one letter:

an catenis,

nobile, laetum

Regulum et Scauros eqs.

The picture is that of carm. III 5, Regulus returning to captivity 'non aliter. . .
quam si clientum longa negotia diiudicata lite relinqueret'. The apposition of the
neuter adjective is familiar: epist. I 6 22 'indignum', epod. 5 87 'magnum',
Verg. Aen. I 251 'infandum', VI 21 'miserum', XI 383 'solitum tibi', georg.
II 30 'mirabile dictu', Ouid. met. III 106 'fide maius', VII 790 'mirum', IX 167
'foedum relatu': Munro pointed out to me as a curiously close parallel Ouid.
am. I 6 1 'ianitor, *indignum*, dura religate *catena*'. *letum* is merely the archetype's
way of spelling *laetum*: unless you follow it in carm. II 1 39 *Dioneo*, 15 17
cespitem, 20 15 *Getulas*, III 12 8 *Liparei*, 29 63 *Aegeos*, epod. 14 3 *Letheos*, serm.
II 3 128 *cedere*, 8 71 and epist. II 1 189 *aulea*, neither need you follow it here.
catenis for *catonis* is a change, but the slightest of changes: see the variants
carm. III 4 16 *forenti* and *ferenti*, IV 4 66 *luctere* and *ductore*, serm. I 2 110 *pelli*
and *tolli*, 4 126 *auidos* and *uides*, 5 78 *torret* and *terret*, II 6 95 *bone* and *bene*, ars
308 *deceat* and *doceat*. Hamacher as I said proposed a similar conjecture 'an
catenis | nobilitatum | Regulum': this of course is further from the MSS, and
I doubt if Horace would approve the rhythm: his other examples are 'Fabri-
ciumque', 'Mercuriusque', 'militiaeque', 'Bellerophontem', || substantives all
four, and three of them proper names. But in v. 34 Hamacher's 'ac superbos'
ought I think to be accepted: we shall thus escape the monotony of 'an'
recurring thrice at the same place in the verse, and gain an admirably appropriate division of the names into three periods: first the founder; next the two

typical kings, lawgiver and conqueror; then the heroes, vanquished and victorious, of the commonwealth.

In v. 31 of this ode I fancy the MSS readings point to 'et minax, sicut uoluere, ponto | unda recumbit'. The vulgate 'quod sic' has no great authority: most MSS offer 'quia sic', a strange piece of perversity if 'quod' was the original. *sicut* is abbreviated *sic̄* and so confused with *sic*; and the variations of the MSS look like attempts to fill up the metrical gap thus left: similarly in Ouid. trist. I 3 87 'talia temptabat *sicut* temptauerat ante' are found the readings *et sic* and *sic et*. Horace's most ancient MS, the old Bernese, actually gives *qui . sic.*

Those who have learnt from Mr Keller that the Horatian archetype belonged to the first century after Christ will enquire whether it is probable that *o* would be written for *e*, or possible that *sicut* could be abbreviated *sic̄*, in a MS of that date. It is therefore necessary to say that this first century archetype is a figment, convenient indeed to an editor who aims at repressing, as far as may be, conjectural alteration of the text, but neither proven nor even, with our materials, susceptible of proof. I am not concerned to maintain that the Horatian archetype was written so late as 700 A.D.; but no one can shew that it was written earlier. Anyhow, when none of the extant MSS are older than the year 800, the onus probandi rests with those who would set the archetype back. I will deal here with the only argument on that side I can even imagine. It may be said that since some of our MSS have the Mavortian subscription while others have it not, therefore the archetype was earlier than the recension of Mauortius, consul 527 A.D. But of course it may be maintained with equal plausibility even a priore that the archetype had the Mavortian subscription, only that certain apographs, from which some of our MSS are descended, omitted it, while others, from which others are descended, copied it out. And happily we are not reduced to arguing a priore. The two || MSS which Mr Keller calls A and *a* are twin brothers descended from a lost MS which Mr Keller calls A′. Now the Mavortian subscription exists in A and therefore existed in A′; yet in *a* it does not exist. But *a* is none the less Mavortian for that: its writer merely omitted to copy out the subscription. The fact then that the subscription is absent from many of our MSS in no way debars us from holding with Bentley that they all belong to the Mavortian recension and all converge in an archetype later than Mauortius.

Carm. II 2 1–4

Nullus argento color est auaris
abdito terris, minuitque lamnae,
Crispe Sallusti, nisi temperato
splendeat usu.

So I should now emend the 'inimice' of the MSS. The difficulty of the vulgate is briefly this. The clause 'nisi splendeat' depends of course on the vocative; so that the sole predication contained in the quatrain is 'nullus argento color est auaris abdito terris'. Now if these words mean, as they naturally should, *silver shines not in the mine*, then the mere statement of this fact is no such enunciation of the theme *thou shalt not covet* as would enable the writer straightway to proceed from his text to his examples with 'uiuet extento Proculeius aeuo' and the rest: the covetous do not propose to leave silver in the *mine*. It therefore becomes necessary with Porphyrion Bentley and most other critics to make 'terris' mean the *burying-place* of treasure. But this interpretation, less natural in itself, seems to be forbidden not only by the parallel carm. III 3 49 sqq. 'aurum *inrepertum*...cum *terra celat*...cogere humanos in *usus*' but above all by the senarius, preserved in Plut. de uit. pud. III p. 148 [533 A = fr. trag. adesp. 389 Nauck], which Horace is here translating: οὐκ ἔστ' ἐν ἄντροις λευκός, ὦ ξέν', ἄργυρος. If then to escape this dilemma resort is had to conjecture, the conjecture should be one which will at the same time restore symmetry to the sentence, four sevenths of which are at present occupied by a vocative trailing after it a string of dependants, three sevenths only by the sentiment enunciated. Regarding 'inimice' therefore as the seat of corruption || I proposed in vol. x of this Journal [this edition p. 1] the conjecture 'minimusque', which I think removes all difficulty. But the correction I now offer is nearer to the MSS, and there is external evidence which appears to shew that it stood for four centuries in the text of Horace: Prud. contra Symm. II 753 'candor *perit* argenti, si defuit usus, | et fuscata situ *corrumpit* uena colorem' is surely neither more nor less than a paraphrase of the verses as written above. The examples in the lexicons of 'minuo' intransitive are confined to the pres. part., but I rely more on the analogy of 'augeo' and on the number of transitive verbs whose intransitive use is found once or hardly oftener. The old and widespread confusion of *qu* and *c* pervades our MSS: see serm. II 1 74, 2 41, 8 48, 52, ars 186 *coquo* and *quoquo*, carm. II 9 7 *querqueta* and *querceta*, III 3 17 *elocuta* and *eloquuta*, 27 7 *cui* and *quid*, IV 8 25 *Aeacum* and *aequum*, c. saec. 22 *cantus* and *quantus*, serm. I 4 19 *hirquinis* and *hircinis*, ars 426 *cui* and *qui*, 456 *secuntur* and *sequuntur*: all the MSS collated by Holder have *quassa* for *cassa* in serm. II 5 36 and *quorsum* for *cursum* in 3 201. As for *minuit* and *inimi*, any sequences of the letters *i, m, n, t, u* (also *l, r,* often *b*) are absolutely interchangeable if the number of downstrokes is the same, as epod. 11 16 *uentis* and *uenus*, serm. I 4 87 *unus* and *imus*, epist. II 1 198 *nimio* and *mimo*, ars 32 *unus* and *imus*: often too a scribe will lose count and write carm. I 15 20 *cultus* for *crinis*, II 6 19 *nimium* for *minimum*, IV 14 28 *minatur* for *minitatur*, serm. I 5 15 *absentem* for *absentem ut*. An almost perfect parallel is Catull. 25 12 *inimica* for *minuta*.

Munro told me that he, feeling the same difficulty as I about 'auaris terris', had jotted down years ago, though without setting much store by it, the conjecture 'abdito thecis'.

Carm. II 18 32–40

Aequa tellus
pauperi recluditur
regumque pueris, nec satelles Orci
35   callidum Promethea
reuexit auro captus. hic superbum
Tantalum atque Tantali ||
genus coercet, hic leuare functum
pauperem laboribus
40   uocatus atque non uocatus audit.

We are apt to think that the 'auro captus' of this passage finds a parallel in
epist. II 2 179 'si metit Orcus | grandia cum paruis non exorabilis auro'; but
look close and the likeness vanishes. When Death is abroad, scythe in hand, and
threatens to mow the rich man down, the rich man may offer his gold for his
life: it is vain, but yet he may offer it; and this is the picture in epist. II 2 179.
But here the picture is quite another one. The word 'reuexit' shews that we
speak of one who is already on the yonder side of Styx: now such a one cannot
offer gold, he has no gold to offer, he has left his riches to other [another *or*
others]: one coin is all that comes to the ferry, no coin crosses. And this is
only the first of the difficulties that beset us here. Why is it said that Prometheus,
of all people in the world, could not find issue from hell by the help of gold?
Croesus or Alcinous or any other type of wealth I could have understood; but
Prometheus is no type of wealth: he is a type of subtlety. And to make matters
worse it is on his subtlety that Horace here insists: 'callidum Promethea' he
calls him: what sort or kind of fitness is there in saying that Prometheus the
subtle could not buy liberty with *gold*? It wants little subtlety to bribe: Midas,
ears and all, is better equipped for bribery than any Prometheus. Then consider
the concluding sentence: 'hic' following immediately on 'captus' refers
naturally, I do not say inevitably, to the substantive with which 'captus'
agrees: that is, not to 'Orci', but to 'satelles Orci', Charon. Now 'Tantalum
coercet' may be said of Charon with truth, but it cannot with truth be said
of him 'leuare pauperem uocatus audit': to relieve people of life is no
business of Charon's: he does but ferry them over when they come dead to the
bank.

Here are three difficulties, severally I think not light, heavy assuredly in
conjunction; and the change of one letter abolishes them all.

nec satelles Orci
35   callidum Promethea ||
reuexit. aure captus hic superbum
Tantalum atque Tantali

> genus coercet, hic leuare functum
> pauperem laboribus
> uocatus atque non uocatus audit.   40

The corruption as I said on I 12 35 is palaeographically of the easiest sort; moreover in this context the scribe's temptation to write 'auro' was manifestly strong, and so perhaps may be the reader's reluctance to part with it. Yet aside from the graver objections already considered it really involves Horace in tautology, for 'nec satelles Orci Promethea reuexit *auro captus*' and 'hic Tantalum coercet' come to just the same thing, 'there is no egress for the great': observe, the presence of 'auro captus' prevents the laying of such stress on 'callidum' as would be necessary for an antithesis between the *calliditas* of Prometheus and the *superbia* of Tantalus. I interpret as follows. 'The grave flings wide its gates for the impartial welcome of high and low, rich and poor; and for him who once has entered, issue there is none, no, not for Prometheus' self, charm he never so wisely.' That is, both rich and poor die: neither, by any art, comes back to life. Now he goes on to make a fresh point: to contrast the hopelessness, even for the mightiest, of return from hell, with the readiness, even for the meanest, of access thither. 'Death holds in prison Tantalus the proud, him and his seed with him, deaf to their prayers: deaf to them, yet keen to hear and succour the poor that call upon him, the poor that call upon him not.' Surely I do not deceive myself in thinking that the contrast thus obtained between 'aure captus' (= surdus)[1] at the opening of the sentence and 'non uocatus audit' at the close is fine and impressive. For this reason, as well as to avoid the difficulty about 'hic', I have placed the stop after 'reuexit'; but the correction 'aure' does not necessitate that change of punctuation, and those whom the difficulty in || question does not trouble may prefer to take 'aure captus' with 'nec satelles Promethea reuexit' as 'deaf to his cajoleries'.

Carm. III 4 9–13

> Me fabulosae Volture in Apulo
> nutricis extra limina pulliae
> ludo fatigatumque somno
> fronde noua puerum palumbes
> texere.

10 *limina pulliae* AaBR, *limina puliae* L, *limen apulliae* τ, *limen apuliae* MCγφψλ/δτπρbuν. No competent metrist now entertains a thought of 'ăpuliae' any more than of 'ăpulicum' in 24 4; and the presence of 'āpulo' in the line above has given pause even to editors whose strength lies elsewhere than in

---

[1] A prose writer no doubt would say 'auribus', but the poets a hundred times over in all manner of connexions use the singular 'auris' when they mean the plural; and compare Liu. IX 29 11 'Appium ...luminibus captum' with Ouid. fast. VI 204 'Appius...lumine captus'.

metre. Clearly 'apuliae' is a conjecture suggested by the word overhead: the hand of Horace must be sought in the 'limina pulliae' offered by four of the best and oldest MSS, which has at least this note of sincerity, that it is quite unmeaning. To help us in the search we get light, for a wonder, from the collection of scholia which bears the name of Acron. They are seldom of use, but every trace of a reading not now found in the MSS deserves close attention; and the scholion 'paruus extra casae limen expositus lauro myrtoque columbis deferentibus tectus' shews that where we read 'pulliae' the scholiast read a word meaning 'casae'. Two or three scholars have independently conjectured 'uillulae': this explains the scholion and comes near enough to the MSS; but Munro's objection seems fatal. From Horace's odes diminutives are virtually exiled: 'puella' and 'uilla' for an obvious reason he admits, and he admits 'parmula' in a humorous passage II 7 10. But 'uillula' is the diminutive of a diminutive; and this the most ambitious of all his odes is the last place where such a word could enter: 'descende caelo et dic age tibia regina longum Calliope melos'! the goddess thus invoked will hardly I think descend to 'uillula'. Try then another solution. The letter *g* is sometimes confused with *b* or *n* or *u* and is then subject to that blending with similar letters of which I spoke on ‖ II 2 2. The following are varied instances of what I mean: carm. I 3 19 *turgidum* and *turbidum*, 9 5 *ligna* and *luna*, epod. 2 18 *agris* and *aruis*, 17 81 *agentis* and *habentis*, serm. I 4 25 *elige* and *erue*, 6 13 *fugit* and *fuit*, II 3 291 *mane* and *magne*, epist. I 10 36 *frenum* and *regnum*, 43 *uret* and *urget*. I believe that even in Virgil we ought to write Aen. I 343 *auri* for *agri* with Huet and VII 543 *peragrans* for *per auras* with Canter; and anyhow in Horace the confusion of *gul* with *ulli* is quite possible. I suggest then that *pulliae* stands for *pgulae*: 'nutricis extra limina pergulae', *without the threshold of the hut that bred me*.

Carm. III 5 31–40

Si pugnat extricata densis
    cerua plagis, erit ille fortis
qui perfidis se credidit hostibus,
et Marte Poenos proteret altero
    qui lora restrictis lacertis
      sensit iners timuitque mortem.
hic, unde uitam sumeret inscius,
pacem duello miscuit. o pudor!
    o magna Karthago probrosis
      altior Italiae ruinis.

35

40

37 *inscius* AaBCMRγτφψλ/π, *aptius* δℨρ*buv* LA2φ2λuar.ψuar. Let me be forgiven if I repeat the words in which I formerly stated as shortly as I could the objections to the above text. 'In this the reading of most MSS and well-nigh all

editions Bentley justly finds fault with the lame climax "timuitque mortem",
and "hic" used where the poet should and might have used "ille": he might too
have added, what sort of writer is Horace if "mortem" and "uitam" here have
nothing to do with one another? But there is this deeper fault in the reading,
that it makes Regulus lose the thread of his argument; for what is he debating?
not what is done and cannot be undone, the surrender of the army, but its
ransom, the matter in hand: his aim is to fence off the pernicies ueniens in aeuum,
the flagitio additum damnum, the probrosae Italiae ruinae, and down to v. 36
he is ‖ speaking straight to the point; but here with a full stop at "mortem" he
loses his way and drifts off into mere exclamation about what is past mending
and will remain the same whether he gains his cause or loses it.' Add that if
'inscius' was the original the senseless variant 'aptius' is nothing short of
inexplicable: an interpolator tries to remove difficulties, not to import them.

The meaning and general form of the sentence were restored, I cannot
doubt, by Bentley: 'timuitque mortem | hinc, unde uitam sumeret aptius, |
pacem et duello miscuit'. The soldier should seek life from battle and his sword:
these soldiers feared death from that quarter and sought life from surrender,
'dedecore potius quam manu salutem quaesiuere' as Bentley quotes from Sallust.
Following Bentley I proposed 'pacemque bello' as nearer the MSS (*be* dropping
out after *ue* and leaving 'pacemquello' to beget the present text) and perhaps
more consonant with the usage of Horace who thrice opposes 'pax' and
'bellum', once 'pax' and 'duella', 'pax' and 'duellum' here only, if here. But
there remains this obvious and unanswerable objection: if Horace wrote 'aptius',
how got 'inscius' into most MSS and those the best?

At last I think I have not only Horace's meaning but the words in which he
put it:

> timuitque mortem
> hinc, unde uitam sumere *iustius*,
> pacemque *be*llo miscuit.

It is scarcely an exaggeration to say that 'iustius' and 'inscius' are the same
thing: to illustrate the error would be mere waste of time. The amendment
'sumeret' was inevitable if only for the metrical reason; but maybe the *t* is
a misunderstood correction of the *c* in the next word. And now it becomes easy
to explain the origin of 'aptius': the corruption 'sumeret inscius' took place
while 'hinc' stood yet in the verse, so that the passage ran nonsensically thus,
'timuitque mortem hinc unde uitam sumeret inscius': plainly a comparative
was wanted in lieu of 'inscius', and 'aptius' fulfilled all requirements. ‖

Carm. IV 6 13–20

Ille non inclusus equo Mineruae
sacra mentito male feriatos
15 Troas et laetam Priami choreis
   falleret aulam,
sed palam captis grauis, heu nefas heu,
nescios fari pueros Achiuis
ureret flammis, etiam latentem
20   matris in aluo.

17 *captis* AaBCRγβ*fh*, omis. φψδ*ζ*πL*ρbt, uictor uv*. It is not merely this conflict of testimony which has thrown doubt on 'captis', but the intrinsic demerits of the word. One could not well devise a stranger way of contrasting the boldness of Achilles with the craft of Ulysses than to call the former *terrible to captives*: to captives, be they palam capti or clam, Ulysses, or for the matter of that Thersites either, might be full as terrible as he: 'captis grauis' indeed, witness the Attic stage, Ulysses preeminently was. The sort of word required is plain, a word to answer 'male feriatos' and 'laetam choreis' just as 'palam' will answer 'mentito' and 'falleret'. Such a word the change of one letter will furnish: Achilles was 'cautis grauis', terrible to forewarned and forearmed opponents: he disdained to take them, like Ulysses, unawares. The δὶς ταυτόν of 'palam' and 'cautis' is intentional and exactly matched by Verg. Aen. I 350 '*clam* ferro *incautum* superat'; but I chiefly put my trust in the following words of Ovid, where the same pleonasm is employed concerning that very Ulysses with whom Achilles is here contrasted by Horace: met. XIII 103 sq. 'quo tamen haec Ithaco? qui *clam*, qui semper inermis | rem gerit et furtis *incautum* decipit hostem.' Horace's MSS have these instances of *u* confused with *p*: carm. III 27 15 *uetet* and *petet*, IV 2 27 *apis* and *auis*, 4 43 *uel* and *per*, epod. 2 25 *riuis* and *ripis*, epist. I 10 18 *diuellat* and *depellat*, ars 378 *uergit* and *pergit*: I should be disposed to add carm. II 10 9 *saepius* for *saeuius*. It is now easier to understand how the word was lost || from so many MSS, for GRAVIS and CAVTIS virtually have five out of their six letters in common: 'uictor' of course is a mere conjecture.

Carm. IV 13 17–22

Quo fugit uenus heu quoue color? decens
quo motus? quid habes illius, illius,
   quae spirabat amores,
20   quae me surpuerat mihi
felix post Cinaram, notaque et artium
gratarum facies?

The old punctuation of v. 21 'notaque, et artium' was exploded by Bentley: we must join together 'nota artium', like II 2 6 'notus in fratres animi paterni'. I see it stated that 'the construction is unexampled': well, Bentley gives four examples of this unexampled construction, and if that is not enough, here is a fifth: Prop. 1 16 2 'ianua Tarpeiae nota pudicitiae'. Yet I hardly think that the present text with 'et' = 'etiam', though almost universally accepted as the lesser evil, can really satisfy many: sure I am that were this a copy of verses one had shewn up at school one would have been told that the 'et' was a lame device to help out the metre. What Horace more probably wrote I fancy is this: 'nota quot artium | gratarum facies': 'quot' seems to be just what is wanted, as it is on the *number* of these 'artes' that the poets are wont to insist: IV 1 15 '*centum* puer artium', Prop. 1 4 13 'ingenuus color et *multis* decus artibus'. This exclamatory use of 'quot' for 'mille' or any indefinitely large number is illustrated by Munro on carm. II 3 11 in vol. IX of this Journal, from whom I take these instances: Mart. XIII 95 'matutinarum non ultima praeda ferarum | saeuos oryx constat *quot* mihi morte canum', Iuu. VI 276 sqq. 'tu tibi tunc, uruca, places fletumque labellis | exsorbes, quae scripta et *quot* lecture tabellas, | si tibi zelo-typae retegantur scrinia moechae.' The corruption of 'quot' to 'que et' is of course easy, *o* and *e* being as we have seen so much alike; but more than this, the very || same error occurs in Ouid. her. 12 17. The best MS there, that known as P, which in age and character is own brother to the principal MSS of Horace, has 'semina iecisset totidem*que et* seminat et hostes': there can be hardly a doubt about the correctness of Madvig's and Palmer's 'semina iecisset, totidem, *quot* semina, et hostes'.

Epod. 8 15–18

Quid quod libelli Stoici inter sericos
iacere puluillos amant?
inlitterati num minus nerui rigent
minusue languet fascinum?

If this precious piece was worth writing I suppose it is worth emending: we need not have it more corrupt than its author sent it forth. To clear the ground for criticism we must first brush aside the extraordinary conjecture 'magisue' in v. 18 which Bentley adopts from Guietus. With virtuous indignation he de-clines to say what he means by it; and later critics one after another profess themselves unable to guess. The fact is he took 'inlitterati' = 'inlitteratorum' and 'fascinum' = ὄλισβος, wrongly of course: the austere divine in a transport of moral severity has thrust upon the passage a much worse meaning than the heathen poet ever intended it to bear. When these misapprehensions are dis-missed, the problem resolves itself to this: sense requires that 'rigent' should mean 'torpent'; language forbids. In this connexion *rigeo, rigor, rigidus* can have only one meaning, and that is the exact reverse of the meaning required. Everything would be set right by Meineke's rather rough alteration 'num magis' for 'num minus' in v. 17; that is 'num propterea nerui mei, qui litteras nesciunt, magis rigent, minusue languet fascinum meum?' But Mr Keller puts forward an interpretation of the MS reading which is worth transcribing entire: 'ei da sehe ich ja gar stoische Bücher in deinem Boudoir; glaubst du denn dass nur wer philosophisch gebildet ist, *neruum bene rigentem* habe, oder dass durch solche Mittelchen mein *fascinum minus languet?*' This is the stage to which four hundred years of editing have advanced the || criticism of Horace. If 'nerui' means nerui inlitteratorum then 'fascinum' can no more mean fascinum meum than it can mean fascinum Luci Titi: possessive pronouns cannot thus be summoned at will from the vasty deep. Admire too the style of the poet: you might think that the 'minus' of v. 17 and the 'minus' of v. 18 had something to do with one another; but no: the former is to mean minus quam litteratorum nerui rigent, the latter is to mean minus quam langueret si libelli inter puluillos non iacerent.

The right and necessary sense, the sense of Meineke's conjecture, I propose to restore by a slighter change than his:

> inlitterati num minus nerui pigrent
> minusue languet fascinum?

The verb no doubt was antiquated in Horace's day, nor would I introduce it into the odes; but in the epodes it will keep company with the 'edit' of 3 3. So rare a word was well-nigh sure to perish; but apart from that, this form of error, in which the transposition of one letter is united with the subtraction or addition of another, has examples everywhere: I take the following almost at haphazard: Lucr. I 741 *casu* and *causa*, II 1169 *caelum* and *saeclum*, V 186 *specimen* and *speciem*, VI 179 *liquescit* and *quiescit*, Hor. carm. III 2 22 *iter* and *ire*, serm. I 3 56 *incrustare* and *incurtare*, II 7 45 *crispini* and *crisipi*, Tibull. II 1 66 *applauso* and *appulso*, 5 70 *pertulerit* and *perluerit*, III 2 27 *casum* and *causam*, pan. Mess. 72 *fera* and *freta*, Prop. I 16 12 *purior* and *turpior*, IV 1 30 *tatio* and *tacito*, 8 39 *crotalistria* and *coralistria*, Ouid. met. I 196 *superi* and *pueri*, VI 77 *fretum* and *ferum*, fast. IV 766 *lupo* and *duplo*. The epodes contain I believe another instance in

13 11–14:   nobilis ut grandi cecinit Centaurus alumno:
> 'inuicte mortalis dea nate puer Thetide,
> te manet Assaraci tellus, quam frigida parui
> findunt Scamandri flumina, lubricus et Simois.'

When one recalls the majesty with which this μέγας ποταμὸς βαθυδίνης is invested by Homer, and the terrific combat it was || to wage with this very Achilles, κυκώμενος, ὑψόσε θύων, μορμύρων ἀφρῷ τε καὶ αἵματι καὶ νεκύεσσιν, the epithet 'parui' assumes an elaborate infelicity which can hardly be surpassed. Orelli offers the amazing defence that the Scamander either shrank or fell into contempt after Homer's time: yes, but Chiron is the speaker; Chiron did not live after Homer's time. What would be thought of a modern poet who should make Chiron tell Achilles that his destination was Troy, excavated by Dr Schliemann's spade? yet that is what Orelli and his followers impute to Horace. I would rather impute it to his copyists. What one most naturally expects is an epithet meaning ξανθός, and so Nic. Heinsius proposes 'flaui', but Bentley with reason rejects this in an author so chary of alliteration. Six or seven years ago I communicated to Munro the conjecture 'raui'; it must not however be set down as mine, as I have since seen it proposed in some foreign journal, where and by whom I unluckily cannot now discover.[1] Forcellini has a passage from Cicero to prove that the word can be applied to the colour of water; but it is to shew its palaeographical probability that I am writing now. Horace uses 'rauos' in epod. 16 33 where the MSS give the following extraordinary array of corruptions: 'flauos, fuluos, saeuos, grauos, prauos': now in our passage the commentator of Cruquius mentions a variant 'praui'. But I especially appeal to Ouid. ars II 659 where everyone reads and must read 'si straba, sit Veneris similis, si raua, Mineruae': well, 'raua' is the correction of Heinsius: the MS has 'parua'.

[1] By Oberdick in the *Neue Jahrbuecher* vol. 123, p. 372.

12

NOTES ON LATIN POETS [I]*

Persius III. 39–43

Anne magis Siculi gemuerunt aera iuuenci
et magis auratis pendens laquearibus ensis
purpureas subter ceruices terruit, 'imus,
imus praecipites' quam si sibi dicat, et intus
palleat infelix, quod proxima nesciat uxor.

'The ghastly inward paleness, which is a mystery, even to the wife of the bosom' Conington. I can imagine no worse nonsense than *inward paleness*. What is paleness? It is one among the outward symptoms of inward disorder: it exists in the complexion, nowhere else in the frame of a living man. When a man is dissected, then his inward parts may have this colour or that: till then they have none at all. And if we are to talk about this inconceivable malady, it will be superfluous and yet at the same time inadequate to say that it is unguessed by the wife of the bosom. It doubtless is: much more than that, it is and must be unguessed by the invalid himself: he cannot possibly know that there is anything the matter with him. I need only mention and dismiss the idea that *palleat* can mean merely *fears*: that sense, if wanted, must be introduced by the emendation *infelix paueat*. Conington in his commentary explains with natural hesitation '*intus palleat*, not a very intelligible expression at first sight, appears to include the notions of *depth* and *secrecy*'; but as those notions are included in the perfectly intelligible expression *quod proxima nesciat uxor*, the other becomes more wonderful than ever.

I suppose that when we read the passage negligently, without pausing to realise how absurd it is, we carry away a vague impression that it means *paleness from an inward cause unknown to the wife of the bosom*. Of course it does not; but it is an almost imperceptible alteration of what does:

et ulcus
palleat infelix, quod proxima nesciat uxor.

The construction is the same as I. 124 *Eupolidem palles*, you are pale from reading Eupolis. The metaphor is frequent enough: take for an instance Cic. *de off.* III. 85 'hunc tu quas conscientiae labes in animo censes habuisse, quae uulnera?'‖

* [[CR 3 (1889), 199–201]]

Martial XII. 3, 1–4

Ad populos mitti qui nuper ab urbe solebas
   ibis, io, Romam nunc peregrine liber,
auriferi de gente Tagi tetricique Salonis,
   dat patrios manes quae mihi terra potens.

'Obwol hier nur das erste und das letzte Wort verdorben zu sein scheinen, ist eine völlig befriedigende Herstellung doch bis jetzt noch nicht gelungen' is Friedlaender's note on v. 4. As to the first word, we shall see presently; but I do not find any intrinsic fault in the last: the old conjecture *parens* which Friedlaender wrongly assigns to Hirschfeld is easy and may be true; yet Lucan x. 324 has the same phrase, 'hinc, Abaton quam nostra uocat ueneranda uetustas, | *terra potens* primos sentit percussa tumultus', and Virgil seems to explain it in *Aen.* I. 531 '*terra* antiqua, *potens* armis atque ubere glaebae'. There can however be no doubt that something is wrong somewhere. The traditional interpretation of the verse was 'in qua scilicet terra conditi sunt cineres meorum parentum, et quae patria mea est'. This would be very good sense; but to extort it from the text is impossible, and to introduce it is difficult: at least I can devise no gentler measures than Gilbert's '*iam* patrios manes quae mihi terra *tegit*' or Munro's '*hac*, patrios manes quae mihi terra *fouet*'.

I doubt then whether this after all is what Martial meant; and since *quae* is given only by one family of MSS while the others read *quod*, I should look for the corruption where the testimony varies, and offer this instead:

dat patrios amnes quos mihi terra potens.

That this use of *dat* is a roundabout way to convey the simple sense *the rivers of my country* I will not at all deny; but here is its fellow from Ovid, *ex Pont.* IV. 16, 43, 'maternos Cottas cui Messallasque paternos, | Maxime, nobilitas ingeminata dedit'. The two words *amnes* and *manes* are much confounded: in Virgil's MSS alone I have counted five examples, *georg.* I. 115, IV. 293, *Aen.* IV. 34, 490, V. 634: Prop. I. 1, 23 I think contains another.

Juvenal IX. 130–4

Ne trepida, numquam pathicus tibi derit amicus
stantibus et saluis his collibus. undique ad illos
conuenient et carpentis et nauibus omnes
qui digito scalpunt uno caput. altera maior
spes superest. tu tantum erucis inprime dentem.

Nothing here is obscure, except this: that when you expect to arrive at the sentiment *your present trade will improve in the future* you come instead to the words *altera maior spes superest*, in which *altera* is quite inexplicable, for the *spes* in question, though *maior*, is not *altera* but *prorsus eadem*. The scholiast sees the difficulty of the word and makes an honest attempt to explain it with 'multos inberbes habes tibi crescentes'; but that is wholly foreign to the matter. Ruperti expounds '*spes altera*, futuri temporis, longe *maior superest* tibi'; but all *spes* is *futuri temporis*: that sense does not reside in *altera*. 'Dir blühen Aussichten in der Zukunft zu einer viel bessern Kundschaft' writes Heinrich: that, as I said, is the sentiment you expect; but *altera* is untranslated, because untranslatable.

But it is hardly worth while to puzzle our brains over a reading which certainly was not the reading of the archetype. It is only one family of MSS that gives the passage thus: the other, represented by our best MS, the Pithoeanus, adds after 134 this verse:

gratus eris, tu tantum faucis inprime dentem.

The variation of the two stocks enables us here as often elsewhere to write down what stood in the common parent of both:

spes superest ⎫
             ⎬ tu tantum erucis inprime dentem.
gratus eris ⎭

Out of this one copyist made two verses by iterating the end of the line; the other made one verse by throwing away the more embarrassing of the two commencements. But a critic, had there been critics in the earth in those days, would have known better than either. Since *altera maior spes superest* merely fails to give a fitting sense, while *altera maior gratus eris* fails to give any sense whatever, it follows that *spes* ‖ *superest* must be dismissed as a conjecture and that *altera maior gratus eris* is the genuine ruin of the words of Juvenal. Those words I suppose were these:

undique ad illos
conuenient et carpentis et nauibus omnes
qui digito scalpunt caput uno: derit amator;
gratus eris. tu tantum erucis inprime dentem.

I will deal first with the palaeographical details. One of the absurdities by which the overworked brain of the copyist avenges itself on the author copied is that inversion of two syllables which transforms d-*er-it* into d-*it-er*. I cite here only the closest of parallels: Ovid *Ibis* 246 *it-er* for *er-it*, *met.* XII. 306 me-*ne-la*-us for me-*la-ne*-us, *trist.* V. 6, 11 po-*li-da*-rius for po-*da-li*-rius, Verg. *Aen.* XI. 711 *ra-pu* for *pu-ra*, Stat. *silu.* IV. 4, 79 e-*ri-ge*-t for e-*ge-ri*-t: in Juvenal, IV. 83 *ge-re*-nti for *re-ge*-nti and VI. 541 o-*ri-si*-s for o-*si-ri*-s might be assigned to the same class. Now the difference between *diteramator* and *alteramaior* is not worth considering, so frequently is *d* confused with *a*, *i* with *l*, and *t* with *i*; and the scribes who when they found at VIII. 148 a hexameter ending with *sufflamine multo consul* altered the order to *multo sufflamine* would not scruple here to write *uno caput* for *caput uno* when metre required it. Buecheler, I ought to say, already suspected the presence of *amator*.

The sense is plain enough: never fear a scarcity of Virrones while the seven hills abide; they will flock over sea and land out of all the world to Rome: it is Naevoli that will be scarce: you will be in high demand: only make you ready against it. The order of the words *caput uno* which I restore is a deliberate imitation of Calvus' notorious epigram, 'Magnus, quem metuunt omnes, digito *caput uno* | scalpit.' The clausula *derit amator* is repeated from the companion Satire II. 168, 'non numquam *derit amator*', and here serves of course as a pointed opposition to the 'numquam pathicus tibi *derit amicus*' of 130.

I may add here two notes on passages which can be dealt with briefly.

VII. 22　　siqua aliunde putas rerum *spectanda* tuarum
　　　　　　praesidia.

This is the reading of P. But *specto* is not thus used; so most editors take *expectanda* from the other MSS. I should think *speranda* nearer to our best authority; and it seems to have been read by the scholiast who writes 'si aliunde magis praesidium *speras* per carmina quam a principe'.

XV. 75　　　terga *fuga* celeri praestant instantibus Ombis.

But P has *fugat*, which points to *fugae*: see for instance Prop. IV. 2, 54, 'turpi terga dedisse fugae': *inst. Omb.* will then be abl. abs.

13

PERSIUS III. 43*

If I recur to this passage it is not so much out of inordinate affection for my own conjectures as because the discussion started by Dr Postgate on p. 275 ⟦CR 3 (1889), 275⟧ may prove interesting to pursue. The 'white liver' of the coward as well as the 'black heart' of the traitor was present to my mind when I objected to 'intus palleat', but I think there is a difference. Cowardice and treachery are qualities, and inherent in the man: the bloodlessness attributed to the craven is with him from his birth and, to be prosaic, may be expected to reveal itself at a post-mortem examination; and so too the traitor's black heart. But I think it is otherwise when one has to speak not of a quality but of an emotion, as here in Persius of guilty fears: emotions may be held to cause by their presence some such internal disorder as the flight of blood from an inward part; but they come and go, and they all depart with life. The difference is of this sort: in the darkness of night a white rose may be called a white rose still, but can a face in the darkness of night be said to turn pale? Next, as to transferring the external signs of a feeling to its internal origin: some signs, a shudder for instance, you can transfer to the inner man because you are not forced definitely to image the inner man when you do so. But if you will transfer thither such signs as the pallor of fear or the blush of shame, which belong not to the whole surface of the body but to the face alone, and owe their significance to that, you must figure the inner man with features and a complexion; and I do not think you can. As for Ovid's 'pectora lacte candidiora', it is very bad, and justly censured by Dr Postgate; but it is of another class. 'Candidus' has a regular and frequent metaphorical meaning, candid: Ovid, writing with his eye on words and not on things, confounds this meaning with the literal one: he often does the like: *met.* XI. 125 contains I think his crowning exploit in this department of folly. But in 'intus palleat', though there is incredible confusion between effect and cause, there is no confusion between a literal and a metaphorical meaning: 'palleo' does indeed sometimes connote fear besides denoting paleness, but it is not then metaphorical. The passage of Ovid would be parallel to ours only if the following rule-of-three sum were correct, *whiteness* : *candour* :: *pallor* : *fear*. On Pindar's λευκαῖς πιθήσαντα φρασίν I dare no more give an opinion than on our old friend φρένες ἀμφιμέλαιναι, though I think that φρεσὶ λευγαλέῃσι πιθήσας is a μέγας

* ⟦CR 3 (1889), 315⟧

ὀφθαλμός. It would however in itself be quite defensible to interpret λευκαῖς as 'blanching the cheek', since many adjectives acquire a similar extension of their use: 'tarda crura', lame legs, 'tarda podagra', laming gout: Persius himself at v. 55 has 'pallentis grana cumini' for 'quod pallidos faciat' as the scholiast there says; but these facts of course are no good for the verb and for 'intus palleat'.

The nearest apparent parallel that I know of is Iuu. I. 166 sq. 'rubet auditor, cui frigida mens est | criminibus, tacita *sudant praecordia* culpa.' But I suppose that 'praecordia' here means what it means in Ovid, *met.* VII. 559, 'nuda sed in terra ponunt praecordia', the external part which is 'prae corde'; so that we should compare Pers. II. 53 sq. '*sudes* et *pectore laeuo* | *excutiat guttas* laetari praetrepidum cor'.

P.S. Since the above was printed I have been allowed to see Mr Morgan's note on the passage [[*CR* 3 (1889), 314–15]]: he urges mainly the points I have discussed, so I will only add a word or two. I. 24 sq. is a metaphor in the regular sense of the word: the heart is riven by poetic travail, masonry by the wild fig: these are two analogous operations, and a term proper to one is rhetorically transferred to the other. But 'intus palleat' is another sort of μεταφορά altogether. It is the transference of an outward sign to the inward seat of feeling, and so far it resembles 'quanta siccum iecur ardeat ira' and 'formidine turpi frigida corda tremant'; but the chilly shudder of fear, as I said above, and also the parching heat of indignation, are signs which can be so transferred without losing their significance, and differ herein from the pallor of fear which owes its meaning to its appearance in the face. Mr Morgan says with truth that Persius is a faulty writer; but when a fault of this sort is laid to his charge by MSS written eight hundred years after his death I think we ought not to lend them too credulous an ear.

14

CONJECTURAL EMENDATIONS
IN THE *MEDEA**

δεινὰ τυράννων λήματα καί πως
120 ὀλίγ᾽ ἀρχόμενοι, πολλὰ κρατοῦντες,
χαλεπῶς ὀργὰς μεταβάλλουσιν.
τὸ γὰρ εἰθίσθαι ζῆν ἐπ᾽ ἴσοισιν
κρεῖσσον · ἐμοὶ γοῦν εἰ μὴ μεγάλως
ὀχυρῶς τ᾽ εἴη καταγηράσκειν.
125 τῶν γὰρ μετρίων πρῶτα μὲν εἰπεῖν
τοὔνομα νικᾷ, χρῆσθαί τε μακρῷ
λῷστα βροτοῖσιν · τὰ δ᾽ ὑπερβάλλοντ᾽
οὐδένα καιρὸν δύναται θνητοῖς,
μείζους δ᾽ ἄτας, ὅταν ὀργισθῇ
130 δαίμων οἴκοις, ἀπέδωκεν.

Here is nothing to arrest us till we come to the τ᾽ of v. 124; but this annihilates all sense and construction in the sentence where it occurs, and is therefore amended to γ᾽ or δ᾽, or, simpler still, discarded: the scribe who inserted it supposed no doubt that he was smoothing away an asyndeton. The words now left possess a meaning, but it is wrong. These verses set forth what the Greeks were never tired of hearing – the praise of the golden mean in disparagement of a high estate; and it flatly contradicts their tenour to say in the midst of them *be it mine to grow old in security if not in grandeur*, for this makes grandeur the prime object of desire and security the second. Mr Th. Barthold corrects ἐπὶ μὴ μεγάλοις, *on modest means*: the recent editors accept this, so I pass to the next sentence.

χρῆσθαί τε λῷστα for αὐτά τε χρῆσθαι λῷστά ἐστιν I will call by no worse name than clumsy; but the expression *overgreatness is tantamount to no profit for mortals* is so strange in itself that Nauck, Prinz, Verrall, and now Wecklein agree to think v. 128 corrupt; and external witness is still more damaging. Mr Verrall has already called attention to an obscure scholion which I present in this amended form: τὰ δ᾽ ὑπερβάλλοντ᾽] αἱ δ᾽ ὑπερβολαί, φησίν, ἀσθενεῖς καὶ οὐ βέβαιοι τοῖς ἀνθρώποις τραχείᾳ (ita scripsi, τῇ ἀρχαίᾳ MSS) μεταβολῇ (*i.e.* ὅταν

* [[CR 4 (1890), 8–11]]

[8

ὀργισθῇ δαίμων v. 129). This note, correct it as I do or leave it as it was, is no comment on our text: the text on which it is a comment I should say with some confidence was this:

τὰ δ' ὑπερβάλλοντ' ἄρρωστα βροτοῖς.

Remember that in any fairly ancient MS ἄρρωστα would be spelt ἄρωστα, and that the scribes omit iota subscript as often as they insert it – indeed it is not recorded whether the MSS have λῷστα or λῶστα here: we then see that the change of ὑπερβάλλοντ' ἄρρωστα to ὑπερβάλλοντα λῷστα is merely λ for ρ, an early and frequent error; and λῷστα βροτοῖσιν τὰ δ' ὑπερβάλλοντ' is a transposition in aid of the metre. For the sense of the corrected verse compare *frag.* 80 [79 Nauck] βροτοῖς τὰ μείζω τῶν μέσων τίκτει νόσους. I take this opportunity of saying that in Soph. *El.* 1070 sq. ὅτι σφὶν ἤδη τὰ μὲν ἐκ δόμων | νοσεῖ, τὰ δὲ πρὸς τέκνων κτλ., where the editors alter νοσεῖ to νοσεῖται or νοσεύει or νοσεῖ δή or νοσώδη or ὀνοστά, and then infer from these corrections of theirs that the antistrophic οἰωνούς is a bacchius, I suspect ἀρρωστεῖ or some such word was the original and νοσεῖ a gloss.

It will be convenient to consider v. 128 next. Mr Verrall observing that one MS gives βροτοῖς for θνητοῖς has suggested that δύναται βροτοῖς is the remains of an explanatory supplement trimmed into measure by the alteration θνητοῖς. I think it now appears that v. 128 is not Euripides at all, but contains a duplicate of the scholion quoted above explaining v. 127. The annotator can hardly have written it as it stands, and its original form I do not undertake to restore, but I guess it to be a blend of two glosses: (1) οὐδὲν δύναται βροτοῖς or θνητοῖς, an interpretation of ἄρρωστα βροτοῖς: (2) καιρόν, a supplement to ὑπερβάλλοντα conveying the ‖ correct information that ὑπερβάλλειν means ὑπερβάλλειν καιρόν, *to overshoot the mark*: this phrase is found in Democritus ap. Stob. *flor.* 18, 36 [vol. i p. 522 Hense] ὅσοι ἀπὸ γαστρὸς τὰς ἡδονὰς ποιεῦνται ὑπερβεβληκότες τὸν καιρόν and Plut. *Ages.* 8 ὑπερβάλλων τὸν καιρόν, and I daresay elsewhere.

The verses 125–6 as my correction leaves them are translatable, or would be thought so if they had been thus handed down, but I do not defend them. It is impossible not to wish away the two dipodiae πρῶτα μὲν εἰπεῖν and χρῆσθαί τε μακρῷ: there would then remain the straightforward sentence τῶν γὰρ μετρίων τοὔνομα νικᾷ | τὰ δ' ὑπερβάλλοντ' ἄρρωστα βροτοῖς: here I do not take ὄνομα to mean *name*, but I take τὸ τῶν μετρίων ὄνομα to be a periphrasis for τὰ μέτρια, as ὄνομ' ὁμιλίας is for ὁμιλία in *Or.* 1082 and τὸ ὄνομα τῆς σωτηρίας for τὴν σωτηρίαν in *I.T.* 905. And I think a piece of external evidence can be adduced to show that the inconvenient words were not originally written where we find them now.

These anapaests, especially the closing verses 129–30, recall a well-known passage of Herodotus, VII. 10, 13 ⟦7 10 ε Hude⟧, ending with the words φιλέει γὰρ ὁ θεὸς τὰ ὑπερέχοντα πάντα κολούειν; and at vv. 125–6 Porson cited another passage of equal celebrity from the same historian, III. 80, 10 ⟦3 80 6 Hude⟧, πλῆθος δὲ ἄρχον πρῶτα μὲν οὔνομα πάντων κάλλιστον ἔχει, ἰσονομίην · δεύτερα δέ, τῶν ὁ μούναρχος ποιέει οὐδέν. Now if in Herodotus it is ἰσονομία which is better than μοναρχία 'on the one hand in name and on the other in practice', while in Euripides it is μετριότης which has this advantage over ὑπερβολή, that in itself need not surprise us. But when in the neighbouring sentence we find ἰσονομία and μοναρχία compared by Euripides also, it must I think surprise us that the antithesis between name and practice should not occur there instead of here; and trusting in Herodotus I place our two dipodiae after v. 122:

> τὸ γὰρ εἰθίσθαι ζῆν ἐπ' ἴσοισιν,
> πρῶτα μὲν εἰπεῖν, χρῆσθαί τε, μακρῷ
> κρεῖσσον.

Examples of πρῶτα μέν thus answered by τε are quoted by Paley from *Hipp.* 996, *Heracl.* 337—40, and Aesch. *supp.* 410: I give the first, ἐπίσταμαι γὰρ πρῶτα μὲν θεοὺς σέβειν, | φίλοις τε χρῆσθαι μἀδικεῖν πειρωμένοις. It is perhaps worth mentioning that Herodotus a few chapters further on, 85, 4 ⟦85 2 Hude⟧, has τοιαῦτα ἔχω φάρμακα, and that the similar words τοιάδ' οἶδα φάρμακα occur in v. 718 of the *Medea*.

Lastly I come to v. 130. Before Mr Verrall editors used to punctuate ὅταν ὀργισθῇ δαίμων, οἴκοις ἀπ.; but as ἀποδιδόναι means to pay and not to inflict a penalty, this cannot be. Mr Verrall therefore places the comma after οἴκοις, but his translation '*when fortune is angered with the house*, that is, *with the increase of it*' shows that οἴκοις wants a good deal of assistance to yield the required sense. I propose then to write

> μείζους δ' ἄτας, ὅταν ὀργισθῇ
> δαίμων ὄγκοις, ἀπέδωκαν.

i.e. μείζους ἄτας ἀπέδωκαν ὄγκοι ὅταν δαίμων ὀργισθῇ αὐτοῖς, *towering fortunes pay a heavier penalty of ruin when heaven is angered with them*: 'celsae grauiore casu decidunt turres.' It would of course be possible, though I should not commend it, to retain ἀπέδωκεν with τὰ ὑπερβάλλοντα for its subject. The sense of ὄγκος is common: a good instance is *frag.* 506 ⟦504 Nauck⟧, ὦ τέκνον, ἀνθρώποισιν ἔστιν οἷς βίος | ὁ σμικρὸς εὐκρὰς ἐγένεθ', οἷς δ' ὄγκος κακόν: the plural however does not seem to be elsewhere found outside technical writers. μείζους ἄτας ἀπέδωκαν ὄγκοι resembles a good deal the last sentence of Sophocles's *Antigone*, with its μεγάλοι λόγοι τῶν ὑπεραύχων μεγάλας πληγὰς ἀποτείσαντες. ὄγκος and οἶκος have been confounded, as was natural, in other places, for instance at *Ion* 15, γαστρὸς διήνεγκ' ὄγκον (Brodaeus, οἶκον MSS), where Cobet ap. Badham adduces Dionys. Hal. *ant. Rom.* III. 11, ἀλλ' ἡ μὲν ὑμετέρα πόλις ἀπὸ μείζονος αὐχήματος ἀρχομένη εἰς ἐλάττονα ὄγκον (οἶκον MS) συνῆκται. Aesch. *Ag.* 961 should be read thus: ἔστιν θάλασσα, τίς δέ νιν κατα-σβέσει; | τρέφουσα πολλῆς πορφύρας ἰσάργυρον | κηκῖδα παγκαίνιστον, εἱμάτων βαφάς. | ὄγκος (Tycho Mommsen, οἶκος MSS) δ' ὑπάρχει τῶνδε σὺν θεοῖς, ἄναξ, | ἔχειν · πένεσθαι δ' οὐκ ἐπίσταται δόμος: here ὄγκος εἱμάτων means a great pile of raiment, as Herodotus has ὄγκος φρυγάνων: 'the sea abounds with purple to dye our vesture, and of vesture for the dyeing we have plenteous store': no fear then of dearth on either hand. Porson's οἴκοις will not serve, for ὑπάρχει τῶνδε fails to convey the notion of abundance.

In conclusion I give vv. 122–30 consecutively in order that their last state may be compared with their first:

> τὸ γὰρ εἰθίσθαι ζῆν ἐπ' ἴσοισιν
> πρῶτα μὲν εἰπεῖν χρῆσθαί τε μακρῷ
> κρεῖσσον · ἐμοὶ γοῦν ἐπὶ μὴ μεγάλοις
> ὀχυρῶς εἴη καταγηράσκειν.
> τῶν γὰρ μετρίων τοὔνομα νικᾷ,
> τὰ δ' ὑπερβάλλοντ' ἄρρωστα βροτοῖς ·
> μείζους δ' ἄτας, ὅταν ὀργισθῇ
> δαίμων ὄγκοις, ἀπέδωκαν. ||

The following passages will not take so long to examine.

24–6   κεῖται δ' ἄσιτος, σῶμ' ὑφεῖσ' ἀλγηδόσιν,
        τὸν πάντα συντήκουσα δακρύοις χρόνον,
        ἐπεὶ πρὸς ἀνδρὸς ᾖσθετ' ἠδικημένη.

The old commentators took συντήκουσα for συντηκομένη, a use without example. The construction is now thought to be συντήκουσα χρόνον, and τήκει βιοτήν v. 141 is quoted as parallel. But parallel it is not: τήκει βιοτήν is a mere equivalent of τήκει ἑαυτήν or τήκεται: αὐανῶ βίον in Soph. *El.* 819 is just the same thing as αὐανοῦμαι in *Phil.* 954, and when Callimachus writes ὤμοσα σὸν βίον Catullus translates it *adiuro te;* moreover if to melt time down meant anything at all it would apparently mean to shorten time or make it pass quickly. Clearly the sense wanted is that which συντηκομένη would give, that of *I. A.* 398, ἐμὲ δὲ συντήξουσι νύκτες ἡμέραι τε δακρύοις; and this Mr Verrall elicits by supplying σῶμα from the preceding verse. Euripides, I think, might have devised something more elegant than this; and I would credit him rather with writing τὸν πάντα συντήκουσα δακρύοις χρόα, comparing 689 τί γὰρ σὸν ὄμμα χρώς τε συντέτηχ' ὅδε and especially *Hel.* 1419, μή νυν ἄγαν σὸν δάκρυσιν ἐκτήξῃς χρόα.

319–20   γυνὴ γὰρ ὀξύθυμος, ὡς δ' αὔτως ἀνήρ,
　　　　　　ῥᾴων φυλάσσειν ἢ σιωπηλὸς σοφός.

Mr Verrall's seems the only possible account of the construction: possible I think it is, though the position of σοφός is curious. But what still perplexes me is the gender of σιωπηλός and σοφός: I do not understand why the parenthetic ὡς δ' αὔτως ἀνήρ exerts this influence, considering especially that the speaker's whole practical concern is with a woman. It is strange if the poet, who already in ὀξύθυμος and ῥᾴων had employed two adjectives suiting masc. and fem. alike, did not end the sentence with a third and write σιωπηλόστομος. These compounds are frequent in tragedy: θρασύστομος, κακόστομος, σεμνόστομος, χαλκόστομος, ἀθυρόστομος, αἰολόστομος, ἐλευθερόστομος.

339   τί δ' αὖ βιάζει κοὐκ ἀπαλλάσσει χερός;

τί δ' αὖ is quite inappropriate and the τί δ' οὖν of one MS is no better: Mr Verrall proposes τί οὖν; but it seems clear that the archetype had τί δ' αὖ, which surely points to τί δαί. Brunck and Porson, as is well known, were for expelling this word from tragedy; but let us weigh the evidence. The text of Aeschylus presents δαί once, at *Prom.* 933, τί δαὶ φοβοίμην; here syntax rejects it and demands δ' ἂν in its stead: we infer then that Aeschylus did not use it. The text of Sophocles presents it once, at *Ant.* 318, τί δαὶ ῥυθμίζεις; here MS testimony is worth nothing, for if Sophocles wrote δέ the scribe had a metrical temptation to an error always easy: we infer then that δαί was not used by Sophocles. If now Euripides did not use it, we might expect his text to offer two or perhaps three suspicious instances; but if instead it offers at least half a dozen which of themselves give no handle to suspicion at all, the inference is obvious.

351–6   προυννέπω δέ σοι,
　　　εἴ σ' ἡ 'πιοῦσα λαμπὰς ὄψεται θεοῦ
　　　καὶ παῖδας ἐντὸς τῆσδε τερμόμων χθονός,
　　　θανεῖ· λέλεκται μῦθος ἀψευδὴς ὅδε.
　　　νῦν δ', εἰ μένειν δεῖ, μίμν' ἐφ' ἡμέραν μίαν·
　　　οὐ γάρ τι δράσεις δεινὸν ὧν φόβος μ' ἔχει.

Verse 356 makes no sense, has few defenders, and is usually now sent into exile with its innocent neighbour 355 for companion; but why it was inserted no one can say. I offer this transposition and amendment:

　　　θανεῖ· λέλεκται μῦθος ἀψευδὴς ὅδε·
　　　μὴ γάρ τι δράσῃς, δεινὸν ὡς φόβος μ' ἔχει.
　　　νῦν δ', εἰ μένειν δεῖ, μίμν' ἐφ' ἡμέραν μίαν.

for I am horribly afraid lest you do mischief. Compare 282 sq. δέδοικά σε. . . μή μοί τι δράσῃς παῖδ' ἀνήκεστον κακόν and *frag.* 608, 4 [605 4 Nauck], φόβος πρόσεστι μὴ δράσωσί τι. If the first letter μ was lost the change of η to οὐ was not difficult: οὐ for ἤ is found at *I. A.* 1189, and at *Med.* 695 we cannot tell whether ἤ should be οὐ or μή. It now becomes possible to believe the hitherto incredible statement of the scholiast that after this verse Didymus read σιγῇ δόμους ἐσβᾶσ᾽ ἵν᾽ ἔστρωται λέχος.

381–3   ἀλλ᾽ ἔν τί μοι πρόσαντες · εἰ ληφθήσομαι
         δόμους ὑπερβαίνουσα καὶ τεχνωμένη,
         θανοῦσα θήσω τοῖς ἐμοῖς ἐχθροῖς γέλων.

I should like some proof that we can say δόμους ὑπερβαίνειν for ὁδὸν ὑπερβαίνειν: the δόμων ὑπερβᾶσ᾽ of *supp.* 1049 will not suffice and is moreover very uncertain. But however this may be, I think that ὑπεσβαίνουσα, which is precisely the σιγῇ δόμους ἐσβᾶσ᾽ of v. 380, will be much more expressive. Bothe has conjectured ὑπεμβαίνουσα.

734–40   πέποιθα · Πελίου δ᾽ ἐχθρός ἐστί μοι δόμος
         Κρέων τε. τούτοις δ᾽, ὁρκίοισι μὴ ζυγεὶς   735
         [ἄγουσιν οὐ μεθεῖς ἂν ἐκ γαίας ἐμὲ]
         λόγοις δὲ συμβὰς καὶ θεῶν ἀνώμοτος, ‖
         ψιλὸς γένοι᾽ ἂν κἀπικηρυκεύματα
         οὐκ ἀντιθεῖο · τἀμὰ μὲν γὰρ ἀσθενῆ,
         τοῖς δ᾽ ὄλβος ἐστὶ καὶ δόμος τυραννικός.   740

'I trust you; but Creon and the house of Pelias are my enemies; and against these, if instead of a binding oath you make only a verbal pact without attestation of gods, you will be left defenceless and unable on your part to retort their diplomatic messages.' Here I have accepted Mr Verrall's ψιλός for φίλος in v. 738, together with his general view of the sense, which seems absolutely necessitated by πέποιθα, v. 734, and strongly though superfluously confirmed by vv. 743–4; then I have altered μὲν to μὴ in v. 735; ejected with Badham the interpolation which μὲν occasioned, v. 736, containing as it does a barbarism if μεθεῖς is kept and a tortured construction if it is changed to μεθεῖ᾽; and amended ἂν πίθοιο in v. 739 to ἀντιθεῖο, which perhaps merely because it is my own I prefer to Verrall's ἀντισοῖο or Leo's and Munro's ὀκνῶν πίθοιο. With τούτοις ψιλὸς γένοι᾽ ἂν καὶ οὐκ ἀντιθεῖο for τούτοις, ψιλὸς γενόμενος, οὐκ ἂν ἀντιθεῖο, compare Soph. *Ant.* 1279 sq. τὰ δ᾽ ἐν δόμοις | ἔοικας ἥκειν καὶ τάχ᾽ ὄψεσθαι κακά.

856–9   πόθεν θράσος ἢ φρενὸς ἢ
         χειρὶ σέθεν τέκνων ⟦τέκνων σέθεν⟧
         καρδίᾳ τε λήψει
         δεινὰν προσάγουσα τόλμαν;

The upshot of the criticism bestowed on this passage is that τέκνων must be replaced by an accusative answering θράσος. Since μένος is not easy nor τέχναν adequate, while σθένος, though it might be absorbed by σέθεν, would not account for τέκνων, I do not see what else the word can have been but κότον, which is confounded now and again with τόκον, and that with τέκνον. Euripides seems to imitate Aesch. *supp.* 65 sqq. παιδὸς μόρον, ὡς αὐτοφόνως ὤλετο πρὸς χειρὸς ἕθεν δυσμάτορος κότου τυχών.

1317   τί τάσδε κινεῖς κἀναμοχλεύεις πύλας;

There is no more innocent-looking verse in all Euripides. But Porson quotes these passages: ὦ καινῶν ἐπῶν κινητὰ καὶ μοχλευτά from Ar. *nub.* 1397, following on an allusion to the *Aeolus* of our poet; τί τούσδε κινεῖς κἀναμοχλεύεις λόγους; from two places in the *Christus patiens*; and τί ταῦτα κινεῖς κἀναμοχλεύεις; τοῦτο δὴ τὸ τῶν τραγῳδῶν from Heliodorus's *Aethiopica*. All this celebrity was never won by anything so simple as our text: Mr Verrall then rightly infers that a strange word or a word strangely used stood here in lieu of πύλας, and he proposes ὀπάς. This will amply account for the notice attracted; but whether it will suit the verse itself is not so sure: it does not seem to me that the ὀπαί or perforations of a door are things one can be said to ἀναμοχλεύειν any more than one unlocks keyholes in English. My own suggestion is πάγας. πηγνύναι means to make fast; and accordingly a right to mean anything that makes or is made fast is the inalienable heritage of πάγη. To show how various may be the meanings of a verbal substantive no better examples could be taken than words of this very family: πάγος, *frost* or *rock*, πῆγμα, *scaffold* or *rennet* for curdling. The liberty of a poet to set colloquial use at naught and impose on πάγη that meaning which specially appears in the related verb πακτοῦν (compare Ar. *Lys.* 265, μοχλοῖς δὲ καὶ κλήθροισιν τὰ προπύλαια πακτοῦν) ought not I think to be doubted; but we can go further. We know that Euripides again bestowed this same meaning in defiance of custom on another cognate of πηγνύναι, and that Aristophanes again laid hold on it as characteristic. In *Acharn.* 479, Euripides, interrupted at home in the writing of a tragedy, has acceded with tolerable urbanity to the endless requests with which he is pestered by Dicaeopolis; but when it comes to σκάνδικά μοι δός, μητρόθεν δεδεγμένος, that is too much, and he ends the interview and returns to the altitudes of tragedy with ἀνὴρ ὑβρίζει · κλῇε πηκτὰ δωμάτων: the point of this we learn from Pollux, x. 27, who informs us that Euripides somewhere or other used the words λῦε πακτὰ δωμάτων, *frag.* 991 〚1003 Nauck〛. Here too then I suppose that Euripides made πάγας mean the fastenings of a door; but πάγη in common parlance meant nothing but a net, and Use and Wont, 'grey nurses, loving nothing new', promptly resented the innovation through the lips of their champion Aristophanes.

If this singular use of πάγη were found in a MS, we should tranquilly record it in our lexicons without suspicion or surprise. Emendations, as is right and natural, are less readily received; but it happens that our lexicons already contain a use of the cognate πῆγμα equally unexampled and equally destitute of MS authority: I mean the ὅρκου πῆγμα γενναίως παγέν restored by Auratus to Aesch. *Ag.* 1198, where πῆγμα has a meaning otherwise unknown, and the MSS have not πῆγμα but πῆμα.

15

REVIEW: T. G. TUCKER, *THE SUPPLICES OF AESCHYLUS**

This edition gives proof of many virtues: common sense, alert perception, lucidity of thought, impatience of absurdity, a rational distrust of MS tradition, and a masculine taste in things poetical. The learner who attacks the play with this commentary will find unfailing help by the way and acquire much information before his journey's end. The old miserable experiences of the classical student who wants to understand what he reads, his lonely fights with difficulties whose presence the editor has never apprehended, his fruitless quest of a meaning in notes where the editor has rendered Greek nonsense into English nonsense and gone on his way rejoicing, are not repeated here. Here on the contrary is a commentator who shares the reader's difficulties, rescues him from some of them, warns him of some existing unperceived, and to tell the truth invents a good many where none exist.

It is Prof. Tucker's main concern, as it must be for an editor of this play, to find || out what Aeschylus wrote; and his administration of this province will decide the value of the book as an original contribution to learning. He has introduced into the text, I reckon roughly, about 200 conjectures of his own. It is the critic's chief duty, and should be his chief pleasure, to commend what is good; so I begin with four emendations which I should call quite certain.

115 (as if our studies were not yet enough perplexed with conflicting numerations Mr Tucker has invented a new one: I ignore this and cite according to Dindorf) τοιαῦτα πάθεα μέλεα θρεομένα δ' ἐγὼ λιγέα βαρέα δακρυοπετῆ, ἰὴ ἰή, ἰαλέμοισιν ἐμπρεπῆ, ζῶσα γόοις με τιμῶ. Whether this means *conspicuous for* or *among dirges*, neither suits, and Dindorf is obliged to translate *decens, aptus*, i.e. to render ἐμπρεπής as if it were ξυμπρεπής. Mr Tucker writes ἐμφερῆ which I find most convincing: the sense is just what one looks for and the error of a common type.

121 [120] πολλάκι δ' ἐμπίτνω ξὺν λακίδι λίνοισιν ἧι Cιδονίᾳ καλύπτρᾳ: in the repetition at 133 [131] αἴνοισιν ἧ. At first this looks like λίνοισιν ἤ, but since ἤ

* [*The Supplices of Aeschylus*, a revised text with Introduction, Critical Notes, Commentary and Translation, by T. G. Tucker. London, Macmillan and Co. 1889. Pp. xxxvii, 228. *CR* 4 (1890), 105–9]

is not at all appropriate they conjecture ἠδέ or λίνοισι καί: Mr Tucker however comparing *Cho.* 27 λινοφθόροι λακίδες proposes ξὺν λακίδι λινοσινεῖ, an admirable correction.

341–4 〖342–5〗

> Β. βαρέα σύ γ᾽ εἶπας, πόλεμον ἄρασθαι νέον.
> Χ. ἀλλ᾽ ἡ δίκη γε ξυμμάχων ὑπερστατεῖ.
> Β. εἴπερ γ᾽ ἀπ᾽ ἀρχῆς πραγμάτων κοινωνὸς ἦν.
> Χ. αἰδοῦ σὺ πρύμναν πόλεος ὧδ᾽ ἐστεμμένην.

'Yes, if she was concerned in the affair at first' is nothing to the point: that Justice was concerned one way or the other there can be no manner of doubt. Or if there is an insinuation that the Danaids were first in the wrong, they cannot afford to ignore it in their reply. Mr Tucker alters ἦν to ἦ, 'that would have force had *I* been originally concerned, but now it is no business of mine', an answer which compels the suppliants to shift their ground; and we are really nearer the MS than before, for in the next verse it gives ἐστεμμένη: the ν was transposed.

> φύλαξαι μὴ θράσος τέκῃ φόβον.
499 > καὶ δὴ φίλον τις ἔκταν᾽ ἀγνοίας ὕπο.

No recorded use of καὶ δή is here in place: Mr Tucker writes ἤδη: one abbreviation of καί is much confused with η, and ἤδη is so appropriate to the sententious aorist that the correction, once made, is obvious.

The following conjectures I select as favourable specimens. 154 εἰ δὲ μή, μελανθὲς ἡδιόκτυπον γένος τὸν γάιον...Ζῆνα...ἱξόμεσθα: Wellauer's ἡλιόκτυπον is generally read, but Mr Tucker objects that κτύπος means *noise* not merely *stroke* and that ὀμβρόκτυπος νιφόκτυπος χιονόκτυπος do not warrant ἡλιόκτυπος = ἡλιόβλητος: he writes with great ingenuity μέλαθρ᾽ ἐς ἡλίῳ στυγούμεν᾽ ὡς τὸν γάιον κτλ.: the sense is excellent and the changes though numerous are all easy: it must however be remarked that the preposition ὡς is not found in Aeschylus. 198 τὸ μὴ μάταιον δ᾽ ἐκ μετώπων σωφρονῶν | ἴτω προσώπων: Mr Tucker writes κατωποσωφρόνων which he compares with such compounds as ἀγνόρυτος and ἀκριτόφυρτος: certainly former conjectures have small likelihood, Porson's least of all. 220 sq. Δ. Ἑρμῆς ὅδ᾽ ἄλλος τοῖσιν Ἑλλήνων νόμοις. | Χ. ἐλευθέροις νῦν ἐσθλὰ κηρυκευέτω: here ἐλευθέροις seems quite irrelevant, and Mr Tucker proposes ἀλλ᾽ εὑρεθεὶς with allusion to Hermes as the god of εὑρήματα: this to be sure gives the verse a point, though hardly perhaps of the sort one looks for after the six foregoing lines. 380 φόβος μ᾽ ἔχει φρένας | δρᾶσαί τε μὴ δρᾶσαί τε καὶ τύχην ἑλεῖν: Mr Tucker's difficulties about ἑλεῖν I share to the full; but when he writes τύχην ἐᾶν, to be construed closely with μὴ δρᾶσαι, the result is not a well-balanced phrase. 405 τί τῶνδ᾽ ἐξ ἴσου ῥεπομένων μεταλγεῖς τὸ δίκαιον ἔρξαι; a man cannot μεταλγεῖν what he has not yet done, so Tournier proposes μ' ἔτ' ἀργεῖς: Mr Tucker's με ταρβεῖς seems better. 480 sqq. σὺ μέν, πάτερ γεραιὲ τῶνδε παρθένων, | κλάδους τε τούτους αἶψ' ἐν ἀγκάλαις λαβὼν | βωμοὺς ἐπ' ἄλλους δαιμόνων ἐγχωρίων | θές: an anacoluthon mended in various ways, as by altering σύ to σοῦ (= ὄρμα) or τε to γε or αἶψ' to αἶρ' or λαβὼν βωμούς to λαβὲ βωμούς τ'. But Mr Tucker further points out what seems to have escaped notice, that τούτους cannot well be right when the Danaids are found still in possession of their κλάδοι at 506, and he removes two difficulties by the easy change of τε τούτους to τοιούτους. 632 θεοὶ διογενεῖς, κλύοιτ' εὐκταῖα γένει χεούσας: γένει seems quite harmless, but in M it is corrected into γένη whence Mr Tucker conjectures τέλη, *offerings*: the word is appropriate and the error common. 834: certain restoration there can be none in this wilderness of ruin, but δύσφρον' ἀνάγκαν for δύσφορα ναὶ κἂν ought to be right. 907 ⟦908⟧ διωλόμεσθα ἑπτάναξ πάσχομεν: it is usual to read ἄελπτ', ἄναξ, πάσχομεν with Robortellus, but Mr Tucker's ἄσεπτ' seems more suitable. 924 ἄγοιμ' ἄν, εἴ τις τάσδε μὴ 'ξαιρήσεται: this weak verse Mr Tucker alters to μάθοιμ' || ἂν εἴ τις τάσδε μ' ἐξαιρήσεται comparing Eur. *And.* 715 ὡς ἂν ἐκμάθω | εἴ τίς με λύειν τῆσδε κωλύσει χέρας: the change cannot be called certain, but to me it is very attractive. 1018 ἴτε μὰν ἀστυάνακτας μάκαρας θεοὺς γανάεντες πολιούχους τε καὶ οἳ χεῦμ' Ἐρασίνου περιναίουσιν: Mr Tucker objects to 'city-gods' comprising both πολιούχους and οἳ χεῦμ' Ἐ. περιναίουσιν, and writes ἄστυδ', ἄνακτας: the meaning of ἄστυ however need not be more restricted here than in ἀστυγειτονουμένας 286: the tragedians, as Strabo viii. p. 356 ⟦p. 506 Meineke⟧ observes, often make no difference between *burgh* and *land*. 1063 ⟦1062⟧ Ζεὺς ἄναξ ἀποστεροίη γάμον: this sense of the verb is unexampled, and Mr Tucker's ἀποστέγοι μοι is as likely as Hartung's ἀποστρέφοι μοι.

Among the residue of the 200 conjectures there may very well be some which will seem more probable to other critics than to me, but there can hardly be many. Mr Tucker's objections to the vulgate are often acute and true: some instances I have given; others are the remarks on σκοπόν 647 and κλύουσά γ' ὡς ἂν οὐ φίλη 718, and the geographical difficulties raised about 254-7. His alterations seldom fail to give a just and straightforward meaning; and the book is almost wholly free of those incredible emendations which consult the *apices codicum* and consult nothing else. There is indeed one extraordinary specimen of this class at 146, where ἔχουσα σέμν' ἐνῶπ' ἀσφαλές is altered into λέχους ἄσεμν' ἐν Ὤπιδι σφάλασα, a reading dependent on two fables, both invented by Mr Tucker, – that Orion assaulted one of Artemis' handmaids named Opis,* and that λέχους ἄσεμνα is Greek for *unholy lust*; but this stands almost alone. What vitiates two thirds of Mr Tucker's conjectures is that despite his professions he takes no due heed to palaeographical probability. 'In the present work', says he in his preface, 'there have been assumed as axioms . . . (iii.) that the

* ⟦See Appendix 4, p. 1257⟧

reading substituted on conjecture must approve its claims by satisfying the conditions of palaeography – as a most natural source of the incorrect reading.' But this is just what an average conjecture of Mr Tucker's does not. True, it seldom sets the MS utterly at naught, and it is usually fortified by a parade of uncial type, the decorative effect of which is often pleasing; but it diverges too far from the *ductus litterarum* to have any convincing force. Possible no doubt it is; but half-a-dozen alternatives are equally possible. We know of course that the scribes did make mistakes as bad as those which Mr Tucker postulates; but when such mistakes have once been made they can never be corrected. It may be that εἴρηται λόγος was the source of εἰθείη Διός, Ἄκμων of Cτρυμών, δηχθῆναι πόθῳ of μιχθῆναι βροτῷ, φοβουμένους of φόβῳ φρενός, διόρνυται ἐς of διορνυμένα, τίς ποτ' οὐ of τις βροτῶν, στυφελώδεις of φυγάδες, κηπωρικὴν λαβοῦσ' ἀνεωσμένην θύραν of καλωρα κωλύουσαν θωσμένειν ἐρῶ; and if the ghost of ever-living Aeschylus has uprisen before Mr Tucker from Acherusian quarters and has begun to shed salt tears and to unfold in words that it was so, well. But if not, then such inventions may indeed convince their inventor, but to the cold world they are offered in vain.

When Mr Tucker's conjectures are not palaeographically improbable they are apt to be causeless and even detrimental. Among the axioms assumed in the preface are the following: 'the reading in the text must hold its place until such cause to the contrary can be shewn as will satisfy a rigidly impartial tribunal. The *onus probandi* lies entirely with the impugner of the text.' 'The conditions of dispossession are these. It must either be proved that the reading is an impossibility, or else that in point of grammar it is so abnormal, or in point of relevance so manifestly inappropriate, as to produce a thorough conviction that the MS is in error.' I for my part should call this much too strict; but these are Mr Tucker's principles. His practice is something quite different: in practice no word, however good, is safe if Mr Tucker can think of a similar word which is not much worse. 180 sq. ὁρῶ κόνιν, ἄναυδον ἄγγελον στρατοῦ. | σύριγγες οὐ σιγῶσιν ἀξονήλατοι: Mr Tucker removes the stop after στρατοῦ and alters οὐ to οὔ. 'The MS reading οὐ', says he, 'causes an asyndeton which can only be explained by a protracted pause after στρατοῦ, while Danaus is awaiting further developments.' Five lines later on we learn that 'Danaus must have paused several times in this speech, commenting from time to time on the further progress of the Argives', so there is an end of that objection: proceed to the next. There is none. There are assertions, possibly true but on the editor's principles irrelevant, that the new reading is better; and that is all. 418 sqq. φρόντισον καὶ γενοῦ πανδίκως εὐσεβὴς πρόξενος · τὰν φυγάδα μὴ προδῷς κτλ.: Mr Tucker removes the colon and writes προδούς. The change is a mere trifle, but it is a trifle for the worse, since the μηδ' ἴδῃς which follows tallies rather better with μὴ προδῷς than with γενοῦ πρόξενος μὴ προδούς: and when Mr Tucker says that προδούς is given ||

on the same obvious ground as that of the change ἐκδῷς to ἐκδούς in 340 [341], he quite misapprehends that obvious ground, which is, if I must explain it, that the question πῶς is more properly answered by a participle than by a finite verb. 517 sqq. ἐγὼ δὲ λαοὺς ξυγκαλῶν ἐγχωρίους | στείχω, τὸ κοινὸν ὡς ἂν εὐμενὲς τιθῶ. | καὶ σὸν διδάξω πατέρα ποῖα χρὴ λέγειν: Mr Tucker puts a comma after τιθῶ and writes διδάξων. Now στείχειν is a necessary preliminary to ξυγκαλεῖν because the λαοί are away in the city, whence ξυγκαλῶν στείχω: to διδάσκειν it is not a necessary preliminary, for Danaus stands by the speaker's side: better then διδάξω than στείχω διδάξων. If we had διδάξων I would not take the trouble to alter it, because the superiority of διδάξω is not worth the change; but superior it is. 606 ὥστ' ἀνηβῆσαί με γηραιᾷ φρενί: Mr Tucker writes γηραιὰν φρένα because the dative would imply that it is the aged heart which makes the speaker grow young again, and because if we are to express the part or respect in which the rejuvenation takes place we must use the accusative: then γήθησε δὲ θυμῷ, for instance, means 'he rejoiced because of his soul'. 935 τὸ νεῖκος δ' οὐκ ἐν ἀργύρου λαβῇ | ἔλυσεν: it occurs to Mr Tucker that λαβῇ and βλαβῇ look much alike and both make sense; the MS gives one, therefore Aeschylus wrote the other. But this method cannot well be avowed, so he looks round for a stone to throw at λαβῇ, and the first that comes to hand is this: 'λαβή is a very common word and always means either a handle or a grasp. We have no authority for treating it as = λῆψις.' Very good; but at 674 we had these excellent remarks on φόρος (which is a very common word and always means tribute, and which we have no authority for treating as = φορά): 'just as τόκος and πρόσοδος had a general meaning before and besides interest and revenue, so φόρος had a general meaning before and besides tribute. The special meaning is the only one in prose, but not in verse. φορά is both tax and crop, and φόρος should be given the same values. Indeed we are apt to insufficiently remember the sound (and etymological suggestion) of Greek words to Greek ears. φόρους = bearings and γᾶς is sufficient definition.' Why then are we not to say that λαβῇ = taking and ἀργύρου is sufficient definition? because φόρους has the luck to be a conjecture and λαβῇ the misfortune to stand in a MS. 961 μονορρύθμους δόμους: 'we can hardly speak of a house having a ῥυθμός...a house cannot even metaphorically have a ῥυθμός': i.e. Mr Tucker, preoccupied with the interests of his conjecture μονορρύμους, has omitted to look out ῥυθμός in the dictionary; just as at 533 he asserts, to recommend his proposal there, that 'rhythm points to a pause at γένος', forgetting that if so, then in the antistrophic verse 526 rhythm points to a pause in the middle of the word τελειότατον. But when one hangs one's criminals first and tries them afterwards, a flaw in the indictment is of no practical consequence.

The emendations of scholars fare no better than the readings of the MS if their place is wanted for a conjecture of the editor's own. Again and again in passages which we all thought had been corrected long ago Mr Tucker proffers another solution, not better but newer, and promotes it, with rigid partiality, to the text. 56 γνώσεται δὲ λόγους τις ἐν μάκει: Mr Tucker very properly objects to μάκει standing alone and alters λόγους to χρόνου. Can he not see that before we bestow a thought on this he must demolish Martin's λόγου which removes the difficulty so much more easily and moreover is clearly what the scholiast read? 74 δειμαίνουσα φόλους, usually amended to φίλους: 'but the o preserved in M can scarcely be accidental' says Mr Tucker, and writes ποιμαίνουσα φόβους: the δ, the ε and the λ can all be accidental, but not the o. 164 κοννῶ δ' ἄγαν γαμετου-ρανόνεικον: Mr Tucker writes γαμετῶν τῶν οὐρανοοίκων. It ought of course to be γαμετᾶν; but apart from that, in what respect is this conjecture not inferior to the γαμετᾶς οὐρανόνικον of Victorius? 229 οὐδὲ μὴ 'ν ῞Αιδου θανὼν | φύγῃ μάταιον αἰτίας πράξας τάδε: this is corrupt, but Mr Tucker's μάταιον αἰτίαν is a conjecture which has no excuse for existing: it means the same as Tournier's ματαίους αἰτίας and comes no nearer the MS, while Schuetz's ματαίων αἰτίας is of course more probable than either. 271 sq. ἔχον δ' ἂν ἤδη τἀπ' ἐμοῦ τεκμήρια | γένος τ' ἂν ἐξεύχοιο καὶ λέγοι πρόσως: Robortellus emends λέγοις πρόσω: for ἔχον δ' ἂν the second hand in M gives γρ. ἔχουσαν: now this second hand collated M throughout with its original and corrected it thence, and pure nonsense like ἔχουσαν cannot be a conjecture: we therefore take this for a foothold, write ἔχουσα δ' with Heimsoeth, and all is clear. The reader now knows how to estimate Mr Tucker's assertion 'the correction of these lines must start with ἔχον δ' ἄν. It is contrary to all the principles of criticism that this should be an error for ἔχουσα δ'. ἔχων is the only rational correction.' Then he goes on 'either λέγοι or ἐξεύχοιο is wrong, and the omission of C from the former is less likely than that of T from the latter'. But ‖ no: nothing in the world is more likely than the omission of σ before π. 'Next, what τεκμήρια has the king given? He has made a statement, but he neither offers nor needs to offer *proofs.*' First Mr Tucker mistranslates τεκμήρια and then declares it corrupt on the strength of his mistranslation: it means here what it means in *Ag.* 352, testimony. All this leads up to the reading ἔχων δ' ἂν ἤδη τἀπ' ἐμοῦ τις ἐν μέρει | γένος τ' ἂν ἐξεύχοιτο καὶ λέγοι τορῶς: and to write ἔχουσα δ' for ἔχον δ' ἂν is contrary to all the principles of criticism! 502 καὶ ξυμβόλοισιν οὐ πολυστομεῖν χρεών: Mr Tucker's κἀν ξυμβολαῖσιν is well enough, only Valckenaer's ξυμβολοῦσιν is much better, and Mr Tucker finds nothing to say against it. 515 σὺ καὶ λέγων εὔφραινε καὶ πράσσων φρενί: we all read φρένα with Heath, against which Mr Tucker can only say that εὔφραινε does not 'require' an object: the rest of the note is a conscience-stricken apology for the demerits of his own conjecture χερί. 744 ἔπλευσαν ὧδ' ἐπεὶ τάχει κότῳ: for these corrupt words Mr Tucker writes ἐπιτυχεῖς σκοποῦ; but if we enquire why this is to be preferred before conjectures so much easier and more attractive as Turnebus' ἐπιτυχεῖ κότῳ or Weil's ἐπικότῳ τάχει, the only reason that can be rendered is Mr Coventry Patmore's: 'Say, how has thy Beloved surpassed So much all others? *She was mine.*'

But to shew what Mr Tucker can do and dare on behalf of his emendations the following example is, as King Pelasgus would say, οὐχ ὑπερτοξεύσιμον. In 137 sqq. ⟦138 sqq.⟧ we read τελευτὰς δ' ἐν χρόνῳ πατὴρ ὁ παντόπτας πρευμενεῖς κτίσειεν, σπέρμα σεμνᾶς μέγα ματρὸς εὐνᾶς ἀνδρῶν, ἑξ, ἄγαμον ἀδάματον ἐκφυγεῖν. Mr Tucker objects to μέγα and alters μέγα ματρὸς to με δάμαρτος: σεμνᾶς δάμαρτος means the august bride of Zeus, the πατὴρ παντόπτας who has just been mentioned. Well, this is very pretty; but unluckily the lines σπέρμα σεμνᾶς κτλ. are iterated at 151 sqq., where they are preceded by the mention not of Zeus but of Artemis, so that σεμνᾶς δάμαρτος will there mean the august bride of Artemis, a discouraging result. Mr Tucker's expedient to avoid this mishap is of a sort that strikes criticism dumb. He silently prints Δίας instead of σεμνᾶς: not as a conjecture, but as if it were the MS reading.

Here I have given proofs enough of the disasters which attend us when we desist from the pursuit of truth to follow after our own inventions. Thus much it was necessary to say, because the many students who will I hope resort to this edition for help and instruction must be warned that they will find not only what they seek but also a good deal which they are not to believe. The book however in spite of its faults is the most useful edition of the *Supplices* we have. The purely explanatory part of the commentary does not contain very much that is absolutely new, and this is well; for it is really a far more venturesome thing, if critics would but understand it, to propose a new rendering than a new reading. Among the most interesting notes are those on 189 ἀγωνίων, 472 ἐκπράξω χρέος, 669 θυμέλαι, 691 πρόνομα, 1071 ⟦1070⟧ δίμοιρον. I mention one or two miscellaneous points which are wrong or doubtful, not that I think them important but because the editor may like to correct or reconsider them. 19 ⟦18⟧: Mr Tucker defends γένος τετέλεσται by Pind. *Pyth.* IV 256, τόθι γὰρ γένος Εὐφάμου φυτευθὲν λοιπὸν ἀεὶ τέλλετο: τέλλετο and τετέλεσται however do not come from the same verb. 167 ⟦168⟧: Mr Tucker proposes a difficult interpretation because he does not observe that δικαίοις means *fitting*. 400: it seems rash to conjecture κάλλοιον when this adjective, so common in prose, is found in tragedy at one place only and makes nonsense there. 503: there can be no cause for Mr Tucker's rendering of ἄγοντας unless it be that a contorted interpretation is better than a plain one. 534: by what artifice can νέωσον εὔφρον' αἶνον be made to mean νέωσον αἶνον ὥστε εὔφρων εἶναι ἡμῖν? 556: Mr Tucker supports his conjecture ἐγκυκλουμένα by Ovid *met.* I 730 'profugam per totum *circuit* orbem': where did he find this reading and how does he construe it? 604: 'we might read ὅτι πληθύεται': no: a pyrrhic cannot constitute the fourth foot of an iambic senarius. 924: the suggestion μοι 'ξαρνήσεται is of course impossible: it is not certain that even μοὐξαρνήσεται would be used by Aeschylus. 1035 [1034]: Mr Tucker is here involved in some confusion: we have ἡμ. β′ coming before ἡμ. α′, and in the note we read of 'the other ἡμιχόριον' though we have hitherto had no ἡμιχόριον at all.

The translation is written with vigour and adroitness, and its rhythm is often admirable. Here and there, chiefly in the stichomythia, are crude phrases, and one or two so afflicting as 'horde of males' for ἄρσενος στόλου. παντὶ σθένει in 147 and ἄτερθε πτερύγων in 782 are left untranslated; ἐφορεύοι in 627 is very freely rendered 'further'; 'lea' at 722 seems meant for 'lee'; and at 966 occurs the comical misprint, 'for thy good deeds mayst thou have thy fill of food, Pelasgian lord'.

16

REVIEW: I. FLAGG, *EURIPIDES'*
*IPHIGENIA AMONG THE TAURIANS**

We have already in this country a very good school edition of the *Iphigenia in Tauris*; but Prof. Flagg's book is also a good one and will be found useful even here, designed as it is for younger students than Mr England's, students who have hitherto read no Greek verse but Homer and are brought to a standstill by each fresh crasis or Doricism. There is therefore none of that ‖ critical matter which occupies Mr England's footnotes, but only an incomplete list of deviations from MS authority at the end of the volume. Mr Flagg has constructed his text with common sense, but yet I think that for boys Mr England's is the better. For scholars of course neither of the two is satisfactory, inasmuch as both are full of conjectures which have no probability at all; but for boys the matter stands otherwise. We cannot always give them what Euripides wrote, for the simple reason that we have it not: the next best thing then is to give them what he might have written, grammar and good sense; and this is what Mr England's freely amended text attempts to do. Mr Flagg's more conservative recension no doubt comes quite as near as Mr England's to what Euripides wrote, but it contains much more which Euripides not only did not write but could not; and the learner's conception of Greek is impaired accordingly. The notes, if we set those aside which explain the various inexplicable things retained in the text, suit their purpose well: they are terse yet not niggardly: especially admirable is the way in which they keep the reader's eye on the progress of the action, and bring to his notice those strokes of art which a schoolboy intent on construing is sure to miss. Here and there the taste of an islander is offended by a style which breathes the ampler ether and diviner air of America, but otherwise it is only details that challenge demur. 250 ‘τοῦ ξυζύγου τοῦ ξένου: *of the stranger who was his mate.* The constr. seems to be like ὁ ἀνὴρ ὁ ἀγαθός, treating ξένου as an adjective.’ But the translation treats ξένου as a substantive, and requires for parallel ὁ ἀγαθὸς ὁ ἀνήρ. 266 ἄκροισι δακτύλοισι πορθμεύων ἴχνος, 'ferrying his track on tiptoe'. 300 ὥσθ' αἱματηρὸν πέλαγος ἐξανθεῖν ἁλός, 'so that the briny deep bloomed forth with gore': we need not encourage boys to translate in this style. 740. Amusing notes have been written on this passage, but none so amus-

* [*Euripides' Iphigenia among the Taurians.* Edited by Isaac Flagg. Ginn & Co. 1889. Pp. 197. *CR* 4 (1890), 160–2]

ing as Mr Flagg's. Iphigenia wishes Pylades to swear that he will carry her letter to Argos; Orestes absurdly stipulates that she on her part shall take oath to send Pylades safely out of the Chersonese, to which she very naturally replies, 'Why, how could he carry my letter unless I did?' Other commentators have remarked on the ineptitude of Orestes; Mr Flagg on the contrary admires the noteworthy cleverness of Iphigenia, and lest we should think that such acumen transcends probability he explains it by the fact that she had not learnt to read and write. 790 'ἐμπεδώσομεν: *will make good; cf.* ἔμπεδον, v. 758.' The student who does compare v. 758 and finds that ἔμπεδον is there translated *binding* will be puzzled to reconcile the two notes. 902. Priestess and victim have been revealed to one another as sister and brother, and forget their peril in transports of emotion; Pylades now interposes to remind them where they stand. Mr Flagg hits off the situation with Columbian vivacity by saying that Pylades 'calls time'. 1152. 'The text', says Mr Flagg, 'is a more than Terpsichorean maze.' It may be, but he should not therefore adopt from J. H. H. Schmidt an emendation which, after violently altering the MSS, produces gibberish. When it comes to introducing an οὐκέτι of which the text has no vestige, and then translating this οὐκέτι as if it were οὔπω, one prefers Terpsichore. 1415. The text gives one punctuation, the note assumes another. 1418 φόνον τὸν Αὐλίδι ἀμνημόνευτον θεᾷ προδοῦσ' ἁλίσκεται: supposing that this meant anything, by what imaginable jugglery could it be made to mean, 'is found guilty of betraying the goddess' trust in that forgotten murderous deed at Aulis'?

The introduction, which covers fifty pages, is a full and interesting account of the legend, plot, artistic structure, and metres of the play. Mr Flagg calls this 'negatively considered, the most faultless of Euripides' extant tragedies', and thinks that 'there remains not another one that is marred by so few of those grave lapses from dramatic propriety and universal good taste to which the poet's mind was subject'. Even negatively considered I should have thought the *Hippolytus* by far the most faultless tragedy of Euripides, if not indeed the most faultless of all tragedies except the *Antigone* alone: what lapses mar it, apart from a certain artificiality in the altercation of Theseus with the hero, I do not know; assuredly none to compare with the see-saw of divine intervention in the ἔξοδος of our play. Mr Flagg defends this machinery as the only way to rescue the chorus, which is one of those excuses which Aristotle calls ridiculous; the poet, as he says, should take care from the outset not to construct his play in such a manner. And when Mr Flagg says that 'the modern reader cannot adequately reproduce the feelings stirred by this final scene in the Athenian spectator's breast', this is to arraign Euripides, not to defend him. It means that he wrote for an age and not for all time: he defaced his drama that he might gladden the eyes of the vulgar with the resplendent stage-properties ‖ of their beloved goddess: a trap to catch applause which does not differ in kind from the tradi-

5

tional sentiment, always welcome to the gallery of our own theatres, that the man who lays his hand upon a woman, save in the way of kindness, is unworthy of the name of a British sailor. On p. 36, where Mr Flagg speaks of the increased employment of a resolved arsis in Euripides' later plays, the terms, 'less care in the finishing', 'deterioration', 'laxity', 'degeneracy', 'looseness', give a wrong impression. We are free to prefer the earlier practice; but the change proceeds from no negligence or failure in craftsmanship. The *Bacchae*, but for the injuries of time, is hardly less exquisite in finish than the *Medea* itself; only it is written on other principles.

The text is printed clearly and, so far as I have observed, accurately, except for the common mistake χἄ, χοὖς, χἅτερον, χὖμῖν, rough breathing for coronis; θοὐμόφυλον however is given correctly.

17

HORACE, *CARM.* iv. 2, 49*

'*io*' *que*, dum procedit, 'io triumphe'
non semel dicemus.

This conjecture of Mr Gow's for *teque* (p. 155 of the April number [[*CR* 4 (1890), 155]]) has a special interest for me, as I had pencilled it in my own margin some while ago. I do not even now feel sure that it is right, for although Ovid often appends *que* in this way to a quoted word, there is no similar instance in Horace; and moreover Meineke's *atque* may well be the true reading. But my purpose in writing is to present Mr Gow with a parallel passage which seems to tell strongly in his favour: Ovid *Trist.* iv. 2, 51 sq. 'tempora Phoebea lauro cingentur "*io*" *que* | miles, "io" magna uoce "triumphe" canet.' This has all the air of a copy from the above text, for Ovid is here in a very imitative mood: the pentameter is taken word for word from Tib. ii. 5, 118, and his next distich, 'ipse sono plausuque simul fremituque calentes | quadriiugos cernes saepe resistere equos', comes from Prop. iii. 4, 14, 'ad uulgi plausus saepe resistere equos'.

Mr Gow's certain emendation *cerebrique* in *Serm.* ii. 3, 208, was forestalled by Horkel, a critic who in a short life did more for the text of Horace than any man since Bentley, though the editors, with the significant exception of Meineke, seldom deign even to record his corrections.

* [[*CR* 4 (1890), 273]]

18

NOTES ON LATIN POETS [II]*

Catullus LXIV. 279–87

Aduenit Chiron portans siluestria dona;
280   nam quoscumque ferunt campi, quos Thessala magnis
montibus ora creat, quos propter fluminis undas
aura aperit flores tepidi fecunda Fauoni,
hos indistinctis plexos tulit ipse corollis,
quo permulsa domus iucundo risit odore.
285   confestim Penios adest, uiridantia Tempe,
Tempe, quae siluae cingunt super impendentes,
Haemonisin linquens doris celebranda choreis.

Before dealing with the last verse I will offer a short defence of the conjecture 'aperit' for 'perit', v. 282, which has already seen the light in Mr Postgate's edition. The vulgate text is 'parit', which a later hand has written in G over the erasure of the original reading; O has the abbreviation which regularly stands for 'perit' but may according to the practice of that scribe signify 'parit' also. If the tradition is 'perit', then 'aperit' since an *a* precedes is an easier change than 'parit'; while even if 'parit' were clearly given by the MSS I should think it hardly suitable: it is surely 'terra' or 'flumen' that 'parit flores', just as 'campi ferunt' and 'ora creat' in the lines above: the function of 'aura' is more properly expressed by 'aperit'. I find this same distinction in vv. 89 sq. 'quales Eurotae *progignunt flumina* myrtos | *aura*ue distinctos *educit* uerna colores': educit quasi obstetrix, I presume; and compare Ovid *fast.* IV. 87 sq. 'uer *aperit* tunc omnia, densaque cedit | frigoris asperitas, *feta*que *terra* patet.' 'fecunda' then will mean not 'fruitful' but 'making fruitful', as it does in Ovid *fast.* II. 427 'fecundae uerbera dextrae' (the blows of the Luperci averting barrenness), and 'aura... fecunda Fauoni' will be exactly the 'genitabilis aura Fauoni' of Lucr. I. 11 where Munro renders 'genitabilis' by 'birth-favouring'.

In v. 287 Heinsius' 'Haemonisin' seems to me a certain correction of 'Minosim': ‖ it is adopted by Baehrens and Postgate, and Ellis now seems well disposed towards it. There remains the corruption in 'doris'. Dorus is the name of a character in Terence, but it is not Latin for Dorian, or at any rate did not become so till hundreds of years after Catullus was dead: Baehrens is now left alone in

* [CR 4 (1890), 340–2]

defending 'Doris' here, and he brings no new evidence to unsettle Lachmann's decision of the question at Lucr. v. 85. The following conjectures have been proposed: claris, doctis, heros, crebris, pulcris, hilaris, duris, floris, diuis, Chlori, solis, solitis, uariis, caris. Statius' 'doctis' and Madvig's 'duris' come nearest to the MSS, but are inappropriate for opposite reasons: 'doctae choreae' seem too artificial for the vale of Tempe; and 'duris', which is said to mean 'rustic' but really means 'clumsy', is not defended but condemned by the parallel of Ovid *fast*. III. 537 where 'ducunt posito *duras* cratere *choreas*' describes a picnic party of tipsy citizens. Several of the more violent conjectures are apt enough, and I do not pretend that the word I am about to offer has any advantage in sense over 'crebris' for instance or 'hilaris'; but it seems to be clearly indicated by the ductus litterarum. Our own Italic type serves very well to shew how easy a mistake it is by which *doris* is written for *acris*: both errors recur at Ovid *met*. VIII. 806 in the variant *ordine*, that is *ordīe*, for *crate*. But all that 'acris' wants is the initial letter it lost through haplography in the verse 'Haemonisin linquens *s*acris celebranda choreis': compare a similar scene in Ovid *met*. VIII. 580 sqq. 'Naides hae fuerant, quae cum bis quinque iuuencos | mactassent rurisque deos ad *sacra* uocassent, | inmemores nostri festas duxere *choreas*.'

Horace carm. II. 3 1–4

Aequam memento rebus in arduis
seruare mentem, non secus in bonis
ab insolenti temperatam
laetitia, moriture Delli.

To smooth away the 'scabrities' of this reading Bentley took from one or two bad MSS the natural and regular 'non secus *ac* bonis', which is accepted also by Peerlkamp and by Horace's most judicious editor Meineke. Mr Keller objects that this 'grammatisch unmöglich ist, weil es vielmehr *atque in bonis* heissen müsste'. It is too much the practice of conservative critics to oppose emendation with assertions of this sort, assertions not meant to be false but thrown off on the spur of the moment with no care taken to ascertain if they are true. It is perfectly good Latin to supply the preposition in this way from the first member of a comparison to the second: take for instance Ovid *met*. XIV. 49 'ingreditur feruentes aestibus undas, | *in quibus* ut *solida* ponit uestigia *terra*.' Possibly therefore *ac* is what Horace wrote, for this word is sometimes confused with *m*, as at Lucr. IV. 241 and VI. 10, and might so be confused with *in*. But perhaps a still easier change will suffice, the restoration of a word continually mistaken for *in*: 'non secus *ut* bonis'. The construction is rare; but Horace has *carm*. III. 25 8 sqq. '*non secus* in iugis Edonis stupet Euhias... *ut* mihi... mirari libet', where Bentley would read *ac*, unreasonably I think, for in Ovid *met*. XV. 180 the most trustworthy MS gives 'assiduo labuntur tempora motu | *non secus ut*

flumen', and Virgil writes *georg.* II. 277 sqq. '*nec setius* omnis in unguem |
arboribus positis secto uia limite quadret | *ut* saepe ingenti bello cum longa
cohortis | explicuit legio.'

Ovid *ars am.* I. 517–18

Nec male deformet rigidos tonsura capillos:
sit coma, sit tuta barba resecta manu.

The epithet 'tuta' is meaningless and no editor retains it: even the interpolators
of the inferior MSS perceived its absurdity and substituted 'docta'; then came
Heinsius with the more scientific amendment 'scita' which is now the vulgate.
But even thus much change is unnecessary: nothing graver has happened than
the common error *u* for *ri*, 'tuta' for 'trita'. The lexicons show that in Cicero
this word means 'practised' and so 'expert', and they supply a perfect counter-
part to its employment here from || Vitr. II. 1 6 '*tritiores manus* ad aedificandum
perficere'.

Ovid is fond of repeating his own phrases, and at *trist.* v. 7 17 sq. he has
a couplet which stands in the editions thus:

uox fera, trux uultus, uerissima Martis imago:
non coma, non ulla barba resecta manu.

He is describing his neighbours at Tomi. Now if one considers it attentively
I think the expression 'non ulla resecta manu' will appear a trifle absurd:
'mortua non ulla lumina clausa manu' is a phrase I can understand; but to say of
a living man that his beard is trimmed 'non ulla manu' will imply, or so it seems
to me, that he has lost the use of his own hands and depends on those of others.
Therefore it may deserve remark that the ductus litterarum of 'ulla' and of
'trita' are practically the same. I anticipate the objection that any such adjective
as 'trita' impairs the sense, inasmuch as the Tomitae of course did not trim their
beards at all, neatly or otherwise; and this is very true if we bring to the reading
of the lines our modern habits of thought. But the ancients were not alive to this
result of adding epithets in negative sentences: to take an example from the
father of them all, when Homer says at δ 566 that in the Elysian fields there is
οὐ νιφετὸς οὔτ' ἄρ χειμὼν πολὺς οὔτε ποτ' ὄμβρος, he does not mean us to infer
that there is χειμὼν μὲν ἀλλ' οὐ πολύς: he means that there are no storms whatever, great or small; only he cannot refrain from ornamenting χειμὼν with
an adjective.

But I do not like to dismiss the distich without a word on the hexameter. It
always struck me as strange that an unkempt savage should be called by a Roman
poet the very image of Mars, a truculent deity to be sure, but a deity still and
father of the founder of Rome, and I thought of a noun which seemed much
better suited to the case; but Riese's apparatus criticus made it appear that the

best MS had 'necis', which afforded me no support but rather the contrary. Now, however, I learn from Mr Owen's edition that the MS which has 'necis' is a poor one, that 'Martis' has no authority but the second hand of another, and that with these exceptions all MSS good and bad concur in reading 'mortis' and so confirm my conjecture, 'trux uultus, uerissima mentis imago': see Cic. *de or.* III. 59 221 'imago animi uultus est' and Ovid *ex Pont.* III. 4 27 'regum uultus, certissima pignora mentis'. At *met.* VI. 629 all MSS give 'mortem' for 'mentem'.

19

HORATIANA [III]*

Serm. 1 2 77–82
Ne paeniteat te,
desine matronas sectarier, unde laboris
plus haurire mali est quam ex re decerpere fructus.
nec magis huic inter niueos uiridisque lapillos
(sit licet hoc, Cerinthe, tuum) tenerum est femur aut crus
rectius; atque etiam melius persaepe togatae.

This reading of the great majority of MSS seems to admit only the punctuation given above: 'sit licet hoc, Cerinthe, tuum' must be a parenthesis. But the relevance or even the meaning of the parenthesis is not discoverable. Reisig and others say 'haec tua res sit, hoc tibi relinquo'; but what is 'hoc' and 'haec res'? Not a predilection for bejewelled matrons: that meaning, as Bentley says and Kiessling the latest editor agrees, 'ex uerbis auctoris nullis tormentis elici nulloque iure subintellegi potest'. A passion for wearing jewellery? of this Bentley says the same, I think with equal justice; but even if the sense be possible it is ludicrously irrelevant: 'a common woman is as good as a matron who wears jewels, although || Cerinthus, who is neither a matron nor a common woman, wears jewels too'! Let us therefore try next the reading found in a few MSS, attested by Cruquius' commentator and approved by Bentley:

nec magis huic, inter niueos uiridisque lapillos
sit licet, hoc, Cerinthe, tuo tenerum est femur eqs.

that is 'nec huic matronae, licet sit inter niueos uiridisque lapillos, hoc (= ideo) femur magis tenerum est tuo, o Cerinthe'. Dillenburger, one of those editors with whom everything is postponed to the duty of resisting Bentley, improvises the objection 'non posse Latine dici *sit licet inter lapillos* pro *licet ornata sit lapillis*'. He is mistaken, for Livy cited by Kiessling has IX 17 16 'Darium... inter purpuram et aurum, oneratum fortunae apparatibus suae,...deuicit'; but the noteworthy point is this, the objection rests on the entirely gratuitous assumption that the subject of 'sit' is 'matrona': obviously there is no reason whatever why the subject should not be 'femur', in which case 'inter lapillos' is correct in Bentley's reading if in Dillenburger's, solecistic in Dillenburger's if in

* [*JPh* 18 (1890), 1–35]

[1–2

Bentley's. But there are other objections of very different weight. This reading supposes Cerinthus to be, as Porphyrion says he was, a 'prostibulum insignis speciei atque candoris': well then, femur Cerinthi will be tenerrimum, crus Cerinthi will be rectissimum; so it becomes not only pointless but senseless to say, by way of disparaging matrons, that femur matronae is not magis tenerum, that crus matronae is not rectius. Further, can one conceive anything more perverse than that Cerinthus, a third term of comparison, should be introduced at all? The question in hand is the relative desirability of the *matrona* and the *togata*; and if reason is to hold her seat 'magis tenerum' must mean 'magis tenerum quam togatae'. Cerinthus then must carry his insignis species back to Porphyrion and permit Horace to write sense:

> nec magis huic, inter niueos uiridisque lapillos
> sit licet aesque, Corinthe, tuum, tenerum est femur aut crus
> rectius; atque etiam melius persaepe togatae. ‖

The *togata* is as good as the *matrona* despite the latter's jewellery and ornaments of the costly alloy known as *aes Corinthium*. The alteration may look formidable at first, but every step of it is easy: *aesquecorinthe* passed through *eccecerinthe* to *hoccerinthe* by mistakes of the commonest sort. I have illustrated the confusion of *ae* with *e* and of *e* with *o* on carm. I 12 35–6, the confusion of *qu* with *c* on carm. II 2 2: it remains only to say that the addition or removal of the aspirate is in MSS like ours absolutely negligible, and that the interchange of *s* and *c* is among the earliest of all corruptions, as Ribbeck's Virgil will abundantly prove. It may be added that one of the Blandinian MSS (we do not know which) had *haec* for *hoc*, which may seem to speak in my favour. Perhaps the *tuo* of two among Holder's MSS and the *tu.m* of a third, for the *tuum* of the majority, point to *tuom* in the archetype.

It may be objected to my history of the corruption that all these changes would hardly occur before the date of Porphyrion, who attests *Cerinthe*. True; but remember that we cannot possibly tell how much of the farrago now going under Porphyrion's name was really written by the 3rd-century commentator. A good deal is demonstrably of far later date; and as I have shewn, I hope, that there is no place for Cerinthus in the text of Horace, I may lawfully assume that this person is a late invention. Collections of scholia, more than any other kind of work, are thus expanded in transcription.

Serm. I 3 38–42

> Illuc praeuertamur, amatorem quod amicae
> turpia decipiunt caecum uitia aut etiam ipsa haec
> delectant, ueluti Balbinum polypus Hagnae.
> uellem in amicitia sic erraremus et isti
> errori nomen uirtus posuisset honestum.

Mr Kiessling paraphrases 'die Moral (*uirtus*) hat dafür nicht wie sie sollte eine lobende Bezeichnung, sondern tadelt es als κολακεία.' The obvious comment on this interpretation is that if 'die Moral' acts otherwise than 'wie sie sollte' it ceases to be 'die Moral'. But further, it is clear that 'uirtus' ‖ is quite the wrong word for the place: to call foibles by pretty names is no function for 'uirtus' or for 'die Moral' either. Other editors avoid this difficulty by mistranslating the word. Thus Prof. Palmer renders 'uirtus' by 'good feeling'; but he will I am sure admit when challenged that 'uirtus' never means anything of the sort, least of all in the passage which he adduces as parallel, carm. II 2 17 sqq. Indeed Horace seems to have written those lines on purpose to refute this interpretation: 'redditum Cyri solio Phrahaten | dissidens plebi numero beatorum | eximit uirtus *populumque falsis* | *dedocet uti* | *uocibus*': there you see the very office of 'uirtus' is to strip away false notions and names: dare you then invite her to ponere nomen honestum errori? Besides, if we allow 'uirtus' to mean 'good feeling', no sense results; for good feeling *does* ponere nomen honestum isti errori, and Horace cannot without absurdity say that he regrets it has not done so. What he could, should, and doubtless did say, is that he regrets good feeling is not more widely diffused, or in other words that he regrets *custom* or *society* has not assigned a nomen honestum isti errori. This sense is restored by Peerlkamp's 'uita imposuisset': 'uita', as he says and the lexicons will prove, is 'consuetudo uulgaris, mos uiuendi, agendi, loquendi'; 'apud alios scriptores *uita decreuit, agnoscit, desueuit, dubitauit* hoc uel illud facere'. But the proposed change is serious and not necessary; for the same meaning may be introduced by altering no more than one letter:

> uellem in amicitia sic erraremus et isti
> errori nomen uictus posuisset honestum.

Cicero and others use 'uita uictusque' in this sense: I have no clear instance of 'uictus' alone for 'mos uiuendi', and I doubt if a prose writer would so use it; but that is just the difference between prose and verse: it is only in poetry that verbal nouns enjoy the width of meaning to which they are entitled by patrimony. The letters *c* and *r*, I know not why, are confused as early as Virgil's capital MSS; but apart from that there is always a perilous likeness between two words which agree in five letters and differ only in the sixth. ‖

Serm. I 3 99–105

Cum prorepserunt primis animalia terris,
mutum et turpe pecus, glandem atque cubilia propter
unguibus et pugnis, dein fustibus, atque ita porro
pugnabant armis, quae post fabricauerat usus,

100

> donec uerba, quibus uoces sensusque notarent,
> nominaque inuenere; dehinc absistere bello,
> oppida coeperunt munire et ponere leges.   105

I imagine no one has read v. 103 without silently wondering why it is that 'uoces', instead of being coupled with their synonyms 'uerba' and 'nomina' as a means of expression, are coupled with 'sensus' as if they were something requiring to be expressed. The commentators dissimulate their amazement as well as they can: Mr Palmer writes '*uerba*, ῥήματα, articulate words, with which men gave meaning and shape to *uoces*, the inarticulate sounds of the savage voice'; but he will not seriously maintain that 'notare' means 'to give meaning and shape'. Astonishing, however, as the sentence appears at first sight, that is nothing to what remains behind. Horace is here reproducing not merely the famous history given by Lucretius of the origin of society, but the very terms in which Lucretius gave it. Lucretius writes v 1041 sqq. 'proinde putare aliquem tum *nomina* distribuisse | rebus et inde homines didicisse *uocabula* prima | desiperest. nam cur hic posset cuncta *notare* | *uocibus* et uarios sonitus emittere linguae?', 1057 sq. 'si genus humanum, cui uox et lingua uigeret, | *pro* uario *sensu* uaria res *uoce notaret*', 1087 sqq. 'ergo si uarii *sensus* animalia *cogunt*, | muta tamen cum sint, uarias *emittere uoces*, | quanto mortalis magis aecumst tum potuisse | dissimilis alia atque alia res *uoce notare*.' There lies Horace's vocabulary before our eyes, *uoces, sensus, notare, nomina*; and *uoces* stand on the one side together with *nomina* as the means of expression, *sensus* on the other as the thing expressed. The phrase which we take for Horace's is perverse enough in itself; but that it should have been penned by a writer who had the fifth book of Lucretius lying open before him as he wrote is a pitch of perversity too wonderful for words; uerba, quibus notetur, non inuenio. Before ‖ I offer my remedy let me premise that the transposition of words for no visible reason, nay sometimes even in defiance of sense and metre, is as common in our MSS as in most others: I open Keller and Holder at random and find epod. 2 18 *agris extulit* and *e. a.*, 5 20 *nocturnae strigis* and *s. n.*, 7 15 *albus ora pallor* and *o. p. a.*, 12 3 *firmo iuueni* and *i. f.*, 13 11 *grandi cecinit* and *c. g.*, serm. 1 1 83 *reddat natis* and *n. r.*, 84 *saluum te uult, t. u. s.* and *t. s. u.*, 3 42 *nomen uirtus* and *u. n.*, 91 *manibus tritum* and *t. m.*, 5 26 *saxis late* and *l. s.*, 6 13 *regno pulsus* and *p. r.*, 69 *uere quisquam* and *q. u.*, 107 *nemo sordes* and *s. n.* – here I desist, not to be wearisome; but it would be easy to treble the tale. In our passage a similar transposition of one word will restore sense and bring Horace into unison with his exemplar:

> donec uerba, quibus sensus, uocesque, notarent,
> nominaque inuenere;

i.e. donec uerba uocesque nominaque inuenere, quibus sensus notarent.

If anyone remarks on this that such an arrangement of words is contorted and unnatural, and wonders how the ancients, lacking our system of punctuation, could understand it at all, I shall cordially agree with him. But let him not suppose that he is advancing any argument against the probability of the emendation. Such dislocations of sentences are a marked feature of many poetic styles in Latin, and none more than Lucretius': now Horace as we have seen was steeped in Lucretius when he wrote these lines. Some notion of the lengths to which a Roman could go in this matter will be given by the following passages, partly taken from Munro's note on the first: Lucr. III 843 'si iam, nostro, sentit, de corpore postquam | distractast, animi natura', IV 1119 'nec reperire, malum id, possunt, quae machina uincat', VI 158 'uentus enim cum confercit, franguntur, in artum, | concreti montes', 176 'fecit, ut ante, cauam, docui, spississcere nubem', V 177 'natus enim, debet, quicumque est, uelle manere | in uita', III 196 'namque, papaueris, aura potest suspensa leuisque | cogere, ut ab summo tibi diffluat altus aceruus', Catull. 44 7 'tussim, | non inmerenti quam ‖ mihi meus uenter, | dum sumptuosas appeto, dedit, cenas', 66 18 'non, ita me diui, uera gemunt, iuerint', Verg. buc. II 12 'at, mecum, raucis, tua dum uestigia lustro, | sole sub ardenti resonant arbusta cicadis', Aen. I 195 'uina, bonus quae, deinde, cadis onerarat Acestes | litore Trinacrio dederatque abeuntibus heros, | diuidit', II 303 'arrectis auribus asto, | in segetem, ueluti, cum flamma furentibus austris | incidit aut rapidus montano flumine torrens | sternit agros sternit sata laeta boumque labores | praecipitesque trahit siluas, stupet inscius alto | accipiens sonitum saxi de uertice pastor' (i.e. arrectis auribus asto ueluti stupet accipiens sonitum pastor: the passage as usually punctuated is incoherent), X 385 'Pallas ante ruentem, | dum furit, incautum, crudeli morte sodalis, | excipit', Hor. serm. I 3 9 'saepe, uelut qui, | currebat, fugiens hostem', 5 71 'sedulus hospes | paene, macros, arsit, dum turdos uersat in igni', II 1 60 'quisquis erit uitae, scribam, color', 3 211 'Aiax, immeritos cum occidit, desipit, agnos', epist. II 2 21 'ne, mea, saeuus | iurgares, ad te quod epistula nulla rediret', Ouid. her. 10 110 'illic, qui silices, Thesea, uincat, habes', amor. III 5 13 'candidior, quod adhuc spumis stridentibus albet | et modo siccatam, lacte, reliquit ouem', ars I 399 'tempora qui solis operosa colentibus arua, | fallitur, et nautis adspicienda putat', met. III 584 'non mihi, quae duri colerent, pater arua, iuuenci, | lanigerosue greges, non ulla armenta reliquit', fast. I 263 'inde, uelut nunc est, per quem descenditis, inquit, | arduus, in ualles et fora, cliuus erat', III 383 'Mamurius, morum fabraene exactior artis, | difficile est, illud, dicere, clausit opus', Ibis 3 'nullaque, quae possit, scriptis tot milibus extat | littera Nasonis, sanguinolenta legi', trist. III 5 23 'si tamen interea, quid in his ego perditus oris, | quod te credibile est quaerere, quaeris, agam', ex Pont. I 1 80 'plus isto, duri, si precer, oris ero', 5 79 'quid tibi, si calidae, prosit, laudere Syenae?', Ter. hecyr. 262 'eo, domum, studeo haec, priusquam ille ut redeat', Luc. Phars. I 13 'heu quantum potuit terrae [[terrae potuit]] pelagique parari | hoc, quem ciuiles

hauserunt, sanguine, dextrae', IX 554 'nam cui crediderim superos arcana datu-
ros | dicturosque magis, quam sancto, uera, Catoni?', 636 'hoc habet infelix,
cunctis impune, Medusa, | quod spectare licet', Mart. XI 97 'una nocte quater
possum; sed, quattuor annis | si possum, || peream, te, Telesilla, semel', Auson.
epigr. 12 [33 Peiper] 1 'cuius opus? Phidiae, qui signum Pallados, eius, | quique
Iouem fecit.'[1] Even in prose are found such examples as Cic. r. p. 1 15 'quae,
uix coniectura, qualia sint, possumus suspicari'.

I take 'uerba', 'uoces' and 'nomina' as all meaning much the same thing:
they are often used quite promiscuously, and Cicero can say at will '*uerba* rebus
impressit' or 'quae res huic *uoci* subiciatur' or 'imponere rebus *nomina*'. Poets in
Latin as in other tongues delight to accumulate synonyms such as 'mortis letique',
'mentem animumque', 'genus alituum uariaeque uolucres'; and so Lucr. IV 533
says 'uoces uerbaque', Hor. epist. 1 1 34 'uerba et uoces', 18 12 'iterat uoces et
uerba cadentia tollit'. Of course in strictness 'uoces' comprises both 'uerba'
(verbs) and 'nomina' (nouns) as well as all the other parts of speech; but just in
the same way Horace writes epist. 1 16 41 'qui *consulta* patrum, qui *leges iura*que
seruat', though strictly 'iura' includes 'leges' and 'consulta' and much more
besides; 'constant autem *iura* populi Romani ex *legibus*, plebis *consultis*, constitu-
tionibus principum, edictis eorum qui ius edicendi habent, responsis prudentium'
is Gaius' definition.

Serm. 1 3 117–24

Adsit

regula, peccatis quae poenas inroget aequas,
ne scutica dignum horribili sectere flagello.
nam ut ferula caedas meritum maiora subire   120
uerbera non uereor, cum dicas esse paris res
furta latrociniis et magnis parua mineris
falce recisurum simili te, si tibi regnum
permittant homines.

This passage is well known as a supposed example of 'uereor ut' = 'uereor
ne'. The use is absolutely unique – Mr Palmer disposes of certain irrelevant
passages cited as parallel – and, to me as to him, absolutely incredible. A lan-
guage in which one || phrase possesses two diametrically opposite senses and
can be employed indifferently in either without anything to tell which is meant,
is not a language in which man can make himself intelligible to his fellow man.
Explanations of a familiar sort are forthcoming: Horace is dead and cannot
protect himself, so we are told that 'ut' coming first makes a difference: his
intellect was not equal to the strain of remembering from one verse to another
how he had opened the sentence: when he began to write he thought he was

[1] These passages supply the answer to Mr Paley's very just remark (vol. XVI of this Journal,
p. 184) that 'uobis' is out of place in the sentence 'tunc ego crediderim et manes et sidera uobis posse
Cytinaeis ducere carminibus.'

going to say 'uerisimile non est' and so wrote 'nam ut ferula caedas': when he
reached the next line he fancied he had written 'nam ne ferula caedas' and so
wrote 'non uereor': what philtre, what hippomanes it was that produced this
'animi caligo et magna obliuio rerum quas modo gessit' we do not learn. He had
thrown off his stupor and regained his memory when in II 1 60 he wrote 'o puer,
ut sis | uitalis metuo'. But Mr Palmer, the first commentator to look the difficulty
in the face, has not restored the text by altering the 'non' of v. 121 to 'nunc';
and when he says that the sense thus obtained is more in keeping with the views
of Horace he is certainly mistaken. The right and the only right sense is that
which other commentators, however illegitimately, extract from the vulgate:
'non uereor ne ferula caedas meritum maiora uerbera subire': Mr Palmer's
'uereor ut ferula caedas meritum maiora uerbera subire' is not the right sense.
The difference between the two is expounded with characteristic lucidity by
Lambinus: 'qui ita loquitur, *uereor ut caedas*, uult caedi et uidetur ita dicere,
uereor ne non caedas. si quis ita loquatur, *non uereor ne caedas*, hoc significat, *ego
non dubito quin non sis caesurus*, uel, *confido te non caesurum*.' Now what cause is
Horace pleading? he is pleading, not that punishment should be *lighter* than the
crime deserves, but that it should be *not heavier* (v. 118 peccatis quae poenas
inroget *aequas*). But Mr Palmer's conjecture 'uereor ut ferula caedas' will make
him say that he wishes a man who has deserved a heavier punishment to receive
the insufficient chastisement of the *ferula*: but that will not be a *poena aequa*:
a too light punishment is just as much *iniqua* as a too heavy one. What Horace
ought to say is not that he wishes the Stoics to be too lenient, but that he feels ||
sure they will not be too lenient: *confido te non ferula caesurum*; and say it I
believe he did, as follows:

adsit

> regula, peccatis quae poenas inroget aequas.
> nam, ut scutica dignum horribili sectere flagello,
> ne ferula caedas meritum maiora subire
> uerbera non uereor, cum dicas eqs.

'for (thought I daresay you will inflict the *flagellum* on one who deserves only
the *scutica*) I am sure from your talk that you will not be content with inflicting
the *ferula* on one who deserves something worse': your theory that one crime
is as bad as another may lead you to punish light crimes heavily but will not lead
you to punish grave crimes lightly: your levelling of punishment will be all in
the direction of severity, not of leniency. I obtain this sense by exchanging the
initial syllables of the two verses. The scribe, I assume, glancing from the one N
to the other, wrote 'ne' when he should have written 'nam ut', and then, not to
spoil his page by an erasure, wrote on, put 'nam ut' in the place of 'ne', and
appended marks of transposition, neglected or not understood by the succeeding
copyist. The same error has been detected by Sanadon in carm. 1 16 5 and 7

where 'non Liber aeque' and 'non Dindymene', as style and sense proclaim, have changed places: again in epist. 1 1 43 and 44 the two final words 'repulsam' and 'labore' are inverted in five of Holder's MSS: again, I do not think anything can be made of carm. 11 5 13–15 until the final 'ferox' of v. 13 is transposed with the final 'fugax' of v. 17 as Wakefield in one of his happy moments suggested: for 'Pholoe ferox' see carm. 1 33 6 'asperam Pholoen'. To conclude: as to the sense of our passage I am at one with the commentators; but I get the sense by transposing two syllables, they get it by translating *ut* as *ne*. Which of these methods is prudence, and which temerity, opinions differ, and, I suppose, will differ as long as men study the classics.

Serm. 1 4 100–3

Hic nigrae sucus lolliginis, haec est
aerugo mera; quod uitium procul afore chartis, ||
atque animo prius, ut si quid promittere de me
possum aliud uere, promitto.

The normal phrase is 'promitto, si quid aliud uere promittere possum.' How then is to be understood and construed the redundant and unexampled 'ut'? O, in a dozen ways: Lambinus makes the sentence stand for 'promitto, ut *quiduis* aliud, si quid *est, quod* de me spondere ac recipere possim'; Doederlein calls it a brachylogy for 'uere promitto, ut *quicquam* aliud, si quid promittere de me possum'; Dillenburger says the construction is 'ita promitto, ut *promitto*, si quid aliud uere de me promittere possum'; Kiessling supposes a blending of two forms 'ut aliquid promittere possum' and 'si quid promittere aliud possum'; and so on, and so on. Against each and all of these profusely furnished explanations a great deal might be said, were it necessary; but it is not: I prefer to rest my case on the sense of the words, which the commentators in their very natural care and trouble about the construction appear to have entirely neglected. If Horace promises that the vice of malice *shall* be absent from his writings, *and first* from his mind, he proclaims, or words have no meaning, that this vice is, at the time of speaking, present both in his mind and in his writings: the future tense with the adverb 'prius' marking two stages can signify nothing else: Lambinus perhaps sees this when he mistranslates 'prius' as 'quod prius est'. That Horace never brought against himself this monstrous charge is of course quite certain; and I think the reader will smile when I point out the perfectly gratuitous manner in which he has been made to bring it. The words Horace wrote are every one of them there, placed as he placed them; only punctuated with a perversity approaching the miraculous. What he said is this:

quod uitium procul afore chartis
atque animo, prius ut, si quid promittere de me
possum aliud uere, promitto.

For the position of 'ut' see I 3 89 'porrecto iugulo historias, captiuus ut, audit'. He promises that malice shall be, as heretofore (ut prius), absent both from his books and from his mind. Verbum non amplius addam. ||

Serm. I 6 100–4

Nam mihi continuo maior quaerenda foret res
atque salutandi plures, ducendus et unus
et comes alter, uti ne solus rusue peregre aut
exirem, plures calones atque caballi
pascendi, ducenda petorrita.

This reading of v. 102, exhibited by all MSS of any account, is not merely indefensible but undefended, which in Horace is another thing. The reading of a single inferior MS, 'peregreue' for 'peregre aut', is accepted by almost all editors; but this gives no adequate explanation of the error. If a scribe offended by the hypermeter had decided to alter the text, he assuredly would not have altered it to anything so strange as 'rusue peregre aut' when it was in his power to write 'rus peregreue': that would have been to create a worse difficulty than he was removing. I will therefore propose another solution:

uti ne aut rus solusue peregre
exirem.

The eye of the copyist glanced from *rus* to *-lus* and he wrote 'uti ne aut rusue peregre', and then on noticing his omission added 'solus' in the margin. His successor had to incorporate 'solus' in the verse: naturally enough it did not occur to him to wrench 'rus' apart from 'ue' and insert 'solus' between them, so he resorted to the rearrangement we now find in the MSS. It is perhaps a point in favour of this conjecture that it introduces the dislocation of words, commonly typified by 'ludo fatigatumque somno', which Horace especially affects. The rather rare correlation of 'aut' and 'ue' is illustrated in the lexicons.

Serm. I 8 33–6

Hecaten uocat altera, saeuam
altera Tisiphonen: serpentis atque uideres
infernas errare canes, Lunamque rubentem,
ne foret his testis, post magna latere sepulcra. ||

The moon, at sight of these sorceries on the Esquiline, blushed and hid her face behind great tombs. To begin with, from all that the ancients tell us of her habits and propensities we should infer that this is the last thing in the world the moon would do. To hide her face behind tombs she must descend to earth from whatever station in the sky she happens at the time to occupy: but that is her special aversion. When sorcerers, instead of confining themselves as here to necromancy, direct their spells upon her, then indeed down she must come whether she will or no, but it is with the worst of graces: the poets again and again depict the scene, 'reluctantem cursu deducere Lunam', 'anhelantes audito carmine bigas', and so on. Passing strange it is then if in order to avoid witnessing magic she does the very thing which when magic constrains her to do it she most abhors. But waive this objection; let the moon be never so eager to hide behind tombs: she could not: there were no tombs on the Esquiline to hide behind. The place was now no longer a burial ground but laid out in pleasure gardens. Mr Palmer indeed observing this difficulty says 'Horace is describing a state of things that is past, before the conversion of the graveyard into a park'; but I prefer to believe Horace himself who says just the contrary, 'nunc licet Esquiliis habitare salubribus atque | aggere in aprico spatiari, qui modo tristes | albis informem spectabant ossibus agrum, | cum mihi non tantum fures. . .curae sunt. . .quantum carminibus quae uersant. . .humanos animos.' But let this objection too be waived: then I go on to say that even before the improvements of Maecenas there stood no 'magna sepulcra' on the Esquiline. The Esquiline, as Horace tells us, was the place of burial for the poor and slaves whose friends could barely afford them a coffin: no great tombs for these: for these the field itself, as he ironically says, 'stabat commune sepulcrum.'[1]

Hide behind great tombs then the moon neither would nor could: Priapus witnessed quite another proceeding: ||

> Lunamque rubentem,
> ne foret his testis, post magna latere crepuscla.

In Lucian Icarom. 21, cited by Peerlkamp, the moon says κἄν τινα ἴδω αὐτῶν μοιχεύοντα ἢ κλέπτοντα ἢ ἄλλο τι τολμῶντα νυκτερινώτατον, εὐθὺς ἐπισπασαμένη τὸ νέφος ἐνεκαλυψάμην: then for 'rubentem' see Stat. Theb. I 105 'per nubila Phoebes | Atracia rubet arte labor'. Ouid. met. XI 596 'exhalantur humo . . .crepuscula' shews that 'crepuscla' can = 'nebulae'. Whether this shorter form of the word occurs elsewhere I do not know, nor does it matter: 'circlos' is quoted only from Verg. georg. III 166, 'spectaclum' only from Prop. IV 8 21 and 56, 'singlariter' only from Lucr. VI 1067, 'coplata' only from ib. 1088. Employing periclum saeclum uinclum hercle as freely as the longer forms, a Roman claimed the right to use this contraction not only where metre might demand or prefer it, as in the examples above, but wherever he chose: Ovid in met. I 321 has 'oracla', Martial in I 41 9 'tomacla', without the least necessity, and it is the prose of Varro that furnishes 'surclus'. He who will object to the cacophony of scl must first emend 'Ascli' in Sil. Punic. VIII 438. Let now the initial c of 'crepuscla' be absorbed by the similar letter e which immediately precedes, as in

---

[1] It is represented to me that perhaps the graveyard had been in remote times a fashionable one and some tombs dating from those days were left standing by Maecenas.

epist. I 2 63 one MS has 'compesce at enis' for 'compesce catenis', there remain
the letters *repuscl*a; and these are the letters of *sepulcr*a. What is the cause of such
vagaries as this, Ouid. trist. I I 83 a*gricol*a for A*rgolic*a, met. II 485 *manet* for
tamen, Catull. 22 5 pal*misep*to for pal*impse*sto, Prop. III 20 title co*mpten*tore for
co*ntemp*tore, Sen. de clem. I 12 3 con*sequemur* for cum *qu̜eremus*, and the like,
I cannot tell; but we must recognise the fact. In this particular instance there is
some excuse for the copyist, as 'repuscla' is no word and the context might
suggest 'sepulcra'. Horace will furnish another example: at least it seems to me
that nothing but Peerlkamp's '*responsi* hic caupo' will restore sense to serm.
I I 29: his instances of 'caupo' thus employed may be supplemented by
Quintilian's similar use of 'institor eloquentiae'. Now *responsi* might by the
easiest palaeographical errors be written ‖ *refpdusi*; and this consists of the same
letters as the MS reading *perfidus*. I will add one more parallel which seems
especially to the purpose. In Prop. IV 1 the astrologer Horos has dilated on the
superiority of astrology to other arts of divination, instancing certain successful
predictions of his own in contrast to the blindness of other prophets such as
Calchas, and thus proceeds, vv. 119 sq.

> hactenus historiae: nunc ad tua deuehar astra.
> incipe tu lacrimis aequs adesse nouis.

Then he goes on to display his proficiency further by giving an accurate account
of where Propertius was born, how he grew up, how Apollo set him verse-
writing and foretold him his fame and his amour; and ends by bidding him fear no
danger except from the sign of Cancer. But *new tears* is no designation of all
this: of the events in question only some are misfortunes, and the misfortunes
are not new but old. It is *new marvels* of the astrological art that Propertius is
told to witness with composure:

> incipe miraclis aequs adesse nouis.

*miracl*is and *lacrim*is are formed out of the same letters; and when the commoner
word had supplanted the rarer, the metre of course cried for the insertion of 'tu'.

Serm. II 2 123–5

> Post hoc ludus erat culpa potare magistra,
> ac uenerata Ceres, ita culmo surgeret alto,
> explicuit uino contractae seria frontis.

The phrase 'culpa potare magistra' is commonly supposed to mean that every
one at the table who committed a fault was condemned, some say to drink a cup
more, some say a cup less, than the rest of the company. Now without remarking
on the singular ambiguity of a phrase which is capable of these two opposite
meanings, without endeavouring to frame in imagination an idea of what would

constitute a 'fault', without speculating how far this remarkable 'ludus' would conduce to the enjoyment of the party, I will only say that there are no ‖ legitimate means of extorting this sense from the words 'culpa magistra'. What was the office of a *magister* or *magistra bibendi* we know very well: he or she determined the strength and measure of the cups to be drunk, and then all the conuiuae drank even: 'culpa magistra' will never mean any such thing as 'culpa multam singulis indicente'. To the alternative explanation mentioned by Mr Palmer, 'each person took as much as he pleased, restricted only by the feeling that excess was culpable', an equal objection must be opposed: 'culpa magistra' cannot be treated as if it were the same thing as 'culpae timore magistro' or 'modestia magistra'. As for Lambinus' 'cuppa', even if it signified a cup, as he supposed, it would hardly give a tolerable sense, and it signifies nothing of the sort. Of Bentley's two suggestions, 'cupa', the hostess of a neighbouring tavern 'crispum sub crotalo docta mouere latus', 'qua et potandi magistra et saltatrice et crotalistria, et siquid amplius uellent, conuiuae uterentur', introduces a figure quite out of keeping with the staid and frugal character of Ofellus or Ofella and his homely festivities. But Bentley's other conjecture 'nulla', though it departs too far from the MSS, gives not merely a just sense but the one sense necessary. Horace is his own best commentator: in a closely similar passage he sketches the 'noctes cenaeque deum' of his own country life, serm. II 6 67 sqq.

> *prout cuique libido est,*
> siccat *inaequalis calices* conuiua *solutus*
> *legibus insanis,* seu quis capit acria fortis
> pocula seu modicis uuescit lentius.

Here the charm of these simple dinner-parties consists precisely in the absence of any arbiter bibendi to make all drink alike whether they can carry liquor or no: the guests drink 'nulla magistra', or in other words

> post hoc ludus erat captu potare magistro

i.e. 'seu quis capit acria fortis pocula seu modicis uuescit lentius'.

If 'captu' became 'culpa' the change of 'magistro' to 'magistra' was in Horace inevitable: in Plautus or Lucretius ‖ it would not be so, since their scribes made no continuous endeavour to understand what they were writing; but Horace was intelligible to his copyists, and when one of them had made a mistake the next one usually carried it further by an attempt at emendation. But now to shew how it was that 'captu' became 'culpa': I will begin at the beginning. The inversion of two consecutive letters is among the commonest of MS errors and hardly wants illustrating, but take carm. I 15 24 *te* and *et*, 31 16 cichor*ea* and cichor*ae*, III 12 6 Lipar*ei* and Lipar*ie*, serm. I 3 90 commix*it* and commix*ti*, epist. I 6 58 *G*argilius and *G*ragilius, II 24 *ut* and *tu*, 18 111 *set* and *est*, ars 36 p*rauo* and p*aruo*, 423 a*rtis* and a*tris*. Less common perhaps on the whole but peculiarly frequent in the MSS of Horace is the inversion of three letters: see carm. II 20 15 *get*ulas and *teg*ulas, III 9 9 *reg*it and *rig*et, 13 11 *uom*ere and *mou*ere, 19 11 Mu*ren*ae and mu*ner*e, epod. 5 15 inp*lic*ata and inp*lac*ita, 16 51 o*uil*e and o*liu*ae, serm. I 2 3 T*ig*elli and T*eg*illi, 3 37 *fel*ix and *fil*ex, epist. I 3 31 *Mun*atius and *Num*atius, 6 18 sus*pic*e and sus*cip*e, to which in my opinion should be added serm. II 3 215 pa*ret* for pa*ter*, epist. II 2 199 *dom*us for *mod*o ut, ars 423 *leu*i for *uel*it: under the same head might be classed serm. I 4 30 *tep*et and p*et*et, 5 79 Tri*uic*i and Tri*ciu*i, II 6 72 nec*ne l*epos and nec *lene* post, epist. I 18 19 do*cil*is and do*lic*is, II 2 203 *loc*o re and *col*ore, ars 223 in*lec*ebris and in*cel*ebris, though these might be assigned with equal reason to another error, the transposition of syllables, in-*le-ce*-bris and in-*ce-le*-bris and so on. Often it will happen that one of the three inverted letters is changed, as carm. III 23 2 Phi*dyl*e and Phi*llid*e, serm. I 1 38 *sap*iens and *pat*iens, 4 30 *tep*et and p*at*et, II 3 21 *uaf*er and *fab*er, epist. I 7 40 p*at*ientis and s*ap*ientis. The exact inversion of four letters is, as might be supposed, a good deal rarer, since inversion is only one out of many ways in which four letters can be rearranged. I formerly quoted an instance from Prop. III 5 24, *inte*gras for *et ni*gras, and some six years ago I was rather elated by hitting on the conjecture '*Roma* quas' for 'quas *amor*' in epod. 2 37, which seems to me absolutely certain; but one's best emendations are always anticipated, and this has been published first by Mr P. J. ‖ Scriverius in *Mnemosyne* for 1887. The converse error was detected by Muretus and Fruterius in Prop. I 12 2 where they restore *amore* for *Roma*. Sometimes one of the four inverted letters is changed, as Ouid. met. XIV 233 *imas* for *Lami*; or two, as ib. 850 p*ositu*m for p*riscu*m. The mistake *culpa* for *captu* is the inversion of four letters and the change of one: I suppose that 'caplu' was first written, *t* and *l* being as common an exchange as there is, and that the scribe then altered the order to get a Latin word.

　　I find an exact parallel in carm. IV 10 2:

　　　　　insperata tuae cum ueniet pluma superbiae
　　　　　et quae nunc umeris inuolitant deciderint comae.

Bentley observes that 'pluma' never means 'lanugo', and that if it did, the 'in faciem uerterit hispidam' which follows would be pointless repetition; 'ut ne addam absurdum esse, quam barbam iam *plumam* hoc est *mollem* uocauerit, eandem e uestigio *hispidam* fieri'. Yet his 'bruma' cannot be right: he says 'passim apud scriptores adulescentia *ueri*, prouectior aetas *autumno* et *brumae* comparatur': yes, but the event here contemplated is not the old age of Ligurinus but his arrival at puberty; a consideration fatal also to Cunningham's 'ruga'. The right and necessary sense is given by the 'poena' of Withof and Lehrs: Tibullus on the same theme writes I 8 71 sqq. 'hic Marathus quondam miseros ludebat amantes | nescius *ultorem* post caput esse *deum*. . .at te *poena* manet, ni desinis esse *superba*'; but I hardly see how in the Horatian archetype 'poena' could become 'pluma'. So I propose to restore the same sense by assuming a more explicable change:

insperata tuae cum ueniet multa superbiae.

The confusion of *t* with *p* is early and frequent, and is found carm. III 6 27 *inpermissa* and *intermissa*, IV 4 6 *propulit* and *protulit*, c. saec. 23 *totiens* and *potiens*, serm. I 2 110 *pelli* and *tolli*, epist. I 16 45 *introrsum* and *inprorsum*, ars 402 *Tyrtaeus* and *Pyrcaeus*: for the rest, 'pluma' is 'mulpa' with its first four letters inverted. The converse corruption I seem to detect in Tibull. [Lygd.] III 6 32 'at nos securae reddamus ‖ tempora mensae: | uenit post multas una serena dies.' Here 'multas' does not any more convey the meaning 'multas nubilas' than the meaning 'multas serenas': Baehrens says with reason '*maestas* uel simile aliquid expectes.' If Lygdamus wrote 'pluuias', that is hardly distinguishable from *plumas*; and the same road led thence to *multas* as from *multa* to *pluma* in Horace.

Serm. II 6 28–31

Luctandum in turba et facienda iniuria tardis.
'quid tibi uis, insane, et quas res agis?' improbus urget
iratis precibus: 'tu pulses omne quod obstat,
ad Maecenatem memori si mente recurras.'

Two conjectures compete for the amendment of the unmetrical v. 29: a very few MSS and most editors omit 'tibi', Bentley changes 'quas res' to 'quam rem'. The great unlikelihood of the former proposal Bentley sets in a strong light: not 'quas res agis' but 'quam rem agis' is the regular phrase; the regular phrase again is not 'quid uis' but 'quid tibi uis', which moreover occurs, as here, in company with 'insane' at Cic. de orat. II 269 'quid tibi uis, inquit, insane?' and Prop. I 5 3 'quid tibi uis, insane? meae [[meos]] sentire furores?' and, most important of all, Pers. v 143, an imitation of this very passage, 'quo deinde, insane, ruis, quo? | quid tibi uis?' But on the other hand in Bentley's conjecture the elision of 'rem' is not legitimate. It will not suffice to say that these sermones, approaching as they do the comic style, admit also the metrical license of comedy: how comes it there is only one example, and that a conjecture? It seems then that both attempts at correction must be abandoned. Now there are two sources whence I see promise of help towards a new essay: one is the imitation of Persius already quoted: the other is the codex Gothanus which gives the verse thus:

'quid tibi uis, insane, et quas res?' improbus urget

omitting 'agis'. This MS is so often the faithful representative of V that its readings, where the reading of V is not recorded, deserve the highest considera-

tion. Here it is not so evident to ‖ me as to Mr Palmer that the omission of
'agis' is a correction: the verb is surely the last word that would be thrown
overboard. On the other hand, if the above is the elder form of the verse, 'agis'
is a very natural supplement to write in the margin. Therefore I would state the
question thus: Persius has 'quid tibi uis', so has Horace; Persius has 'insane', so
has Horace; Persius has 'quo ruis': can we elicit from the 'quas res' of the
Gothanus something to answer this? I think so. The inversion of two letters
I have already illustrated, the confusion of *f* with *s* I need not illustrate; but the
combination of these errors in ars 294 may be quoted: the MSS give both p*re*-
*s*ectum and p*erf*ectum. Exactly parallel is the mistake qua*s*res for qua*fe*rs.[1] But
'qua fers' is just the same thing as 'quo ruis': true 'ferri' and 'se ferre' are
commoner in this sense, but Forcellini cites even from the prose of Nepos an
instance of the intransitive 'ferentem', and Lucr. VI 299 has 'tulit' = 'se tulit'.

Epist. I I 53–60

'O ciues, ciues, quaerenda pecunia primum est,
uirtus post nummos': haec Ianus summus ab imo
55   prodocet, haec recinunt iuuenes dictata senesque,
laeuo suspensi loculos tabulamque lacerto.
est animus tibi, sunt mores et lingua fidesque,
sed quadringentis sex septem milia desunt:
plebs eris. at pueri ludentes 'rex eris' aiunt
60   'si recte facies'.

V. 56 recurs at serm. I 6 74 'magni | quo pueri magnis e centurionibus orti, |
laeuo suspensi loculos tabulamque lacerto, | ibant octonos referentes Idibus
aeris'. This says nothing against it, as the repetition of a verse is not uncommon
with Horace: it is for its entire inappropriateness that Guietus and so many
others condemn it. Dr Wilkins thinks though doubtfully that it may be defended 'as heightening the irony: old and young all repeat the same lesson, like
a pack of schoolboys, on their way ‖ to school'. Even if 'young and old, satchel
and tablet on shoulder' were a tolerable method of conveying that meaning
instead of an intolerable failure to convey it, still such a metaphor would here
be out of place, because we presently have the 'dictata' of these 'iuuenes senesque' contrasted with the 'nenia' of real schoolboys, those who really do carry
satchel and tablet. Yet how can the verse be spurious? what should possess an
interpolator to insert anything so wholly inopportune?

Now it is undoubted that there has been some disturbance here, for the next
two verses, 57 and 58, occupy in almost all MSS the reverse position, 58, 57,
leaving 'sed' without sense. I believe then that v. 56 is merely out of its due

---

[1] In Verg. Aen. IV 438 the Medicean gives *fretque refretque* for *fertque refertque*.

order. Placed three lines lower down, this torment of the critic will fit its context perfectly:

> at pueri ludentes 'rex eris' aiunt   59
> laeuo suspensi loculos tabulamque lacerto   56
> 'si recte facies'.   60

The boys repeat the jingle 'rex eris si recte facies, si non facies non eris' at play on their way to and from school. I do not pretend to greatly admire the way in which the quoted sentence is thus broken apart; but if the MSS put the verse here and I proposed on that score to remove it, how much attention should I receive?

Epist. I 2 27–33

> Nos numerus sumus et frugis consumere nati,
> sponsi Penelopae nebulones Alcinoique
> in cute curanda plus aequo operata iuuentus,
> cui pulchrum fuit in medios dormire dies et   30
> ad strepitum citharae cessatum ducere curam.
> ut iugulent hominem, surgunt de nocte latrones:
> ut te ipsum serues, non expergisceris?

I summarise Bentley's arguments against the above reading of v. 31 presented by most MSS. In the first place 'cessatum ducere' is itself a strange and scarcely intelligible substitute for 'lenire' or 'solari'; secondly the youth of Phaeacia did ‖ not 'bring care to cease' (if that is what the words mean), inasmuch as they knew nothing of care except from hearsay; thirdly to soothe care by music is no reproach to anyone, and Horace himself carm. IV 11 35 asks for a song because 'minuentur atrae carmine curae'. Further it may be said that 'curam' here can hardly be dissociated from 'cute curanda' in v. 29; so that it will apparently mean 'curam cutis' and give a very absurd result. We turn then to the other reading 'somnum' found in V, in its follower the Gothanus, in the important Emmerammensis and in another of Holder's MSS, and attested by Acron's note 'quia adhibemus sonitum citharae ac lyrae ut facilius sopiamur'. Now 'somnum' cannot be a correction of 'curam', for it makes obvious nonsense: 'curam' may be a correction of 'somnum', for the nonsense which it makes is less obvious. Science therefore bids us take 'somnum' as a relic of truth and seek for an emendation of the now indefensible 'cessatum'. The sense required is clear from the context and especially from vv. 32 sq.: the Phaeacians artificially created or prolonged sleep by the sound of the lyre: see carm. III 1 20 'non auium citharaeque cantus somnum reducent' (to tyrants), Seneca ap. Bentl. 'somnus per symphoniarum cantum ex longinquo lene resonantium quaeritur.' Bentley's 'cessantem' (with 'ducere' = 'inducere') and Munro's 'recreatum' (with 'ducere' = 'producere') are entirely satisfactory in point of meaning, but neither approaches the MSS so closely as to enforce assent: the following is nearer, and seems the best word in the language for the thing:

ad strepitum citharae *ar*cessitum *in*ducere somnum.

The lexicons quote '*somnum* medicamentis *arcessere*' from Celsus and '*quies* molli strato *arcessita*' from Livy: add Prop. III 17 13 sq. 'quod si, Bacche, tuis per feruida tempora donis | *accersitus* erit *somnus* in ossa mea'. The loss of *ar* after *ae* is easy, capital R and E being a good deal confused: the further change from 'cessitum' to the nearest Latin word 'cessatum' was sure to happen in this much-read and often-copied author, and is probably deliberate; yet I find the accidental exchange of *i* and *a* in carm. I 28 3 *litus latus* and *latum*, III 10 6 *satum* ‖ and *situm*, epist. I 7 82 *ambagibus* and *ambigibus*, 15 46 *uillis* and *uallis*, ars 249 *fricti* and *fracti*, 327 *Albini* and *Albani*. The whole corruption has a close parallel in Lucr. III 978 where the best MSS give *atque ea nimirum* as Lucretius wrote; but the one *e* was absorbed by the other, leaving *atqueanimirum*, from which certain later MSS elicit *atque animarum* by the change of *i* to *a*. I have written 'inducere' because the loss of *in* after *m* is so common that MS authority is worth nothing on the point, and the verse has thus a smoother rhythm. I think it however quite possible that the writer of serm. II 3 134 'an tu reris eum occisa insanisse parente', 181 'uestrum praetor is intestabilis et sacer esto', ars 87 'cur ego si nequeo ignoroque poeta salutor' and 263 'non quiuis uidet inmodulata poemata iudex' wrote also 'ad strepitum citharae arcessitum ducere somnum': the verse is harsher than the other four to my ear, but that proves nothing for Horace's.

Epist. I 5 8–11

Mitte leuis spes et certamina diuitiarum
et Moschi causam: cras nato Caesare festus
dat ueniam somnumque dies: inpune licebit
aestiuam sermone benigno tendere noctem.

A summer night on the eve of the equinox is alienis mensibus aestas with a vengeance: by the Julian calendar summer ended and autumn began on the 11th of August, six weeks before. I assume as a matter of course that the birthday meant is Augustus': there was more than one Caesar in Rome and there is more than one Victoria in England, but as certainly as 'Victoria's natal day' is the 24th of May to an English poet, so certainly was 'nato Caesare festus dies' the 23rd of September to Horace. Dr Wilkins says that 'Horace and most of his friends would not be likely to be in Rome at all during the unhealthy month of September'; but epist. I 7 shews us August ended and Maecenas in Rome expecting a visit from Horace. Yet Meineke's 'festiuam', found in a few late MSS, cannot be right with 'festus' just above; and Lucian Mueller adds 'abstinent fere dactylici adiectiuo quod est festiuus.' || I propose 'festinam'. The exact counterpart of 'festinam tendere noctem' appears in carm. II 7 6 '*morantem* saepe *diem* mero *fregi*': there the dragging day is curtailed by an early dinner hour, here the too fleet night is lengthened by carousing on into the day. The first letter of a verse is of course in a post of peril: thus in epod. 7 12 all the MSS have *umquam* for *numquam*; and here one of the best, Holder's A, reads *estiuā*. Of *n* confused with *u* I say nothing.

Epist. II 2 87–90

Frater erat Romae consulti rhetor, ut alter
alterius sermone meros audiret honores,
Gracchus ut hic illi, foret huic ut Mucius ille.
qui minus argutos uexat furor iste poetas?

It is no longer attempted to defend this reading of v. 87 against the censures of Dan. Heinsius and Bentley. Horace has indeed a peculiar use of 'ut' in serm. I 7 13 'ira fuit capitalis, ut ultima diuideret mors' and II 3 1 'si raro scribes, ut toto non quater anno | membranam poscas'; but there 'tam' is readily supplied to 'capitalis' and 'raro', they being an adjective and adverb of quality: 'frater' is nothing of the kind. Again, there is not a word in the text to tell you that this rhetor and lawyer did not thoroughly deserve one another's praise; but unless the praise was groundless and preconcerted, the anecdote is beside the mark, and their behaviour no parallel to that of the 'arguti poetae'. Yet again: if they were brothers, their mutual admiration was natural and pardonable, no subject for ridicule or blame. Here then are three faults to be removed: now consider the various conjectures. Meineke supposes the loss of a verse in this way: 'frater erat Romae consulti rhetor, *uterque* | *alterius laudum sic admirator*, ut alter | alterius sermone meros audiret honores.' To this Dr Wilkins objects that 'the combination *uterque alterius* is very dubious Latin'; but this doubt will be dispelled by Mart. VII 38 4 'quod si fera monstra duorum | iunxeris, *alterius* fiet *uterque* timor'. The true objection, I conceive, is that the proposal removes only the first, not the second or third, of the || faults enumerated above; and the objection to Schuetz's 'fautor' for 'frater' is that though it removes the first and third it leaves the second. All three faults are removed by Bentley's 'pactus erat Romae consulto rhetor' which exactly fulfils the requirements of the sense; but the corruption is hardly to be explained. Palmer's 'auctor...consulto' has the same merit and demerit; Hamacher's 'suasor...consulto' is perhaps a trifle more probable.

But in reading this passage I have always been arrested by a fourth stumbling-block. When Horace relates an anecdote of what happened elsewhere than at Rome, he often names the place where the scene is laid: serm. I 1 64 'quidam memoratur Athenis', II 3 168 'Seruius Oppidius Canusi', 5 84 'anus improba

Thebis', epist. II 2 128 'fuit haut ignobilis Argis'. But when he relates an anecdote of what happened at Rome, and he relates many, never save here does he introduce it with a 'Romae'; and no wonder, for surely 'erat Romae' would sound as strange a beginning to Romans as 'there was a man in England' to Englishmen, without it were necessary for the understanding of the tale. At least, I have always felt this difficulty, and did not invent it merely to recommend the following conjecture, which will probably strike the reader as more violent than Bentley's or any of the others:

> praemostrator erat consulto rhetor, ut alter
> alterius sermone meros audiret honores.

The loss of the initial letter left *raemo strator*: the change of *raemo* to *romae* (*remo* to *rome*) may be an instance of that inversion which I illustrated at serm. II 2 123, or may be due merely to that continual exchange of *e* for *o* which together with the confusion of *st* and *f* (ars 249 *fricti* and *stricti*, Ouid. trist. IV 10 86 *structos* and *fructos*, Prop. III 20 17 *constringit* and *confringit*, paneg. Messal. 87 *facilis* and *stabilis*) reduced *strator* to *frater* and so necessitated *consulti*. If I am asked why 'Romae' was transposed, I suspect it was to give the verse the Ovidian flow which copyists prefer: thus some of them in serm. I 5 67 alter '*nilo deterius* dominae ius esse: rogabat' to *deterius nihilo* and in 3 117 'et qui nocturnus *sacra diuum* legerit. adsit' ‖ to *diuum sacra*: but it may be the pure accident which I exemplified fully on serm. I 3 103. Horace got the word 'praemostrator', like so much else, from his friend Terence: haut. 875 'auditor meus et monitor et praemonstrator Chremes'. The spelling *mostro* is well attested, e. c. by the Medicean MS of Virgil in georg. I 19 'mostrator aratri', and should be restored to our texts wherever traces of it occur: thus in epist. I 2 65 we should take *mostret* from the excellent codex A. Very much to my purpose is the variant *formare* for *monstrare* in ars 49: *mostrare* became *mofrare* as *strator* here became *frater*, and then the letters *mofr-* were arranged as *form-*.

   Conjectures which assume a chain of errors like this, even when each error singly is a slight one, are apt to meet with incredulity. Well, suppose that Horace were preserved to us only in those MSS which exhibit carm. I 13 18–20 in this form: 'quos inrupta tenet copula nec malis | *diuolsusque prementibus* | suprema citius soluet amor die'. Suppose that a critic conjectured *diuolsus querimoniis*, and explained that through the confusion of *qu* with *p*, *o* with *e*, and *i* with *t*, *querimoniis* became *perimentis*; that *que*, written above as a correction, was attached by mistake to *diuolsus*; that *perimentis* by the transposition of one letter and the subtraction of another became *prementis*; and that this was stretched to metrical length by the alteration *prementibus*: that conjecture, I imagine, might also meet with incredulity. Yet it would be right.

Ars poet. 60–3

Vt siluae foliis priuos mutantur in annos,
prima cadunt, ita uerborum uetus interit aetas
et iuuenum ritu florent modo nata uigentque.

I have accepted Bentley's 'priuos' for 'pronos' in v. 60, not understanding how anyone can read his note and refuse. Dr Wilkins observes, as if answering Bentley, that '*in annos* stands very well by itself for *each year* as carm. II 13 14 *in horas* = *every hour*'. Quite true; but that is just Bentley's point. *In annos*, if it stood by itself, would stand very well: the objection to the || vulgate is that *in annos* does not stand by itself but stands with *pronos*. To the phrases *in annos*, *in dies*, *in horas*, used in this sense, the Romans do not add descriptive epithets: they add *singulus* or *priuus* or no epithet at all. I am told that 'pronos' is very poetical: I reply, That question does not yet arise. Bentley has not denied that it is poetical; he has denied that it is Latin. Prove it to be Latin, then we will consider whether it be poetical or no: till then, to call it either poetical or unpoetical will be meaningless.

Less valid however are the further objections by which Bentley seeks to bring in an unmetrical alteration. Thus 'foliis mutantur' seems to be quite defensible and rightly explained by Dr Reid as *are parted from their leaves*: 'mutari finibus' comes to the same thing as 'mutare fines', 'foliis mutantur' as 'folia mutant'. Again, when Bentley says 'cum *folia* hic, non *siluae*, cum *uerbis* comparentur, oportet utique ut id uocabulum casu recto efferatur et ducat sententiam', he is quite mistaken. Ovid, as if to refute him beforehand, wrote these exactly parallel verses: met. III 729 'non citius *frondes* autumni frigore tactas | iamque male haerentes alta *rapit* arbore *uentus* | quam *sunt membra* uiri manibus *direpta* nefandis', not *frondes rapiuntur uento*; and so Horace himself in epod. 15 5 says 'artius atque *hedera* procera *adstringitur ilex* | lentis *adhaerens* bracchiis', not *hedera adstringit ilicem*.

But there remains this very real objection to the text: that after 'prima cadunt' a corresponding member such as 'subeunt altera' is imperatively demanded. The difficulty is recognised by all, and is not smoothed away by the irrelevant passages which Vahlen and Keller adduce. Now the tractatus Vindobonensis on this poem has here 'prima, scilicet folia, cadunt, *noua succrescunt*; ita uetus aetas uerborum, id est uerba in uetere aetate inuenta, intereunt, et modo nata … florent', and Lehrs has suggested that a verse is lost containing the word 'succrescunt': say 'prima cadunt *porroque cadentibus altera primis* | *succrescunt*; ita uerborum' cet. Prof. Nettleship in support of his own similar hypothesis refers to Bentley's citation from Jerome, 'postquam … alia uenerit generatio primisque cadentibus foliis uirens silua succreuerit'. Certainly at first sight it looks as if || 'succrescunt' must have stood in the text; but on reflexion I do not find the evidence convincing. It is clear that if the Viennese commentator had our Horace before him he would in his paraphrase be impelled and even constrained to supplement the manifest defect in the sense by some such words as 'noua succrescunt'; nor do I see why those exact words should not occur to him. Mr Nettleship indeed says that '*succresco* is a word of the true classical stamp, and not at all likely to have been used *suo Marte* by a medieval commentator'; but even in the middle ages they did not rigidly exclude a word merely because it was classical; and *succresco*, I should think, is the word which would naturally present itself to any-one, medieval commentator or modern schoolboy. As for Jerome, I doubt if his words are from Horace at all: 'uirens silua succreuerit' seems rather to come straight from the great original, φύλλα τὰ μέν τ' ἄνεμος χαμάδις χέει, ἄλλα δέ θ' ὕλη | τηλεθόωσα φύει. And furthermore there is the gravest reason against in-serting any such words as 'noua succrescunt'. I said above that some such words were imperatively demanded by what precedes, and so they are; but then they are inexorably rejected by what follows. If Horace wrote 'prima folia cadunt, noua succrescunt', he might go on 'ita uerborum uetus interit aetas et florent modo nata uigentque'; but that he should add 'iuuenum ritu' is an impossibility. The human simile, if employed simultaneously with the simile of leaves, which would be bad enough, must at the very least appear in each part of the comparison. Before a man writes treatises concerning the art of poetry, let him acquire its rudiments: if at the 61st verse he gives this specimen of his proficiency few will be found so covetous of misinformation as to read him further. *As leaves perish and spring anew, so words perish and spring anew like young men*: there yawns an abyss of literary incapacity into which by no accident can Horace have stumbled. Horace? no, nor Meuius.

Surely the cure for all this trouble is very simple. Nothing wants changing but the stops:

> ut siluae foliis priuos mutantur in annos,
> prima cadunt ita uerborum. uetus interit aetas
> et iuuenum ritu florent modo nata uigentque. ||

As each year's leaves are shed from the trees, so perish the earliest words. Then, with a fresh image: the old generation of them dies, and the newly born, like young men, flourish and thrive.

Ars poet. 101–4

> Vt ridentibus adrident ita flentibus adsunt
> humani uoltus: si uis me flere, dolendum est
> primum ipsi tibi: tunc tua me infortunia laedent,
> Telephe uel Peleu.

Commentators who tell us that *adesse* means to support with sympathy tell us what is quite true but no way relevant to the defence of 'adsunt' here. Of course Horace could say (though the remark would have no connexion with the context) 'ut ridentibus ita flentibus adsunt'; but he did not: he began with 'ut ridentibus adrident', to which 'ita flentibus adsunt' forms no sort of contrast or parallel. But the most serious objection to 'adsunt' is that the notion of 'supporting' is quite foreign to the matter in hand: Horace's point is that whatever emotion you would fain create in your audience, that emotion you must yourself exhibit; and so he goes on 'si uis me flere, dolendum est primum ipsi tibi'; but in this connexion 'flentibus adsunt' is quite incoherent, for no one pretends that *adesse* means *flere*. If you impress it on the young playwright as a general truth that mankind *adsunt flentibus*, you will have him introducing all his dramatis personae in tears on all occasions, because success will then be sure. It is therefore very natural that many critics should alter 'adsunt' to 'adflent', which Bentley supports with his usual resourcefulness by Sen. de ira II 2 5 'inde est quod *adridemus ridentibus* et *contristat* nos turba *maerentium*' and Ouid. met. III 459 'cum *risi, adrides*; *lacrimas* quoque saepe notaui | me *lacrimante* tuas'. This no doubt gives Horace's thought; but not his words. It is a poor stylist who having used 'ad*flent*' in v. 101 proceeds with 'si uis me *flere*' in v. 102. There is no offence in 'flentibus' v. 101 followed by 'flere' v. 102, because they who *flent* in the former verse are the actors while he who *flet* in the latter is the spectator; but there would be offence || in 'dolentibus' v. 101 followed by 'dolendum est' v. 102; and there is offence in 'adflent' thus followed by 'flere'. Horace's words therefore seem to have been these:

> ut ridentibus adrident ita flentibus adsunt
> umiduli uoltus.

adsunt umiduli = adflent. Our archetype usually spells the cognates of *umor* correctly, and so does the archetype of Lucretius; but he slips once and writes *humorem* VI 523, and I suppose some ancestor of ours slipped once and wrote *humiduli* here; just as at serm. II 5 86 we find *humeris*, but no repetition of the blunder in the other places where Horace uses *umerus*. Now with *d* changed to *a* by too short a stroke, and with the customary absence of a dot over the letter *i*, *humiauli* becomes *humani* by the confusion I illustrated on carm. II 2 2. By a very similar error *inaignum* became *magnum* in serm. II 5 79, if Bentley's *indignum* is right, as it ought to be.

Ars poet. 391–401

> Siluestris homines sacer interpresque deorum
> caedibus et uictu foedo deterruit Orpheus,
> dictus ob hoc lenire tigris rabidosque leones.
> dictus et Amphion, Thebanae conditor urbis,
> saxa mouere sono testudinis et fide blanda   395
> ducere quo uellet. fuit haec sapientia quondam,

publica priuatis secernere, sacra profanis,
concubitu prohibere uago, dare iura maritis,
oppida moliri, leges incidere ligno.
400   sic honor et nomen diuinis uatibus atque
carminibus uenit.

'Orpheus awed savage men from bloodshed and filthiness, and was therefore said to tame lions and tigers. Amphion was said to lead stones with his music whither he would. Wisdom once upon a time consisted in discriminating public property from private, things sacred from things profane, in forbidding roving licence'. . . where are we? What has all this about primitive wisdom, which by the way seemingly differs little from modern wisdom, to do with Amphion and Orpheus? And ‖ then he goes on 'sic honor et nomen diuinis uatibus atque carminibus uenit': poets and their songs won renown because wisdom once upon a time consisted in discriminating public property from private etc.! And then, as suddenly as he introduced this digression from Orpheus and Amphion, so suddenly does he forget all about it, and proceeds (v. 401) 'post hos (Orphea et Amphiona) insignis Homerus | Tyrtaeusque' eqs.

Now not only have we here a shower of information which we do not expect in the least, but we are defrauded of information which we do expect. Horace's theme from v. 391 to v. 407 is this, that poets are the authors of civilisation: 'ne forte pudori | sit tibi Musa lyrae sollers et cantor Apollo'. To shew forth this truth he rationalises ancient legend: Orpheus, he declares, was said to tame lions and tigers because he softened the rudeness of savage men; Amphion was said to make stones follow his music – now, surely, we are about to hear, of Amphion as of Orpheus, why he was said to do so. And Horace told us thus:

dictus et Amphion, Thebanae conditor urbis,
saxa mouere sono testudinis et fide blanda
ducere quo uellet, fuit huic sapientia quando
publica priuatis secernere, sacra profanis eqs.

Amphion was said to make stones follow his music and build up Thebes, because he was the architect of social order. Then we go on: thus, through the humanising power of Orpheus and the constructive power of Amphion, did poets and poetry win renown.

huic is often confused with hic, and hic in Horace's MSS must be accommodated to the gender of 'sapientia'. The alteration of quando to quondā is an instance of that curious but not uncommon freak by which two letters in order to exchange places overleap the intervening part of the word without disturbing it: the most frequent example is the variation flagro and fraglo found at serm. I 4 125 and hundreds of years older than any MS of Horace: here are others: epist. I 2 5 distenet and destinet, Ter. haut. 535 uersaret and seruaret, Lucr. VI ‖

1122 qua gra*d*itur and quadragitas, Verg. Aen. 1 264 cont*u*ndet and contend*u*nt, Ouid. met. VI 234 *d*antem and *t*andem, fast. V 507 exsuscitat and excus*s*it ab, Prop. III 3 35 *n*eru*i*s and *u*erni*s*, 13 11 m*a*trona and m*o*trana, IV 1 129 *u*ersarent and *s*eruarent, 6 34 eg*e*ss*i*t and eg*i*sset, Iuu. X 294 uergin*i*a and u*i*rginea. This very confusion of *quando* and *quondam* recurs in Prop. II 21 11 and, I believe, not forty verses away in the ars poetica itself. The following is the vulgate text of vv. 354–60:

> ut scriptor si peccat idem librarius usque,
> quamuis est monitus, uenia caret, et citharoedus   355
> ridetur, chorda qui semper oberrat eadem,
> sic mihi, qui multum cessat, fit Choerilus ille
> quem bis terue bonum cum risu miror; et idem
> indignor quandoque bonus dormitat Homerus;
> uerum operi longo fas est obrepere somnum.   360

The misquotation 'aliquando bonus dormitat Homerus' has become a household word, so it never occurs to us to marvel at the insolence of the epithet 'bonus' coming from Horace to Homer; but if an English critic wrote about 'the good Milton' I think we should ask him to keep his condescension for Dr Watts: the word in fact is the technical term by which in literary matters we express tolerance for mediocrity. Even if this is not recognised it must yet be thought strange that the modest elevation to which Choerilus now and then rises and the majestic altitude habitual to Homer should here be designated by the same adjective. But further, v. 359 is a flat contradiction of what he said only eight lines above: he said in vv. 351 sq. 'ubi plura nitent in carmine, non ego paucis | offendar maculis', but now it seems he has altered his mind. And further still, 'idem' has not a shred of meaning; there is no semblance of an opposition: 'when Choerilus chances on a good verse my feeling is amused surprise, and *yet* I am impatient when Homer nods': excogitate a sense for that *yet*, et eris mihi magnus Apollo. Now these latter objections are removed by placing a full stop after 'indignor', a punctuation supported by the florilegium Nostradamense which begins its quotation || with 'quandoque'. Both 'idem' and 'indignor' are thus quite right: the few happy lines of Choerilus move the reader to amused surprise yet do not mitigate his impatience of the poetaster's performance. But the next sentence is worse than ever: 'bonus' is unremoved, and 'quandoque', which must now mean 'aliquando', is precluded from that sense by Augustan usage. We require then an appropriate adverb in lieu of 'quandoque', an appropriate adjective in lieu of 'bonus'. And here comes to the rescue an authority four hundred years older than any of our MSS. Jerome, who quotes from memory '*interdum magnus* dormitat Homerus', is not giving the words which Horace wrote: metre forbids 'interdum', 'magnus' may be merely

a reminiscence of serm. I 10 52 'tu nihil in magno doctus reprehendis Homero';
but he found a full stop after 'indignor' and an adverb meaning 'aliquando' in
place of 'quandoque'. I suggest that what he found was this:

> sic mihi, qui multum cessat, fit Choerilus ille,
> quem bis terue bonum cum risu miror et idem
> indignor. quondam nauos dormitat Homerus;
> uerum operi longo fas est obrepere somnum.

quondam I regard as certain, *nauos* only as probable: I would try to commend it
by the following considerations. In the first place it is just the word wanted,
forming as it does a good contrast to 'dormitat', a perfect antithesis to 'qui
multum cessat'.[1] Secondly it will explain the MS text: I gave under serm. II 2 123
several corruptions which may be classed as transpositions of syllables: certainly
so to be classed are carm. I 36 17 *pu-tres* and *tres-pu*, III 8 27 *ra-pe* and *s-pe-ra*:
for a combination of this error with the ubiquitous interchange of *u* and *b* see
Stat. silu. IV 5 17 *la-ua*-nt for *ba-la*-nt: thus then might *na-uo*-s become *bo-na*-s,
and out of *quando bonas* the necessities of metre and grammar would elicit
quandoque bonus. Thirdly it may be the origin of Jerome's *magnus*, for *nauus* is
probably to be restored for *magnus* in Prop. II 7 16, and *magnus* in IV 8 41 of the
same poet is universally corrected to *nanus*. ‖

Ars poet. 431–7

> Vt qui conducti plorant in funere dicunt
> et faciunt prope plura dolentibus ex animo, sic
> derisor uero plus laudatore mouetur.
> reges dicuntur multis urgere culullis
435 > et torquere mero quem perspexisse laborant
> an sit amicitia dignus: si carmina condes,
> numquam te fallent animi sub uolpe latentes.

Orelli's note on v. 437 is embellished with a number of passages Greek and
Latin from Archilochus onwards in which a fox is said to be crafty or to hide
behind something else; and this to elucidate a passage of Horace in which
something else is said to hide behind a fox or the skin of a fox! Strangest of all
it is to see how Pers. v 116 'fronte politus | astutam uapido seruas in pectore
uolpem' continues to be quoted: if that verse was imitated from this it proves
our MSS here to be desperately corrupt; so totally do the two passages differ in
meaning and in everything else except the mere mention of a fox. But to consider Horace's words by themselves: what creature, desiring to conceal his guile,
would try to do so with a fox's skin of all things in the world? what possible

---

[1] Compare v. 140 'nil molitur inepte', 148 'semper ad euentum festinat et in medias res | non
secus ac notas auditorem rapit.'

disguise could excite livelier suspicion than the coat of this proverbial trickster? 'A bad heart under a cunning face' is Macleane's rendering; but if the face is cunning then the bad heart is ill concealed. Dr Wilkins, if I understand him, supposes the 'uolpes' to be the 'derisor' himself: but 'animi sub uolpe latentes' cannot stand for 'animi uolpis sub eius pectore latentes': who ever said 'sub me celo' meaning 'sub meo pectore'? 'curae sub imperatore' for 'sub pectore imperatoris'?

The required sense is clear: kings ply with wine those whose real character they seek to discover: you will find the recitation of your own verses an equally infallible touchstone to detect a 'derisor'.

> si carmina condes,
> numquam te fallent anguis sub uepre latentis

or anguis in uepre. This is not all conjecture, for the old ‖ Bernese, the best of Horace's MSS in the matter of spelling, has retained the 'latentis' which I adopt: the nom. plur. termination -is in i-nouns and present participles is frequently preserved by our great authorities for orthography, such as the MSS of Virgil and Lucretius. The difference between 'angui' and 'animi' is next to nothing, as I shewed at carm. III 4 10: exanguis and exanimis are confused in Ouid. Ibis 142 and 505. The change of 'uepre' to 'uolpe' involves the change of o to e (see on carm. I 12 35) and of r to l: this is very early and common: see carm. III 10 4 plorares and ploralis, 12 11 arto and alto, IV 4 41 alma and arma, serm. II 3 235 uerris and uellis, epist. II 2 123 carentia and calentia, ars 371 aulus and aurus: then conjecture would inevitably alter 'uople' to 'uolpe' if accident did not. Virgil's 'latet anguis in herba' will occur to every one: a still closer parallel will be Pompon. ap. Non. 231 13 [p. 343 16 Lindsay] 'uipera est in ueprecula' if that is the true correction of the MS reading 'uepra est ueprecula'. The following too has some relevance: Theogn. 599–602 οὔ μ' ἔλαθες φοιτῶν κατ' ἀμαξιτόν, ἦν ἄρα καὶ πρὶν | ἠλάστρεις, κλέπτων ἡμετέρην φιλίην. | ἔρρε, θεοῖσίν τ' ἐχθρὲ καὶ ἀνθρώποισιν ἄπιστε, | ψυχρὸν ὃς ἐν κόλπῳ ποικίλον εἶχες ὄφιν.

20

EMENDATIONS IN OVID'S
*METAMORPHOSES**

I 237–9

fit lupus et ueteris seruat uestigia formae.
canities eadem est, eadem uiolentia uultus,
idem oculi lucent, eadem feritatis imago est.

The eyes of a homicide transformed into a wolf may well be said to *flagrare,*
ardere, scintillare or the like, but 'lucent' is quite inadequate and should I suspect be replaced by 'lurent'. The adjective 'luridus' is of course common, the
substantive 'luror' very rare, the verb 'lureo' unknown to lexicographers: once
however it has been preserved, and that once in the metamorphoses. At II 776
our MSS give 'nusquam recta acies, liuent rubigine dentes'; but this verse is
found by Mr Ellis in a Bodleian codex of excerpts (MS Digby 65, saec. XII) with
'lurent' for 'liuent', and not only is it intrinsically improbable that the unique
word should be a corruption of the common one, but 'lurent' is supported by
Hor. *carm.* IV 13 10 'luridi dentes'. Again in Plaut. *Menaech.* 828 'uiden tu illi
oculos uirere? ut uiridis exoritur colos' cet., where 'uirere' cannot well be right
with 'uiridis' following and one MS gives 'iurere', Ritschl has conjectured
'lurere'. Once more, in Sen. *Herc. fur.* 766 sq. Charon is thus described:
'inpexa pendet barba, deformem sinum | nodus coercet, concauae lucent genae'
(for 'lucent' one family of MSS has 'squalent', but that comes from 'squalidus'
in 765): here again the verb is miserably weak, especially if compared with
Virgil's 'stant lumina flamma', and here too I propose 'lurent'. Finally at *met.*
IV 715 'praebentem Phoebo liuentia terga draconem' in our best MS the
Marcianus ‖ (M) 'liuentia' is corrected by the hand of a contemporary reviser
into 'lucentia': either of the two is unimpeachable and may be right, but if the
phenomena require us to seek for an unfamiliar word which looked like 'liuentia' at a first glance and 'lucentia' at a second, it will be 'lurentia'.

* [*TCPhS* 3 (1890), 140–53: summarized in *PCPhS* 1889, 8–9]

I 345
crescunt loca decrescentibus undis.

loca do not *crescere*, nor can the word signify dry land in opposition to water: Plautus *mil.* 413 speaks of the sea as 'locis Neptuniis', Ovid *her.* VII 57 sq. writes 'nec uiolasse fidem temptantibus *aequora* prodest: | perfidiae poenas exigit *ille locus.*' The proper word to contrast with 'undis' will be 'sola': Catull. 63 40 '*sola* dura, *mare* ferum'. Again in *met.* VII 57 'notitiamque loci melioris et oppida, quorum | hic quoque fama uiget, cultusque artesque locorum', 'soli' should be read for 'loci' with Heinsius on account of 'locorum' in the next verse: see too XIV 681 'haec loca sola colit' where 'sola' has dropped out through its likeness to 'loca' and the MSS have put 'magna' in its place. How the confusion of the two words comes about may be seen from the error 'lose' for 'sole' in Verg. *georg.* II 512.

I 441–4
hunc deus arcitenens, et numquam talibus armis
ante nisi in dammis capreisque fugacibus usus,
mille grauem telis, exhausta paene pharetra,
perdidit effuso per uulnera nigra ueneno.

It was first observed by Heyne on Tibull. IV I 39 how strangely 'et' is employed to couple two such notions as 'arcitenens' and 'numquam talibus armis ante usus': he proposed 'non umquam': Polle would alter 'et' to 'sed', but even that is forced; and there remains 'talibus', which ought to be 'eis'. I propose therefore 'numquam letalibus', 'letalibus' having been corrupted first I suppose to 'te talibus', and then 'te' as often to 'et'. 'fatalibus' I should think less likely. ||

I 632*
frondibus arboreis et amara pascitur herba.

'*amara* corruptum?' asks Riese with some cause, for grass is not bitter, and if Ovid means that it was bitter to Io because unfamiliar I should have expected some similar epithet with 'frondibus' instead of the simple 'arboreis'. But I find 'herba' the suspicious word, since 'gramen' occurs in the very next verse, and I suggest 'amaro pascitur eruo': vetches are bitter, the word is often spelt 'heruum', and *u* is everywhere confused with *b*.

* [[See Appendix 4, p. 1257]]

II 275–8

sustulit oppressos collo tenus arida uultus
opposuitque manum fronti magnoque tremore
omnia concutiens paulum subsedit et infra
quam solet esse fuit sacraque ita uoce locuta est.

Instead of 'sacra' which no editor I think defends, some interpolated MSS have 'sicca' which has become the vulgate; Schenkl proposes 'rauca'. It will be equally appropriate and much nearer to the text to write 'fracta': *f* is endlessly confounded with *s*, *ct* very frequently with *c*, and *r* is oftener transposed than any letter of the alphabet but *h*.

II 688

Battum uicinia tota uocabant.

'uicinia tota' is found in a few late MSS, but our better authorities vary thus: 'uicinaque' M with 'tota' added by the second hand in an erasure, 'uicinia rura' N, 'uicina hunc rura' λ and Harl.: these divergences point to 'uicinia cuncta'.

II 855 sq.

cornua parua quidem, sed quae contendere possis
facta manu, puraque magis perlucida gemma.

Heinsius objects to 'parua' that 'alta cornua et spatiosa laudantur in tauro' and writes 'uara'. Haupt replies that several works of ancient art represent Europa's bull with ‖ small horns. So far so good; but now what are we to make of 'quidem' and 'sed'? what contrast exists between small size and perfection of finish? none at all, but rather the reverse. And in this respect Heinsius' 'uara' is no better; nor would 'curua' or 'panda' furnish the required opposition: I propose to obtain it by writing 'torua'. Lucan 1 612 has 'cornua torua', and the epithet is applied to bulls by Ovid in *met.* VI 115, VIII 132, and X 237; but the following passages are especially to the point because they refer to the rape of Europa: Sen. *Phaedr.* 303 sq. '*fronte* nunc *torua* petulans iuuencus | uirginum strauit sua terga ludo' and Sil. XV 61 sq. 'illa ego sum, uerti superum quae saepe parentem | nunc auis in formam, nunc *torui* in *cornua tauri*': compare also [Sen.] *Oct.* 766 sq. 'per fluctus raptam Europen | taurum tergo portasse *trucem*'. There is of course no inconsistency between 'cornua torua' and the ensuing lines 'nullae in fronte minae nec formidabile lumen: | pacem uultus habet.' 'toruus' and 'paruus' are confused in Lucr. VI 131 'saepe ita dat *toruum* sonitum displosa repente' Munro, *paruum* MSS, and Stat. *silu.* II 6 40 '*paruo*que uirilis | gratia' editors, *toruo* or *torua* MSS.

III 660 sq.

stetit aequore puppis
haut aliter quam si siccum nauale teneret.

It may be fancy, but I think Ovid would have written 'siccam'; and certainly
if he wrote it nothing but a miracle could save it from the alteration. Compare
Hor. *carm.* 1 4 2 'trahuntque siccas machinae carinas', Ovid *ex Pont.* 1 4 17 sq.
'soluetur in aequore nauis | quae numquam liquidis sicca carebit aquis', *met.*
XI 455 sq. 'eductam naualibus aequore tingui...pinum iubet'.

III 721–5

illa, quis Actaeon, nescit, dextramque precantis
abstulit: Inoo lacerata est altera raptu.
non habet infelix quae matri bracchia tendat,
trunca sed ostendens deiectis uulnera membris
'aspice mater' ait. ||

'deiectis' can mean 'struck off' with a sword or the like but is quite out of
place here, and most editors have taken 'disiectis' from a few late MSS: it
accords better both with the context and with the ductus litterarum to read
'dereptis'.

IV 663

clauserat Hippotades aeterno carcere uentos.

'aeternus carcer' of course can mean a prison of imperishable material; but
you cannot say 'claudo aliquem aeterno carcere' without implying that the
imprisonment as well as the prison is eternal. Hence many conjectures, of
which Haupt's 'alterno' is no better than the MS reading, and the others, 'inferno', 'terreno', 'Tyrrheno', 'aerato', 'hesternos', 'aduersos', are all further
from the text than what I offer, 'Aetnaeo': it appears from Verg. *Aen.* VIII 416
sqq. 'insula Sicanium iuxta latus Aeoliamque | erigitur Liparen...quam subter
...antra Aetnaea tonant' that this epithet extends to the Lipari islands: Aetna as
the chief mountain of that volcanic district lends its name to the whole.

V 117 sq.

concidit et digitis morientibus ille retemptat
fila lyrae casuque fuit miserabile carmen.

This is a miserabile carmen itself: instead of this languid 'fuit' with its change
of tense no wonder that Heinsius preferred even so violent an alteration as
'canit'. But a very slight amendment restores one of those rare phrases which the
copyists labour to exterminate: 'casuque ferit miserabile carmen': compare
trist. IV 10 50 'dum *ferit* Ausonia *carmina* culta lyra', Prop. II 1 9 'siue lyrae
carmen digitis *percussit* eburnis'.

VI 61–4

illic et Tyrium quae purpura sensit aenum
texitur et tenues parui discriminis umbrae,
qualis ab imbre solet percussis solibus arcus
inficere ingenti longum curuamine caelum. ||

The rainbow is absurdly described as arising from sunbeams struck by rain instead of rain struck by sunbeams: the editors perceive this, and some of them endow 'percussis' with the new meanings 'fractis' or 'repercussis', while others make the alteration 'percussus' which is futile after all, since it is not the rainbow but the rain which the sunbeams strike. Restore sense thus:

qualis sole solet percussis imbribus arcus
inficere cet.

The error perhaps began with the absorption of 'sole' in 'solet' and its addition in the margin, but these interchanges occur where there is no such excuse: VIII 762 'sanguine cortex' for 'cortice sanguis', XIII 495 'meum tua' for 'tuum mea', 374 'capiendo...feci' for 'faciendo...cepi', Verg. *buc.* IV 18 'nulla...primo' for 'prima...nullo'. Lest 'sole solet' should be thought cacophonous compare for instance II 639 'arcana canebat'.

VII 554 sq.

uiscera torrentur primo, flammaeque latentis
indicium rubor est et ductus anhelitus igni.

'In Glut gezogener Athem = heisser Athem' says Haupt; but 'in Glut gezogener' no less than 'ductus igni' is a wondrous way of conveying that sense. The old editors altered 'igni' to 'aegre' which is at any rate much better than Zingerle's insufferable 'ingens'; but neither breath which is 'ductus aegre' nor breath which is 'ductus ingens' (if that were Latin) is necessarily any 'indicium flammae latentis': 'igni' in fact has every sign of genuineness and the corruption lies elsewhere. I propose to write 'et anhelitus aridus igni': $a = d$, $ri = u$, $d = ct$: the resultant 'anhelitus ductus' must then be transposed for the metre; and we have many less excusable instances of metrical transposition: for example at VII 234 'et iam nona dies' the copyist took it into his head that 'et iam' was 'etiam' and accordingly wrote 'nona dies etiam'. For 'anhelitus aridus' see X 663 '*aridus* e lasso ueniebat *anhelitus* ore'. That the next sentence is 'aspera lingua tumet tepidisque *arentia* || uenis | ora patent' need not disquiet us, especially in this unfinished poem: the Romans are not careful to avoid such repetition where a full stop intervenes: compare Verg. *georg.* II 125 sq. 'et gens illa quidem sumptis non *tarda* pharetris. | Media fert tristis sucos *tardum*que saporem' cet.

VII 741 sq.

exclamo 'male fictor adest: male fictus adulter
uerus eram coniunx: me perfida teste teneris.'

'male fictor' has no sense, nor can 'fictor' be right with 'fictus' following.
Korn writes 'fictus' for 'fictor', a slight change, but improbable, because scribes
are more apt to assimilate than to dissimilate: the other conjectures are somewhat
violent, as Merkel's 'manifesta rea est' and Zingerle's 'iamne ultor adest', or
unprofitable, as Ellis's 'mala, fictor adest'. I have no doubt that *malefictor* stands
for *simulator*: much earlier than our archetype this would be very like *fimalector*:
then *fi-male-ctor* becomes *male-fi-ctor* by a transposition of syllables which has
a parallel as good as a hundred in XIV 254 where *s-tet-imus-que* has become
s-imul-at-que; but here are a few more: Plaut. *mil.* 356 *me-mini* for *minu-me*,
Catull. 58 5 magna a-*mire-mi-ni* for magna-*ni-mi remi*, Hor. *carm.* 1 36 17 *tres-pu*
for *pu-tres*, Ovid *trist.* IV 2 31 *in host*-ibus for *host-il*-ibus, Pers. 1 114 dis-*seuit*
cedo for dis-*cedo secuit*, Stat. *silu.* 1 praef. *est ual*-enti for *ual-esc*-enti, III 5 57
in-trac-ia for *trach-in*-ia, Nonius p. 94 3 ⟦133 3 Lindsay⟧ *co-bus* for *bus-to*,
heptat. Lat. *gen.* 420 ⟦474 Peiper⟧ *terni-qua* for *qua-terni*. In Val. Fl. II 191 'sua
cuique furens festinaque coniunx | adiacet', where I hardly understand *fest-in*-a,
I should write *in-fest*-a. In Hor. *carm.* III 4 50 'fidens iuuentus horrida bracchiis'
either 'fidens' or 'horrida' can be spared and 'bracchiis' wants an epithet
which ought I suspect to be obtained by altering *fi-den*-s to *den-si*-s.

VII 864 sq.

Aeacus ingreditur duplici cum prole nouoque
milite, quem Cephalus cum fortibus accipit armis.

There is no fault to find with 'cum fortibus', for the ‖ repetition of 'cum' is
but a trifle: 'consortibus' however has more special fitness in this place, and
palaeographically the difference is nothing: see on the one hand XIII 184 *sortes*
and *fortes*, on the other 1 705 *cum prensam* and *compressam*, VI 243 *cum tento* and
contento, XIII 610 *consonus* and *cum sonus*, 819 *me coniuge* and *mecum iuge*, 944
conbiberant and *cum biberant*.

VIII 237

garrula ramosa prospexit ab ilice perdix.

The partridge of course is not arboreal in its habits, and Ovid himself ex-
pressly tells us so: 256 sqq. 'non tamen haec alte uolucris sua corpora tollit |
nec facit in *ramis* altoque cacumine nidos: | propter humum uolitat ponitque in
saepibus oua | antiquique memor metuit sublimia casus.' Instead therefore of
'ramosa...ilice' most recent editors adopt from the auctor de dubiis nominibus
in *gramm. Lat.* Keil v 587 the reading 'limoso...elice'; and as to the substan-

tive I think there can be no doubt. But the corruption in our MSS would be better explained if Ovid's adjective were 'lamoso'. Nonius p. 489 11 ⟦785 11 Lindsay⟧ quotes from Lucil. III ⟦109 Marx⟧ the verse 'praeterea omne iter est hoc labosum atque lutosum' and absurdly derives 'lābosum' from 'lăbos': Mr Keller comparing a line of Ennius ⟦*ann.* 568 Vahlen⟧ quoted by the pseudo-Acron at Hor. *epist.* 1 13 10, 'siluarum saltus, latebras *lamas*que *lutosas*', suggests with high probability that the word should be 'lamosum'. In Prop. IV 7 81 the MSS give 'ramosis Anio qua pomifer incubat aruis' where 'ramosis' is utterly indefensible, and Mr Ellis perhaps rightly proposes 'lamosis'. If Horace uses 'lama', 'lamosus' cannot well be denied to Propertius or Ovid.

X 169 sq.

dum deus Eurotan inmunitamque frequentat
Sparten.

For 'inmunitam' M has 'immutatam', written 'immutā̆' just as at 285 'tractata' is written 'tractā̆'; and this points rather to 'immuratam'. The lexicons contain neither this ‖ word nor any example of 'muratus' earlier than Vegetius and Jerome; but at *ciris* 105 the MSS give 'stat Megara Alcathoi quondam *mutata* labore', whence Ellis restores '*murata*' rather than the vulgate '*munita*'; and in Cic. *ad Att.* IV 16 7 'constat enim aditus insulae esse *miratos mirificis molibus*' Tyrrell emends '*muratos*'. Seneca in *Med.* 79 describes Sparta as 'muris quod caret oppidum'. That 'immuratus' is not found elsewhere gives me no concern at all: the number of adjectives beginning with *in*- which make their first or their only appearance in Ovid is very large: illabefactus illimis imperfossus imperiuratus inambitiosus inattenuatus inconsumptus incruentatus indefletus indeiectus indeploratus indesertus indetonsus indeuitatus ineditus inexperrectus innabilis inobrutus insolidus intumulatus.

X 202 sq.

atque utinam merito uitam tecumque liceret
reddere.

'merito tecumque' is a ridiculous coordination: some editors read 'pro te. . . tecumue', 'pro te' from inferior MSS, 'ue' from M, which is good sense but does not explain the corruption 'merito'. I propose

atque utinam tecumque mori uitamque liceret
reddere.

Some trace of the displacement perhaps remains in N which seems to have read originally 'merito tecumque uitam'. For the tautology of 'mori' and 'uitam reddere' compare Verg. *Aen.* III 339 'superatne et uescitur aura?'

x 636 sq.

dixerat, utque rudis primoque Cupidine tacta,
quid facit, ignorans, amat et non sentit amorem.

The 'quod facit' of the old editions amends the solecism but leaves the inappropriate verb, for *facio* = *patior* belongs to colloquial styles. 'quidque agat' Heinsius, 'quid uelit' Nick, 'dissidet' Korn, are all violent alterations: I propose 'quid fuat, ignorans': the changes of *u* to *a* and of *a* to *ci* ‖ are both common; the archaic form, imitated no doubt from Virgil, is at any rate no more surprising than 'moriri' in xiv 215; and the scribes who altered 'moriri' to 'morique' there were not likely to have more tolerance for 'fuat' here. It may be worth mentioning that 'qui foret, ignorans' occurs at xi 719.

x 731–3

sic fata cruorem
nectare odorato sparsit, qui tractus ab illo
intumuit.

For the 'tractus' of M the other MSS have 'tactus' which may be right. But *ra* is practically the same thing as *in*, and 'tinctus' appears to be supported by the parallel passage in iv 250 sqq. 'nectare odorato sparsit...*imbutum* caelesti nectare'. At Sen. *Phoen.* 257 the MSS vary between 'tinctas' and 'tractas'.

xi 180 sq.

ille quidem celare cupit, turpique pudore
tempora purpureis temptat uelare tiaris.

In this reading 'pudore' must mean 'through a sense of shame'; but it is admitted that the epithet 'turpi' has then no sense, unless like Riese in his former edition you invent a new one for the occasion, 'turpitudine moto'; for however disgraceful it may be to have the ears of an ass, to be ashamed of having them is not disgraceful but eminently natural. If 'pudore' could here signify, as at viii 157 and elsewhere, *a shameful thing, a dishonour*, then indeed would the epithet 'turpi' become appropriate; but this with the present text is impossible. To bring about the desired result the Italians of the renascence altered the MS reading, some of them very clumsily to 'turpemque pudorem' in apposition with 'tempora', others very audaciously to 'celat, turpique onerata pudore ‖ tempora' etc. which was long the vulgate.

This is critically a most instructive passage, because the change of a single word will so transmute the sentence that ‖ the whole trouble disappears, and yet the single word in question has every outward sign of soundness. What could look more beautifully appropriate than 'uelare'? yet emend it and see what happens:

> ille quidem celare cupit, turpique pudore
> tempora purpureis temptat releuare tiaris

'and essays to disembarrass his brows of their foul dishonour by means of a purple turban'. The syllable *re* is always falling out and here fell out the easier because *le* followed: just so at IX 318 N has *leuare* for *releuare*. Now the change from *leuare* to *uelare* is the same inversion precisely as VI 354 re*uel*are N for re*leu*are and XIV 97 *leu*ato M for *uel*atos: see also II 415 me*lan*on for mae*nal*on, III 725 ac*cip*e for as*pic*e, VI 556 for*pic*e for for*cip*e, XI 28 *num*era for *mun*era, 489 *reg*untur for *ger*untur, 506 sus*cip*ere for sus*pic*ere, XIII 731 re*mou*it for re*uom*it, XIV 86 ippo*dat*e for hippo*tad*ae, 89 i*ran*imen for i*nar*imen, XV 705 cau*nol*a for cau*lon*a, 818 *loc*etur for *col*atur.

XI 270–2

> hic regnum sine ui sine caede regebat
> Lucifero genitore satus patriumque nitorem
> ore ferens Ceyx.

Heinsius observed that *regnum rego* is not Ovidian Latin, and he proposed 'tenebat'; but much the easiest alteration to make will be 'gerebat'. The exchange of 'gero' and 'rego' is in Latin MSS what the exchange of βαλεῖν and λαβεῖν is in Greek, the commonest of those inversions of three letters which I have illustrated above: in this poem there are three more examples, VII 655, XI 489, XV 834.

There is a fellow to our passage in Sen. *Phaedr.* 617 sqq.

> mandata recipe sceptra, me famulam accipe.
> te imperia regere, me decet iussa exsequi:
> muliebre non est regna tutari urbium.

'imperia regere' is rendered so peculiarly obnoxious by the occurrence of 'ciues imperio rege' three lines further on that ‖ Peiper and Leo expel verse 618 from the text. For 'regere' write 'gerere'.

XI 523

> fulmineis ardescunt ignibus ignes.

The verse, describing a storm at sea, stands thus in M: the inferior MSS amend the obvious corruption of the last word by the rough conjecture 'undae'. Write 'imbres': the same error is found in Lucr. 1 784 sq., Catull. 62 7, Tibull. 1 1 48, and elsewhere.

XII 24–6

> permanet Aoniis Nereus uiolentus in undis
> bellaque non transfert; et sunt qui parcere Troiae
> Neptunum credant, quia moenia fecerat urbi.

The god of the sea should not be called Nereus in one breath and Neptunus in the next; nor has 'permanet Nereus' any significance, since Nereus always 'permanet', storm or no storm: I suppose Ovid would hardly say 'permanet uiolentus' for 'permanet in uiolentia'. The letters of 'nereus' come by customary changes from those of 'boreas', πνοαὶ ἀπὸ Cτρυμόνος μολοῦσαι as Aeschylus says: 'eurus' would be less accurate and further from the MSS.

XIII 601–3

corruit igne rogus nigrique uolumina fumi
infecere diem, ueluti cum flumina natas
exhalant nebulas, nec sol admittitur infra.

Anything more wretched than 'natas' I never read; and when our best authority does not give the passage thus, why should we endure it? M omits 602 and reads 'uolumine' in 601 and 'exalat' in 603. The omission is a mere blunder due to the likeness of the penultimate words in 601 and 602; but 'exalat' requires attention, and the error 'uolumine' might suggest that in 602 the exemplar had not 'flumina' but 'flumine'. If then we try what can be done with 'ueluti cum flumine natas | exhalat nebulas' it is clear that NATAS conceals a nominative singular: this can be nothing but NAIAS. Ovid of course spelt the word ǁ 'Nais', but the scribes have again introduced the longer form against metre at XIV 557 and 786.

XIII 724–7

tribus haec excurrit in aequora pinnis,
e quibus imbriferos est uersa Pachynos ad austros,
mollibus expositum zephyris Lilybaeon, ad arctos
aequoris expertes spectat boreamque Peloros.

All editors read 726 thus; 'expositum' however has but poor MS authority, as both M and N have 'impositum'. Ovid wrote neither, but 'oppositum': *op* was lost before *po* as again at XIV 768 where N has 'positas' for 'oppositas': then to fill out the metre some copyists borrowed *im* from 'imbriferos' just above and others *ex* from 'expertes' just below. Compare Catull. 26 1 sq. 'uillula uostra non ad austri | flatus opposita est.'

XIV 200

crudelesque manus et inanem luminis orbem.

This is a faultless verse and may very well be what Ovid wrote. But M has 'orbum' for 'orbem'; and as 'luminis orbus' is an Ovidian phrase, recurring at III 517 sq., XIV 189 and *Ibis* 258 [260], it is also possible that this should be retained and 'inanem' altered into a substantive. Now the terminations -*nem* and -*men* are much confounded, in 'crinem' and 'crimen' for instance; and *ia* is much like *lu*: the original then may have been 'lumen luminis orbum' *his eye bereft of eyesight*, which whether right or wrong is Ovid all over: compare I 720 'quodque in tot *lumina lumen* habebas | extinctum est'.

XV 622–5

pandite nunc Musae, praesentia numina uatum,
(scitis enim, nec uos fallit spatiosa uetustas)
unde Coroniden circumflua Thybridis alti
insula Romuleae sacris adgeicerit urbis.

Any attempt to amend 625 must rest on the 'adgeicerit' of h, our best MS for this book: a comparison of this with the 'deiecerat' of Priscian where he quotes this verse puts entirely out of court the 'accerserit' or 'arcesserit' of some ‖ MSS which has come from 640, the 'accesserit' of others which is a corruption of that, and the 'acciuerit' of others yet. Palaeographically then nothing could be better than Riese's 'adiecerit', but this is not a very appropriate verb, and is now abandoned by its author. I propose 'adlegerit': the word is a rare one, LEG is readily confused with IEC, and the reading of h seems to come from a superscript G intended to repair this mistake. See Sen. *Ag.* 813 sq. 'meruit...adlegi caelo magnus Alcides.'

21

THE NEW FRAGMENT OF EURIPIDES*

* [*Academy* 1891, March 14 p. 259, March 28 p. 305]

[I]

The fragment of the *Antiope* published by Prof. Mahaffy in the last number of *Hermathena* is emended in this month's *Classical Review* by two distinguished Grecians. Their emendations are numerous and intrepid. Dr Rutherford 'would restore' to Euripides the senarius σὺ μὲν χερῶν τὸ πνεῦμ' ἐκ πολεμίων λαβών, which Euripides, I think, would restore to Dr Rutherford. Prof. Campbell proposes to enrich the tragic vocabulary by the importation of ἄχρι, in accordance with his opinion that it is not yet 'time to cease from guessing and to begin the sober work of criticism'. When that time arrives it will occur to someone that l. 18 of fragment C [35 p. 20 Arnim, 59 p. 66 Page], ὁλκοῖς γε ταυρείοισιν διαφερουμένη, is neither verse nor Greek, and should be amended ταυρείοισι διαφορουμένη: there is, of course, no such verb as διαφερῶ. It surprised me that the first editor did not correct this obvious blunder, and I looked to see it removed by the first critic who took the fragment in hand; but our scholars seem just now to be absorbed in more exhilarating sport, so I will perform this menial office, at the risk of incurring Prof. Campbell's censure for premature sobriety.

[II]

If Prof. Campbell will turn to v. 1100 of the *Aiax* of Sophocles, he will see what comes of assuming that any correction, however trivial, can be 'too much a matter of course to be worth mentioning'. He will find that he and his brother-editors – Dindorf, Wunder, Schneidewin, Nauck, Jebb, Blaydes, Wecklein, Paley, and, in short, the whole goodly fellowship – have printed in that verse the non-existent word λεῶν. They mean it for the gen. plur. of λεώς; but the gen. plur. of λεώς is λεών. And it looks as if another false accentuation were about to gain a foothold in our fragment of Euripides. The text is given in *Hermathena* without accents or breathings, but Frag. B has been twice invested with these perhaps superfluous ornaments – in the *Athenaeum* of January 31, and again by Prof. Campbell in the *Classical Review* for March; and in both places v. 4 [4 p. 18 Arnim, 4 p. 62 Page] begins with ἴκται. Now ἴκται is the nom. plur. of ἴκτης, and makes no sense whatever: the word meant is ἵκται. The reason why I do not descend so far as to correct the spelling of vv. 40 ⟦57 p. 21 Arnim, 78 p. 68 Page⟧ and 57 ⟦74 Arnim, 95 Page⟧ in Frag. C is that Nauck or Wecklein, whichever gets hold of the fragment first, can be trusted not to miss the chance of observing 'ἄστεως scripsi' and 'εὐνατήριον scripsi', and they derive more pleasure from these achievements than I do.

The further fragments of Prof. Campbell's *Antiope* (a drama which I much admire and hope to see completed), published in last week's *Academy*, have been slightly corrupted by the scribes, and I would venture to restore the poet's hand by the following emendations: for ποῦσθ' read ποῦ 'σθ', for στεγή read στέγη, for ἔνοντας read ἐνόντας, and for ἰθαγένους read ἰθαγενοῦς.

22

ADVERSARIA ORTHOGRAPHICA*

I

Nothing is much better known in the province of Plautine metric than H. A. Koch's paper in the *Neue Jahrbuecher* for 1870, vol. 101, headed *uoxor = uxor* There are ten or twelve verses in Plautus, spoilt by hiatus as they stand, which would be rid of this disfigurement if *uxor* began with a consonant: in such places Koch would introduce the form *uoxor*, which is actually proffered by B, the codex uetus Camerarii, at *truc.* 515 and *trin.* 800. Ritschl in the preface to his second edition of the *trinummus* praises the ingenuity of this suggestion and suspends judgment; but I do not encounter the apparition of *uoxor* in any text published during the twenty years since 1870, and here I shall attempt to lay the ghost, for a ghost it is.

The two verses in which B gives the form are these:

truc. 515
Márs peregre adueniéns salutat Nérienem *uxorém* suam.
trin. 800
uxorem quoque ipsam hanc rem ut celes face.

This is of course corrupt, and Ritschl writes:

uxórem quoque eampse hánc rem uti celés face.

uoxorem B in both places.

Now even if we concede to Koch that Plautus wrote *uoxor* in other verses, where it does not appear, it nevertheless is quite certain that in these two verses, where it does appear, he did not write it. In *truc.* 515 it will not scan, and there is an end of the matter. In *trin.* 800 it makes no difference to the scansion, and there is an end of the matter again. For after we have fathered *uoxor* on Plautus as often as Mr Koch desires there will still remain a great majority of instances where *uxor* alone is admitted by the metre; and this means that *uxor* was the normal form with Plautus, and that *uoxor*, if he employed it at all, he employed for metrical convenience only. But for metrical convenience he cannot have employed it at *trin.* 800, since it commences the verse. How strange now is this: that *uoxor*, which has thrust itself into two verses where Plautus did not write it, should have vanished from a dozen verses where he did.

* ⟦*CR* 5 (1891), 293–6⟧

But what then is *uoxorem*? for there it stands in B. VOXOREM is the ghost of VCXOREM. There are four ways of spelling this word, *uxor*, *ucxor*, *uxsor*, *ucxsor*; but if we want to find the three last forms preserved we must go to stone records or the best and most ancient of our MSS. In Virgil we have *georg.* IV. 491 *respecxit* M, *Aen.* I. 108, 109 *sacxa* c, 398 *cincxere* G, II. 56 *arcx* M², IV. 682 *extincxti* M², XII. 353 *prospecxit* M, 671 *respecxit* M, 734 *aspecxit* M, and XI. 860 *duxsit* P, XII. 266 *dixsit* P, 300 *reluxsit* P. But in MSS less excellent than Virgil's it is rare to find these forms intact, as at Lucr. III. 1044 *restincxit* A (oblongus), Ovid *met.* I. 353 *iuncxit* Mλ, II. 554 *texsta* λ. Never doubt that other writers used them as often as Virgil; but their scribes have substituted simple *x* when they recognised what was meant. Here and || there however they have not recognised this, and we may detect the old orthography under some such disguise as *uoxorem*. Thus in Hor. *serm.* I. 2, 47 I would write *mercx* for *mercs* Bφλ, in Sen. *Oed.* 227 and *Ag.* 562 *arcx* for *arsx* E. In Prop. IV. 4, 10 we have the variants *facta* O, *saxa* N, in Ovid *met.* II. 326 *fa∗tum* (*factum*) N, *saxum* cett., in XIII. 567 *iactum* MN, *saxum* cett.: write *sacxa* and *sacxum*. In Catull. 68, 143 Schwabe restores *dexstra* for the *deastra* of V; and at 64, 237 of the same poet I think I see a similar form under a deeper disguise. Aegeus charges his son to hoist white sails if he return –

> quam primum cernens ut laeta gaudia mente
> agnoscam, cum te reducem aetas prospera sistet.

I do not flatter myself with the hope of many converts, so I will be brief, and will merely refer to Baehrens for the objections to *aetas*, which Avantius very suitably replaces by *fors*. Now *fors* is not at all like *aetas* but very like *pros*: it may be then that *aetas prospera* is an attempt to emend *pros aetaspera*, which in its turn is a letter-for-letter corruption of *fors decxstera*.

II

Virgil *Aen.* VII. 703–5:

> nec quisquam aeratas acies ex agmine tanto
> misceri putet, aeriam sed gurgite ab alto
> urgueri uolucrum raucarum ad litora nubem.

'*ex agmine tanto* seems to go with *misceri*, to be made up, or massed, out of that great multitude: a poetical variety for *hoc agmen tantum aeratas acies esse*' Conington. These are two explanations, not one; they are irreconcilable with one another, and they are both untenable. The former renders the Latin correctly and is nonsense: there is no difficulty at all in believing that armed ranks can be made up out of a great multitude: the difficulty is to believe that the multitude can be made up out of armed ranks. The second explanation gives the sense needed, the sense of the Greek original οὐδέ κε φαίης | τόσσον νηίτην στόλον ἔμμεναι, ἀλλ' οἰωνῶν | ἰλαδὸν ἄσπετον ἔθνος ἐπιβρομέειν πελάγεσσιν, but obtains it by ignoring *ex*: 'hoc agmen tantum aeratas acies esse' is the equivalent of 'aeratas acies agmine tanto misceri', 'that those who are mingling together in such a multitude are armed ranks', which is not what we have in the text. Ladewig expounds 'dass aus einer solchen Masse sich eherne Schaaren bilden und mit dem Feinde handgemein werden würden': except for the wealth of inappropriate meaning bestowed on *misceri* this is the former of the two explanations confused by Conington.

Now turn to *Aen.* II. 725–8:

> ferimur per opaca locorum;
> et me, quem dudum non ulla iniecta mouebant
> tela neque aduerso glomerati ex agmine Grai,
> nunc omnes terrent aurae.

Heyne, Wagner, and Ladewig give what I conceive to be the correct translation of 'aduerso glomerati ex agmine Grai': 'a troop of Greeks collected out of the hostile army'. But other editors feel, what is very true, that this falls far beneath the sense required; so once again they ignore *ex* and render 'the hostile mass of Greeks', *i.e.* 'aduerso glomerati agmine Grai'. Twice over then, it seems, has Virgil written *ex* where he did not mean it. Why, in both these places, does the word which follows happen to be *agmine*? The coincidence is the key to the riddle.

Of Virgil's capital MSS *Aen.* II. 727 is contained in two, MP, VII. 703 in three, MPR. All these, after the wont of capital MSS, are written without punctuation or interspaces between word and word. P has been sparsely pointed by a later hand: R is profusely besprinkled, also by a later hand, with dots which often fall in the most absurd situations; but as originally written these MSS offer in each line an unbroken row of equidistant letters. The difficulty therefore of these two verses lies wholly at the door of the editors or the scribes of later MSS. The reading of the capital codices in both lines is EXAGMINE, and it is perfectly right: 'aduerso glomerati *exagmine* Grai': 'aeratas acies *exagmine* tanto | misceri'. *exagmen* is the word with which we are more familiar in the form *examen*. The older spelling is preserved or indicated by M or by γ in the following passages: *buc.* IX. 30 *exacmina* M, *georg.* II. 452 *exacmine* M, IV. 21 *exagmina* M, 103 *exagmina* γ, *exacmina* M, *Aen.* XII. 725 *exagmine* γ. The other MSS have in those places substituted the common form, and the only reason why *exagmine* has survived in *Aen.* II. 727 and VII. 703 is that the || context led the obtuse copyists to mistake the end of the word for *agmine*. But they were not all obtuse, and at VII. 703 two late codices, the Leidensis and the Hamburgensis alter, put the editors of Virgil to shame by writing *examine*.

An exact parallel to these phenomena appears in *Aen.* III. 483 'picturatas auri subtegmine uestes': *subtegmine* G, *subtecmine* Mγb, *subtemine* Pac: the simple Servius regardless of sense and deaf to admonition observes '*sub tegmine*... nam male quidam *subtemen* stamen accipiunt.'

III

Ovid *trist.* IV. 10, 95 sq.:

<blockquote>
postque meos ortus Pisaea uinctus oliua
abstulerat deciens praemia uictor eques.
</blockquote>

There were no jockeys at Olympia, so *eques* is wrong, and Bentley at Hor. *carm.* IV. 2, 17 restores *equus*, shewing after Spanheim from Theocritus and Plutarch that the winning horses in the chariot-race were crowned with wreaths. But the corruption *eques* means that Ovid wrote *equos*, as I can prove by adducing the very passage from which he borrowed *uictor equos*, spelling and all: Prop. II. 34, 38 'tristia ad Archemori funera *uictor equos*', for so the MSS give it. That Ovid sometimes at any rate employed this form of the nom. sing. we know chiefly from the codex reginensis of the *fasti* which offers III. 228 *auos*, 273 *riuos*,

IV. 46 *auos*, 824 and 836 *nouos*: at II. 316 it has *riuu̯es*, i.e. *riu̯os*; also *soluont* at IV. 333: the Harleian at *met.* II. 186 has *suos* and at 456 *riuos*, the Amplonianus prior *flauos* at III. 617: at XIV. 589 for *paruum* the Marcianus has *paruo*, i.e. *paruom*. This *uo* is presented by the MSS not of Augustan writers merely but even of Martial: therefore when in [Sen.] *Herc. Oet.* 1219 we find *reuulsus* in E and the corruption *reuersus* in A we need not doubt that the common origin of both was *reuolsus*. Nor is Ovid *trist.* IV. 10, 96 the only place where a puzzled scribe has changed *equos* to *eques*: Prop. IV. 10, 19 will furnish another example, though to discuss that passage would involve a long digression. But lest any one at Hor. *epod.* 16, 12 'urbem | *eques* sonante uerberabit ungula' should be tempted to propose an alteration because the hoof is the horse's and not the horseman's, I would point out that the MS reading is defended by Virg. *georg.* III. 116 sq. 'equitem docuere sub armis | insultare solo et gressus glomerare superbos' and Luc. VI. 81 sqq. 'pabula terrae, | quae currens obtriuit eques, gradibusque cita-tis | ungula frondentem discussit cornea campum.' There is however I believe in the text of Horace at least one place where the termination -*u̯os*, which his MSS so often preserve, still lurks undetected: *carm.* IV. 7, 14 sqq.:

<blockquote>
nos, ubi decidimus,
quo pius Aeneas, quo Tullus diues et Ancus,
puluis et umbra sumus.
</blockquote>

Whether *diues* belongs to Tullus or to Ancus it is the least appropriate epithet which the Latin vocabulary contains, for both these kings are expressly cited by

Juvenal v. 57 as examples of antique poverty. I would write *saeuos*, and trace the corruption through *saluos aluos diuos*. It may be that Juvenal's 'Tulli census *pugnacis* et Anci' comes from this very line.

IV

At Lucr. I. 125 'lacrimas effundere salsas' the oblongus (A) has *effundere*, the quadratus (B) *et fundere*. Lachmann observes '*ecfundere* libri nostri non exhibent: horum autem scribendi rationem reddere satis habeo.' But neither do the MSS of Catullus exhibit this form; yet when they offer *et futura* at 6, 13 it is Lachmann himself who restores *ecfututa*, and rightly. Only once even in Virgil is *ec* preserved, *Aen.* IX. 632 *ecfugit* b, where PRγ²c accordingly give *etfugit* and Servius attests *et fugit*; Ribbeck however restores it at *Aen.* VII. 440 where M has *etfeta*, and it ought to be restored also at *georg.* IV. 450 *etfatus* M, *Aen.* II. 657 *etferre* M, v. 317 *etfusi* M, XII. 499 *etfundit* P. Therefore at Lucr. VI. 258, where the MSS give *et fertus* and the sense demands Lachmann's *effertus*, the form indicated is surely *ecfertus*. But if I. 125 and VI. 258 are not thought evidence enough for *ec* in Lucretius I bring forward a stronger proof. The verse I. 70 is preserved by Priscian p. 879 [*GLK* vol. ii p. 499] in the form 'inritat animi uirtutem *effringere* ut arta', but the MSS of Lucretius give *confringere* against metre: why? because he wrote *ecfringere* and *ec* was mistaken for *cō*.

Restore *ec* again in Ovid *met.* II. 144 *et fulget* MSS, *effulget* Heinsius, Pers. III. 20 *et fluis* α C, *effluis* B, Juv. IX. 150 *et fugit* P, *effugit* ω. In Hor. *ars* 111 we have the variants *effert* α γ C δ ε L u v, *efferet* B, *et certi* R φ ψ λ l z π: write *ecfert*.

Sometimes *ec* is deeper concealed. Hor. ‖ *epist.* I. 10, 9 'quae uos ad caelum *fertis* rumore secundo' most MSS, *effertis* V and some others: Pauly has seen that this means *ecfertis*: it has been modernised on the one hand to *effertis*, on the other it has been corrupted as usual to *et fertis* and *et* has then been thrown away because it gave no sense. Turn to Prop. III. 9, 9 and you have the same variation: 'gloria Lysippo est animosa *effingere* signa' N, *fingere* O: write *ecfingere*. Ovid *met.* I. 71 'sidera coeperunt toto *efferuescere* caelo' M, *feruescere* λ, *ecferuescere* Ovid; Sen. *Thy.* 987 sq. 'admotus ipsis Bacchus a labris fugit | circaque rictus ore decepto *effluit*' A, *fluit* E, *ecfluit* Seneca.

All this will serve as preface to the consideration of Hor. *serm.* II. 3, 171 sqq.:

postquam te talos, Aule, nucesque
ferre sinu laxo, donare et ludere uidi,
te, Tiberi, numerare, cauis abscondere tristem,
extimui, ne uos ageret insania discors,
tu Nomentanum, tu ne sequerere Cicutam.
quare per diuos oratus uterque penates
tu caue ne minuas, tu ne maius facias id
quod satis esse putat pater et natura coercet.

On this passage the editors continue to comment as if they had not read Bentley, nay as if they had not read Horace. I do not wish to be unfair, so I will quote one of the best among their number: '*ludere*, gamble; sc. *iis* with them, in which there would be the risk of losing them – a risk the cautious brother would not face.' This father then is alarmed for Aulus' future and fears he will prove a spendthrift, because the boy applies nuts and knucklebones to the very use for which boys have nuts and knucklebones given them! Then again: 'a risk the cautious brother would not face'; 'the serious Tiberius would not gamble at all'. Indeed? then how was he to swell his hoard? and if he did not swell his hoard what makes his father afraid 'ne maius faciat id quod satis esse' etc.? and wherein resides his likeness to Cicuta? Cicuta gambled: he was a money-lender, and therefore a gambler by profession. Briefly *ludere* is impossible for two reasons: it signifies that Tiberius did not play, which is false, and that Aulus ought not to have played, which is false again. Bentley, who demonstrated this, offered only the hasty conjecture *perdere*: I believe that ETLVDERE stands for ETFVDERE, in which we shall now recognise *ecfundere*; and *effundere* has already been proposed by Hamacher.

V

Cicero, says Quintilian, wrote *aiio* and *Maiia*, and so did many others beside Cicero; the scribes however view the practice with disfavour, and these forms have seldom escaped them except in masquerade. The following are passages where they have not yet been stripped of the disguises which saved them.

Hor. *epist.* I. 15, 45 'uos sapere et solos *aio* bene uiuere', *alio* φ ψ λ l z ε π L: write *aiio*, comparing Lucr. I. 477 where Lachmann restores *Graiiugenarum* from the *Graliugenar* of A.

Sen. *Tro.* 69 sq. 'ex quo tetigit | Phrygius *Graias* hospes Amyclas', *gratias* excerpt. Thu.: write *Graiias*. So in Catull. 66, 58 Baehrens restores *Graiia* for *gratia*, and I have pointed out elsewhere that in Prop. IV. 1, 7 the *Tarpetius* of N means *Tarpeiius*.

Sen. *Tro.* 146 sq. 'nec feret umquam | uicta *Graium* ceruice iugum', *granum* excerpt. Thu.: write *Graiium*, and see Virg. *Aen.* VII. 386 where γ has *manus*, i.e. *maiius*, for *maius*. At Sen. *Tro.* 551 'libera *Graios*' there is the variant *nos*, which signifies that an original *Graiios* was corrupted to *granos*, and *gra* absorbed by the preceding *era*.

Pers. v. 147 '*Veientanum*que rubellum', *Vellentanum* C: write *Veiientanum*: at Juv. IV. 113, where this MS gives *Vellento*, Buecheler has observed that *Veiiento* is indicated; and in Prop. IV. 4, 1 and 15 I have restored *Tarpeiiae* and *Tarpeiia* for the *Tarpelle* and *Carpella* of F.

Juv. IV. 13 sq. 'nam quod turpe bonis Titio *serio*que decebat | Crispinum': Calderinus emends *Seio*; but write *Seiio*.

23

THE *OEDIPVS COLONEVS*
OF SOPHOCLES*

263-9

κἄμοιγε ποῦ ταῦτ' ἐστίν; οἵτινες βάθρων
ἐκ τῶνδέ μ' ἐξάραντες εἶτ' ἐλαύνετε
ὄνομα μόνον δείσαντες· οὐ γὰρ δὴ τό γε   265
σῶμ' οὐδὲ τἄργα τἄμ'· ἐπεὶ τά γ' ἔργα μου
πεπονθότ' ἐστὶ μᾶλλον ἢ δεδρακότα,
εἰ σοι τὰ μητρὸς καὶ πατρὸς χρείη λέγειν,
ὧν εἵνεκ' ἐκφοβεῖ με.

So long as vv. 266 sq. stand in every edition of Sophocles as they stand above I hardly comprehend why the editors should alter the MS reading anywhere. Once let me steel myself to endure ἔργα πεπονθότα μᾶλλον ἢ δεδρακότα and the scribes might do their worst: I could always murmur τέτλαθι δή, κραδίη· καὶ κύντερον ἄλλο ποτ' ἔτλης. The sense is to be Shakespeare's 'I am a man more sinned against than sinning': that the Greek words may yield it, either τὰ ἔργα μου must mean ἐγώ, or else πεπονθότα μᾶλλον ἢ δεδρακότα must mean ὑπενηνεγμένα μᾶλλον ἢ δεδραμένα or, as some prefer to put it, πεπονθότος μᾶλλον ἢ δεδρακότος. To state such propositions is to explode them, one would fancy; yet they are entertained, because critics will acquiesce in solecisms which they think they cannot emend: durum, sed leuius fit patientia quidquid corrigere est nefas. The correction here, though simple, is not obvious, so the editors, instead of resolving to find it, content themselves with collecting what they take for parallels; and a survey of the collection will suggest that their discriminating faculties have been a trifle numbed, as is not surprising, by the Gorgonian terrors of their text. ‖

I have first to clear the air of matter so irrelevant that I cannot even guess by what confusion of thought it is brought into this connexion. A common method of forming abstract substantives in Greek is to prefix the article to the neuter of an adjective: ἀνδρεῖος *courageous*, τὸ ἀνδρεῖον *courage*. Participles are adjectives, and from them, as from other adjectives, abstract substantives are formed by this

* [*AJPh* 13 (1892), 139–70: the Corrigenda (*AJPh* 13 (1892), 398) have been, where possible, silently incorporated in the text]

method: θαρσῶν *confident*, τὸ θαρσοῦν *confidence*. Thus Sophocles at Phil. 674 sq. has τὸ νοσοῦν *sickness*, Euripides or his interpolator at I. A. 1270 τὸ κείνου βουλόμενον *his wish*; in Thucydides examples are frequent, I 36 τὸ δεδιὸς αὐτοῦ and τὸ θαρσοῦν *apprehension* and *confidence*, 90 τὸ βουλόμενον καὶ ὕποπτον (the participle side by side with another adjective which is not a participle) τῆς γνώμης *wish* and *suspicion*, II 59 τὸ ὀργιζόμενον τῆς γνώμης *irritation*, III 10 ἐν τῷ διαλλάσσοντι τῆς γνώμης *change*, v 9 τοῦ μένοντος *stand*, VI 24 τὸ ἐπιθυμοῦν τοῦ πλοῦ *eagerness*, VII 68 τῆς γνώμης τὸ θυμούμενον *fury*. Accordingly, when the MSS of Sophocles give τὸ ποθοῦν at Trach. 196, that, though it makes no sense in its context, is Greek for *desire*; and if at O. C. 1604 they gave what they do not give, τοῦ δρῶντος, that would be Greek for *activity*. The reader will be asking me what all this has to do with the matter in hand; and truly I do not know. But Prof. Campbell, in the essay on the language of Sophocles prefixed to his edition, adduces several of these examples and then bewilders me by proceeding thus, 'In the following instances the action is similarly identified with the agent or subject, although a *state* is not described': here follows our passage. Similarly identified! τὸ μὲν ἐπιθυμοῦν τοῦ πλοῦ οὐκ ἐξῃρέθησαν *they were not deprived of their eagerness for the voyage*: is the action (or the state) here identified with the agent or subject? does it mean *they were not deprived of themselves*? Yet Prof. Jebb says the same thing over again: 'The agent's activities (τὰ ἔργα μου) here stand for the agent himself... *So* [my italics] a particular activity of a person's mind is sometimes expressed by the active participle (neut.) of a verb to which the person himself would properly be subject'; and he quotes Thuc. I 36, 90, II 59, given above. I cannot even conjecture where the analogy is imagined to lie. Is it meant that in Thuc. II 59, for instance, 'the agent's activities stand for the agent himself', and that ἀπαγαγὼν τὸ ὀργιζόμενον τῆς γνώμης *having removed the irritation of their mind* stands for ἀπαγαγὼν αὐτοὺς ὀργιζομένους? I suppose not; and yet, if not, what are these quotations doing in a note which professes to show that τὰ ἔργα μου means ἐγώ? ‖

A traditional parallel is O. t. 1214 sq. γάμον τεκνοῦντα καὶ τεκνούμενον; and though it is not really a parallel, it is nevertheless an analogous phenomenon. τεκνοῦντα καὶ τεκνούμενον *begetter and begotten in one* are words properly applicable to Oedipus himself, and not to his marriage, yet to his marriage they are applied; similarly, it may be said, πεπονθότα and δεδρακότα, though properly applicable only to Oedipus himself, can be applied to his deeds. But, in the first place, if you mean to match the absurdity of ἔργα δεδρακότα, γάμος τεκνούμενος will not serve: it asks nothing short of γάμος γεγαμηκώς. And, secondly, it is no private suspicion of mine, but the general opinion, that O. t. 1214 is corrupt. The whole passage runs thus: ἐφηῦρέ σ᾽ ἄκονθ᾽ ὁ πάνθ᾽ ὁρῶν χρόνος. | δικάζει τὸν ἄγαμον γάμον πάλαι | τεκνοῦντα καὶ τεκνούμενον. This breakneck asyndeton is accepted, I think, by no modern editor but Prof. Jebb. The vulgate is Hermann's δικάζει τ' ἄγαμον, which rids us indeed of the asyndeton, but defaces the metre in the process. I have little doubt that the truth has been recovered by Prof. Campbell, δικάζει τ' ἐν ἀγάμῳ γάμῳ (perhaps -οις -οις) πάλαι κτλ. With τ' ἐν once altered to τὸν, the other change would follow easily; and now the anomalies of diction and connexion disappear together. But even in its corrupt form, as I said above, the phrase was not a parallel to ἔργα δεδρακότα.

Now turning from the attempts to make τὰ ἔργα μου mean ἐγώ, I approach the attempts to make πεπονθότα μᾶλλον ἢ δεδρακότα mean ὑπενηνεγμένα (or πεπονθότος) μᾶλλον ἢ δεδραμένα (or δεδρακότος); and here again there is confusion to be dispelled. There exists in Greek, as in other languages, a cata-chresis of the participle which is well illustrated by El. 1231 γεγηθὸς ἕρπει δάκρυον ὀμμάτων ἄπο. The tear does not rejoice: the participle means not *rejoicing* but *betokening joy*: we render in English *a tear of joy*. In this modified sense participles signifying any mental state are placed in agreement with substantives signifying any sign of that mental state, oftenest with substantives meaning *words*: Phil. 1045 sq. βαρεῖαν ὁ ξένος φάτιν | τήνδ' εἶπ', Ὀδυσσεῦ, κοὐχ ὑπείκουσαν κακοῖς *showing a spirit that does not yield*, O.C. 74 ὅσ' ἂν λέγωμεν, πάνθ' ὁρῶντα λέξομεν *words of a seeing soul*, 1281 sq. ῥήματ' ἢ τέρψαντά τι | ἢ δυσχεράναντ' ἢ κατοικτίσαντά πως *evincing anger or pity*;[1] and finite verbs are also thus employed, as at Aesch. sept. 425 ὁ κόμπος δ' οὐ κατ' ἄνθρωπον φρονεῖ, Eur. Cycl. 58 sq. ποθοῦσί σ' || ἀμερόκοιτοι βλαχαὶ σμικρῶν τεκέων. On this analogy ἔργα μαινόμενα would be Greek for *acts of a madman*, *acts bewraying madness*: thus we find ὁρμῇ and ἔριδι and ἐλπίδι μαινομένη. Whether ἔργα πεπονθότα will thus have anything to be called a meaning I hardly feel sure and do not stay to consider, because about ἔργα δεδρακότα at least there can be no mistake. δεδρακώς and participles of that signification are never thus used, because the occasion for such use can never arise; and if they were thus used they still could not be joined to ἔργα or substantives of that significa-tion except to raise a laugh. γεγηθὸς δάκρυον justifies ἔργα μαινόμενα: it will be time to think of ἔργα δεδρακότα when they find us γεγηθυῖα γηθοσύνη.

Mr Blaydes quotes μαινομένοις ἄχεσιν from Aiax 957 ἦ ῥα κελαινώπαν θυμὸν ἐφυβρίζει | πολύτλας ἀνήρ, | γελᾷ δὲ τοῖς μαινομένοις ἄχεσιν | πολὺν γέλωτα. If this phrase were sound it would be extraordinary, although no parallel to ἔργα δεδρακότα: that wants μαινομέναις μανίαις. But turn to Mr Blaydes' own edition of the Aiax and we find him writing 'The expression μαινομένοις ἄχεσιν has always seemed to me open to suspicion': 'mit Grund' says Nauck. I conceive there is a sense in which the words are Greek: the imaginary woes of a madman who fancies that he has committed the Unpardonable Sin, or that he is an hourglass

---

[1] I assume for the nonce, with most editors, what I think very doubtful, that these two verbs are not transitive.

which wants inverting because its sand has run through, are μαινόμενα ἄχη *woes arguing madness*. But the participle cannot signify, as the scholiast would have it and as the context requires, διὰ τὴν μανίαν συμβεβηκόσιν, the dishonour and death of Aiax brought to pass by his frenzy. Now, no editor reads this verse as it runs in the MSS, for it fails to answer the strophic 911 ἐγὼ δ᾽ ὁ πάντα κωφὸς ὁ πάντ᾽ ἄιδρις: they alter τοῖς either to τοῖσι, with Triclinius, or better, with Elmsley, to τοῖσδε. When a verse presents false metre and anomalous phrase together it appears to crave an emendation emending both, such as γελᾷ δὲ τοῖσδ᾽ ἰαινόμενός γ᾽ ἄχεσιν | πολὺν γέλωτα: γε marks the ascent from less to greater, as in Ar. ran. 562 ἔβλεψεν ἔς με δριμὺ κἀμυκᾶτό γε, Soph. Phil. 1296, etc.: δ is early confused with λ, and λι later with μ: observe that Tecmessa replies 961 οἱ δ᾽ οὖν γελώντων κἀπιχαιρόντων κακοῖς | τοῖς τοῦδ᾽. But take this conjecture or leave it, μαινομένοις ἄχεσιν falls short of ἔργα δεδρακότα.

They quote O. C. 239 sq. ἔργων ἀκόντων and 977 ἄκον πρᾶγμα where ἄκων has the sense *unintentional* which is commonly expressed by ἀκούσιος. But how naturally ἄκων assumes this meaning, if indeed it does not rather possess it by nature, may be || seen from the identical use of the corresponding words in Latin and English: Ovid ex Pont. II 1, 16 writes 'inuita saepe iuuamur ope' *a boon not meant for me*, and we talk of an unwitting injury or an unwilling consent. And still more striking in this connexion is the fact that just as Sophocles uses ἄκων for ἀκούσιος, so does he use ἑκούσιος conversely for ἑκών: Phil. 617 sq. οἴοιτο μὲν μάλισθ᾽ ἑκούσιον λαβών, | εἰ μὴ θέλοι δ᾽, ἄκοντα and Trach. 1123 οἷς θ᾽ ἥμαρτεν οὐχ ἑκουσία. If, then, ἔργων ἀκόντων justified ἔργα δεδρακότα = ἔργα δεδραμένα, ἥμαρτεν οὐχ ἑκουσία would equally justify ὁ δρασθείς = ὁ δράσας; but, since the copyists do not happen to have soiled our texts with this solecism, it will not find defenders.

Then they quote τὸν εὖ πράττοντα τοῖχον from Ar. ran. 536 sq. μετακυλίνδειν αὐτὸν ἀεὶ | πρὸς τὸν εὖ πράττοντα τοῖχον *the prosperous side of the ship*, i.e. the side where the sailors are prosperous. Why this is cited, and why, if cited, it is cited alone out of the scores and hundreds of passages where the character of a place's tenants is given to the place, I will not try to divine. If this is a parallel, the literature teems with parallels: Eur. Alc. 566 sq. τἀμὰ δ᾽ οὐκ ἐπίσταται | μέλαθρ᾽ ἀπωθεῖν οὐδ᾽ ἀτιμάζειν ξένους, etc., etc.: any one who cared could fill a book with them. Sophocles himself has a very curious instance which I benevolently proffer to the editors, not indeed as apposite, but as less strangely inapposite than most of their citations: frag. 176 ⟦174 Pearson⟧ εὐναῖος εἴη δραπέτιν στέγην ἔχων *a runaway abode*, i.e. a hare's form. And finally they quote a phrase occurring in Libanius' declamation Φιλάργυρος ἀποκηρύττει, vol. IV, p. 626, 22, ed. Reiske ⟦vol. vii p. 87 Foerster⟧, λαμβάνων, αἰτῶν, εἰσπράττων, ἀγείρων, πάντα εἰς τὴν κερδαίνουσαν πήραν ὠθεῖν ἀξιῶν and explained by the Phrynichus Bekkeri anecd. Gr., vol. I, p. 39, 27 εἰς τὴν κερδαίνουσαν πάντα ὠθεῖν πήραν· τὸ ἐκ παντὸς τρόπου κερδαίνειν σημαίνει. Because the pouch into which gains are put is called *the gain-getting pouch*, therefore *my deeds have suffered rather than acted* means... I discern no end to the sentence.

Behold the evidence on which contemporary commentators take τὰ ἔργα μου for ἐγώ and active participles for passive! More will be forthcoming, never fear, when the conservatives find the text assailed and fly to arms in its defence; and, of course, I can no more foresee their next array of parallels than I could have foreseen the medley which I have here been trying to sort for them. But there occurs now and again, both in Greek and in Latin, an idiom which will hardly escape their notice in the general ransack; and on this I will put in a word beforehand. It ‖ is not frequent, and some apparent instances are, in my judgment, corrupt, as O. C. 658 and Ant. 1135; but here are two clear examples: Aesch. sept. 348 sqq. βλαχαὶ δ' αἱματόεσσαι τῶν ἐπιμαστιδίων ἀρτιτρεφεῖς βρέμονται, and Enn. ann. ap. Varr. ling. Lat. VII 104 [531 Vahlen] 'clamor ad caelum uoluendu' per aethera uagit.' The βρόμος is not made by the βληχαί but it *is* the βληχαί, the 'uagitus' is not made by the 'clamor' but it *is* the 'clamor'; and yet the poets have written as we see. What hinders, then, that another poet should write ἔργα δεδρακότα, though the δρᾶμα is not done by the ἔργα but *is* the ἔργα? Well, an answer which satisfies me is that the one phenomenon is exampled and the other is not. But if you will have a reason, I suppose it is that voices are far more readily separable in conception from the speaker than are acts from the doer. The uttered sound flies away like a thing possessing a life and an initiative of its own, and so in these phrases it comes to be conceived as a cause, when in truth it is only an effect. Any one, I think, may convince himself by trial that *voice* calls up in his mind a more vivid and definite notion than *deed*; and however it may be with us, it certainly was thus with the ancients. Words in Homer are fledged with wings and break loose from the fence of the teeth, they leap on high in Aesch. cho. 846, they hover in a living swarm round the murderer at Soph. O. t. 482. Deeds are not found exhibiting these signs of independent vitality; and similarly, while cries are said to wail and wails to cry, deeds are not said to act.

One real parallel to δεδρακότα = δεδραμένα I know: Musgrave long ago quoted Apoll. Rhod. IV 156 ἀρκεύθοιο νέον τετμηότι θαλλῷ, whence it clearly appears that τετμηότι means τετμημένῳ in Apollonian, a picturesque dialect but depraved. The editors of Sophocles quote this no longer, considering, I suppose, that the fact, though interesting, is unimportant. We have not the means of tracing how the Alexandrians fell into all their blunders, but here one might guess that Apollonius misconstrued some passage in the elder literature where τετμηότα or τετμηκότα governed θαλλόν.

It is duly noted by Hermann, though recent editors do not repeat it, that our text is at least as old as the second century after Christ: Aristid. ὑπὲρ τῶν τεττάρων, vol. II, p. 231 Jebb, vol. II, p. 304 Dindorf, ἐκείνων μὲν γὰρ καὶ ἡμεῖς αἴτιοι τὸ μέρος, τούτων δὲ οὐδὲ μικρόν· ἀλλὰ ταῦθ', ὡς ἔφη Σοφοκλῆς, πεπονθότα ἐστὶ μᾶλλον ἢ δεδρακότα. This piece of evidence has its use, since it warns the emender to presume such errors only as might befall before the date of ‖ Aristides. It is nothing strange that the text should already be corrupt in the sixth century after Sophocles' death: Didymus a hundred and fifty years earlier found v. 4 of the Antigone in its present condition. And it is nothing strange that Aristides should accept the active participles for passive without demur: Didymus interpreted ἄτης ἄτερ to signify ἀτηρόν; and Aristides' contemporaries habitually said ἀνέῳγεν ἡ θύρα when they meant ἀνέῳκται.

Before correcting the error I have one more point to urge. To grasp the full perversity of the phrase imputed to Sophocles you must remember that he more than once repeats this same idea; that to convey it he employs these same verbs or others of the same meaning; and that he employs them not as here, but correctly. In the immediate context comes 271 παθὼν μὲν ἀντέδρων, 274 ὑφ' ὧν δ' ἔπασχον, εἰδότων ἀπωλλύμην: then 538 sq. ΧΟ. ἔπαθες ΟΙ. ἔπαθον ἄλαστ' ἔχειν. ‖ ΧΟ. ἔρεξας ΟΙ. οὐκ ἔρεξα, 962 sqq. φόνους...καὶ γάμους καὶ συμφορὰς... ἃς ἐγὼ τάλας ‖ ἤνεγκον ἄκων, 1196 πατρῷα καὶ μητρῷα πήμαθ' ἄπαθες. Nay, more: the phrase itself is not new, not Sophocles' own. His words are borrowed from Eur. frag. 711 παθόντες οὐδὲν μᾶλλον ἢ δεδρακότες, a verse already familiar, already mimicked by Aristophanes thesm. 518 sq. κᾆτ' Εὐριπίδη θυμούμεθα, ‖ οὐδὲν παθοῦσαι μεῖ̃ζον ἢ δεδράκαμεν. Was such jargon as ἔργα πεπονθότα μᾶλλον ἢ δεδρακότα the likelier to please the Attic audience when they recognized in it the words of a well-known verse suddenly instinct with unknown meanings?

I suppose Sophocles to have written

ἐπεὶ τά γ' ἔργα με
πεπονθότ' ἴσθι μᾶλλον ἢ δεδρακότα.

πεπονθότα and δεδρακότα are acc. sing. masc. ἴσθι με πεπονθότα μᾶλλον ἢ δεδρακότα is the well-known emphatic periphrasis for πέπονθα μᾶλλον ἢ δέδρακα: *I tell you that as for my deeds, I did them not, but suffered them.* Lest it be thought that ἴσθι creates any difficulty in view of εἴ σοι...χρείη λέγειν, let me remind the reader that vv. 266 sq., alike in the old reading and in mine, are not the apodosis to that protasis: the apodosis is not expressed at all, but understood, '*quod intelligeres*, si...tibi exponere mihi liceret', Wunder: vv. 266 sq. are an independent statement and no part of a conditional sentence. ΙϹΘΙ in uncials is hard to tell from ΤϹΕΙ, which four letters are those of ΕϹΤΙ with the first and third transposed. This is a type of error which I have often illustrated but need not illustrate here, because it suffices to cite an interchange ‖ of the same two words from Eur. Bacch. 808 καὶ μὴν ξυνεθέμην τοῦτό γ', ἴσθι, τῷ θεῷ: ἴσθι

Musgrave, ἔστι MS. Since the σοι of 268 stands nearer than the δείσαντες of 265, I prefer ἴσθι to ἴστε.

Whether the conclusion to which I have been led will seem probable or improbable to others I cannot foresee; but this long disputation will have achieved its main purpose if it induces the editors to think.

357–60

νῦν δ' αὖ τίν' ἥκεις μῦθον, Ἰσμήνη, πατρὶ
φέρουσα; τίς σ' ἐξῆρεν οἴκοθεν στόλος;
ἥκεις γὰρ οὐ κενή γε, τοῦτ' ἐγὼ σαφῶς
ἔξοιδα, μὴ οὐχὶ δεῖμ' ἐμοὶ φέρουσά τι.

This, too, I fear must be a long discussion, and through no fault of mine. The scholars whose names follow have earned a title to respect which is not forfeited even by such notes as they have written on this passage. But of the notes themselves it would be hard to speak too severely. They are vicious to a degree which well-nigh protects them from refutation. So intricate is the tangle of error that I scarce know where to begin the task of unravelling it and half despair of making all its convolutions clear: the spectacle of such confusion almost dizzies the brain. If the argument proves tedious, I ask the reader to lay the blame on the right shoulders and remember that making mistakes is much quicker and easier work than showing that mistakes have been made. The comments to be considered can have given little trouble to those who wrote them, but for that very reason they impose the more labour on him whose duty it is to examine them.

'The somewhat vague οὐ κενή γε', says Schneidewin, 'is more closely defined by μὴ οὐχὶ δεῖμ' ἐμοὶ φέρουσά τι.' Here is a promising commencement. οὐ κενή means *bringing something*, and if it is 'more closely defined', the words which define it are δεῖμ' ἐμοὶ φέρουσά τι *bringing some terror for me*; therefore the explanation comes to this, that the words μὴ οὐχί mean exactly nothing. But let us give our editor another chance and suppose him to have meant that κενή, not οὐ κενή, was defined by this clause. Then the οὐ of v. 359 is to be understood before μὴ οὐχὶ κτλ., and the sentence is ἥκεις οὐ κενή, τουτέστιν ἥκεις οὐ μὴ οὐχὶ δεῖμ' ἐμοὶ φέρουσά τι. When we have sufficiently admired this row of negatives (οὐ μὴ οὐχὶ φέρουσα = φέρουσα) we shall desire to learn what function μή ‖ performs in a clause which defines an adjective not hypothetical in sense, κενή. Vain to ask of Schneidewin, for it never occurs to him that μή requires explanation: quite otherwise, he sets about explaining οὐχί, and this is how he does it: 'μὴ οὐχί, since the sense is *non ades quin feras*. Compare note on El. 107.' Mark first that this commentator, who undertakes to explain v. 360, does not know the contents of v. 359: he fancies it contains words meaning *non ades*, when in fact it contains nothing of the sort, but, on the contrary, ἥκεις οὐ κενή *ades non sine nuntio*. Secondly, if the sense is *non ades quin feras*, the sense is nonsense, for those words are not Latin. To express the invariable concomitant of a recurring event, *you never come without bringing*, the Romans employ *quin* with the subjunctive, *numquam uenis quin feras*. The particular accompaniment of a single event, *you are not come without bringing*, they do not express thus, but regularly by a participial construction such as *non ades nullum adferens metum*. Would you learn why Schneidewin imports the Latin *quin* into the matter? turn, as he bids you, to his note on El. 107. El. 107 exhibits the construction of μὴ οὐ with the *infinitive*, οὐ λήξω θρήνων μὴ οὐκ ἠχὼ προφωνεῖν: *this* construction has its counterpart in a Latin use of *quin* with the subjunctive which he there illustrates from Sall. Cat. 53, 6 'quos silentio praeterire non fuit consilium, *quin* utriusque naturam et mores aperirem'. Therefore, when we encounter ἥκεις οὐ κενὴ μὴ οὐ δεῖμα φέρουσα, we are expected, so lightly are our wits esteemed, to accept *quin* here also as equivalent to μὴ οὐ and never to notice that φέρουσα is not φέρειν!

Wunder, too, avails himself of this serviceable *quin*: 'neque enim uacua huc uenisti, certo scio, quin aliquid terroris mihi afferas, id est, neque enim ad me uenisti, quin aliquid afferas, quod quidem, ut fert fortuna mea, non potest non esse aliquid terribile.' First he translates as if the Greek were ἥκεις οὐ κενὴ μὴ οὐχὶ δεῖμ' ἐμοὶ φέρειν τι. Then, *quin* having served its turn by lulling to sleep our suspicions of μὴ οὐχί, he proceeds with 'id est' to offer us, as if identical, a paraphrase in which 'neque enim ad me uenisti, *quin* aliquid afferas' translates (into ungrammatical Latin, but no matter) the Greek ἥκεις οὐ κενή, and not μὴ οὐχί at all. The note ends with a reference to O. t. 12 sq. δυσάλγητος ἂν εἴην μὴ οὐ κατοικτίρων, where μή, as usual, is conditional, and the only matter calling for any comment is the unnecessary οὐ: a reference, it will be observed, not only irrelevant to our text, but also incongruous with the pretence at explanation which we have just perused. ‖

Prof. Jebb begins by saying that 'μὴ οὐχὶ...φέρουσα explains the special sense of κενή. You have not come empty-handed, i.e. *without bringing* some terror for me': it will be seen that this is what Schneidewin probably intended, ἥκεις οὐ κενή, τουτέστιν οὐ μὴ οὐχὶ φέρουσα. But Mr Jebb goes on to do what Schneidewin left undone and to essay an explanation of μή. 'μὴ οὐ properly stands with a partic. in a negative statement only when μή could stand with it in the corresponding affirmative statement: thus (*a*) affirmative: βραδὺς ἔρχει μὴ φέρων, you (always) come slowly, *if* you are not bringing: (*b*) negative: οὐ βραδὺς ἔρχει, μὴ οὐ φέρων, you never come slowly, *unless* you are bringing. Here μὴ οὐ is irregular, because the affirmative form would be ἥκεις οὐ (not μὴ) φέρουσα, a simple statement of fact; and so the negative should be οὐχ ἥκεις οὐ φέρουσα.' Here is another editor who has forgotten v. 359 by the time he comes to v. 360. There is no οὐχ ἥκεις: the affirmative form would not be ἥκεις. What we have is ἥκεις οὐ κενή: the affirmative form would be ἥκεις κενή. But commentators engaged on v. 360 descry v. 359 half lost in the distance, indistinctly perceive an οὐ there, and imagine that it qualifies ἥκεις. If we correct this oversight, Mr Jebb's remarks will look very strange, for they will run as follows: 'Here μὴ οὐ is irregular, because the affirmative form would be ἥκεις κενή, οὐ (not μὴ) φέρουσα, a simple statement of fact; and so the negative should be ἥκεις οὐ κενή, οὐ φέρουσα.' The negative, of course, should be ἥκεις οὐ κενή, φέρουσα. However, let us push forward: Mr Jebb is about to account for μή. 'But *bringing bad news* is felt here as a *condition* of her coming. Hence μὴ οὐ is used as if the sentence were *formally* conditional: οὐκ ἂν ἦλθες μὴ οὐ φέρουσα.' I ask whether this statement of cause and effect really depicts any process which ever took place in the mind of man. I for my part have no experience of the perturbation of thought in which such things are possible, and I will not thus lightly impute it to my betters. You are come, and I feel *bringing bad news* to be a condition of your coming: well, I have no difficulty whatever in expressing that feeling: I can say 'you are come, so I know you bring bad news': nay, it would suffice to say 'you are come bringing bad news', ἥκεις φέρουσα δεῖμα or ἥκεις οὐ κενὴ ἀλλὰ φέρουσα δεῖμα. It needs more proof, though no more is supplied, than the mere word of a modern editor, to assure us that Sophocles, because he felt bringing bad news as a condition of Ismene's coming, therefore employed language which conveys with perfect clearness not this sense but another. ‖

For, to crown everything, the task before the editors is not merely to invest the sentence with meanings which it has not, but to divest it of a meaning which it has. ἥκεις οὐ κενὴ μὴ οὐχὶ δεῖμ' ἐμοὶ φέρουσά τι is Greek for 'you are not come empty-handed unless you bring some terror for me', i.e. 'you bring some news unless you bring bad news, in which case you bring no news': utter nonsense, true, but that is what the words mean; and it is useless to yearn that they would mean something else or to make believe that they do.

I have endeavoured to display the editorial comments in their true futility, and it now remains to try if the passage whose corruption provoked them can be amended. Grammarians will hardly smile on an attempt to rob them of a bone which they have long mumbled in the past and doubtless hope to mumble in the future; but this is what I propose:

ἥκεις γὰρ οὐ κενή γε, τοῦτ' ἐγὼ σαφῶς
ἔξοιδα· μή που δεῖμ' ἐμοὶ φέρουσά τι;

num forte. . .? H and Π are easily and early confused, and the absorption of this in that leaves οὐ for the next scribe to alter to οὐχί. The verb ἥκεις is mentally supplied from above as at Trach. 316 μὴ τῶν τυράννων;

478–81

ΟΙ. ἦ τοῖσδε κρωσσοῖς οἷς λέγεις χέω τάδε;
ΧΟ. τρισσοῖς γε πηγάς· τὸν τελευταῖον δ' ὅλον.
ΟΙ. τοῦ τόνδε πλήσας θῶ; δίδασκε καὶ τόδε.
ΧΟ. ὕδατος, μελίσσης· μηδὲ προσφέρειν μέθυ.

'θῶ', writes Prof. Jebb on v. 480, 'has raised needless doubts. The operator is to fetch water from the spring in the grove (469), fill the bowls which he will find ready, and *place* them in a convenient position for the rite.' If the text of Sophocles really contained this direction to the operator, which Mr Jebb emphasizes with italics, to place the bowls in a convenient position, or any direction to place them in any position, our doubts would indeed be needless. But our doubts spring from the fact that the text of Sophocles contains not a syllable of the sort. In the whole context the sole allusion to the placing of the bowls is this disputed θῶ, which, since it proceeds from the lips of the operator himself, cannot possibly form part of any directions as to what the operator is to do. We have been listeners to the entire colloquy between Oedipus and his instructors; nothing has reached his ears which ‖ has escaped ours; and neither he nor we have heard a word about placing the bowls. Mr Jebb, from information privately received, knows that 'the operator is to place them in a convenient position for the rite'; but Oedipus does not. Why, then, instead of inquiring 'wherewith shall I fill it', does he say 'wherewith shall I fill it ere I set it down'? for the matter now in hand is not setting down but pouring out. This is the question we ask ourselves and cannot answer, and therefore resort to conjectural emendation, Meineke proposing πλήρη θῶ and Wecklein, less appropriately, πλήσας φθῶ. I prefer a slighter alteration than either, merely to cancel Θ as a dittography of C:

τοῦ τόνδε πλήσας ὧ; δίδασκε καὶ τόδε.

See Ant. 1067 ἀντιδοὺς ἔσει, O. t. 90 προδείσας εἰμί, 1146 σιωπήσας ἔσει.

I will seize this opportunity of restoring a similar periphrasis to the defective verse Aesch. cho. 124:

κῆρυξ μέγιστε τῶν ἄνω τε καὶ κάτω,
124   Ἑρμῆ χθόνιε, κηρύξας ἐμοί,
τοὺς γῆς ἔνερθε δαίμονας κλύειν ἐμὰς
εὐχάς.

The metre lacks a foot and a half, the sense requires an optative or imperative verb. Most editors place the gap at the beginning of the line, and prefix Klausen's ἄρηξον or the like. But the words Ἑρμῆ χθόνιε occur again in this play at v. 1, and they commence that verse; hence a slight presumption that they commence this verse too, and that Canter rightly marked the hiatus after χθόνιε. I propose to write

Ἑρμῆ χθόνιε, ⟨γένοιο⟩ κηρύξας ἐμοί.

The loss of γένοιο after χθόνιε, from which it hardly differs except in the position of ν, was very easy: for the locution compare Phryn. trag. frag. 20 μή μ' ἀτιμάσας γένῃ, Soph. O. t. 957 αὐτός μοι σὺ σημήνας γενοῦ, Aiax 588, Phil. 773. The conjecture is confirmed by the opening of the play, Ἑρμῆ χθόνιε. . .σωτὴρ γενοῦ μοι: with κῆρυξ. . .γένοιο κηρύξας ἐμοί compare sept. 145 Λύκει' ἄναξ, Λύκειος γενοῦ στρατῷ δαΐῳ.

515–16

μὴ πρὸς ξενίας ἀνοίξῃς
τᾶς σᾶς πέπονθ' ἔργ' ἀναιδῆ.

Bothe's generally accepted restoration of the metre by altering πέπονθ' to the vocative πέπον is very properly scouted by Hermann ‖ and Jebb: the latter excellently observes on this word, which never once occurs in tragedy, that it 'always marks familiarity: there is a touch of household intimacy in it, as when Polyphemus says to his ram, κριὲ πέπον (Od. 9. 447)'. The rival amendment is Reisig's ἃ πέπονθ' ἀναιδῆ, and I do not doubt that his addition of ἃ is a true correction. But there are now two difficulties. The first, common to both readings but worse in this, is the word ἀναιδῆ, which Prof. Jebb quite mis-translates in 'bare not the *shame* that I have suffered'. ἀναιδής means not *shameful* but *shameless*, and the translation accordingly ought to be 'bare not the *shamelessness* that I have suffered'. ἔργ' ἀναιδῆ *shameless deeds* are words, as Nauck remarks, unsuitable to the ignorant acts of Oedipus, which were ἀνόσια, if you will, but not ἀναιδῆ. But when ἔργα disappears and leaves ἃ πέπονθ' ἀναιδῆ, this is too preposterous, that he should describe his parricide and incest as *shameless treatment* which he has received: who treated him shamelessly, and how? The second difficulty is peculiar to Reisig's reading: it is the difficulty, or rather impossibility, of explaining how ἔργ' found its way into the text. Mr Jebb's account is not plausible: 'ἔργ' was inserted in the MSS to explain that ἀναιδῆ referred to his own acts.' Scribes are not wont to be thus solicitous, and the insertion of ἔργ' does not effect its supposed purpose.

ἔργ' ἀναιδῆ comes from this:

ε ργ
αναιδη

ε ρ γ are the letters required for correcting ἀναιδῆ to the word from which it was corrupted by the three errors α for ε, ι for ρ, and δ for γ, the first not uncommon and the other two very easy in uncials.

μὴ πρὸς ξενίας ἀνοίξῃς
τᾶς σᾶς, ἃ πέπονθ', ἐναργῆ.

The adjective is part of the predicate: *lay not bare to the light the things I have endured.*

527–8

ἦ μητρόθεν, ὡς ἀκούω,
δυσώνυμα λέκτρ' ἐπλήσω;

I think ἐπλήσω grotesque and Nauck's ἐπάσω certain; but the two readings have the same general sense, and that sense I assert to be this: *didst thou, as I hear, marry thy sister?* Oedipus did not marry his sister, nor could any such report have reached ‖ Colonus: the world rang with the true tale that he had married his mother. But to woo this meaning from the text the commentators exert themselves in vain. 'ματρόθεν is substituted for ματρός', says Prof. Jebb, 'by a kind of euphemism: that was the quarter from which the bride was taken.' Renuit negitatque Sabellus. Iocasta, I submit, was not the quarter from which Iocasta was taken. Nor can I imagine with what aim Mr Jebb proceeds 'cp. Aesch. *Theb.* 840 οὐδ' ἀπεῖπεν | πατρόθεν εὐκταία φάτις (the curse of Oed. on his children).'

You may obtain the true sense by altering μητρόθεν to ματέρος with Nauck, or λέκτρ' to τέκν' with Gleditsch, or by writing with me

ἦ πατρόθεν, ὡς ἀκούω,
δυσώνυμα λέκτρ' ἐπάσω;

i.e. didst thou wed thy father's widow? a euphemism which would be much praised if it stood in the MSS. This is the change of one letter, προθεν for μροθεν; and at Ant. 980 the Laurentian has πατρός for ματρός. There was here much temptation to the error, for the scribe's mind would be running on Oedipus' mother, and it might well escape him, as it has escaped a long series of editors, that by importing the name he expelled the person.

720–1

ὦ πλεῖστ' ἐπαίνοις εὐλογούμενον πέδον,
νῦν σοι τὰ λαμπρὰ ταῦτα δὴ φαίνειν ἔπη.

The above is the Laurentian text and cannot be construed: later MSS write δεῖ for δή and so obtain a construction of doubtful Atticism: the most of recent editors retain δή and change σοί to σόν, which is Nauck's conjecture, or rather the half of Nauck's conjecture. Both alterations are ineffectual, because φαίνειν does not mean what it is wanted to mean. The real signification of φαίνειν is easy to know, for the phrase is twice, if not thrice, elsewhere employed by Sophocles:

Ant. 621 κλεινὸν ἔπος πέφανται, O. t. 525 τοὖπος δ' (τοῦ πρόσδ' L) ἐφάνθη, 848 ὡς φανέν γε τοὖπος ὧδ' ἐπίστασο: it means to *utter* a saying. But the λαμπρὰ ἔπη, the praises of Athens, are already uttered: the question is, will they be made good. Accordingly, the editors for the most part explain φαίνειν as *rata facere*, and refer with Hermann to Trach. 239 εὐκταῖα φαίνων, where, however, φαίνων, as in Hom. o 26, is simply πορσύνων and the phrase signifies *making votive oblation*. ‖ Prof. Jebb, on the other hand, refusing to confer a new meaning on φαίνειν, bestows one instead on λαμπρὰ ἔπη: 'φαίνειν τὰ λαμπρὰ ἔπη = φαίνειν τὰς ἀρετὰς δι' ἃς ἐπαινεῖσθε': but in lieu of essaying to prove this equation, he quotes a parallel to the phrase φαίνειν ἀρετάς, which is hardly what we ask for.

If we accept the whole of Nauck's conjecture, νῦν σὸν τὰ λαμπρὰ ταῦτα δὴ κραίνειν ἔπη, sense is restored; but the following comes a trifle nearer the text:

νῦν σ' ὀρθὰ λαμπρὰ ταῦτα δεῖ φαίνειν ἔπη.

now it behooves thee to show that this praise is true. For φαίνειν ὀρθά see O. t. 852 sq. οὔτοι ποτ', ὦναξ, τόν γε Λαΐου φόνον | φανεῖ δικαίως ὀρθόν; for ὀρθὰ ἔπη, Ant. 1178 ὦ μάντι, τοὖπος ὡς ἄρ' ὀρθὸν ἤνυσας. Often in uncials the curved line of P bears much the same proportion to the upright stroke as the volute of an Ionic capital to the column which supports it, and it needs care to distinguish the letter from Ι: the change of θ to τ I should guess to be intentional, though it sometimes happens by accident.

755–60

> ἀλλ' οὐ γὰρ ἔστιν τἀμφανῆ κρύπτειν, σύ νιν   755
> πρὸς θεῶν πατρῴων, Οἰδίπους, πεισθεὶς ἐμοὶ
> κρύψον, θελήσας ἄστυ καὶ δόμους μολεῖν
> τοὺς σοὺς πατρῴους, τήνδε τὴν πόλιν φίλως
> εἰπών· ἐπαξία γάρ· ἡ δ' οἴκοι πλέον.
> [δίκῃ σέβοιτ' ἄν, οὖσα σὴ πάλαι τροφός.]   760

Strike out v. 760. I do not insist on the fact that Corinth, and not Thebes, was properly the τροφός of Oedipus: it is enough to note the grammatical blunder of σέβοιτο in a passive sense and the obviousness of the interpolator's motive. The sentence ἡ δ' οἴκοι πλέον looked incomplete at a first glance, though the defect is apparent only: the sense is 'speak Athens fair, for she deserves it; but Thebes deserves it more'. φίλως εἰπών, like χαῖρε itself, is applicable equally to the courtesies of farewell and of greeting: Athens is worthy that Oedipus should speak her friendly at parting, Thebes still more worthy that he should greet her fair at his return. The meaning is not obscure, but it asked more thought than a scribe is commonly willing to expend. As for v. 759, it will be retained unaltered by those who can stomach the phrase ἡ οἴκοι πόλις; others may write

7

ἐκεῖ with Wecklein; others ‖ again may prefer a slighter change which the dele-
tion of v. 760 renders possible, οἱ δ᾽ οἴκοι πλέον.

811–15

OI. ἄπελθ᾽, ἐρῶ γὰρ καὶ πρὸ τῶνδε, μηδέ με
    φύλασσ᾽ ἐφορμῶν ἔνθα χρὴ ναίειν ἐμέ.
KP. μαρτύρομαι τούσδ᾽, οὐ σέ· πρὸς δὲ τοὺς φίλους
    οἷ᾽ ἀνταμείβει ῥήματ᾽, ἤν σ᾽ ἕλω ποτέ, –
OI. τίς δ᾽ ἄν με τῶνδε συμμάχων ἕλοι βίᾳ;

The traditional interpretation of 813 sq., which descends to us from Musgrave
and Brunck, I present in Prof. Jebb's words: 'These men – not thee – call I to
witness; but, as for the strain of thine answer to thy kindred, if ever I take
thee –.' But hardly an editor outside England has let this go by without signi-
fying incredulity. Whether such an aposiopesis be tolerable is a question rather
for the taste than for the reason, so I set that aside. But, to begin with, I must
ask what in the world it is that Creon calls the men of Colonus to witness, for
not a suggestion does the context afford. 'Nempe iniuria se affici' interpolates
Hermann: so be it; treat Sophocles like an infant learning to talk, and put into
his mouth the words he cannot find for himself; but now δέ, as Nauck remarks,
'stört den Zusammenhang' by promising a transition to a fresh subject, instead
of which we find only the same thing in another form, 'but as for your language
to me'. But these are small matters beside the bewildering absurdity of μαρτύρομαι τούσδ᾽, οὐ σέ. 'οὐ σέ ist sinnlos: denn unmöglich kann Oid. selbst zum
Zeugen seiner Ungerechtigkeit genommen werden', Nauck. Had Oedipus even
hinted that Creon was calling him to witness anything at all? Is it in the category
of imaginable things that when you are quarrelling with a man you should call
that man himself to witness how he is behaving? Does there exist a notion to
which such words correspond? my mind frames none.

    I would emend the verses thus:

    μαρτύρομαί σου τούσδε προσθέτους φίλους
    οἷ᾽ ἀνταμείβει ῥήματ᾽, ἤν σ᾽ ἕλω ποτέ.

*I take these new allies of yours to witness how you answer me, in case I ever lay
hands on you*: that my conduct may be justified. If the sentence were οἵδε μάρτυρες
ἔστων οἷ᾽ ἀνταμείβει ῥήματ᾽, ἤν σ᾽ ἕλω ‖ ποτέ it would be exactly parallel to
Hom. Α 338 sqq. τὼ δ᾽ αὐτὼ μάρτυρες ἔστων | πρός τε θεῶν μακάρων πρός τε
θνητῶν ἀνθρώπων | καὶ πρὸς τοῦ βασιλῆος ἀπηνέος, εἴ ποτε δή[1] αὖτε | χρειὼ
ἐμεῖο γένηται ἀεικέα λοιγὸν ἀμῦναι | τοῖς ἄλλοις. The difference is that in our
passage the apodosis is not set out in words, but only suggests itself to the mind

---

[1] δή Bekker, La Roche, Ameis, Rzach, Monro, Leaf, δ᾽ MSS.

as a sequel of μαρτύρομαι, as thus: μαρτύρομαι τούσδε ⟨ἵνα μάρτυρες ὧσιν⟩ ἥν σ' ἕλω ποτέ. Such suppression of an apodosis is common enough: see, for instance, Thuc. III 21 εἶχε μὲν (τὸ τεῖχος) δύο τοὺς περιβόλους, πρός τε Πλαταιῶν καὶ εἴ τις ἔξωθεν ἀπ' Ἀθηνῶν ἐπίοι 'the circumvallation consisted of two lines, one towards the besieged, the other *for protection* in case of any attack on the outside from Athens'. The sense of the adjective in πρόσθετος φίλος answers to the verbal προστίθεμαι φίλον: Her. I 69 τὸν Ἕλληνα φίλον προσθέσθαι, and compare too v. 1332 of this play, οἷς ἂν σὺ προσθῇ, τοῖσδ' ἔφασκ' εἶναι κράτος: there is allusion to the words of Oedipus just above, 811 ἐρῶ γὰρ καὶ πρὸ τῶνδε; and he has τῶνδε συμμάχων in his reply 815. I do not know that πρόσθετος is thus employed elsewhere, and Sophocles may have been the first or even the only writer to use it so; but the use itself is no less legitimate than his employment, perhaps also for the first time, of the cognate προσθήκη in the same sense at O. t. 38 προσθήκη θεοῦ, schol. συμβουλῇ, ἐπικουρίᾳ. δ for θ is not one of the commonest errors, but neither is it uncommon: for the rest, σου τούσδε and τούσδ' οὐ σέ are the same letters: I should guess that their transposition arose from the false division σ' οὐ τούσδε.

887–90

τίς ποθ' ἡ βοή; τί τοὔργον; ἐκ τίνος φόβου ποτὲ
βουθυτοῦντά μ' ἀμφὶ βωμὸν ἔσχετ' ἐναλίῳ θεῷ
τοῦδ' ἐπιστάτῃ Κολωνοῦ; λέξαθ', ὡς εἰδῶ τὸ πᾶν
οὗ χάριν δεῦρ' ᾖξα θᾶσσον ἢ καθ' ἡδονὴν ποδός.

For the ποδός of 890 Nauck would substitute ἐμοί or else expel the verse. The addition of a genitive to the adverbial phrases καθ' ἡδονήν and πρὸς ἡδονήν is, to say the least, not customary, and this particular genitive is altogether inappropriate. Running does not tire the foot: it tires first the lungs, then the thighs and the arms; but a man may run till he drops and never feel the least distress in his feet. Walking exerts the muscles of the feet ‖ more than running, and even in walking one must go many miles to be footsore; but Theseus has never been out of earshot. I think we have here an example of that confusion between α and ος which Porson illustrates at Eur. Hec. 782 [794], and I would alter ποδός to πόδα. For ᾄσσω with an accusative see Porson on Eur. Or. 1427 [1430], where he quotes Soph. Aiax 40 ᾖξεν χέρα, Eur. Hec. 1071 πόδ' ἐπάξας, and the phrases βαίνω, προβαίνω and ἐμβαίνω πόδα, as well as the passive ᾄσσεται in v. 1261 of this play. This reading, and not the vulgate, is correctly rendered by Prof. Jebb's translation 'since therefore have I sped hither with more than easeful speed of foot'.

978–81

μητρὸς δὲ τλήμων οὐκ ἐπαισχύνει γάμους
οὔσης ὁμαίμου σῆς μ’ ἀναγκάζων λέγειν
οἵους ἐρῶ τάχ’· οὐ γὰρ οὖν σιγήσομαι
σοῦ γ’ εἰς τόδ’ ἐξελθόντος ἀνόσιον στόμα.

‘εἰς τόδ’. ἐξελθ ἀνόσιον στόμα, having gone to such lengths of impious speech . . . ἀνόσιον στόμα agrees with τόδ’, depending on εἰς. Since στόμα was familiar to poetry in the sense of λόγος (cp. O. T. 426), this version is clearly preferable to taking εἰς τόδ’ separately and ἀνόσ. στ. as accus. of respect’, Jebb. Preferable, perhaps, but it is a choice of evils. I demur to the statement that στόμα was familiar to poetry in the sense of λόγος, and there is not the least excuse for interpreting it so in the passage to which Prof. Jebb refers, O. t. 426 sq. πρὸς ταῦτα καὶ Κρέοντα καὶ τοὐμὸν στόμα | προπηλάκιζε: ‘os suum uates contumeliae haberi indignatur’, says Ellendt. Liddell and Scott, to be sure, quote, after Stephanus, several examples, but they are all from Sophocles and all false: most of them are correctly explained by Ellendt, so I notice only one or two. In O. t. 671 sq. τὸ γὰρ σόν, οὐ τὸ τοῦδ’, ἐποικτίρω στόμα | ἐλεινόν thy lips are piteous and move compassion in me, not his, of course speech would come to the same thing as lips, but Ellendt has no more cause for translating στόμα by loquella in that place than in O. t. 426, 706, O. C. 603, Ant. 997, where he rightly resists this rendering. The fragment 844 〚930 Pearson〛, adduced as parallel also in the Schneidewin–Nauck edition, κλέπτων δ’ ὅταν τις ἐμφανῶς ἐφευρεθῇ | σιγᾶν ἀνάγκη, κἂν καλὸν φορῇ στόμα, means ‘even though he carry a specious tongue in his head’. In O. C. 131 sqq. τὸ τᾶς εὐφάμου στόμα φροντίδος ἱέντες, whatever view you take of it, the interpretation which I am combating is quite impossible. ‖ ‘στόμα ἱέναι pro φωνὴν ἱέναι dicitur’, says Wunder; and the required meaning is οὐχ ἱέντες φωνήν! Mr Jebb, with more regard for the sense but some violence to the Greek, renders ‘moving the lips’; I agree with Nauck that ἱέντες is corrupt and a word of opposite meaning wanted in its place, say πρίοντες: frag. 811 〚897 Pearson〛 δάφνην φαγὼν ὀδόντι πρῖε τὸ στόμα. But to come back to v. 981: the interpretation λόγον is not more precarious than gratuitous.

οὐ γὰρ οὖν σιγήσομαι
σοῦ γ’ εἰς τόδ’ ἐξελθόντος, ἀνόσιον στόμα.

ἀνόσιον στόμα is vocative, O impious tongue. στόμα is naturally preferred to κάρα or λῆμα or the like, because it was in speech that the ἀνοσιότης of Creon displayed itself; just so at 794 we had τὸ σὸν δ’ ἀφῖκται δεῦρ’ ὑπόβλητον στόμα.

1016–38

ΘΗ. ἅλις λόγων· ὡς οἱ μὲν ἐξειργασμένοι
      σπεύδουσιν, ἡμεῖς δ' οἱ παθόντες ἕσταμεν.
ΚΡ. τί δῆτ' ἀμαυρῷ φωτὶ προστάσσεις ποεῖν;
ΘΗ. ὁδοῦ κατάρχειν τῆς ἐκεῖ, πομπὸν δ' ἐμὲ
      χωρεῖν, ἵν', εἰ μὲν ἐν τόποισι τοῖσδ' ἔχεις   1020
      τὰς παῖδας ἡμῶν, αὐτὸς ἐκδείξῃς ἐμοί·
      εἰ δ' ἐγκρατεῖς φεύγουσιν, οὐδὲν δεῖ πονεῖν·
      ἄλλοι γὰρ οἱ σπεύδοντες, οὓς οὐ μή ποτε
      χώρας φυγόντες τῆσδ' ἐπεύξωνται θεοῖς.
      ἀλλ' ἐξυφηγοῦ· γνῶθι δ' ὡς ἔχων ἔχει   1025
      καί σ' εἷλε θηρῶνθ' ἡ τύχη· τὰ γὰρ δόλῳ
      τῷ μὴ δικαίῳ κτήματ' οὐχὶ σῴζεται.
      κοὐκ ἄλλον ἕξεις εἰς τόδ'· ὡς ἔξοιδά σε
      οὐ ψιλὸν οὐδ' ἄσκευον ἐς τοσήνδ' ὕβριν
      ἥκοντα τόλμης τῆς παρεστώσης τανῦν,   1030
      ἀλλ' ἔσθ' ὅτῳ σὺ πιστὸς ὢν ἔδρας τάδε.
      ἃ δεῖ μ' ἀθρῆσαι, μηδὲ τήνδε τὴν πόλιν
      ἑνὸς ποῆσαι φωτὸς ἀσθενεστέραν.
      νοεῖς τι τούτων, ἢ μάτην τὰ νῦν τέ σοι
      δοκεῖ λελέχθαι χὤτε ταῦτ' ἐμηχανῶ;   1035
ΚΡ. οὐδὲν σὺ μεμπτὸν ἐνθάδ' ὢν ἐρεῖς ἐμοί·
      οἴκοι δὲ χἠμεῖς εἰσόμεσθ' ἃ χρὴ ποεῖν.
ΘΗ. χωρῶν ἀπείλει νυν.

What meaning have the words in v. 1028, κοὐκ ἄλλον ἕξεις εἰς τόδ' (al. τάδ')?
'Recte Dindorfius', says Wunder, 'neque quicquam ǁ tibi proderunt, quos tecum
adduxisti. Tum ἐς τάδε est ἐς τὸ τὰ δόλῳ τῷ μὴ δικαίῳ κτήματα σῴζεσθαι.' These
are two eminent scholars, but no number of scholars, whatever their eminence,
can bring it to pass that *thou shalt have none other for this purpose* should mean
the same thing as *those whom thou hast brought shall avail thee nothing*. Schneidewin and Jebb translate the Greek correctly, though they are obliged to eke it
out with supplements of their own: '*auch wirst du nicht einen andern* als Beistand
haben für diesen Zweck (das σῴζειν κτήματα, die Behaltung der Mädchen in
Gewalt)', Schneidewin; 'and you will not have another (to aid you) with
a view to this (i.e. to the removal of the captives)', Jebb. But the words are false.
Creon did have others to aid him. He had his guards, in whose custody the
captives at that instant were, and who afterwards fought a pitched battle for
him during the performance of the next stasimon. Now we see what forced
Dindorf and Wunder to their mistranslation: the sentence gives no right sense
unless it is mistranslated. Nor does Prof. Jebb render it any the more endurable

by pointing out, what is indisputably true, that in the following verses down to 1033 Theseus declares his suspicion that Creon has an accomplice[1] at Athens. If the words 'you will not have another (to aid you) with a view to this' are to mean, as Mr Jebb apparently desires, that Creon will not have the aid of this Athenian accomplice, they must be further eked out by a second parenthesis such as '(except your guards)'. And, now that the sense has been thus augmented by the eleemosynary contributions of the charitable, what triviality is this, to tell Creon that in his attempt at 'the removal of the captives' or 'die Behaltung der Mädchen in Gewalt', he will not have the aid of this one additional friend. He has his guards: one man more or less will not affect the issue. And how will Theseus prevent this undetected accomplice from rendering help? He may have joined the guards already, for aught that Theseus knows. I do not wonder, then, that Nauck should say 'κοὐκ ἄλλον uerba corrupta', though we shall presently find that the fault is not in κοὐκ ἄλλον.

Six lines more and I am arrested again. You have an abettor in Athens, says Theseus: this I must look to, and not let a single ‖ traitor defeat the common will: νοεῖς τι τούτων *do you recognize this?* Recognize it! what does it, what can it matter, whether Creon recognizes or fails to recognize that Theseus must take these steps? Mr Jebb wrongly translates 'dost thou take my drift': the meaning of νοεῖς is fixed by the alternative ἢ μάτην... δοκεῖ λελέχθαι: it signifies *perceive, recognize as true.* And what is there in common between this alleged necessity for investigations at Athens and τὰ τότε λεχθέντα ὅτε ταῦτα ἐμηχανῶ 'the remonstrances and menaces of the Chorus, 829 ff.' (Jebb), that Theseus proceeds 'or do you think my views on domestic polity as empty as you thought the remonstrances addressed to you when you were carrying off the girls?' No; the question νοεῖς τι τούτων can only follow on the utterance of some ethical proposition bearing on Creon's act; such, for instance, as τὰ δόλῳ τῷ μὴ δικαίῳ κτήματ' οὐχὶ σῴζεται.

And so it did. Since neither νοεῖς τι τούτων nor κοὐκ ἄλλον ἕξεις εἰς τόδ' is permitted to yield sense by the context in which it stands, I propose to find a new context for each by transposing the six verses 1028–33 from their present seat to another.

КР.   τί δῆτ' ἀμαυρῷ φωτὶ προστάσσεις ποεῖν;
1019   ΘΗ.   ὁδοῦ κατάρχειν τῆς ἐκεῖ. πομπὸν δ' ἐμὲ
1028   κοὐκ ἄλλον ἕξεις εἰς τόδ'· ὡς ἔξοιδά σε
                οὐ ψιλὸν οὐδ' ἄσκευον ἐς τοσήνδ' ὕβριν

---

[1] Mr Jebb says *accomplices*; but though the singular number ἔσθ' ὅτῳ cannot be pressed, the ἑνὸς φωτός of 1033 shows that Theseus contemplates the existence of a single accomplice only. Let it be remarked that ἑνὸς φωτός must mean *one private Athenian citizen* and cannot signify Creon, or it constitutes no antithesis to πόλιν. The worsting of Athens by Creon (or of Thebes by Theseus) is not the worsting of a city by one man, but of one city by another city. Theseus says that he cannot suffer the public will to be thwarted by a private counterplot.

ἥκοντα τόλμης τῆς παρεστώσης τανῦν,
ἀλλ' ἔσθ' ὅτῳ σὺ πιστὸς ὢν ἕδρας τάδε.
ἃ δεῖ μ' ἀθρῆσαι, μηδὲ τήνδε τὴν πόλιν
ἑνὸς ποῆσαι φωτὸς ἀσθενεστέραν.   1033
χωρεῖν, ἵν', εἰ μὲν ἐν τόποισι τοῖσδ' ἔχεις   1020
τὰς παῖδας ἡμῖν, αὐτὸς ἐκδείξῃς ἐμοί·
εἰ δ' ἐγκρατεῖς φεύγουσιν, οὐδὲν δεῖ πονεῖν·
ἄλλοι γὰρ οἱ σπεύδοντες, οὓς οὐ μή ποτε
χώρας φυγόντες τῆσδ' ἐπεύξωνται θεοῖς.
ἀλλ' ἐξυφηγοῦ· γνῶθι δ' ὡς ἔχων ἔχει
καί σ' εἷλε θηρῶνθ' ἡ τύχη· τὰ γὰρ δόλῳ
τῷ μὴ δικαίῳ κτήματ' οὐχὶ σῴζεται.   1027
νοεῖς τι τούτων, ἢ μάτην τὰ νῦν τέ σοι   1034
δοκεῖ λελέχθαι χὦτε ταῦτ' ἐμηχανῶ;

'What do you bid a helpless man to do?' 'To lead the way yonder. And to escort you on your road you shall have me and no one else; no one else, I say, for sure I am that there was some || one here on whom you counted when you went to these lengths.' Instead of the Athenian accomplice whom Creon might expect to conduct him through Athenian territory, he shall have only Theseus for his escort. Then χωρεῖν in 1020 is infinitive for imperative; so 481 προσφέρειν, 484 ἐπεύχεσθαι, 490 ἀφέρπειν, Ant. 151 θέσθαι, 1143 μολεῖν, O. t. 462 (El. 9, Phil. 1411) φάσκειν, 1466 μέλεσθαι, Phil. 57 λέγειν, 1080 ὁρμᾶσθαι. Lastly, at 1034 the words νοεῖς τι τούτων 'dost thou apprehend this truth?' come just where they should. I declare, when I look at the new face this speech has now put on, I can hardly refrain from unbecoming exclamations of delight. The transposition adopted is not the only way to achieve the prime end of bringing 1028 into juxtaposition with 1019, and 1034 with 1027: the verses might be arranged 1018, 1020–4, 1019, 1028–33, 1025–7, 1034 sqq.; but the method I have chosen is simpler and seems generally preferable. In 1021 I have accepted Elmsley's slight but very uncertain alteration, ἡμῖν for ἡμῶν, though I think G. H. Mueller's αὐτὸς ἡγεμὼν δείξῃς really more probable, and I have also conjectured τὼ παῖδ' Ἀθηνῶν, the genitive depending on τόποισι: see Aiax 437 sq., O. t. 1134 (where I would read τοῖς Κ. τόποις, adopting Mr Margoliouth's admirable correction of 1136), Aesch. Pers. 447. For ἐγκρατεῖς in 1022 I should much prefer οὔγκρατεῖς: I would make a similar change in Eur. frag. 166, reading τὸ μῶρον αὐτῷ τοῦ πατρὸς νόσημ' ἔνι· | φιλεῖ γὰρ οὕτως οὐκ κακῶν εἶναι κακός (ἐκ...κακούς MSS, κακός Wagner).

In v. 1036 Prof. Jebb retains the MS reading which most critics now think corrupt; 'nam sensus non ὤν sed ὄντι flagitat', says Wecklein. 'But', says Mr Jebb, 'the vulgate is right. " *While here* ", said of Theseus, means " since this is your own realm, in which you have force at command."' This remark shows no apprehension of the difficulty. Creon says that he will not object to any words uttered in Attica by Theseus. A coherent sequel to this would be that, if Theseus utters such words outside Attica, Creon will object to them. But neither this nor any coherent sequel follows. There follows, with no sort of pertinence, the statement that Creon, when returned to Thebes, will know how to act. Perhaps; but what of that? His attitude towards the words uttered by Theseus will still remain unchanged; for he has made the general statement that he will object to none of them. What, then, is the meaning of δέ? What is the connexion, or what the opposition, between the two predications linked by this particle? It is such as we find in the verse of a modern poet: || 'A fool is bent upon a twig, *but* wise men dread a bandit.' The statement that Creon, when returned to Thebes, will know how to act, would follow coherently upon the statement that his freedom of action is hampered while he, Creon, stands on Attic soil; and this is what Wecklein means by saying 'sensus non ὤν sed ὄντι flagitat'.

Therefore Blaydes conjectures ἐνθάδ' ὄντ' ἐρεῖς ἐμέ: Wecklein and Tyrrell, Pfluegl having already proposed μεμπτὸς ἐνθάδ' ὤν ἐρεῖς, confine themselves to a change of fascinating simplicity, ὧν for ὤν, i.e. οὐδὲν ὧν σὺ ἐρεῖς μεμπτὸν ἐμοὶ ἐνθάδε; and they well defend the hyperbaton. What discontents me with these emendations is the χἠμεῖς of 1037. 'Here I shall object to nothing you say, but at home I shall know how to act', οἴκοι δ' εἰσόμεσθ' ἃ χρὴ ποεῖν, is thoroughly satisfactory: the contrast is between Creon in Attica and the same Creon in Thebes. Introduce χἠμεῖς, 'but at home I *too* shall know how to act', and you disturb this contrast. Or shift the point of view: suppose we had been shown the verse οἴκοι δὲ χἠμεῖς εἰσόμεσθ' ἃ χρὴ ποεῖν and told to guess the sense of the verse above it, we should never have guessed ἐγὼ ἐνθάδε οὐδὲν μέμψομαι ὧν σὺ ἐρεῖς: we should have guessed something like σὺ μὲν ἐν τῇ σῇ χώρᾳ δεινὸς εἶ. And I believe we should have been right.

For the wisest words on this passage which I have anywhere found are Nauck's: 'ἐνθάδ' ὤν ist *in der jetzigen Form der Rede* unpassend.' The question is whether the fault lies with ἐνθάδ' ὤν or with the context. Now, if one scans the words to consider which look sound and which corrupt, surely what first catches the eye is the exact correspondence between σὺ . . . ἐνθάδ' ὤν and οἴκοι . . . χἠμεῖς: here, I say to myself, is a relic of the sentence's pristine form showing the lines on which to reconstruct it: the comparison is between Theseus at his home and Creon at his. Looking round for the seat of corruption, one observes that what most obscures this comparison is the emphatic form of the pronoun ἐμοί distracting attention from σύ; this, then, should be altered, and as little as possible beside. I write

οὐδὲν σὺ μεμπτὸν ἐνθάδ' ὤν αἴρεις μένος·
οἴκοι δὲ χἠμεῖς εἰσόμεσθ' ἃ χρὴ ποεῖν.

i.e. you are a terrible fighting-cock on your own dunghill; but I too, when my foot is on my native heath, shall know how to bear myself with proper spirit. I rely much on the closely parallel phrase of Aiax 1066 πρὸς ταῦτα μηδὲν δεινὸν ἐξάρῃς μένος; for ‖ the adverbial οὐδέν with μεμπτόν see too Eur. Ion 1519 καὶ τὸ γένος οὐδὲν μεμπτόν ἐσθ’ ἡμῖν τόδε. The words μένος οὐδὲν μεμπτόν mean a rage nowise to be sneered at, that is, formidable. The use of the verb from which this use of the adjective springs is found in Aesch. frag. 199 [326 Mette], 1 sqq. ἥξεις δὲ Λιγύων εἰς ἀτάρβητον στρατόν· | ἔνθ’ οὐ μάχης, σάφ’ οἶδα, καὶ θουρός περ ὤν, | μέμψει, man of war though you are, you will find the fighting no laughing matter: the adjective itself is thus used at Plat. legg. 716 B in a context which explains the meaning clearly: the lawless man ὑποσχὼν τιμωρίαν οὐ μεμπτὴν τῇ Δίκῃ ἑαυτόν τε καὶ οἶκον καὶ πόλιν ἄρδην ἀνάστατον ἐπόησε, a punishment not to be made light of. The Medea of Euripides plays on the two senses of the word when at v. 958 of the play she says concerning the envenomed gifts οὔτοι δῶρα μεμπτὰ δέξεται (ἡ νύμφη): the scholiast rightly observes τοῦτο διπλῆν ἔχει τὴν ἔννοιαν, μίαν μέν, ἣν ὁ Ἰάσων ἐκδέχεται, ὅτι οὐκ ἀπόβλητα αὐτῇ τὰ δῶρα, ἀλλὰ θαυμαστά, ἑτέραν δέ, ἣν αὐτὴ κρύπτει, ἀντὶ τοῦ οὐ γελάσει τὸ δῶρον ὡς ἀσθενές, ἀναιρήσει γὰρ αὐτήν. The corruption came to pass, I should suppose, through the loss of the final ς at the margin and the rearrangement of μένο as ἐμόν; though other ways are also conceivable.

1132–6

καίτοι τί φωνῶ; πῶς σ’ ἂν ἄθλιος γεγὼς
θιγεῖν θελήσαιμ’ ἀνδρός, ᾧ τίς οὐκ ἔνι
κηλὶς κακῶν ξύνοικος; οὐκ ἔγωγέ σε,
οὐδ’ οὖν ἐάσω· τοῖς γὰρ ἐμπείροις βροτῶν   1135
μόνοις οἷόν τε συνταλαιπωρεῖν τάδε.

Prof. Jebb writes ‘βροτῶν is changed by Nauck to κακῶν, and by Dindorf to ἐμῶν (“my affairs”), on the ground that ἐμπείροις needs definition. But if the preceding words leave any need for such definition, it is supplied in the next v. by συνταλαιπωρεῖν τάδε.’ This understates the offence by one half. True it is that ἐμπείροις wants defining by an objective genitive, expressed or understood, because, in default of such a genitive, it means *skilful* and makes nonsense; and I with Nauck regard as impracticable the artifice of supplying τῶνδε from below, which commends itself to Mr Jebb. The absence of an objective genitive is half the depravity of the vulgate: the other half is the presence of βροτῶν in that genitive’s stead. βροτῶν, you will notice, is quite useless: take it away and the passage means what it meant before: no reason can be invented why Sophocles should add it except to complete the ‖ trimeter. Imagine him now, when ἐμπείροις cried for a defining genitive and the last foot of the senarius lay empty for the defining genitive’s reception, imagine him not merely refusing it but proffering in its place a genitive which does not define nor perform any office whatsoever except to ensnare the reader in the momentary delusion that the phrase before him has its natural meaning, *those who know men*. Is such writing reconcilable with perfect soundness of intellect? Great wits are sure to madness near allied, but not to fatuity.

Instead of ἐμῶν or κακῶν I would put forward this conjecture:

> τοῖς ταλαιπώροις βροτῶν
> μόνοις οἷόν τε συνταλαιπωρεῖν τάδε.

In the progress of error I should impute γαρεπώροις to accident and the rest to design.

1201–5

> ἀλλ' ἡμὶν εἶκε · λιπαρεῖν γὰρ οὐ καλὸν
> δίκαια προσχρήζουσιν, οὐδ' αὐτὸν μὲν εὖ
> πάσχειν, παθόντα δ' οὐκ ἐπίστασθαι τίνειν.
> ΟΙ. τέκνον, βαρεῖαν ἡδονὴν νικᾶτέ με
> λέγοντες · ἔστω δ' οὖν ὅπως ὑμῖν φίλον.

'βαρεῖαν ἡδονὴν νικᾶτέ με singulari breuitate dictum hoc sensu: νικᾶτέ με νίκην βαρεῖαν ἐμοί, ἡδεῖαν δ' ὑμῖν': singular indeed. 'Grievous (for me) is the gratification (to yourselves) in regard to which ye prevail over me by your words... ἡδονήν is a bold acc. of respect with νικᾶτε, suggested by the constr. with a cognate acc., νίκην νικᾶτε, since the pleasure is secured by the victory': very bold. The plain meaning of the words is not this but 'ye conquer me by mentioning a calamitous self-gratification', i.e. the indulgence of Oedipus' angry temper, to which Antigone attributes his misfortunes. But I have little doubt that what Sophocles wrote was the much simpler and apter βαρεῖαν πημονήν, in support of which I quote the words of Antigone to which reference is made, 1195 sq. σὺ δ' εἰς ἐκεῖνα, μὴ τὰ νῦν, ἀποσκόπει | πατρῷα καὶ μητρῷα πήμαθ' ἅπαθες · | κἂν κεῖνα λεύσσῃς, οἶδ' ἐγώ, γνώσει κακοῦ | θυμοῦ τελευτὴν ὡς κακὴ προσγίγνεται. | ἔχεις γὰρ οὐχὶ βαιὰ τἀνθυμήματα | τῶν σῶν ἀδέρκτων ὀμμάτων τητώμενος. Oedipus answers 'Child, ye vanquish me by the heavy affliction ye recall; so, then, have it as ye will.' 'δ' οὖν: cp. Ai. 115 σὺ δ' οὖν... | χρῶ χειρί, well, then, (if thou must)': this is Prof. Jebb's reference, which I gratefully accept, though with some || perplexity as to his motive in giving it, since he himself translates δ' οὖν 'however'. The corruption may have arisen from the loss, here as at 360, of Π beside H. I present the conservative garrison with the defensive argument that Antigone only, and not Theseus also, had in fact made mention of the πημονή or πήματα.

1249–53

AN. καὶ μὴν ὅδ᾽ ἡμῖν, ὡς ἔοικεν, ὁ ξένος
    ἀνδρῶν γε μοῦνος, ὦ πάτερ, δι᾽ ὄμματος   1250
    ἀστακτὶ λείβων δάκρυον ὧδ᾽ ὁδοιπορεῖ.
ΟΙ. τίς οὗτος; AN. ὅνπερ καὶ πάλαι κατείχομεν
    γνώμῃ, πάρεστι δεῦρο Πολυνείκης ὅδε.

'Genetiuus ἀνδρῶν ab μοῦνος, quod pro μονωθείς dictum sit, pendere creditur. Quod Graecis lectoribus non facile erat in mentem uenturum', Dindorf. The obvious sense of the words is 'he and none other', but γε then means nothing. The sense 'having no man with him', as Dindorf says, is not obvious; and γε, if it has a meaning, then means that he has women or children or some other escort with him, of which we hear nothing in the sequel. Hence scholars have conjectured ἀνδρῶν ἔρημος (ἐρῆμος) or μονωθείς or δίχ᾽ ἄλλων. I do but transpose a couplet and add one letter at the end of a line:

AN. καὶ μὴν ὅδ᾽ ἡμῖν, ὡς ἔοικεν, ὁ ξένος –   1249
ΟΙ. τίς οὗτος; AN. ὅνπερ καὶ πάλαι κατείχομεν   1252
    γνώμῃ, πάρεστι δεῦρο. ΟΙ. Πολυνείκης ὅδε;   1253
AN. ἀνδρῶν γε μοῦνος, ὦ πάτερ· δι᾽ ὄμματος δ᾽   1250
    ἀστακτὶ λείβων δάκρυον ὧδ᾽ ὁδοιπορεῖ.   1251

ἀνδρῶν γε μοῦνος *yes, he and none other*, the common use of γε in confirmatory answers. I am shy of praising my own handiwork, but if it were a scribe of the eleventh century, and not I, who had written the verses thus, I would point out, or rather the editors would have saved me the trouble by pointing out already, the dramatic merit of this broken dialogue.

1354–9

ὅς γ᾽, ὦ κάκιστε, σκῆπτρα καὶ θρόνους ἔχων,
ἃ νῦν ὁ σὸς ξύναιμος ἐν Θήβαις ἔχει,   1355
τὸν αὐτὸς αὑτοῦ πατέρα τόνδ᾽ ἀπήλασας
κἄθηκας ἄπολιν καὶ στολὰς ταύτας φορεῖν,
ἃς νῦν δακρύεις εἰσορῶν, ὅτ᾽ ἐν πόνῳ
ταὐτῷ βεβηκὼς τυγχάνεις κακῶν ἐμοί. ‖

Of ἐν πόνῳ κακῶν Prof. Jebb offers only a half-hearted defence which will not bear scrutiny. 'πόνῳ...κακῶν = πολυπόνοις κακοῖς, the gen. being added to define πόνῳ more closely. Since πόνος was a word of such general meaning, the phrase, though unusual, seems defensible. Cp. such phrases as δυσοίστων πόνων | ἄθλ᾽ (Ph. 508), πόνων | λατρεύματ᾽ (Tr. 356), ἄεθλ᾽ ἀγώνων (ib. 506).' Well, to begin with, however general the meaning of πόνος may be, the meaning of κακά is more general still, and κακῶν, therefore, is a singularly useless word for defining πόνῳ more closely. Secondly, by way of defending a phrase in which the meaning of πόνος is said to be so general that it wants another word to define it more closely, it is rather injudicious to quote two phrases in which the meaning of πόνος is so little general that it is used to define more closely the meaning of another word.

Reiske would alter πόνῳ to βυθῷ, Martin to κλόνῳ, Bergk to πότμῳ: the first alone procures good sense, and it has no plausibility. Mr Wecklein's conjecture ὅτ᾽ ἐν κακῶν | ταὐτῷ βεβηκὼς τυγχάνεις κλυδωνίῳ exhibits vividly the distress, the κλυδώνιον κακῶν, in which that accomplished critic is plunged. Mr Tournier proposes ἄκων for κακῶν: this is the easiest of changes, and if ἄκων stood in the MSS it would be zealously defended by those who now defend κακῶν. Critics who study to think as the ancients thought would object that ἄκων imports a notion irrelevant to the speaker's theme. That Polynices could not help his plight is true, but not to the purpose; and the classics, unlike the moderns, are careful to eschew such details as divert attention from the main concern. It would not be much use to urge these considerations if ἄκων were the MS reading, but since it is only a conjecture, they will probably be entertained. I believe the true text is this:

ὅτ᾽ ἐν πόνῳ
ταὐτῷ βεβηκὼς τυγχάνεις ἴσων ἐμοί.

ἴσων has nothing to do with πόνῳ, nor τυγχάνεις with βεβηκώς: the words τυγχάνεις ἴσων ἐμοί mean *eadem sortiris atque ego*: see El. 532 οὐκ ἴσον καμὼν ἐμοί. ΙϹΩΝ was mistaken for ΚΩΝ and then expanded to ΚΑΚΩΝ. The same error has come to pass at Aesch. sept. 945, where Weil restores πικρὸς δὲ χρημάτων ἴσος δατητὰς Ἄρης ἀρὰν πατρῴαν τιθεὶς ἀλαθῆ for κακός.

1472–4

ΟΙ.   ὦ παῖδες, ἥκει τῷδ᾽ ἐπ᾽ ἀνδρὶ θέσφατος
       βίου τελευτή, κοὐκέτ᾽ ἔστ᾽ ἀποστροφή.
ΧΟ.   πῶς οἶσθα; τῷ δὲ συμβαλὼν ἔχεις; ‖

So L, quinarius pro senario: most other MSS complete the trimeter by inserting τοῦτο, some before τῷ δέ, some after. Hermann pointed out the fact, which his successors neglect to notice, that Suidas has τῷ δὲ τοῦτο συμβαλὼν ἔχεις· ταυτὸν τῷ, τῷ τοῦτο κρίνεις, τουτέστι, τίνι τεκμηρίῳ νοήσας καὶ στοχασάμενος. This agreement of Suidas with sundry of our MSS might seem to render the vulgate τῷ δὲ τοῦτο συμβαλὼν ἔχεις secure in spite of L.

But it is to be remembered that L is probably* older than Suidas. These phenomena have a parallel in Ant. 1037. Some of our MSS read ἐμπολᾶτε τὸν

* [‘L is not “probably” older than the main body of Suidas: possibly it is, but the probability is the other way’, Corrigendum p. 398]

πρὸς Cάρδεων | ἤλεκτρον, and so does Eustathius twice over, pp. 368 30, 1483 27. But neither τὸν ἤλεκτρον nor πρὸς Cάρδεων can possibly be imputed to Sophocles. L offers τα προσάρδεων, whence Mr Blaydes elicits τἀπὸ Cάρδεων: this excellent emendation we all accept, undeterred by the consent of other MSS with Eustathius. Here too, in spite of Suidas, L must be considered. For, in the first place, there is no apparent reason why τοῦτο should disappear. Secondly, one of the tokens which oftenest enable us to expel from a classical text a word which has no business there is that the MSS which combine to offer it will disagree in placing it. Here this token is present: half the MSS which have τοῦτο place it after οἶσθα, half after τῷ δέ: the best MS omits it: away with it, say I, for a metrical correction.

Dindorf adds πάτερ at the end of the verse, which he assigns, perhaps rightly, to Antigone. I would suppose an easier loss. η is confused with υ and α with β more times than can be told; no wonder, then, if συμβ absorbed σημα.

πῶς οἶσθα; τῷ δὲ ⟨σῆμα⟩ συμβαλὼν ἔχεις;

by what means hast thou interpreted the sign? the thunders and lightnings, to wit: 1511 sq. αὐτοὶ θεοὶ κήρυκες ἀγγέλλουσί μοι | ψεύδοντες οὐδὲν σημάτων προκειμένων. To which passage we will next proceed.

1510–15

ΘΗ. τῷ δ᾽ ἐκπέπεισαι τοῦ μόρου τεκμηρίῳ;
ΟΙ. αὐτοὶ θεοὶ κήρυκες ἀγγέλλουσί μοι
       ψεύδοντες οὐδὲν σημάτων προκειμένων.
ΘΗ. πῶς εἶπας, ὦ γεραιέ, δηλοῦσθαι τάδε;
ΟΙ. αἱ πολλαὶ βρονταὶ διατελεῖς τὰ πολλά τε
       στρέψαντα χειρὸς τῆς ἀνικήτου βέλη. ||

The nominatives βρονταί and βέλη are anacoluthic, but the passage is not to be deemed corrupt on that account: see O. t. 740 sqq. τὸν δὲ Λάιον φύσιν | τίν᾽ ἔτυχε, φράζε, τίνα δ᾽ ἀκμὴν ἥβης ἔχων; | IO. μέγας, χνοάζων ἄρτι λευκανθὲς κάρα, O. C. 1500 sqq. τίς αὖ παρ᾽ ὑμῶν κοινὸς ἠχεῖται κτύπος; . . . μή τις Διὸς κεραυνὸς ἤ τις ὀμβρία | χάλαζ᾽ ἐπιρράξασα; I quote these passages to show that no such alteration as Reiske's δηλοῦσι for αἱ πολλαί is demanded by grammar. Inferior MSS and most editors read αἱ πολλά: I prefer the text of L. It contains a false quantity, true; but there are worse things on earth than false quantities, and the vulgate reading of this verse is one of them. The unusual order of words for αἱ πολλὰ διατελεῖς βρονταί is successfully defended by Prof. Jebb. But a verse in which πολλά comes twice over – first as an adverb meaning *very* and then as an adjective meaning *many* – is a verse which I, who am not one of the world's greatest poets, should be ashamed to set my name to; and to find Mr Jebb saying 'the reiterated πολλά is effective' would be astounding if one had not often observed that a conservative critic writing for a conservative public is apt to grow careless how he defends a text which most of his readers are willing and even eager to accept without any defence at all. However, I put this question by and content myself with pointing out the simple fact that πολλὰ διατελεῖς is not Greek. πολλὰ δεινοί, πολλὰ μοχθηρός, πλεῖστα μῶροι, πόλλ' ἀέκων, Mr Jebb's examples, are all correct and all inapposite. Cleverness, misery, folly, reluctance, are conceptions admitting the notion of more and less; and a man can be clever, miserable, foolish, or reluctant, in the positive, the comparative, or the super-lative degree. But either a thing is διατελές or it is not διατελές, and when a thing is διατελές no other thing can be more διατελές than it: there are no degrees of the quality; and πολλὰ διατελής is no more Greek than *multum perpetuus* is Latin. When Mr Jebb translates 'the long-continued thunderings' he is deceived by an idolon fori residing in the English word *continued*. *Long-continued* means *long-protracted*; but διατελής does not mean *protracted*: it means *uninterrupted*, and πολλὰ διατελεῖς would mean *very uninterrupted*. Which being ridiculous, I propose this substitute:

$$\text{Δῖαί τε βρονταὶ διατελεῖς τὰ πολλά τε}$$
$$\text{πρέψαντα χειρὸς τῆς ἀνικήτου βέλη.}$$

See 95 βροντήν τιν' ἢ Διὸς σέλας, 1460 sq. Διὸς πτερωτὸς ἥδε μ' αὐτίκ' ἄξεται | βροντὴ πρὸς Ἅιδην, 1502 Διὸς κεραυνός. Let the ΤΑΙ of ΔΙΑΙΤΑΙ be absorbed by the ΙΑΙ, and the ΔΙ of ΔΙΑΙ by the ‖ ΑΙ, αἱ βρονταί remains, and some one inserts πολλαί, suggested by the πολλά at the end of the verse.

In 1515 I have altered στ to ϖ, στρέψαντα to πρέψαντα *which shone forth*: for the form see Plat. Charm. 158 c. στρέψαντα is not defended: the vulgate is, or was till lately, Pierson's στράψαντα, to which it is objected that the Attic form is ἀστράπτω and that στράπτω occurs no earlier than Apollonius Rhodius. 'In cases of this kind', pleads Mr Jebb, 'we should always recollect how incomplete is our knowledge of the classical Attic vocabulary, and allow for the likelihood that the learned Alexandrian poets had earlier warrant for this or that word which, as it happens, we cannot trace above them. With ἀστράπτω and στράπτω, cp. ἀστεροπή and στεροπή, ἀσπαίρω and σπαίρω, ἀσταφίς and σταφίς, ἄσταχυς and στάχυς, and many other instances in which the longer form and the shorter both belong to the classical age.' This is ignoratio elenchi: we are not concerned with the classical age, but with the dialogue of Attic tragedy. The classical age extends from Homer to Demosthenes, and includes Herodotus and Pindar; and even when we know a word to have been used in the classical age, we do not on that account admit it into tragic senarii. στράπτω we do not know to have been so used; only we are encouraged by Mr Jebb to hope that it was, because it would be unlucky for Pierson's conjecture if it were not. Mr Jebb's examples are unhappily chosen: as for ἀστεροπή and στεροπή, neither of them is Attic;

ἀσπαίρω is Attic, but σπαίρω is not; there is no evidence that ἀσταφίς and σταφίς are both Attic; στάχυς is Attic, but the only ground for thinking ἄσταχυς so appears to be the grammarian at anecd. Bekk., p. 453 27, who supports his statement by a quotation from the illustrious Athenian poet Homer. στράψαντα therefore being highly improbable, some recent editors adopt Forster's σκήψαντα, which has much less palaeographical likelihood. Mr Jebb further remarks, with some truth, that 'the thought is of the lightning-flash breaking forth as a sign in the sky (φλέγει, 1466), rather than of its descent on earth'. On the other side Nauck observes with equal justice that 'βέλος σκῆψαν dem Sprachgebrauch besser entspricht als βέλος ἀστράψαν.' It will be seen that πρέψαντα escapes both these objections.

1744–7

AN. μόγος ἔχει. ΧΟ. καὶ πάρος ἐπεῖχεν.
AN. τοτὲ μὲν ἄπορα, τοτὲ δ' ὕπερθεν.
ΧΟ. μέγ' ἄρα πέλαγος ἐλαχέτην τι.
AN. αἰαῖ, ποῖ μένωμεν, ὦ Ζεῦ; ‖

Prof. Jebb thinks that 'πέλαγος, without κακῶν, or the like, is excused by the familiarity of this metaphor in Greek.' This I do not concede; but it is here superfluous to discuss the question, because even the presence of κακῶν, or the like, would not redeem so incongruous an expression as πέλαγος λαγχάνω. The metaphor πέλαγος κακῶν, as Mr Jebb says, is familiar, but it is familiar in another guise than this: Aesch. Pers. 433 sq. κακῶν δὴ πέλαγος ἔρρωγεν μέγα | Πέρσαις, supp. 470 sq. ἄτης δ' ἄβυσσον πέλαγος οὐ μάλ' εὔπορον | τόδ' ἐσβέβηκα, κοὐδαμοῦ λιμὴν κακῶν, Eur. Hipp. 822 sqq. κακῶν δ', ὦ τάλας, πέλαγος εἰσορῶ | τοσοῦτον ὥστε μήποτ' ἐκνεῦσαι πάλιν, H. f. 1086 sq. τί παῖδ' ἤχθηρας ὧδ' ὑπερκότως | τὸν σόν, κακῶν δὲ πέλαγος ἐς τόδ' ἤγαγες; Men. arreph. 1 5 sq. [59 5 sq. Koerte] ἀληθινὸν | εἰς πέλαγος αὑτὸν ἐμβαλεῖς γὰρ πραγμάτων: so too πέλαγος πλούτου, Pind. [124b Snell] ap. Athen. XI 782 D πελάγει δ' ἐν πολυχρύσοιο πλούτου | πάντες ἴσα (fort. ἴσον) νέομεν ψευδῆ πρὸς ἀκτάν. Small warrant here for the phrase *you have gotten a great sea*! Aeschylus at sept. 690 sq. writes ἴτω κατ' οὖρον κῦμα Κωκυτοῦ λαχὸν | Φοίβῳ στυγηθὲν πᾶν τὸ Λαΐου γένος, i.e. *with hell for its portion to dwell in*, and so Homer Ο 190 ἔλαχον πολιὴν ἅλα ναιέμεν αἰεί, but that is not to the purpose. This verse of Sophocles I would emend

μέγ' ἄρα πένθος ἐλαχέτην τι.

Sophocles has πένθος λαγχάνω at frag. 598 1 [659 1 Pearson] and μέγα πένθος at Aiax 616: the latter occurs also at Aesch. cho. 300 and seven times over in Homer. The ελαγ of the corrupt reading may be an anticipation of the following ελαχ; but I incline rather to derive πέλαγος from

ΑΛΓΟΣ
ΠΕΝΘΟΣ

i.e. the gloss ἄλγος mistaken for a correction of -νθος to -λαγος. I do not find πένθος explained by ἄλγος either in Hesychius, who has πένθος· συμφορά, θρῆνος, λύπη, or in the Byzantine lexicons; nor in the tragic scholia have I met anything nearer than Eur. Hipp. 138 κρυπτῷ πένθει· ἀντὶ τοῦ ὑπὸ τῆς ἀλγηδόνος καὶ τῆς νόσου τῆς κρυπτῆς. But the possibility of such a gloss may be shown as follows. Hesychius has ἄλγος· πόνος, πένθος. At first you might think that πένθος is not likely to be explained by ἄλγος when ἄλγος is explained by πένθος. But observe that ἄλγος is also explained by πόνος: now turn to πόνος and you find it explained by ἄλγος: the article runs πόνος· ἄλγος, ἐνέργημα ὀδύνης. Nothing forbids, then, that ἄλγος, a ‖ common word in late as in early Greek, should be similarly employed as a gloss to πένθος. It is a trifle, yet perhaps worth mention, that the verse now tallies precisely, which formerly it did not, with the accepted reading of the strophic line 1734 ⟦1733⟧ ἄγε με καὶ τότ᾽ ἐπενάριξον.

24

SOPHOCLEA*

Ant. 69–70

οὔτ᾽ ἂν κελεύσαιμ᾽ οὔτ᾽ ἄν, εἰ θέλοις ἔτι
πράσσειν, ἐμοῦ γ᾽ ἂν ἡδέως δρῴης μέτα.

The only correct translation of these words is Seyffert's, *nor, were you willing to help me, would you enjoy it*: ἡδέως, that is to say, can mean nothing but ἡδέως σαυτῇ. But that Seyffert and Wecklein should think this rendering a defence of the text is strange. It is precisely the inaptness, not to say ineptitude, of this sentiment that drives most editors to make ἡδέως mean ἡδέως ἐμοί and to give the apt but inadmissible translation *nor, were you willing to help me, would I willingly suffer you.* Prof. Jebb supports this version with such examples as Ar. nub. 79 πῶς δῆτ᾽ ἂν ἥδιστ᾽ αὐτὸν ἐπεγείραιμι; i.e. ἥδιστ᾽ αὐτῷ: examples which certainly demonstrate something. They demonstrate that when you have, for instance, δρᾷς τάδ᾽ ἡδέως ἐμέ, then ἡδέως can mean either ἡδέως ἐμοί or ἡδέως σαυτῇ, which you will: naturally; for a transitive verb is related as closely to its object as to its subject, and so accordingly is any adverb which qualifies that verb: if any one has denied this, Mr Jebb refutes him. But to a substantive or pronoun attached by the link of a preposition the verb, and consequently its adverb too, is related much less nearly: the feasibility therefore, in the sentence ἐμοῦ γ᾽ ἂν ἡδέως δρῴης μέτα, of supplying ἐμοί to the exclusion of σαυτῇ must be demonstrated, if at all, from other examples than these. Meanwhile I shall suspect that we are debating over a mere error for ἐμοῦ γ᾽ ἂν ἵλεω δρῴης μέτα. Since ι had the sound ‖ of η and Λ the look of Δ we should expect to find the scribes confounding these two words, nor do they disappoint us. At Aiax 1011 the Laurentian and its older apographs have ὅτῳ πάρα | μηδ᾽ εὐτυχοῦντι μηδὲν ἵλεων γελᾶν, later MSS ἥδιον. In Eur. I. A. 1596 the words ἡδέως τε τοῦτ᾽ ἐδέξατο καὶ πλοῦν οὔριον | δίδωσιν ἡμῖν will never perhaps regain their pristine form, but Weil's ἵλεως is a most specious correction of the initial cretic. In Eur. Bacch. 188 ἐπιλελήσμεθ᾽ ἡδέων | γέροντες ὄντες sense is commonly restored by Milton's ἡδέως, and I would not set up my own conjecture against it; yet I am not at all sure that ἵλεωι is not really as near the MSS.

* [*JPh* 20 (1892), 25–48]

Ant. 437–40

τὸ μὲν γὰρ αὐτὸν ἐκ κακῶν πεφευγέναι
ἥδιστον, ἐς κακὸν δὲ τοὺς φίλους ἄγειν
ἀλγεινόν. ἀλλὰ πάντα ταῦθ᾽ ἥσσω λαβεῖν
ἐμοὶ πέφυκε τῆς ἐμῆς σωτηρίας.

But all these things are to me less worth winning than my own safety. All what things? Beside τὸ αὐτὸν ἐκ κακῶν πεφευγέναι, which is of course the same as ἡ ἐμὴ σωτηρία, mention has been made of one thing only; and what is that one thing? it is ἐς κακὸν τοὺς φίλους ἄγειν: all such things then as bringing one's friends to grief are less worth winning than one's own safety! This absurd result Prof. Jebb avoids by one road in his translation and in his commentary by another. In the commentary he paraphrases 'all such objects as the *safety* of friends'; but *safety* is just the reverse of ἐς κακὸν ἄγειν. In the translation this method is impracticable and he gives "'tis my nature to make all such things *of less account* than my own safety'. But this is a version which in the commentary Mr Jebb himself expressly condemns, for the sufficient reason that it is no proper rendering of ἥσσω λαβεῖν. Instead of a text which puts us to these shifts Mr Blaydes procures a simple sense by altering ταῦθ᾽ to τἄλλ᾽, which Nauck accepts and Mr Jebb calls attractive but palaeographically improbable. To this objection I will add that in Sophocles the phrase is always τἄλλα πάντα (Oed. Col. 609, ‖ Phil. 610, 1442, El. 657, 741, Aiax 1398, though I think this last corrupt), not πάντα τἄλλα. Write the words in their usual order and it will give us that palaeographical probability which Mr Jebb requires: ἀλλὰ τἄλλα πάνθ᾽ ἥσσω λαβεῖν: τἄλλα was lost in ἀλλὰ and a solicitous metrist then expanded πάνθ᾽ to πάντα ταῦθ᾽ without heeding the context.

I take this opportunity of emending a very similar error in Stob. ecl. 1 4 2 b p. 71 2 [[vol. i p. 71 Wachsmuth]] = Eur. frag. 299 Nauck ed. 1889:

πρὸς τὴν ἀνάγκην πάντα τἄλλ᾽ ἔστ᾽ ἀσθενῆ.

ἔστ᾽ in this position is metrically inadmissible: see Elmsley Eur. Bacch. 246 and Nauck Euripideische Studien 1 pp. 46 sq. Write

πρὸς τὴν ἀνάγκην τἄλλ᾽, ὅσ᾽ ἔστιν, ἀσθενῆ.

οσ is absorbed in εσ, and scribes never care whether they write ἔστιν or ἔστ᾽: this leaves τἄλλ᾽ ἔστ᾽, and some one inserts πάντα to make a senarius. πάνθ᾽ ὅσ᾽ ἔστιν I should think hardly so probable.

Ant. 548

καὶ τίς βίος μοι σοῦ λελειμμένη φίλος;

When Sophocles had written the first five feet of this senarius, *how can I live without you*, he had written a vigorous sentence adequate to the situation:

compare 566 τί γὰρ μόνη μοι τῆσδ' ἄτερ βιώσιμον; One iambus was lacking, and his native language proffered him iambic words in plenty to complete the verse without impairing its vigour. Who believes that he set them all aside and chose instead a word which enfeebles the sentiment to *how can I enjoy life without you?* Wecklein's μόνη and Hense's μένει are both of them words he might have used, and either of the two would easily merge in -μένη and leave a gap for the scribes to fill with this nerveless φίλος. But a simpler correction than either, surely the simplest possible, is καὶ τίς βίος μοι σοῦ λελειμμένη, φίλη; Misapprehended vocatives are a perennial fount of error in ancient MSS which do not employ our devices of punctuation: I take two kindred instances from the Hippolytus: 199 λέλυμαι ‖ μελέων ξύνδεσμα, φίλαι, corrupted to φίλων, and 364 sq. ὀλοίμαν ἔγωγε πρὶν σᾶν, φίλα, | κατανύσαι φρενῶν, τὸ σὰν φίλαν.

Ant. 746
ὦ μιαρὸν ἦθος καὶ γυναικὸς ὕστερον.

μιαρόν! what has Haemon said or done to earn this epithet? 'O dastard nature' Jebb; but this is no translation of μιαρόν, which means *bloody* or *filthy* or *ruffianly*. It is only the least self-respecting of disputants who can choose a term so openly devoid not merely of truth but of verisimilitude: pointless abuse of this sort hurts none but those who utter it, and no heat of anger will reconcile it with the lofty character of Creon. I propose to replace the word by μάργον *lustful* (Aesch. supp. 741, Eur. El. 1027), precisely the taunt which can most plausibly be levelled at a man who interferes with the course of justice to save the forfeit life of his affianced bride. And sure enough it is this reproach that Haemon in the next verse repels with οὔ τᾶν ἕλοις ἥσσω γε τῶν αἰσχρῶν ἐμέ. MAPION is the halfway-house between the two readings.[1]

Ant. 1019–22
κᾆτ' οὐ δέχονται θυστάδας λιτὰς ἔτι
θεοὶ παρ' ἡμῶν οὐδὲ μηρίων φλόγα,
οὐδ' ὄρνις εὐσήμους ἀπορροιβδεῖ βοὰς
ἀνδροφθόρου βεβρῶτες αἵματος λίπος.

ἀπὸ τοῦ ἑνικοῦ ἐπὶ τὸ πληθυντικὸν μετέβη says the scholiast; and really that is all there is to say about ὄρνις ἀπορροιβδεῖ βεβρῶτες: succeeding commentators can add nothing, no palliation, no parallel; unless any easy-tempered reader will accept for parallel the common and regular correlation of ὅστις with οὗτοι, or οὐδέν πω κακόν γ' ἀπώλετο | ἀλλ' εὖ περιστέλλουσιν αὐτὰ δαίμονες, or ὡς ὥρα πάντα μὲν ἄνδρα σβεννύντα τὸ πῦρ, δυναμένους δὲ οὐκέτι καταλαβεῖν. And ‖ then

---

[1] Prof. Palmer in Hermathena vol. VI pp. 291 sq. brings the same objection against μιαρόν, and adds that no other senarius in this play begins with a dactyl or anapaest. He proposes μωρόν (μῶρον).

the form βεβρῶτες? It is true, as shewn by Mr Rutherford at Babrius 33 3, that even the comedians abused the analogy of ἑστώς by figments no less absurd than βεβρώς for βεβρωκώς; but each supposed example, and more especially a ἅπαξ εἰρημένον like this, must be narrowly scanned, and here any doubt which may be kindled by the metaplasm will hardly be quenched by the false concord. The joint force of the suspicions converging on this word from the diverse quarters of accidence and syntax every one will measure for himself: I am led to guess that the original was οὐδ᾽ ὄρνε᾽ εὐσήμους ἀπορροιβδεῖ βοὰς | ἀνδροφθόρου βεβρωκόθ᾽ αἵματος λίπος: Mr Blaydes has already conjectured ὄρνε᾽. Let the one ε absorb the other, the remnant ὄρν᾽ would most readily suggest ὄρνις: βε-βρωκΕϹ for βεβρωκΟΘ is a short step on the road of error and βεβρῶτες an unlucky effort to retrace it. ὄρνεον, though not found in the tragic texts, is at once Attic and poetical, and Dr Verrall's restitution of τέθνηκεν οἷσπερ ὀρνέοις θνῄσκειν καλόν to Aesch. sept. 1011 on the strength of the scholion appears to have high probability.

Oed. tyr. 216–18

αἰτεῖς· ἃ δ᾽ αἰτεῖς, τἄμ᾽ ἐὰν θέλῃς ἔπη
κλύων δέχεσθαι τῇ νόσῳ θ᾽ ὑπηρετεῖν,
ἀλκὴν λάβοις ἂν κἀνακούφισιν κακῶν.

Because in English we sometimes speak of ministering to a sickness when we mean the very opposite, fighting the sickness and ministering to the sick man, it does not follow that the Greeks were equally inaccurate. Latin examples are to be found, though not many; and all that I have noted are post-Augustan, as Stat. Achill. II 445 'auxiliantia morbis | gramina', for it is on other grounds improbable that Horace wrote 'podagram' at epist. I 2 52. But in Greek it appears that the editors of Sophocles can find no parallel at all, since the single passage they adduce, El. 1306 οὐ γὰρ ἂν καλῶς | ὑπηρετοίην τῷ παρόντι δαίμονι, speaks of furthering a toward chance, not of mending a cross one. Prof. Jebb very fairly allows that according to common use νόσῳ ὑπηρετεῖν would mean to indulge || a malady, as in the τῇ ἑαυτοῦ παρανομίᾳ προθύμως ἐξυπηρετῶν which he quotes from Lysias. Nauck therefore writes τῷ θεῷ for τῇ νόσῳ; but the context points another way. Recall how often Sophocles likens a city to a ship: 694 ἐμὰν γᾶν φίλαν ἐν πόνοις σαλεύουσαν κατ᾽ ὀρθὸν οὔρισας, Ant. 163 τὰ μὲν δὴ πόλεος ἀσφαλῶς θεοὶ | πολλῷ σάλῳ σείσαντες ὤρθωσαν πάλιν, 994 δι᾽ ὀρθῆς τήνδ᾽ ἐναυκλήρεις πόλιν, Aiax 1082 ταύτην νόμιζε τὴν πόλιν χρόνῳ ποτ᾽ ἂν | ἐξ οὐρίων δραμοῦσαν ἐς βυθὸν πεσεῖν: compare in particular 22 sqq. of our play, πόλις γάρ...ἄγαν | ἤδη σαλεύει κἀνακουφίσαι κάρα | βυθῶν ἔτ᾽ οὐχ οἷά τε φοινίου σάλου, with the ἀνακούφισιν of the passage we are now considering: does not the nautical metaphor of ὑπηρετεῖν invite the citizens to render aid neither τῇ νόσῳ nor τῷ θεῷ but to the *city*? γῇ θ᾽ ὁμῶς ὑπηρετεῖν *to serve your country with one accord.* One form of ν is μ, merely μ without its last stroke; the ι which with us is subscript is as often omitted as expressed in MSS earlier than 1200 A.D.: the error here then is μοσωθ for θομωσ, a transposition of letters; for the confusion of γῆ and τῆ is not worth mentioning.

Oed. tyr. 596–8

νῦν πᾶσι χαίρω, νῦν με πᾶς ἀσπάζεται,
νῦν οἱ σέθεν χρήζοντες αἰκάλλουσί με,
τὸ γὰρ τυχεῖν αὐτοὺς ἅπαν ἐνταῦθ' ἔνι.

Nauck seems to be the only modern editor who retains this reading of the last verse, and he retains it only because it is not yet emended. Inferior MSS give αὐτοῖσι πᾶν: if this unscientific conjecture were made by a scholar of these days it would be despised as it deserves, but because it occurred to an unlettered scribe before the dawn of criticism it becomes the vulgate. The following strikes me as not only easier but more satisfactory: τὸ γὰρ τυχεῖν σοῦ, τοῦθ' ἅπαν ἐνταῦθ' ἔνι *their gaining your ear depends wholly on me*: compare Eur. Hipp. 328 μεῖζον γὰρ ἢ σοῦ μὴ τυχεῖν τί μοι κακόν; Aesch. supp. 161 μὴ τυχοῦσαι θεῶν Ὀλυμπίων. This resumptive use of τοῦτο has a good example in Trach. 458 τὸ μὴ πυθέσθαι, τοῦτό μ' ἀλγύνειεν ἄν. Porson at Eur. Hec. 782 [794] gives many ‖ instances of οσ confused with α, and the similar corruption of σο is little less easy.

Oed. tyr. 1275–9

τοιαῦτ' ἐφυμνῶν πολλάκις τε κοὐχ ἅπαξ
ἤρασσ' ἐπαίρων βλέφαρα. φοίνιαι δ' ὁμοῦ
γλῆναι γένει' ἔτεγγον, οὐδ' ἀνίεσαν
φόνου μυδώσας σταγόνας, ἀλλ' ὁμοῦ μέλας
ὄμβρος χάλαζά θ' αἱματοῦσσ' ἐτέγγετο.

The scholiast takes the object of ἐπαίρων to be βλέφαρα, which is unavoidable but absurd: modern editors mostly supply περόνας or χεῖρα, which is appropriate but impracticable. I will therefore propose without more ado ἤρασσε περόναις βλέφαρα: compare 1268 sqq. ἀποσπάσας…περόνας…ἄρας ἔπαισεν ἄρθρα τῶν αὐτοῦ κύκλων. If the termination -αις were represented by one or other of its abbreviations and so lost, the resultant ηρασσεπερον would be really the same thing as ηρασσεπαιρων; or this corruption may have taken place first and extruded αις; or αις may have been lost through its likeness, which in some handwritings would be very strong, to the following βλε.

I should like further to upbraid modern editors, or most of them, with the form in which they present 1279: ὄμβρος χαλάζης αἱματοῦς Wunder Wecklein Campbell Jebb, ὄμβρος χαλάζης αἱμάτων Schneidewin Nauck. You can say ὄμβρος χαλάζης for hail, the genitive defining the exact substance which you mean when you use the generic term ὄμβρος: you can say ὄμβρος αἱματοῦς or χάλαζα αίματοῦσσα or αἱμάτων for a downpour of blood, the genitive or adjective defining the substance of which the so-called ὄμβρος or χάλαζα really consists: these things are credible in themselves and are proved by the examples which the editors adduce. But that when you have already defined the substance of the ὄμβρος as being χάλαζα you can then contradict yourself and define it anew as being not χάλαζα but αἷμα, this requires to be proved by examples which never have been adduced and I prophesy never will be. ‖

Oed. tyr. 1349–53

ὄλοιθ᾽ ὅστις ἦν, ὃς ἀπ᾽ ἀγρίας πέδας
νομάδος ἐπιποδίας ἔλαβέ μ᾽ ἀπό τε φόνου
ἔρυτο κἀνέσωσεν, οὐδὲν εἰς χάριν πράσσων.

The second half of the first verse has one syllable too many for a dochmiac, so the editors reject ἀπ᾽. This entails altering ἔλαβέ μ᾽ to ἔλυσ᾽ and κἀνέσωσεν with Campbell to κἀνέσωσέ μ᾽: these changes may be right, for the latter is very easy and the former has whatever authority attaches to an ancient correction ἔλυσεν in L. What cannot be right is to reject ἀπ᾽ without making these changes and to say as Schneidewin and other German commentators do that ἀπό can be understood before πέδας from the ἀπό φόνου which follows. To prove this they quote 734 Δελφῶν κἀπὸ Δαυλίας ἄγει, and of course I could add twenty similar citations of equal irrelevance which would become pertinent if the passage on its trial were πέδας μ᾽ ἀπό τε φόνου ἔρυτο or πέδας ἔλαβέ μ᾽ ἀπό τε φόνου: but the would-be defenders of πέδας ἔλαβέ μ᾽ ἀπό τε φόνου ἔρυτο must produce Δελφῶν ἄγει κἀπὸ Δαυλίας φέρει, which they cannot.

The next verse is still more difficult: here the first half has one syllable over dochmiac measure and the strophe leaves us doubtful whether or no the measure ought to be dochmiac. The answering verse 1330 appears in L as ὁ κακὰ τελῶν τάδ᾽ ἐμὰ πάθεα, whence it is proposed to delete ἐπιποδίας here. But since there was no adequate motive for inserting that word it is more likely that each verse should consist of a brace of dochmiacs, though whether at 1330 the ancient correction in L ὁ κακὰ κακὰ τελῶν ἐμὰ τάδ᾽ ἐμὰ πάθεα gives what Sophocles wrote must be quite uncertain. To restore a dochmiac in 1350 Elmsley alters νομάδος, which has no known meaning suitable to the place, into νομάδ᾽, which however has no suitable meaning either. I feel no doubt that Prof. Jebb's conjecture μονάδ᾽ is correct so far as it goes; but I propose to reconstitute the passage with slighter changes than these four of ὅς for ὃς ἀπ᾽, μονάδ᾽ for νομάδος, ἔλυσ᾽ for ἔλαβέ μ᾽ and κἀνέσωσέ μ᾽ for κἀνέσωσεν; to wit as follows: ‖

ὄλοιθ᾽ ὅστις ἦν, ἀπ᾽ ἀγρίας πέδας
μονάδ᾽ ὃς ἐπὶ πόας ἔλαβέ μ᾽ ἀπό τε φόνου
ἔρυτο κἀνέσωσεν.

ἐπὶ πόας, by which μονάδα gains a good deal to my fancy, is Prof. Campbell's: the alteration ἐπιποδίας was suggested I suppose by the scribe's knowledge of the story. When μονάδ' ὅς coalesced into μονάδος or νομάδος it of course became necessary to insert ὅς somewhere, and its most natural place was where we find it in the MS, at the beginning of the clause. If L's original reading of 1330 be retained and ἐπιποδίας ejected from 1350 I would still write the other words as above, ἀπ' ἀγρίας πέδας | μονάδ' ὅς ἔλαβέ μ' ἀπό τε φόνου | ἔρυτο, counting the last syllable of φόνου as long.

Aiax 784–5

ὦ δαΐα Τέκμησσα, δύσμορον γένος,
ὅρα μολοῦσα τόνδ' ὁποῖ' ἔπη θροεῖ.

The coryphaeus might call Tecmessa δύσμορον Τελεύταντος γένος: Teleutas himself perhaps might call her δύσμορον γένος without adding ἐμόν: but neither she nor any other person can be addressed as γένος except it be with a reference to her or his descent. Here there is no question of Tecmessa's ancestors or of any woe with which they have aught to do; and editors who quote Z 180 where the Chimaera is said to have been θεῖον γένος οὐδ' ἀνθρώπων prove that they are easily satisfied, but nothing else. Tecmessa is called unhappy because her husband is in peril of his life; no name therefore can suit her better than δύσμορον λέχος *unhappy wife*: she is δύσμορος νύμφη at 894 and λέχος δουριάλωτον at 211. The exchange of λέχος and γένος is not difficult and in fact occurs at other places: I have noted down Eur. Or. 1154 where the MSS are divided between the two: in O. t. 1362 ὁμογενής seems just defensible but Meineke's ὁμολεχής right.

Aiax 795–802

ΑΓ.	ἐκεῖνον εἴργειν Τεῦκρος ἐξεφίεται σκηνῆς ὕπαυλον μηδ' ἀφιέναι μόνον. ‖	795
ΤΕΚ.	ποῦ δ' ἐστὶ Τεῦκρος, κἀπὶ τῷ λέγει τάδε;	
ΑΓ.	πάρεστ' ἐκεῖνος ἄρτι· τήνδε δ' ἔξοδον ὀλεθρίαν Αἴαντος ἐλπίζει φέρειν.	
ΤΕΚ.	οἴμοι τάλαινα, τοῦ ποτ' ἀνθρώπων μαθών;	800
ΑΓ.	τοῦ Θεστορείου μάντεως, καθ' ἡμέραν τὴν νῦν, ὅτ' αὐτῷ θάνατον ἢ βίον φέρει.	

'Teucer gives charge to confine Aiax in the tent and let him not go forth *alone*.' But the messenger's first version of Teucer's charge at 741 contained no such limitation: there it was simply to let him not go forth, ἔνδοθεν στέγης | μὴ 'ξω παρήκειν πρὶν παρὼν αὐτὸς τύχοι: and that moreover was the charge given to Teucer by Calchas at 753, εἶρξαι κατ' ἦμαρ τοὐμφανὲς τὸ νῦν τόδε | Αἴανθ' ὑπὸ σκηναῖσι μηδ' ἀφέντ' ἐᾶν. The spaced words are surely a plain fingerpost to the correction of our passage thus: ἐκεῖνον εἴργειν Τεῦκρος ἐξεφίεται | σκηνῆς ὕπαυλον μηδ' ἐᾶν ἀφειμένον. Compare for additional confirmation Ant. 578 sq. εὖ δὲ τάσδε χρὴ | γυναῖκας εἶρξαι μηδ' ἐᾶν ἀνειμένας:[1] the phrase recurs in another sense at Eur. El. 379 κράτιστον εἰκῇ ταῦτ' ἐᾶν ἀφειμένα. εαναφει and αφιεναι have six letters in common out of seven.

I will not add another to the conjectures heaped on 799, but proceed to 801 sq. The MS reading now has few to defend it: it will apparently mean 'he heard it from Calchas this day, wherein it (ἡ ἔξοδος comes over from 798 to govern the verb) brings either death or life to Aiax', i.e. death if it takes place, || life if it does not. This is incapably expressed: much better is the translation given of Jacobs' τὴν νῦν ὅς αὐτῷ, 'who announces death or life to Aiax this day'; only it does not appear that the translation is legitimate unless φέρει is altered as Nauck suggests to θροεῖ or the like: Prof. Jebb quotes Aesch. Pers. 249 [248] φέρει σαφές τι πρᾶγος, and the immediate context here supplies a similar instance in 789 φέρων | Αἴαντος ἡμῖν πρᾶξιν ἣν ἤλγησ' ἐγώ: but θάνατόν τινι φέρειν would naturally and regularly mean something quite different. It must be generally felt that the sense we desire and expect is that which some inferior MSS regardless of metre procure by altering ὅτ' to ἥ, 'on this very day, which brings either death or life to Aiax'; and I propose to obtain it thus: καθ' ἥλιον | τὸν νῦν, ὅς αὐτῷ κτλ. This poetical use of ἥλιος for ἡμέρα recurs at Eur. El. 654 and Hel. 652, but is rare enough to invite the gloss which I suppose to have ousted the genuine word: the necessary change of τόν to τήν offered no difficulty, but to substitute ἥ for ὅς required more nerve, and ὅτ' served instead.

Aiax 1393–9

σὲ δ', ὦ γεραιοῦ σπέρμα Λαέρτου πατρός,
τάφου μὲν ὀκνῶ τοῦδ' ἐπιψαύειν ἐᾶν,

1395   μὴ τῷ θανόντι τοῦτο δυσχερὲς ποιῶ·
                τὰ δ' ἄλλα καὶ ξύμπραττε, κεἴ τινα στρατοῦ
                θέλεις κομίζειν, οὐδὲν ἄλγος ἕξομεν.
                ἐγὼ δὲ τἄλλα πάντα πορσυνῶ· σὺ δὲ
                ἀνὴρ καθ' ἡμᾶς ἐσθλὸς ὢν ἐπίστασο.

---

[1] Whether εἴρξαι or εἶλαι (ἶλαι) should here be read is not certain, but they come to the same thing: Hesych. ἐλλόμενον· εἰργόμενον. Αἰσχύλος Βασσάραις. I have given the passage after Dindorf's emendation as perfected by Madvig: the MS has ἐκ δὲ τάσδε χρή | γυναῖκας εἶναι τάσδε μηδ' ἀνειμένας. Certainly I cannot entertain a thought either of Engelmann's ἐκδέτας δὲ χρή, which in iambic dialogue ought at least to be ἐκδέτους, or of the old unscientific ἐκ δὲ τοῦδε χρή which is still the vulgate. 'Henceforth they must be women, and not range at large', as Prof. Jebb renders it, sounds very well till we look at the context, which proceeds φεύγουσι γάρ τοι χοἰ θρασεῖς, ὅταν πέλας | ἤδη τὸν Ἅιδην εἰσορῶσι τοῦ βίου, 'for verily even the bold seek to fly, when they see Death now closing on their life' (Jebb): this reflexion with its inferential particle is quite incoherent unless there has preceded a command to imprison the sisters; and even if μὴ ἀνειμένας εἶναι ('not to range at large') could by itself signify imprisonment, it certainly cannot when coordinated with γυναῖκας εἶναι, as if forsooth women were not women unless imprisoned.

'In the burial I am loth to let you have a hand lest I displease the dead; but in all else help us and welcome, and if you will bring any other man of the host we shall be nothing vexed.' Interpreted thus the lines 1396 sq. seem defensible: the presence of the hated Odysseus would outrage the dead, but if he cares to provide a representative in token of respect, well and good. Were it necessary to accept the version which against Sophoclean usage makes κομίζειν mean *bury* and so elicits the jocular sentiment 'if you like to bury any one else it ‖ will not annoy us at all', then indeed we must concede to Schneidewin that the two verses are interpolated; and the interpolator was another Aristophanes. But to expel the lines involves further changes and appears as I said to be unnecessary if they are understood aright. With this preface then I go on to my present concern, the words τἄλλα πάντα in 1398. These words mean the burial; but in what a way do they come to mean it! τὰ ἄλλα in 1396 means τὰ ἄλλα πλὴν τάφον τόνδε: τἄλλα πάντα in 1398 means τὰ ἄλλα πλὴν τὰ ἄλλα πλὴν τάφον τόνδε, *everything except everything except the burial = the burial*: an admirably correct equation, I admit. Rauchenstein's τἀμὰ πάντα and Schneidewin's ταῦτα πάντα are better than the text because anything is better, yet the former is little suitable and the latter not the easiest of changes: I should write ἐγὼ δὲ τἀλλείποντα προσυνῶ *I will make good what lacks*, in support of which I will only remind the reader that ει compendiously written has been mistaken times out of number for α, and refer him to the words of Odysseus in 1378 sqq. καὶ τὸν θανόντα τόνδε συνθάπτειν θέλω ‖ καὶ ξυμπονεῖν καὶ μηδὲν ἐλλείπειν ὅσων ‖ χρὴ τοῖς ἀρίστοις ἀνδράσιν πονεῖν βροτούς: the offer to συνθάπτειν is rejected in 1394, the offer to ξυμπονεῖν accepted in 1396, and here in 1398 is dispelled all fear of an ἔλλειμμα. And now that 1379 has helped to emend 1398 the latter in its turn shall help to emend 1380: πονεῖν after ξυμπονεῖν in the line above can hardly be right, and our τἀλλείποντα προσυνῶ suggests καὶ μηδὲν ἐλλείπειν ὅσων ‖ χρὴ τοῖς ἀρίστοις ἀνδράσιν πορεῖν βροτούς: ρ like μ is easily confounded with ν.

El. 453–60

αἰτοῦ δὲ προσπίτνουσα γῆθεν εὐμενῆ
ἡμῖν ἀρωγὸν αὐτὸν εἰς ἐχθροὺς μολεῖν,
καὶ παῖδ' Ὀρέστην ἐξ ὑπερτέρας χερὸς   455
ἐχθροῖσιν αὐτοῦ ζῶντ' ἐπεμβῆναι ποδί,
ὅπως τὸ λοιπὸν αὐτὸν ἀφνεωτέραις
χερσὶ στέφωμεν ἢ τὰ νῦν δωρούμεθα.
οἶμαι μὲν οὖν, οἶμαί τι κἀκείνῳ μέλον
πέμψαι τάδ' αὐτῇ δυσπρόσοπτ' ὀνείρατα. ‖   460

In regard to the phrase χερσὶ στέφωμεν αὐτόν a scruple is suggested by the fact that in the 17 other examples of στέφειν or στεφανοῦν τινά τινι which the tragic lexicons offer, Aesch. Eum. 44, Soph. El. 53, Ant. 431, Aiax 93, frag. 492 5

⟦535 5 Pearson⟧, Eur. Bacch. 81, 101, 106, 112, 177, 341, Alc. 759, Tro. 576, Hec. 126, frag. 282 24, 369 3, 530 2, the dative is always the dative of the material composing the στέφος. It is only when στέφειν takes another construction, as in Aesch. sept. 50 μνημεῖα… πρὸς ἄρμα… χερσὶν ἔστεφον, that we find χερσίν added. Now if anyone bearing in mind the στέφωμεν and δωρούμεθα of our passage will then remember these, Eur. Or. 117 Ἑλένη σ᾽ ἀδελφὴ ταῖσδε δωρεῖται χοαῖς, 1321 sq. τάφον | στέψασα καὶ σπείσασα νερτέροις χοάς, Soph. El. 51 sqq. τύμβον …λοιβαῖσι…στέψαντες, 440 sq. χοάς…τῷδ᾽ ἐπέστεφεν and finally Ant. 431 χοαῖσι τρισπόνδοισι τὸν νέκυν στέφει, I shall be rather disappointed if he does not agree with me in restoring ἀφνεωτέραις | χοαῖς στέφωμεν ἢ τανῦν δωρούμεθα. There remains the question whether ἀφνεός, like most words which mean *rich*, πλούσιος ὄλβιος *diues beatus*, can have the sense *abundant* which is now required but for which the lexicons cite no earlier authority than Oppian: if not, I think we must read ἀφθονωτέραις or ἀφθονεστέραις: Aesch. frag. 72 ⟦106 Mette⟧ has ἀφθονεστέραν λίβα. To assist the defender of ἀφνεωτέραις χερσί I will remind him that ἀφνειᾶς χειρός occurs in Pind. Ol. VII 1.

In 459 for μέλον, which is thought to mean μέλον εἶναι, read μετόν: τι then is the subject of πέμψαι: 'I think that this dream was sent by some cause in which he (as well as the powers to whom dreams belong) has a part.' There is one form of τ much like the λ which we commonly employ.

El. 537–41

   ἀλλ᾽ ἀντ᾽ ἀδελφοῦ δῆτα Μενέλεω κτανὼν
   τἄμ᾽, οὐκ ἔμελλεν τῶνδέ μοι δώσειν δίκην;
   πότερον ἐκείνῳ παῖδες οὐκ ἦσαν διπλοῖ;
540 οὓς τῆσδε μᾶλλον εἰκὸς ἦν θνήσκειν, πατρὸς
   καὶ μητρὸς ὄντας, ἧς ὁ πλοῦς ὅδ᾽ ἦν χάριν. ‖

Professors Jebb and Campbell have no note on ἧς in 541, and of course it looks easy to English the sentence by 'being the children of the father and mother for whose sake the fleet sailed', because *whose* is English for ἧς and οἷν and ὧν alike. But the only proper translation is 'being the children of a father, and of the mother for whose sake' etc.: two reasons then are given why Menelaus' children should have been sacrificed rather than Iphigenia: they, unlike Iphigenia, were born of Helen, and they, unlike Iphigenia, had a father. The editors who have notes help us little. ἧς, says Wunder, is employed instead of ὧν 'cum inuidia quadam Helenae'. Grant that this was the aim in view: how easy to attain it. How easy *not* to write πατρός at all, but simply μητρὸς ὄντας ἧς. There is not one of us, οἳ νῦν βροτοί ἐσμεν ἐπιχθόνιοι, but could excite the desired 'inuidia' *without* violating a concord, *without* leaving πατρός to hang in the air sans grammar or meaning: was Sophocles so much our intellectual inferior that he could not?

When Nauck conjectures πάρος for πατρός he displays his customary acuteness: the two words are often confounded, as at Eur. H. f. 930, and the pleonasm μᾶλλον πάρος is very idiomatic: see for instance O. C. 418 sq. πάρος | τοὐμοῦ πόθου προὔθεντο τὴν τυραννίδα. But then with a lack of art which unhappily is no less habitual he goes on to eject the next verse; as if an interpolator, any more than Sophocles himself, would have written ἧς when he meant ὧν. All the change now wanted is the substitution of a breathing for an accent. ε before κ dwindles to an almost invisible volute at the head of the upright stroke and thus often vanishes altogether: hence ἐκ appears as κ̇ and is taken for κ̇ the abbreviation of καί: O. C. 792 ἐκ L, καί al. I should write therefore οὓς τῆσδε μᾶλλον εἰκὸς ἦν θνῄσκειν πάρος, | ἐκ μητρὸς ὄντας ἧς ὁ πλοῦς ὅδ᾽ ἦν χάριν.

El. 708–11

Βοιωτὸς ἄλλος, δέκατον ἐκπληρῶν ὄχον.
στάντες δ᾽ ὅθ᾽ αὐτοὺς οἱ τεταγμένοι βραβῆς
κλήρους ἔπηλαν καὶ κατέστησαν δίφρους,
χαλκῆς ὑπαὶ σάλπιγγος ᾖξαν. ||

I start from Wunder's correction, adopted I think by all modern editors except Prof. Campbell, κλήρους for the MS κλήροις in 710: this renders the sentence intelligible, and the construction κλήρους ἔπηλαν αὐτούς for ἐκλήρωσαν αὐτούς, harsh as it is, has yet parallels to defend it, though after all one may wonder with Mr Blaydes why the poet did not write αὐτοῖς. But there remains the stumbling-block of ὅθ᾽. It was Elmsley at Eur. I. T. 35 who first pointed out that ὅθι is not elsewhere employed in tragic dialogue, and that even in those parts of tragedy where it is employed it is never elided. Sophocles therefore if he wanted an adverb of that meaning would here have used ἵν᾽, which Nauck bravely sets in the text. He observes that Homer's MSS vary between ὅθι and ἵνα at Θ 83, δ 85, 3 210; but in those places it seems reasonable to suppose that the rarer ὅθι is the original and ἵνα the substitute: here we must assume the reverse, which is not likely. Prof. Jebb proposes ὅτ᾽, i.e. ὅτε in the sense which it often has of ἐπεί postquam; and although the change of a common word into a strange one does not easily happen, yet here it is merely the change of one letter, and that is always possible. But Mr Jebb does not seem to perceive that this will involve a further alteration of στάντες, which is left pitiably naked when the adverb of place is taken away. I agree however that ὅτε was the poet's word; only ὅθ᾽ is quite right and the mistake is elsewhere: πάντες δ᾽, ὅθ᾽ ἁγνοὺς οἱ τεταγμένοι βραβῆς | κλήρους ἔπηλαν καὶ κατέστησαν δίφρους, | χαλκῆς ὑπαὶ σάλπιγγος ᾖξαν, *when the appointed judges had cast incorrupt lots*. The confusion of π with στ is very well known; the change of ἁγνους to στυους was easy and the correction to αυτους certain: ὅθ᾽ ἁγνούς explains the MS reading much better than would ὅτ᾽ αὐτοῖς, better even than ὅτ᾽ αὐτούς.

El. 930–1

οἴμοι τάλαινα· τοῦ γὰρ ἀνθρώπων ποτ' ἦν
τὰ πολλὰ πατρὸς πρὸς τάφον κτερίσματα;

'τάφον and not τάφῳ, since κτερίσματα implies προσφοραὶ κτερισμάτων' writes Prof. Jebb, and compares, I do not know ‖ why, ἀπαγγέλλειν πρός τινα: similarly Prof. Campbell 'the accusative, because of the notion of bringing implied in κτερίσματα'. Words will imply a good deal when our exigencies require it of them; but the notion of bringing which we now discover to be resident in κτερίσματα would have remained unthought-of to the end of time had not this passage put the spur to our wits. If Sophocles could and would use acc. for dat. in this way it is really impossible to say why he refrained from using it in fifty other places, φῦλον θακεῖ πρὸς Παλλάδος διπλοῦς ναούς ('ναούς and not ναοῖς, since θακεῖ implies προσελήλυθεν'), νηλέα γένεθλα πρὸς πέδον κεῖται ('the accusative, because of the notion of falling implied in κεῖται'), etc., etc.: for a writer in verse the convenience of two strings to his bow is exceedingly obvious: yet the only parallel these dramas offer is the corrupt and unmetrical line Phil. 23. Mr Blaydes therefore writes τάφῳ, which is regular and simple; but no scribe would intentionally alter this to τάφον, and the change is not one of those which easily occur by accident. Comparing 894 sq. νεορρύτους | πηγὰς γάλακτος and 901 νεώρη βόστρυχον τετμημένον I think the sense would receive a welcome though not necessary addition if one wrote τὰ πολλὰ πατρὸς πρόσφατα κτερίσματα, or perhaps rather πρόσφατον. Adverbs of time, νῦν πρίν τότε πάλαι ἀρτίως νεωστί, are freely used with the article in lieu of adjectives, and πρόσφατον is an adverb at Pind. Pyth. IV fin. πρόσφατον Θήβᾳ ξενωθείς. In O. t. 668 Nauck restores metrical correspondence and a familiar antithesis by writing τάδ' εἰ κακοῖς κακὰ προσάψει τοῖς πάλαι τὰ πρόσφατα, but there too the MS reading προσφῶιν seems to indicate πρόσφατον. But whether it was φατ̇ (φατον) or φατ̄ (φατα) that the scribe mistook for τάφον, either way the change was easy: I gave in vol. XVI of this Journal, p. 261 [this edition p. 68], many instances from this Laurentian MS of three letters reversed, to which I will here add O. C. 1105 τόδε for δότε, Trach. 810 προὔλαβες for προὔβαλες, Phil. 423 κἀξεκήρυξε for κἀκ' ἐξήρυκε and 1416 κατηρετύσων for κατερητύσων: at O. t. 1350 we have already met νομάδος for μονάδ' ὅς.

I hesitate however between this and πρὸς τάφοις, a slighter change than τάφῳ: the use of the plural is common. ‖

El. 1466–7

ὦ Ζεῦ, δέδορκα φάσμ' ἄνευ φθόνου μὲν εὖ
πεπτωκός· εἰ δ' ἔπεστι νέμεσις, οὐ λέγω.

I have given 1466 with Tyrwhitt's exquisite emendation of εὖ for οὐ, accepted by Musgrave Brunck Matthiae Wunder and Blaydes: 'uideo spectaculum felici casu (modo absit inuidia uerbo) oblatum: at, si Nemesis insequatur, non dico' as Musgrave renders it. Jebb and Campbell retain the MS lection; Nauck Mekler and Wecklein prefer Gomperz's ἄνευ θεοῦ μὲν οὐ which Nauck, always civil to Gomperz, calls 'treffliche': my present concern is with a point independent of this question, so I will only observe that both readings are confuted by the presence of μέν, for in both of them the sentence εἰ δ' ἔπεστι νέμεσις οὐ λέγω must be regarded as an afterthought and therefore cannot have had its way prepared before its face by that particle. What occupies me now is the phrase φάσμα πεπτωκός. Whether πεπτωκός means *fallen* like a cast of the dice or *fallen* like a dead body, in neither sense is it applicable to φάσμα *a spectacle*: φάσμα πεφηνός as Nauck suggests would serve, and so would φάσμα πεσόντος; but as for *a fallen sight*, there is no such thing. Better however than a violent change in the one word is a slight change in the other: ὦ Ζεῦ, δέδορκα σφάλμ' ἄνευ φθόνου μὲν εὖ (or οὐ or θεοῦ μὲν οὐ if you will) πεπτωκός. σφάλμα *an overthrow* here means *one overthrown*, as πτῶμα and πέσημα mean *one fallen*. Λ dropping out after Α left σφάμ', no word; and I presume δέδορκα suggested the transposition of σ which gives φάσμ'. These errors are similar: Aiax 292 αἰβά for βαιά, 1243 ἤρκεσεν for ἤρεσκεν, Ant. 452 οἳ τοῦσδ' for τοιούσδ', O. C. 1742 βουλόμεθ' for μολούμεθ', Phil. 701 ἕρπει for εἶρπε, Aesch. supp. 22 ἱεροστέπτοισι for ἐριοστέπτοισι, Eur. Med. 138 ἐπεί for εἶπέ, Bacch. 817 θέλῃς for ἔλθῃς, Ion 651 ἐλθών for θέλω, Alc. 1089 χηρεύεις for χηρεύσει, Andr. 290 [[289]] δολίοις for αἰόλοις, frag. 187 2 παρειάσει for παρεὶς ἑᾷ, 593 2 ῥόμβῳ and ὄμβρῳ, 835 3 τις ἀνήρ for πονηρά, Ar. pax 415 ἁρματωλίας for ἁμαρτωλίας: καινός and ἱκανός are interchanged more than once. ||

σφάγμα *a sacrifice* is also possible: the word is not found, but compare the compound πρόσφαγμα and the similar use of θῦμα.

Trach. 141–6

πεπυσμένη μέν, ὡς ἀπεικάσαι, πάρει
πάθημα τοὐμόν· ὡς δ' ἐγὼ θυμοφθορῶ,
μήτ' ἐκμάθοις παθοῦσα, νῦν τ' ἄπειρος εἶ.
τὸ γὰρ νεάζον ἐν τοιοῖσδε βόσκεται
χώροισιν αὑτοῦ, καί νιν οὐ θάλπος θεοῦ   145
οὐδ' ὄμβρος οὐδὲ πνευμάτων οὐδὲν κλονεῖ.

The two reasons for which most editors esteem 145 corrupt are, first, the lack of any relative to answer τοιοῖσδε, a void which is filled after a fashion by understanding ἐν οἷς ἄπειρόν ἐστι from what has gone before; secondly the phrase χώροισιν αὑτοῦ, which apparently if it meant anything would mean 'districts of itself' but has to be translated 'places of its own'. The first difficulty vanishes at Musgrave's change, which is no change, of χώροισιν to χώροις ἵν': the second has been assailed with many conjectures of no diplomatic probability such as Wunder's ἵν' αὐαίνοντος and Blaydes' ἵν' οὐ ψῦχός νιν. I offer ἐν τοιοῖσδε βόσκεται | χώροις, ἵν' οὐκ αὐγαί νιν, οὐ θάλπος θεοῦ κτλ.: αὐγαὶ θεοῦ is just the ἀκτῖνες of Homer ε 479 τοὺς μὲν ἄρ' οὔτ' ἀνέμων διάει μένος ὑγρὸν ἀέντων | οὔτε ποτ' ἠέλιος φαέθων ἀκτῖσιν ἔβαλλεν | οὔτ' ὄμβρος περάασκε διαμπερές. The likeness of Γ to Τ often turns αὐγή into αὐτή as at Phil. 1199: then ουκ-αυτ-αι and αυτ-ουκ-αι are the same syllables with their order changed. These errors are strange, but they happen: Eur. I. A. 694 συν-ισχ-άν-ει and συν-αν-ίσχ-ει, Ar. Lys. 331 στιγ-μα-τίαις and μα-στιγ-ίαις, Hom. Ν 78 δὲ πο-σσίν and πό-δε-σσιν, Thuc. v 115 4 χρή-σι-μα for χρή-μα-σι-ν, Aeschin. Tim. §35 ἀν-ηκ-έστ-ως for ἀν-εστ-ηκ-ώς, Ael. nat. an. xiv 25 λου-σί-ρῳ for σι-λού-ρῳ: I have given some kindred blunders from Latin MSS in the Classical Review vol. iii p. 201 [this edition p. 108] and the Transactions of the Cambridge Philological Society vol. iii p. 146 [p. 167]. ||

Trach. 232–5

ΔΗΙ. ὦ φίλτατ' ἀνδρῶν, πρῶθ' ἃ πρῶτα βούλομαι
δίδαξον, εἰ ζῶνθ' Ἡρακλῆ προσδέξομαι.
ΛΙΧ. ἔγωγέ τοί σφ' ἔλειπον ἰσχύοντά τε
καὶ ζῶντα καὶ θάλλοντα κοὐ νόσῳ βαρύν.

Tell me, says Deianira, *will Heracles come home alive?* and she receives the answer *Well, I left him strong and alive and hale and free from sickness.* At what a place in this enumeration does *alive* occur! If Lichas had said at the outset that Heracles was alive, his listener might well care to hear further, as from the messenger who in 182 sq. says καὶ ζῶντ' ἐπίστω καὶ κρατοῦντα κἀκ μάχης | ἄγοντ' ἀπαρχάς, that he was not only alive but hearty; but after hearing that a man is ἰσχύων one scarcely craves to be told that he is ζῶν. No support to such a derangement of epithets can be sought from οὐ νόσῳ βαρύν at the end, for that is merely the figure of rhetoric, occurring πολλάκις τε κοὐχ ἅπαξ, which repeats for emphasis in a negative form what has already been said in the affirmative. Wunder's excuse is that 'gratum quid facturus Deianirae quam plurimis uerbis saluum esse Herculem affirmat; quod cum faciat παθητικῶς, nihil fere attinet quo ordine singula proponantur'; Schneidewin thinks the offence diminished by the fact that the words are an answer to δίδαξον εἰ ζῶντα προσδέξομαι, a fact which to me on the other hand seems to concentrate attention on the fault; Campbell refers to instances of 'natural sequence inverted' such as Ant. 281 ἄνους τε καὶ γέρων ἅμα but to no example where the first epithet says all that is said in the second and a great deal more into the bargain.

Now in Aesch. Ag. 676 sq. this same MS to which we owe both Aeschylus and Sophocles has the words εἰ δ' οὖν τις ἀκτὶς ἡλίου νιν ἱστορεῖ | καὶ ζῶντα καὶ βλέποντα: Toup however, finding in Hesychius the gloss χλωρόν τε καὶ βλέποντα· ἀντὶ τοῦ ζῶντα, deduced thence the generally accepted inference that χλωρόν τε and not καὶ ζῶντα was what Aeschylus wrote. I find it hard not to believe that here likewise χλωρόν τε καὶ || θάλλοντα was written by Sophocles and corrupted by the evidently traditional gloss: certainly χλωρόν suits θάλλοντα well. Other causes may have had their share in the result: that ζῶντα stands overhead in Deianira's question; that καὶ ζῶντα begins v. 182; that ζῆν and θάλλειν are elsewhere coupled in more appropriate situations, as Eur. I. A. 1225 ζῶσάν τε καὶ θάλλουσαν and frag. 898 13 ζῆ τε καὶ θάλλει.

Trach. 575–7

ἔσται φρενός σοι τοῦτο κηλητήριον
τῆς Ἡρακλείας, ὥστε μή τιν' εἰσιδὼν
στέρξει γυναῖκα κεῖνος ἀντὶ σοῦ πλέον.

If ὥστε μὴ στέρξει is Greek we may burn our grammars. We turn for help to the commentators, and they receive us, some with silence, others with profuse illustration of μή cum fut. indic. in *relative* clauses! Sophocles wrote μή τιν' εἰσιδὼν ποτε | στέρξῃ γυναῖκα. One form of π, as Badham somewhere says, is just ω with a lid to it, so that ϖοτε and ὥστε have little to discriminate them: then the unmetrical ὥστε migrates to the only place in the verse which will receive it. According to Prof. Campbell στέρξῃ was actually the original reading of L; but the itacistic error is so common that this is not worth insisting on.

Phil. 348–9

ταῦτ', ὦ ξέν', οὕτως ἐννέποντες οὐ πολὺν
χρόνον μ' ἐπέσχον μή με ναυστολεῖν ταχύ.

You can withhold a man from sailing at once, and you can withhold him a long time from sailing; but how you are to withhold him a long time from sailing at once I cannot imagine: well may Nauck say 'ταχύ suspectum'. And the diction is of a piece with the sense: what sane writer repeats με in this way at two words' interval? Schneidewin can find no better parallel than O. C. 1278 ὡς μή μ' ἄτιμον, τοῦ θεοῦ γε προστάτην, | οὕτως ἀφῇ με: no one will cite Phil. 945 ὡς ἄνδρ' ἑλών μ' ἰσχυρὸν ἐκ βίας μ' ἄγει, for there the one με is object to the participle, the other to the verb, and moreover Suidas quotes the || verse without the former μ'.[1] It cancels both offences to write οὐ πολὺν | χρόνον μ' ἐπέσχον μὴ νεναυστοληκέναι, or μὴ οὐ if that is necessary: we have had μ and μ confused

---

[1] I assume that the editors purposely refrain from quoting the exceptional and uncertain ἰδού μ' ἀναταράσσει εὐοῖ μ' ὁ κισσός of Trach. 218 sq.

already: after the detachment of με the further corruption at the end of the verse was partly due I suppose to the fact that there is no such word as ναυστοληκέναι, partly to the perils which environ whatever comes next the margin.

Phil. 424–5

κεῖνός γε πράσσει νῦν κακῶς, ἐπεὶ θανὼν
Ἀντίλοχος αὐτῷ φροῦδος, ὅσπερ ἦν γόνος.

The words ὅσπερ ἦν γόνος are almost universally regarded as corrupt: the sense *his son* is suitable enough, but the phrase is contemptible. The fourteen conjectures enumerated by Nauck are either slight changes which do no good or improvements obtained by violence; so I add my stone to the cairn. ὅσπερ ἦν differs from ὃν σπείρει in little but the position of ν: the trajection of a letter has been illustrated already at El. 1466, but examples more closely resembling this are Aesch. supp. 272 λέγοι πρόσως for λέγοις πρόσω and 417 δοκεῖν δεῖ for δοκεῖ δεῖν. The expression Ἀντίλοχος αὐτῷ φροῦδος, ὃν σπείρει, γόνος, pleonastic though it seems to us, is nevertheless very characteristic of the tragic style: Aiax 1172 πατρός, ὅς σ’ ἐγείνατο, El. 261 μητρός, ἥ μ’ ἐγείνατο, Eur. El. 964 τὴν τεκοῦσαν, ἥ μ’ ἐγείνατο, Alc. 16 ἥ σφ’ ἔτικτε μητέρα. The present tense of the verb is again idiomatic: O. t. 437 τίς δέ μ’ ἐκφύει βροτῶν; Eur. H. f. 252 οὓς Ἄρης σπείρει ποτέ. Finally take a passage which tallies with this in both peculiarities: Eur. supp. 986 Εὐάδνην, ἣν Ἶφις ἄναξ παῖδα φυτεύει.

Phil. 606–9

Ἕλενος, ὃν οὗτος νυκτὸς ἐξελθὼν μόνος,
ὁ πάντ’ ἀκούων αἰσχρὰ καὶ λωβήτ’ ἔπη,
δόλιος Ὀδυσσεὺς εἷλε δέσμιόν τ’ ἄγων
ἔδειξ’ Ἀχαιοῖς ἐς μέσον, θήραν καλήν.

After saying of a man that he is called by every term of ‖ disgrace and contumely it is a very tame sequel and seriously impairs the force of what has been said to select a single term, by no means so disgraceful and contumelious as many another that could be thought of, and to call him by that, δόλιος. I should therefore reverse the letters ιο and write δόλοις Ὀδυσσεὺς εἷλε: ἑλεῖν δόλοις and δόλῳ recur at 948 and 1228 of the play. In this Journal vol. xvi p. 253 ⟦this edition p. 62⟧ I gave examples of this transposition taken from the Laurentian MS, to which I add, as especially similar to the above, the following from other sources: Eur. supp. 925 ἰοκλέους for οἰκλέους, Aesch. frag. 31 ⟦61 Mette⟧ δαίδας for διάδας, Ar. eccl. 288 ἐνδούμεναι for ἐνδυόμεναι.

This is all the change needed, so I make no more. It is however quite possible that what Sophocles really wrote was λόχοις: see Procl. chrest. p. 459 ⟦p. 106 Allen⟧ Ὀδυσσεὺς λοχήσας Ἕλενον λαμβάνει: at Rhes. 17 and 92 the MSS of Euripides vary between λόχος and δόλος.

Phil. 984–5

ἔμ', ὦ κακῶν κάκιστε καὶ τολμήστατε,
οἵδ' ἐκ βίας ἄξουσιν;

Not only are contracted forms of adjectives in -ήεις and -όεις (and -όεις except the feminine -οῦσσα[1]) unknown to tragic dialogue but according to Nauck no other example of -ήστατος for -ηέστατος occurs anywhere at all. Prof. Jebb quotes instances, not from tragedy, of -ησ- for -ηεσ-, and says that 'in O. T. 1279 it is almost certain that Soph. used αἱματόεις'; but if there is anything in what I have already written on that passage it is almost certain that Sophocles there used no form of that adjective except the legitimate αἱματοῦσσα, with which compare κεροῦσσα frag. 86 [[89 Pearson]] and Eur. frag. 857. How the portent came here I would propose to explain as follows. If ever there stood in a MS of Sophocles the verse ἔμ', ὦ κακῶν κάκιστε καὶ τολμηστέρας, a copyist encountering those words could hardly choose but see that the last was wrong. The contraction would not trouble him, but it would naturally strike him that this adjective side by side with κάκιστε ought to be vocative not genitive or accusative in case, masculine not ‖ feminine in gender, and superlative not comparative in degree: τολμήστατε instead of τολμηστέρας. He might not so readily perceive that all he had to do was duly to separate the letters and write ὦ κακῶν κάκιστε καὶ τόλμης τέρας.

I register without discussion a few more conjectures which seem to have either less certainty or necessity or moment than some of the foregoing.

O. t. 420 sqq. βοῆς δὲ τῆς σῆς ποῖος οὐκ ἔσται [λιμήν], | ποῖος Κιθαιρὼν οὐχὶ σύμφωνος τάχα, | ὅταν καταίσθῃ τὸν ὑμέναιον, ὃν δόμοις | ἄνορμον εἰσέπλευσας εὐπλοίας τυχών; write ὅταν καταίσθῃ τὸν λιμένα, τὸν ἐν δόμοις | ἄνορμον εἰσέπλευσας: hence came the meaningless λιμήν of 420. For the rhythm compare 826 μητρὸς ζυγῆναι καὶ πατέρα κατακτανεῖν, Eur. Bacch. 731 ἡ δ' ἀνεβόησεν· ὦ δρομάδες ἐμαὶ κύνες.

O. t. 602 οὔτ' ἂν μετ' ἄλλου δρῶντος ἂν τλαίην ποτέ: Heimsoeth writes δρᾶν τόδ', but δρῶν τόδ' suffices: see El. 943 τλῆναι δρῶσαν, Aesch. sept. 754 σπείρας ἔτλα.

O. t. 685 γᾶς προπονουμένας: perhaps πεπονημένας.

O. t. 866 sq. ὑψίποδες, οὐρανίαν | δι' αἰθέρα τεκνωθέντες: write οὐρανίᾳ 'ν | αἰθέρι, with ἀκρότατα γεῖσ' ἀναβᾶσ' | ἀπότομον ὤρουσεν in the antistrophe. ΔΙ seems to be a dittography of ΑΙ. I may remark that the ἀποτμοτάταν conjectured by K. Schnell in 876 [[877]] and adopted by Wecklein is a form unexampled in tragedy and ought to be ἀποτμωτάταν.

O. t. 1031 τί δ' ἄλγος ἴσχοντ' ἐν καιροῖς ⟨με⟩ λαμβάνεις; for ἐν καιροῖς write εἰς χέρας.

---

[1] πτερoῦντα is found in a suspected passage Aesch. supp. 1000.

　　　　　　　　　　　　　　　　　　　　　　　　G H C

O. t. 1242 sq. ἵετ' εὐθὺς πρὸς τὰ νυμφικὰ | λέχη: the conjecture εὐθύ is inadmissible: ἐς for πρός may be right, but so may εὐθὺς πρὸς τὰ νυμφίχ' ἵετο.

O. t. 1382 sq. τὸν ἀσεβῆ, τὸν ἐκ θεῶν | φανέντ' ἄναγνον καὶ γένους τοῦ Λαΐου: write τὸν εἰς θεοὺς . . .καὶ γένος τὸ Λαΐου: the whole corruption flowed from the error ἐκ for ΕΙΣ.

O. t. 1494 sq. τοιαῦτ' ὀνείδη λαμβάνων, ἃ τοῖς ἐμοῖς | γονεῦσιν ἔσται σφῷν θ' ὁμοῦ δηλήματα: write ἃ τοῖσιν οἷς | γόνοισιν ἔσται σφίν θ' ὁ. δ.: for σφιν see O. C. 1490: γόνοισιν has been proposed before.

O. t. 1505 sq. μή σφε παρίδῃς | πτωχὰς ἀνάνδρους ἐγγενεῖς ἀλωμένας: write μή σφε δὴ παρῇς. ‖

Aiax 1100 λεῶν: there is no such word: write λεών. When Arcadius p. 94 4 ⟦244 32 Lentz⟧ says that τὰ εἰς ΩΣ 'Αττικὰ ὁμοτονοῦσιν ἐκείνοις ἀφ' ὧν ἐσχηματίσθησαν, ναός νεώς, λαός λεώς, he speaks only of nominatives: inflexions are not treated till p. 127 10 ⟦406 1 Lentz⟧.

Aiax 1310 sqq. ἐπεὶ καλόν μοι τοῦδ' ὑπερπονουμένῳ | θανεῖν προδήλως μᾶλλον ἢ τῆς σῆς [ὕπερ | γυναικὸς ἢ τοῦ σοῦ θ' ὁμαίμονος] λέγω: delete the bracketed words and for λέγω write γάλω.

El. 475 εἶσιν ἁ πρόμαντις Δίκα: this comes from μάντις in 473: write προμαθίς (Aesch. supp. 700) or προμαθής.

El. 800 sq. οὔτ' ἐμοῦ καταξίως | πράξειας οὔτε τοῦ πορεύσαντος ξένου: for οὔτε write οὔτ' ἂν, comparing for the postponement of ἂν Ant. 664: αν becomes αι and then ε.

El. 841 πάμψυχος ἀνάσσει: I and Nauck before me once proposed παμοῦχος: better perhaps δαμοῦχος.

El. 1327 πότερα παρ' οὐδὲν τοῦ βίου κήδεσθ' ἔτι; for παρ' perhaps γάρ.

El. 1394 νεακόνητον αἷμα χειροῖν ἔχων: χερὶ νεακονῆ μάχαιραν φέρων Heimsoeth after Heath: for the last word write νέμων, comparing the same error at Aesch. sept. 590.

Trach. 256 τὸν ἀγχιστῆρα τοῦδε τοῦ πάθους: perhaps ἐγχρωστῆρα: see Arist. eth. Nic. 11 3 8 πάθος ἐγκεχρωσμένον τῷ βίῳ.

Phil. 83 sqq. νῦν δ' εἰς ἀναιδὲς ἡμέρας μέρος βραχὺ | δός μοι σεαυτόν, κᾆτα τὸν λοιπὸν χρόνον | κέκλησο πάντων εὐσεβέστατος βροτῶν: for ἀναιδές write ὄνειδος, comparing κέκλησο 85 and 967 sq. μὴ παρῇς | σαυτοῦ βροτοῖς ὄνειδος.

Phil. 760 δύστηνε δῆτα διὰ πόνων πάντων φανείς: write δυσπόνων πόνων, comparing Ant. 1276 for the phrase and O. t. 1214 for the cacophony.

Phil. 1048 νῦν δ' ἑνὸς κρατῶ λόγου: the sense required is ἐν ἀρκέσω λέγων.

Phil. 1443 sq. ἡ γὰρ εὐσέβεια συνθνήσκει βροτοῖς, | κἂν ζῶσι κἂν θάνωσιν, οὐκ ἀπόλλυται: if we might alter συνθνήσκει to θρήσκοισιν it would save the next verse, which οὐ γὰρ ηὐσέβεια does not save.

25

REMARKS ON THE VATICAN GLOSSARY 3321*

Professor Nettleship's notes on this glossary in vol. XIX of the Journal of Philology, pp. 113–28, 184–92, 290–5, contain many certain corrections: the following are a few places where I dissent from his proposals and have suggestions of my own to offer in their stead. What oftenest dissatisfies me with Mr Nettleship's conjectures is their failure to bring about a correspondence in meaning between the explanation and the word explained: here and there too I grudge the rather profuse hospitality with which new words are made welcome to the lexicons.

4 44 *absono absurdum uel prospero*. 'Read perhaps *absurdo uel aspero*' N. For *prospero* rather *praepostero*.

12 18 *aepas horientalis*. 'Read *eous*' N. Yes; but *aepas* is *aetas*, and these are the remnants of two glosses, ⟨*aeon*⟩ *aetas* and ⟨*eous*⟩ *orientalis*: compare 63 39 *aeon, aetas uel tempus*, followed by 40 *eous, lucifer*.

17 40 *angiportum androna uiformium uel callem*. 'Perhaps *angiportum callem. androna uirorum* [*aedes*]' N., rightly no doubt: *uiformium* however is not a corruption of *uirorum* but part of a third gloss, ⟨*ancipitium*⟩ *biformium*.

21 8 *aruas demonas*. 'Read *heroas*' N. Read *laruas*, comparing 105 5 *larualis demoniosus*.

22 22 *aufertice ablatiuus*. 'I can find no other instance of this bastard Greek term' N. It seems to be a mistake for *aferetice* = ἀφαιρετική.

29 37 *camba cauis*. 'Perhaps *cumba nauis*' N. One might also propose *gambae, calcis*; but nearer than either to the ductus litterarum is *corbula, corbis*.

51 1 *depalata deuoluta designata delinita*. 'Probably *depalata deuelata. designata delineata*' N. There can be no doubt that ‖ the first gloss was what Mr Nettleship restores, *depălata, deuelata*; but the reason why the two are mixed up together is that the second was *depālata, designata, delimitata*. So in 51 2 *depopulatio desinatio* where Mr Nettleship says 'probably *dissignatio*' I would write *depālatio, designatio*; and in 53 11 *deuolato designato* where he proposes *deuelato dissignato* I suspect that we have once more the two glosses ⟨*depălato*⟩ *deuelato* and ⟨*depālato*⟩ *designato*.

* ⟦*JPh* 20 (1892), 49–52⟧

53 12 *decoratio dehonestatio.* 'Read *decoriatio*' N. The explanation then is very euphemistic. Read *dedecoratio.*

61 35 *eligit affligit.* 'Read *elidit*' N. Read *fligit,* F for E.

62 24 *emptorium locus ubi negotiationes exercentur.* 'Add the word *emptorium* to the lexicons' N. I am afraid it is nothing but *emporium.*

63 7 *enhermis sine arma uel sine mensura.* 'Read *inermis sine armis. enormis sine mensura*' N. Read *enormis, sine norma uel sine mensura.*

65 29–30 *erga id uacuum. egregium circa hoc.* 'Read *erga id, circa hoc. egregium magnum*' N. *uacuum* I suspect indicates a third gloss ⟨*egenum*⟩ *uacuum.*

65 41 *estidram quam ueteres canapum nominarunt.* 'Perhaps *oestrum* (or *asilum?*) *quem ueteres tabanum nominarunt*' N. Loewe prodrom. p. 403 amends *estidram* with more probability to *excetram* comparing gloss. Bodl. auct. t. II 24 *excreante* (= *excetra*) *plena malitia, hoc est ira* (= *hydra*) *quam ueteres canopum nominarunt*: see Mr Ellis in this Journal vol. XII pp. 259 sq. I conjecture that the one gloss is a decapitated form of the other and that *estidram* stands for *est hydra.*

65 47 *eutum sonum.* 'Perhaps ἦχον' N. Read *accentum,* comparing 5 40 *accentus, sonus.*

65 50 *euirat examinat.* 'Read probably *exarmat*' N. Read *euitat, exanimat.*

68 44 *exaceruabit aflecauit.* 'Perhaps *exacerbauit adflictauit*' N. These two words are very diverse in meaning: for the latter I offer *asperauit.*

68 46 *exercita exporrecta eleuata.* 'Read *exerta*' N. But as *exerta* does not mean *eleuata* we must make the further alteration *deuelata* or *reuelata.* ||

75 21 *feminalis pandi femoribus immoluti.* 'Read *feminales panni femoribus inuoluti*...The word *feminalis* should be added to the lexicons' N. It is no less easy to write *feminalia, panni f. i.*; and this entails no addition to the lexicons.

75 54 *fenium coccinum.* 'Probably for *minium*' N. The gloss is evidently identical with the *fenicum cocimum* of the Epinal glossary p. 9 col. A l. 34, for which Mr Nettleship in this Journal vol. XIV p. 37 proposed *phoeniceum coccinum.*

80 24 *fulcrum sustentatum.* 'Read *fultum*' N. It is a slighter change to retain *fulcrum* and write *sustentaculum.*

82 19 *gener initium foris.* 'Possibly *genae initium barbae*' N. Read *genesis, initium, fons*: in *genesisinitium* one *si* absorbed the other and *genes* then became *gener.*

85 42 *herosui uiri fortes.* 'Perhaps *heroes sunt u. f.*' N. I should write *neruosi uiri, fortes.*

86 48 *hiliesatus in silua natus.* 'Perhaps *siluisatus*; though I can find no instance of this word' N. *hiliesatus* is the same thing as *uilicsatus,* i.e. *siluaticus* with its elements in disorder.

94 17 *infusum destinatum.* 'Perhaps *infixum*' N. *destillatum* is a slighter change and produces a better accord between γλῶσσα and γλώσσημα.

94 22 *indutia utilitas.* 'Perhaps *industria*' N. Does *industria* mean *utilitas?* I propose *indusia, tunicas*; for *tunicas* and *utilitas* are the same thing.

94 26 *inertia stupor dentium.* 'Read *inedia*' N. If I remember right I have met this gloss elsewhere in the form which Mr Nettleship gives it; but that too must be corrupt. The phrase 'stupor dentium' is almost too absurd to exist, if it existed it could not mean 'inedia', and if it did mean 'inedia' no one would dream of employing it to explain that word. I would write, following exactly the ductus litterarum, *amentia, stupor, delirium*: to read *ineptia* for the lemma would be no less easy, but the explanation would then be less accurate.

97 15 *inploratum inspiratum.* 'Perhaps for *inoptatum insperatum*' N. Accepting *insperatum* I propose *inopinatum*, which I imagine was first corrupted to *inoplratum* and then emended as we see by the transposition of *o*.

100 19 *inuado insecuro.* 'Probably for *insequor*' N. Read *in uado, in securo*: Ter. And. 845 etc. ‖

103 21 *kategoriam dilatinominis.* '*a* reads *delatatio*, which I would correct to *denotatio*' N. Read *delationem nominis*.

108 32 *licanus candidatio dicitur.* 'Perhaps *lychinus candelabrum d.*' N. Read *Libanus*: Augustine on psalm 72 16 'mons est *Libanus* excelsas arbores habens, et nomen ipsum interpretatur *candidatio.*'

109 28 *lisymmachus solutus uel litis.* 'Perhaps *lysimachus solutor litis*' N., which is clearly right so far as it goes; but read *solutor ⟨belli⟩ uel litis*: *uelli* absorbed *belli*.

113 17 *manda deceptio uel fraus.* 'Read *menda*' N. *menda* however means neither *deceptio* nor *fraus*: those words I suspect were an explanation of *manticulatio*, for *manticulare* is glossed as *decipere* and *fraudare*: see Lachmann Lucr. p. 108. Whether *manda* is a corruption of *manticulatio* or a fragment of another gloss is harder to say.

118 41 *modestare regere.* 'Add *modestare* to the lexicons' N. I would not venture: *r* and *st* are too much alike.

126 50 *nudi pedalia.* 'Read *nodi*, and add this use of *pedale* to the lexicons' N. This is a trifle precipitate: what we have here is merely the γλῶσσα *nudipedalia* without its γλώσσημα.

128 40 *obnixius humilissimus missus.* 'Perhaps *obnoxius humilissimus; obnixus nisus*' N. Rather *obnoxius, humilis, summissus*. The confusion of *obnoxius* and *obnixius* recurs at 129 15.

132 16 *oloser crini.* Mr Nettleship proposes *holoserica*: to me it looks like *olores, cycni*.

132 26 *omnitens omnipotens.* 'Perhaps *omnituens*' N. Read *omnitenens*.

136 26 *papitans timens*. 'Read *palpitans*' N. Read *pauitans*: the explanation will then be correct.

143 23 *pix tracxit uelba marina*. 'Read *pistrices beluae marinae*' N. Read *piscatrix, belua marina*: the creature meant is the angler or sea devil described by Cicero n. d. II 49 125 and Oppian hal. II 86–98, τὸν βάτραχον τὸν ἁλιέα in Arist. hist. an. p. 620 B 11, the lophius piscatorius of modern zoologists, Pliny's 'rana quae in mari *piscatrix* uocatur'.

26

SOPH. *OED. COL.* 527*

In the *American Journal of Philology*, vol. XIII. p. 152 [this edition p. 192],
I proposed to write here ἢ πατρόθεν, ὡς ἀκούω, δυσώνυμα λέκτρ᾽ ἐπάσω; and
I added *i.e. didst thou wed thy father's widow?* No. XIX. of *Hermathena* contains
an article by Prof. Tyrrell, full of his usual kindness and generosity, in which the
following remarks occur (p. 307):

'But what is most puzzling to me is to guess why... Prof. Housman
thinks that he has improved the sense by reading πατρόθεν for ματρόθεν, and
how he has persuaded himself that πατρόθεν λέκτρα could mean "his father's
widow", unless πατρόθεν can take the place of πατρός; and if it can, then
ματρόθεν = ματρός, and ματρόθεν λέκτρα means "thy mother's bed", and
there is no difficulty in the passage.'

I take πατρόθεν with the verb: ἢ πατρόθεν λέκτρ᾽ ἐπάσω means *came thy bride
unto thee from thy father's arms?* My paraphrase *didst thou wed thy father's widow?*
is in sense the exact equivalent of this; but since its form has misled Prof. Tyrrell,
and may therefore mislead others, into thinking that I took πατρόθεν λέκτρα to
mean *thy father's widow*, I desire to make this explanation.

* [CR 7 (1893), 449]

27

THE MANUSCRIPTS OF PROPERTIUS [I]*

Nimium altercando ueritas amittitur

CARDINAL MANUSCRIPTS[1]

N. Codex *Neapolitanus*, no. 224 inter Gudianos in the ducal library at Wolfen-buettel, first collated by N. Heinsius at Naples, assigned to the 13th century by Lachmann and Hertzberg, to the 13th or 12th by Keil, to the 14th or rather the 15th by Lucian Mueller, and by Baehrens to a date not earlier than 1430. It wants the leaf which contained the verses IV xi 17–76.

A. Codex *Vossianus* Latinus no. 38 at Leyden, collated in Burmann's edition as Vossianus secundus, assigned by Baehrens to a date near 1360. It contains only the first book and the first 63 verses of the second.

F. Codex *Laurentianus* plut. 36 49 at Florence, first collated by Baehrens for his edition of 1880 and assigned by him || to the beginning of the 15th century. It is complete. It contains many corrections by

f, a hand a little later than the first.

D. Codex *Dauentriensis*, no. 1792 in the public library at Deventer, collated in Burmann's edition as alter codex meus, assigned by Baehrens to a date between 1410 and 1420. It wants the first elegy and the first 13 verses of the second.

V. Codex *Ottoboniano-Vaticanus* no. 1514 at Rome, first collated by Baehrens for his edition of 1880 and assigned by him to the end of the 14th century but to a date near 1450 by Messrs Stevenson fils Maurice Faucon and Pierre de Nolhac (Plessis, études critiques sur Properce p. 21). It is complete. It contains many corrections by

v, several hands of the 15th century.

---

* [*JPh* 21 (1893), 101–60]

[1] Since this paper was written Mr Carl Hosius has published in the Rheinisches Museum vol. XLVI pp. 575–88 some notes of his researches among the Italian MSS of Propertius. His conclusion (p. 582) is that only one deserves adding to our apparatus criticus, Neapolitanus 268, which is near akin to A and F and will make some amends for the absence of A from II i 63 onwards. I attach value also to another, Vrbinas 641, which agrees more closely than any other MS with N and will therefore have its use at any rate in IV xi 17–76 where N is not extant. Of these two MSS I shall speak further at the end of this paper: at present I will only say that they do not disturb the classification here proposed.

THESIS

In this paper I intend to establish the following propositions.

1. NAFDVfv are authorities independent of one another and therefore are one and all to be employed in the reconstruction of the archetype.

2. The relationship of these MSS is the following.

The codices DV together form one family, and the codices AF another, both which families are wholly derived from a common parent now lost which following Baehrens I call O. N is a MS deriving its readings from three sources: partly from a MS of the same family with AF, partly from a MS of the same family with DV, and partly from a lost MS which I shall call Z, a MS entirely independent not only of those two families but of their parent O. From this codex Z are also derived many of the readings given by f and v.

These relations are expressed by the following stemma, in which lost MSS stand within brackets. ||

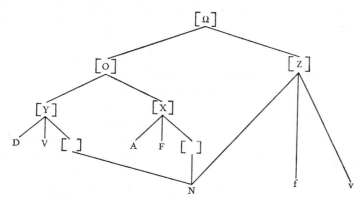

How far these conclusions agree with those of my predecessors, or differ from them, will be made plain by the following review of the dispute.

HISTORICAL SURVEY

In the year 1816 Karl Lachmann published at Leipzig the first scientific recension of Propertius. As for the textual criticism of his predecessors, it resembled nothing so much as the condition of mankind before the advent of Prometheus: ἔφυρον εἰκῆ πάντα. The younger Burmann's great edition of 1780 presents an imperfect and inaccurate collation of some five and twenty MSS good bad and indifferent: the authority for this reading or that, if reckoned at all, is ascertained by the simple process of adding up the codices which offer it: if one MS weighs heavier than its fellows, that is because it has had the luck to be collated twice over under the different names of Mentelianus and Leidensis primus and accordingly counts as two. To the conjectural emendation of the text the critics of the 17th and 18th centuries rendered immortal services; two of them at least, Heinsius and Schrader, achieved in this province far more than Lachmann: but towards the formation of a critical apparatus they did nothing but amass a chaos of ‖ material and leave it to be set in order by this young man of twenty-three.

Lachmann singled out from the crowd of witnesses the codices Groninganus and Neapolitanus and made these two the pillars of his recension: the Groninganus he reckoned first in merit, the Neapolitanus second, the other MSS he employed but sparingly or discarded altogether. He did well – I will here assume as proven what I shall prove hereafter – to select the Neapolitanus, which remains today an authority second to none: he did well also to select the Groninganus, which though now superseded contains nevertheless much truth which the Neapolitanus does not contain. He erred, though the error was of no great moment, in setting the Groninganus highest, misled by specious interpolations which he mistook for genuine: he erred more gravely and disastrously in neglecting the MS known to him as the alter codex Burmanni and to us as the Dauentriensis, whose honest and independent witness he mistook for interpolation.

Lachmann's right opinions had the strength of truth; his wrong opinions were sustained by his genius and growing authority; right and wrong together they took captive the learned world and held sway unchallenged till 1843. Keil in that year published his observationes criticae in Propertium and there corrected Lachmann's less important error by demonstrating that the Neapolitanus must be set at least on a level with the Groninganus. Hertzberg, whose elaborate edition was then in publication, still held wholly with Lachmann; but from this date onward the Neapolitanus gained more and more in honour as the Groninganus lost, and the chief critics and editors down to 1880, as Haupt Mueller and Palmer, took N for their mainstay and made but subsidiary use of the Groninganus or of any MS beside.

But 1880 like 1816 began a new era. In this year the late Emil Baehrens published a recension founded on four MSS, two of them, A and D, already known in part from Burmann's edition under the names of Vossianus secundus and alter codex meus, two now first collated, F and V. From these four alone, A and F forming one family, D and V another, Baehrens ‖ proposed to reconstitute the archetype: all other MSS, N included, were to be set aside, and their testimony, where it dissented from AFDV, was to be deemed interpolated.

The edition of Baehrens placed in our hands all the materials for restoring the text of Propertius which are yet known to exist:[1] that he himself should not employ them rightly was excusable enough, since men are apt to be overmuch enamoured of their own discoveries. His four MSS were really of high import-

---

[1] See note on p. 101 [this edition p. 232].

ance and superseded not only the Groninganus but all known MSS excepting N; N however they did not supersede, and Baehrens was further mistaken in ascribing to interpolators certain readings, often agreeing with N, which are offered by f and v the correctors of F and V. Somewhere, it might have been thought, in the world of scholarship there would be found the candour and the perspicacity to welcome his distinguished services, correct his demonstrable mistakes, and establish without more ado on a sure foundation the textual criticism of Propertius.

But Baehrens was envied for his talents and disliked for his vanity and arrogance; many of his contemporaries, not all of whom deserved it, he had assailed with abuse; and by his lack of due servility towards the deified heroes Lachmann and Haupt he had affronted the school of philologers now regnant in Germany. Accordingly it was not to be borne that valuable MSS unknown to Haupt or Lachmann should be discovered by Baehrens; and the task of proving that his MSS were valueless was promptly undertaken in the Rheinisches Museum of the same year 1880, vol. xxxv pp. 441–7, by Mr Friedrich Leo. Mr Leo is known from his services to Plautus and Seneca for a very competent critic; but Baehrens two years before had described him with foolish scurrility as an 'asinus sub Leonina pelle'.[1]

Mr Leo successfully demonstrated that in discarding the Neapolitanus Baehrens erred: his proofs are not invariably cogent and we shall see hereafter that they can be largely reinforced, but they sufficed. This however was not enough; || and having corrected the error of Baehrens Mr Leo must next proceed to put himself no less in the wrong by asserting, not proving, for that was impossible, that 'AFDV omnino nihil ualent', and returning to the rubbish-heap of old MS materials superseded by Baehrens' discoveries. Into the relationship of the MSS to one another he made no investigations, and indeed he could hardly have made any without upsetting his conclusion.

A few months later Mr Ellis published in the American Journal of Philology, vol. I pp. 389–400, a paper on 'the Neapolitanus of Propertius'. Considered as a defence of that MS the article was by no means equal to Mr Leo's in completeness method or precision; but it was quite untouched by faction or prejudice, and the author was content to vindicate N without disparaging AFDV. Like Mr Leo he held that certain of the vulgar codices were not yet superseded, and like Mr Leo he propounded no theory of the relations existing between the MSS.

In 1882 appeared the most elaborate work yet published on the subject, a dissertation de codicibus Propertianis by Mr Richard Solbisky of Weimar. Rightly ignoring all MSS but N and AFDV Mr Solbisky addressed himself to

---

[1] Haec prius fuere: in 1891 Mr Leo on p. 21 of his edition of the culex writes kindly and justly of Baehrens.

comparing the merits and defining the relations of these. He concluded that for practical purposes N and the family DV are our only authorities, both necessary but N the better of the two: the family AF may be set down as useless. The MSS are related thus: N descends from one apograph of the archetype, the family DV from another; the family AF is blent from both these apographs and contains no other element of genuine tradition but only errors and interpolations with a few happy conjectures; f and v have derived readings from a MS resembling N. The treatise is written with admirable diligence adequate learning and entire freedom from the spirit of faction: its faults spring partly from a deficiency, I will not say in critical faculty, but certainly in critical experience; partly, it seems, from the fact that though party spirit is absent preconceived opinion is not. One finds conclusions, correct in themselves, supported by proofs which prove nothing; ‖ false or doubtful propositions are stated as self-evident; the codices AF are disparaged in a manner not only erroneous but arbitrary; and for his genealogy of the MSS, which I shall shew to be quite impossible, Mr Solbisky neither adduces nor pretends to adduce any evidence at all.

The études critiques sur Properce of Mr Frédéric Plessis published in 1884 contain two chapters, pp. 1–45, devoted to the MSS. The book is written with French lucidity and more than French diligence; but Mr Plessis, it must be said, is no critic. His conclusions, which since he shews no argument for them appear to be intuitive, are these: the MSS to be employed in constructing the text are NAFDV the Groninganus and Hertzberg's Hamburgensis: there are two families: the first comprises two branches of which N is the better and AF the worse: the second family consists of DV and is inferior to N but equal to AF. f and v derive from N the readings which they have in common with that MS: Mr Plessis, who as I have said is no critic, adds that the agreement of Nfv 'équivaut presque à une certitude', i.e. a reading found in N is rendered more probable if two scribes have copied it thence. The Groninganus and Hamburgensis have combined the readings of the two families already mentioned, but are nevertheless to be employed in constructing the text.

In 1887 Mr C. Weber published a disquisition de auctoritate codicum Propertianorum in which after a painstaking examination confined to the first book he came to the following conclusions: N is by far our best authority but AFDV with f and v are also of service: of the two families AF and DV the former is akin to N but the latter is nevertheless the better: f and v have derived readings from a MS resembling N but interpolated. Mr Weber's conclusions then, so far as they concern the relations of NAFDV, are virtually those of Mr Plessis.

I subjoin, for comparison with my own, the stemmata codicum which I have drawn up from the statements of the four scholars who have formulated their opinions on the relationship of the MSS. ‖

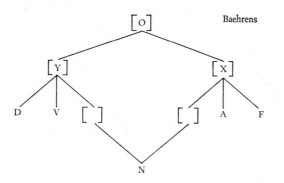

Baehrens

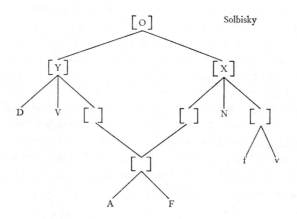

Solbisky

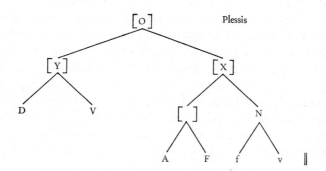

Plessis

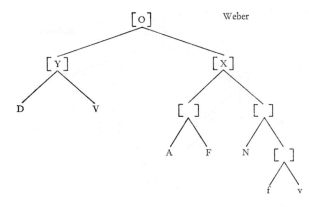

Controversy is inseparable from the discussion of our subject, and the ensuing pages will of necessity contain a certain amount of polemical matter; but my purpose is not in the main controversial. My purpose is to establish my own theory: to demolish the theories of others is only a necessary incident in the process. Therefore I shall not examine point by point the conclusions of my predecessors and controvert them severally: I shall develope my own views in what appears to be the most natural sequence, pointing out from time to time how this or that error of former critics is refuted by the evidence adduced.

The mass of facts which I am about to pass in review is much greater than would be needed merely to demonstrate the thesis which I have proposed. But side by side with the demonstration of my thesis I pursue a second aim: to amend or elucidate as far as may be those passages in our author where his MSS are not unanimous and where it becomes our business to extract from their conflicting testimony the reading of the Propertian archetype. ||

N AND O

§ 1. *N better than O [= AFDV in agreement]*

First I set out to demonstrate the existence in N of a genuine element not derived from O the common archetype of AFDV but from a MS which I call Z, the brother of O and its coequal in authority. To demonstrate this is to vindicate against Baehrens the merit of N; and so far I am fighting side by side with Messrs Leo Ellis Solbisky Plessis and Weber. But concerning the nature and origin of the merit of N Messrs Leo and Ellis have formed, or at any rate have pronounced, no opinion, while Messrs Solbisky Plessis and Weber have pronounced an opinion opposite to mine, they affirming[1] and I denying that N derives its merit from the common archetype of AFDV.

To refute Baehrens, I say, is an aim we have in common; and wherever

---

[1] Solbisky p. 194, Plessis p. 44, Weber p. 16.

I borrow a weapon from my comrades in arms I shall take care to acknowledge the debt. But I will here explain why I discard as futile a great portion of the armoury employed by Messrs Solbisky and Weber. Our adversary has never denied that N has many true readings which AFDV have not: only he has asserted that those true readings are conjectural emendations. Therefore when Messrs Solbisky and Weber adduce I iii 28 sqq. where AFDV have wrongly 'obstipui uano credulus auspicio, | ne qua tibi insolitos portarent uisa timores | neue quis inuitam *cogerit* esse suam' and N has rightly *cogeret*, they beat the air. No scribe who attended to what he was writing and knew the elements of Latin grammar could fail, with *portarent* overhead, to make the correction *cogeret* if he found *cogerit* in his exemplar. Such errors as *cogerit* occur in the best MSS in the world, such corrections as *cogeret* in the very worst. The virtue for which we esteem a MS is not correctness but integrity; and for the integrity of N a reading like this says nothing. And the use || of these brittle weapons will seem less than ever excusable when I point to the invincible evidence which lies ready to our hand.

The fact is, though it looks a paradox, that no true reading and no number of true readings are proof positive of a genuine element in the MS which offers them. Not even the 'te uaria laudaui saepe figura, | ut, quod non *esses*, *esse* putaret amor' given by N at III xxiv 6 where DV have *esset saepe* and F *essem saepe*, not even a reading so manifestly true and so hard to find by guessing as this, can beat a determined opponent from the position that all the truth which N possesses it owes to the divination of correctors. Improbable to the last degree it renders his opinion, yet not impossible. But a deadly weapon would be this: if we could find passages where O is corrupt and where N gives, not the true reading, but a corruption standing half way between the true reading and the corruption in O. Take from another author an instance of what I mean: when in Catull. 67 42 'loquentem | solam cum *ancillis* haec sua flagitia' we find the Oxoniensis giving *concillis* and the Sangermanensis *conciliis*, we say that the former is here superior in integrity to the latter; for not only is *conciliis* a worse corruption than *concillis* but it is a corruption of that corruption, and *concillis* being meaningless cannot be conjectural. It is evidence of this incontrovertible sort that I shall now employ against Baehrens: I shall adduce passages where N exhibits a corruption in its early stage and O exhibits a later stage of that same corruption. Now if I had but a single instance, that would not suffice to prove my case, for it is conceivable that a single instance might spring from a freak of chance: for example, I do not doubt that in Prop. II xxxiii 12 the true reading is Prof. Palmer's elegant emendation 'mandisti et stabulis *arbita* pasta tuis', and here while ON have *abdita* the Cuiacianus has *abbita* which is nearer the truth by one letter; but from the whole of the Cuiacianus, as we shall see hereafter, there has been adduced no other peculiar reading which has even the semblance of integrity, and *abbita* must accordingly be imputed to accident. But from N

I adduce not one such instance but the following list. || First I set down the reading recognised as true by the consent of modern critics, Baehrens himself included; then the corruption found in N; then the further corruption of that corruption found in O. Wherever f or v agrees with N I note the fact, since I am concerned to prove that these as well as N preserve a genuine tradition independent of O.

I vi 3

cum *quo Rhipaeos* possim conscendere montes.
coripeos N
corripeos O

N presents the regular palaeographical equivalents for *qu, rh* and *ae*: O inserts a second *r* to make the word more like Latin.

I xviii 16

lumina *deiectis* turpia sint lacrimis.
delectis Nv
dilectis O

II xxxiv 59

me iuuet *hesternis* positum languere corollis.
externis Nf
eternis F
aeternum DV

O clearly had *eternis* or *aeternis*.

III v 6. Adduced by Leo.

nec miser *aera* paro clade, Corinthe, tua.
aere N
ire O

III vii 49

sed Thyio thalamo aut *Oricia* terebintho.
orythia N
corythia DV
corinthia F

O had *corythia* or *corithia*. ||

IV i 106. Adduced by Leo.

umbra*ue quae* magicis mortua prodit aquis.
ne quę N
que ne O

IV iii 55. Adduced by Leo.

Glaucidos et catulae uox est mihi grata querentis.
Graucidos N
Grancidos O

IV vii 61. Adduced by Leo.

> qua numerosa fides *quaque aera rutunda* Cybelles.
>> *qua quaerar ut unda* Nv
>> *qua quaerat ut unda* D V
>> *qua quaerat nuda* F

IV xi 97

> et bene habet: numquam mater *lugubria* sumpsi.
>> *lubrigia* Nv
>> *lubrica* O

Here then falls to earth the system of Baehrens; and the further evidence to be brought against him is in its controversial aspect no more than a slaying of the slain. But my purpose, as I said, is not in the main controversial; so our enquiry proceeds. We have established the existence in N of a genuine element not derived from O: we now go on to investigate its magnitude.

§2. *N better than O: continued*

I begin with certain evidence which is closely akin to the above though as an offensive weapon against Baehrens it has not the same irresistible cogency: it consists of passages where the reading which I think true and shall try to prove so appears slightly corrupted in N and worse corrupted in O, but where Baehrens dissents as to the truth of the reading. The example however which I place first is really no less certain than those just enumerated. ||

IV viii 37   Lygdamus ad cyathos, *uterque* aestiua supellex.

uterque O, *utrique* Nfv. Baehrens proposes *craterque*; Mr Rossberg retaining *uterque* explains *ūter* as the wine-skin. Scaliger with the assent I think of all scholars but these restored '*uitrique* aestiua supellex' from copa 29 'si sapis, *aestiuo* recubans te prolue *uitro*': the copa is full of parallels to this poem and the emendation seems placed beyond dispute.

II xiii 47–50
> cui si tam longae minuisset fata senectae
>> Gallicus Iliacis miles in aggeribus,
> non *ille* Antilochi uidisset corpus humari
>> diceret aut 'o mors, cur mihi sera uenis?'

O has *ille* which N omits. 'suspectum fraudis pronomen, cum absit ab N neque causa defectus appareat. repone illud *aut*, quod quam facile potuerit absorberi sequente *ant* nemo non uidet' Lucian Mueller. The *ille* of O then will be a metrical correction of the reading of N. That Propertius wrote *aut* is an hypothesis which explains the facts before us: that he wrote *ille* is not. But Mr Palmer at III xi 17 contends that the scribe of N ejected *ille* because he pronounced Antilŏchi; and that in IV iii 1 'haec Arethusa suo' *haec* was lost not because it

stood next the margin but because the scribe pronounced Ārēthusa; and that in
II xxxiv 40 'aut Capanei magno grata ruina Ioui' the scribe of O omitted
magno because he pronounced Cāpānēi. I have the greatest difficulty in setting
before my mind's eye a conception of these scribes, who first invent for themselves, with no motive and on no foundation and against the metre of the verse
they are transcribing, a false scansion of a word, and then adhere with such
tenacity to this causeless baseless and embarrassing fiction that instead of
reforming their pronunciation as the verse suggests they deform the verse to
keep their pronunciation unreformed.

II xxv 1–3

> unica nata meo pulcherrima cura dolori,
>   excludit quoniam sors mea 'saepe *ueni*',
> ista meis fiet notissima forma libellis. ||

ueni O, *uenit* N. This surprising punctuation, invented by Jacob and adopted by
all subsequent editors but Mr Palmer, is deservedly scouted by Madvig in his
adversaria critica: 'in illa, quae fingitur, inuitandi formula peruerse abundat
saepe, neque is dolor erat, quod non saepe uenire iuberetur, sed quod non reci-
peretur et quod excluderetur a puella. codex optimus (Neapolitanus) a prima
manu habet *uenit*. fuerat: "*excludi* quoniam sors mea saepe uenit", hoc est, quod
saepe mihi ea sors obuenit, ut excludar.' The conjecture was anticipated by
Scaliger. It is open I think to the objection of Baehrens, that you would expect
mihi: to remove this scruple I would alter with Lachmann one letter more and
write

> *excludi* quoniam sors mea saepe *uehit*.

III vi 21–2

> ille potest nullo miseram me linquere facto?
> *aequalem nulla* dicere habere domo?

So O. Cynthia complains to the slave Lygdamus that Propertius has forsaken
her for another. The pentameter is senseless; and Heinsius proposed 'aequalem
nullam dicere habere *domi*'. *domi* may well be accepted, since 'habere domi' is
a regular phrase in this connexion: Q. Cic. de pet. cons. 2 8 'quo tamen in
magistratu amicam quam *domi* palam *haberet* de machinis emit', Auson. epigr.
120 [78 Peiper] 1 sq. 'lambere cum uellet mediorum membra uirorum | Castor
nec posset uulgus *habere domi*'. But the rest of the conjecture, to mention one
objection only, is subverted by the fact that neither in III viii 21 nor anywhere
else does *aequalis* mean *riualis*. Turn to N, and you find that for *aequalem nulla*
it offers *et qualem nullo*, from which Mr Palmer has recovered the truth: no more
brilliant and certain correction was ever made in the text of Propertius:

> ille potest nullo miseram me linquere facto
> et, qualem *nolo* dicere, habere domi?

i.e. 'puellam uilem, cuius quaestum nolo dicere, domi habere'. Mr Palmer compares Iuu. VIII 275 'aut pastor fuit aut illud quod *dicere nolo*' and Catull. 67 45 'quendam, quem *dicere nolo* | || nomine'. *nolo* was corrupted by the *nullo* just above, and the error *equalis* for *et qualis* recurs in the MSS of Tib. II 4 17.

III vi 41–2

> quid mihi si tanto felix concordia bello
> extiterit, per me, Lygdame, liber eris.

quid mihi si O, *quod nisi et* N. All editors accept as is necessary the *quod* of N, and the *e* which Lachmann elicits from *et* makes the meaning plainer. And since the 'bellum' in question is a quarrel between Propertius and Cynthia it does not appear why *mihi* is used where *nobis* would be better; so that *nisi* too demands attention. Mr Lucian Mueller altering very slightly the reading of N writes '*quodsin e tanto*' cet.: the unfamiliar word, used also by Valerius Flaccus v 667, was easily changed to *quod nisi*, and the scribe of O mistook *nisi* for *ṁsi*, i.e. *mihi si*.

III viii 19–20. Adduced by Leo.

> non est certa fides quam non *iniuria* uersat.
> hostibus eueniat lenta puella meis.

iniuria O, *iniurgia* N. The hexameter may be interpreted either with Broukhusius 'nihil potes tibi polliceri de fide puellae tuae, nisi eam uariis iniuriis lacessiueris' or with Burmann 'one cannot love one's mistress faithfully unless she outrages one's love'. Either of these very diverse sentiments may be true, but neither has any connexion with the theme of the poem. This elegy celebrates an outbreak of Cynthia's temper: it begins 'dulcis ad hesternas fuerat mihi rixa lucernas | uocis et insanae tot maledicta tuae', and then proceeds to explain: 'nimirum ueri dantur mihi signa caloris, | nam sine amore graui femina nulla dolet. | quae mulier rabida iactat conuicia lingua, | haec Veneris magnae uoluitur ante pedes': its argument is that one's mistress by such outbreaks of temper displays the truth of her affection. This consideration together with the *iniurgia* of N has conducted Mr Vahlen to the following conjecture: 'non est certa fides quam non *in iurgia uertas*', 'that love is not sure which cannot be provoked to a quarrel': the || context admits no other sense than this, and the indications of N seem to leave no doubt that these were the very words which expressed it.

III xv 31–4. Adduced by Ellis.

> ac, ueluti, magnos cum ponunt aequora motus,
> eurus *in aduersos* desinit ire *notos*,
> litore sic tacito, sonitus rarescit harenae,
> sic cadit inflexo lapsa puella genu.

in aduersos...notos O, *sub aduerso...notho* N. It at once appears that the former is easier explained as a correction of the latter than the latter as a corruption of the former. Lachmann therefore is followed by most editors when he writes *ubi aduerso...noto*. The construction of the sentence seems to be this: ac, ueluti sonitus harenae, cum aequora, ubi eurus aduerso noto ire desinit, magnos motus ponunt, litore sic [= in ea rerum condicione] tacito, rarescit, sic cadit puella. But the passage is uncertain, and I will say that to my mind Lachmann's conjecture though generally accepted partakes of its uncertainty.

IV X 41–2

> genus hic Rheno iactabat ab ipso
> nobilis *effecti* fundere gaesa rotis.

effecti O, *erecti* Nf, whence Passeratius *e rectis* which seems clearly right: compare Verg. Aen. XII 671 'eque *rotis* magnam respexit ad urbem'. *rectis* = quas ipse regebat: Virdomarus is extolled for the skill with which at one and the same time he held the rein and hurled the javelin, as Hertzberg explains quoting Caes. bell. Gall. IV 33 'per omnes partes perequitant et tela coniciunt.' Baehrens' *e uectis* can pretend to no merit but the merit of disregarding N; and after all it is as near to N as to O.

II xiii 1–2

> non tot Achaemeniis *armantur* Etrusca sagittis,
> spicula quot nostro pectore fixit Amor.

armantur O, *armatur* N: which of these is true or nearer truth we cannot tell till we have emended the corrupt *Etrusca*; ‖ but Hertzberg justly observes that a scribe was likelier to write plural for singular, taking 'Etrusca spicula' for the nominative, than singular for plural. The best conjecture yet proposed, Volscus' *Susa* (see Lucan II 49 'Achaemeniis...Susis'), demands *armantur*: many read *Itura*, which they mean for *Ituraea*; but since they do not know whether this figment of theirs is fem. sing. or neut. plur. they cannot tell which form of the verb to choose: Ellis would write *armatur Atusa*, which is nearer to the MSS but yet not very near. I offer this:

> non tot Achaemeniis *armatus Eruthra* sagittis.

Eruthra or *Erythra* is Ἐρύθρας, that fabulous king of the east who left his name to the Red Sea and the Persian Gulf. For the Latinised inflexion compare a verse the counterpart of this, II xiv 1 'non ita Dardanio gauisus *Atrida* triumpho'; also *Marsyă* Hor. serm. I 6 120, Ovid met. VI 400, Sil. VIII 503, *Peliă* Sen. Med. 201 and 276, *Tiresiă* Oed. 289. Velius Longus 2215 [*GLK* vol. vii p. 49] tells us that Verrius Flaccus regarded Greek υ and Latin *u* as equivalent, and this transliteration seems from the best MSS, Virgil's especially, to have been common enough in Augustan writers: in late MSS like Propertius' the scribes have sub-

stituted *y* wherever they recognised what was meant, but traces of *u* survive in such corruptions as I xx 4 *minius* for *Minuis* or III ix 14 *nuros* for *Muos*, or this which I have just emended. The confusion of -*atus* and -*atur* is perpetual.
II xxvii 1–10

> at uos incertam, mortales, funeris horam
>   quaeritis, et qua sit mors aditura uia;
> quaeritis et caelo, Phoenicum inuenta, sereno
>   quae sit stella homini commoda quaeque mala,
> seu pedibus Parthos sequimur seu classe Britannos,   5
>   et maris et terrae caeca perinde uia est.
> rursus et obiectum *flemus* caput esse tumultu,
>   cum Mauors dubias miscet utrimque manus.
> praeterea domibus flammam domibusque ruinas
>   neu subeant labris pocula nigra tuis.   10

flemus O, *fletus* N. No person is mentioned to whom the 'tuis' || of v. 10 can refer. They say that Propertius here diverts his address from mankind in general to an imaginary individual; and so he doubtless does. But this transition can only be effected by means of a vocative or of a personal pronoun: a possessive pronoun cannot serve for the purpose. That is to say, it does not so serve in the writings of authors whose MSS are good and ancient: the late and corrupt MSS of Propertius supply two parallels, one in III iv 4 which I shall shortly have occasion to discuss, the other in II xxv 47 where after '*uidistis* Argiuas', '*uidistis* nostras', we come to 'haec atque illa mali uulneris una uia est, | cum satis una *tuis* insomnia portet ocellis | una sit et cuiuis femina multa mala.' But here the sense is no better than the diction: either woman works hurt, *because* one woman works hurt enough to you or to anyone! Coherency of thought and expression may be restored by inserting before 'cum satis' cet. some such couplet as this: 'quin *tu* uulgares, *demens*, compescis amores | in poenamque uagus desinis esse tuam'. To return then to II xxvii: 'tuis' has no meaning; nor is it rendered any the more tolerable by Mr Lucian Mueller's emendation of v. 9 'praeterea domibus flammam *metuis*que ruinas'. The emendation in itself I think right and necessary: it delivers us from the absurd 'fleo flammam domibus', and I would support it with M. Sen. contr. II 9 12 [p. 112 Müller] 'ut anxii interdiu et nocte *ruinam ignemque metuant*': the scribe's eye glancing from *etui* to *erui* he wrote *flammameruinas* which was afterwards expanded to the length required by the metre. But still neither 'tuis' nor 'metuis' has any person to whom it can be referred. Therefore from the *fletus* of N we are to elicit, not the vulgate *fletis* which is no more help than *flemus*, but *fles tu*, transposing one letter. O has further corrupted *fletus* to *flemus*, seduced by the *sequimur* which stands above.

II xxxii 3–6 (Solbisky pp. 163 sq.)

> nam quid Praenesti dubias, o Cynthia, sortes,
> quid petis Aeaei moenia Telegoni?
> *cur uatem* Herculeum deportant esseda Tibur?
> Appia cur totiens te uia ducit anum? ‖

cur uatem O, *curua te* N. The second distich is evidently corrupt, and in going about to amend it the *cur uatem* of O is altered by all editors but one. Mr Palmer however, unluckily remembering II iv 15 sq. 'nam cui non ego sum fallaci praemia *uati*? | quae mea non deciens somnia uersat *anus*?', retains this reading, changes *te uia* in the next verse with one interpolated MS into *deuia*, which singularly inappropriate epithet he bestows on the Appian highway, and explains the passage thus: 'Cynthia ad suam domum Tiburtinam uatem prae-sagum, anum fatidicam deportari essedis iubet ut futura exponant.' The Via Appia does not lead to Tibur; but that is a trifle: if the couplet means what Mr Palmer says it means, then it is a fragment of some other poem and has no business in this context, where Propertius complains to Cynthia, that *she* is always quitting Rome for Praeneste, for Tusculum, for Aricia, and concludes that '*ista* tui furtum *uia* monstrat amoris: | non urbem, demens, lumina nostra *fugis*': all which has nothing to do with sooth-sayers and old women who are summoned to Tibur and expect to get there by the Appian way. The two verses therefore, if they belong to this elegy, enquire why Cynthia so often visits Tibur and some other place in the neighbourhood of Rome; and I will give them at once in what I believe to be their genuine form:

> *curnam te* Herculeum deportant esseda Tibur?
> Appia cur totiens te uia *Lanuuium*?

The brilliant emendation of the pentameter seems to be Jortin's: *la* was lost in *ia*, *uianuuium* suggested *uia anum*, and *ducit* was thrown in for the metre: in IV viii we find Cynthia driving along the Appian way to Lanuuium in the company of a rival lover. The *curnam te* which I have written in the hexameter is based on the *curua te* of N and seems to me the simplest correction: Baehrens' *cur tua te*, likewise based on N, that N to which he denies all authority, is no less easy palaeographically, but the juxtaposition of the pronouns lays a stress on 'tua' for which no reason is apparent. If Mr Lucian Mueller's *cur aut te* be accepted, that again is nearer to N than O. The old vulgate *curue te in* is unmetrical. ‖

III iv 1–6

> arma deus Caesar dites meditatur ad Indos
> et freta gemmiferi findere classe maris.
> magna, uiri, merces: parat ultima terra triumphos;

> *Tigris* et Euphrates sub tua iura fluent,
> Seres et Ausoniis uenient prouincia uirgis;
> adcrescent Latio Partha tropaea Ioui.
> ite agite cet.

Tigris O, *Tygris* N. This is the passage to which I alluded under II xxvii 1–10. 'tua iura' in v. 4 is said to mean 'thy rule, O Caesar', though one line above you have the vocative 'uiri' and three lines below the plural imperatives 'ite agite': another of those 'Propertian' peculiarities which are peculiar not to Propertius but to those authors whose MSS are late and bad. 'istud *tua*' says Broukhusius most truly 'non habet quo referatur', and he conjectures *sua*, i.e. 'eiectis regibus erunt sui iuris et liberi'; but this accords ill with the context, which prophesies the subjugation of the East to Rome. The antitheses of the next distich point to the sense required, and Heinsius' *noua* is better; but the following seems to have much more point:

> parat ultima terra triumphos,
> *Thybris*, et Euphrates sub tua iura *fluet*.

How easily Euphrates would transform *Thybris* to *Tigris* is evident; and the *Tygris* of N may be a vestige of the change: how easily *fluet* would then become *fluent* is evident again. For *Thybris* instead of *Thybri* compare III vii 68 'et tu, materno tacta dolore *Thetis*'; and indeed nominative for vocative in the poets is not uncommon. For the ascription of 'iura' to the Tiber I would adduce Verg. Aen. VIII 77 'corniger Hesperidum fluuius regnator aquarum', Ovid met. II 259 'cuique fuit rerum promissa potentia, Thybrim', fast. V 641 'quem nunc gentes Tiberim noruntque timentque', Stat. silu. III 5 111 'ductor aquarum | Thybris'; for the antagonism imputed to the rivers of different lands Prop. II xxxiii 20 'cum Tiberi Nilo gratia nulla fuit', III xi 42 'Tiberim Nili cogere ferre minas', Val. Fl. I 5 17 sq. 'quid barbarus amnibus ullis | Phasis... obstat?' ||

III xxii 1–4

> frigida tam multos placuit tibi Cyzicus annos,
> Tulle, Propontiaca qua fluit Isthmos aqua,
> Dindymus et sacra fabricata *iuuenta* Cybelle
> raptorisque tulit quae uia Ditis equos.

iuuenta O, *inuenta* N. The conjecture of Isaac Voss *sacrae fabricata iuuenca Cybebae*, once much admired, is now consigned to the neglect it merits: the only author who vouches for the existence of a 'fabricata iuuenca' at Cyzicus is Voss himself, and the sacrifices of heifers which did take place there were made not to Cybebe but to Proserpina. Haupt (index lectionum Berlin 1854–5, pp. 12 sq.) draws attention to ancient authorities who tell us of one thing at any rate at Cyzicus which was 'fabricata': Strab. XII p. 575 [p. 808 Meineke] Δίνδυμον... ἱερὸν ἔχον τῆς Δινδυμήνης μητρὸς θεῶν, ἵδρυμα τῶν Ἀργοναυτῶν, Apoll.

Rhod. I 1117 sqq. ἔσκε δέ τι στιβαρὸν στύπος ἀμπέλου ἔντροφον ὕλη, | πρόχνυ γεράνδρυον· τὸ μὲν ἔκταμον, ὄφρα πέλοιτο | δαίμονος οὐρείης ἱερὸν βρέτας· ἔξεσε δ’ Ἄργος | εὐκόσμως. καὶ δή μιν ἐπ’ ὀκριόεντι κολωνῷ | ἵδρυσαν: hence he proposes *sacra fabricata e uite*, adding 'quod siquis audaciam nostram reprehendet, gaudebimus si protulerit quod et propius absit a codicum litteris et rei aeque conueniat'. Comparing the letters of the MSS with the ἐπ’ ὀκριόεντι κολωνῷ of Apollonius I conjecture 'sacra fabricata *in caute* Cybelle'. The letters of *caute* are those of *uecta*, and *-uecta* is commonly confused with *-uenta*: this gives us the reading of N, and O corrupts one letter more. The ill attested form *Dindymus* with the asyndeton it involves should be removed by substituting with Mr Palmer the adjective *Dindymis*.

IV i 31–2

> hinc Titiens Ramnesque uiri Luceresque *coloni*,
> quattuor hinc albos Romulus egit equos.

coloni O, *soloni* N. The Luceres were no more devoted to agriculture than were the other tribes; so Hertzberg explains *coloni* as a reference to the tradition that they were brought to Rome from Etruria by Lucumo. Thus interpreted the word is defensible || in itself but indefensible in its place; for the juxtaposition 'Ramnesque uiri Luceresque coloni', just as it signifies that the Luceres were and the Ramnes were not *coloni*, will signify also that the Ramnes were and the Luceres were not *uiri*. This objection can only be removed by replacing *coloni* with some laudatory title for the Luceres which shall be virtually synonymous with that bestowed on the Ramnes; and the ridiculous *soloni* of N points to just such a word: *seueri*.[1] At II iii 7 our MSS vary between *seueris* and *serenis*; at Lucr. V 1190 'noctis signa *serena*' is restored by Candidus instead of *seuera* which however pretty to a modern taste could have no meaning for a Roman; at IV 460 of the same poet I would similarly alter '*seuera* silentia noctis' to *serena*: now then *sereni* is palaeographically almost identical with *soloni*, and would also be no less easily confused with *coloni* than *serenda* with *colenda* in the MSS of Tib. II 3 8. The epithet is often applied to the early Romans, as in Verg. Aen. VIII 638 'Curibus seueris', and it tallies very well with *uiri*, which has the same force as *mares* in Hor. epist. I i 64 'maribus Curiis'.

IV ii 1–2

> qui mirare meas tot in uno corpore formas,
> accipe Vertumni signa *petenda* dei.

petenda O, *paterna* Nfv. 'signa petenda' are words which no one I think has ever attempted to explain. It is curious to note that they recur in Ovid ars I 114 'rex populo praedae *signa petenda* dedit' (the signal for the rape of the Sabine

---

[1] It is some confirmation of this conjecture that Vrbinas 641 (see note on p. 101 [this edition p. 232]) has *seloni*.

women) where it seems necessary to write *petita* with Bentley and Madvig. In our passage the *paterna* of Nfv is adopted by all editors but Baehrens, and they explain with Passeratius thus: 'notas, quibus possis eum agnoscere, audi et intellege. alludit enim ad γνωρίσματα comicorum. et *paterna* pro *patriis* uidetur dixisse, sequitur enim *Tuscus ego.*' Yes, but no 'signa paterna' or 'patria', no marks of the origin of Vertumnus, follow: what follows is first of all the plain assertion 'I am a Tuscan', and then the god's autobiography and a list of his || varied accomplishments; but about marks of his origin never a word. Nor in Baehrens' *signa petita* can I interpret either the substantive or the participle. In brief, only one sense will the context suffer; 'Tuscus ego et Tuscis orior' answers the question 'what is Vertumnus' origin', not 'what are the marks of his origin' nor anything else: write 'accipe Vertumni *regna paterna* dei', 'learn the native land of Vertumnus'. At [Sen.] Herc. Oet. 1160 the MSS vary between *regna* and *signa*; in Prop. IV vi 78 v gives *signa* for *regna*, though that may be a mere conjecture and not an honest mistake.

IV V 21–4

> si te Eoa *derorantum* iuuat aurea ripa
>   et quae sub Tyria concha superbit aqua,
> Eurypylisque placet Coae textura Mineruae
>   sectaque ab Attalicis putria signa toris.

derorantum O, *doroʒantum* N. In place of these meaningless rows of letters they have conjectured the names of many eastern nations, *Doanarum*, *Areiʒantum*, *Domaʒanum* and I know not what besides. The parallels of Tib. II 4 27–30 'o pereat quicumque legit uiridesque *smaragdos* | et niueam *Tyrio murice* tingit ouem. | hic dat auaritiae causas et *Coa* puellis | *uestis* et e rubro lucida concha mari' and [Sen.] Herc. Oet. 661 sqq. 'nec gemmiferas detrahit aures | *lapis Eoa* lectus in *unda*, | nec *Sidonio* mollis *aeno* | repetita bibit lana rubores' point in quite another direction, and *ʒmaragdorum* suggests itself; but Propertius himself brings more light: take II xvi 17 sq. 'semper in Oceanum mittit me quaerere *gemmas* | et iubet ex ipsa tollere dona *Tyro*' with 43 sq. 'quascumque tibi uestes, quoscumque smaragdos | quosue dedit *flauo lumine chrysolithos*' and set these verses beside our passage and its '*aurea* ripa': then say if *topaʒorum*, topazes or chrysoliths, is not the word to restore. Its letters I should guess were wrongly ordered *poroʒatum*, and thence corrupted by the confusion of P with D to *doroʒātum*. The form *topaʒontum* seems less likely and is really further from the MSS.

I conclude this list with an example which is a very effective argumentum ad hominem against Baehrens. ||

II xxii 29–34

> quid? cum e complexu Briseidos iret Achilles
>   num fugere minus Thessala tela Phryges?

quid? ferus Andromachae lecto cum surgeret Hector
bella Mycenaeae non timuere rates?
ille uel hic classes *poterat* uel perdere muros:
hic ego Pelides, hic ferus Hector ego.

poterat O, *poterant* N. Although Baehrens is mistaken in saying that 'ille' in the above text must refer to Achilles and 'hic' to Hector (see for instance II i 38), it is nevertheless true that the verse appears to contemplate either hero performing either feat, and that this is absurd. Baehrens therefore seems to be right in proposing '*illi uel* classes *poterant* uel perdere muros'; but then his theory of the MSS receives a shock from his own hand. After 'ille uel hic' a scribe was not very likely to change singular to plural, but rather the reverse.

§3. *N better than O: continued*

I now come to treat of passages where N is right or virtually right and O is wrong. These, as I said above, are not, like the examples I set in the forefront, invincible evidence for the genuineness of N, since it might be maintained without impudence though not without perversity that N here owes its superiority to conjectural emendation. I shall begin however with several instances of a peculiar sort, whose persuasiveness attains almost to cogency.

II xxxiii 37. Adduced by Leo.

cum tua praependent *demissa* in pocula *serta*.

demissa...*serta* O, *demissae*...*sertae* N. Which is right we learn from Charisius p. 107 25 Keil [p. 137 Barwick] 'serta neutro genere dicuntur...sed Propertius feminine extulit sic: tua praependent *demissae* in pocula *sertae*.' This accordingly has always been reckoned one of N's chief titles to esteem, and Baehrens is generally and deservedly ridiculed for his note '*demissae*...*sertae* Charisius et (ex hoc interpolatus) N'. θεοῦ θέλοντος, remarks Mr Leo, κἂν ἐπὶ ῥιπὸς πλέοις. ||

II xxiii 21–2. Adduced by Leo.

et quas Euphrates et quas mihi misit Orontes
me *capiant*.

capiant O, *iuuerint* N, 'interpolate' says Baehrens. This 'interpolate' is a mere formula to which the writer himself can have attached no definite meaning: why any scribe should find *capiant* difficult, why if he found *capiant* difficult he should find *iuuerint* easier, why he should replace a verb in one tense which will scan by a verb in another tense which will not, are questions to which no answer is even imaginable. And it is especially indiscreet of Baehrens to talk of interpolation here, because if ever a word had all the outward air of an interpolation it is *capiant*. It almost proclaims itself to be what every other critic thinks it, an obvious conjecture to amend the unmetrical *iuuerint*, *iuuerint* being in truth a corruption of the rare form *iǔerint* employed by Catullus at 66 18 and similarly corrupted there.

III i 24–8

> maius ab exequiis nomen in ora uenit.
> nam quis equo pulsas abiegno nosceret arces
>   fluminaque Haemonio comminus isse uiro
> Idaeum Simoenta Iouis *cunabula parui*,
>   Hectora per campos ter maculasse rotas.

Thus does O present v. 27; and Lachmann and Haupt (index lectionum Berlin 1854–5) have shewn long ago that its reading is impossible. Propertius might adopt if he chose the less common fable which made Jove to have been nursed on the Trojan and not the Cretan Ida; but even if Trojan Ida was Jove's cradle, Idaean Simois was not, and a much graver difficulty arises from the context. Propertius here prophesies that his reputation will redouble after his death, and confirms this forecast by the reminder that Troy owes its fame to its fall: had it not perished there would have been no Iliad, and we should never have heard of the things which that poem relates. But from μῆνιν ἄειδε to Ἕκτορος ἱπποδά-μοιο not one word has the Iliad to say about Jove's cradle on Ida; and our information ‖ or misinformation concerning that matter cannot in any conceivable way depend on the fall of Troy. When therefore Mr Palmer writes 'Idaeos montes Iouis incunabula parui' he provides the infant deity with a drier cradle, but he does nothing to cure the verse of its entire inconsequence. Now N omits the words *cunabula parui*, and it is too much to suppose that it does so because its scribe apprehended the absurdity to which modern scholars with Lachmann and Haupt to teach them still shut their eyes. If one compares Homer's Ξάνθου δινήεντος ὃν ἀθάνατος τέκετο Ζεύς it will seem that Gustav Wolff has restored the very words of Propertius by writing 'Idaeum Simoenta Iouis *cum prole Scamandro*'. It appears that in the archetype the end of the verse was torn away to the letters *cu* which in N are omitted as unintelligible but in O are conjecturally expanded to *cunabula parui*.

IV vii 7–8. Adduced by Ellis.

> *hosdem* habuit secum, quibus est elata, capillos,
>   *hosdem* oculos.

So O: the true reading in both verses is of course *eosdem*. Now N gives *hosdem* in v. 7 and *eosdem* in v. 8, a singular trait of genuineness, for an interpolator who emended one would have emended both.

II vii 1–3

> gauisa es certe sublatam, Cynthia, legem,
>   qua quondam edicta flemus uterque diu,
> *ni* nos diuideret.

ni N, *quis* O, from which Baehrens prefers to elicit *quod*, never asking himself whether it is the wont of interpolators to adorn a poet's pages with such things as this rare yet correct use of *ni* = *ne*, nor caring to notice how easily *ni* would be absorbed in the following *n* and leave a gap for some thoughtless emendator to fill with *quis*.

II ix 19–22. Adduced by Ellis.

> at tu non una potuisti nocte uacare,
>   impia, non unum sola manere diem. ||
> quin etiam multo *duxisti* pocula risu,
>   forsitan et de me uerba fuere mala.

duxisti O, but N *duxistis*, i.e. you and your paramour drank: of two readings equally correct, science bids us take the less obvious and more exquisite.

II xxxiv 43   incipe iam angusto uersus *componere* torno.

componere O, *includere* Nv. That *componere* is wrong there is no doubt, and no doubt whence it comes, for v. 41 runs 'desine et Aeschyleo *componere* uerba co*turno*', and O has *turno* for *torno* in our verse. There is no question, I say, that *componere* is wrong: the question is whether *includere* be right. It may be thought that Baehrens' *compescere* is more plausible; but in places where a scribe has repeated a word from overhead the ductus litterarum are a foundation on which nothing can be built. For '*angusto* uersus *includere torno*' I adduce what seems to me a striking and decisive piece of external evidence: Gell. noct. Att. IX 8 'hanc sententiam memini a Fauorino inter ingentes omnium clamores *detornatam inclusamque uerbis his paucissimis.*'

III xxiv 5–6

> mixtam te uaria laudaui saepe figura,
>   ut, quod non *esses*, *esse* putaret amor.

esses esse N, *essem saepe* F, *esset saepe* DV. That N is right is undisputed and indisputable; and as Ellis observes (p. 399) 'to ascribe to a copyist of the early xvth century a felicity of correction worthy of a Bentley or a Lachmann is a somewhat dangerous experiment'.

IV iii 51–2. Adduced by Leo.

> nam mihi quo? Poenis *tibi* purpura fulgeat ostris
>   crystallusque *tuas* ornet aquosa manus.

tibi...tuas O, *te...meas* N. Arethusa writes to her absent husband that she cares not for gaiety or finery while he is away; and from these verses, after they have been subjected to the above punctuation, it is desired to extract the following sense: || 'what profit is it to me? for you let the purple of [my] Tyrian raiment shine and the watery crystal deck [my] hands which are yours.' The feasibility of this astounding interpretation, to borrow a phrase of Lachmann's, 'exemplis docendum erat, non optandum et fingendum'. The words really mean 'let your raiment shine and the crystal deck your hands', and are very absurdly addressed to a soldier at the wars. The *meas* of N is now accepted by most editors, and its obvious corruption *te* appears to be the origin of the *tibi* in O : the passage should seemingly be written thus:

> nam mihi quo Poenis *nunc* purpura fulgeat ostris
> crystallusque *meas* ornet aquosa manus?

'why should I bedeck myself while you are away?' *nunc* is not seldom confused with *tunc*, and *tunc* is abbreviated *t͞c*. Compare Ovid her. XIII 37 sq. 'scilicet ipsa geram saturatas murice lanas, | bella sub Iliacis moenibus ille gerat?'

I xiii 11   haec tibi uulgares istos *compescet* amores.

compescet Nfv, *componet* O. *compescet* is accepted by Baehrens as by all other editors; he however must regard it as a conjecture. Yet *componet* was quite simple and in no way invited correction; nor was *compescet* at all an obvious word for the corrector to hit on.

II viii 15   *ecquandone* tibi liber sum uisus?

ec quando ne N, *et quando ne* DV, *et quando ue* F. Observe that N, which gives the letters correctly, shews by its division of them that the scribe did not understand what he wrote. Baehrens apprehends that his theory is thus jeopardised, and accordingly says 'grauius haec corrupta', but shews no argument.

II viii 37–8

> at, postquam *sera* captiua est reddita poena,
> fortem illum Haemoniis Hectora traxit equis.

sera Nfv, *sacra* DV, om. F. Nothing is easier than the exchange || of these two words with *saera* for the mediating form: thus Horace's MSS at serm. I 10 21 give *seri saeri* and *sacri*. All we have to consider then is which of the two suits better the restoration of Briseis to Achilles; and the answer of course is *sera*. Baehrens is able to prefer *sacra* here because it is not nonsense; but presently he comes to II xxxiv 25:

> Lynceus ipse meus *seros* insanit amores.

seros Nfv, *sacros* O. Here even he is forced to desert O for N; a lesson which should not be neglected at II viii 37.

II xix 19–20

> incipiam captare feras et reddere pinu
> cornua et audaces ipse *monere* canes.

monere N, *mouere* O and Baehrens. But no: mouet uenator feras; canes monet.

II xxv 41–2
uidistis pleno teneram candore puellam,
uidistis fusco: *ducit* uterque color.

ducit N, *dulcis* O. The former, as Mr Leo points out p. 446, is confirmed by the
'utraque forma *rapit*' of v. 44, and the latter is somewhat discountenanced by the
'quantum sic cruciat lumina uestra dolor' of v. 40.

II xxvi 15   et tibi *ob inuidiam* Nereides increpitarent.

ob inuidiam Nv, *prae inuidia* O, which solecism Baehrens introduces into the
text of Propertius. It is pretty generally known that in Augustan Latin *prae*,
when it signifies cause, signifies only a hindering cause, and that 'prae inuidia
increpito' though good for Plautus or Liuius Andronicus is not good for
Propertius or his contemporaries. N's reading accounts for O's: in *tibiobin-
uidiā* the syllable *bi* comes twice over, whence the error *tibinuidia*, of which
O gives the unhappy correction (Palmer Hermathena IV p. 53). Mr Solbisky
however is much mistaken in saying (p. 170) that the elision of *prae* is inad-
missible: he refers to Lucian Mueller de re metr. p. 283 but does not appear ||
to have read that page, which deals with the elision of *prae* and other mono-
syllables before a short syllable.

II xxviii 9–10 (Solbisky pp. 154 sq.)

num sibi collatam doluit Venus *ipsa paremque?*
prae se formosis inuidiosa dea est.

This has been the vulgate since Lachmann who found v. 9 thus in the Groninganus. Lachmann himself perceived that the acceptance of that reading involved
the alteration of *prae se* in the next line, 'quomodo enim nunc formosa prae
Venere quae antea *par* ei dicebatur?' but his followers are less sensitive and
retain the contradiction. Now for *ipsa* both O and N have *illa*; *paremque* is in
F, D has *pareque* and so apparently had V which has now suffered erasure: N on
the other hand gives *per aequae*, that is *peraeque* which is offered by v. Take this
and there is no need to alter *illa*:

num sibi collatam doluit Venus? *illa peraeque*
prae se formosis inuidiosa dea est.

This, the old vulgate, correctly explained by Passeratius 'aequaliter et pariter in
omnes inuidiosa', seems now on the way to restoration, and is defended by
Messrs Vahlen Palmer and Solbisky. *peraeque* has the excellent authority of
Catullus and Cicero yet is too rare to be a likely interpolation.

II xxxiv 3–4
expertus dico: nemo est in amore fidelis:
formosam raro non sibi quisque petit.

formosam Nv, *et formam* O. Baehrens points out with truth that Propertius sometimes uses 'forma' = 'femina formosa'; but the ambiguity of 'formam sibi petit', which naturally means 'seeks personal beauty for himself', is here intolerable.

II xxxiv 9–10

> Lynceu, tune meam potuisti *tangere* curam?
> *perfide,* nonne tuae tum cecidere manus?

So O, but Nv make *tangere* and *perfide* change places. I do not pretend that this is any improvement, but I say that the ‖ very aimlessness of such an alteration proves that the reading of Nv is not introduced by conjecture: what corrector takes the trouble to make such resultless transpositions? If it is an error it is an accident; but it seems to be true because less simple than the other order.

III iv 19   ipsa tuam *serua prolem,* Venus.

serua prolem Nv, *prolem serua* O. The separation of adjective and substantive is less obvious and more workmanlike.

III xi 13–14

> ausa ferox ab equo quondam obpugnare sagittis
> *iniectis* Danaum Penthesilea rates.

iniectis O, which is well enough; but N has *Meotis,* i.e. *Maeotis*: the geographical epithet is clearly to be preferred in an Augustan poet.

IV i 27–8

> nec rudis infestis miles radiabat in armis:
> miscebant usta proelia *nuda* sude.

nuda Nv, *facta* O without meaning, whence Baehrens *ficta* which has no relevance to the context. In favour of *nuda* Passeratius quotes Stat. Theb. I 413 'exsertare umeros *nudam*que lacessere *pugnam*': add Sil. VI 46 'abstulerat fors arma; tamen *certamine nudo* | inuenit Marti telum dolor' and Sen. Phaedr. 544 sqq. 'tum primum *manu* | *bellare nuda,* saxaque et ramos rudes | uertere in arma.' It seems that *nuda* was lost in *sude* and the scribe filled up the gap with the first word that occurred to him.

IV i 141–2

> et, bene cum fixum *mento* decusseris uncum,
> nil *erit* hoc: rostro te premet ansa tuo.

mento Nfv, *merito* O. *erit* Nv, *premit* O which is obviously an anticipation of the following *premet*. But rather than accept the reading of N Baehrens writes *iuuet,* and for the sake of his theory imputes to the dead and defenceless Propertius this sentence: 'cum decuss*eris,* nil iuu*et*: prem*et* ansa.' ‖

IV ii 43–4

>caeruleus cucumis tumidoque cucurbita uentre
>me *notat* et iunco brassica uincta leui.

notat Nfv, *necat* O. The peculiar aptness of *notat* will be shewn by comparing III xi 48 'Tarquinii. . .nomine quem simili uita superba *notat*' i.e. stamps with the name Superbus: so here do these fruits of the seasons stamp the god who receives them with the name Vertumnus, deus *uertentis anni* (v. 11). If then the scribe of N was an emendator he knew his craft better than Baehrens who writes *grauat*.

IV iv 29–30

>et sua Tarpeia residens ita fleuit ab arce
>uulnera, uicino *non patienda* Ioui.

non patienda Nv, *compatienda* O: *comperienda* Baehrens, which is both less forcible and further from O.

IV v 37–8

>supplex ille sedet: posita tu scribe cathedra
>*quidlibet.* has artes si pauet ille, tenes.

quidlibet Nf, *quilibet* O: *quoilibet* Baehrens, which comes no nearer to O and is furthermore absurd. The old woman is instructing the young one how to manage her lover: to excite his jealousy she is to sit down and write – not to *anyone*, which would be superfluous and aimless, but merely to scribble *anything*; and he will fancy it is a love letter.

IV vii 15–16

>iamne tibi exciderunt uigilacis *furta* Suburae
>et mea nocturnis trita fenestra dolis?

furta N, *tecta* O: it is a singular testimony to the superiority of *furta* that Baehrens who rejects it here should five lines lower down introduce the word by such an alteration as *furtaque* for *pectora*. The corruption *tecta*, if we care to trace it, passed through these stages: *furta* is perpetually altered to *facta*; *f* is absorbed by a preceding *s*, and this will leave *acta*; *a* is much confused with *ce* or *te*, and there is *tecta.* ‖

IV vii 40–2

>haec nunc aurata cyclade signat humum,
>et grauiora *fundit* iniquis pensa quasillis,
>garrula de facie si qua locuta mea est.

fundit O, *rependit* Nfv, *iniungit* Baehrens. Palaeographically there is little to choose between these two last, and the sense of either is equally good and practically the same: the nominative to *rependit* will be the antecedent of 'si qua' (serua), to *iniungit* the nominative will be 'haec' (domina). What turns the scale for *rependit* is Ovid her. ɪx 78 'formosae *pensa rependis* erae'. Mr Postgate suggests that *fundit* may come from *refundit*, in its late Latin sense, written over *rependit* as an explanation.

IV X 45–6

causa Feretri,
omine quod certo dux ferit ense ducem.

omine Nv, *crimine* O, i.e. *c̊mine*, the simplest of errors, on which Baehrens builds the conjecture *numine*. The letters are further from O than *omine* is, and the sense is no better.

In the passages which follow the correctness of N is universally recognised and no argumentation is needed.

I iii 33 *compositos* leuibus radiis patefecit *ocellos: compositos...ocellos* Nfv, *compositis...ocellos* DV, *compositis...ocellis* AF.   I vii 20 nec tibi subiciet carmina *serus* amor: *serus* NfVcorr., *uerus* O.   I ix 31 illis et *silices* et possunt cedere quercus: *silices* Nv, *salices* O.   I xviii 19 uos eritis testes, si quos habet *arbor* amores: *arbor* Nv, *ardor* O.   II xxvi 44 me licet unda ferat, te *modo* terra tegat: *modo* Nv, *quoque* O.   II xxx 18 turpia cum faceret *Palladis* ora *tumor*: *Palladis* N, *pallidus* O; *tumor* Nv, *timor* O.   III i 5 dicite, quo pariter carmen *tenuastis* in antro: *tenuastis* N, *tenuistis* O.   III v 34 solis et *atratis* luxerit orbis equis: *atratis* N, *attractis* O.   III xiii 23–4 hoc genus infidum nuptarum; *hic nulla* puella | nec fida Euadne nec pia Penelope: *hic nulla* Nv, *nupta* F, *innupta* D : V has suffered erasure.   III xiii 43 et leporem, quicumque uenis, *uenaberis*, hospes: *uenaberis* Nv, *ueneraberis* O. ‖   III xiii 58 delapsis *nusquam* est Amphi-araus equis: *nusquam* Nfv, *nūquam* F, *nunquam* D, *nunc* V.   III xvi 30 *non* iuuat in media nomen habere uia: *non* Nfv, *me* O.   III xxii 27 at non squamoso *labuntur* uentre cerastae: *labuntur* N, *lambuntur* O.   IV i 144 gutta *quoque* ex oculis non nisi iussa cadet: *quoque* Nv, *quidem* O.   IV ii 26 iurabis nostra gramina *secta* manu: *secta* N, *facta* O.   IV ii 64 unum *opus* est, operi non datur unus honos: *opus* Nfv, *usus* O.   IV iii 59 siue in *finitimo* gemuit stans noctua tigno: *finitimo* Nfv, *furtiuo* O.   IV v 25 *docta* uel Hippolytum Veneri mollire negantem: *docta* Nfv, *nocto* F, *nocte* DV.   IV v 25 *seu quae* palmiferae mittunt uenalia Thebae: *seuq;* (= *seuque*) N, *seu quam* O.   IV vi 79 hic referat *sero* confessum foedere Parthum: *sero* Nfv, *ferro* O.   IV vii 84 quod currens *uector* ab urbe legat: *uector* Nf'V corr.' (? = v), *uictor* O.   IV viii 11 ille sibi admotas a uirgine *corripit* escas: *corripit* Nv, *colligit* O.   IV viii 34 et Venere ignota furta *nouare* mea: *nouare* Nfv, *notare* O.

§4. *Origin of N's superiority*

As I said at the beginning of the last section, most of the true readings there quoted from N might be explained as conjectures if there were any reason to doubt the integrity of their origin; but there is none: quite otherwise. We began by proving the existence in N of a genuine element which it does not share with

9

AFDV; and now that we come to consider the lections just enumerated nothing debars us from the conclusion which their number and excellence naturally suggest, that they too are part of this genuine element.

But I have undertaken not only to prove against Baehrens that N has genuine readings of its own but also to prove against Messrs Solbisky Plessis and Weber that it does not derive those genuine readings from the parent (O) of the codices AFDV. I now therefore proceed to shew how this is proved by the facts we have just surveyed.

Such is the inherent impossibility of the theory propounded ‖ by Messrs Plessis and Weber that nothing more conclusively demolishes it than their own practice. From their genealogy of the MSS it follows as a necessary consequence that whenever the family DV agrees with the family AF (or with F where A is absent) in the reading offered, and N differs, then, except the difference be palaeographically infinitesimal, the reading of AFDV must have stood in the archetype, and the reading of N must be wrong; for AF and DV, according to the stemmata of these scholars, are two independent witnesses to the reading of the archetype, and the consenting testimony of two independent witnesses must be believed against the dissent of one. Now I have just been filling pages with passages where this phenomenon occurs: do Messrs Plessis and Weber accept the consequence? No: they habitually in these passages prefer the reading of N. For instance: in I xiii 11 both AF and DV give 'nec tibi uulgares istos componet amores', and instead of nec...componet N gives haec...compescet: this latter lection Mr Plessis (p. 38) and Mr Weber (p. 14) adopt. And they do well; but there is an end of their theory. For turn to the stemmata codicum of these scholars and consider what this phenomenon means if they have divined aright the relationships of the MSS. It means in the first place – and this is quite credible – that haec...compescet, which stood in O, was correctly copied into X but was corrupted to nec...componet in Y: this, I say, is quite credible. But now behold a portent. While haec...compescet, which stood in X, was correctly copied into N, the scribe of the parent codex of AF not only blundered in copying from X but pitched upon that very blunder which was made by the scribe of Y in copying from O: – wrote nec for haec and componet for compescet. Now it is not impossible that two independent scribes, copying from different MSS, should once or twice coincide in error if that error be diplomatically very slight. But the theory of Messrs Plessis and Weber demands of our credulity that this coincidence in error shall have occurred not once or twice but fifty times over, and in places where the error is not slight but extraordinary. The thing is inconceivable. Imagine two several copyists from diverse exemplars mistaking ni for quis (II vii 3), ob inuidiam for prae inuidia (II xxvi 15), modo for ‖ quoque (II xxvi 44), includere for componere (II xxxiv 43), nuda for facta (IV i 28), erit for premit (IV i 142), opus for usus (IV ii 64), furta for tecta (IV vii 15), rependit for *fundit* (IV vii 41)! Such phenomena as these passages present are explicable to Baehrens who holds N to be interpolated, explicable to me who recognise in N an element not derived from O: to Messrs Plessis and Weber they would be inexplicable if those critics apprehended their own theory. But they do not: they have propounded it without perceiving what it meant.

The theory of Mr Solbisky escapes this objection. The two families DV and AF are not, in his stemma, as they are in the stemmata of Messrs Plessis and Weber, absolutely independent witnesses to the reading of O: he has provided a channel by which AF may have derived readings from DV, and he is thus enabled to explain the agreement of the two families in places where Messrs Plessis and Weber cannot explain it. It is when the facts under discussion are considered in another aspect that they overthrow the system of Mr Solbisky. Let any one peruse the foregoing pages and mark the lections adduced from N, their number, and not their excellence merely but in very many cases the obviousness of that excellence: then let him take in hand Mr Solbisky's stemma codicum and ask himself by what malignity of fate it happens that all these manifestly true readings, which Mr Solbisky supposes to have stood in O, have twice missed the chance which was twice offered them of finding their way into AF. It is comprehensible that they should find their way into one only of the two apographs of O, into X and not into Y. But how strange it is that when X in its turn became the parent of apographs the same thing should happen over again: that all these obviously correct readings, while finding their way safely from X into N as they did from O into X, should fail to find their way from X into AF as they failed to find it from O into Y. And marvel accumulates on marvel when we consider in this connexion the nature, as represented by Mr Solbisky, of the family AF. That family, he holds, was formed by blending the tradition of Y with the tradition of X. Now the tendency of MSS which blend two strains of tradition is to choose the easier of any two readings proffered ‖ by their two sources.[1] But we are fresh from the perusal of passages, which though numerous are only a selection from a much greater number, where N gives a reading not merely true but obviously so, DV a reading not merely false but unintelligible, and yet AF always sides with DV. Take one representative instance, IV ii 64, and consider what it is that Mr Solbisky would have us believe: that the scribe who wrote the codex whence AF descend, having before him the two versions 'unum *opus* est, operi non datur unus honos' (N) and 'unum *usus* est, operi non datur unus honos' (DV), set aside the former, which is simplicity itself, and adopted the latter, which can neither be scanned nor construed; and that habitually throughout his task he thus chose the evil and refused the good. Incredible: the fact that all these true and simple readings are

---

[1] Thus in the instance immediately to be quoted, IV ii 64, only four of the thirty-nine MSS examined by Mr Hosius have *usus*, all the rest *opus*.

found in N only, and not in AF, means that they were inaccessible to AF; that they were not in X any more than in Y; and consequently that N did not derive them from X. There will be more to say against Mr Solbisky's theory when I come to deal particularly with AF; but this suffices to demonstrate his error in the matter of N. And in order that due weight may be attached to my arguments against his theory it must be remembered that he himself has put forward no argument in its favour. He has adduced evidence to support his estimate of the various MSS, but to support his view of the relationship subsisting between them he has adduced none.

If any one should fabricate the theory, untenable for many reasons, that N is derived straight from O, not through X, it would still be impossible to maintain that N derives from O the readings we have been considering, because, as I have said, when two independent witnesses, such as X and Y, consent in their testimony to the reading of their archetype, that consent outweighs the contrary testimony of a single witness. There remains therefore no alternative to the position which I defend, that N possesses a genuine element not derived from O the archetype of AFDV. ||

§5. *N better than AFDV in disagreement*

I now bring forward a certain number of passages where N presents a correct reading which is not preserved in A or F or D or V but which, by comparing the testimony of AF with that of DV, we infer to have existed in their common parent, which I call O. The bearing of these phenomena I shall discuss after I have exhibited them.

I iv 21–2

et te circum omnis alias irata puellas
differet.

differet Nfv, *differt* AF, *deferet* DV.

I x 25   *irritata* uenit, quando contemnitur illa.

irritata N, *irritatura* AF, *iritata* DV.

II ix 26   cum capite hoc Stygiae iam *poterentur* aquae.

poterentur N, *potarentur* F, *peterentur* DV.

II xiii 46–50 (Solbisky pp. 167 sq.)

Nestoris est uisus post tria saecla cinis.
cui si tam longae *minuisset* fata senectae
Gallicus Iliacis miles in aggeribus,
non aut Antilochi uidisset corpus humari
diceret aut 'o mors, cur mihi sera uenis?'

Here in v. 47 I have accepted the 'cui si tam longae' of Liuineius and Santen for the 'quis tam longaeuae' of the MSS; but whether you read thus, or 'cui si longaeuae' with others, or even 'quoi stamen longae' with Baehrens, makes no difference, any more than does the corrupt 'Gallicus' of v. 48, to the question we are now to consider. *minuisset* is the reading of Nfv, *iurauisset* of F, *meminisset* of DV. Now this divergence of F and DV makes it plain that, whatever was written by Propertius, *minuisset* was read by O. *min-uisset* is diplomatically ‖ indistinguishable from *iura-uisset*; *me-minisset* is a metrical correction of *minisset*, i.e. *minuisset* with its *u* absorbed by the neighbouring *n*. But because *minuisset* is in N Baehrens prefers to write *renuisset*.

II xxii 6   seu uarios *incinit* ore modos.

incinit N, *incūt* F, *inicit* DV. O clearly had *incīit* = *incinit*.

II xxii 22   *haut* umquam est culta labore Venus.

haut N, *hoc* F, *haud* DV. The *c* of F appears to indicate a *t*, not a *d*, in O.

II xxx 16   hic locus est in quo, tibia docta, *sones*.

sones Nf, *senes* F, *sonet* DV.

III v 6   nec miser aera paro *clade*, Corinthe, tua.

clade Nf, *pace* F, *classe* DV. Both *pace* and *classe* would arise more easily from an original *clade* than either of the two would arise from the other.

III x 15–16   *dein, qua* primum oculos cepisti ueste Properti,
                    indue.

dein qua N, *denique* F, *de qua* D, *te qua* V.

III xvi 17   saeua canum rabies morsus *auertit* hiantis.

auertit N, *aduertit* F, *auertat* DV.

III xxi 5–6   omnia sunt temptata mihi, quacumque fugari
                    possit; *at* ex omni me premit ille deus.

at Nf, *ad* F, *et* DV. ‖

IV v 35–6   ingerat Apriles Iole *tibi, tundat* Omichle
                    natalem Mais idibus esse tuum.

tibi tundat N, *circumdat* F, *tibi tondat* DV. It seems clear from the divergence of F and DV that O had what N has, and it further seems clear that this rare and idiomatic *tundat* is right: Passeratius quotes Donatus on Ter. hec. 123 'tundere est saepius idem repetere.' Baehrens adopts *contendat*, one of Heinsius' many conjectures on this passage; but there is no call for the handmaid to *maintain* this fact or fiction, as if any one were disputing it: she has only to din it into the lover's ears, lest it be forgotten.

The following example differs from those above in that the reading which N has and O had is not the correct reading but an early form of the corruption.

IV x 40–1 (Leo p. 445)

> Belgica cui uasti parma relata ducis
> *Virdomari.*

Virtomane N, *Dutomani* F, *Vncomani* DV. O had *Virtomani*: FDV have all corrupted the *ir*; F has corrupted the *V* and preserved the *t*; DV have corrupted the *t* and preserved the *V*.

What is the source from which N derived these readings? Several answers are possible and therefore none is certain.

With two exceptions, these readings may have been derived, as Baehrens would contend, from conjecture based on a comparison of MSS belonging to the two families AF and DV. The two exceptions are the *haut* of II xxii 22, a form which no scribe of the early 15th century would dream of introducing, and the *Virtomani* of IV x 41, which cannot be a conjecture as it means nothing.

Or the readings may have been derived from O, not through either of the families AF and DV, but by some such channel as the stemmata of Messrs Solbisky, Plessis and Weber display. I ‖ have shewn however that those stemmata are on other grounds incredible.

Or, as I think likely, the readings may have been derived from that source whose existence I have been demonstrating, Z as I call it, a brother-codex of O, here preserving lections which were also preserved in O but corrupted in O's descendants AFDV.

But there is yet another possibility. With two exceptions again, N may have derived these readings, as it certainly derived much else, from a MS of the family AF. It will be observed that in our examples, excepting the two which head the list, that family is represented by F alone because A is three parts lost. Now F was written by a most ignorant man who added many mistakes of his own to those he found in his exemplar, so that when A is absent we cannot be sure whether the errors F presents are peculiar to itself or belong to its family. It is conceivable that if A contained the 2nd 3rd and 4th books we should find it giving, in the eleven last examples, the same reading as N.[1] But in the two first examples, I iv 22 and x 25 where A is extant, the tradition of the family AF is ascertained, and we see that N has not derived its reading thence.

I incline therefore to suppose that N derived these thirteen readings from Z,

---

[1] There is room for hope that a collation of Mr Hosius' Neap. 268 may dispel this doubt.

but I have thought myself bound to point out that other opinions are tenable. And of course some of the thirteen may have come from one source and others from another.

§6. *N better than O: spelling*

I now come to deal with a matter in which Baehrens himself is constrained to admit the frequent superiority of N over AFDV, its spelling. This superiority he explains as follows, prolegg. p. IX:

> 'in sola re orthographica fieri potest ut libri N testimonia singularia fidem mereantur, cum in illa uel fidelissimi ‖ cetera librarii saepius suam secuti sint consuetudinem minimeque sibi constiterint. quare in his Neapolitani scribam haud indoctum certisque usum normis interdum meliora seruasse non inepte sumes.'

On this I remark in the first place that Baehrens' theory of the MSS requires not one such scribe as he here imagines but two at the least. For according to him N was not copied straight from O but from a descendant of O belonging to the family AF: therefore the writer of that MS too must have been 'haud indoctus' etc.

But the scribe imagined by Baehrens is such a scribe as never was on sea or land. There breathed no man in the 15th century, for that is the date to which Baehrens assigns him, who knew what he is supposed to have known. Facts about Latin orthography which have only been ascertained in our own century, facts which are yet unknown to half the scholars in Europe, facts which Baehrens himself never learnt to his dying day, were in the possession, it appears, of this copyist of the renascence. And the man who thus forstalled in the 15th century the discoveries of the 19th was a man who filled his pages with such barbarisms as *michi, sompnus, contempno, solatia, iocundus* and *humidus*!

I shall enumerate the principal instances in which N alone gives the true spelling, or gives the better of two spellings, or, where two spellings are equally good, gives that one which had fallen out of use in the middle ages and was unknown or disapproved at the renascence. I begin with a crucial example.

IV ix 36   et caua *succepto* flumine palma sat est.

succepto N, *suscepto* O. Caper orth. p. 98 Keil [*GLK* vol. vii] '*suscipimus* ad animum et mentem refertur, *succipimus* corpore', Velius Longus [*GLK* vol. vii] p. 34 'aliud est amicum *suscipere*, aliud aquam *succipere*.' The distinction laid down in these passages, which I borrow from Prof. Nettleship, Journal of Philology vol. XIII p. 80, is recognised by the MSS of Lucretius at IV 1250 and V 402 and of Virgil at Aen. I 175, IV 391, and VI 249, where the form *succipio* is employed in the physical sense. But at Aen. XI 806 ‖ even the capital MSS of

Virgil err; and that so late a MS as N should preserve the true spelling is a trait of singular excellence.

II iv 5 *nequiquam* N, *nequicquam* O; III xvii 23 *nequiquam* N, *nequisquam* F, *nequicquam* DV.

IV i 7 *Tarpetius* N, *Tarpeius* DV, *Tarpeus* F. The *Tarpetius* of N is a relic of the form *Tarpeiius*.[1]

I ii 3 *murra* N, *mirra* AF, *myrra* V; III x 22 *murreus* N, *mureus* O; IV v 26 *murrea* N, *mirrea* F, *murea* DV.

II v 23 *conexos* N, *connexos* O.

IV i 13 and iv 63 *bucina* N, *buccina* O.

III xxii 35 *pelice* N, *pellice* O.

IV viii 79 *querellae* N, *querelae* O.

II xxxiv 68 *harundinibus* N, *arundinibus* O; IV ii 33 *harundine* N, *arundine* O.

III iii 23 *harenas* N, *arenas* O.

II iii 18 *euhantes* Nv, *euantes* DV, *eufaues* F.

III xiii 24 *Euhadne* N, *Euadne* O.

IV viii 48 *ei* N, *hei* F, *heu* DV.

IV x 47 *umeris* N, *humeris* O.

III xxi 5 *temptata* N, *tentata* O.

II xxviii 56 *omnis* (acc. plur.) N, *ōms* F, *omnes* DV.

III v 13 and vii 35 *haut* N, *haud* O.

II xviii 21 *deminuo* N, *diminuo* O.

III i 22 *duplicei* N, *duplici* O.

III xiii 64 *equm* N, *equum* O; IV iii 36 *equs* N, *equus* O.

III xx 17 *pignera* Nf, *pignora* DV, *pignita* F.

IV v 52 *saluere* Nv, *saliere* O.

II xxxiii 1 and III x 31 *sollēpnia* N, *solemnia* O, telling instances against Baehrens because N while correctly preserving the *ll* has spelt the rest of the word barbarously.

§7. N and O equidistant from archetype

Here I approach the end of my enquiry into the independent strain of genuine tradition existing in N. The last ‖ proofs of its existence which I shall offer are not less cogent than any which have gone before but I have postponed them till now because they serve at once to conclude this part of the discussion and to introduce the next. Not only do they prove that N has a genuine element independent of O but they prove equally that O has a genuine element independent of N. They are passages where N and O have alike deserted the truth but have deserted it by divergent paths: where the reading of O is not a further corruption of N, nor the reading of N a further corruption of O, but both stand

---

[1] So I said in this Journal in 1888 [this edition p. 37]. Mr Hosius now finds *Tarpeiius* in Vrb. 641.

equidistant from their common archetype. Here then in closing my defence of N against Baehrens I begin my defence of O against Mr Leo.

II xxviii 35   deficiunt magico torti sub carmine *rhombi*.

bombi N, *rumbi* DV, *nimbi* F which is merely a further corruption of *rumbi*: *rumbi* was clearly the reading of O, as again at III vi 26:

staminea *rhombi* ducitur ille rota.

bombi N, *rumbi* O. Of the archetypal *rombi*, N has in both places changed the first letter but kept the second, O has changed the second but kept the first.

III vi 3   *num* me laetitia tumefactum fallis inani?

non N, *dum* O, each preserving a part of the truth.

III xii 14   *sic redeunt*, illis qui cecidere locis.

si credunt N, *si credent* O, each omitting one letter. It is difficult to say which of several reasons induces Baehrens to write *si redient*: whether that it recedes further from both MSS, or that *redient* is used by no Augustan writer, or that *sic redeunt* is supported by Ovid met. XI 727 sq. '*sic*, o carissime coniunx, | *sic* ad me, miserande, *redis*.'

III xiv 17   qualis et Eurotae Pollux et Castor *harenis*. ||

habenis Nfv, *athenis* O. Here N is a trifle nearer the truth than O, which has not only altered one letter but transposed another. It appears however that the reading in O is separately derived from the archetype and is not a corruption of the reading in N, since *t* arises much more easily from *r* than from *b*.

IV viii 21   *spectaclum* ipsa sedens primo temone pependit.

ibid. 56   *spectaclum* capta nec minus urbe fuit.

spectaculum N, *spectandum* O, in both places. Each scribe had *spectaclum* before him: the one recognised what was meant and substituted the common form to the ruin of the metre; the other mistook *cl* for *d* and substituted the nearest Latin word with like disaster to the sense.

IV viii 39   Nile, tuus tibicen erat, *crotalistria* Phyllis.

eboralistria N, *coralistria* O (F has *colistria* which comes from this by the omission of the compendium for *ra*). O omits one letter and transposes another: N neither omits nor transposes but corrupts three letters, writing *e* for *c*, *b* for *r*, *r* for *t*.

To these certain examples I add others which in my opinion display the same relationship of the MSS.

II xviii 5–6

> quid *mea si* canis aetas *canesceret* annis
> et faceret scissas languida ruga genas?

mea si...canesceret N, *si iam...mea caneret* O. The reading of N is usually accepted with Heinsius' change of *canesceret* to *candesceret*. But scientific criticism can hardly come to any other conclusion than that *canesceret* is an attempt to emend the unmetrical *caneret*; and Bentley did better to accept the reading of O with the change of *caneret* to *curreret*. I think however that I can recover the true text from Ovid. This distich is followed by the words 'at non Tithoni spernens Aurora senectam' and eleven more lines which treat of that legend: comparing Ovid's address to Aurora, am. I 13 41 'cur ego plectar ‖ amans, si uir tibi *marcet ab annis*', and also Lucr. III 946 'si tibi non *annis* corpus iam *marcet*' and Sil. XV 743 'senex *marcentibus annis*', I propose the following[1] as best explaining what we find in our MSS:

> quid mea si canis aetas *marceret ab* annis?

mea caneret comes from *marcaberet*, i.e. *marceret ab* with the *ab* transposed: it was absorbed in the following *an-* and afterwards inserted above the line. Now we have to choose between *si iam* and *mea si*, and must prefer the latter, since *mea* is needed to save the sense from ambiguity. The Propertian archetype therefore should seem to have given the verse thus:

> quid *mea si* canis aetas *mea caneret* annis?

O avoids the repetition of *mea* by writing *si iam*: N more cleverly emends the false quantity at the same time by substituting *canesceret* for *mea caneret*.

III ix 9   gloria Lysippo est animosa *effingere* signa.

effingere N, *fingere* O. This is a divergency often found in MSS, and readily to be explained. It means that Propertius wrote *ecfingere*. In N this has been recognised for what it was and has been translated to the commoner form *effingere*. In the other stock *ec* was corrupted as usual into *et*, and then this importunate conjunction was omitted. Compare Hor. epist. I 10 9 *fertis* most MSS, *effertis* Bland. uet., *ecfertis* Pauly; Ovid met. I 71 *feruescere* some MSS, *efferuescere* others, write *ecferuescere*; Sen. Thy. 988 *fluit* E, *effluit* cett., write *ecfluit*.

III xiv 19–20

> inter quos Helene nudis *capere arma papillis*
> fertur nec fratres erubuisse deos.

capere arma papillis N, *armata capillis* O (F inserts *est* before *armata*). The *papillis* of N is of course right: see IV iii 43 'felix Hippolyte, nuda tulit arma

---

[1] Mr Palmer has conjectured *marceret et*, Heinsius *marcesceret*.

papilla'. But if *capere arma* was the original there is nothing to account for the *armata* ‖ of O, whereas *armata* will excellently account for *capere arma*: *ta* was lost in the following *pa* or *ca*, and *capere* was inserted to prop the metre. Read then, partly from N and partly from O, 'nudis *armata papillis* | fertur, nec fratres erubuisse deos'. This idiomatic coordination of participle with infinitive, 'fertur armata (esse) nec erubuisse', is not uncommon: compare Ovid fast. II 551 sq. 'bustis *exisse* feruntur | *et* tacitae *questi* tempore noctis aui', Prop. I x 5 sq. 'cum te complexa *morientem*, Galle, puella | uidimus *et* longa *ducere* uerba mora'. I must add that O's good faith is here more certain than N's, for the emendation *papillis* would not be hard to find if the scribe had *capillis* before him.

IV iii 11–12

> haecne marita fides, *hae sunt pactae mihi* noctes,
> cum rudis urgenti bracchia uicta dedi?

hae sunt pactae mihi DV, *et pacate mihi* F, *et parce auia* N. In the reading above and in most of the conjectures proposed, such as Haupt's 'et pactae in sauia noctes', it is not so much their grossness which I blame, gross though they are, as their entire incongruity with the pentameter. As if the bride who according to her own account 'dedit bracchia uicta urgenti' can represent herself as there and then bargaining for 'noctes'! There remains Mr Lucian Mueller's '*pactae et* mihi *gaudia noctis* | cum' cet.: he explains 'pactae noctis' to mean 'noctis nuptialis'; but the interrogation 'haecne sunt gaudia noctis nuptialis?' addressed by Arethusa in Italy to Lycotas in Parthia seems little better than nonsense, and the variations of the MSS are not accounted for. Let us try first to find the reading of O: when DV have *hae sunt pactae mihi* and F *et pacatae mihi*, this may mean either that O had *hae (et) sunt pacatae mihi* and that its two apographs tried different ways of compression, or that it had *hae (et) pactae mihi* and that its two apographs tried different ways of expansion. To decide between these alternatives let us turn to the *et parce auia* of N: the reading most like this is *et pactae mihi*, which therefore I suspect to have been the reading of O. Now for the reading of the common archetype of O and N: I suggest that *et prae mia* ‖ stands half way between them, and that Propertius wrote 'haecne marita fides *et ⟨primae⟩ praemia* noctis | cum' cet., *primae* falling out before *praemi*: 'is your desertion the reward I merit for my surrender to your embraces?'

IV iv 9–10

> quid tum Roma fuit, tubicen uicina Curitis
> cum quateret lento murmure *saxa* Iouis?

saxa Nfv, *facta* O. Here N preserves the right word but O indicates that Propertius spelt it *facxa*. So at Ovid met. II 326 we find the variants *saxum* and *factum*, at XIII 567 *saxum* and *iactum*, and the explanation I believe to be the same.

§8. *O better than N*

Evidence is now to be adduced which will prove that O in its turn is often a more faithful witness than N. Here I shall be controverting the assertion of Mr Leo that 'AFDV [= O] omnino nihil ualent', and I shall have on my side Baehrens and, for the most part though not in all details, Mr Solbisky and Mr Weber. I shall begin with cases where the reading of N is inferior to the reading which, from the consent of the two families AF and DV, we know to have been the reading of O. The enumeration of these cases will not exhaust the merits of O, for there are many places where only AF or only DV present the true reading; and in those places we must of course conclude that this true reading was found in O, and must add those instances to the proofs of O's superiority over N. But such cases will be more conveniently dealt with when I come to appraise the relative value of the families AF and DV as witnesses to the tradition of O. Let it be borne in mind therefore that O is superior to N not only in the passages which I now bring forward but in others to which I shall duly call attention at a later stage of the enquiry.

At the head of these passages I set three which have peculiar significance. They are passages where the reading of O is corrupt and N has corrupted that reading further: they therefore prove the superior integrity of O with the same || invincible cogency as was possessed by the evidence with which I began the defence of N.

III ii 3–4   Orphea *detinuisse* feras et concita dicunt
                    flumina Threicia sustinuisse lyra.

detinuisse Nv; but clearly neither this nor any compound of 'teneo' is tolerable with 'sustinuisse' in the next line. D is also corrupt and gives *te tenuisse*; but the consent of F and V, witnesses from each family, tells us that O had *detenuisse*, from which we easily elicit the generally received correction *delenisse*. Here then N has made a bad attempt at amending the slight and honest error of O.

III vi 9   *sicin eam* incomptis uidisti flere capillis?

sicut eam O, *si causa* N. The scribe of N had before him the *sic̄ eā* (= *sicut eam*) of O: he mistook it for *si cā* (= *si causa*).

III xviii 24 (Solbisky p. 176)

              scandenda est *torui* publica cumba senis.

torti O (DF: V is erased), *troci* N. All editors now read *torui* which is doubtless right; O then errs in one letter only; N has corrupted the corruption by changing *t* to *c* and transposing *r*. Mr Leo's 'scandenda *atrocis*' is further even from N than *torui* is. I would not conjecture *taetri*, though Juvenal III 265 writes '*tae-trum*que nouicius horret | porthmea'.

II iii 27　　　　　non non humani *sunt partus* talia dona.

sunt partus O, *partus sunt* Nf.

II xxxiv 23　　　sed numquam uitae *me fallet* ruga seuerae.

me fallet O, *fallet me* N.

These two passages bear striking witness to the sincerity of O. Lucretius and Catullus with their contemporaries were much enamoured of the heavy and stately rhythm imparted ‖ to an hexameter whose fourth foot is a spondee by making that spondee consist of a single word: 'quae mare nauigerum, quae *terras* frugiferentis', 'surgere iam tempus, iam *pinguis* linquere mensas.' In the Augustan age fashion changed and this rhythm was oftenest avoided: 'arma uirumque cano, Troi*ae qui* primus ab oris', 'hanc tua Penelope len*to tibi* mittit, Vlixe', not 'qui *Troiae*' or 'tibi *lento*'. Throughout the later literature the Augustan cadence kept its vogue, and it was thus more familiar and acceptable to the ears of medieval copyists. But the Augustan poets understood well enough the value of variety, and they accordingly diversify their numbers by recurring now and then to the antiquated rhythm. Propertius, to believe the consenting testimony of our MSS, employs it in fourteen instances where he might without detriment to sense or rhetoric – I omit cases where either of these would suffer – so have transposed his words as to give his usual cadence: II ii 13 'quas *pastor* uiderat', iii 5 'si *posset* piscis', 19 'cum *temptat* carmina', 33 'si *flagret* nostra', v 1 'te *ferri* Cynthia', xxiii 7 'quos *dicit* fama', xxiv 1 'iam *noto* fabula', xxix 1 'cum *potus* nocte', 19 'iam *certos* spondet', xxxiv 29 'tibi *prosunt* carmina', III xi 1 'si *uersat* femina', xviii 1 'qua *ludit* pontus', xx 7 'sunt *castae* Palladis', IV vii 89 'nox *clausas* liberat'. But the scribes preferred the customary rhythm and sometimes took upon themselves to restore it; so we find two passages, noted by Baehrens prolegg. p. xiv, where the MSS differ: I ix 31 'illis et silices et *possunt* cedere quercus' and III i 19 'mollia, Pegasides, date *uestro* serta poetae': in these two cases both O and N agree in ordering the words as above, while inferior MSS give 'possunt et' and 'uestro date'. Now just as N and O in these two cases shew themselves superior to other MSS, so does O in the two verses from which I started shew itself superior to N.

II xxx 21　　　*spargereque* alterna communes caede penates.

spargereque O, *spargere et* N. Here is a like instance. The attachment of *que* to a short *e* is eschewed by Virgil and Ovid who set the fashion to posterity and accordingly is discountenanced ‖ by the scribes. But it is Propertian: at III xxi 13 both O and N agree in the exact parallel 'iungiteque extremo'; and Tib. 1 3 34 quoted by Burmann has 'reddereque antiquo'. O then has here preserved a characteristic reading in the face of a strong temptation to which N has succumbed.

II xxxii 33–6

> ipsa Venus, *quamuis* corrupta libidine Martis,
>   nec minus in caelo semper honesta fuit,
> quamuis Ida [Parim] pastorem dicat amasse
>   atque inter pecudes accubuisse deam.

'Parim' is of course corrupt; but we are now concerned with v. 33 where O has *quamuis*, N *fertur*. There is no more open interpolation than *fertur* in any MS of any author. O gives a recondite yet perfectly correct construction of the sort which grammarians call hyperbaton or ἀπὸ κοινοῦ: in its most natural form the sentence would be 'Venus non minus honesta fuit quamuis corrupta libidine Martis et quamuis Ida pastorem dicat amasse deam', but since the apodosis appertains equally to either protasis it may no less legitimately be placed in juxtaposition with the second, in the order 'Venus, quamuis corrupta libidine Martis, et non minus honesta fuit quamuis Ida dicat' etc., an arrangement especially dear to Horace but frequent also throughout Latin poetry: then the words 'et non' are replaced by their equivalent 'nec'.[1] But this was too subtle for the scribe of N, and he thought to simplify matters by substituting *fertur*, which is indignantly ejected by all modern editors but Mr Palmer who says 'cur ab optimo libro subito desciscam non uideo': the answer is 'quia subito fit pessimus'. Here is the case in a nutshell: will *quamuis* account for *fertur*? Yes. Will *fertur* account for *quamuis*? No.

II i 2   unde meus ueniat mollis in *ora* liber. ‖

ora O, *ore* N. The latter though retained by Hertzberg and Palmer is incorrect: the Romans, as Burmann observes, said 'esse in ore' (Ovid fast. VI 528, her. XVI [[XVII]] 34) but 'uenire in ora' (Prop. III i 24, ix 32, Catull. 40 5, Hor. epist. I 3 9).

II xx 7–8   nec tantum Niobe bis sex ad busta superbe
                 sollicito *lacrimans* defluit a Sipylo.

lacrimans O, *lacrimas* N. Mr Lucian Mueller seems to have reason in saying that 'tam uetusto tamque bono scriptori non conuenit uerbum defluendi cum accusatiuo iunctum.' It was not until the Augustan age that even 'mano' began to be thus used: to find a similar employment of 'fluo' and its compounds Lachmann has to descend to Claudian. *lacrimans* therefore is preferable to *lacrimas*. The distich however needs emendation, and the usual change of *superbe* to *superba*

---

[1] It may be that 'nec minus' = 'et', as at I iii 5, xv 7, II xxxii 59, in which case the form of the hyperbaton will be simpler.

does not emend it. It is correct to say of a liquid that it 'defluit a monte', and so it would be correct to say here, as Heinsius proposed, 'nec tantum Niobae (dat.) ...lacrimae (gen.) defluit a Sipylo'; but a solid body which streams or drips with a liquid does not 'defluere *a* monte' but '*in* monte' (Sen. Herc. fur. 390 sq. 'riget superba Tantalis luctu parens | maestusque Phrygio *manat in Sipylo* lapis'), and 'Niobe defluit a Sipylo' cannot be defended. Now *Niobe...superbe* would in our archetype be the same thing as *Niobae...superbae*, which indeed some of the later MSS restore: I would confine alteration therefore to the inappropriate *a* and write 'nec tantum Niobae bis sex ad busta superbae | sollicito lacrimans defluit *os* Sipylo.'

II xxv 41–4

uidistis pleno teneram candore puellam,
uidistis fusco: ducit uterque color.
uidistis quandam Argiua *prodire* figura,
uidistis nostras: utraque forma rapit.

prodire Nfv, *prodente* O. The former can be construed and the latter can not; but this very fact will seem to favour *prodente* and stamp *prodire* as a conjecture when one considers how unsatisfactory the construable reading is: how inappropriate || is *quandam* and how ill the singular is opposed to the plural *nostras*. In moret. 32 I find the following words which at once confirm *prodente* and shew us how to emend the context: 'Afra genus, tota patriam *testante figura*'. Write accordingly 'uidistis *patriam* Argiua*s prodente* figura, | uidistis nostras'. *patriam* is no violent alteration, for *p* is much confused with *qu*, as also is *tr* with *cl* (in *trudo* and *cludo* perpetually) and *cl* with *d*.

II xxx 19 (Solbisky pp. 173–5)

num tu, dura, paras Phrygias nunc ire per undas?

nunc tu dura paras DV and so doubtless O: F omits *tu*. Scaliger restored *num* for *nunc*, and it is probable that *dura* should be altered to *dure*. But N has the extraordinary and meaningless reading *non tamen inmerito*. These words occur, as Mr L. Mueller praef. p. VII has pointed out, in III xix 27 '*non tamen inmerito* Minos sedet arbiter Orci': the scribe saw before him n̄c̄ tu (= *nunc tu*) which he mistook for nō tn̄ (= *non tamen*); the other verse came into his head and he carelessly added *inmerito* instead of *dura paras*. I could quote many similar errors, but let one from the immediate context suffice: at 36 D gives 'Bistoniis olim rupibus *ingemuit*' for '*accubuit*' because I i 14 'saucius Arcadiis *rupibus ingemuit*' was running in the copyist's mind. See then the foundation of sand on which Mr Leo constructs his conjecture '*num tamen ingredior*'! But although O is clearly faithful and N corrupt, nevertheless to call the latter 'interpolated' here with Baehrens is to use language at random: its blunder is stupid, but transparently honest.

II xxxiv 29–30   aut quid *Crethei* tibi prosunt carmina lecta?
nil iuuat in magno uester amore senex.

Crethei O, *Erechti* N, whence v invents *Erechthei*, and this absurd conjecture
has become the common reading. Absurd I call it, because 'the old Athenian
poet' designates no one in the world. No city was ever so rich in poets as
Athens, and all her greatest poets lived to old age. Now *Erechti*, which has ||
prompted this foolish guess, is simply a disarrangement of the seven letters
which form *Crethei* and which O has kept in their proper order. And *Crethei* is
the medieval way of spelling *Cretaei*: the person designated is the philosopher
Epimenides, just the poet whom the philosopher Lynceus would study, and
certainly one who 'nil iuuat in amore'. But there is one word more to say:
whether we write *Cretaei* or *Erechthei*, Propertius could use neither of these
words as a substantive, and the substantive must be sought in *lecta*. I believe
that Mr Palmer has discovered it: *plectri*: compare Sil. VIII 594 'Smyrnaeis
aemula plectris' = rivalling Homer.

II xxxiv 31–2   tu satius *musis memorem* imitere Philetam
et non inflati somnia Callimachi.

musis memorem O, *memorem musis* N. Both readings are meaningless but O's is
unmetrical into the bargain: probably therefore it is the more genuine of the
two and N gives an attempt at correction. The simplest emendation no doubt is
the *Musis meliorem* (= meliorem Musarum iudicio) found in some interpolated
MSS; but *meliorem* is tautological after *satius*, and we seem rather to require an
epithet balancing the 'non inflati' of the pentameter, which shall indicate some
characteristic of these erotic poets distinguishing them from the philosophical or
epic or tragic writers whom Lynceus has studied hitherto: this is one reason for
rejecting Jacob's ingenious *Meropem musis* based on N. A very slight change
then will be Santen's *leuiorem*: 'leuis' is almost a technical description of amatory verse: II xii 22 'haec mea Musa leuis': *musis* then means 'carminibus' as in
Verg. buc. I 2 and often elsewhere. No wider alteration is needed, for the construction 'satius imitere' for 'satius est ut imitere' is well defended with examples
by Mr L. Mueller.

III i 23   *omnia* post obitum fingit maiora *uetustas*.

omnia . . . uetustas O, *fame . . . uetustae* N, which seems to be a mere blunder: the
reading of O is irreproachable, and no || editor has accepted or is likely to accept
Mr Heimreich's conjecture 'fama post obitum fiunt maiora uetusta'. Perhaps too
the following fact speaks for O: Friedlaender, Martial p. 81, tells us that
Martial's MS Q (Arondellianus Gronouii) at v 10 gives in the margin a distich
whose origin he does not appear to recognise: 'omnia post fatum fingit maiora

uetustas: | maius ab exsequiis nomen in ora uenit.' That MS belongs to the 15th century, so that the quotation may have been made from memory by a scribe who had read Propertius in one of the codices descended from O; but on the other hand the variant *fatum* for *obitum* may indicate some source independent of O and N alike.

III vii 43–6

> quod si contentus patrios boue uorteret agros
> uerbaque duxisset pondus habere mea,
> uiueret ante suos dulcis conuiua penates,
> pauper, at in terra nil *ubi* flere potest?

So N. This reading can only be punctuated as above and explained with Mr Palmer 'poor I grant, but where in the world is it possible to have no cause of sorrow?' In another poem the words might have that sense; but this elegy is devoted to contrasting the security of the land with the risks of the sea, and 'terra' must here perforce mean 'dry land' and nothing else: it is impossible without ruinous ambiguity to use 'ubi in terra' or even 'in terris' for 'ubi gentium'. Other critics, that 'terra' may have its due meaning, write 'pauper, at in terra, nil ubi *flare* potest', 'where blowing is powerless', others again 'nil ubi, *Caure, potes*'; from all which one turns with some impatience to the reading of O. This is *nisi* instead of *ubi*; and Baehrens has founded on it one of the finest corrections ever made in this poet's text: 'pauper, at in terra nil *nisi fleret opes*', 'poor I grant, but on dry land his poverty would have been his only grief'. 'opes' is one of those words which the grammarians call μέσα: it takes its colour from the context and means 'riches' or 'poverty' as that requires: for the latter sense, overlooked by lexicographers, see Ovid fast. III 56 'nec taceam uestras, Faustule *pauper, opes*', II 302, Ibis 420. || The error in all our MSS arose from the transposition 'flere*potes*': *nisi* and *ubi* are confused at Cic. de fin. II 14 44 and Luc. IX 578.

III xi 25   duxit et Euphraten medium *quam* condidit arces.

Semiramis building Babylon is the theme. O has *quam* without sense: N gives *qua* which is generally read. But 'duxit medium qua condidit' is a vague and clumsy expression, and far inferior to what Baehrens following Heinsius has restored from the reading of O: 'medium, *quam* condidit, *arcis*', 'through the midst of the stronghold she built': the arrangement of the words, for which compare Ovid met. XIII 916 'innitens, quae stabat proxima, moli', laid a trap for the copyists.

III xiii 55–6

> te scelus accepto Thracis Polymestoris auro
> nutrit in hospitio non, Polydore, *tuo*.

tuo O, *pio* N. Baehrens rightly accepts *tuo*, the idiomatic use of the possessive pronoun in the sense of 'fausto'. Of two readings which are equally good we prefer the less obvious.

III xiv 27–8

> non Tyriae uestes errantia lumina fallunt
> est neque *odoratae* cura molesta domi.

odoratae O, *adoratae* N. The reading of N was retained only by Hertzberg, who himself believed in it so little that he offered in its stead two or three conjectures too absurd for mention. Canter's correction '*odoratae* c. m. *comae*' is now generally accepted, and the following facts seem to render it certain: Ovid, who in fast. II 357 has imitated the hexameter with 'fallentes lumina uestes' and employs 'odoratae...comae' at ars II 734, evidently imitates the whole couplet when in med. form. 18 sq. he writes 'uultis inaurata corpora *ueste tegi*, | uultis *odoratos* positu uariare *capillos*'. ||

III xxii 11–14

> tuque tuo Colchum propellas remige Phasim
> Peliacaeque trabis totum iter ipse legas,
> qua rudis *Argoa* natat inter saxa columba
> in faciem prorae pinus adacta nouae.

Argoa N, with which the editors have found no fault; nor is it indefensible, though the 'Peliaca trabs' and the 'pinus' are none other than Argo, so that the sentence virtually amounts to 'natat Argo, Argoa columba duce'. But we look rather for some such epithet as 'Iasonia'; and we find it in the *Argea* of O. *Argeus* is Ἀργεῖος the adjective of Ἄργος, that is, not of τὸ Ἄργος *Argos* the city but of ὁ Ἄργος *Argus* the builder of Argo. And here is strong confirmation: Propertius at II xxvi 39 sq. has these words, 'uenti...qui mouistis montis duo, cum ratis *Argo* | dux erat ignoto missa *columba* mari'. The editors could not construe this, and altered *Argo* to the genitive *Argus*; but Mr Ellis (Univ. Coll. prof. dissert. 1872–3) has pointed out that *Argo* is Ἄργῳ, the dative of Argus, who not only built the vessel but had it under his care throughout the voyage: Val. Fl. I 477 'Arge, tuae tibi cura ratis'. When these two passages, with the 'columba' in each of them, are set side by side, it seems to be placed beyond possibility of doubt that *Argea* is the truth.

III xxiii 11–15

> forsitan haec illis *fuerint* mandata tabellis:
> 'irascor, quoniam es, lente, moratus heri.
> an tibi nescio quae uisa est formosior? an tu
> non bona de nobis carmina ficta iacis?'
> aut dixit 'uenies hodie, cessabimus una.'

fuerint N and editors, even Baehrens; *fuerant* O. Now Propertius twice (II ix 22, xv 54) has 'forsitan' with the indicative; in a third place (III xx 6) the MSS are divided between indicative and subjunctive; here they are divided again. It seems then that in both these last places we ought to follow those MSS which give the indicative. But in this passage there is more to be said; for observe that in v. 15 he ‖ goes on 'aut *dixit*': that surely settles the question. It is of course possible that Propertius wrote *fuerunt*.

III xxiii 19–20

>   me miserum, his aliquis rationem scribit auarus,
>   et ponit *duras* inter ephemeridas.

duras O, *diras* N with ludicrous over-emphasis.

IV v 57–8

>   qui uersus, Coae dederit nec munera uestis,
>   istius tibi sit surda sine *arte* lyra.

arte O, *aere* N. 'surda sine *arte*', says Lachmann, 'nihil significat.' It signifies 'unmusicianly and so tuneless': compare Lucr. v 841 'muta sine ore etiam, sine uoltu caeca', 'mouthless and so dumb', 'eyeless and so blind'. *aere* looks very pretty as long as one does not attend to the context, and is adopted by most editors since Lachmann. See the result: 'if a lover brings you verses only and no Coan robe, deem his lyre tuneless – *unless he brings you money*'! To have said 'qui *munera* non dederit, istius surda sit lyra sine *muneribus*' would have been clumsy iteration but nothing worse: in 'qui *uestem* non dederit, istius surda sit lyra sine *aere*' absurdity is superadded.

IV x 45   *haec* spolia in templo tria condita.

haec O (DF: V is erased), *nunc* N. He has related the stories of 'arma de ducibus trina recepta tribus', and *haec* is very appropriate in summing up at the end: *nunc* is at best superfluous.

Five passages follow in which words or verses omitted by N are preserved by O.

II xxxiv 81–4

>   non tamen haec ulli uenient ingrata legenti,
>   siue in amore rudis siue peritus erit,
>   nec minor his animis aut sim *minor ore canorus*
>   anseris indocto carmine cessit olor. ‖

N omits *minor ore canorus*. The explanation doubtless is that the scribe saw that the line was nonsense and desisted from finishing it. That the words are substantially genuine is not doubted by the editors: an interpolator would have given us something easier. Let us try to emend the verse: the poet has been praising the bucolics and georgics of Virgil: he now proceeds 'but yet light poems such as I write will please all readers, lovers or no; nor –' then comes the corruption. The sense, it is generally recognised, must be 'nor is Virgil less inspired (minor animis) in poems of this kind than in his more important works': the simplest restoration seems to be the following, 'nec minor *hic* (= in his scriptis: cf. *haec* in v. 81) animis, *ut sit* minor ore, canorus | anseris indocto carmine cessit olor', 'and the melodious swan, displaying equal genius though less stately diction in these light verses, has not retired with the tuneless strain of a goose'. *hic* is printed by accident in Lachmann's second edition.

III ix 35   non ego uelifera tumidum mare findo carina.

This verse is omitted by N, but the editors rightly retain it. The only handle it gives to objectors is *findŏ*, the earliest example in Latin poetry of a spondee transformed into a trochee by the shortening of a final *o*. But every change must have a beginning; and it is in Propertius that we might expect to find the fashion started which becomes common in Ovid: thus his elder contemporaries Horace and Tibullus with their *Poliŏ* and *desinŏ* are the first who by a similar shortening transform cretics into dactyls. I may further point out that Ovid seems to imitate this verse in met. xv 719 'huc ubi *ueliferam* nautae aduertere *carinam*' and ex Pont. III 2 67 'cum duo *uelifera* iuuenes uenere *carina*', and pseudo-Ovid in her. xv [xvi] 31 sq. 'nec me crede *fretum* merces portante *carina* | *findere*'.

28

THE MANUSCRIPTS OF PROPERTIUS [II]*

III X 15–18

dein, qua primum oculos cepisti ueste Properti,
indue, nec uacuum flore relinque caput.
et pete, qua polles, ut sit tibi forma perennis,
inque meum semper stent tua regna caput.

N omits the second distich for a plain reason: the two pentameters end with the same word and begin with two words almost the same, and the scribe's eye glanced from the one to the other. No doubt is cast on the lines by the recurrence of *caput*, a negligence very common in Roman elegy: see p. 187 [this edition p. 296].

III xi 57–8

septem urbs alta iugis toti quae praesidet orbi
femineas timuit territa Marte minas?

N omits the pentameter.

IV iii 7   te modo uiderunt iteratos *Bactra per ortus.*

So O: N omits the three last words. It is admitted I think by all critics but N's most fanatical devotee Mr Heimreich that this can be no interpolation: Mr Solbisky p. 181 well asks 'quomodo librarius, si in exemplari suo nihil nisi *te modo uiderunt iteratos* inuenisset, in uoces illas satis quidem quaesitas incidere potuit?' O then is better than N; but the line can hardly be right as it stands. For an explanation of 'iteratos per ortus' some refer us with extreme irrelevance to Ovid fast. VI 199 'mane ubi bis fuerit Phoebusque *iterauerit ortus*': Propertius then makes a wife in Rome write to her husband in Parthia and tell him that he has recently been at Bactra for ‖ two days! Others take 'ortus' for the East and 'iteratos' for 'iterum peragratos' comparing Hor. carm. I 7 32 'cras ingens iterabimus aequor'; but the one phrase is no warrant for the other, and the meaning, even if possible, is most obscure: Mr L. Mueller has reason for saying of this passage 'nec uero quisquam satis expediuit'. The true reading I suspect to be 'te modo *Ituraeos uiderunt* Bactra per *arcus*': compare Verg. georg. II 448 '*Ituraeos* taxi torquentur in *arcus*', Luc. VII 230 '*Ituraeis* cursus fuit inde *sagittis*', 514 sq. 'tunc et *Ituraei* Medique Arabesque, soluto | *arcu* turba minax, nusquam rexere *sagittas*', bell. Afr. 20 '*sagittariis*...*Ituraeis*'.

* [*JPh* 21 (1893), 161–97]

I conclude with a selection of examples in which the error of N is obvious and undefended. They are of no great significance, but deserve mention among the other instances of O's frequent superiority.

II xxxii 8 tibi me credere turba *uetat*: *uetat* O, *uocat* N: none will propose *uotat*. II xxxiii 9 cum te iussit habere puellam cornua *Iuno*: *Iuno* O, *humo* N. III i 36 illum post cineres auguror ipse *diem*: *diem* O, *deae* N. III v 7 o prima infelix *fingenti* terra Prometheo: *fingenti* O, *frangenti* N. III ix 37 non *flebo* in cineres arcem sedisse: *flebo* O, *phebo* N. III xiii 33–4 his tum blanditiis furtiua per *antra* puellae | oscula siluicolis empta dedere uiris: *antra* O, *rara* N. III xvi 9 peccaram semel, et totum sum *pulsus* in annum: *pulsus* O, *portus* N. IV ix 38 Alciden terra *recepta* uocat: *recepta* O, *suscepta* N.

§9. *O better than N: spelling*

I give separately the cases where O shews itself N's superior in matters orthographical.

II xv 20, xxii 6, III xiv 5, IV iv 28, vii 66 and viii 67 *bracchia* O, *brachia* N.

II xxviii 23 *Calisto* O, *Callisto* N: see Baehrens in Fleckeisen's annual for 1883, p. 787.

II xiv 2 *Laumedontis* O, *Laomedontis* N.

IV i 108 *petunda* O, *petenda* N.

III xviii 5 *mortalis* (acc. plur.) O, *mortales* N. ||

§10. *Doubt between N and O*

Further evidence redounding to the credit of O and the discredit of N will be forthcoming, as I said above, when we treat of the two families AF and DV. But we are already in a position to weigh with perfect impartiality the testimony of N and O where they conflict; and I will here examine certain passages in which it is hard to decide between them.

I viii 43–6

> nunc mihi summa licet contingere sidera palmis:
> siue dies seu nox uenerit, illa mea est;
> nec mihi riualis *certos* subducit amores:
> ista meam norit gloria canitiem.

certos Nf and V, with which no fault can be found. But the reading of O was something quite different, for AF have *summos* and D *somnus*: V, which as I shall shew in an appendix has been much tampered with, is not a witness to be believed against these three MSS when we are enquiring what stood in O. Now it is possible that *certos* may be right and that the *summa* of v. 43 may have caused an error *summos* in v. 45. But it is equally possible that *summos* is the corruption and *certos* the gloss of *firmos*, which Mr Rossberg proposes to restore: see

Ovid ars II 385 'hoc *firmos* soluit *amores*'. *firmos* is virtually the same thing as *fūmos* from which *somnus* arises by the transposition of the vowels: it is identical in meaning with *certos* but much less frequent in elegiac poetry, and the more familiar word may have been written above as an explanation; or *certos* may be a mere conjecture in lieu of *summos*, suggested by II xxix 19 'iam *certos* spondet *amores*'.

II viii 13–15

> ergo tam multos nimium temerarius annos,
> 　improba, *qui* tulerim teque tuamque domum,
> ecquandone tibi liber sum uisus?

qui O, perhaps rightly: *quin* N, from which Mr Lucian Mueller, perhaps rightly, elicits *qum*. ‖

II xiii 58　　　nam mea *quid* poterunt ossa minuta loqui?

quid O, *qui* N, between which there is nothing to choose; but Mr Mueller points out that at IV i 86 N gives *qui* where *quid* is necessary: a fact which shakes its witness here.

II xviii 21–2

> quin ego deminuo curam, quod saepe Cupido
> 　*nunc* malus esse solet, cui bonus ante fuit.

nunc O, *huic* Nfv: I prefer the latter, but either is defensible.

II xxviii 21　　Andromede monstris fuerat *monstrata* marinis.

monstrata O, an obvious corruption caused by *monstris*. *deuota* Nfv, which we may hope to be the genuine reading, like the *includere* which in similar circumstances Nv preserve at II xxxiv 43 against the *componere* of O. But here we have no such confirmation as is there supplied by the words I quoted from Gellius, and our hope is no more than a hope: we have learnt that N is not free from interpolation.

II xxxiv 1–2

> cur quisquam faciem dominae *non credit* amori?
> sic erepta mihi paene puella mea est.

non credit O, *iam credat* Nfv. Propertius reproaches his friend Lynceus for making love to Cynthia. Clearly then the reading of O is nonsense; and N's is no better till *amori* has been changed with the Italians into *amico*, for no lover was ever so foolish as knowingly to trust his mistress 'amori', i.e. to one who is in love with her. Supposing that *amico* is a true correction one may either accept *iam credat*, or may regard *non credit* as a corruption of *nunc credit* (Post-gate) or of *concredit*: this hypothesis will explain *iam credat* as an attempt at correction while the other will hardly explain *non credit*; yet *iam* is favoured by v. 24 'omnes *iam* norunt quam sit amare bonum.' But *amico* with all the readings which contain || it is open to the objection that though 'credere dominam amico' is an excellent phrase, the phrase 'credere *faciem* dominae amico' is not so easy to accept; and it may be that we ought rather to prefer with Baehrens the *non credit* of O and alter *amori* with v into *amari*: the confusion of *amare* and *amore* is frequent in our MSS. The sense will be then 'why does any lover shut his eyes to the fact that his mistress' face makes others fall in love with it?' Yet again it must be admitted that 'cur quisquam...credit amico' leads up better to the 'nemo est in amore fidelis' of v. 3; and I for my part am altogether at a loss to decide between the various readings.

II xxxiv 39–40
>   non Amphiaraeae prosint tibi fata quadrigae
>   aut Capanei *magno* grata ruina Ioui.

The simplest amendment of the hexameter is to strike out *non* with Munro and make the sentence interrogative: see a similar corruption at III xiii 35, *atque hinuli* for *hinulei*. In the pentameter N has *magno*, O omits it. Now *magno* is well enough, and Propertius writes 'magno...Ioui' at II xxxii 60, but it is hard to see why it should fall out; and there is more diplomatic probability about Heinsius' *irato*: this word is a good deal confused, as at I vi 10, with *ingrato*, which would easily be lost between *i* and *grata*; and it manifestly has more peculiar appropriateness than *magno*, which may have been suggested to an interpolator by II xxxii 60 quoted above: Ovid Ibis 469 sq. referring to Capa-neus writes 'aut *Iouis infesti* telo feriare trisulco | ut satus Hipponoo'. It is how-ever uncertain whether Propertius would venture to elide this diphthong in a Greek name. Seeing that even before a short syllable he employs the very rare elision of a long Greek vowel in II xxviii 19 'Ino etiam', he may be thought capable of eliding before a long syllable even the diphthong, which after all is not a Greek diphthong: but it is perhaps safest to suspend judgment.

III v 39   sub terris sint iura deum et tormenta *gigantum*. ||

gigantum is given by O, omitted by N. Haupt (ind. lectt. Berlin 1854–5) raises some factitious objections to the presence of 'gigantes' in hell, and then proceeds to demolish them by quoting Stat. Theb. IV 533 and VIII 42, to which Ellis adds Sil. XIII 590. But Haupt goes on to say with some truth that 'iura deum' and 'tormenta' point in another direction. When Propertius grows old he says he will turn philosopher and enquire whether what we hear about hell is true 'an ficta in miseras descendit fabula gentis | et timor haut ultra quam rogus esse potest': now the tales which strike terror into mankind are not so much the punishments of the giants but rather of human malefactors: the bad man fears the doom which has overtaken other bad men. Haupt therefore accepted Lobeck's conjecture *nocentum*, which seems an improvement to the sense but explains neither the blank in N nor the *gigantum* of O. If the scruple suggested above be thought sufficient cause for deserting O, I would rather propose *reorum*: let this be corrupted to *deorum* and the scribes will have before them the manifestly absurd phrase 'iura *deum* et tormenta *deorum*': small wonder that one of them should omit the last word and the other should substitute the antithetic name *gigantum*. The expression 'tormenta reorum' is employed in the same connexion at Ovid Ibis 187 [189].

III vii 25–6

> reddite corpus humo, posita*que* in gurgite uita
> Paetum sponte tua, uilis harena, tegas.

So O: 'posita *est* in gurgite uita' N, which is rather abrupt and perhaps less pleasing.

III xii 1–4

> Postume, plorantem potuisti linquere Gallam
>   miles et Augusti fortia signa sequi?
> tantine ulla fuit spoliati gloria Parthi,
>   ne *facias*, Galla multa rogante tua?

facias O, *faceres* Nfv: either is defensible, according as we take *potuisti* and *fuit* to be true perfects or past aorists. ||

III xiii 51–4

> torrida sacrilegum testantur limina Brennum,
>   dum petit intonsi Pythia regna dei.
> at *mons* laurigero concussus uertice *diras*
>   Gallica Parnasus spargit in arma niues.

mons…diras Nv, *mox…duras* O. *diras* of course is right: of *mons* and *mox* I incline to the latter as more significant.

III xvi 7   at si *haec distulero* nostro mandata timore.

So O, *distulero haec* N: either elision is admissible, and a modern ear is incapable of judging which an ancient would prefer.

III xxiv 28 [xxv 8]

> tu bene conueniens non sinis *esse* iugum.

esse O, *ire* Nv. If *esse* is right, 'iugum' will mean the yoke; if *ire*, the yokefellows. I see nothing to choose.

IV i 73–4

> accersis lacrimas cantans: *auersus* Apollo:
> poscis ab inuita uerba pigenda lyra.

auersus Nv, *aduersus* O: the two words come to the same thing, though perhaps *auersus* harmonises better with 'inuita'.

IV iv 57–8

> si minus, at raptae *non* sint impune Sabinae:
> me rape, et alterna lege repende uices.

So O: N has *ne*: 'at, raptae *ne* sint impune Sabinae, me rape' is smoother than the other reading; yet it may be said that the somewhat rare and poetical use of *non* in prohibition (cf. Ovid ars III 133) is less likely to have come from a scribe.

IV vii 19–20

> saepe Venus triuio commissa est: pectore mixto
> fecerunt tepidas *pectora* nostra uias.

pectora O, which cannot be right after 'pectore' and may have come thence: *pallia* Nv (*palia* f) which may be a mere || conjecture and if so is a most miserable one. Mr Rossberg building on *pectora* proposes *corpora* which is often confused with that word and may be true. On *pallia* is based the conjecture *proelia* mentioned by Mr Luetjohann, which perhaps is no less probable; for the objection that the word is inappropriate to a stealthy encounter does not seem very heavy, and it is worth noting that in [Tib.] IV 3 3 [III 9 3 Postgate] where the best MS gives *praelia* the others have *pectore*.

THE DESCENDANTS OF O

§11. *DV better than AF*

I shall now examine the respective value of the families AF and DV as witnesses to the reading of their common parent O. In the cases about to be considered N exhibits the presence of no element independent of O but agrees with one or other of the two families AF and DV or with one or more of those four MSS: oftenest with AF or, where A is wanting, with F, but frequently also with DV against F or AF. The nature and significance of its vacillation will appear in the course of the enquiry; but the chief aim proposed in this part of my treatise is to shew that the families AF and DV are practically equal in value, and that if we would discover the reading of O we can dispense with neither.

And first I will take the places in which DV shew themselves superior to AF. We shall find, as I said, that N agrees more often with AF than with DV; and in every case where this happens, and DV are right, one more instance is added to those already collected in which O is superior to N.

In maintaining the value of DV I am at one with Baehrens, with Mr Solbisky, and probably with all post-Baehrensian critics but Mr Leo.

I ii 26 uni si qua placet, *culta* puella sat est: *culta* DVN, *una* AF: *c* was absorbed by *t*, leaving *ulta*.

I ii 29   unica nec desit iucundis gratia *dictis*.

dictis DV, *uerbis* AFN. The superior vigour of *dictis* is evident; || and the question is settled by Ovid's imitation met. XIII 127 'neque abest facundis gratia dictis'.

I iv 9–10 nedum, si leuibus *fuerit* collata figuris, | inferior duro iudice turpis eat: *fuerit...eat* DVN, *fuerat...erat* AF.   I viii 1 tune igitur demens, nec te mea *cura* moratur? *cura* DVN, *culpa* AF.

I viii 7–8
>   tu pedibus teneris positas fulcire *pruinas*,
>   tu potes insolitas, Cynthia, ferre niues?

pruinas DV, *ruinas* AFN. Because Lucretius has 'ruina grandinis', Virgil and Silius 'caeli ruina', and Valerius Flaccus 'ruina poli', Scaliger should not have inferred that 'positas ruinas' without any such genitive can mean fallen snow; and so Gronovius observes. The corruption is due to 'fulcire': see Luc. VIII 528 'potes Magni *fulcire ruinam*.'

I viii 17–20
>   sed, quocumque modo de me, periura, mereris,
>   sit Galatea tuae non aliena uiae;
>   *ut te*, felici praeuecta Ceraunia remo,
>   accipiat placidis Oricos aequoribus.

So read AFN, and thereby confer on the past participle 'praeuecta' the absolutely solecistic sense 'O thou who art about to sail by'. Some would escape this solecism by means of another, and take the vocative 'praeuecta' as an accusative 'praeuectam', a device which Mr Vahlen, 'ueber zwei Elegien des Propertius' Berlin 1882, p. 9, seeks to defend by a collection of passages partly misunderstood and all irrelevant. These I pass by: the nearest parallel I myself can find, and it is quite inadequate, is Luc. V 231 'secreta tenebis | litoris Euboici memorando *condite* busto', an incorrect expression into which the poet has been betrayed by the common practice of employing, for metrical convenience, vocative instead of nominative in such apostrophes as Stat. Theb. IV 620 sq. 'funera belli | pande uel *infensus* uel res *miserate* tuorum': a practice so common that the distinction between the two cases is at length obliterated, and 'tenebis condite', which strictly interpreted is || nonsense, since the person addressed is not yet buried nor dead, comes to be exactly the same as 'tenebis conditus'. But there exists no practice of substituting vocative for *accusative* which should lure Propertius into writing 'te, praeuecta, accipiat' for 'te praeuectam accipiat':

hence all the best critics of the author have held this verse to be corrupt and essayed to amend it; and amongst them Eldick at the end of the last century proposed *utere* for *ut te*: 'praeuecta' then becomes nominative and at the same time Latin: for 'utere remo' compare Ovid trist. 1 1 91 'remis utaris', ex Pont. II 6 37 'remo tamen utor in aura'. We now learn that *utere* is the reading of D and evidently was the reading also of V which at present has *ut te* with the second *t* in an erasure and with another erasure between the two words; and since Baehrens' publication of this fact in 1880 the new reading is well on its way towards acceptance. The omission of 'te' in the next verse, whether we like it or no, is quite Propertian: Mr Solbisky compares 1 vi 22 'nam tua non aetas umquam cessauit amori, | semper at armatae cura fuit patriae' sc. tibi.

I viii 27   hic *erit*, hic iurata manet: rumpantur iniqui.

erit DV, *erat* AFN. Mr Palmer alone reads *erat*, which, he says, means 'she was here all the while'. It does; but that is why all other critics reject it.

I xi 15   ut solet *amoto* labi custode puella.

amoto DV, *amota* AFN. The latter, accepted by Haupt and Palmer, is shewn by the context to be unsuitable: 'custos' means here a jealous lover like the poet himself.

I xii 10 lecta Prometheis *diuidit* herba iugis: *diuidit* DVN, *diuitis* AF.   I xiii 5 dum tibi deceptis augetur *fama* puellis: *fama* DVN, *forma* AF.   I xiii 7–8 *perditus* in quadam tardis pallescere curis | incipis: *perditus* DVN, *queritis* AF.   I xiii 16 et flere *iniectis*, Galle, diu manibus: *iniectis* DV, *inlectis* N, *in lectis* AF.   I xvi 18 quid mihi *tam* duris clausa taces foribus? *tam* DV, *iam* AFN.   I xix 10 *Thessalis* antiquam uenerat umbra domum: *Thessalis* DV, *Thessalus* AFN. ||

I xx 11   nympharum *cupidas semper* defende rapinas.

cupidas semper DV, *semper cupidas* AFN. Propertius prefers that order which places the substantive in one half of the hexameter and its adjective in the other.

I xx 13–14 ne tibi sit, durum, montes et *frigida* saxa, | Galle, neque expertos semper adire lacus: *frigida* DVN, *turbida* AF.

II v 3   haec merui sperare? dabis *mihi*, perfida, poenas.

mihi DV, *mi* FN. Propertius never uses the latter form except under metrical necessity.

II ix 11–12   et dominum lauit maerens captiua cruentum
                appositum flauis in Simoenta uadis.

appositum DV, *propositum* FN. Briseis is laving the dead body of Achilles. Before we judge between the two readings we must remove a difficulty common to both. For 'in Simoenta' Passeratius refers us to the phrase 'in possessionem esse', and he might add III ix 60 'in partes...fuisse tuas'; but this Roman vulgarism is confined to native inflexions, and its extension to Greek forms is a thing unheard of. Guietus therefore proposed 'apposito...Simoente' and Paley 'ad Simoenta': it suffices to write 'Simoente' without further change, leaving the accusative participle, the cause of the error, to agree with 'dominum'. Now with *appositum* the construction will be 'dominum flauis uadis appositum lauit in Simoente', which seems irreproachable sense. But *propositum* has no fit meaning and apparently has never found any partisans but Perreius and Mr Palmer, the latter of whom adduces the damaging citation Ovid trist. III 9 29, where we read how Medea *exposed* on a rock the mangled limbs of Absyrtus. The corruption is easy to explain: the initial *a* was torn away with the margin or left blank for the rubricator, and *ppositum* was then mistaken for *ppositum*.

II x 21–2 ut caput in magnis ubi non est tangere signis | ponitur *hic* imos ante corona pedes: *hic* DV, *hac* FN. ‖ II xi 1–2 scribant de te alii, ne sis ignota, licebit; | *laudet*, qui sterili semina ponit humo: *laudet* DV, *ludet* FN.   II xiii 24 plebei paruae funeris *exequiae*: *exequiae* DV, *obsequiae* FN; but in N the mistake is corrected by the same hand which made it.   II xv 8 sicine, *lente*, iaces? *lente* DV, *lecte* FN.

II xvi 11–12

> Cynthia non sequitur fasces nec curat honores:
> semper amatorum ponderat *illa* sinus.

illa DV, *una* FN. These words are both of them easily confounded with *ulla* and therefore with one another: all we have to consider in choosing is the sense; and the sense of *illa* is not and cannot be impugned. But *una* is in the worshipped Neapolitanus; and it is accordingly accepted both by Mr Palmer, though he appears to apprehend correctly its irrelevant meaning ('Cynthia is not lured by the pomp of office: it is the purse of her lovers that she always weighs *with unrivalled accuracy*'), and by Mr Vahlen, who, justly intolerant of this, chooses, rather than take the faultless *illa*, to construe *una* as acc. plur. masc. agreeing with 'sinus' (Monatsbericht der königl. Akademie der Wissenschaften zu Berlin, 7 April 1881, pp. 342 sqq.).

II xxiii 1–2

> cui fuit indocti *fugienda* semita uulgi,
> ipsa petita lacu nunc mihi dulcis aqua est.

fugienda DV, *fugienda et* FN. '*et* uerum est' writes Mr Palmer; '*etiam* semitam qua utebatur uulgus Propertius dicit sibi fugiendam fuisse': i.e. Propertius says

'I, who formerly held that amours *even* with low women (much more then with ladies) were to be shunned, now find pleasure in amours with the lowest.' Because this is incoherent in itself and subverts the argument of the poem, in which Propertius explains why, having formerly consorted with ladies, he now consorts with low women instead, other editors alter *et* to *haec*; but it cannot be denied that the pronoun would be better away, and with DV before us it seems impossible to doubt that *et* is merely a metrical stopgap. Baehrens therefore proposes the transposition ‖ and alteration 'cui fuerit fugienda indocti semita'; but if we transpose the words aright no further change is needed:

> cui fugienda fuit indocti semita uulgi.

For 'fuīt' see IV i 17 'nulli cura fuit externos quaerere diuos'.

II xxiv 45–6

> iam tibi Iasonia uecta est Medea carina
> et modo *ab infido* sola relicta uiro.

uecta in the hexameter is Heinsius' slight and necessary correction of *nota*. In the pentameter DV have *ab infido*, F omits these words, N gives *seruato* in their stead. As to sense there is little to choose; though inasmuch as this poem deals with the fickleness of men, not their ingratitude, the balance inclines a trifle to *ab infido*. For when Messrs Leo and Solbisky assert on the other side that 'modo' has no sense without *seruato*, they err: in the sentence 'iam tibi (tibi = 'look you' as in Lucr. v 805 etc.) uecta est et modo relicta', 'iam' and 'modo' answer one another, as 'nunc' and 'modo' perpetually do, in the sense of 'modo… modo'. But what must settle the question in favour of *ab infido* for any impartial judge are palaeographical considerations. It is quite clear, as Baehrens prolegg. p. XII pointed out, that the scribe of the parent codex of the one family glanced from the *do* of *modo* to the *do* of *infido* and so left a metrical gap which F honestly preserves and which N fills up with the conjecture *seruato*. When therefore Mr Solbisky p. 168 declares that '*ab infido* temera est coniectura' his assertion is as irrational as his language is solecistic. This passage, be it observed, is a very striking addition to our proofs of O's superiority over N.

II xxvii 13–14

> iam licet et Stygia sedeat sub harundine remex
> *cernat* et infernae tristia uela ratis.

So FN. But though it would be appropriate enough to say of a ghost approaching the banks of Styx that he 'descries' the sail of the ferry-boat, the word is absurd when used of one who is seated oar in hand in that very vessel. DV have *seruat*: ‖ the confusion is easy and recurs for instance at Ovid trist. IV 2 14. Now of two unsatisfactory readings that one is likely to be nearer truth which is the more obviously unsatisfactory; and from *seruat*, which is not even grammatical, Broukhusius elicits *soluat*: for *o* confused with *e* as well as *l* with *r* compare I xvi 23 p*l*ena for *prona*; and see IV xi 69 sq. 'mihi cumba uolenti | soluitur'.

II xxviii 29–30

> et tibi Maeonias *inter heroidas omnis*
> primus erit nullo non tribuente locus.

Thus FN, but the lengthening of -*er* is unexampled in Propertius. DV give *omnis herodias inter*: this order of the words is confirmed as Baehrens says by Ovid trist. I 6 33 'prima locum sanctas *heroidas inter* haberes'.

II xxxii 7–8 hoc utinam spatiere loco, quodcumque uacabis, | Cynthia; sed *tibi me* credere turba uetat: *tibi me* DV, *time* N, *timeo* F.

II xxxiv 11–12

> quid si non constans illa et tam certa fuisset?
> *posses in* tanto uiuere flagitio?

posses in N, *posset et in* F, *posses et in* DV. The vulgate *posses in* is well enough in itself but affords no scientific explanation of the other readings: *posses in* and *posset et in* appear to be alternative corrections of the unmetrical *posses et in*. But we shall prefer the correction of a competent scholar, Heinsius' '*posses tun* tanto uiuere flagitio': 'tu' in opposition to 'illa' adds much force to the sentence, and indeed would in a prose writer be necessary.

III ii 5–6 saxa *Cithaeronis* Phoebeam agitata per artem | sponte sua *in muri* membra coisse ferunt: *citeronis* DV, *ciceronis* FN: *in muri* DV, *ī mineri* F, *in numeri* N.

III v 23–4

> ubi iam Venerem grauis interceperit aetas
> *sparserit et nigras* alba senecta comas.

sparserit integras DV, inverting the order of the letters *etni*; || *sparsit et integras* F, a further error; *sparserit et integras* N, a conflation of the two erroneous readings. Therefore when Mr Leo enquires, p. 446, 'tu uero ubi pristinam scripturam fidelius seruatam credis, in DV qui *sparserit integras*, an in F qui *sparsit et integras*, an in N qui praebet *sparserit et integras*?' we shall return him without hesitation the unexpected answer: 'in DV'.

III v 35 (Solbisky p. 190)

> cur serus uersare boues et *plaustra Bootes*.

plaustra bootes DV; *flamma palustra* F, which two words are both corruptions of *plaustra*, the latter by the transposition of a letter, the former through the likeness of *p* to *f* and of *st* to *n* and of *flaunra* to *flamma*; *flamma boon* N. Everyone accepted the reading of DV until Baehrens in his edition exalted those MSS above N, after which it became necessary for Mr Leo to conjecture, p. 447, 'cur serus uersare Bootes flammea plostra'; and this conjecture after all is based not on that N which Mr Leo is concerned to defend, but on that F of which he says, on the very same page, that it 'omnino nihil ualet'.

III xi 51 fugisti tamen in timidi *uaga* flumina Nili: *uaga* DV, *uada* FN.   III xiii 32 aut uariam plumae *uersicoloris* auem: *uersicoloris* DV, *uiricoloris* FN.   III xiii 53 mons *laurigero* concussus uertice: *laurigero* DV, *aurigero* FN.

III xiv 11–14

gyrum pulsat equis, niueum latus ense reuincit
 uirgineumque cauo protegit aere caput,
qualis Amazonidum nudatis bellica mammis
 Thermodontiacis turba *lauantur* aquis.

lauantur DV, *lauatur* FN: the plural, as Baehrens remarks, being equally correct (III xvii 28 '*potant* Naxia turba merum') is to be preferred as less obvious than the singular. Since much trouble has been caused here by the neglect of a common idiom it may be well to add that 'protegit caput qualis Amazonidum turba lauantur' (or 'lauatur') does not in the least imply that the Amazons wear helmets while bathing. It ‖ merely means that the Spartan girl wears a helmet as the Amazons do; and it occurs to the poet to mention by the way that the Amazons bathe in Thermodon. 'quales Amazonides lauantur' = 'quales sunt Amazonides, quae lauantur': compare Verg. Aen. III 641 sqq. 'nam qualis quantusque cauo Polyphemus in antro | lanigeras claudit pecudes atque ubera pressat, | centum alii curua haec habitant ad litora uolgo | infandi Cyclopes et altis montibus errant.'

III xv 14 molliaque *immites* fixit in ora manus: *immites* D, *ī mites* V, *immittens* F, *inmittens* N.   III xv 27 saepe uago *Asopi* sonitu permota fluentis: *asopi* DV, *esopi* F, *ęsopi* N.

III xx 6   forsitan ille alio pectus amore *terit*.

terit DV, *terat* FN. As I said above[1] on III xxiii 11, the MSS of Propertius are twice agreed on the indic. with 'forsitan', twice divided between indic. and subj.: the indic. then should be preferred.

III xxii 23–6

hic Anio Tiburne fluis, Clitumnus ab Vmbro
 tramite, et aeternum Marcius umor opus,
Albanus lacus et *socii* Nemorensis ab unda
 potaque Pollucis lympha salubris equo.

[1] pp. 158 sq. [this edition pp. 274–5].

So N, unintelligibly. Francius therefore read *socia*; Scaliger retaining *socii* altered *Albanus lacus et* to *Albanusque lacus*; but these emendations rest on the fiction that those two lakes have a common fount, and that fiction in its turn rests on these emendations. Therefore Hertzberg emends Scaliger's emendation by further altering *ab* to *et*; but 'Albanusque lacus, socii Nemorensis et unda' is now a great way from the MSS. In place of *socii* F has *sotii* and DV have the very noticeable variant *sotiis* which bears every sign of originality: a scribe who took 'Nemorensis' for gen. might alter *sotiis* to *sotii*, but there was nothing to prompt the converse change. *sotiis*, by the very common exchange of *f* for *s* and *l* for *t* (both mistakes occur together at II vii 2 *stemus* for *flemus*), stands for *foliis*: Propertius wrote ||

> Albanus lacus et *foliis* Nemorensis *abundans*,

and the two last letters were lost through injury to the margin. The lake of Aricia 'silua praecinctus opaca' (Ovid fast. III 263) was called 'Nemorensis' after the grove of Diana known κατ' ἐξοχήν as 'Nemus' (Prop. II xxxii 10) which stood on its banks.

III xxiv 9–10 quod mihi non patrii poterant auertere amici | *eluere* aut uasto Thessala saga mari; *eluere* DV, *fluere* FN.   IV iii 1 *haec* Arethusa suo mittit mandata Lycotae: *haec* given by DV, omitted by FN.   IV iv 32 et *formosa* oculis arma Sabina meis: *formosa* DV, *famosa* FN.

IV iv 71–2   illa ruit, qualis celerem prope Thermodonta
              Strymonis *abscisso* fertur aperta sinu.

abscisso DV, *absciso* FN. To begin with, the pentameter as Lachmann says is neither Greek nor Latin until we supply 'aperta' with an acc. respectus by writing either with Broukhusius *abscissos* (or *abscisos*)...*sinus*, or else *pectus* for *fertur* with Hertzberg. In favour of the latter Hertzberg cites Ovid fast. I 408 'dissuto *pectus aperta sinu*', to which I will add epist. Sapph. 122 'lacero *pectus aperta sinu*', Tib. I 6 18 'laxo *pectus aperta sinu*', Ovid met. XIII 688 'apertae *pectora* matres', Stat. silu. V 5 13 'aperto *pectore* matres'. Now for the question between *abscisso* and *absciso*. The latter is supposed to signify that mutilation from which the Amazons were thought to derive their name, and it may be dismissed at once: *sinus* is not *mamma*, and 'abscidere sinum' is a thing impossible. *abscisso sinu* will of course refer to the torn folds of the dress over the bosom, and may be supported by Ovid fast. IV 448 'ipsa suos *absciderat*que *sinus*' and Prop. III viii 8 'fac mea *rescisso pectora nuda sinu*'.

IV vi 75   ingenium *potis* irritat Musa poetis.

potis DV, *positis* FN. The former is obviously right: the next verse is 'Bacche, soles Phoebo fertilis esse tuo'. ||

IV vii 7   eosdem habuit secum, quibus est elata, *capillos*.

capillos DV, *capillis* FN. Either is correct, but *capillos* best accords with the poet's custom of placing a substantive in one half of the verse with its adjective in the other; and moreover the change of *capillos* to *capillis* through the neighbourhood of *quibus* is easier explained than the converse error.

IV viii 38   et Methymnaei *Graeca* saliua meri.

greca FN, *grata* DV. Propertius never uses the form 'Graecus', and Roman poets in general prefer 'Graius'; most editors therefore accept the *Graia* which Palmerius built on *grata*. But since neither *Graia* nor *Graeca* conveys anything which is not already conveyed in 'Methymnaei' it may well be that *grata* itself is the true reading, = 'iucunda': see Mart. XIII 21 'spina...non erit...*gratior* asparagis' and especially Plin. h. n. XIV 1 3 §16 'aliis (uuis) *gratiam*, qui et *uinis*, affert fumus fabrilis' and ib. XXIII 1 22 §40, quoted by Passeratius, 'sua cuique *uino saliua* innocentissima, sua cuique aetas *gratissima*.'

IV viii 71–2 supplicibus palmis tum demum ad foedera ueni,
          cui uix tangendos praebuit illa pedes.

cui DV, *cur* F, *cum* N. *cui*, as less obvious, is to be preferred to *cum*, which seems due to the 'tum' above.

IV viii 85   imperat et totas iterum mutare *lacernas*.

lacernas DV, *laternas* F, *lucernas* N. This is perhaps a case where DV are superior, not to the family AF, but merely to the extant representatives of that family: it is possible that A, if it were here present, would stand halfway between F and N and give, like DV, the true reading.

IV ix 40   et numquam ad *uacuas* irrita tela feras.

uacuas DV, *natas* F, *uatas* N, all three utterly impossible. The Italians proposed *uastas* which has some support in II xix 21 '*uastos* ausim temptare leones'; but Santen's *nocuas* appears to be the best correction: this word courted corruption by its rarity and was perilously like *uocuas*, which form the scribes would alter as usual to *uacuas*: the likeness of *c* to *t* || accounts for the further errors. I suspect that this adjective should again be restored to Propertius at III vii 60 by writing 'attulimus NOCVAS in freta uestra manus?' which was corrupted I imagine to NOGLAS and thence by transposition of letters to LONGAS.

IV x 17   urbis *uirtutum*que parens sic uincere sueuit.

uirtutum DV, *uirtutem* F, *uirtutis* N. The unusual plural is not likely to be a correction yet is perfectly correct: Baehrens compares Cat. 68 90 'Troia, uirum et uirtutum omnium acerba cinis': see too Verg. Aen. 1 566 'uirtutesque uirosque'.

IV xi 7–8

uota mouent superos: ubi portitor aera recepit
obserat *umbrosos* lurida porta rogos.

umbrosos DV, *erbosos* F, *herbosos* N. If *herbosos* stood in all the MSS, it would
not surprise one to find it defended as 'Propertian', i.e. absurd. But here the
MSS are divided; and it is not yet a recognised canon, even in the criticism of this
author, that 'commodae lectioni praestat inepta'. 'rogus' has no known meaning
but a funeral pile, and funeral piles are not grassy. Grant, though the evidence
produced is worthless, that it could mean 'Orcus' or 'manes': these are not
grassy either. *umbrosos* on the other hand is applicable to *rogos* alike in the
known meaning of that substantive and in the unknown meaning 'Orcus' or
'manes' which the context here requires. The context I say requires it; for if we
grant, again on no evidence, that 'rogus' could mean a grave and could so be
called grassy, we are in no way helped, since grassy graves are not shut in by the
gate of hell. And in fact *herbosos* is inapplicable to any substantive of which
'obserat lurida porta' can be said: the superiority of *umbrosos* is therefore
assured, whether we retain *rogos* in its unexampled meaning, or alter it with
Markland to *locos*, an easy change recurring for instance at Sen. Oed. 61, Herc.
fur. 508, 512. The confusion of *umbra* with *herba* is found elsewhere, as at
IV viii 35. ‖

§12. *DV better than AF: spelling*

The following are passages where DV excel the other family by giving the true
spelling, or the better spelling of two, or the less known of two good spellings.

II vii 4, xvi 16, 48, xxii 25, xxvi 42, xxviii 1, xxxiii 14, III ix 15, xi 28, IV i 54,
82, iv 85, vi 14 and x 15, *Iuppiter* DV, *Iupiter* FN.

II xvi 24, xx 9, xxii 15, III vii 69, xiv 9, xxi 24, IV iii 12, iv 67, *bracchia* DV,
brachia FN; II i 70 *bracchia* D, V doubtful, *brachia* N, *brachide* F.

I xviii 29 *querellae* DV, *querelae* AFN.

II xix 22 *comminus* DV, *cominus* FN.

IV ii 21 *opportuna* DV, *oportuna* FN.

I iv 21 *omnis* (acc. plur.) DV, *omĩs* F, *omnes* AN; xiii 25 and II i 57 *omnis* DV,
omnes AFN; I x 7 *labentis* DV, *labentes* AFN; II xv 51 *arentis* DV, *arentes* FN.

I xx 45 *quoius* DV, *cuius* AFN; II xxiv 3 *quoi* DV, *cui* FN. In III viii 29 where
FN have *cum* DV have *quo* pointing to *quom*. In II vi 26, a verse which ought I
believe to be written 'si *quoiuis* nuptae *quoilibet* esse licet' though some prefer
quidlibet, the MSS vary thus: *cuiuis* N, *cuius* F, *quoius* D, *quouis* V; *quoilibet* DV,
cuilibet F, *quidlibet* N.[1]

---

[1] In the latter half of the 15th century it became a common affectation with Italian scribes to use the
archaic forms; but the parent codex of DV was probably earlier than 1400 and certainly not much
later, so that its witness in the matter can safely be taken as sincere.

III iii 33 *diuorsae* (i.e. *diuorse*) DV, *diuerse* F, *diuersae* N.

II xxvii 12 *nec hic* DV, *neque hic* FN: the former is likelier to be true, as less approved by the vulgar.

II iii 5 and IV viii 76 *harena* DV, *arena* FN; IV vi 83 *harenas* DV, *arenas* FN.

II xxii 23 *percontere* DV, *percuntare* F, *percunctere* N.

II xiv 16 *condicio* DV, *conditio* F, *condito* N.

I iv 23 *contemnet* DV, *contempnet* AFN; vii 25 *contemnas* DV, *contempnas* AFN; II v 29 *contemnas* DV, *contempnas* FN. Baehrens prolegg. p. xi states that he has not recorded all the ‖ places where this verb is rightly spelt in DV and wrongly in FN, or where DV have *somnus* and FN *sompnus*. He also says that DV generally give *proelia* and FN *praelia*.

§13. *AF better than DV*

Pursuing our investigation into the relative value of the families AF and DV as witnesses to the reading of O we shall now set out in their turn the principal passages where AF shew themselves superior to DV. I must preface the list with a word of explanation. The codex A, our best representative of its family, contains only the first book and the first 63 verses of the second: for the rest of the elegies our knowledge of the family is derived only from F and from N. Now N, as we have seen and shall see, contains much which comes from other sources than the family AF; and F, whose scribe was a most ignorant man, is defaced by a hundred blunders which were not in the exemplar whence it was copied. But where F and N agree, there we have the reading of the family AF. And again, where F, even standing alone, gives the true reading, there too must we suppose that reading to be the reading of the family; for the scribe of F, it is abundantly plain, was quite incapable of conjectural emendation: F's false readings may be its own, but its true readings must be those of its exemplar.

In upholding the importance of the family AF and placing it on a level with DV I am in particular controverting Mr Solbisky.

I iii 27–9

> et quotiens raro duxit suspiria motu
> obstipui uano credulus auspicio,
> ne qua *tibi* insolitos portarent uisa timores.

tibi AFN, *sibi* DV, a solecistic attempt to escape the change from third person to second in 'duxit...tibi'. The true emendation was later found in *duxti*. ‖

I iii 43–4

> interdum *leuiter* mecum deserta *querebar*
> externo longas saepe in amore uias.

leuiter...querebar AFN, *grauiter...loquebar* DV. *querebar* is clearly right: between the adverbs the choice is harder, but perhaps the editors do well in preferring *leuiter* the less obvious. Mr Solbisky taking the other side reminds us of Cynthia's violent temper and asks 'nonne igitur absurdum fere est, si Propertio, quippe cui irascatur, dicit se leuiter tantum questam esse?' I should reply, no, not absurd that she should *say* so: to *represent* herself as meekly enduring his neglect is an effective artifice enough. Mr Solbisky further argues that the *loquebar* of DV comes from a misunderstood *le* written over *grauiter* in the archetype. If this were so it would say nothing for *grauiter*, since the *le* might well have been a true correction due to renewed examination of the exemplar; but the fact is that the confusion of *queror* and *loquor*, which we shall meet again at I viii 22, is too common to serve as a ground for his suspicion.

I iv 15–16 quo magis et nostros contendis soluere amores | hoc magis accepta *fallit uterque* fide: *fallit uterque* AFN, *fallis utrumque* DV.

I vi 15–18

> ut mihi deducta faciat conuicia puppi
> Cynthia, et insanis ora notet manibus,
> osculaque opposito dicat sibi *debita* uento,
> et nihil infido durius esse uiro.

debita AFN, *dedita* DV. All modern editors rightly read *debita*; but since they explain the verse in various and as I think impossible ways I ought to say how I understand it. I take 'opposito...uento' (or rather 'ponto' with Fonteine) as abl. abs. like 'deducta...puppi' in the preceding hexameter, and understand Cynthia to be represented as crying to Propertius 'my kisses bring again!' when now his ship has left the shore and the wind (or sea) forbids return. ||

I vi 25   me sine, quem *semper uoluit* Fortuna iacere.

semper uoluit AFN, *uoluit semper* DV. 'semper' belongs to 'iacere' and therefore in accordance with the metrical principles of Propertius should stand in the first half of the verse to balance 'iacere' at the end.

I vi 32 Lydia Pactoli *tingit* arata liquor: *tingit* N, *tinguit* AF, *cingit* DV. I viii 22 quin ego, uita, tuo limine uerba *querar*: *querar* AFN, *loquar* DV.

I viii 25–6

> et dicam, licet Atraciis considat in oris
> et licet *Hyleis*, illa futura mea est.

Hyleis AF, *Hileis* N, *Ellaeis* DV. Cynthia was starting for Illyria, so it has been usual to write *Hylleis*, the name of an Illyrian tribe. Then arises the difficulty that *Atraciis* now must also signify some part of Illyria, only it does not: therefore it is usually altered to *Autaricis*. But another sense in no way inferior to this is procured by retaining *Hyleis*, i.e. *Hylaeis*, and merely transposing one letter of *Atraciis*. Hylaea was a land beyond Scythia, Herod. IV 9, 54, 55, 76: if then we introduce the name of another very distant country we shall have the sense 'though she sail to the ends of the earth she shall be mine': Mr Palmer accordingly in the hexameter restores *Artaciis*, referring to Apoll. Rhod. Arg. I 954 sqq., Orph. Arg. 496 [494 Abel].

I xiii 6 certus et in nullo quaeris amore *moram*: *moram* AFN, *uiam* DV from m̊am.

I xix 7–10

> illic Phylacides iucundae coniugis heros
> non potuit caecis inmemor esse locis,
> sed cupidus falsis attingere gaudia palmis
> Thessalis antiquam *uenerat* umbra domum.

uenerat AN, F has not the verse, *uerberat* DV. *uenerat*, pluperfect with past aorist sense as often in Propertius, is faultless: *uerberat* is soon explained as an attempt to correct the easy mistake *ueberat*: there is no cause or defence then for ‖ Baehrens' suspicion *peruolat*, or for Mr Rossberg's surprising *uerterat*.

I xix 13–14

> illic formosae *ueniant* chorus heroinae
> quas dedit Argiuis Dardana praeda uiris.

ueniant AFN, *ueniat* DV misled by 'chorus'. The verse however requires emendation. It is not Latin to say 'formosae heroinae, chorus': chorus caterua turba manus and similar words are not placed in apposition without an adjective in agreement; and *formosae* must be changed to *formosus*.

I xx 51 his, o Galle, tuos *monitus* seruabis amores: *monitus* AFN, *monitis* DV.

I xxi 6–10

> haec soror acta tuis sentiat e lacrimis,
> Gallum per medios ereptum Caesaris enses
> effugere ignotas non potuisse manus;
> et, *quaecumque* super dispersa inuenerit ossa
> montibus Etruscis, haec sciat esse mea.

quaecumque AFN, *quicumque* DV. These lines are a message from the dying Gallus to his sister, so *quicumque* is clearly wrong: Gallus has no concern with 'whosoever finds bones on the Etrurian mountains'. *quaecumque* is accepted I think by everyone but Mr Postgate, whose objections to it rest on a not unnatural misconception which I will try to remove. *quaecumque* and *haec* are not relative and antecedent. *haec* is purely demonstrative and means 'these bones here': the antecedent to *quaecumque* is suppressed, and 'quaecumque inuenerit' is equivalent to 'licet sescenta alia inuenerit' or the like. There is a similarly deceptive collocation of the two words in Lucr. 1 670 sq. 'nam *quodcumque* suis mutatum finibus exit, | continuo *hoc* mors est illius quod fuit ante', where *hoc* refers not to *quodcumque* but to the notion of that clause, τὸ *exire*.

II iii 23–4

> *num* tibi nascenti primis, mea uita, diebus
> *candidus* argutum *sternuit* omen Amor? ||

num F, *non* N, *nunc* DV. *candidus . . . sternuit* is preserved by Macrobius GLK v p. 626 17; FN have *ardidus . . . sternuit*, the initial *c* having been lost and *n* altered to *r*; DV corrupt this to *aridus . . . stertuit*.

II vi 1–2

> non ita complebant Ephyreae Laidos aedes,
> ad cuius iacuit Graecia tota *fores*.

fores FN, *pedes* DV. The latter is satisfactory and has been supported by Ovid her. III 84 'et iacet ante tuos Graecia maesta pedes'. But *fores* the more exquisite reading is plainly the original and *pedes* the interpolation; and to settle the question Passeratius quotes Anth. Gr. VI 1 1 sq. ἡ τὸν ἐραστῶν | ἑσμὸν ἐνὶ προθύροις Λαῖς ἔχουσα νέων.

II vii 7–8

> nam citius paterer caput hoc discedere collo
> quam possem nuptae perdere *more* faces.

more FN, *amore* DV. *amore* is the vulgate, but for external reasons it is the less probable reading, since it may come from the 'nil in *amore* ualent' of v. 6. And its meaning too is unsatisfactory: the event here contemplated is the enforced and unwilling marriage of Propertius, whose heart is given to Cynthia, with some other woman; not at all the transference of his affections. *more*, preferred by Baehrens and Postgate, makes good sense: 'to relinquish my passion for you in obedience to the will of a bride': Ter. And. 152 (Pamphilus is supposed to speak of the coming time when he must marry) 'prope adest, quom *alieno more* uiuendumst mihi: | sine nunc *meo* me uiuere interea *modo*.'

II ix 17 (Solbisky p. 150)

> tunc igitur *castis* gaudebat Graecia natis.

castis DV, *uiris* FN. Baehrens' correction of the irrelevant *natis* to *nuptis* is accepted even by Mr Vahlen. The question of the adjective is soon settled: *uiris*, as the Italians saw, is a corruption of *ueris*, and *castis* is a gloss explaining the peculiar signification, which *ueris* here has, of faithfulness in love: see || II xxix 34 'uel tu uel si quis *uerior* esse potest'. Thus the discrepancy has a solution: none, if *castis* be preferred with Baehrens.

II x 11–12 (Solbisky p. 159)

> surge, anima, ex humili iam *carmine*; sumite uires,
> Pierides; magni nunc erit oris opus.

carmine DVN: some editors retaining the same reading punctuate 'ex humili; iam carmine sumite uires, | Pierides'. But F gives *carmina*, which in itself has an air of genuineness, since its corruption to *carmine* through the neighbourhood of 'humili' is likelier than the contrary change; and it renders the verses more symmetrical when they are punctuated thus:

> surge, anima, ex humili; iam, *carmina*, sumite uires;
> Pierides, magni nunc erit oris opus.

Three vocatives and three exhortations. This is the reading of Burmann Lachmann Baehrens and Palmer, and it is accepted by F's worst enemy Mr Solbisky.

II xi 1–4

> scribant de te alii, *uel* sis ignota, licebit;
> laudet, qui sterili semina ponit humo:
> omnia, crede mihi, tecum uno munera lecto
> auferet extremi funeris atra dies.

uel DVN, *ne* F, which I with Baehrens prefer. The choice perhaps is a subtle matter, but I will try to make it plain as follows. The reading of F means 'scribant de te alii, laudet alius'; that of DVN means 'scribant de te alii *uel nemo*, laudet alius': it will be felt I think that in the former the pentameter follows more harmoniously. Then consider too the next couplet with its 'omnia...munera... auferet': this does not look as if the contingency 'licebit sis ignota' had been entertained, for there would then be no 'munera' for death to take.

II xii 19 intactos isto *satius* temptare ueneno: *satius* FN, *potius* D, *pocius* V.

II xiii 46   Nestoris est *uisus* post tria saecla cinis. ‖

uisus FN, *iussus* DV. This confusion, which may arise from the spelling *uissus*, is perpetual: *iussus* will not serve to build conjectures on.

II xv 23–6 (Solbisky pp. 159 sq.)

> dum nos fata sinunt, oculos satiemus amore:
> nox tibi longa uenit nec reditura dies.
> atque utinam haerentes sic nos uincire catena
> *uelles*, ut numquam solueret ulla dies.

Let me clear the way for the consideration of this passage by two remarks. First, the occurrence of 'dies' at the end of two consecutive distichs (though I do not myself believe that these two distichs were originally consecutive) is no ground for suspecting the word in either place: see I viii 42–4, II xx 24–6, xxiv 30–2, 36–8, xxxii 24–6, III x 16–18, xxiv 2–4, IV ix 16–18. Secondly, the verses are imitated by or from Sulpicia, Tib. IV 5 15 sq. [III 11 15 sq.] 'sed potius ualida teneamur uterque catena: | nulla queat posthac nos soluisse dies', a parallel which refutes many of the conjectures put forward. The sole difficulty resides in *uelles*. Two renderings are possible: one makes 'catena' vocative, so that Propertius with extreme absurdity addresses himself to the imaginary 'bond' of love; the other, taking 'catena' as ablative and 'nos' as 'me', supposes Cynthia to be addressed: but a lover's prayer that he may be constant is beyond his mistress' ability to fulfil and can only be granted by superior powers. Now instead of the *uelles* found in DVN, F has *uellet*; and Baehrens accepting this removes all the trouble by altering *ut* to *uti*: for this common error compare, if it is worth while, Ovid rem. 333.

II XV 43   non ferrum crudele *neque esset* bellica nauis.

neque esset FN, *esset neque* DV. The case is clear: DV have softened the masculine rhythm of Propertius, for which see II i 51 'seu mihi sunt tangenda nouercae pocula Phaedrae'.

II xviii 11 *illum* ad uicinos cum amplexa quiesceret Indos: *illum* FN, *illa* DV which comes from v. 13.   II xviii 31–2 si caeruleo quaedam sua tempora *fuco* | tinxerit: *fuco* FN, *succo* DV. ||

II xix 26   niueos abluit unda *boues*.

boues FN, *pedes* DV from an untimely reminiscence of I xx 8 'tinxerit unda pedes' or IV xi 16 'inplicat unda pedes'.

II XX 11   in te ego *et aeratas* rumpam, mea uita, catenas.

et aeratas FN, *ferratas* DV from 'ferratam' in the next verse.

II XX 21–6
             septima iam plenae deducitur orbita lunae,
                 cum de me et de te compita nulla tacent:
             interea nobis non *numquam* ianua mollis,
                 non *numquam* lecti copia facta tui.
             nec mihi muneribus nox ulla est empta beatis:
                 quidquid eram, hoc animi gratia magna tui.

numquam F, *umquam* DVN: the context demands the former which is accepted by Lachmann Hertzberg Haupt Mueller and Palmer. Keil however rejects the couplet altogether, for the reason, unintelligible to me, that 'numquam non' is what the sense requires: Baehrens reads *umquam* and having thus rendered the passage incoherent declares that vv. 21–4 are a fragment from some other poem.

II xxii 29–30 quid? cum e complexu Briseidos iret Achilles, | *num* fugere minus Thessala tela Phryges? *num* F, *non* DVN.   II xxiii 10 captus et *inmunda* saepe latere casa: *inmunda* FN, *in nuda* DV.   II xxvi 9–10 *quae* tum ego Neptuno, *quae* tum cum Castore fratri | quaeque tibi excepi, iam dea Leucothoe: *quae* FN, *quem* DV.

II xxvi 53   crede mihi, nobis *mitescet* Scylla.

mitescet FN, *mutescet* DV. Baehrens prefers *mutescet*, to which Mr Solbisky objects that the verb is not found earlier than Appuleius. A heavier objection, it seems to me, may be brought against its sense: if Scylla *mutescet* she will then be even more dangerous than before, since mariners will no longer be warned of her whereabouts.

II xxvii 7   rursus et obiectum flemus *capiti* esse tumultum.

So DV; a sentence which will mean, as I conceive, 'we lament || that we are personally accused of causing broils': assuredly it will never signify what the context requires, 'we lament that our life is jeopardised by broils'. That meaning is obtained by taking the *caput* of FN and altering *tumultum* with Mr Lucian Mueller to *tumultu*,[1] a form of the dative which greatly perplexes copyists: then compare Stat. Theb. I 652 'obiecisse caput fatis', Verg. Aen. II 751 'caput obiectare periclis', Sil. III 121 'obiectasque caput telis', Sen. Phoen. 407 'armis obuium opponam caput', Ag. 946 'ultro uulneri opponam caput', Luc. V 770 sq. 'ruinae... praestare caput'.

II xxviii 47 haec tua, Persephone, *maneat* clementia: *maneat* FN, *moueat* DV. II xxix 10 *dixit, et* in collo iam mihi nodus erat: *dixit et* FN, *dixerat* DV.

II xxxi 7   atque aram circum *steterunt* armenta Myronis.

steterunt F, *steterant* DVN. Either is admissible, but the former is more likely to be the original, since the 3rd pers. plur. perf. in -*ĕrunt* is perpetually altered into the pluperf. by scribes who do not know that this scansion is correct. The same error is found in I xi 29 *fuerant* for *fuerunt*, II viii 10 *steterant* for *steterunt*, III xxiv 20 and IV vii 15 *exciderant* for *exciderunt*: those editors who in these places retain the MS reading shew themselves ignorant of the fact that the pluperfect, though it can be used for the imperfect or for the past aorist, cannot be used for the perfect.

II xxxi 9–10 templum | et patria Phoebo *carius* Ortygia: *carius* FN, *clarior* DV.

II xxxii 7   hoc utinam *spatiere* loco, quodcumque uacabis.

spatiere F, *spaciere* N, *spatiare* DV. The error is trifling and would not deserve mention but for the extraordinary fact that Baehrens, forgetting in his enthusiasm for DV to what conjugation the verb 'spatior' belongs, has placed *spatiare* in his text.

---

[1] I find this correction in cod. Brit. mus. 23766.

II xxxii 29–30 (Solbisky p. 145)

> sin autem longo nox una aut altera *lusu*
> consumpta est, non me crimina parua mouent. ‖

lusu FN, *luxu* DV. Propertius is here extenuating the delinquencies of Cynthia, and *lusu* is therefore to be preferred as the less offensive term.

II xxxiv 85 haec quoque perfecto *ludebat* Iasone Varro: *ludebat* FN, *laudabat* DV.   III ii 4 flumina Threicia *sustinuisse* lyra: *sustinuisse* FN, *detinuisse* DV from *delenisse* in the line above.   III iii 11 Hannibalemque *lares* Romana sede fugantes: *lares* F, *lacies* N, *alacres* D, *lacres* V with an erasure before the first letter.

III vi 27–9

> illum turgentis ranae portenta rubetae
> et lecta *exectis* anguibus ossa trahunt,
> et strigis inuentae per busta iacentia plumae.

The pentameter is corrupt, but corrupt in one word only: *anguibus* is defended against such conjectures as *exsuccis unguibus* or *ex atris ignibus* by the 'ranae' which precedes and the 'strigis' which follows; and the construction 'legere ossa anguibus', i.e. 'ex anguibus', is well illustrated in the lexicons under 'lego'. But *exectis*, which the editors who keep it apparently take to mean 'cut open', means 'cut out', and therefore, so far as this passage is concerned, means nothing. Now the same word is given by most of Horace's MSS at epod. 5 37 '*execta* uti medulla et aridum iecur | amoris esset poculum' in a similar context: there some MSS have *exucta* which seems to be the true reading; and here '*exuctis* anguibus', the dried bodies of snakes, ought I think to be restored. If so, then F, which has *exactis*, comes nearer the truth than DVN with *exectis*, since nothing is easier than the confusion of *u* with the open form of *a*.

III vi 36 hac eadem *rursus*, Lygdame, curre uia: *rursus* FN, *cursu* DV.   III vi 39 me quoque *consimili* inpositum torquerier igni: *consimili* F, *cum simili* DV, *consuli* N.   III viii 1 dulcis ad *hesternas* fuerat mihi rixa lucernas: *hesternas* FN, *externas* DV.   III viii 34 *in te* pax mihi nulla placet: *in te* FN, *uitae* DV. ‖

III xi 21–4

> Persarum statuit Babylona Semiramis urbem
> ut solidum cocto tolleret aggere opus,
> et duo in aduersum missi per moenia currus
> *ne* possent tacto stringere ab axe latus.

So DV and most editors. Propertius says then that Semiramis built the walls of Babylon in such a manner that two chariots driven in opposite directions along the top of them *could not* touch. This is not only false but manifestly absurd: let Semiramis build her walls a mile thick, there will be nothing to *prevent* the two chariots from touching if you drive them against one another: to *prevent* this she must erect a partition, of which however history tells us nothing. What Semiramis did, according to history, was to build her walls so thick that two chariots could meet and pass, without touching, on the top of them. Now FN give *nec* for *ne*: taking this and Prof. Tyrrell's *mitti* for *missi* in v. 23 we get the required sense, 'et duo in aduersum *mitti* per moenia currus | *nec* possent tacto stringere ab axe latus', i.e. possent mitti nec stringere, could be driven past without grazing: the verb 'possent' is deferred by an artifice familiar to Latin poetry: see for instance Ovid met. XIII 360 'manu fortes nec sunt mihi Marte secundi', i.e. sunt fortes nec secundi.

III xi 44 baridos et *contis* rostra Liburna sequi: *contis* FN, *cunctis* DV.   III xi 48 nomine quem simili uita superba *notat*: *notat* FN, *uocat* DV.

III xiii 37   pinus et incumbens *lentas* circumdabat umbras.

lentas DVN; but the boughs of a pine are not pliant as Hertzberg and others assert them to be, nor if they were would that be any defence of 'lentas circumdabat *umbras*'. *letas* F, i.e. *laetas*, 'luxuriant': this word is perfectly appropriate, and *laetus* is confused with *lentus* times out of number, even so early as Virgil's capital MSS at buc. VII 48. Baehrens' conjecture *lentis* departs further from *lentas* and disturbs the Propertian balance of adjective against substantive. ‖

III xv 45–6   fabula nulla tuas de nobis *concitet* aures:
                              te solam et lignis funeris ustus amem.

concitet (*consciet* F originally) FN, *conciet* DV. Propertius is here trying to lay the suspicions of a jealous mistress who has doubted his fidelity. Whether then the *conciet* which Baehrens alone accepts be meant for the present of 'concieo', or whether for the future of 'concio', in the former case he asserts what is ex hypothesi false, in the latter he foretells what he cannot pretend to foresee.

III xvi 29 aut *humer ignotae* cumulis uallatus harenae: *humer ignotae* F, *humeri ignotae* N, *ignotae humor* DV.   III xviii 19–20 Attalicas supera uestes atque omnia magnis | *gemmea* sint ludis: ignibus ista dabis: *gemmea* FN, *semina* DV. III xxi 11 nunc agite, o socii, propellite in *aequora* nauem: *equora* F, *aequore* DVN.   IV i 65–6 scandentes quisquis *cernet* de uallibus arces, | ingenio muros aestimet ille meo: *cernet* F Lachmann Hertzberg Haupt Mueller Baehrens, *cernit* DVN Palmer.   IV i 129 tua *cum* multi uersarent rura iuuenci: *cum* FN, *non* DV.

IV ii 19–20   mendax fama, *noces*: alius mihi nominis index.
                              de se narranti tu modo crede deo.

noces N and most editors. But the erroneous derivations of the name Vertumnus from 'uersus amnis' and 'uertens annus' which false report has noised abroad are no way *injurious* to the god: they are merely incorrect. DV offer *uaces* which is accepted by Baehrens and makes very good sense, 'give over, lying rumour', 'be quiet': 'uacare' means much the same as 'cessare', cf. Sen. Ag. 87 'licet arma uacent cessentque doli'. But F gives what is obviously the parent of both readings, *uoces*: this is the older way of spelling *uaces*, and probably the only way Propertius knew, for 'uacare' first appears in inscriptions of Domitian's time. Our MSS indicate the same form through the slight disguise of *uorans* at II xxvi 54. ||

IV ii 33–4

cassibus inpositis uenor; sed harundine sumpta
Faunus plumoso sum deus aucupio.

So DV; but it is not apparent how 'plumoso aucupio' can be explained either as dative or as ablative. F has *fauuor* and N *fauor*, both very unreasonable corruptions of *Faunus*: and Mr Rossberg hence proposes *fautor*. 'deus plumoso aucupio fautor' I regard then as an allusive description of Faunus, giving the supposed ἔτυμον of his name. Mr Solbisky objects to this correction that 'ne ad sensum quidem apta est, cum deum non fautorem siue patronum aucupum dici oporteat, sed eum ipsum arundine sumpta aucupari'. Why not both? see III xiii 44–5 'si forte meo tramite quaeris auem...me Pana tibi *comitem* de rupe uocato.'

IV ii 52 atque Sabina feri *contudit* arma Tati: *contudit* FN, *contulit* DV.

IV vi 21–2

altera classis erat Teucro damnata Quirino
pilaque feminea turpiter *acta* manu.

acta DV, *apta* FN. At first sight the former may seem to get some support from Mart. spect. 6 6 'haec iam feminea uidimus acta manu', where however 'acta' has quite a different meaning. But the context decides: Propertius here depicts the two fleets as they confronted one another before the battle of Actium: the battle does not begin till v. 55 where it is opened by the shafts of Apollo and then 'proxima post arcus Caesaris hasta fuit'. *acta* therefore is premature: we must read *apta*, and therewith Markland's *femineae*: the dative 'manu' was misunderstood as usual: compare II i 66 '*Tantaleae* poterit tradere poma manu', *Tantalea* MSS.

IV vi 25 tandem aciem geminos Nereus *lunarat* in arcus: *lunarat* F, *limarat* DVN.   IV vii 9 et solitum digito beryllon *adederat* ignis: *adederat* FN, *ademerat* DV.

IV vii 85   sed *Tiburtina* iacet hic aurea Cynthia ripa.

Tiburtina F, *Tiburna* DN, V is erased. The reading generally || received and doubtless right is 'hic Tiburtina iacet aurea Cynthia ripa': the meaningless *sed* of the MSS is an accidental repetition from the preceding verse '*sed* breue, quod currens uector ab urbe legat'. F then has merely transposed *hic*: the other MSS have carried the error further by a blundering attempt to mend the metre.

IV viii 44 *reccidit* inque suos mensa supina pedes: *reccidit* N, *recidit* F, *decidit* DV.

IV viii 83–4

> dein, quemcumque locum externae tetigere puellae,
>   *suffiit ac* pura lumina tergit aqua.

The exact reading must be doubtful: *suffiit et* and *suffit et a* have also been proposed: but about the verb there can be no question; so that FN with *sufficat* are nearer the truth than DV with *suffocat et.*

IV ix 45–6

> sin *aliquam* uultusque meus saetaeque leonis
>   terrent.

aliquam F and modern editors except Palmer, *aliquem* DVN. Hercules is addressing women and proceeds to explain why women need not fear him: better then the distinctive form.

IV ix 52 puniceo canas stamine *uincta* comas: *uincta* F, *iuncta* DVN.   IV xi 20 in mea sortita *uindicet* ossa pila: *uindicet* F (N has not the verse), *iudicet* DV.

IV xi 101–2

> moribus et caelum patuit: sim digna merendo
>   cuius honoratis ossa uehantur *aquis.*

aquis FN, *equis* DV. Had Caligula made his horse a consul as he threatened, the world would then have seen what in fact it never saw, a 'honoratus equus': for 'honoratae aquae' no signification can even be imagined. But *aquis* serves for the base of Heinsius' correction *auis*, which was clearly read by the author, whoever he was, of the consolatio ad Liuiam 329 sq. 'ille pio, si non temere haec credun- tur, in aruo | inter *honoratos* excipietur *auos.*'‖

§14. *AF better than DV: spelling*

The following are passages in which the family AF gives a better or less vulgar spelling than the other. Baehrens prolegg. p. xi, describing certain character- istics of the MSS which his apparatus criticus does not record, mentions that the words *namque iamque quicumque* are spelt thus or with $\bar{u}$ in AFN while DV give *nanque* etc.; that AFN spell the compounds of *iacio* correctly, *traicio* etc. while DV write wrongly *traiicio* etc.; that AFN have *maestus* and *felix*, DV *moestus* and *foelix.*

I iii 15 *temptare* AFN, *tentare* DV; iv 25 *temptatur* AFN, *tentatur* DV; II iii 19 *temptat* FN, *tentat* DV; xii 19 and xix 21 *temptare* FN, *tentare* DV.

I iii 38 *ei* AN, *hei* DV (and also F, by an error which is its own and not its family's, as we know from A).

IV vi 40 *umeris* F, *humeris* DVN; x 11 *umeris* FN, *humeris* DV.

I viii 11 and xvii 8 *harena* AFN, *arena* DV; III xviii 3 *harena* FN, *arena* DV.

II xxxi 13 *Parnasi* FN, *Parnassi* DV; III xiii 54 *Parnasus* N, *Parnasi* F, *Parnassu* V, *Parnassi* D.

IV viii 3 *tutela* FN, *tutella* DV.

IV iv 1 *Tarpelle* F which points to *Tarpeiiae*, *Tarpeiae* DV, *Tarpelae* N; 15 *Carpella* (i.e. *Tarpeiia*) F, *Tarpeia* DV, *Tarpela* N.

IV x 29 *bucina* FN, *buccina* DV.

II i 10 *facilis* (acc. plur.) AFN, *faciles* DV; xxxiii 43 *absentis* F, *absentes* DVN; III v 45 *gentis* FN, *gentes* DV.

I vii 26 *fenore* AFN, *foenore* DV; III i 22 *fenore* FN, *foenore* DV.

I xi 28 *discidium* AFN, *dissidium* DV; II xxiv 32 *discidium* FN, *dissidium* DV.

II xxix 25 *ostipui* (for *obstipui*) F, *obstupui* DVN.

III iii 22 *cumba* F, *cymba* DVN.

IV i 120 *equs* (for *aequs*) F, *aequus* DVN. ||

III xix 19 *Clitemestrae* (for *Clytaemestrae*) N, *Clitemestre* F, *Clytaemnestrae* DV; IV vii 57 *Clytemestre* N, *Clitemestre* F, *Clytaemnestrae* DV.

§15. *Defence of AF*

At this point I pause for a moment to note how the facts which we have just surveyed confute Mr Solbisky's depreciatory estimate of AF and demolish his theory that this family is blent from the two stocks of N and of DV. To make the matter quite clear I will here enumerate the instances in which we have found F (A being absent from II i 63 onwards) giving the true lection, or the lection nearest to truth, while both N and DV give a false lection, or a lection further from truth. They are these: II iii 23 *num* F, *non* N, *nunc* DV; x 11 *carmina* F, *carmine* DVN; xi 1 *ne* F, *uel* DVN; xv 26 *uellet* F, *uelles* DVN; xx 23–4 *numquam* F, *umquam* DVN; xxii 30 *num* F, *non* DVN; xxxi 7 *steterunt* F, *steterant* DVN; III iii 11 *lares* F, *lacies* N, *alacres* D, *lacres* V; vi 28 *exactis* F, *exectis* DVN; 39 *consimili* F, *consuli* N, *cum simili* DV; xiii 37 *letas* F, *lentas* DVN; xxi 11 *equora* F, *aequore* DVN; IV i 65 *cernet* F, *cernit* DVN; ii 19 *uoces* F, *noces* N, *uaces* DV; vi 25 *lunarat* F, *limarat* DVN; vii 85 *Tiburtina* F, *Tiburna* ND, V erased; ix 45 *aliquam* F, *aliquem* DVN; 52 *uincta* F, *iuncta* DVN: and in the matter of orthography these: II xxix 25 *ostipui* F, *obstupui* DVN; xxxiii 43 *absentis* F, *absentes* DVN; III iii 22 *cumba* F, *cymba* DVN; IV iv 1 *Tarpelle* F, *Tarpelae* N, *Tarpeiae* DV; 15 *Carpella* F, *Tarpela* N, *Tarpeia* DV; vi 40 *umeris* F, *humeris* DVN. From this list I will subtract III vi 28 *exactis*, because this is a place where the lection which I have commended is a conjecture of my own; and I will subtract II xi 1 *ne*, II xx 23–4 *numquam*, III xiii 37 *letas*, and IV ii 19 *uoces*, because these are places where Mr Solbisky (pp. 154, 157, 166) expressly rejects the reading of F. There remain nineteen instances in which the family AF, represented by F, has alone preserved the truth or the clue to the truth. Now the enquirer who turns to ‖ Mr Solbisky's treatise in hopes of learning how he squares these nineteen instances with his pronouncement (p. 161) 'familiam AF nullius fere momenti habendam esse. ubicumque enim ueram lectionem nobis tradit, Neapolitani consensus accedit', – that enquirer will be surprised. He will find that Mr Solbisky quotes (pp. 159 sq.) four of the number, II x 11 *carmina*, II xv 26 *uellet*, III xxi 11 *equora*, and IV ix 45 *aliquam*, and admits that in these cases F alone is right, but considers them unimportant. About the remaining fifteen Mr Solbisky says not one word, and the plain fact is that he has overlooked them; for it neither is nor can be disputed that at any rate in the majority of these instances F gives the certain truth. The falsity of Mr Solbisky's conclusions regarding AF is thus very simply explained: it proceeds from his negligence in collecting his facts. And I fully expect that Mr Solbisky, a most candid disputant, will renounce his error when he is confronted with the evidence which has hitherto escaped him. For among our examples there are very striking tokens of integrity: the recondite *lunarat*, *Tiburtina* retained despite the metre, the form *Tarpeiia* disguised but thinly, the form *cumba* preserved. Though none in truth is more striking than the retention at II xv 26 of the unmetrical *uellet* which alone puts into our hands the clue to the genuine reading, a trait of sincerity whose significance Mr Solbisky does not apprehend.

Further evidence to prove the value of AF and the error of Mr Solbisky will be forthcoming in the next section.

29

REVIEW: K. P. SCHULZE,
*CATVLLI VERONENSIS LIBER**

The first edition of Baehrens' Catullus, which now that the second has appeared will fetch fancy prices, was in the rigour of the term an epoch-making work. But it exhibited a text of the author much corrupted by unprovoked or unlikely or incredible conjecture; so that the task of revision was delicate, and the choice of a reviser was not easy. It was not easy; but scholars who are acquainted with the history of Catullus' text and with the metres he wrote in, who know how to edit a book and how to collate a manuscript, who are capable of coherent reasoning or at all events of consecutive thought, exist; and to such a scholar the task might have been allotted.

It has been allotted to Mr Schulze, who says, 'Munus nouae huius libelli editionis post praematuram Aemilii Baehrensii mortem curandae ita suscepi, ut quoad fieri posset quam plurima eorum, quae ille ad Catulli carmina et recensenda et emendanda contulisset, retinerem ac seruarem.' Out of Baehrens' conjectures Mr Schulze has found it possible to retain six. The first of these is the merely orthographical correction 2 6 *lubet* for *libet* or *iubet*. Two more are specimens of Baehrens' most despicable trifling: 6 9 *heic et illeic*[1] for *hec et illo*, as if forsooth that were a less and not a greater change than the old *hic et ille*; and 21 13 *nei* for *nec* instead of the usual *ne*, as if *nec* were not a perpetual corruption of *ne* in the MSS of authors who never wrote *nei* in their lives. The three others, 68 139 *concipit*, 100 6 *egregie est*, 111 2 *ex nimiis*, are ‖ somewhat above the low average of Baehrens' conjectures.

But the emendations which place Baehrens next to Haupt among the post-Lachmannian correctors of Catullus are the things which Mr Schulze has not found it possible to retain. Take for shortness' sake the 64th poem only. I will not be unreasonable and complain that Mr Schulze omits Baehrens' correction of v. 73 *illa ex tempestate ferox quo tempore*; because I know that Mr Schulze has never seen or heard of that correction. It occurs in Baehrens' commentary, and Mr Schulze has not read Baehrens' commentary. That I affirm securely: if you ask 'whence then did Mr Schulze learn (p. 97) that Baehrens had proposed

---

* [*Catulli Veronensis liber*, recensuit Aemilius Baehrens. Noua editio a K. P. Schulze curata. Lipsiae, Teubner, 1893. Pp. lxxvi, 127. *CR* 8 (1894), 251–7]

[1] The text has *illei*, whether from a misprint or from an improvement of Mr Schulze's.

prompta at 68 39?' I reply that he learnt it from Schwabe's edition of 1886; and if you ask 'how does he know (p. v) that Baehrens abandoned in the commentary some of his earlier conjectures?' I reply that he knows it from Iwan Mueller's *Jahresbericht*. For if he had read the commentary he would not merely know that Baehrens abandoned some conjectures but he would know which those conjectures are; and he does not. He still represents Baehrens as proposing *quaecumueis* at 64 109, though Baehrens in the commentary said 'quam formam minime latinam non debui olim exemplis male fidis deceptus recipere'. And this barbarous and repudiated depravation, and the frivolous *heic* at 269, are all of Baehrens that Mr Schulze finds it possible even to mention within the 400 verses of the 64th poem. The transposition of 216 and 217, *nascente* in 275, *incultum cano . . . crinem* in 350, *residens* in 387, *Amarunsia* in 395, – these may be found at least recorded in the editions of other scholars, but not in this book which bears on its front 'recensuit Aemilius Baehrens.' The transposition is accepted both by Riese and by Postgate, the emendation of 350 by Riese Postgate and Schwabe, the emendation of 387 is approved by Schwabe and accepted by Riese and Schmidt: but no vestige of these corrections survives in the monument reared to their author's memory by the Oedipodean piety of Mr Schulze.[1]

Baehrens' are not the only emendations which Mr Schulze finds it impossible to retain or even to record. Which is the finest correction ever made in Catullus I will not undertake to say; but one of the first half-dozen is Froelich's 'non est sana puella nec rogare | qualis sit solet *aes* [*et* MSS] imaginosum', which Baehrens of course accepted. Mr Schulze ousts it for 'nec *rogate* | qualis sit: *solide est imaginosa*'. But no reader is likely to waste a glance on these Berlin goods if Froelich's restoration is left glittering in the apparatus criticus; so Mr Schulze does not leave it there: he suppresses it. *Quaecumque adeo possunt afferre pudorem*, says Ovid, *illa tegi caeca condita nocte decet*.

One clue Mr Schulze appears to possess: if he sees the name of Lachmann he follows it, 'errabunda regens tenui uestigia filo'. I say advisedly *the name*. At 63 5 he expels the emendations of Auantius and Bergk and writes 'deuolsit *ile*': it is not sense, but it is Lachmann's. A still more pleasing instance of simple faith occurs at 63 74 where Mr Schulze reads with Lachmann 'roseis ut huic labellis sonitus abiit *celer*'. Lachmann himself, 'uir egregius' as Haupt calls him 'et multo quam imbecilli capiunt maior', had a reason for adding *celer*: his theory of the pagination of the archetype made this verse the 18th line on the 41st page, while the 18th line on the 39th page was 'aliena quae petentes uelut exules loca *celeri*', whence he took the hypermetrical word to repair the deficiency here. But Mr Schulze does not hold Lachmann's theory, for on p. lxiv he retains a note of Baehrens' which says 'tota ista numerorum singularum in V paginarum paginarumque uersuum computatio a Lachmanno instituta et ab Hauptio

---

[1] 'Tam bene de poeta suo meruit, ut dignus sit, cuius memoria pie colatur', p. v.

[quaest. Cat. p. 39–49; op. 1 28 sq.] multis defensa ad nihilum recidit'; nor is it through inadvertence that he retains this note, for he has taken the trouble to write 'ab Hauptio' where Baehrens wrote 'a Hauptio' and to add the reference to the opuscula. He has abandoned then the basis of Lachmann's conjecture, but to the conjecture he adheres; and why not? its merit is not that he thinks it has a basis but that he knows it is Lachmann's. Again, when Lachmann has amended a passage, Mr Schulze allows no one to improve Lachmann's emendation, because he does not know whether the improvement is an improvement and he does know that it is not Lachmann's. At 66 58 the MSS have '*gratia* Canopieis incola litoribus', Lachmann emended *Graia*, and Baehrens improved this to *Graiia*, which Lachmann of course would have adopted, as any one can see who turns to his note on Lucr. 1 477 or remembers, as Haupt says, 'quotiens ex antiquae scribendi consuetudinis recordatione maxime Lachmannus in Catulli carminibus fructum ceperit.' But no painting of ‖ the lily for Mr Schulze, who ejects *Graiia* and replaces *Graia* in the text. I do not know all the salutations with which his idol will hereafter welcome him to Elysium, nor durst I write them down if I did; but from what happened to Eichstaedt and Forbiger I can tell that *mancipium* and *simius* are two of them. At the end of the note however Mr Schulze ventures on a suggestion of his own: 'fortasse *grata*'. It is news then to this editor of Catullus that for 300 years no text was printed with any other reading than *grata*: history for him begins with 1829: he supposes Scaliger and Heinsius and Bentley and the rest of them went on content with *gratia* till Lachmann came upon earth to tell mankind that it was a trisyllable.

This brings us to Mr Schulze's own emendations. One of these, *monendum est te* for *monendum est* at 39 9, is no worse than the *monendum te est* and *monendus es* of others, so that the odds against it are only two to one. Then in several places he writes *uoster* where the MSS are divided between *uester* and *noster*. Catullus may of course have used that form, but this divergency of the MSS affords not the slightest ground for thinking that he did: *uester* and *noster* are interchanged not in his text only, but in all authors whose MSS are medieval; and they are interchanged not because those authors wrote *uoster* but from the cause exhibited in Mr Schulze's own note at 71 3: 'u̅r̅m̅ VM: n̅r̅m̅ g.' At 10 25 sqq. Mr Schulze punctuates 'quaeso, inquit, mihi, mi Catulle, paulum | istos: commoda nam uolo ad Serapim | deferri', but omits to say whether this means 'I wish my emoluments to be carried to Serapis' or 'I wish to be carried to Serapis in an obliging frame of mind.' Finally he emends 29 20 thus:

hunc Galliae timent, timet Britannia.

Two metrical solecisms in one line.

Baehrens' spelling, which was bad, Mr Schulze has corrected as well as he knows how. He knows how to spell *sicine nequiquam* and *condicio*; so these words are rightly spelt. He does not know how to spell *umidus iucundus sodalicium* or *multa*; these words therefore retain their Baehrensian forms.

Baehrens' apparatus criticus was, as usual, a model of lucidity and order. Take a few examples of what it now is. At 68 140 the text has 'noscens omniuoli plurima furta Iouis', where 'furta' is an old and generally accepted correction for the 'facta' of the MSS. An editor who knows his trade expresses this fact by writing 'furta *uulgo*, facta V.' Mr Schulze's note is 'plurima facta VM plurima furta *uulgo*': to occupy the printer he writes 'plurima' twice where it ought not to be written at all; to delay the reader he puts the note wrong end foremost. At 113 2 is a still wilder scene: text, 'Maeciliam: facto consule nunc iterum': note of a competent workman, 'Maeciliam *Lachmannus*, Meciliā G, Mecilia O, Maecilia *uulgo*, Mucillam *Pleitnerus*': note of Mr Schulze, 'Mecilia OM Meciliā G | facto VM | Maecilia: facto *uulgo* Maeciliam: facto *Lachmannus* Mucillam: facto *Pleitnerus*.' Another revelation of the amateur encounters us in such places as 64 386: the text is 'saepe pater diuum templo in fulgente reuisens', which is the MS reading, so that of course there should be no note at all unless some conjecture is to be mentioned: Mr Schulze writes 'reuisens VM'. Why not 'saepe VM, pater VM, diuum VM, templo VM, in VM, fulgente VM'? Elsewhere Mr Schulze's ignorance of how things are done and inability to learn have made his notes completely unintelligible, and a reader who wants to know what the MSS give must consult another edition. Take 61 46 sq.: text, 'quis deus magis est ama-|tis petendus amantibus': note, 'amatis VM magis a magis *Scaliger* ancxiis *Hauptius* magis est ama-tis *Bergkius*': problem, what is the MS reading? From other editions you learn that it is 'magis amatis est'. These are the sights which may now be seen in what was once the apparatus criticus of Baehrens: for appropriate comments I refer the reader to Cic. *Phil.* ii c. 41 ⟦104–5⟧.

Now for the prolegomena. The prolegomena, I need not say, were the kernel of Baehrens' edition. In them he demonstrated, what no one suspected before but every one acknowledges now, that the Oxoniensis (O) and the Sangermanensis (G) are the authorities on which the text of Catullus rests. All that is now in dispute is whether the other MSS are quite useless, as Baehrens held, or only almost useless, as his opponents hold. His prolegomena are thus the chief landmark in the criticism of Catullus' MSS, and there were two reasons why they should have been kept intact: their intrinsic merit, and their historical interest. Errors they may contain; and Bentley's Horace and Lachmann's Lucretius contain errors, but Mr Schulze has not yet been invited to revise those works.

Baehrens held that G and O are the only ‖ copies ever made of the lost archetype V, and that the other MSS (ς) are all derived from G. His disputation ran as follows. When G and O disagree, ς almost always side with G; and they side with it not only in corruptions but in false conjectures which its corrector has introduced and which they cannot have got from any ancient MS: therefore ς are derived from G. On the other hand all ς, or nearly all, often agree in one reading when G and O agree in another: therefore ς, except perhaps the Datanus, are not derived straight from G but from an apograph of G containing conjectures. The few instances where ς agree with O against G are partly due to true conjectures in this apograph, partly, where the difference is very minute, to accident: the Santenianus (L) has marginal readings taken from O, but whether O was ever transcribed entire he doubts. Where G and O and ς all three differ, the reading of ς is conjectural. As to the Datanus (D), which has at least one interpolation from Thomas Seneca, none of its readings (*posquam, demostres*, etc.) are necessarily genuine but may be sham-antique: sometimes, like almost all other MSS, it gives better readings than GO, but these are conjectures: it is so interpolated that he does not trouble to decide whether it comes straight from G or through the same apograph as the others, for from G it comes: else why does it agree with G in error where O preserves the truth, and why, above all, does it reproduce almost every reading of G's corrector? questions which also apply to the rest of ς. He then discusses the marginal variants found in G: these must have been in the archetype because the scribe of G says he had only one exemplar: many of them appear in ς, which shows that they had most of them been copied into the apograph of G from which ς are derived.

Baehrens' arguments are now expunged, and in their place stands printed matter composed by Mr Schulze. He sets out to demonstrate that all our MSS come from a single codex, and fills more than two pages with passages which prove, or do not prove (the very first is 'I 5 *est* pro *es* codd. omnes sinceri' where of course 'sinceri' just begs the question), what might have been proved in two lines: I notice that this form of exercise is now much in vogue with amateurs who wish to be critics and think this is the way. The archetype, he holds, was four times transcribed: one transcript is O, another G: 'librorum OG praestantiam magnus numerus locorum ostendit, quibus *soli* [my italics] ueram lectionem aut certe meliorem quam ceteri *omnes* [mine again] codices praebent.' The list begins 'I 9 *quod* OG ς plerique: *quidem* ς complures', and contains '42 22 *nobis* OG ς plerique: *uobis* ς pauci' and '61 100 *uolet* OG ς plerique: *nolet* D, *nollet* AL': Mr Schulze is proving what is indisputably true and denied by nobody, and yonder is how he proves it. Then follow a number of places where ς agree with g (i.e. the corrector of G) in opposition to OG, and then (p. xliii) these incredible words: 'uel hac re eorum opinio refutatur, qui, ut Baehrensius et qui eum secuti sunt, omnes ς ex G fluxisse opinentur. nam cum codd. ς saepe cum G facere supra uideremus, qua re illi ut ς ex G descriptos esse putarent inducti sunt, hic non minorem numerum locorum congessimus, quibus ς cum g consentiunt.' And pray what is g? simply the corrector of G: the fact then that ς agree with the corrections found in G proves that Baehrens was wrong in supposing ς to be derived from G! This is no malevolent fiction of mine: it is what Mr Schulze has written and Messrs Teubner printed. But in the next sentence Mr Schulze faintly remembers what g is, so he says that if the corrections in G are derived, as he holds, from some lost copy of the archetype, 'manifestum est fieri potuisse ut etiam ς non ex G, sed ex eodem illo codice correcto fluerent': *fieri potuisse*! so evaporates our refutation of Baehrens. 'Atque adeo g ς inter se conspirant, ut ex eodem codice interpolato descripti esse uideantur': yes, and Abraham and Isaac were so much alike that they appear to have been brothers.

Next we have places where ς agree with OG against g; then 'Og ς saepius contra G facere uidemus', and of this 'frequent' phenomenon five examples are given, one of which is an example where it happens, and four of which are examples where it does not happen; then passages where D and the rest of ς desert G and agree with O are quoted, legitimately, though in stupefying disorder, to prove that ς are not derived from G. Some of these are places where G is wrong and ς are right, on which Mr Schulze remarks (p. xlvi) 'qua in re ut sane concedendum est facile fuisse librariis uitia illa corrigere, ita mirum est, quamuis sescenties in transcribendis corruptelis scribas summa religione uti uideamus, illas a *cunctis* [Mr Schulze's italics] felicissime esse correctas.' *Cunctis*! why, who ever dreamed of maintaining that each of the scribes made these corrections for himself? Baehrens, as ‖ I have related, held that ς were all derived from a single apograph of G, and that all corrections common to all ς were derived from that apograph. But because Messrs Teubner allow Mr Schulze to maul Baehrens' work out of all recognition, he appears to think that he can with equal ease obliterate it from human memory. Then passages are quoted where ς have the reading which by comparing O we infer to have been G's original reading now erased by the corrector g. All these examples of ς agreeing with O against G are of course valid *prima facie* objections to Baehrens' theory. Baehrens' answer was 'talia, si falsa sunt, mero casui adtribuas: sin recta, aut casui aut Italorum ingenio.' This perhaps is not plausible; but on the other hand Mr Schulze has no ground for concluding 'praeter duo illa apographa codicis V, G et O, tertium sumendum est, ex quo deriuati sunt g ς, uel potius, cum inter hos quoque D quidem et qui cum eo consentiunt et M insignem obtinere locum uideamus, quartum.' All readings which ς share with O they may have derived from O.

But in order to prove that ς are authorities independent of O and G Mr Schulze now quotes a page and a half of readings from ς which he thinks better than O's and G's. They are all obvious conjectures, except one which is an exploded corruption, one in which he misreports the MSS, one which is probably interpolated from Quintilian, and the following two: '65 16 *Battiadae*] *bactiade* B ς pauci: *actiade* O, *acciade* G. 66 5 *sub Latmia*] *sublamia* B: *sublamina* O, *sublimia* G ς plerique.' But *bactiade* may be a conjecture, as that was one of the many ways they spelt this name in the 15th century; and *sublamia* may be no more than a corruption of *sublamīa*. Therefore Mr Schulze is mistaken in saying 'nonnulla ea habent expressae sinceritatis signa, ut facere non possimus quin eis fidem habeamus.' Against the view that the good readings in ς are conjectures he has this notable argument: 'nemo quidem credet, eundem correctorem, quem aliis locis hominem indoctum cognouimus, hic illic mira sagacitate optimas correcturas suo ingenio inuenisse.' *Eundem correctorem*! Remember that on p. xlvi it suited him to assume that readings common to all ς must, if conjectures, have been made by each scribe for himself: now, when for instance at 64 120 he finds one MS and one only giving *praeoptaret*, and giving it merely in the margin, he assumes that this reading must, if a conjecture, have been made by the scribe of the common archetype of all ς.

Then we deal particularly with the two MSS which Mr Schulze regards as holding an 'insignem locum' among ς. First D, which 'ceteris codicibus hisce praestat locis': the places are 23 in number (and in several of them, since the list is of Mr Schulze's making, other MSS read just the same as D), some of them obvious conjectures, some bad corruptions, one probably interpolated from Seneca, one in which Mr Schulze contradicts his own apparatus criticus, and these two, – 1 2 *arrida*, 25 11 *insuta*, the latter of which is worth something if it is really in the MS; but these two readings are not found in D by other collators and rest on the testimony of Mr Schulze; and if any one, after hearing what I shall shortly say about M, chooses to accept Mr Schulze's testimony, let him. Then follow passages, proving nothing, where D 'optima tradidit' in company with OG or O or ς; then our old friends the 'priscae uerborum formae' which are no doubt D's most plausible feature; but Mr Schulze has drawn up the list, so it contains eleven which are also found in G or O or both: it is true that what he set out to prove was that D is not derived from O or G but from a separate apograph of V; but that was some pages back, so he has forgotten it. Lastly, crown of glory, 'uersum 65 9 paene solus tradidit', *alloquar audiero numquam tua loquentem*. Then are duly enumerated D's faults, its blunders and interpolations, among the latter 68 47 *omnibus et triuiis uulgetur fabula passim*, which would do D even greater credit than *alloquar audiero* but for the mischance that we know it was written by Thomas Seneca.

'Neque minus insignem locum inter ς codex M tenere mihi uidetur, qui et ipse magnum numerum bonarum lectionum praebet': this is the Venetus excerpted by Ellis. There follow two pages of these 'bonae lectiones', many of which of course are bad (one of them is 68 50 where M has the false *alii* and the right reading *Alli* is in O!), while of those which are not bad only one is peculiar to M. True, the reader would never guess this, for Mr Schulze only notes the agreement of other MSS in about a third of his examples, and leaves you to draw the false inference that in the other two thirds, where he does not note their agreement, they do not agree: in another writer this suppression of facts would argue fraud, but no such hypothesis is necessary in the case of Mr Schulze. ‖ Not one of the readings quoted has any sign of genuineness. But 'accedunt priscae formae': e.g. *Bithynia, Phrygii, coetus, labyrintheis, cachinni*! Others of these are not peculiar to M but found also in O or G or both or ϛ: the reader has guessed, before I tell him, that Mr Schulze sometimes states this fact and some-times conceals it. Others contradict his apparatus criticus, as 23 1 *seruos*. *Neptumnus* at 31 3 and *antemne* at 64 234 are not the readings of M but merely Mr Schulze's interpretation of its readings: it has *neptŭnus* and *antĕne*, which are identical with the *neptunnus* and *antenne* of other MSS. 'Etiam in his lectionibus complures sunt quas non ingenio scribae deberi manifestum est, ut' – then one of Mr Schulze's lists, comprising for instance 76 18 *extrema*, which is undis-guisedly a conjectural accommodation of G's and O's *extremo* to the gender of *morte*; and 25 5 *oscitantes*, which is in G, so that Mr Schulze need not be at all afraid of our imputing it 'ingenio scribae'. These readings, he placidly continues, are confirmed by the fact that most of them are found in other MSS (such is the 'insignis locus' occupied by M), 'whence we may readily infer that the good readings peculiar to M are also derived from V'. On this logic it is the less necessary to comment, because there are only two good readings peculiar to M. They are *thuniam* for *thimiam* at 31 5 and *hinsidias* for *insidias* at 84 2. And these two – does my reader flatter himself that he has lost by this time the power to wonder at anything? I promise to amaze him now – these two readings, the only two good readings peculiar to M which Mr Schulze can find, are not in M at all. They are figments of Mr Schulze's. A facsimile of M has been issued by Count Nigra and may be seen at the British Museum: the handwriting is beauti-fully clear and the ink is beautifully black: and M gives *thimiam* and *insidias* just like any other MS. We see then that Mr Schulze the collator is in no way inferior to Mr Schulze the critic, Mr Schulze the metrist, and Mr Schulze the logician. And with such a collation of such a MS has Mr Schulze sullied Baehrens' apparatus criticus from end to end. Worse: whereas he says that M is derived from V, he exhibits it throughout as an independent authority, and you find 'arido VM' at 1 2 and you find 'dabis VM' at 116 8 and you find 'VM' on every page between.

Last comes the question of marginal variants in the archetype. Mr Schulze has taken Baehrens' list of the variants in G, and has mixed up with it all the variants he can find in ϛ and especially in his precious M; and he, who has himself collated that codex, has done so without discovering what is patent to every one who sets eyes on the facsimile, that nine tenths of its variants are from a later hand. It is clear, he then proceeds to say, that these variants found their way into M and ϛ not from G but from some other MS: 'nam cum G octoginta omnino praebeat atque inde ab c. lxvii nullas, M 155 per totum librum Catullianum aequaliter distributas habet.' If you say you have three sons at a school where there are 100 boys, Mr Schulze will ask whether you are the father of the remaining 97, and if you disclaim the honour he will tell you that in that case you cannot really be the father of the three. But he has another argument: 'quodsi omnes ς ex G descripti essent, ponendum est singulares codicum O, M, B, L, aliorum duplices lectiones a scribis horum librorum fictas esse; id quod uel propterea fieri non potest, quod multae earum in textu aliorum extant codicum.' First, observe the ratiocination: because many of the variants in OMBL etc. are found in the text of other codices, therefore the variants in OMBL etc. which are not found in the text of other codices cannot have been invented by the scribes of OMBL etc. Secondly, it is not true that the hypothesis which derives ς from G compels us to suppose that these marginal variants have been invented by the scribes of the MSS in whose margins they occur: what one naturally supposes is that the variants in the margins of MBL etc. (I do not know what O is doing here, nor does Mr Schulze) have been taken from those other MSS in whose texts they occur; and this is what Mr Schulze must disprove before he will persuade any one that these variants come from the archetype. But he cannot disprove it: all he can do is to say 'nam si [30 9] in B *inde* al *idem*, in GDL *inde*, in O *idem* legitur, quis dubitet, quin in communi archetypo, codice V, duplex illa scriptura fuerit?' That V had the dittography is possible, since O has one reading and G the other; but B proves nothing unless Mr Schulze can show that it did not get its *inde* from G and its *idem* from O. He however, as if he had proved his point, sails away with 'iam cum M et B neque ex O neque ex G fluxisse certum sit...', and concludes 'itaque ea quoque, quae de uariis lectionibus codicum Catullianorum exposuimus, etiam codices deteriores quos uocant in recensendis poetae carminibus adhibendos ‖ esse aperte docent.' Yes, and if I had been in Venice a week before Mr Schulze and had scribbled conjectures of my own in the margin of M while the librarian's back was turned, Mr Schulze, who cannot tell one handwriting from another, would have copied them all into his list, and they would now adorn pp. liv–lix of his prolegomena, and he would be maintaining that M got them from the archetype.

Such are the contents of a book which carries on its title-page the name of Aemilius Baehrens and the monogram of B. G. Teubner.

30

THE MANUSCRIPTS OF PROPERTIUS [III]*

§16. *DV and AF equidistant from O*

I have now established that DV often preserve the reading of O where AF corrupt it, and on the other hand that AF often preserve it where DV corrupt it: here follow passages where the reading of O is preserved by neither family but is diversely corrupted in each and must be recovered by comparing the two. These examples constitute additional evidence for my contention that neither DV nor AF can be dispensed with.

I ii 23–4

>non illis studium uulgo *conquirere* amantes:
>illis ampla satis forma pudicitia.

conquirere DVN, *aquirere* AF. Propertius in this poem reproves Cynthia for the richness of her dress: beauty is best unadorned: it was not by any such finery that the heroines of story won their lovers but by their native charms; and then follow the above lines. What 'uulgo conquirere amantes' would mean we can see from Ter. haut. 446 sq. 'ea coacta ingratiis | postilla coepit uictum uolgo quaerere': the sense of the hexameter will be that the ancient heroines were not streetwalkers, Cynthia is! small wonder that Eldick altered *uulgo* to *fuco*. The pentameter and the whole tenour of the context shew what sense is wanted: the heroines did not try to win lovers by any addition to their beauty: we require something like the 'mercatus cultus' of v. 5 'naturaeque decus mercato perdere cultu' and the 'falsus candor' of v. 19 'nec Phrygium falso traxit candore maritum...Hippodamia'. Now the source of the divergency of the MSS I find in *anquirere*, corrupted on ‖ the one hand into *conquirere* by the frequent error *co* for *a*, on the other into *aquirere* by the abbreviation *ā* for *an*. Then for *uulgo*, remembering that *f* and *u* are often confused (IV ix 34 *uana* for *fana*) and that the compendium for *re* is often omitted (Sen. Ag. 161 *lango* for *languore*), I propose *fulgore*:

>non illis studium fulgore anquirere amantes.

I xii 19

>mi neque amare aliam neque ab hac *desistere* fas est.

* [*JPh* 22 (1894), 84–128]

desistere F, *dissistere* AN, *discedere* DV. Either the first or the last may be right, but it is perhaps most scientific to seek the origin of these variations in Heinsius' *desciscere*.

II xiv 5   nec sic Electra, *saluum cum* aspexit Orestem.

saluum cum FN, *suum saluum* DV: the latter is of course corrupt but probably points to the order *cum saluum*: this rhythm, the third foot ending with the end of a word, is common enough in Propertius but avoided by the Ovidian school with whose principles the copyists are imbued.

II xiv 29–32   nunc ad te, mea lux, ueniet mea litore nauis
                       seruata. *an* mediis sidat honusta uadis?
                   quod si forte aliqua nobis mutabere culpa
                       uestibulum iaceam mortuus ante tuum.

an FN, *in* DV. *quod* DVN, *quae* F. Propertius in this poem exults over the past night which has reconciled him to Cynthia after a long exclusion: he promises to render thankofferings at the shrine of Venus: then follow these verses and conclude the elegy. The above pointing, with its absurd interrogation, is Hertzberg's: I forbear to quote his long paraphrase since it is sufficiently refuted by the fact that it obliges him to render the *quod* of v. 31 (*quae* is of course impossible with his reading) as if it were *nam*. Baehrens punctuates 'nunc ad te, mea lux, ueniet, mea litore nauis | seruata an mediis sidat honusta uadis', which will apparently mean 'nunc ad te ueniet mea nauis, siue litore seruata sidat siue mediis uadis honusta sidat'! ‖ The conjectures, some of which assume that 'uenire litore' can mean 'uenire ad litus', are very numerous, but only those of Heinsius and D'Orville are any improvement on the text: I give the latter as the less violent: 'nunc *in* te (sc. 'est' or 'stat'), mea lux, *ueniat sua litora* nauis | seruata, an mediis sidat honusta uadis': the sense is good but the changes very improbable. I think the variation of the MSS between *an* and *in* will help us to a much easier emendation:

           nunc *a*[1] te, mea lux, *pendet*, mea litore nauis
               soluat, an in mediis sidat honusta uadis.

Propertius is now embarked on a new voyage of love: it rests with Cynthia whether his ship as it starts shall clear the shore or founder in the shoals. The error *ueniet* for *pendet* comes from the frequent confusion of *p* with *u* even in MSS much older than ours, Horace's for instance; the interchange of *soluo* and *seruo* is easy and probably recurs at II xxvii 14; then when *seruatanin* became *seruata an in* the metre required the extrusion of one word, and the one family omitted *in*, the other *an*. In the next verse I read *quae* with F: this connexive use of the relative is not common when it denotes the first or second person, but it

---

[1] *a* is given by one interpolated MS.

is nevertheless quite correct: Ovid met. IX 64 '*qui* postquam...*sinuaui* corpus', 382 sqq. 'care uale coniunx, et tu, germana, paterque. | *qui* (altered, just as in Propertius, to *quod* by the second hand of one MS), si qua est pietas,...frondes *defendite* nostras.' The *quod* of DVN appears to be irreconcilable with all readings of vv. 29 sq. yet proposed.

II xxii 49–50   et rursus puerum quaerendo audita fatigat,
                   quem, quae scire timet, quaerere *plura* iubet.

plura DV, *fata* F, N omits the verse. The lines describe the conduct of a lover 'speranti subito si qua uenire negat'. The 'quaerere' of the pentameter has plainly come from the 'quaerendo' overhead and has ousted some such word as 'promere': the suspicious lover questions his messenger again and again as ‖ to what he has observed at the lady's house. The *plura* of DV is faultless, but that will not content a scientific critic who notices that F has *fata*: he requires the common parent of the two readings; and this Mr Palmer finds in *furta*. The words *furta facta fata* are so much confounded in medieval MSS that when our text gives one we may take whichever we please of the three: at II ii 4 N has *fata* for *furta*. Then on the other hand *furta* closely resembles *purla* which would infallibly be altered to *plura*. The appropriateness of the word, 'infidelities', is evident.

II xxix 41   sic ego tam sancti *custos recludor* amoris.

custos recludor DV, *custodis rector* F, *custode reludor* N: none of these is defensible and the conjectures proposed are many. Propertius is relating how he stole to Cynthia's bedside to see if she were alone: she was, and on awaking upbraided him with his suspicions, 'quid tu matutinus, ait, speculator amicae? |me similem uestris moribus esse putas?' and so on. Burmann proposes *custos eludor*: perhaps *custos deludor* will best explain the phenomena in the MSS: 'thus I prove a fool for my pains in spying on my virtuous mistress': this sense of 'custos' is abundantly illustrated in the lexicons.

II xxxii 33–40   ipsa Venus, quamuis corrupta libidine Martis,
                   nec minus in caelo semper honesta fuit,
                   quamuis Ida [Parim] pastorem dicat amasse
                   atque inter pecudes accubuisse deam.
                   hoc et Hamadryadum spectauit turba sororum
                   Silenique senes et pater ipse chori,
                   cum quibus Idaeo legisti poma sub antro
                   subposita excipiens Naica dona manu.

hoc DVN, *non* F. In this passage as it stands the 'legisti' of v. 39 is nonsense: this poem is addressed to Cynthia; but Cynthia never went applegathering on

Ida with Silenus and the Hamadryads and the rest. Venus did; and therefore it is rightly held that Propertius here diverts his address to Venus; but the mode in which the MSS make him do so is wrongly ‖ defended, and is libellously described as 'Propertian'. From the practice of authors whose MSS are good and early we learn that either a vocative or a personal pronoun is required in such cases; and here instead of *hoc* or *non* I would write *uos*: 'thou, Venus, and thy lover were seen by the Hamadryads...with whom thou gatheredst' etc. The same correction of *hoc* to *uos* is to be made in Cat. 36 9: 'annales Volusi, cacata charta, | uotum soluite pro mea puella. | nam...uouit...electissima pessimi poetae | scripta tardipedi deo daturam...et *hoc* pessima se puella uidit ...uouere.' 'pessima' here can have no other meaning than 'pessimi' just above, that is to say it must be neut. plur. and mean 'pessima scripta': *hoc* therefore cannot be right. But neither can the old correction *haec*. Catullus began by addressing the 'annales', and not until v. 11 'nunc, o caeruleo creata ponto' does he divert his address to anyone else: thenceforward he addresses Venus throughout seven verses, and at v. 18 with 'at uos interea' returns to the 'annales' again. The poem is short and is composed with much artifice; and I call it incredible that at v. 9 he should so have lost his way as to forget he was addressing the 'annales' and to speak of them in the third person. *hoc* then should be *uos*.

II xxxiv 51–4
    harum nulla solet rationem quaerere mundi,
        nec cur fraternis luna laboret equis,
    nec si post Stygias aliquid *restauerit undas*,
        nec si consulto fulmina missa tonent.

restauerit undas DV, *restabit erūpnas* F; *restabit* N, whose scribe knew the quantity of *erumpnas* or *aerumnas* and accordingly left it out. *undas* of course is right, but the form *restauerit* is impossible in an Augustan writer. The vulgate is Wassenberg's *restabimus undas*, a very rough alteration; and instead of the harsh 'aliquid restabimus' one would look for something more like the 'si tamen e nobis aliquid nisi nomen et umbra | restat' of Ovid amor. III 9 59 or the 'si tamen extinctis aliquid nisi nomina restat' of trist. IV 10 85. Now the divergency of the MSS would be explained to perfection by ‖ supposing that the archetype had *restabiterundas*: DV then will have altered *b* to *u* and transposed the syllables *it* and *er*; F avoiding these errors will have altered *d* to *p* and transposed it with *n*. But this hypothetical reading wants but one letter to make good sense: Munro restores 'nec si post Stygias aliquid *rest arbiter undas*', 'whether there is really any such thing as the judge on the yonder side of Styx': the indicative amidst subjunctives is very characteristic of Propertius, see III v 25–46. Compare Ovid met. VI 542 sq. 'si numina diuum | sunt *aliquid*', amor. I 12 3 'omina sunt *aliquid*', III 3 23 'aut sine *re* nomen deus est', ex Pont. IV 1 17 'da mihi, *si quid* ea est, hebetantem pectora Lethen', 14 11 '*Styx* quoque, *si quid*

ea est', Cic. n. d. III 53 'qui hos deos ex hominum genere in caelum trans-
latos non *re* sed opinione esse dicunt', pro Sest. 71 'respirasse homines
uidebantur nondum *re*'; also Prop. IV vii 1 'sunt *aliquid* manes' and III v 39
sqq. 'sub terris sint iura deum...an ficta in miseras descendit fabula gentis | et
timor haut ultra quam rogus esse potest', and finally III xix 27 'Minos sedet
arbiter Orci', which suggested to Jacob the conjecture 'aliquis sedet arbiter' on
which Munro's is based.

III ii 23–4   aut illis flamma aut imber subducet honores
                annorum aut *ictu pondera* uicta ruent.

ictu pondera F, *ictu pondere* N, *ictus pondere* DV. The objection to the above
reading, the vulgate, as also to N's 'ictu, pondere uicta, ruent', is the singular
'ictu' where the sense requires the plural: hence the conjectures 'ipso pondere'
and 'tacito pondere'. But the *ictus* of DV will help us here: it is nom. plur., and
'ruent' is transitive as in Virgil and Horace. It would be possible to accept the
reading of DV entire, the 'strokes of years will overthrow them, crushed by their
own weight'; but the construction will be clearer and the corruptions better
explained if we adopt *ictus* from DV and *pondera* from F: 'annorum aut ictus
pondera uicta ruent', 'the strokes of years will overcome the massy piles and
cast them down': ‖ scribes unacquainted with the transitive use of 'ruo' found
this unintelligible and emended it as they could.

IV ii 5   *haec me* turba iuuat, nec templo laetor eburno.

haec me FN, *nec mea* DV: each family gives one word right and one wrong.

IV iv 55–8   sic, hospes, *pariamne* tua regina sub aula?
                dos tibi non humilis prodita Roma uenit.
                si minus, at raptae non sint impune Sabinae:
                me rape et alterna lege repende uices.

pariamne N, *patriaȵne* F, *patiare* DV. It does not appear to me that either 'sic' or
'hospes' is suspicious: 'sic' signifies 'on condition of my betraying Rome' as
she has just proposed; 'hospes' here as in many other passages duly registered
in the lexicons means merely 'stranger', and it is natural that Tarpeia should
call Tatius so rather than 'hostis'. But *pariam* on the lips of a Vestal virgin
overcome by first love is much worse than premature; and this reading is therefore surrendered by some of N's keenest partisans, as for instance by Mr Leo.
patiare, accepted by Baehrens, demands the alteration of other words which as
I said are not in themselves suspicious: he writes 'sim compar patiare', and no
slighter change seems adequate, for 'sospes' is refuted by the 'si minus' of the
next distich. The most probable correction proposed is Heinsius' *spatiorne*,
though perhaps *spatierne* is preferable: compare Verg. Aen. I 46 'incedo regina':

if the *s* were absorbed by the final *s* of 'hospes', it is clear that *patierne* might easily give rise to the variants we find in the MSS. Heinsius' 'dic' for 'sic' may also be right, though it does not seem necessary.

IV xi 69–70   et serie fulcite genus: mihi cumba uolenti
                     soluitur, *uncturis* tot mea fata meis.

uncturis DV, *nupturis* F, neither defensible; N is wanting here. The true reading was recovered long ago by the Italians, *aucturis*: compare Tib. 1 7 55 sq. 'at tibi succrescat proles, quae facta parentis | *augeat*', whence it also appears that we ought || here to write *facta* for *fata* with Kindscher and Postgate. In the first letter of the participle all our MSS are wrong; the second is preserved in F and corrupted in DV, the third preserved in DV and corrupted in F.

See also the passages quoted in vol. XXI pp. 139–41 [[this edition pp. 260–2]].

§17. *Doubt between D V and A F*

It has been established that the two families AF and DV possess equal authority as witnesses to the reading of their lost original. We shall therefore approach without prejudice the consideration of the following passages in which it is hard or impossible to tell which of the two is right.

I iii 31–3   donec diuersas *percurrens* luna fenestras,
                     luna moraturis sedula luminibus,
                     compositos leuibus radiis patefecit ocellos.

percurrens DV, *praecurrens* AFN. The former is read by nearly all editors and is quite satisfactory: 'luna' will then mean the beams of the moon. But if 'praecurrere' could mean 'praeter currere', to run past or in front of a stationary object, *praecurrens* would be still better: 'luna' will then mean the orb of the moon, hurrying along its path in the sky with the officious haste imputed to it in the pentameter. The lexicons quote no instance of 'praecurrere' in this sense: it means to run on in front of another runner or the like; but I agree with Mr Weber, p. 9, that we cannot with confidence deny to 'prae' in this verb the sense of 'praeter' which it has in praeuehor praegredior praeferor praelabor and praefluo.

I viii 11–16   nec tibi Tyrrhena soluatur funis harena
                       neue inimica meas eleuet aura preces

             .   .   .   .

             .   .   .   .

                       et me defixum uacua patiatur *in ora*
                       crudelem infesta saepe uocare manu. ||

in ora is the reading signified by the *in hora* of AF and the *in aͦura* of N. DV have *arena* which looks at first like a mere repetition from v. 11, and so it may be. But there is something to be said for the conjecture of the elder Burmann who read *harena* here and proposed *ab ora* for v. 11. His aim was to avoid the Leonine jingle 'Tyrrhena...harena', which however has a parallel in I xvii 5 'quin etiam absenti prosunt tibi, Cynthia, uenti': what most favours the conjecture is its introduction of the phrase 'uacua...harena', for which compare II xxv 7 'putris et in *uacua* requiescit nauis *harena*', Luc. VIII 62 'lustrat *uacuas* Pompeius *harenas*', Stat. Theb. III 334 '*uacua* iacet hostis *harena*'.

I ix 20 infernae *uincula nosse* rotae. *uincula nosse* AFN, *noscere uincla* DV: there is nothing to choose.   I ix 27 quippe ubi non liceat uacuos *seducere* ocellos. *seducere* AFN, *subducere* DV: none but factitious reasons can be given for preferring one to the other.

I xvii 25–6   at uos, aequoreae formosa Doride natae,
                         candida felici soluite uela *choro*.

choro AFN, *noto* DV: either is excellent, and the change is easy both ways. *coro tono noto* or *noto roco coro*. Mr Solbisky who prefers *choro* ingeniously suggests that *coro* was mistaken for *Cōro* and altered to the name of another wind for the sake of the verse.

I xviii 20   fagus et Arcadio pinus *amica* deo.

amica AFN, *amata* DV. They support the former with Claud. rapt. Pros. II 108 'quercus amica Ioui', the latter with Ovid trist. III 1 39 sqq. 'cur tamen opposita uelatur ianua lauro?...num quia perpetuos meruit domus ista triumphos? | an quia Leucadio semper amata deo est?'

II i 19–20   Ossan Olympo | *impositum*.

impositum DV, *impositam* AFN. Either is correct: perhaps however, as Hertzberg says, it is more likely that the termination of 'Ossan' should have led a scribe to substitute fem. for masc. than that the opposite change should have been made. ||

II v 21   nec tibi *periurae* scindam de corpore uestes.

periurae DV, *periuro* FN. *periurae* is clearly the simpler and better; and Volpi compares II xix 6 'nec tibi clamatae somnus amarus erit'. Yet it may be argued on the other hand, as by Mr Solbisky p. 144, that *periuro* is more probably genuine because less obvious. The accidental exchange however of *e* and *o* is so common that no great weight can be assigned to this plea.

II vi 20   nutritus *duro*, Romule, lacte lupae.

duro DVN, *dure* (= *durae*) F. It is hard to choose; and we cannot say for certain whether F speaks for the family AF or only for itself.

II viii 4   ipsum me iugula, *segnior* hostis ero.

segnior DV, *lenior* N, *leuior* F. I see no way to decide between *segnior* and *lenior*; unless we are to prefer the former because scribes are more prone to shorten words than to lengthen them.

II xv 49   tu modo, dum *lucet*, fructum ne desere uitae.

lucet N, *l̆icet* F, *licet* DV. The metaphor of *lucet* is poetical to a modern taste but hardly possible in a Latin writer unless there has preceded something leading up to it; I think it certain however that in this elegy many distichs are out of place, and probable that this line originally followed the couplet (23–4) 'dum nos fata sinunt, oculos satiemus amore: | *nox* tibi longa uenit, nec reditura *dies*.' On the other hand *lucet* may well be only a metrical correction of *licet* which Mr Solbisky supports with I xix 25 'quare, *dum licet*, inter nos laetemur amantes'; and possibly the true emendation is to insert 'o' before 'fructum' with Mr Lucian Mueller.

II xix 3–4
      nullus erit castis iuuenis corruptor in agris,
          qui te blanditiis non sinat esse *probam*.

probam FN, *meam* DV. The former is generally accepted; I am inclined however to prefer *meam* as conveying the same || meaning in a less obvious way. I would compare I xi 7 sq. 'an te nescio quis simulatis ignibus hostis | *sustulit e nostris*, Cynthia, *carminibus*', i.e. has seduced you and so removed you from my heart and consequently your name from its place in my songs; II viii 5 sq. 'possum ego in alterius positam spectare lacerto? | *nec mea dicetur, quae modo dicta mea est?*'; Ovid am. III 12 5 sq. '*quae modo dicta mea est*, quam coepi solus amare, | cum multis uereor ne sit habenda mihi'; Cat. 8 17 'quem nunc amabis? *cuius esse diceris?*'

II xxi 13 sic a Dulichio iuuene est *elusa* Calypso. *elusa* FN, *delusa* DV.

II xxiv 30–1
      iam tibi de timidis iste proteruus erit,
          qui nunc se in *tumidum* iactando uenit honorem.

So DVN; i.e. 'qui nunc se iactando uenit in tumidum honorem', a sentence by no means so contorted as many others which Latin poetry will supply: see for instance Munro on Lucr. III 843. But F has *tumide*, and it is possible that we ought to transpose *in* with Paley and read 'qui nunc se *tumide* iactando *in*uenit honorem': for a similar transposition of *in* see Pers. I 131 where instead of 'nec qui abaco numeros et secto *in* puluere metas' one family of MSS gives 'nec qui *in* abaco numeros et secto puluere metas'.

II xxxii 13   et *platanis creber pariter* surgentibus ordo.

So N, *creber platanis pariter* F, *creber pariter platanis* DV: all have *urgentibus* for *surgentibus*. Between N's arrangement and F's there is little to choose: that of DV is decidedly bad. But it explains better than the others how *surgentibus* lost its *s*; and Baehrens therefore may be right in reading *crebris pariter platanis*: for the construction he compares II xiii 23 'desit *odoriferis ordo* mihi *lancibus*'.

II xxxii 23–4   nuper enim de te nostra me laedit ad *aures*
                   rumor et in tota non bonus urbe fuit.

aures DVN, *aure* F. Schneidewin's *maledixit* seems the most ‖ probable emendation of the corrupt *me laedit*. But whether we should retain *aures* and alter *nostra* to *nostras* with most editors, or whether with Baehrens we should take the *nostra...aure* of F to signify *nostram...aurem*, is a separate question and hard to decide.

IV i 89 cum geminos produceret *Arria* natos. *Arria* FN, *Accia* DV: both are Roman names.

IV iii 7–8   te modo uiderunt iteratos Bactra per ortus,
                te modo munitus *hericus* hostis equo.

hericus FN, *heṅricus* V, *hernicus* D. The name of an eastern nation is wanted. Beroaldus proposes *munito Sericus*, Jacob *munito Neuricus*, and doubtless one or the other is right. If Beroaldus, then the *s* of *sericus* adhered to the foregoing word and changed it through *munitos* to *munitus*, leaving *ericus*, to which FN have merely prefixed the aspirate while D has further corrupted *hericus* into the well known name of an Italian people, V into a well known personal name of medieval times. If Jacob, then V is nearest the truth, D next, FN furthest away: the error *munitus* for *munito* will then be ascribed to the confusion of *o* with ꝯ the abbreviation of *-us*.

IV xi 25–6   Cerberus et nullas hodie petat inprobus umbras,
                et iaceat tacita *laxa* catena sera.

laxa DV, *lapsa* F, N has not the passage. The choice is a question of taste: I myself prefer *laxa*; and F is so carelessly written that we cannot be sure whether *lapsa* is the reading of its family or only a freak of its own.

§18. *N as a representative of O*

I shall here investigate the value of N considered as a representative of O the common parent of AFDV, and the nature and significance of its fluctuation between the two families AF and DV. ‖

We have seen that although N most commonly sides with AF there are nevertheless very many places where it deserts that family to range itself with DV. And we cannot help noticing that in most cases the side which N takes, be it AF or DV, is the right side: not in all cases, but in most. From this fact a hasty observer might infer that N is the most trustworthy representative of O.

But a little reflexion would teach him better. Take any good modern edition, say Lachmann's: we shall find that it, like N, sides now with AF, now with DV; we shall find that it, like N, usually takes the right side; and we shall find that it takes the right side much oftener than N does. But this virtue of correctness of course confers no authority on Lachmann's edition, neither does N's similar virtue confer any authority on it. For it is explicable by the hypothesis that N too is, so to speak, an edition, and has formed its text, as Lachmann formed his, by selection, achieving thereby the merit for which we praise an edition, correctness, and forfeiting the merit for which we praise a MS, integrity. The facts, I say, on the face of them admit this explanation; and when we examine them we shall find that they demand it.

I will first state the truth of the matter and then proceed to prove it true. N, so far as it is a descendant of O, has derived its text mainly from a codex of the family AF; but where it found the readings of that codex unsatisfactory it has resorted to a codex of the family DV and taken readings thence. For proof, I will begin at 1 ii 14, the first verse where all five MSS are present, and pursue the vacillations of N between the two families: the case will soon be clear.

19 '*nec* Phrygium falso traxit candore maritum' AF, *non* DV: the reading of AF is probably true and certainly void of offence, so N adheres to it. 23 'non illis studium uulgo *aquirere amittes (amictes* F)' AF, hiatus false quantity and nonsense: N cannot tolerate this, resorts to the other family, finds *conquirere amantes* there, is satisfied and adopts it. But I shall be disappointed if I am not thought to have made it probable, in my discussion of this passage above,[1] that *conquirere* too is ‖ false and that O had *anquirere*: if that is so, we learn here that N had not access to O itself but only knew the readings of O, as we do, through the two families AF and DV. 24 'illis *forma satis ampla* pudicitia' AF: N is disturbed by the false quantity, turns for help to the other family and takes thence the true reading *ampla satis forma*. 26 'uni si qua placet, *una* puella sat est' AF: another false quantity and nonsense too: DV proffer the true reading *culta* and N borrows it. 29 'unica nec desit iucundis gratia *uerbis*' AF: this is inoffensive, so N accepts it. But all the while DV give the true reading *dictis* which Ovid imitates at met. XIII 127 'neque abest facundis gratia dictis'. Can anything be plainer? when N agrees with DV in the truth, that is because N has been driven to DV by the manifest falseness of AF: when the reading of AF,

[1] p. 84 [[this edition p. 314]].

though false, is tolerable, N is contented with it and DV are left to tell the truth alone.

Here we are arrived at the end of the elegy: all this evidence against the integrity of N has been amassed within eleven verses. But consult the apparatus criticus where you will, its lesson is always the same: no fact presents itself which is inexplicable by my hypothesis: facts present themselves in abundance which are explicable by no other. If N has not formed its text as I assert, why does it never once agree with DV against AF in places where DV give the ill-looking true reading and AF the specious false one? Why does it desert AF for DV in places where the former are right though they seem wrong and the latter are wrong though they seem right? – such places as II xv 26 *uellet* F, *uelles* DVN, or IV vii 85 *Tiburtina* F, *Tiburna* DN? These phenomena are the tokens of an edition: an edition founded mainly on the text of AF and often adhering to that text where, though wrong, it is not obviously wrong; usually deserting that text where it is obviously wrong, and sometimes deserting it where, though right, it is not apparently right; adopting from DV many readings which are both easy and true, some easy readings which are not true, but never one true reading which is not easy.

Equally reconcilable with this hypothesis are certain phenomena ‖ which at first sight might possibly be thought to discountenance it. The fact that N not seldom agrees with AF in an obvious corruption where DV offer the obvious truth might seem to indicate that N had not access to the text of DV: for instance at III xiii 32 FN give *uiricoloris*, clearly wrong, DV give *uersicoloris*, clearly right: why did not N adopt it? But the answer is easy: operi longo fas est obrepere somnum: the editor's industry flagged or his attention wandered. Indeed, if we consider the difficulty of such a task in such an age, we shall rather wonder that these oversights occur no oftener than they do. Other phenomena which might be thought to conflict with my supposition are such as IV vi 25 *lunarat* F, *limarat* DVN: here F's reading is clearly the better, DV's clearly the worse: why has N adopted the latter? The answer is to be found in the fact that wherever this phenomenon occurs, and it occurs very seldom, the two readings are palaeographically almost identical. N has not deliberately chosen the false reading: it has merely made the same easy mistake in copying from the text of AF as was made by the parent of DV in copying from the text of O.

I hope therefore to have demonstrated the truth of Baehrens' assertion (prolegg. p. viii) that N, so far as it derives its text from the archetype of AFDV, derives it through MSS of the two families of AF and DV, not through an independent channel. To demonstrate this is to demonstrate the falsity of the stemmata codicum proposed by Messrs Solbisky Plessis and Weber: but that has been demonstrated already by other methods. Here I desire only to insist on the corollary that N, as a witness to the reading of O, is less deserving of credence than any one of the four codices AFDV. Wholly useless it is not, even in those books where A fails us N often serves to confirm the testimony of F and so to assure us better what the reading of the family AF really was. But the element of singular and transcendent merit which N possesses is derived, not from the archetype of AFDV, but from that other source which I denominate Z. ||

§19. *AFDV considered severally*

I will now examine the few instances in which one alone of the four codices AFDV preserves a true reading or a trace of the truth. From this list I exclude the unique readings presented by F in the absence of A which have been already considered and which would presumably be found in A also if that MS were entire.

A

It curiously happens that A exhibits, in the whole of the verses it contains (I 1 to II i 63), only one true reading not known to us from FNDV. This is the correct spelling *solacia* in I v 27 'non ego tum potero *solacia* ferre roganti' where the rest have *solatia*. And this solitary distinction loses something of its effect when we observe that A gives *cum* for *tum* in the same verse: it may well be that the archetype after all had the false form *solatia* and that A has merely blundered into the right way through its carelessness about *t*'s and *c*'s. In every other place where A gives a true reading, that true reading is also given by F or by N or by both.

The fact however remains that A is the most faithful representative of its family; and the following examples will display the nature of its value to us. The codex N, as we have seen, frequently deserts the family AF to side for the nonce with DV: now in these cases it is often only the presence of A that enables us to discover what the reading of the family AF really is. For F is most negligently written, and we cannot tell whether its blunders are derived from its exemplar or peculiar to itself unless we have A to set beside it. Thus at I ii 26 *culta* DVN, *una* AF, viii 1 *cura* DVN, *culpa* AF, xii 10 *diuidit* DVN, *diuitis* AF, xiii 5 *fama* DVN, *forma* AF, the presence of A informs us that F got these errors from X and did not itself originate them; and on the other hand at xi 6 *restat* DVNA, *monstrat* F, xvii 13 *uela* DVNA, *bella* F, xviii 31 *mihi* DVNA, *tibi* F, xix 4 *exequiis* DVNA, *obsequiis* F, || we learn that F's mistakes are its own. But so soon as A disappears we are left without a test, and we are taught its value by the perplexity in which its absence plunges us. Most of all do we miss it in sundry places where F omits a word about which DV on one side and N on the other bear contradictory witness. Take IV i 15 'nec sinuosa *cauo* pendebant uela theatro': *cauo* N, *suo* DV, om. F. Whence did N derive the true reading *cauo*?

and what was the reading of O? no answer is possible. Suppose now that A were present. If A gave *cauo* we should know *cauo* to be the reading of X, accidentally omitted by F, and also the reading of O, corrupted to *suo* by Y the parent of DV. If A gave *suo* we should know that *suo* was the reading of X and of O, and that N therefore derived its *cauo* from Z. If A omitted the word we should know that X omitted it, and though we should not know what the reading of O was, we should have little doubt that at any rate it was not *cauo*. And whatever A exhibited, it must necessarily teach us something which now we do not know. We suffer a like uncertainty through its absence at III xxii 23 sq. '*Clitumnus* ab Vmbro | tramite' (*litumnus* N, *liciminus* D, *liciinnus* V, om. F) and IV ii 28 'corbis *in* inposito pondere messor eram' (*in* N, *ab* DV, om. F).

Thus much in defence of A, lest any one should despise it because of the accident that in one place only is it the sole preserver of a true reading.

F

There is at least one passage in which F displays a striking superiority not only over the opposite family DV but over its own near relatives A and N: II i 31–2.

> aut canerem Aegyptum et Nilum, cum *attractus* in urbem
>   septem captiuis debilis ibat aquis.

attractus AN, which is indefensible; *tractus* DV, which will not explain the corruption. Baehrens and Palmer have independently arrived at the correction *atratus* which is accepted by Solbisky and others and will probably become the vulgate: ‖ the similar error *attractis* for *atratis* occurs at III v 34. Now F outshines A and N by giving *atractatus*, that is *atractus*: merely *ct* for the *t* of the true reading, and even this error corrected.

At I iii 40 it seems that F rightly gives *qualis* (acc. plur.) where ANDV have *quales*. Still more noteworthy is F's retention of this form in *leuis* at II i 49, where the agreement of DV shews it to be correct, while F's own brethren A and N have altered the inflexion to *leues*.

There is one more place where F alone exhibits what I strongly suspect to be the hand of Propertius; but this I fear is no more than a lucky accident: I viii 35–6.

> dotatae regnum uetus Hippodamiae
>   et quas Elis *opes* ante pararat *equis*.

opes...*equis* ANDV, *equis*...*opes* F: the latter arrangement, distributing adjective and substantive, 'quas' and 'opes', between the two halves of the pentameter, is preferred by the elegiac poets in general and Propertius in particular. But it appears incredible that so wanton an alteration as the transposition of the two words should have been made independently by A and by the parent of DV; and we are accordingly bound to suppose that *opes...equis* was the reading of O, and that F has only by an accident restored the correct order, if correct it be.

The above examples, let me say once more, are all drawn from that portion of the text which is contained by A as well as F, and exclude a large number of true readings, already considered, in which the singularity of F seems due merely to the absence of A.

D

D alone preserves the true reading in the seven passages which follow.

II iii 42 hic dominam exemplo ponat in *arte* meam. *arte* D, *ante* VFN.   II iii 51 turpia perpessus uates est uincla *Melampus*. *melampus* D, *nylampus* VN, *inlampus* F.   II ix 2 ‖ hoc ipso *eiecto* carior alter erit. *eiecto* D, *electo* VFN.   II xiii 12 auribus et *puris* scripta probasse mea. *puris* D, *pueris* VFN. It is possible that this divergency indicates *pureis*.   III xvi 25 di faciant, mea *ne* terra locet ossa frequenti. *ne* D, *nec* VFN.   III xxiv 33 [xxv 13] uellere tum *cupias* albos a stirpe capillos. *cupias* D, *cupies* V, *capias* FN.   IV v 36 natalem *Mais* Idibus esse tuum. *maiis* D, *malis* VFN.

There are also three places in which D has retained an old spelling which the other MSS have modernised: II i 23 *Karthaginis* D, *Carthaginis* VAFN; III vii 43 *uorteret* D, *uerteret* VFN; IV x 44 *gula* D, *gyla* VFN.

But the greatest service rendered us by D singly is I think in IV i 17–19, a passage which the other MSS exhibit thus:

> nulli cura fuit externos quaerere diuos,
>   cum tremeret patrio pendula turba sacro,
> annuaque accenso *celebrare* Palilia faeno.

That is, in ancient times no one troubled to seek after foreign gods and no one troubled to celebrate the Palilia; which is absurd, for of course every one cele-brated the Palilia: Lachmann accordingly restores sense by writing *annua at* for *annuaque*. But D points the way to an easier correction when instead of *celebrare* it offers *celebrate*, that is to say *celebrāte* or *celebrante*. The construction is 'cum tremeret turba, faenoque Palilia celebrante' = 'tremente turba faenoque P. celebrante' or 'cum tremeret turba faenumque P. celebraret': for a similar co-ordination of temporal clause with ablative absolute see Ovid met. v 362 sq. '*postquam exploratum* satis *est*, loca nulla labare, | *depositoque metu*'. The figure by which the lighted 'faenum' instead of those who set it alight is said to celebrate the Palilia is the same as occurs in v. 23 'lustrabant compita porci'.

D moreover, like A, makes its value felt by the inconveniences which attend its absence. It lacks the first elegy and the first 13 verses of the second; and within this small portion of the text there are at least three differences of reading which we cannot track to their source for want of D to help us. They are cases where a contradiction occurs between AF on the one hand and VN on the other: I i I *fecit* AF, *cepit* VN; 13 || *arbore* AF, *uulnere* VN; 22 *placeat* AF, *palleat* VN. These variations are susceptible of two explanations: that N has deserted, as it often does, the family AF and adopted the reading of the family DV; or that V, as it does not infrequently,[1] has deserted the tradition of O and adopted, apparently from the source which I call Z, the reading which also presents itself in N. If D were here and gave *cepit uulnere palleat*, we should know that the former explanation was right; if it gave *fecit arbore placeat*, the latter; but now we must rest in doubt.

V

V alone preserves the true reading in III i 26:

fluminaque Haemonio comminus isse uiro.

isse V, *esse* DN, *ille* F.

The case is less clear in III iii 41–2.

nil tibi sit rauco praeconia classica cornu
flare nec Aonium cingere Marte nemus.

cingere V, *tingere* DF, *tinguere* N. *cingere* is read by Lachmann Hertzberg and Baehrens, *tinguere* by Haupt Mueller and Palmer: I see no solid ground for a decision.

In IV viii 23,

Serica nam taceo uolsi carpenta nepotis,

if this generally accepted emendation of Beroaldus' is right, V comes nearest the truth with *sirica nam*: D has *si riga nam*, FN *si riganam*.

In two places V seems to preserve the genuine spelling: III vii 39 *triumphalis* (acc. plur.) V, *triumphales* DFN; II xxviii 49 *aput* V, *apud* DFN.

There is one passage more where V has perhaps retained a fragment of truth which the other MSS have obliterated; and I gladly seize the opportunity of discussing it by reason of its great interest and difficulty: IV v 19–20.

exorabat opus uerbis ceu blanda perure
saxosamque ferat sedula culpa uiam. ||

This gibberish should describe how an old procuress poisons the mind of the poet's mistress with her insidious counsels. In the first place the unmeaning *exorabat*, which some editors alter with no good result into *exornabat*, should be written *exercebat*: *o* for *e* and *a* for *ce* are common mistakes. Now what is the simile? plainly the wearing away of a hard substance by gentle and continuous friction. Three words at least, *perure ferat* and *culpa*, must be corrupt. *ferat*, for which *terat* and *terit* were formerly proposed, is corrected with certainty by

---

[1] pp. 115 sq. [[this edition pp. 337–8]].

Messrs Rossberg and Palmer to *forat*. Instead of *culpa* v gives *talpa*, and the same conjecture had occurred to Mr Rossberg who writes 'ceu blanda*que rura* | saxosamque *forat* sedula *talpa* uiam', most unhappily: if it is meant that moles burrow holes in stones, that is false; if this is not meant, 'saxosam' misleads and the simile comes to naught; nor is it any less ridiculous to say in Latin that a mole 'forat blanda rura' than to say in English that it tunnels the smiling landscape. Turn then from *talpa* to Jacob's conjecture *gutta* (*lympha* had been already proposed) which in capital letters is easily confused with *culpa*: we have now the favourite image of the water wearing the stone, employed again by Propertius at II xxv 16, as also by Lucretius Tibullus and Ovid. *perure* remains: *perurit* and *pererrat* are quite inappropriate verbs, and *terebrat* recedes too far from the ductus litterarum; moreover 'blanda', if it is to be an epithet of 'gutta', is absurd: I propose therefore to remodel the passage with these very minute alterations:

exercebat opus, uerbis *heu* blanda, *perinde*
saxosam *atque* forat sedula gutta uiam.

For 'uerbis blanda' see [Phaedr.] appendix fabularum 23 18 [p. 390 Burman (Leiden 1745)] 'qui, *uerbis blandus*, fraudem celat pectore', Hor. epist. II 1 135 'docta prece blandus': for the confusion of *perinde* with *perure* compare Ovid her. VII 86 where the MSS are divided between *inde* and *ure*. If now I am right in this restoration, V is perhaps to be commended as preserving a trace which has perished from the other MSS: instead of *saxosamque ferat* it gives *saxosam feratque*, which may mean that the change of *atque* to *que* came to pass through the transposition *ferat atque* || and the consequent absorption of one *at* by the other. But the change occurs in other places where no such explanation is possible, as at Verg. georg. IV 139 *idem atque* M, *idemque* P.

APPENDICES

f and v

We saw that, in many of the places where N gives a better reading than O, that same better reading is also given by f or v or both. It is therefore necessary to enquire whether f or v preserves any element of a genuine tradition which has not found its way into N. Here we must advance with extreme caution; for it is abundantly evident that many of the readings given by f and very many of those given by the various hands in V which Baehrens denotes all together by the sign Vm.2, and to which I am thus obliged to assign the single tally v, are the merest conjectures. Those only therefore among the lections of f and v can we reckon as genuine for certain, which preserve not the truth but a vestige of the truth, and which since they make no sense cannot be ascribed to conjectural emendation. But if we find that there are in f and v such lections as these, then we shall be disposed to refer to the same untainted source certain true readings in f and v which though they may be conjectural are nevertheless by no means easy or obvious conjectures.

In the following passages we recover the truth from relics preserved by f or v.

I XX 51–2

> his, o Galle, tuos monitus seruabis amores,
> formosum nymphis credere *uisus* Hylam.

'nunc tu seruabis amorem, cum hucusque nymphis puerum tuum credere uisus sis' Hertzberg; but if the poet had meant this he would have made more of it: we should have heard of Gallus' negligence at the beginning of the poem, not in the very last verse, where it takes us quite by surprise. Therefore acuter critics, as Lachmann and Baehrens, have held the line ‖ corrupt, and the latter after enumerating the conjectures *tutus nisus cautus fisus* concludes 'nondum uerum repertum est'. Nondum, in the spring of 1880; but it was found in the autumn. Instead of *uisus* v reads *rursus*, which, mark, being meaningless is therefore no conjecture, and would consequently demand attention even if no scruple were suggested by *uisus*. Mr Palmer hence emended 'formosum *ni uis perdere rursus* Hylam', 'unless you wish to repeat the loss of Hylas': *p* and *c* are commonly interchanged, so are *u* consonant and *f*, and *nīfis* means *nymphis*. But from the *uisus* of O and N we learn that Propertius spelt the adverb *rusus*: this form is often preserved in the best MSS of the best writers, as in Virgil's at georg. II 232 and III 335.

II i 27–35

> nam quotiens Mutinam aut ciuilia busta Philippos
>   aut canerem Siculae classica bella fugae
> euersosque focos antiquae gentis Etruscae
30   et Ptolomaeeae litora capta Phari,
> aut canerem *Aegyptum* et Nilum, cum atratus in urbem
>   septem captiuis debilis ibat aquis,
> aut regum auratis circumdata colla catenis
>   Actiaque in Sacra currere rostra Via,
35   te mea musa illis semper contexeret armis.

I have given what I hold to be the true reading of v. 31. I will at first mention only the variants of AFNDV: *cyptum* AN, *ciptum* F, *cyprum* DV. Cyprus is here quite out of place: the fact that Antonius transferred that island to the kingdom of Egypt is very poor cause for numbering it among the triumphs of Augustus: *cyprum* then is an attempt to make sense of the earlier corruption *cyptum*. To this therefore we turn; and I assert that palaeographically the old conjecture *Aegyptum* is easier than Baehrens' *Coptum*, since the loss of one *e* in the sequence *canereēgyptum*, and the change of G to C, together constitute a slighter alteration than is *y* for *o*. But it is objected that *Aegyptum* is bad in sense; 'neque enim' says Mr Solbisky p. 147 'nudum nomen eius terrae, quam poeta uerbis *Ptolomaeei litora capta Phari* et Nilo significauit, || medium inter haec interpositum esse potest.' Now as to 'litora capta Phari', this is that same misapprehension of the passage which led Schrader to write *aut* for *et* in v. 30 and *et* for *aut* in v. 31 in order that Pharos and the Nile might not be disjoined. All this will be refuted by the observation that vv. 27–30 refer to the *wars* of Augustus, vv. 31–4 to his *triumphs*: the point of disjunction is at the end of v. 30, and the contents of that verse may therefore be banished from our mind while we are emending v. 31. We have only to consider whether both Egypt and the Nile would appear in the triumphal pageant; and this question is easy to solve: Ovid trist. IV 2 41 sqq. 'cornibus hic fractis, uiridi male tectus ab ulua, | decolor ipse suo sanguine *Rhenus* erat. | crinibus en etiam fertur *Germania* passis', ars I 223 sqq. 'hic est *Euphrates*, praecinctus harundine frontem: | cui coma dependet caerula, *Tigris* erit: | hos facito Armenios: haec est Danaeia *Persis*', Sil. xvii 635 sqq. 'mox uictas tendens *Carthago* ad sidera palmas | ibat, et *effigies orae* iam lenis *Hiberae*, | terrarum finis *Gades*, ac laudibus olim | terminus Herculeis *Calpe*, *Baetis*que lauare | solis equos dulci consuetus fluminis unda, | frondosumque apicem sub-igens ad sidera mater | bellorum fera *Pyrene*, nec mitis *Hiberus* | cum simul illidit ponto quos attulit amnes.' I claim then that there is no excuse for refusing to *Aegyptum* its place in the text. And if *Aegyptum* is right, then f, which gives *giptum*, has preserved more of the truth than any other witness; for *i* and *y* may be considered the same thing in MSS like ours.

IV vi 25–6

> tandem aciem geminos Nereus lunarat in arcus,
> armorum *et* radiis picta tremebat aqua.

Instead of *et* v gives *q;* (= *que*) which contravenes the metre and is motiveless as an interpolation. A possible suggestion would be *armorumque radis*, for Pro-pertius has not only the genitives *Mari Deci Tati* but the nominative *Gabi*. But *picta* is unsatisfactory: to describe the water as 'picta' by the reflexion of the brightly coloured prows of ships would be a correct use of the word; but the reflexion of light from weapons || is virtually of one colour with the reflexion from water, and water which catches the light from weapons suffers no change of hue. Dausqueius and Heinsius therefore conjectured *icta*: the corruption is explained if we write 'armorum radiisque icta': for the elision compare I v 32 'non inpune illa rogata uenit' and III xxii 10 'Herculis Antaeique Hesperidum-que choros'. *q; icta* was taken for *picta: q;* was afterwards written overhead as a correction and then inserted in the wrong place, where only v preserves it: ON finding it incompatible with the metre alter it to *et*.

IV xi 29–30   si cui fama fuit per auita tropaea decori,
            et Numantinos regna *loquuntur* auos.

So DV; F omits v. 30, and N has lost the page which contained it. The line is nonsense and 'Nūmantinos' is a false quantity. Now f reads thus: '*aera* Numantinos regna *locuntur* auos'; and *aera* is also given by v. *locuntur* is not the spelling of a renascence corrector, and Baehrens is clearly right when with heinous infidelity to his principles he adopts it. *aera* again is no interpolation, since it cannot be construed; and *era* will explain the corruption *et*. Now as to the original sense of the verse there can be no doubt: it was '*nobis* fama per auita tropaea decori est': the 'si cui' of the hexameter, as Baehrens says, admits no other sequel. We may write   *aera* Numantinos *nostra* locuntur auos,

'the spoils of armour in our house tell of our ancestors who took Numantia'. The three first letters of '*nos*tra' might be absorbed in the three last of 'Numant*inos*', and the remaining *tra* corrected into the first word that came to hand. The above emendation was formerly proposed by Mr Palmer who afterwards abandoned it for the incoherent *Afra*. . .*regna* of Scaliger. Perhaps however a better way of obtaining the required sense is to read with Baehrens

        nostra Numantinos *signa* locuntur auos.

aera may well be a relic of *nostra* or *ñra*, as *sera* is at Ovid fast. III 738; and we had *signa* and *regna* confused in Prop. || IV ii 2 (vol. XXI pp. 123 sq. [[this edition pp. 248–9]]), where add Ovid fast. V 152. I should add that our singular indebtedness to f and v in this passage does not prove so much for their singular merit as did the instances adduced before; for it is very likely that if we could recover the lost page of N we should find *aera* there also.

    In the passages which now follow it appears that v or f has preserved the true reading corrupted by all our other witnesses. I exclude a great many instances in which the reading of v or f, though peculiar to themselves and indisputably true, may be plausibly explained as a conjectural emendation. For example, even the 'nigraque funestum *concinit* omen auis' of v at II xxviii 38 where the other authorities give *condidit*, even this reading, which is proved to be true by Ovid am. III 12 2 'omina non albae concinuistis aues' and was by no means easy to recover by conjecture, may yet be a conjecture after all. But in the cases here to be adduced this hypothesis is impossible or else highly improbable; and we have learnt from the evidence above that f and v contain at any rate some element of truth which is not drawn from conjecture.

III xv 7   tertius *haut* multo minus est cum ducitur annus.

haut v, clearly the source of *haud* O and *aut* N; and imagine a renascence interpolator of V, where *haud* stood in the text, spontaneously altering this approved form into the then unfashionable *haut*!

1 xi 9–12

> atque utinam mage te remis confisa minutis
> paruula Lucrina cumba moretur aqua,
> aut teneat clausam tenui *teutantis* in unda
> alternae facilis cedere lympha manu.

teutantis DVN, *tuetantis* AF, *teutrantis* v, i.e. *Teuthrantis*. This generally accepted reading is I think very plausibly defended by Hertzberg: Teuthras was king of Mysia, and from him the south-west of that country derived the name Teuthrania: now on that coast lay the Aeolic Cyme which was thought to have shared in founding the Campanian Cumae; '*Teuthrantis* ‖ lympha' (*Teuthrantis* a feminine adjective) therefore means 'Cumana lympha', probably the lacus Acherusius, just as 'Lydus' and 'Maeonius' often stand for 'Tuscus'. There may be some significance in the fact that Silius XI 288 bestows the name of Teuthras on a native of Cumae. It is worth mentioning further that in Sen. Herc. fur. 477 some MSS have *teutantis*, like DVN, where they evidently mean *Teuthrantis*, and that in Ovid her. IX 51 *Teuthrantia* is corrupted to *teuthantia* and in trist. II 19 to *teutantia* also. The verse wants no more change: when Baehrens prolegg. p. XXII enquires 'quid hoc noui est, per deos te oro, *in unda lympha te teneat?*' we reply that it is nothing new at all, any more than 1 xxii 6 sqq. '*puluis* Etrusca...*tu* nullo miseri contegis ossa *solo*' or the similar examples collected by Dr Postgate, Select Elegies p. lxviii.

1 xx 25–8

> hunc duo sectati fratres, Aquilonia proles,
>   hunc super et Zetes, hunc super et Calais,
> oscula suspensis instabant carpere *palmis*,
>   oscula et alterna ferre supina fuga.

After the vain attempts of others to make out that *palmis* can stand for *alis*, Hertzberg explains 'suspensis palmis' by the remark 'pendere et suspensum esse de omni uolucrum parte dicitur'. Perhaps; but when a man walks along the street, except he goes on all fours, his 'palmae' are no less 'suspensae' than if he flew: in order that Zetes and Calais may be described as flying, the epithet 'suspensae' must be applied to some part of the body which is not 'suspensum' except in flying. Thus Statius silu. II 7 4 with the words 'pendentis ungulae' depicts Pegasus as a flying horse: 'pendentis caudae' would not have that effect. Here instead of *palmis* v offers *plantis*, which should be accepted even if a conjecture; but a conjecture it cannot be unless we are to confess that an interpolator of the fifteenth century considered the passage with more attention than a long series of modern editors. I would compare Stat. Theb. VI 638 sqq. 'uix campus euntem | sentit, et exilis *plantis* interuenit aer, | raraque non fracto *uestigia* puluere *pendent*.' ‖

II ii 3–4

> cur haec in terris facies humana moratur?
> Iuppiter, *ignoro* pristina furta tua.

'Jove, I am ignorant of your old amours' may be instantly dismissed as non-sense. Hence Broukhusius Volpi Huschke and Hertzberg render *ignoro* as 'nihili aestimo', taking 'furta' to mean 'puellas amatas'. *ignoro* has no such meaning: it possesses, in some passages quoted by these scholars, the meaning 'I disregard' = 'I refuse to recognise' possessed by the English 'ignore': it does not possess the meaning 'I disregard' = 'I contemn'. When it is proposed to make the verse an interrogation, and asserted that 'am I ignorant of your old intrigues, Jupiter?' is Propertius' way of saying 'are they myths or realities?', I can only reply that, if so, it might be Propertius' way of saying anything. There is an end to all these desperate devices if we take the *ignosco* proffered by v and by the second hand in N: now that Propertius has seen how beautiful a mortal woman can be, he forgives the old amours of Jove with the daughters of men. The construction of 'ignosco aliquid' without an 'alicui', like the similar use of 'inuideo', is rare but not unexampled. *sc* is confused with *r*, and some MSS at Ovid trist. IV 4 8 give *ignoras* for *ignoscas*.

II xii 17–18

> quid tibi iucundum est siccis habitare medullis?
> si *puer* est alio traice *puella tuo.*

puer...puella tuo ON, *pudor...tela puer* v. The *tela* of v is universally accepted, for the *bella* of some late MSS will not serve; *pudor* too is adopted by all modern editors except Baehrens and Mueller; but at the end of the verse all read *tua*. Baehrens followed by Mr Lucian Mueller writes 'i, puer, en alio traice tela tua.' I assert that neither this nor the 'si pudor est, alio traice tela tua' of the vulgate explains the apparition *puella tuo* in ON. Such meaningless and unmetrical words are no interpolation but a dull and honest mistake: how did it arise? The change of *tela* to *puella* may have been caused, it is barely possible, by the *puer* preceding; but why *tua*, protected by the similar inflexion of *tela* or *puella*, should ‖ have been altered to *tuo*, it is hard to conceive. I shall essay to defend the reading of v; and I will begin at the beginning of the verse. Mr Lucian Mueller impugning 'si pudor est' says that 'priorem uersum respicienti non erit dubium quin Propertio, si apte uellet loqui, potius fuerit dicendum *si sapis*'. I reply by citing an epigram of Martial's in which the phrase is used with precisely the same shade of meaning as here: I insert in brackets parallel verses from this elegy of Propertius: Mart. x 90 'quid uellis uetulum, Ligella, cunnum? [Prop. 17 quid tibi iucundum est siccis habitare medullis?] | quid busti cineres tui lacessis? [Prop. 20 non ego, sed tenuis uapulat umbra mea] | tales munditiae decent puellas [Prop. 19 intactos isto satius temptare ueneno]...erras, si tibi cunnus hic uidetur | ad quem mentula pertinere desit [again Prop. 20 non ego sed...umbra mea]. | quare, *si pudor est*, Ligella, noli | barbam uellere mortuo leoni.' The formula is employed not merely in serious objurgation as at Iuu. III 153 sq. 'exeat, inquit, | *si pudor est*, et de puluino surgat equestri', but in mild or playful remonstrance, as at Prop. I ix 33 'quare, *si pudor est*, quam primum errata fatere', Ovid am. III 2 23 sq. 'tua contrahe crura, | *si pudor est*, rigido nec preme terga genu', Verg. buc. VII 44 'ite domum pasti, *si quis pudor*, ite iuuenci.' Mr L. Mueller makes the further objection that 'nisi antiquitus traditum fuisset illud *puer*, uix ac ne uix quidem in N [et O] pro *tela* scriptum esset *puella*'; and this is an effective argument against the vulgate but will lose all its force if we accept the whole reading of v. For then we shall hold that *puer* was not only 'antiquitus traditum' but placed where it had much more power to produce *puella* than at the beginning of the verse. In *traice tela puer* the letters *te* were lost after *ce* and then added above or in the margin; then from the elements *puer* and *la* and *te* the scribe constructed *puel-la te* and altered *te* to *tuo* for the metre. The reading of v, if not genuine, is a surprisingly subtle conjecture.

II xxix 35–6

> apparent non ulla toro uestigia presso,
> signa *uoluptatis*, nec iacuisse duos. ‖

uoluptatis DV, which is satisfactory enough, and of which the *uoluntatis* found in FN may be a corruption. But f gives *uolutantis*, which is approved by Lipsius and Heinsius and by Lachmann, who however thinks it may be a 'felix error'; and so indeed it may. An interpolation it can hardly be, since the word and the form are a far less obvious correction of *uoluntatis* than *uoluptatis* would have been. The postponement of *nec* (or *non* as O reads) is one of those concessions to metre so frequent in Latin pentameters: compare III xxi 16 'qualiscumque mihi tu*que*, puella, uale'. Hertzberg objects that the verb *uoluto* is too coarse for the occasion; but this, as Baehrens says, is to forget that Cynthia wounded by unjust suspicion is here speaking in anger and contempt.

IV iv 63–4

> et iam quarta canit uenturam bucina lucem
> ipsaque in Oceanum sidera *lapsa* cadunt.

With *lapsa* the addition of 'ipsa' is senseless: '*even* the stars have fallen': then something else has fallen; and what is that something else? the context gives no reply. *lassa* v, which immediately invests 'ipsa' with a meaning: 'the stars, weary like me'. Compare Sen. Herc. fur. 125 sq. 'iam rara micant *sidera* prono | *languida* mundo.' Again in I iii 45,

> dum me iucundis *lapsam* sopor inpulit alis,

one enquires 'unde quo lapsam?' and gets no answer: *lassam*, given by 'corr. V' (? = v), is intelligible.

I will now enquire what relation subsists between fv on the one hand and N on the other.

Baehrens prolegg. p. IX asserts that where Nfv agree together N has copied its reading from f or v. The assertion is baseless, for it is not yet established that even F and V, far less f and v, are older than N. And Baehrens himself is constrained to admit immediately afterwards that many of N's readings, where it differs from O, are not derived from f or v but from some other source: then why not all? Obviously his assertion will not bear serious criticism: it is only a surreptitious attempt to prejudice the reader against N. ||

Mr Plessis p. 39, opposing Baehrens' opinion, asserts that 'le contraire est certain, si F et V, comme je crois l'avoir établi, sont postérieurs d'un siècle et demi à N', a characteristic example of Mr Plessis' ratiocination: because f and v are later than N, therefore they are copied from N. This conclusion, to judge from the facts which we have just surveyed, is no less false than it is irrational; but I pause a moment to signalise the futility of the argument with which it is impugned by Mr Leo, who says p. 445 that the corrections of f and v are certainly not derived from N: 'satis hoc probat IV 11, 17–76 locus in N omissus'. Now the fact is that those verses are absent from N simply because the leaf on which they were written is now torn out. But assume what this very fact shews to be false: assume that N originally omitted them: what would that prove? merely that the readings of f and v *in those verses* are not derived from N. But we knew already, without this proof, that hundreds of the readings of f and v in all the four books are not derived from N: 'permulta' confesses Mr Leo himself 'ab N aliena a correctoribus in V et F interpolata, alia recte emendata sunt.' So even when we have granted Mr Leo his false premiss we find that it will not help him to his conclusion. Yet premiss and conclusion alike are accepted by Mr Solbisky p. 172.

But from the tedious though necessary task of refuting what ought never to have been written I return to the question in hand: what relation subsists between fv on the one hand and N on the other? In the passages just considered we find f or v or both together preserving elements of genuine tradition which N does not preserve: here at least then f and v are not derived from N. On the other hand at the beginning of this treatise we found N preserving elements of genuine tradition (I vi 3, III v 6, IV i 106, iii 55 etc.) which are preserved neither by f nor by v: there at least then N is not derived from f or v. Therefore, in those places where elements of genuine tradition are preserved by Nfv in common, we have no ground for supposing either that N derives them from fv or that fv derive them from N.

The simplest hypothesis is that which I have embodied in || my stemma codicum: that f and v derive these elements from the same lost MS whence N derives them. This supposition is consistent with all the facts before us. We have seen that Nfv often present the same genuine reading: that is natural, if their source is the same. We have seen that less frequently N presents a genuine reading not given by fv, or fv present a genuine reading not given by N: that is easily explicable: it means that for the nonce N has been copying more carefully than fv, or fv more carefully than N, the text of the exemplar. If however any one should prefer to say that f and v derive their genuine readings not from the same exemplar as N but from another MS closely resembling it, I should be unable to confute his opinion, just as he would be unable to substantiate it.

Agreement of V with N

I shall here bring together certain passages in which V quits DF, its fellow-descendants of O, and ranges itself with N.

II iv 17 hostis si quis erit nobis, amet *ille* puellas. *ille* NV, *ipse* DF.   II vi 11 me *laedit* si multa tibi dedit oscula mater. *laedit* Itali, *laedet* NV, *laedes* DF.   II x 10 *nunc* aliam citharam me mea Musa docet. *nunc* NV, *nāque* F, *nanque* D.   II xii 12 nec quisquam ex illo uulnere sanus *abit*. *abit* NV, *erit* DF.   II xiv 11 at, *dum* demissis supplex ceruicibus ibam, | dicebar sicco uilior esse lacu. *dum* NV, *cum* DF.   II xx 10 sint mea *uel* Danaes condita membra domo. *uel* NV, *nec* DF.   II xxii 16 et Phrygis insanos *caeditur* ad numeros. *caeditur* NV, *quaeritur* DF.   II xxx 1–2 tu licet usque | ad *Tanain* fugias. *tanain* N, *tanaim* V, *tantam* DF.   II xxxiv 30 nil iuuat in magno *uester* amore senex. *uester* NV, *noster* DF.   III iv 22 me sat erit *Sacra* plaudere posse Via. *sacra* NV, *media* DF.   III v 11–12 hostem | quaerimus atque armis *nectimus* arma noua. *nectimus* NV, *quaerimus* DF.   III xxiv 38 [xxv 18] euentum *formae* disce timere tuae. *formae* N, V in ras., *dominae* DF.   IV v 39–40 semper habe morsus circa tua colla recentes, | dentibus *alterius* quos putet esse datos. *alterius* DF, *alternis* NV. ‖

Now to consider the meaning of these phenomena. I hold that the reading in which D and F, representatives of both families, concur, was the reading of O, and that the scribe of V has employed for the emendation of his text the same codex Z whence N derived so much, or, if you will, another codex closely resembling Z. I think it unlikely that this hypothesis, which seems at any rate simple and adequate, will encounter much opposition; but I may call attention to one circumstance which tells strongly in its favour and against the explanation which might conceivably be offered, that the dissension between V and DF arises from a dittography in their parent O. The fact I speak of is this: except in the passage last quoted, where the divergency is so minute that it is probably a mere accident, the readings given by V are always the true, or at any rate the apparently true readings; and this is no slight indication that the scribe of V adopted them as I have suggested, with the deliberate intention of improving his text. In short I can hardly doubt that the fact is as I say; but since from the nature of the case no proof is possible I have refrained throughout the treatise from employing any of these passages to support my arguments.

The vulgar manuscripts

I shall here defend the thesis that all the known MSS of Propertius except NAFDVfv are worthless. So far as most of them are concerned this assertion is not denied, or at any rate no attempt is made to oppose it by evidence or argument. But some have had their champions; and it is the claims of these that I now essay to controvert.

First comes the codex *Groninganus* and its chief defenders Mr Luetjohann and Mr Heydenreich. I should observe that these scholars published their defences of this MS before the year 1880, and that possibly they now agree with me that it has been superseded by Baehrens' MSS, just as I agree with them that it had some value while Baehrens' MSS were yet unknown. ||

The following are the lections adduced as witnesses to the independent value of G by Mr Heydenreich, quaestiones Propertianae pp. 38 sq., from the first three books, and by Mr Luetjohann, commentationes Propertianae p. 6, from the fourth. I pass them singly in review.

I iii 27–9

> et quotiens raro *duxit* suspiria motu
> obstipui uano credulus auspicio,
> ne qua tibi insolitos portarent uisa timores.

duxti G. Easily explicable as a conjecture.

I viii 21–2

> nam me non ullae poterunt corrumpere, *de te*
> quin ego, uita, tuo limine uerba querar.

taedae G. Probably wrong; certainly unnecessary.

I xvi 23–4

> me mediae noctes, me sidera *plena* iacentem,
> frigidaque Eoo me dolet aura gelu.

prona G. A good, but not a difficult conjecture.

I xix 5   non adeo leuiter *noster* puer haesit ocellis.
nostris G. Given also by v.

II xii 18   si *puer* est alio traice *puella tuo.*

pudor…tela tua G. *pudor* and *tela* are also given by v; *tua*, I have above[1] attempted to shew, is wrong.

[1] pp. 111 sq. [this edition pp. 334–5].

II xv 47   *nec* certe merito poterunt laudare minores.

haec G. Given also by f.

II xvi 18   et iubet ex *ipso* tollere dona Tyro.

ipsa G. An obvious emendation.

II xvi 33–4

tot iam abiere dies, cum me nec cura theatri
nec tetigit Campi, nec mea *mensa* iuuat.

musa G. Explicable as a conjecture. ‖

II xxi 11–12

Colchida sic hospes quondam decepit Iason,
eiecta est *tenuis* namque Creusa *domo*.

tenuit . . . domum G. This reading, if right, is an easy conjecture; but it is probably wrong. That Propertius wrote

eiecit Aesonia namque Creusa domo

is in my opinion established by the following imitations: Ovid her. XII 134 'ausus es, *Aesonia*, dicere, cede *domo*', XVI [XVII] 229 sq. 'omnia Medeae fallax promisit Iason: | pulsa est *Aesonia* num minus illa *domo* ?', ars III 33 sq. 'Phasida, iam matrem, fallax dimisit Iaso: | uenit in *Aesonios* altera nupta *sinus*': compare also Prop. III xi 12 'iret ut *Aesonias* aurea lana *domos*', I vi 4 'ulteriusque *domo* uadere *Memnonia*', II iii 54 'mox *Amythaonia* nupta futura *domo*'. The classical but unfamiliar *eiĕcit* (= *eicit*) was naturally misapprehended by the scribe.

II xxii 45–50

hic unus dolor est ex omnibus acer amanti,
speranti subito si qua uenire negat.
quanta illum toto uersant suspiria lecto,
cum recipi *quae* non nouerit *illa uetat*,
et rursus puerum quaerendo audita fatigat,
quem, quae scire timet, prodere furta iubet.

quem . . . ille putat G. This reading (*ille* is given also by FN) is adopted by most modern editors and makes very good sense:

cum recipi, *quem* non nouerit, *ille putat*.

Certain however it cannot be called; and it may quite well be conjectural.

II xxviii 9–10

num sibi collatam doluit Venus? *illa peraeque*
prae se formosis inuidiosa dea est.

ipsa paremque G. I have already[1] discussed this passage and endeavoured to shew that *illa peraeque*, accepted by the latest editors Palmer and Vahlen, is the true reading. *paremque* is given by F as well as G. ‖

II xxxiv 33   nam *rursus* licet Aetoli referas Acheloi.
cursus G. An easy conjecture.

II xxxiv 59–62

> me iuuet hesternis positum languere corollis,
>   quem tetigit iactu certus ad ossa deus;
> Actia *Virgilio* custodis litora Phoebi
>   Caesaris et fortes dicere posse rates.

Virgilium G. A very obvious conjecture, and probably wrong: it seems more scientific to retain the dative *Vergilio* in v. 61 and write *mi lubet...posito* in v. 59: when *mi lubet* was corrupted to *me iuuet* the scribe changed the adjacent *posito* into the accusative but forgot to alter the distant *Vergilio*, which survives to indicate the truth.

III v 47   exitus hic uitae *superest* mihi.
superet G. Explicable as a conjecture.

III xii 35   ueteres arcus *lecto* renouasse procorum.
leto G. An obvious conjecture.

III xv 3   ut mihi praetexti pudor est uelatus *amicus*.
amictus G. Given also by DV.

III xvii 11–12

> semper enim uacuos nox sobria torquet amantes
>   spesque timorque *animo* uersat *utroque modo*.

animum...utrinque meum G. Explicable as a conjecture, and a bad conjecture: *meum* impairs the sense. The text can be emended by the simple substitution of *e* for *o*:   spesque timorque *animae* uersat utroque modo,

'hope and fear toss them to and fro like a wind': 'utroque' is the adverb (Ovid rem. 443 'secta bipertito cum mens discurrit utroque'), and 'animae modo' = 'aurae ritu' (Ovid am. III 4 14 'fulminis ire modo').

III xvii 30   *cingit* Bassaricas Lydia mitra comas.
cinget G. Given also by v. ‖

III xxii 5–6

> si te forte iuuant Helles Athamantidos urbes,
>   *et* desiderio, Tulle, mouere meo.

nec G. Explicable as a conjecture.

---

[1] vol. XXI p. 131 [this edition p. 254].

IV i 36   hac ubi Fidenas longa erat *isse* uia.

ire G. Given also by FDV.

IV ii 3   Tuscus *ego* Tuscis orior.

ego et G. An obvious metrical emendation: thus other of the inferior MSS insert *a*.

IV ii 58   haec spatiis ultima *creta* meis.

meta G. An obvious conjecture, but unnecessary and probably wrong: *creta* is defended by Plin. h. n. VIII 42 65 § 160 'peracto legitimo cursu ad cretam stetere'.

IV v 19–20

      exorabat opus uerbis ceu blanda *perure*
      saxosamque ferat sedula culpa uiam.

'*pererrat* G' says Mr Luetjohann. G does not give *pererrat*, which moreover is an absurd reading: it gives *perurat*, which is given also by v.

IV vii 65–6

      haec *summa aeternis* queritur liuere catenis
      bracchia nec meritas frigida saxa manus.

sua maternis G. A most elegant emendation, but not hard to find for anyone who was acquainted with the well known story of Andromeda. G apparently belongs to the latter half of the 15th century and was written in Italy, which by that date contained many scholars quite capable of the correction.

IV viii 68–9

      Lygdamus, ad plutei fulcra sinistra latens,
      eruitur, geniumque meum *protractus* adorat.

prostratus G. Again a good emendation. Mr Luetjohann argues that this can hardly be a conjecture, because there was no necessity for altering the text; but Italian MSS of this ‖ date are replete with unnecessary alterations, some wrong, some right.

IV viii 77–8

      colla caue inflectas ad summum obliqua theatrum,
      aut lectica tuae *sudet* aperta morae.

'*sudet* G, *sidet* N; ubi e G scriptura Kochius in symb. ph. B. p. 328 haud improbabiliter enucleauit *nudet operta*' writes Mr Luetjohann. He is mistaken: *sudet* is given by N, and by FDV into the bargain.

IV ix 21   dixerat; at sicco *torquet* sitis ora palato.

torret G. The alteration is not only unnecessary but detrimental: extreme thirst, as is well known, distorts the mouth into a grin.

IV ix 22   terraque non ullas *feta* ministrat aquas.

festa G, whence Mr Luetjohann would read *tosta* with Keil. It is true that *feta* is obscure and *tosta* appropriate; but the emendation is quite uncertain, and no editor has yet adopted it.

IV ix 38   Alciden terra *suscepta* uocat.

recepta G. Given also by FDV.

To these examples I add one more, put forward by Mr Ellis p. 393: II iii 21–2.

> et sua cum antiquae committit scripta Corinnae
> carminaque *quiuis* non putat aequa suis.

lyrnes G, whence Volscus conjectured *Erinnes*. Admitting for the sake of argument that the conjecture is right, I remark that G displays no peculiar merit, since v gives *lyrines* which is nearer yet.

We see then that the proofs of G's sincerity adduced by its defenders are ineffectual. They fall into three classes: readings which are false; readings which are explicable as conjectures; and readings which are given not only by G but by one or other of the witnesses NAFDVfv. Is it asked, Why may not G, in respect of the readings which it shares with NAFDVfv, be just as sincere as are NAFDVfv in respect of the readings || which they share with G? the answer is ready to hand in the simple fact that, while NAFDVfv give scores of sincere readings which are not in G, G gives no sincere reading which is not in one or other of NAFDVfv. This fact of course has only one explanation: G is derived from these MSS, or from some of them or from one of them, and possesses no genuine element drawn from any other source. The particular MS from which G does in point of fact derive the greater number of its readings is V corrected by v, as has been already observed by Baehrens prolegg. p. x.

Next I come to the *Cuiacianus* or *Perusinus*, perhaps the worst MS of Propertius in the world. It was written at Perugia in 1467, came into the possession of Cujas, was lent by him to Scaliger, exerted a deleterious influence on Scaliger's recension, and then disappeared from sight: for some two hundred and fifty years it remained 'inrepertum et sic melius situm', till in 1874 Mr Palmer had the ill luck to discover it in the library of a friend. The following are the passages, few enough, in which he has accepted its readings or built conjectures on them.

I xx 52   formosum nymphis credere *uisus* Hylam.

rursus P in marg., whence Mr Palmer elicits the admirable emendation which I have accepted in my previous discussion of the passage:[1] *ni uis perdere rursus*. But *rursus* is given also by v.

II vi 20   nutritus *duro*, Romule, lacte lupae.

durae P. Given also by F.

---

[1] pp. 105 sq. [this edition p. 330].

II xiii 55–6

> illis formosum *iacuisse* paludibus, illuc
> diceris effusa tu, Venus, isse coma.

lauisse P. Explicable as a conjecture and accepted by no modern editor but Mr Palmer.

II xiv 15–16

> atque utinam non tam sero mihi nota fuisset
> condicio! *cineri* nunc medicina datur. ‖

emeriti P, whence Mr Palmer proposes '*emerito cineri* nunc' cet., an alteration which deprives the hexameter of all relevant sense. The reading of P is due to the fact that *cineri* and *emeri* are palaeographically almost identical.

II xxxii 45   haec eadem ante *illam* inpune et Lesbia fecit.

illam iam P. An obvious and perhaps unnecessary conjecture. The MSS offer two more examples, II xv 1 and III vii 49, of hiatus at the caesura.

II xxxiii 11–12

> a quotiens quernis laesisti frondibus ora,
> mansisti stabulis *abdita* pasta tuis.

abbita P, whence Mr Palmer brilliantly recovers the truth: '*mandisti* et stabulis *arbita* pasta tuis'. I have fully admitted above[1] that *abbita* is a most extraordinary freak and has all the tokens of sincerity if considered in itself. But a freak and no more we are in reason bound to deem it, when we find it absolutely alone in a wilderness of depravity.

IV iii 11–12

> haecne marita fides et pactae *iam* mihi noctes,
> cum rudis urgenti bracchia uicta dedi.

This reading of P is accepted by Mr Palmer. If there is anything in my discussion of the passage above,[2] the sense is unsatisfactory; nor are the variations *hae sunt pactae mihi* and *et parce auia* easily deduced from this original.

IV xi 21–2

> assideant, fratrem iuxta Minoia *sella, et*
> Eumenidum intento turba seuera foro.

So Mr Palmer, taking *sella et* from P. It is given also by V, and is wrong: *et* is placed at the end of an hexameter by the satiric poets alone (Lachmann on Lucr. II 502).

In these passages only has even Mr Palmer assigned any weight to the readings of the Perusinus. The Perusinus then is judged. ‖

---

[1] vol. XXI p. 111 [this edition p. 239].   [2] vol. XXI pp. 148 sq. [p. 267].

The only other MS specifically patronised by any writer since Baehrens is the *Hamburgensis*: its patron is Mr Plessis, whose words I transcribe because such things must be seen to be believed: they occur on p. 41 of his études critiques sur Properce.

'Je trouve que le Hamburgensis n'est guère inférieur aux manuscrits de M. Baehrens et que Hertzberg n'avait pas tort de l'admettre dans sa récension. M. Baehrens lui-même accorde au Hamburgensis une mention honorable. Il dit que, parmi les manuscrits contenant Catulle et Tibulle avec Properce, c'est le seul qui mérite d'être cité [what Baehrens says is 'fortasse memorari meretur'] parce qu'il est transcrit d'après F ayant, il est vrai, déjà souffert des corrections. Cette dernière circonstance diminue la valeur du Hamburgensis aux yeux de M. Baehrens, qui n'en relève les variantes que de loin en loin avec celles d'autres manuscrits interpolés, sous le signe commun ϛ; d'après l'opinion de M. Léo et la mienne sur AFDV, le copiste de H a, au contraire, bien fait de tenir compte des corrections de F.'

Mr Plessis therefore admits that the Hamburgensis is copied from F, and yet would have us receive it into our apparatus criticus.

It remains only to notice the assertion of Mr Leo, p. 447, where after extolling N as the mainstay of Propertian criticism he proceeds 'librarii errores arguere ualebit e melioribus uulgaris notae libris quicumque eligetur. uerum AFDV omnino nihil ualent.' We have just tried and condemned the only three among the vulgar MSS which have been selected by any recent critic. When Mr Leo specifies his selections it will be possible to examine their merits: till then it must suffice to say that I have scrutinised the mass of critical material collected by Burmann and Hertzberg without discovering a fragment of genuine tradition unknown to us from NAFDVfv.[1]||

CONCLUSION

I hope that I have now made good the promises with which I set out. It has been demonstrated, against Baehrens, that N contains a genuine element which AFDV do not contain,[2] and it has been demonstrated, against Messrs Solbisky

---

[1] This is the place to speak as I promised, vol. XXI p. 101 [[this edition p. 232]], of the MSS to which Mr Hosius has called attention since this treatise was written. A collation of his Neapolitanus 268 has been obtained by Dr Postgate, who has been kind enough to inform me of its readings in a number of passages which I selected as tests. Mr Hosius' estimate seems altogether correct: the MS is one from which we shall get nothing new: at the utmost it may help to settle the tradition of the family AF when A is absent and F dissents from N. The same may be said of another new MS, Holkhamicus 333, an account of which was read by Dr Postgate before the Cambridge Philological Society on May 11. I expect more from Mr Hosius' Vrbinas 641 and from a closely similar Paris codex, the Memmianus of Passerat, my knowledge of which I owe to Dr Postgate. These two MSS are akin to N and on the whole decidedly inferior to it; but I think it possible that they here and there preserve the Z element even better. I base this opinion chiefly on the *Tarpeiius* quoted from both at IV i 7: another example will be their *seloni* at IV i 31 if my conjecture *seueri* is true.

[2] vol. XXI pp. 110 sqq. [[pp. 238–57]].

Plessis and Weber, that this genuine element in N is not derived from the archetype of AFDV but from an independent source[1] whence f and v have also derived a genuine element not possessed by AFDV.[2] It has further been shewn that N contains a second element drawn from a MS of the family AF, and a third and smaller element drawn from a MS of the family DV.[3] It has been demonstrated, against Mr Leo, that AFDV contain a genuine element which N does not contain,[4] and it has been demonstrated, against Mr Solbisky, that the two families AF and DV deserve equal credence as witnesses to the reading of their archetype O.[5] It has been shewn also that each one of the four codices AFDV preserves fragments of truth peculiar to itself.[6]

It is proved therefore that the cardinal MSS are related to one another as I asserted in my second thesis. Hence follows as a necessary consequence the truth of my first thesis: that the seven authorities NAFDVfv are independent witnesses and must all be employed if we would reconstruct the Propertian archetype. ||

Finally it has been shewn that the residue of the MSS exhibit no element of genuine tradition not possessed by one or other of these,[7] whence it follows that they are derived from these, and are therefore to be cast aside.

I add a few remarks on certain matters connected with our subject.

In my stemma codicum, following the accepted practice, I have expressed the threefold origin of N in the simplest form by three lines converging on that MS from its three sources. I am not however to be understood as implying that N was copied directly from these: that indeed I think incredible: but since it is impossible to say how many steps separate N from each of its ancestors, any more detailed scheme would be purely conjectural and almost certainly wrong. Here however I will indicate one method by which the text of N may have been formed. Let us imagine a codex α of the family AF: there comes a scribe who employs this as his exemplar but has also at hand a codex β of the family DV to which he turns for help when α puzzles him: thus equipped he executes a copy which we will call γ. The owner of γ lights upon the codex Z which has an unmistakable air of high antiquity, and he reverentially copies thence a great number of readings into his own codex γ, just as v has copied a great number of them into V. Then comes a scribe who employs γ as his exemplar and, in transcribing it, incorporates in his copy the readings of Z appearing in the margin, which he takes to be meant for corrections, just as the Groninganus, in transcribing V, has incorporated many of the readings of v. The copy thus

---

[1] vol. xxi pp. 135–8 [[this edition pp. 257–60]].   [2] pp. 105–15 [[pp. 329–37]].
[3] pp. 95–8 [[pp. 322–5]].   [4] vol. xxi pp. 149 sqq. [[pp. 268–78]].
[5] vol. xxi pp. 168 sqq. [[pp. 282 sqq.]].   [6] pp. 99–105 [[pp. 325–9]].
[7] pp. 116–24 [[pp. 338–44]].

formed is our N. All this is a mere flight of the imagination; but my aim is to leave nothing obscure, and to shew that, although we cannot trace how the confluence into N of the three streams of tradition actually came to pass, that confluence itself is a matter of no difficulty.

It will be observed that in discussing the merits and the faults of N I have eschewed all reference to the vexed question || of its date. This I have done for two reasons. First, the date of N, being still in dispute, cannot legitimately be made the foundation of an argument. Secondly, the date of N is immaterial to our estimate of its worth. If it were proved to belong, as Messrs Keil and Plessis contend, to the 12th century, that would indeed confute Baehrens' estimate of it; but then I think I have confuted Baehrens' estimate already without this help. If on the other hand it were proved to be written, as Baehrens contends, later than 1430, that fact would not one whit discredit the proofs of its sincerity amassed in these pages, because those proofs are intrinsic. I myself however incline, I confess, to suspect that N is not earlier than the 15th century, for the following reason. Mr Lucian Mueller praef. p. ix, while conceding that its handwriting in some respects though not in all resembles that of the 12th or even the 11th century, has the words 'quid quod ipsae membranae saeculum xv potius quam XIII referre uidebantur?'; and Baehrens too prolegg. p. viii says 'certe ipsae cartae non priores saeculo xv'. Now this statement, true or false, has never been contradicted. Mr Plessis devotes a whole chapter, pp. 6–18, to this MS: he has much to say on the antique aspect of its writing; but not by one word does he so much as attempt to refute the assertion that the parchment on which it is written is of the 15th century. If then I give, as I am bound to give, equal credence to the two parties in the dispute, I must deem the date assigned to N by Mueller and Baehrens the more probable; since it seems easier for a man living in the 15th century to imitate the writing of the 12th than for a man living in the 12th to imitate the writing materials of the 15th.

Which is the best MS of Propertius? There is no best MS of Propertius. But if we were compelled to choose two MSS, and to construct our text from them alone, the choice would be easy: they should be N and D, because they best supply one another's defects. D is not only the best representative of the family DV but it is the best representative of O; for, though the family AF is quite equal to the family DV, neither A nor F || represents its family so well as D represents the other, since A is mutilated and F is carelessly written by an illiterate man. N on the other hand, exceedingly untrustworthy as a representative of O, contains a large element of truth derived from Z to which D had no access, and moreover has drawn even from O, through the family AF, a great deal which serves to supplement the testimony of D. Possessing these two MSS we should still lack many true readings of the family AF which F alone preserves, and many true readings from Z presented only by f or v; but no other two MSS would leave us lacking so little.

To conclude: I design this treatise for a defence of eclecticism, but of eclecticism within scientific bounds. The student of an ancient text has two enemies. There is the devotee of system who prefers simplicity to truth, and who having half learnt from Madvig and Bekker the great lesson of our century, *magnam et inconditam testium turbam ad paucos et certos esse redigendam, a quibus ceteri rem acceperint*, selects his few witnesses without ascertaining if they were really the informants of the rest, constructs a neat apparatus at whatever cost to the text of his hapless author, and seeks to overawe the timid by sonorous talk about 'sanae artis praecepta omnia'; and there is the born hater of science who ransacks Europe for waste paper that he may fill his pages to half their height with the lees of the Italian renascence, and then by appeals to the reader's superstition would persuade him to hope without reason and against likelihood that he will gather grapes of thorns and figs of thistles. Here is my attempt to fortify against delusion on either hand the student of at least one Latin author.

31

A NOTE ON VIRGIL*

Virgil Aen. I 393–400

Aspice bis senos laetantis agmine cycnos,
aetheria quos lapsa plaga Iouis ales aperto
turbabat caelo: nunc terras ordine longo
aut capere aut captas iam despectare uidentur.
ut reduces illi ludunt stridentibus alis
et coetu cinxere polum cantusque dedere,
haut aliter puppesque tuae pubesque tuorum
aut portum tenet aut pleno subit ostia uelo.

395

400

'I am not a bird' said the Irishman 'to be in two places at once'; and it is
another injustice to his distressful country that we call this speech a bull. The
bird which is in two places at once is the Virgilian swan. Aeneas is bidden to
behold these fowl alighting or alighted on the earth, and with the same breath
is told that even as they are sporting together in the zenith, so are his scattered
ships united in the harbour or the harbour-mouth. To evade the contradiction
they propose to give the perfects in v. 398 the force which the perfect has for
instance in 'fuimus Troes', and to interpret the line 'and have ceased from
circling the sky and from singing'. This interpretation is so obscure to its own
inventors that they cannot agree when it was that the circling and singing took
place, Ladewig and Wagner putting it before the swoop of the eagle, Weickert
and Forbiger afterwards. But this doubt may be set on one side: it is apparent
that unless the verse forms one picture with the verse preceding it, and describes,
as that describes, the present doings of || the swans, it has no part to play in the
simile and tallies with nothing in the apodosis introduced by 'haut aliter' which
describes the present doings of the ships and not what the ships have ceased to
do. Accordingly Ladewig professes himself dissatisfied with his own explanation, and Weidner declares that he can make nothing of the verse and would
willingly strike it out. Conington offers the remark that the words 'coetu
cinxere polum' are 'evidently ornamental and only vaguely descriptive'. To

* [TCPhS 3 (1894), 239–41: summarized in PCPhS 1892, 6–7]

say that swans are doing what they are not doing may be ornamental, but I deny that it is even vaguely descriptive.

Now it will be seen that if *terras* in v. 395 were altered to some such word as *nubes* the contradiction would vanish and the verses would give no difficulty.[1] A while ago the swans were pursuing their voyage overhead, when an eagle swooped from the empyrean and scattered them abroad; but now with their column formed anew they are soaring to the – clouds, let us say, – and above the clouds: even as they are reunited and rejoicing in the sky, so are the ships in the haven. And it must further be reckoned as a point in favour of some such change that 'terras captas iam despectare', or 'respectare' as the Palatine has it, is a phrase which has caused great dissension and perplexity, whereas the words 'nubes aut capere aut captas iam despectare', 'scaling the clouds or looking down on the clouds they have scaled', appear straightforward and simple. If then the place of *terras* is to be taken by some word signifying the sky, that word can hardly be other than *stellas*. Ribbeck in his prolegomena quotes from Virgil's capital MSS thirteen clear instances of *l* confused with *r*, and the list is not exhaustive: it may be an error of the ear, but the shapes of the two letters are much alike in the ancient cursive which has left its few remains at Pompei and on certain cinerary urns of the Augustan epoch. In this script also the resemblance between *s* and *c* is close enough to render easy the loss of the first letter in *stellas* after the last in *nunc*: of this ‖ confusion Ribbeck gives sixteen examples. The hyperbole to my taste is frigid, but unhappily it has many frigid hyperboles to keep it company. In the georgics and bucolics such things are not found; but of the Aeneid I can only say with Markland 'plurima esse in isto Poemate, quae, si ego (pessimus omnium poeta) uersus scriberem, nollem in meis conspici'. Virgil never meant them for our eyes: Donatus or rather Suetonius relates of him that 'ne quid impetum moraretur, quaedam imperfecta transmisit, alia leuissimis uersibus ueluti fulsit, quos per iocum pro tibicinibus interponi aiebat ad sustinendum opus, donec solidae columnae aduenirent.' Lucretius too is full of this temporary scaffolding, but in him such verses are apt rather to be crude and prosaic; in Virgil they oftenest have a false intensity, and this is not the only passage where he soars too near the stars: compare III 423 'Charybdis...sidera uerberat unda', 567 'ter spumam elisam et rorantia uidimus astra', 619 'ipse arduus altaque pulsat | sidera'. Our instance, softened as it is by 'uidentur', is less extravagant than these and approaches rather V 517 (columba) 'decidit exanimis uitamque reliquit in astris | aetheriis' or X 193 'Cycnum...linquentem terras et sidera uoce sequentem'. The closest parallel I have anywhere found among the ancients is Ovid met. IV 788 sq. where

---

[1] Peerlkamp removes the contradiction by altering *polum* in v. 398 to *lacum*.

Perseus relates his flight through the air, 'quae freta, quas terras sub se uidisset ab alto | et quae iactatis tetigisset sidera pennis'. To quote parallels from modern poetry either in defending a classical text or in recommending a conjecture is not as a rule a legitimate proceeding; between Tennyson and Virgil however there is so much resemblance, perhaps in other respects but certainly in this habit of using language too grand for the occasion, that I do not feel myself debarred from adducing in conclusion these lines from the fourth book of *The Princess*: 'at eve and dawn With Ida, Ida, Ida, rang the woods; The leader wildswan in among the stars Would clang it'.

32

THE MANUSCRIPTS OF PROPERTIUS [IV]*

In a recent instalment of the *Transactions of the Cambridge Philological Society* (vol. IV, Part I) Dr Postgate has issued a pamphlet of eighty-two pages 'on certain manuscripts of Propertius'. It includes a collation and discussion of cod. Holkhamicus 333, henceforth to be called L, a MS written in 1421 and containing nearly two-thirds of the author, from II xxi 3 to the end; excerpts and briefer notices of several other codices; and a disputation on the value and relationship of Propertius' MSS in general. My name is scattered through the treatise, and I hasten to acknowledge the invariable benignity with which Dr Postgate reproves me, sometimes for doing what I have not done, and sometimes for doing what it was my bounden duty to do.

To make clear what follows, let me premise that hitherto the only MSS of Propertius which count for anything have been NAFDV with f and v the correctors of F and V: AF form one family (which Dr Postgate calls Φ), DV another (which he calls Δ); the agreement of these two families is signified by the letter O;[1] N has something in common with each family but also something derived from neither, and this third element appears too in f and v. The codex A leaves off at II i 63, and thus through four-fifths of the elegies Φ is represented only by F and N, the former of which is full of blunders and the latter of foreign elements: when the two agree they probably give us Φ's reading, but when they differ we are often in doubt concerning it: another scion of this stock was therefore much desired. The new L is a MS agreeing often with DV, often with Nfv, but still belonging in the main to this family Φ.

Dr Postgate adduces (p. 37) nine places where he says L has a better reading or spelling than the other MSS. It has II xxv 7 *harena*, IV i 103 *harenosum*, vii 25 *harundine* (III xv 33 *harene* should apparently be added) for the forms without *h*; but since the *harenosum* and *harundine* are found also in Neap. 268 which Dr Postgate on pp. 50 sq. maintains with reason to be a copy of F, these spellings are no proof of independence. The same then is to be said of III xviii 15 *uicesimus* for *uigesimus*: the former is the better spelling, but there is no cause to doubt that the archetype had the latter: the same again would have to be said of

---

* [*CR* 9 (1895), 19–29]

[1] Students who use Dr Postgate's collation should be warned that in noting the agreement or disagreement of the other MSS with L he habitually employs the letter O to mean FDVN, though throughout the rest of the pamphlet it regularly means (A)FDV as opposed to N.

anubin for *anubim* at III xi 41 if that were a better spelling. Three more examples, II xxv 17 *sub limine* for *sublimine* or *sub lumine*, III iii 52 *philetea* for *philitea*, xi 23 *per menia* for *permenia*, are explicable as emendations of the most obvious sort. There remains only IV vii 65 *suma eternis* for *summa eternis*, one letter nearer to the true *sua maternis*; and if any of the other readings were clearly genuine this might be thought genuine too: but now one can only point to the similar corruption *suma* for *summam* appearing in this same MS at III ix 11. L therefore brings nothing new and true to the constitution of the text: these readings are much inferior in merit to the list collected by Messrs Luetjohann and Heydenreich from the now discarded Groninganus.[1]

In the next place then, as L has nothing good of its own, does it confirm F, the chief representative of Φ, in any good reading hitherto unconfirmed? In that portion of the poems which L contains, F gives about eighteen readings unconfirmed as yet[2] and seemingly right and genuine. Of these eighteen L gives only five, none important, II xxii 30 *num*, xxvi 57 *quod*, III vi 39 *consimili*, IV ii 19 *uoces*, vi 40 *umeris*. It also supports F in one reading which may be right, II xxxii 13 *creber platanis pariter*; and further it agrees with F alone in some four places where F, though not better than DVN, preserves or may preserve one part of the truth while they preserve another, II xxii 50 *fata*, xxxii 37 *non*, xxxiv 53 *restabit erūpnas*, IV iii 11 *et pacate mihi*.[3]||

L therefore confirms F in very few good readings; and the question arises, Is *confirm* the word to use? Is L an independent witness to the Φ tradition, or is it merely derived from F? Probably the former: the indications are few, far fewer than Dr Postgate imagines, but they seem enough. At IV vii 92 F omits the word *onus* altogether, L gives, not the word *onus*, but the letter *o*: the two appear to have copied from the same exemplar. There is moreover at least one place where L seems to have preserved alone a corrupt reading of Φ, a place, that is to say, where it stands midway between the true reading of DV and the corrupt reading of F, and F's reading seems to be a further corruption of L's: III xix 6 *fontis* DV (and N) rightly, *fontes* L, *montes* F. There is another place where L may indicate what corrupt reading stood in Φ or even in O: IV x 41 *Vncomani*

---

[1] Dr Postgate (p. 39) bases or essays to base a conjecture on an unsupported reading of L at III iv 22 'me sat erit *sacra* plaudere posse uia' NV, *media* DF, uoc. om. L, where he proposes 'me sacra sat erit'.   [2] v has three of them, but that does not count as confirmation.

[3] There are also two places where Dr Postgate (pp. 39–41) builds conjectures, as he is quite entitled to do, on the joint testimony of F and L; but the conjectures themselves appear to have no advantage over the proposals of earlier critics. At III xii 34 'Sirenum surdo remige adisse *lacus*' F has *latus* (*s* in ras.), L *latreus*, Dr Postgate accepts *latus* and alters *Sirenum* to *Sicanium*: if the vulgate needs changing, this change is no easier than Schrader's *locos* or than transposing *lacus* with the *domos* of the hexameter. At III xvii 17 'dum modo purpureo *spument* mihi dolia musto' *spument* is an old correction, DVN have *numen*, F *numine*, L *numerē*, Dr Postgate offers *cumulem* which is not likely to oust the vulgate: *st* and *sc* are both confused with *n*, and the corruption of *sp* is only a trifle harder; then the archetype will have had *nument*, altered on the one hand to *numen*, on the other to *numene* whence *numine* and *numerē*.

DV, *Butoniam* D marg., *Dutomani* F, *Vntoniani* L: Φ probably and O possibly had *Vntomani*. Once perhaps L even preserves alone a corrupt reading of O: if at III xiii 27 we compare the *illius munus decussa* of D (V has seemingly suffered correction) with the *illis*. . . . . (gap of five letters) *decussa* of F, the *illis munus decussa* of L looks like the origin of both. Apart from the above examples must be set the two following: II xxxiv 4 *formosam* N rightly, *formam* L, *et formam* FDV; III vii 68 *thetis* N rightly, *petis* L, *pedis* FD (V is erased). Here L is less corrupt than FDV, but there is no reason to think that it preserves the reading of Φ or of O: the consent of F with the other family is a reason for thinking otherwise.[1] In these two instances – as perhaps in a third III xi 14 *Meotis* (= *Maeotis*) N rightly, *Iniectis* FDV, *Nectis* L, where *Iniectis* and *Nectis* seem severally derived from *Mectis* – L may be exhibiting traces, as it does elsewhere, of the undiscovered source Z whence Nfv are in part derived; or after all these may be mere freaks of the pen, stumblings backward towards truth. But after subtracting these three passages the above evidence makes it likely that L independently preserves a small fragment of the tradition of Φ and is not derived from F.

I have selected most of the above examples from a great number which Dr Postgate (pp. 21 sqq.) presents as proofs but which are not proofs at all. For instance, he begins reasonably enough 'If L was copied from F, it must have been copied from F corrected', and then, to show that it was not copied from F corrected, proceeds 'whereas it often sides with the first hand against the corrector's', as if that were any objection: MSS copied from a corrected MS whose first hand is not erased invariably waver in this way. Then he goes on to prove that 'L is not derived from F in any stage of its existence' by pointing out that L, though it often has the same omissions as F, does not omit *de* at II xxii 12, *tu* at xxx 19, *est* at III iii 24, and *linque* at IV ix 54, while F does; quite overlooking the fact that in three of these four places it is only the first hand of F which omits the words, while the second hand inserts them, and also that L's composite text is derived in part from other sources, known to us, whence these omissions of F could easily be repaired. Again, Dr Postgate will have it that L cannot be derived from F because it often deserts F where F's reading would have been satisfactory, so he affirms, to the scribe of L. That may perhaps disprove that L is copied straight from F; but it admits the explanation, equally fatal to L, that L is copied from a copy of F, in which copy these alterations had been made by a scribe less easy to satisfy. The same reply invalidates another proof which Dr Postgate makes a great deal of: that L often gives the syllable

---

[1] To show my meaning I take parallels from N: when at II xxxii 8 DV give rightly *tibi me*, N *time*, F *timeo*, we judge from comparing DV with F that N has here kept the corrupt reading of Φ while F has corrupted it further, just as we judged at III xix 6 that L had kept and F corrupted the *fontes* of Φ; but when at III vi 41 FDV give *quid mihi si* and N *quod nisi et* we do not infer that N preserves the reading of Φ or O, since FDV consent against it and N had elsewhere to draw from.

us instead of *er*, obviously from confusing the compendia, whereas in every place the syllable *er* is written at length in F. 'I infer then', says Dr Postgate, 'that *L* is *not derived* from F': so do I, but not from evidence like this.

The use of L is therefore the following. Where it agrees with F, there the common reading of the two will generally be the reading of Φ; not always, for at II xxxii 8 they both have *timeo*, but generally. But where L dissents from F, that fact in itself tells us nothing about Φ and shakes F's testimony not a whit. Take examples. When at II xxxii 37 DVN give *hoc* and FL *non*, that means that *non* was in Φ and is ‖ not a mere blunder of F's. But when at IV vii 25 DVNL give *fissa* and F *fixa*, no conclusion can be drawn respecting Φ. Maybe Φ had *fissa* and F, as often, blundered; maybe Φ had *fixa* and L, as often, stole from the other sources: no one can say. Only in such a case as III xix 6 already cited, where L stands halfway between F and DV, is there ground for thinking that it has preserved the reading of Φ against F. The adherence of L to N is absolutely weightless as witness to the tradition of Φ:[1] both steal from other sources, and one of the sources whence L steals may very well be N itself: F remains the sole untainted channel of the family tradition when A is absent. The adherence of L to DV is equally unimportant: the tradition of that family is seldom doubtful, so that a third witness is superfluous, especially so poor a witness as L: only a case like III xxiv 33 [[xxv 13]] *cupias* DL, *cupies* V, *capias* FN, where D and V are at odds, may deserve mention. With that exception, L should never be cited in an apparatus criticus unless it agrees with F and dissents from N, or else presents a reading peculiar to itself. Its agreements with F against N confirm F; its unique readings, though never important, are sometimes interesting and perhaps contain fragments of the lost source whence f and v derived what virtue they possess. If I were editing Propertius I should mention L in about thirty places.[2]

The intrinsic value of L being thus insignificant, it occurs to Dr Postgate to

---

[1] Dr Postgate on the contrary says (p. 66) 'we have seen that the concurrent testimony of L and N as to the reading of the family outweighs the dissent of F'. I suppose the reference is to p. 33 where he quotes examples of agreement in spelling between N and L which he thinks must have been in Φ because 'it is most improbable that correctors of this period would have troubled about trifles like *equm*, *tinguere*, *pignera*, *murrea* and so forth'. The example of f and v would alone suffice to show that correctors write in the margin many readings which are in no sense corrections but merely variants, often insignificant, sometimes senseless, which have caught their eye in other MSS: then the next copyist stolidly incorporates them in his text. But it too often happens that scholars, instead of acquiring by observation a knowledge of what scribes were, prefer to frame from considerations of probability a notion of what scribes must have been.

[2] Dr Postgate occupies two pages, 35–7, in demonstrating what he calls the honesty of L. He finds that L contains few readings which can be imputed to the conjecture of its scribe; he compares D, which Baehrens and I have praised for its honesty, and finds that D contains more readings of this sort; and he concludes 'in honesty then it is clear that L is superior to D'. Even if the term *honesty* is thus restricted, the amount of such conjecture in D is so small that this superiority of L's is evanescent; and an honesty which is compatible with such adulteration of the text as appears in L is not much to boast about.

enhance its relative value by dragging down F as near to the same level as may be. I collected examples of F's singular merit in the *Journ. of Phil.* XXI p. 196 [this edition pp. 303–4]. Dr Postgate observes (p. 27):

> 'In most of the instances alleged by Mr Housman the difference between the various readings is very slight, and in many of them it seems more likely that F is accidentally right, has in fact blundered into a correction, than that one and the same corruption should have appeared independently in all the other manuscripts.'

He instances III iii 11: *lares* F rightly, *lacres* L, *lacies* N, *lacres* V, *alacres* D. In this particular passage – it is a pleasure to acknowledge a real correction – Dr Postgate's remark is just: if *lares* was in Φ it is hard to see why the intrusive *and sense-destroying* letter *c* appears in N and L; for those two MSS, though they steal from the source of DV, display some judgment in their thefts. But my list, after subtracting *lares* and the *absentis* falsely reported by Baehrens at II xxxiii 43 and some disputable examples, numbered nineteen, and may be raised to twenty-one by adding II xxii 50 *quem quae* F, *quae quoque* DVL, uers. om. N, and IV xi 20 *uindicet* F, *iudicet* DVL, pag. om. N; and among these twenty-one there is no instance open to the same objection as *lares*. In four of them F is now confirmed by L, so Dr Postgate must confess that in those four I was right, and that F did not blunder into a correction; though I on my part am quite willing to admit that this might sometimes happen. But I had spoken of five instances, among others, as very striking tokens of integrity. Dr Postgate objects (p. 28):

> 'I find it difficult to understand why such readings, as "the recondite *lunarat*" (IV vi 25) and "*Tiburtina*, retained despite the metre", are such "very striking tokens of integrity". For some MSS they would be; for F they prove nothing. F abounds in strange words and unmetrical lines; and, as the motive to alter on these grounds is completely absent, no conclusion can be drawn from its not operating in a particular case.'

My head goes round: does not Dr Postgate perceive that the absence of motive to alter strange words and unmetrical lines, and the abstention from such alteration which results from that absence of motive, *are* the 'integrity' of F and constitute its merit? and that a particular case in which F has so abstained is a token of that integrity? and that a striking case is a striking token? Does he suppose that when I talk about integrity I picture the devil at the scribe's || elbow prompting him to write *limarat* for *lunarat* and the scribe prevailing against him by prayer and fasting? I simply mean that the scribe has copied faithfully what most scribes would have altered and the other scribes did alter: there stands *lunarat* saved: that is integrity. 'And why should the retention of "lunarat" here be deemed more noteworthy than the corruption of "innabant" to "lunabant" in a majority of the MSS of Silius Italicus xii 448?' To this enquiry I readily return the answer it expects: the retention of 'lunarat' is not more noteworthy, but less. Both phenomena are noteworthy, but the retention by one MS of a rare word which its fellows have corrupted into a commoner one is less noteworthy than the corruption of a commoner word into a rarer. I have given the desired reply; and I should like to see what Dr Postgate can do with it.

But now let me point out that if Dr Postgate could shake the solitary witness borne by F he would land himself in a conclusion at which he does not desire to arrive. In the first place, his method of degrading F does not really bring F's level nearer to L's: L is degraded *pari passu*. If he denies genuineness to the unsupported readings I quote from F, he must in common fairness renounce genuineness for the unsupported readings he quotes from L, which are so far inferior in apparent merit. In the second place, to depreciate F is to depreciate the whole family Φ (as distinct from N); for all the important readings peculiar to that family are found in F alone. From i i i to ii i 63, where A leaves off, AF have no important reading which is not in N or DV. From ii i 63 to xxi 3, F stands alone and *is* the family, and on its sole authority rest the readings ii x 11 *carmina* and xv 26 *uellet* (a 'very striking token of integrity') which even the foe of the family Mr Solbisky is constrained to accept. From ii xxi 3 onwards we have F and L: L supports F in five or six true readings, none of them important, out of eighteen or so; but the *lunarat* and *Tiburtina* mentioned already, the *cumba* iii iii 22 which I also quoted as a striking token of integrity, and the *equora* iii xxi 11 and *aliquam* iv ix 45 accepted by Mr Solbisky, are not in L but in F only. Therefore when Dr Postgate says on p. 26 'we cannot trust F unconfirmed' he is saying that the family Φ is practically worthless, though on p. 61 he commends me for maintaining the contrary against Mr Solbisky. And at the bottom of p. 28 he himself becomes aware whose game he is playing, and checks his career with the words 'I have however no wish to decry F', which he has been doing for two pages and a half.[1]

---

[1] Dr Postgate writes on p. 27 'Mr Housman's advocacy of the value of F's isolated witness involves him in a curious inconsistency. He follows Baehrens in maintaining that A "is the most faithful representative of its family" *Journal of Phil.* xxii p. 99 [this edition p. 325]. It certainly then "happens curiously" that in the poems in which we have both A and F, A should give of itself but one true reading "solacia" i v 27, which Mr Housman thinks after all may be an accident, and F three (or four), *ib.* p. 100 sq.' The only reason why I appear to Dr Postgate to be involved in a curious inconsistency is that he has forgotten the facts, which are these. A gives a far greater number of true readings than F, but wherever it gives a true reading that reading is also given either by F *or by N* or by both. F, which gives a far less number of true readings than A, gives two or three true readings which are given neither by A nor by N. I set three boys twelve sums: Tom does the first nine, Dick the first seven, and Harry the last eight; and I say Tom has done most, although every sum done by him has also been done by Dick or Harry or both, and although the three last sums have been done only by Harry; and I do not expect any one but Dr Postgate to tell me that I am thus involved in a curious inconsistency.

Thus much I have written to adjust Dr Postgate's partial estimate of his new codex L. But on pp. 61–74 he discusses the relations and comparative value of Propertius' MSS in general. I hoped I had done with this matter for a long time to come; for after all, Propertius' MSS are not the only things in the world. But apparently, like Nehemiah's builders, one must carry the sword to protect the labours of the trowel. When Baehrens Leo Solbisky and I with some thought and pains have got this rather uninteresting garden of the Muses into decent order, here is Dr Postgate hacking at the fence for no discoverable reason unless it is the hope of boasting 'liquidis immisi fontibus apros'. I feel it a hardship, but I suppose it is a duty, to withstand this inroad. Dr Postgate makes his mistakes with a tranquil air of being in the right which is likely enough to satisfy students not possessing my weary familiarity with the subject; so here I put it at their service.

In confusing anew the relations of the MSS Dr Postgate has two principal aims: to exalt N and to disparage DV. It was easy to foresee that the next writer on Propertius' MSS would disparage DV: Baehrens had disparaged N, Mr Leo had disparaged O, Mr Solbisky had disparaged AF, I had defended one and all; so to disparage DV was the only way left of being original. Idolatry of N, on the other hand, is nothing new. ‖

'It is in his treatment of the Neapolitanus' says Dr Postgate (p. 63) 'that I find Mr Housman least satisfactory'; and he proceeds to explain why: 'though not the enemy of N, he is its most discriminating friend.' I had said, in my discriminating and unsatisfactory way, that there is no best MS of Propertius. 'The critics of the future' writes Dr Postgate (p. 73) 'will, unless I am much mistaken, pronounce on the contrary that the Neapolitanus *is* the best MS of Propertius, best as being the oldest of our witnesses' – but age is no merit. Age is merely a promise of merit, which experience may ratify or annul. The hoary head is a crown of glory, says Solomon, *if it be found in the way of righteousness*. Till we have examined two rival MSS, we presume that the older is the better. When we have examined them, we judge them by their contents. Till we have examined the Ambrosian fragment of Seneca's tragedies (saec. v) and the codex Etruscus (saec. XI–XII) we presume that the former has the purer text. When we have examined them we find that it has not. Just so in the first decade of Livy: the MS which is by five or six centuries the oldest is not the best. The worst texts of Euripides yet known to man were written in classical antiquity itself. Useless then to call the Neapolitanus 'best as being the oldest of our witnesses', unless you can keep it out of our reach. But Dr Postgate continues 'best again as the one that presents the greatest amount of truth with the smallest amount of falsehood'. Then if I set a clerk to copy out the Teubner text the result will be in Dr Postgate's opinion a still better MS than the Neapolitanus, because it will present a greater amount of truth with a smaller amount of falsehood. How often must I repeat that the legitimate glory of a MS is not correctness but integrity, and that a MS which adulterates its text, as N does, forfeits integrity in direct proportion as it achieves correctness? Give us our ingredients pure: we will mix the salad: we will not take it ready made from other cooks if we can help it. We have the Φ element pure in AF and the Δ element pure in DV and we can blend them for ourselves much better than N has blent them.[1] The merits which I recognise in N are not the age and correctness which Dr Postgate expects the critics of the future to admire, but these two: the lesser, that it usefully supplements the pure but imperfect witness of AF to the tradition of Φ; the greater, redeeming all its vice, that it contains in its adulterated text a third ingredient which we nowhere possess in a pure form.

This brings me to speak of a cause to which N owes more blind worshippers than to either its age or its correctness. Dr Postgate writes (pp. 62 sq.) 'a doubt, greater or less according to circumstances, must rest upon all unsupported lections in any of the manuscripts AFLDV. There is in fact only one known manuscript of Propertius whose unsupported evidence is to be taken into serious account in any considerable number of passages. I mean of course the Neapolitanus.'[2] That is to say, each of the other MSS mentioned is so lucky as to possess a near relative which confirms and checks its witness: N has the singular misfortune to possess none. For this whimsical reason do many people call N the best MS of Propertius. Perhaps the simplest way to dispel the error is the following. Suppose that all extant MSS, with one exception, exhibited a text akin to N's, and that the one exception were our D: those who now on the above grounds call N the best MS would then be bound by parity of reasoning to call D the best. And, I assure them, they would do so: they would forget all D's faults just as they now forget N's. Yet of course D would not really be a jot better than before. The confusion of thought is here: we do right to rejoice that we possess N rather than a second F or D or V; but we find a wrong vent for that joy when we call N the best MS: the proper vent is to thank providence. Iron is plentiful in England, so we would rather have the Borrowdale blacklead-mine than one iron-mine more; but we do not therefore call blacklead a better mineral than iron. If however any one is of opinion that the good readings found in N and not in F or D outweigh the good readings found in F or D and not in N, *plus* the excess of F's or D's integrity over N's, then he has a right to call N best MS of Propertius. But since I do not see how such a comparison can be carried out with any approach to precision I prefer to state what is roughly true and say that there is no best MS. ‖

---

[1] Dr Postgate disputes the proposition that N has borrowed from Δ, but I shall come to that point presently.

[2] I should add F, from II i 63 onwards, because it is there the only respectable representative of the family Φ; but with that exception I subscribe to Dr Postgate. I attach little weight to F's unsupported readings from I i 1 to II i 63, or to the unsupported readings of D which I cite *J.P.* XXII pp. 101–3 [this edition pp. 327–8].

Now for the relation of N to DV. They have many readings in common: Baehrens and I account for this by the hypothesis that N derived them from a MS of the Δ family. This will never do if DV are to be brought low and N exalted, so Dr Postgate says (p. 66) –

'Now I do not intend to examine the evidence which Mr Housman adduces in support of these statements,' – I had been pointing out how the phenomena of N's text tallied with the hypothesis, – 'for the following reason. He assumes *without proof* that the common readings of N and Δ (DV) were derived by N from Δ, not derived by Δ from N nor by both from a common source. Until that proof be furnished, to discuss separate passages would be a waste of time. For what if Δ arose from a codex not differing very much from AF to start with, into which readings had been copied from N or some cognate manuscript and also from another source, say W, whence come the characteristic DV readings?'

Very good. Now on the next page, 67, Dr Postgate has these words: 'The agreements between N and AF (and L) are sufficient to warrant us in believing that N in great part is derived from a MS of the Φ family.' Suppose that some scholar, who bears to Φ the ill will which Dr Postgate bears to Δ, observes in Dr Postgate's own fashion –

'Now I do not intend to examine the evidence which Dr Postgate adduces in support of his statements, for the following reason. He assumes *without proof* that the common readings of N and Φ (AFL) were derived by N from Φ, not derived by Φ from N nor by both from a common source. Until that proof be furnished, to discuss separate passages would be a waste of time. For what if Φ arose from a codex not differing very much from DV to start with, into which readings had been copied from N or some cognate manuscript and also from another source, say K, whence come the characteristic AFL readings?'

What reply can Dr Postgate give? None: he has sealed his own lips: there is not a pin to choose between that theory of N's relation to Φ and the theory he has himself suggested of N's relation to Δ: both are equally possible and equally improbable. But observe that the only one of the two which occurs to Dr Postgate is the one which jumps with his own prepossessions: I had considered and rejected both before ever I set pen to paper. Two obvious reasons against his improvised account of N's relation to Δ are the following. First, the text of N, Dr Postgate himself admits it, is compounded from at least two elements, while there is no visible indication that the text of Δ contains more than one. What perversity then, in order to avoid assuming that the MS known to have blent two elements has blent a third as well, to assume that the MS not known to contain more than one element contains three! That is the first reply: the second is this. The simplest hypothesis which will account for any given facts is held to be the likeliest hypothesis: it is not the practice to complicate affairs by gratuitous and unhelpful suppositions of 'another source, say W', or of five other sources, say W, U, T, S, R. At the date of its publication, what visible superiority had Copernicus' account of the planetary movements over Ptolemy's? Its simplicity: years had to pass before Galileo's telescope confirmed it. The College of Cardinals rejected the simple account because it seemed to threaten Holy Writ. Dr Postgate rejects the simple account because it is derogatory to the scarce less sacred Neapolitanus.

Again, Dr Postgate thinks, like many scholars, that N belongs to the 13th or 12th century, as, for aught I know, it may; and against my hypothesis, Baehrens' rather, that N has borrowed from a MS of the DV family he writes thus (p. 65) –

> 'For the antiquity of the parent codex of DV Mr Housman claims only a moderate antiquity; in vol. 21, p. 180 note [[this edition p. 291]], he says "it was probably earlier than 1400 and certainly not much later". Let us however place this codex anywhere he likes in the 14th century; and should N be of the 13th this portion of his edifice will still collapse.'

When I claimed for Δ the date 1400, that was merely my modesty: I claimed no more than I wanted for the point I was then discussing. But nothing ties down Δ to the 14th century or near it: it can easily be older than any date yet assigned to N: it has the valuable advantage of being inaccessible, so that no one can ask awkward questions about the date of its parchment. Moreover this objection invites the retort that, should N be older than Φ, that portion of Dr Postgate's edifice will collapse which derives N from Φ. In fact, the only imaginable reason why Dr Postgate does not say against Φ everything which he here says against Δ is that he has taken no dislike to Φ.

Thus, when he concludes (p. 67) that 'the origin of the readings which N has in common with DV is unknown', any one will be ready with the supplement that it is no more unknown than the origin, which Dr Postgate believes to be known, of the readings which N has in common with AF. And again, when he says (p. 74)

> 'the evidence of the Δ family must be separated into three: (*a*) evidence confirmed by Φ for which O can be used as an algebraical expression, (*b*) evidence ‖ confirmed by L' – pretty confirmation – 'or N, (*c*) evidence confirmed by neither. The last, though certainly not to be neglected, must be carefully sifted and received with caution until it is confirmed from some undiscovered source' –

there is no *must* about the matter except the necessity of gratifying Dr Postgate's private enmity to Δ; and if he had conceived that enmity against Φ instead, he would here be writing 'the evidence of the Φ family must be separated into three: (*a*) evidence confirmed by Δ for which O can be used as an algebraical expression, (*b*) evidence confirmed by N, (*c*) evidence confirmed by neither. The last... must be carefully sifted and received with caution until' etc.

In short, every word that Dr Postgate says against Baehrens' account of the relation between N and Δ can be turned against his own account of the relation between N and Φ. All the tools he employs are two-edged, though to be sure both edges are quite blunt.

But Dr Postgate further engages to show that DV are more interpolated (interpolated by conjecture, that is) than N. His method is the good old rule, the simple plan, of 'heads I win, tails you lose'. N and DV commit just the same offences: he extenuates them in N and denounces them in DV. His divers weights and divers measures may escape the eye in his pamphlet because they are there arranged on separate pages; but I shall bring them together, and in juxtaposition I fancy they will astonish even their owner.

At III ii 1 [3] sq., where editors read after Ayrmann 'Orphea *delenisse* feras et concita dicunt | flumina Threicia sustinuisse lyra', FV have *detenuisse*, Nv *detinuisse*, D *te tenuisse*. I had said that the consent of F and V, witnesses from each family, showed that O had *detenuisse*; and that N had made a bad attempt at amending the slight and honest error of O. Dr Postgate comments (p. 69) in this derisive vein –

'Now observe, to change one letter and to insert a second and to write "detenuisse" for "delenisse" is a slight and honest error. But to confound two letters already three times confused within the book of which this is the 41st line, and so alter a spelling, is a serious and dishonest one.'

These words, though meant in irony, are almost the literal truth. To write the 'uox nihili' *detenuisse* (the term is somewhat too harsh but it is Dr Postgate's own) for the Latin word *delenisse*, is a slight and a transparently honest error. As to the change of *detenuisse* into *detinuisse*, when critics find a 'uox nihili' altered into a Latin word they do not call it confounding two letters but they call it a conjecture. And Dr Postgate himself does as critics do when he has no motive for doing otherwise. D has here committed the very offence which he palliates in N: it has altered the 'uox nihili' into Latin by the change of one letter, *te tenuisse*: and Dr Postgate on pp. 36 sq., where he was impugning D's honesty, threw this in its teeth: 'Now to turn to the honest D. It is clear that its scribe took an interest in his subject, and allowed his mind to work upon it. Hence...at III ii 1 [3] the uox nihili "detenuisse" becomes "te tenuisse".' There you hear the truth about the crime because the judge is no friend to the criminal. But to come again to p. 69: Dr Postgate goes on –

'Well, be it so: Mr Housman has still to explain how it is that the MS which wilfully alters "detenuisse" here, reads "detenere" for "tenere" against the metre at II xxx 26.'

Turn back to p. 37 and the dishonesty of D: 'Metre...is the ground for the impudent alteration in IV viii 58 "Teia petebat aquas" for "clamat", the scansion Tēĭă being unknown to the scribe.' If I disputed as Dr Postgate disputes I should reply 'Dr Postgate has still to explain how it is that the MS which wilfully alters "Tēĭă" here, retains "Tēĭă lucos" at IV viii 31'; but I know better. There is no discrepancy. Scribes are sometimes awake and sometimes asleep: the scribe of D was awake when he wrote 'Teia petebat' and asleep when he wrote 'Teia lucos'; the scribe of N was awake when he wrote 'detinuisse' and asleep when he wrote 'detenere'.

On p. 37 Dr Postgate quotes it as an instance of dishonesty in the scribe of D that 'at II xxx 36 he has allowed himself to write "ingemuit" for "accubuit" from I i 14'. Only seventeen lines from that spot, at II xxx 19, the scribe of N has done just the same thing, has allowed himself to write 'inmerito' for 'dura paras' from III xix 27.[1] Turn then to p. 68, where Dr Postgate enumerates 'the only examples in Mr Housman's collection of the corruptions of N or outside it, in which I find the hypothesis of interpolation certain, reasonable or plausible' and see if he quotes this passage. No; nor do I blame him, for the hypothesis of interpolation is neither certain, reasonable nor plausible: I only invite attention to the transparent iniquity of his ‖ procedure. On the very next page, 69, among places where 'the reading of Δ is either interpolated or open to grave suspicion', he adduces just such another, II xix 26 'pedes' Δ for 'boues' from I xx 8 or IV xi 16. And much else does he adduce in lieu of evidence, which is not evidence at all but mere uncharitable imputation. Here is a specimen: 'I xix 10 "Thessalis antiquam uenerat umbra domum"] Δ, not understanding the acc., makes the ghost knock, "uerberat", before he enters!' The note of exclamation is Dr Postgate's, but I echo it with all my heart. He even quotes against Δ's good faith such customary errors as 'laudabat' for 'ludebat' and 'externas' for 'hesternas'. I declare, Dr Postgate's entire observations on DV remind me of nothing so much as the famous soliloquies, described by Coleridge as 'the motive-hunting of a motiveless malignity', in which Iago tries to explain to himself why he hates Othello. By p. 70 he has so incensed himself against the odious MSS that he finally writes –

'Should any one press this evidence in favour of the theory thrown out above that Δ descends from a corrected copy of Φ, I confess I do not see how he is to be refuted; and when to the interpolations of Δ are added the interpola-

---

[1] Baehrens, disliking N as Dr Postgate dislikes DV, promptly remarked 'interpolate': I in *J.P.* XXI p. 154 [this edition p. 271] resisted him as I am here resisting Dr Postgate.

tions of D, of which a portion have been already cited, I seem to discern some justification for what Mr Housman calls the grave and disastrous error of Lachmann in neglecting the Daventriensis "whose honest and independent witness he mistook for interpolation".'

The *tu quoque* to which Dr Postgate habitually exposes himself is once more available: should others collect the similar evidence against the good faith of Φ, which he refrains from collecting, and press it in favour of the theory that Φ descends from a corrected copy of Δ, refutation would be about as difficult or about as easy.

But Dr Postgate has thus shown to his own satisfaction (p. 71) 'that Δ is much more deeply interpolated than N, and that where Δ contradicts N as to the word to be supplied in a lacuna of Φ, N is to be believed rather than Δ'. At II xxiv 45 sq. 'iam tibi Iasonia uecta est Medea carina | et modo *ab infido* sola relicta uiro' DV have *ab infido*, N *seruato*, FL omit the words or word. Dr Postgate writes –

> 'of course one of the two must be an interpolation. In deciding which, we ask first which gives the easier construction; and the answer is *ab infido*; and secondly which presents the more obvious sense and the answer, as we see from another supplement "fallaci" in D, is again *ab infido*.'

Strange, that any one could pen these words and not foresee the inevitable retort. If the supplement 'fallaci' shows that *ab infido* presents the more obvious sense, then it equally shows that *seruato* gives the easier construction. If it does not show that *seruato* gives the easier construction, then neither does it show that *ab infido* presents the more obvious sense. Nor indeed does there appear to be any tangible difference in obviousness between the two senses or in ease between the two constructions; and I suggest that Dr Postgate should remodel his words so as to run 'of course one of the two must be an interpolation. In deciding which, we ask only which is in DV.' But I had said 'what must settle the question in favour of *ab infido* for any impartial judge are palaeographical considerations. It is quite clear, as Baehrens prolegg. p. xii pointed out, that the scribe of the parent codex of the one family glanced from the *do* of *modo* to the *do* of *infido* and so left a metrical gap which F honestly preserves and which N fills up with the conjecture *seruato*', and I added that for Mr Solbisky to call *ab infido* a random conjecture was irrational. But Dr Postgate, because he breaks the laws of reason himself, will not allow any one else to keep them, and rebukes me as follows (p. 72) –

> 'It is quite clear however that F and its family often omit words without any glancing of the eye, as at II xxi 5, 7   xxxiv 55   III i 38   iii 21   xi 21' – he means 58 – 'IV iii 9   xi 64, 68; and Mr Housman would have done well to examine the apparatus criticus before stigmatising as "irrational" the statement that "ab infido" is a conjecture.'

Three of these nine examples which I should have found if I had examined the apparatus criticus are examples where the word omitted is *est*, i.e. no word at all but the single letter *ē* or the dotted line of the compendium; a fourth is *q.*, a fifth is *te*. But grant, as I do grant freely, that words are sometimes omitted without assignable cause not only in F and its family but in most other MSS: rational enquirers nevertheless prefer suppositions which explain phenomena to suppositions which leave phenomena unexplained; and when a word is missing they consider – I am ashamed to enunciate such truisms, but what is one to do? – that the likeliest cause is the recurrence of similar syllables. So does Dr Postgate, when rational enquiry suits his plan: at III iv 22 'me sat erit *sacra* plaudere posse uia' we have a precise parallel: NV give *sacra*, FD *media*, L omits the word: Dr Postgate says (p. 39) –

> 'It would appear...that an epithet of "uia" was omitted...Was this epithet "sacra" or "media"? ‖ I prefer "sacra" for two reasons. First it is a less obvious word to choose; and secondly it explains the omission better, the scribe's eye slipping from "sac" to "sat".'

Shall I then reply 'Dr Postgate would have done well to examine the apparatus criticus' etc.? Not I: I commend him for following in this instance the dictates of reason, and encourage him to follow them elsewhere, even when it serves no cherished end.

Another interpolation of N's is defended by Dr Postgate on an earlier page, 24. At III xiv 19 sq. N has 'inter quos Helene nudis *capere arma* papillis | fertur nec fratres erubuisse deos', O has 'nudis *armata* capillis' (*est armata* F). I had said that *armata* was the original, *ta* was absorbed by the following *pa* or *ca*, and *capere* then inserted by N to prop the metre. L has since been collated, and it exhibits the very stage of corruption which I postulated: 'nudis *arma* capillis'. Now hear Dr Postgate –

> 'There has occurred one of the transpositions of words which...abound in Latin manuscripts. And the readings of O are derived from "*arma cape capillis*" (for *papillis* is found only in N), that of FDV *armata* by the loss of *pe* before *pi* [he means "the loss of *pe* before *capi*"] and the change of *c* to *t* (F further intruding an *est*), that of L by the loss of one *ca* out of two [he means "the loss of *cape*"].'

That zeal for N could enslave the reason and warp the judgment we knew; but apparently it can even cloud the perceptions: Dr Postgate with evident sincerity calls this 'a more excellent way' and seriously says that I should have adopted it if I had only remembered the compendium for *per*.[1] I trust my mental

---

[1] In the same paragraph I am told, with a compliment to soothe my vanity, that at II xxviii 9 I have not sufficiently regarded manuscript abbreviations, because, the true reading being *peraeque*,

balance would have sustained even that recollection. The slips of the pen which I correct within square brackets are quite of a piece with the whole.

I return to p. 72 –

'In the much-canvassed omissions of N I find no evidence of design. III x 17–18 were obviously omitted through homoioteleuton, "caput" ending 16 and 18. The omission of III xi 58' – he might add II xxii 50 – 'must have been a pure accident...And if so, why should we assume design at III ix 35? Mr Housman does not; and yet of II xxxiv 83, one out of two places where N omits the end of a line, the part most liable to injury, he says that "the scribe saw the line was nonsense and desisted from finishing it".'

The places where N omits the end of a line are not two but five: II xxxiv 53 nec si post Stygias aliquid restabit *erumpnas*, 83 nec minor his animis aut sim *minor ore canorus*, III i 27 Idaeum Simoenta Iouis *cunabula parui*, v 39 sub terris sint iura deum et tormenta *gigantum*, IV iii 7 te modo uiderunt iteratos *Bactra per ortus*. In one, III i 27, the reading of O is certainly, in another, III v 39, possibly interpolated; so that N's omissions may there be placed to its credit. In the three others the omitted words present obvious difficulties; and I inferred that N omitted them because of those obvious difficulties. It never occurred to me to reason, as Dr Postgate does, that a MS which omits some things by accident is not likely to omit other things on purpose: when a man is charged with murder it is not thought much of a defence to say that he has frequently committed homicide by misadventure. But to proceed: when I write 'the scribe saw the line was nonsense and desisted from finishing it', Dr Postgate thinks it an answer to remark 'Presumably then he was not the same scribe who a few pages on at III v 35 writes "cur serus uersare boues et *flamma boon*".' There is no support for any such presumption. When Dr Postgate on p. 37 wrote of D 'Metre is the ground for the impudent alteration in IV viii 58 "Teia petebat aquas" for "clamat", the scansion Tēiă being unknown to the scribe', I did not answer 'Presumably then he was not the same scribe who twenty-seven lines above had

I quoted N's *per aequae* as an example of its superiority to the other MSS, of which D has (and V probably had) *pareque* and F *paremque*. 'But' says Dr Postgate 'the original of the readings of all our MSS is neither "pereque' nor "pareque" but "peque' which L presents.' It pleases Dr Postgate to say so, but the statement has no other ground. That the readings of DVF are due to *peque*, which their common parent O had misinterpreted as *pareque*, is probable; but I do not know what Dr Postgate means by saying that *peque* was the original of N's *per aequae*: N, as he is aware, derives scores of readings from an older source than O, and there is not a hint that this source had *peque* rather than *peraeque*. The *peque* of L no more tells for that opinion than the *pereque* of v for the contrary. But suppose I concede the point, what follows? that 'N is here no better than D, V or F [Dr Postgate does not really mean "or F"]; for it has misdivided the word, while they have wrongly expanded the abbreviation.' Then N is better, because truth is more obscured by wrongly expanding the abbreviation than by misdividing the word. It will be observed that Dr Postgate's zeal for N has here succumbed to his tenderness for L.

On p. 23 an equally baseless charge of neglecting abbreviations is brought against Mr Leo and supported only by flat contradiction.

written "Tēiă lucos"'; nor do I now say that presumably the Dr Postgate who wrote p. 37 of this treatise was not the same Dr Postgate who wrote p. 72. ||

This *flamma boon* reappears on p. 66. Baehrens and I consider that all which N derives from O it derives through Φ or through Δ and not through a third independent channel. Dr Postgate is anxious, in the interests of N, to believe the contrary; so he cites III v 35 where DV have rightly 'cur serus uersare boues et *plaustra Bootes*', FL *flamma palustra*, N *flamma boon*, and comments as follows –

> 'Unless N's unintelligible and unmetrical reading was "reverentially copied" from the unknown Z, we must suppose it was derived either from Δ or from Φ, that is *flamma boon* from *plaustra bootes* or from *flamma palustra!*, or else admit that N may be, what Baehrens and Mr Housman say it is not, an independent witness to the reading of O.'

This is no way to argue, 'unless *a* is true, either *b* or *c* must be true, but *b* is absurd, therefore let us hope that *c* is true': a logician would attempt to show some reason against *a*. But that is what Dr Postgate cannot even attempt; for he believes that many of N's readings were reverentially copied from Z. Nor is this the only flaw in the reasoning. To suppose that *flamma boon* was derived from *flamma palustra* is doubtless absurd; but it is not therefore absurd to suppose that it was derived from Φ. Baehrens and Dr Postgate and I are all agreed that N is an independent witness to the reading of Φ; and the phenomena here will be perfectly explained by supposing that Φ had *flamma boones* (*boones* is in Par. 8233 and Vrb. 641) with *plaustra* in the margin as a correction of *flamma*, and that in one apograph *plaustra* was mistaken for *palustra* and substituted not for *flamma* but for *boones* and so produced the *flamma palustra* of FL, while in another apograph the correction was neglected and *flamma boones* descended with only the loss of the last syllable into N. The explanation, though I do not pledge myself to it, is absolutely perfect, and Dr Postgate's ingenuity, which fabricated on N's behalf the wonderful scheme to justify *nudis capere arma papillis*, was quite equal to devising it; but apparently he will not take so much trouble unless he sees hope of arriving thereby at some welcome conclusion.

This ends what I have to say on Dr Postgate's spirited attempt (pp. 61–74) to re-establish chaos amongst Propertius' MSS. He calls it (p. 74) 'a toilsome though necessary examination of the past in Propertian criticism'. The attempt to find grounds for groundless opinions is likely to be toilsome; but the necessity seems to have been purely subjective.

If it were not for the humour of the situation I might well resent the tone of placid assurance in which I, who think before I write and blot before I print, am continually admonished by the author of this pamphlet. Hitherto I have noticed only those references to myself which are connected with the tenour of these remarks; but I will here cite two more, because they show, better perhaps than anything yet quoted, what a bewildering disputant Dr Postgate is. The question is asked, whence did f and v derive their genuine readings which often agree with N? Dr Postgate writes on p. 60 that they 'seem to be derived from a source similar to N', and adds this note:

'Mr Housman says these readings were derived "from the same lost MS whence N derives them". This cannot be proved or disproved and comes in the end to the same thing, that is identity of source.'

A reader who finds this minute observation standing in a note all by itself, and sees words of mine quoted within inverted commas, will probably suppose that I really did say what Dr Postgate imputes to me. Perhaps I should have been right if I had; but it so happens that I did not. I transcribe the sentences which Dr Postgate had under his eyes, *J.P.* XXII pp. 114 sq. [[this edition pp. 336–7]]:

'The simplest hypothesis is that which I have embodied in my stemma codicum: that f and v derive these elements from the same lost MS whence N derives them... If however any one should prefer to say that f and v derive their genuine readings not from the same exemplar as N but from another MS closely resembling it, I should be unable to confute his opinion, just as he would be unable to substantiate it.'

Not only therefore did I not say what Dr Postgate represents me as saying, but I did say, before him, what he represents as being a criticism of his own, that 'this cannot be proved or disproved'. His mis-statement is harmless, and I acquit him of any intention either to garble or to plagiarise; but he has done both.

The second example is more injurious. Mr Leo, who in 1880 denied all value to AFDV, said that any vulgar MS of the better sort would serve to check the testimony of N by: 'librarii errores arguere ualebit e melioribus uulgaris notae libris quicumque eligetur.' I said 'We have tried and condemned the only three [Groninganus, Perusinus, Hamburgensis] among the vulgar MSS which have been selected by any recent critic. When Mr Leo specifies his selections it will be possible to examine their merits: till then it must suffice to say that I have ‖ scrutinised the mass of critical material collected by Burmann and Hertzberg without discovering a fragment of genuine tradition unknown to us from NAFDVfv.' Dr Postgate (pp. 74 sq.) first imputes to Mr Leo an opinion which he has never expressed, 'that ς [= the vulgar MSS] may yet have some revelations in store for us', and then represents my remarks as an unsuccessful attempt to combat that opinion –

'Mr Housman, criticising this opinion', – which I had never heard of, – 'declares that "he has scrutinised the mass of critical material collected by Burmann and Hertzberg without discovering a fragment of genuine tradition unknown to us from NAFDVfv". To scrutinise a collection as inaccurate as Hertzberg's would appear to be a waste of time; and a scrutiny of Burmann's edition did not save Lachmann, according to Mr Housman, from "erring grievously and disastrously". Dismissing then this argument, if argument it be', and so on.

The misrepresentation is of course unintentional and only proceeds from indistinctness of thought: but could an unluckier occasion have been chosen for this air of triumph?

Neither the conception nor the execution of the pamphlet entitles it to so long a criticism; but it is the work of a scholar who has done much better work before, and to whom Propertius and I are both of us considerably indebted. I should add that pp. 42–58 give interesting information about various MSS, and that the excerpts from Parisinus 8233 and Vrbinas 641, as I conjectured in *J.P.* XXII p. 125 [[this edition p. 344]] that they would be, are even valuable and seem to show that the former at any rate deserves collation quite as much as L.

33

REVIEW: J. P. POSTGATE,
*SEXTI PROPERTI CARMINA**

Since the annus mirabilis 1880 there has appeared no edition of Propertius but Mr Vahlen's insignificant revision of Haupt in 1885. So long ago however as 1881 Dr Postgate in his Select Elegies furnished one fourth of the poems with the best explanatory commentary they yet possess; and among the many critics who have handled this author in the last fifteen years he has been one of the busiest. He now issues, as part of his Corpus Poetarum and simultaneously in a separate form, this recension and apparatus: a work full as important for the criticism of the text as any edition of the century after Lachmann's, Baehrens' and Palmer's.

Dr Postgate's own emendations are over a hundred in number. The best in the book is at IV i 93 'quippe Lupercus, *aui* (*equi* MSS) dum saucia protegit ora, | heu sibi prolapso non bene cauit equo', which is admirably neat: now at length one can form a picture of what happened, and Lupercus has something sensible to die for, like his brother Gallus who 'in castris dum credita signa tuetur | concidit ante aquilae rostra cruenta suae': *auis* is corrupted to *equis* at IV xi 102. The correction of II vii 20, already published in the Select Elegies, 'hic erit et patrio *nomine* (*sanguine* MSS from 14) pluris amor', seems certain: and so does IV ii 12 'seu, quia uertentis fructum praecerpimus anni, | Vertumni rursus *credis id* (*credidit* MSS) esse sacrum', and the minute correction III xix 6 'flamma per incensas citius sedetur aristas | fluminaque ad fontis *sunt* (*sint* MSS) reditura caput'. II xxiii 22 'nolim furta *pigenda* (*pudica* MSS) tori' is convincing to me and superior to Baehrens' conjecture *pudenda* which ought however to be mentioned. II xiii 55 'illis *formosus* (*formosum* MSS) iacuisse paludibus, illuc | diceris effusa tu, Venus, isse coma' is attractively simple and favoured by κεῖται καλὸς Ἄδωνις ἐν ὤρεσι, though it must be allowed that 'formosum *lauisse*' or '*ciuisse*' is more strictly pertinent to the context. II xxiv 1 'tu *quereris* (*loqueris* MSS) cum *sis* (so codd. recc. for *sit*) iam noto fabula libro' seems more satisfactory than Baehrens' transposition '*sic* loqueris, ‖ cum *tu*', and one or the other must be right. IV xi 101 'moribus et caelum patuit: *sis* (*sim* MSS) digna merendo, | cuius honoratis ossa uehantur auis' is in my judgment a true correction: certain

* [*Sexti Properti carmina* recognouit Joh. Percival Postgate. London, G. Bell and Sons: Cambridge, Deighton, Bell and Co. 1894. *CR* 9 (1895), 350–5]

I hesitate to call it because it depends for its validity on my transposition of 67 sq. and 71 sq. to precede this couplet: perhaps too the right reading may be *fi*. At II xxix 27, in the MS text 'ibat et *hinc castae* narratum somnia Vestae', the *hinc* is meaningless and Jacob proposed *in*; but this ellipse, as I think Dr Postgate himself has somewhere observed, does not appear to allow a descriptive epithet: he reads *intactae*, which may well be right, though *incanae* (Verg. A. v 744 canae penetralia Vestae) would be as near the MSS. In III xi 56 the reading 'non haec, Roma, fuit tanto tibi ciue uerenda, |*dixi, aut* (*dixit et* MSS) assiduo lingua sepulta mero' seems as good as any yet suggested; and in 58 '*femineo* (*femineas*) timuit territa Marte minas' is likely enough, though Dr Postgate does not improve it by writing *extimuit*. At IV i 57 '*munera* (*moenia* MSS) namque pio conor disponere uersu' is at any rate a lighter change than Mr L. Mueller's *munere...uersus*. II ix 44 'nunc quoque *erit*, quamuis sis inimica, *nihil*' (*eris...mihi* MSS) and IV x 19 'idem eques, *e* (*et* MSS) frenis idem fuit aptus aratris' are worth considering. At I xii 10 the conjecture 'num me deus obruit? an quae | lecta Prometheis *diuidis* herba iugis' accounts well for the MS variants *diuidit* and *diuitis*, though *diuidit* is better in itself. In II xxxiv 13–16 the MSS have 'tu mihi uel ferro *pectus* uel perde ueneno; | a domina tantum te modo tolle mea. | te socium uitae, te *corporis* esse licebit, | te dominum admitto rebus, amice, meis.' The phrase 'socium *corporis*' is unintelligible, and Dr Postgate writes *pectoris* in 15 and *corpus* in 13: *pectus* however is there a better word than *corpus*, and the fault is easier mended by transposing the *socium* and *dominum* of 15 and 16, 'te *dominum* uitae, te corporis esse licebit, | te *socium* admitto rebus, amice, meis'.

In a good many places however Dr Postgate's conjectures have no apparent advantage over his predecessors'. Thus at I ii 13 'litora natiuis *persuadent* picta lapillis' his *resplendent* is to say the least neither nearer to the text nor apter to the sense than Baehrens' *praefulgent*. At IV ix 3 'uenit *et aduictos* pecorosa Palatia montes' his *ad intactos* is further from the MSS than Lachmann's *ad eductos*, which he does not mention, and has no superiority in meaning. In III xxi 19 sq. the vulgate 'cum fessa *Lechaeo* | sedarit placida uela phaselus aqua' was amended by Guietus to *Lechaei*: Dr Postgate writes *Lechaea* (adj.). The earlier conjecture is the more probable: scribes would have less temptation to alter *Lechaea*, especially with so many similar terminations in the neighbourhood to protect it. At III xiii 39 sq. 'corniger atque dei uacuam pastoris in aulam | dux aries saturas ipse reduxit oues' some interpolated MSS, wrongly as it seems, have *cornigerique*, which Palmerius explained to mean Pan; Dr Postgate alters this further to *crinigerique* and refers to Tib. II iii 11 sqq. where Apollo is described as keeping the herds of Admetus. What in the world have the herds of Admetus to do with this picture of the primitive pastoral life of mankind? At II xxx 20 'et petere Hyrcani litora *nota* maris' Dr Postgate writes *muta* and adds 'coll. Sen. H.F. 540'. It cannot be pretended that *muta* is nearer to the MSS than Lachmann's *nuda* or so near as Hertzberg's *nauta*: its superiority must depend on the support it gets from Seneca. Sen. H.F. 540 (536) is 'et *mutis* tacitum *litoribus* mare'. Because Seneca applies *mutus* to the shores of one sea, does it follow that Propertius applied it to the shores of another? Besides, Lachmann quoted *litora nuda* from Statius: why does not that prove that Propertius wrote *nuda*? II xxxii 33–6 runs as follows: 'ipsa Venus, quamuis corrupta libidine Martis, | nec minus in caelo semper honesta fuit, | quamuis Ida *Parim* pastorem dicat amasse | atque inter pecudes accubuisse deam.' There is no such story about Venus and Paris, so editors regard *Parim* as a mistaken gloss and generally understand Anchises to be meant: Schrader proposes *Phrygem*, Haupt *palam*, Baehrens *suum*. Dr Postgate mentions none of these, but writes 'fuit, | quamuis Ida, *Rhea*, pastorem dicat amasse' cet., and says in the *Cambridge University Reporter* 6 Dec. 1892 'the reference is to the fable preserved in Theocr. xx 40 καὶ τύ, ʽΡέα, κλαίεις τὸν βου-κόλον, Tertullian ad nat. I 149 Cybele pastorem suspirat.' But others, as we have seen, think that the reference is to the fable preserved in Iliad B 820 sq. Αἰνείας, τὸν ὑπ' ᾽Αγχίσῃ τέκε δῖ' ᾽Αφροδίτη | ῎Ιδης ἐν κνημοῖσι θεὰ βροτῷ εὐνηθεῖσα, Theocr. I 105 εἴ λέγεται τὰν Κύπριν ὁ βουκόλος, ἕρπε ποτ' ῎Ιδαν, | ἕρπε ποτ' ᾽Αγχίσαν, xx 34 sq. ὅτι Κύπρις ἐπ' ἀνέρι μήνατο βούτᾳ | καὶ Φρυγίοις ἐνόμευσεν ἐν ὤρεσι: Dr Postgate must ‖ therefore give some reason why he believes that the person meant is Rhea, whose name is not in the MSS, rather than Venus, whose name is; and it must be a strong reason, if it is to justify a dislocated order of words which has no parallel in Propertius for violence unless you accept Dr Postgate's emendation of III xix 19 sq. At II xxxiv 39 the MSS have '*non Amphiareae* prosint tibi fata quad-rigae',which Munro simply emended '*Amphiaraëae* p. t. f. quadrigae?' Dr Postgate writes '*Amphiarea tibi non prosint* fata quadrigae', to which there is no objection except the needless violence of the change. But then he adds in his note 'alii alia aut numeris durissimum uersum aut *Amphiaraeae* nouum uerbum excudentes'. It is not a 'nouum verbum' but occurs in Strabo IX p. 399 ⟦p. 564 Meineke⟧ τὸ ᾽Αμφιαράειον μαντεῖον: that however is not the point: the point is that the proper adjective in -ειος from ᾽Αμφιάραος is ᾽Αμφιαράειος and nothing else, whether it occurs or not; just as the proper adjective from Μενέλαος is Μενελάειος (Prop. II xv 14). Because Euphorion chooses to frame ᾽Αμφιάρειος out of ᾽Αμφιάρης the normal formation is not therefore outlawed from that day forth. Dr Postgate himself at Catull. 68 74 reads '*Protesilaeam* Laudamia domum' in the teeth of the MSS, which have *Protesileam*, and adds no note about 'nouum uerbum'.

Some of Dr Postgate's alterations are to be blamed as needless. For example, at IV vii 85 'hic *Tiburtina* (al. *Tiburna*) iacet aurea Cynthia ripa' he writes *Tiburne tua*, which means just the same as *Tiburtina* and is further away from all the MSS: he says indeed on p. 78 of his pamphlet 'On certain MSS of Proper-tius' that *Tiburtina* is post-Augustan, but that is an error. Another conjecture of this sort he defends at praef. p. vii. IV x 41 sq. describe the encounter of

Claudius and Virdomarus: 'genus hic Rheno iactabat ab ipso, | nobilis e rectis
fundere gaesa rotis. | illi uirgatis iaculantis ab agmine bracis | torquis ab incisa
decidit unca gula': Dr Postgate in 43 writes 'illi, *ut* uirgatis *iaculans it* ab a.
bracis, | torquis' cet. This conjecture removes no real fault which the MS reading
possesses. The text is both grammatical and intelligible. The verb *decĭdo* serves
as the passive of *decīdo*, and such verbs can take the constructions of a passive:
Ovid met. v 192 'a tanto cecidisse uiro', Sil. iv 543 'huic cadit infelix niueis
Varenus in armis'. *illi* then is dative of the agent (or if you like of the recipient)
and signifies Claudius, which nothing forbids, for Virdomarus has just been
called *hic*. All danger of mistaking *illi* for the possessive dative and referring it
to Virdomarus is precluded by the presence of the genitive *iaculantis*. The
verses therefore mean 'illi (Claudio) torquis iaculantis (Virdomari) decisa est ab
incisa gula'. There is indeed a difficulty in *uirgatis bracis*; but Dr Postgate's
conjecture does not remove it.

Some alterations are even injurious. iii ix 37 sq. 'non flebo in cineres arcem
sedisse paternos | Cadmi, nec semper proelia clade pari.' Propertius will not
mourn over the fort of Cadmus collapsed into the ashes of the last generation,
and the fight where the slaughter was one-sided at length: nec semper pari = et
non semper pari = et tandem impari. This is that sack of Thebes by which the
Epigoni broke the precedent of Καδμεία νίκη set by the Sparti and followed by
the sons of Oedipus. Thebes was sacked so often that the words 'cineres
paternos' are useful if not needful to tell us that the sack by the Epigoni is meant;
and I should have thought too that this was poetical, to say that the falling
fortress blent her ashes with those of her former defenders. But if the significant
paternos is to go, what does Dr Postgate put in its place? *repentes*: a useless
epithet and a form not known to exist. For an inflexion of *repens* he can only cite
repenti; and that from Lucretius. iii xvii 1–4 'nunc, o Bacche, tuis humiles
aduoluimur aris: | da mihi pacato uela secunda, pater. | tu potes insanae ueneris
compescere fastus, | curarumque tuo fit medicina mero.' In 2 Dr Postgate writes
placatus for *pacato*, in 3 he proposes either *infensae* or *fluctus*: these conjectures
are all unnecessary and the first is downright harmful. The second distich means
as it stands 'thou canst quell the disdain of the frantic fair (exhibited for instance
at iv viii 72), and thy liquor heals the lover's grief': wine can make an angry
mistress kind or a slighted lover tranquil: this is tersely repeated in the next line
'per te iunguntur, per te soluuntur amantes'. What Propertius now seeks from
Bacchus is the second of these boons, tranquillity; therefore when he says 'da
mihi uela secunda' he specifies the favour asked by adding 'pacato'. Dr Postgate
refers to Ovid fast. iii 789 sq. 'mite caput, pater, huc placataque cornua uertas | et
des ingenio uela secunda meo': but if that passage shows that Propertius wrote
placatus it also shows that he wrote *mitis*. ||

At ii xvii 11 sq. the MSS have 'quem modo felicem inuidia *admirante* ferebant, | nunc decimo admittor uix ego quoque die'. Dr Postgate writes *adridente* and says 'corr. nos cf. Mart. v 6 5'. Martial there invokes on a friend the extravagant blessing 'sis inuidia fauente felix', may you be prosperous but escape envy; just as Ovid Ibis 121 sq. invokes on an enemy the extravagant curse 'sitque, quod est rarum, solito defecta fauore, | fortunae facies inuidiosa tuae', may you incur envy though wretched. Whether Propertius when prosperous escaped envy I do not know and it does not matter, for certain it is that he never said so here. If he were lamenting the loss of general goodwill, there would be some sense in the remark that he was formerly unenvied. But what he is lamenting here is the loss of Cynthia's favour; so the remark would be not merely irrelevant but perverse, because in real life envy is the measure of prosperity, and the way to describe supreme felicity is not to say that you were not envied but to say that you were: usque ad inuidiam felix. The sense therefore requires the very opposite of *adridente* (Ovid depicting Inuidia in met. II 775 sqq. writes 'risus abest, nisi quem uisi mouere dolores'), some such word as Heinsius' *maerente*. If the meaning and the ductus litterarum were all we had to think about I should confidently propose *lacrimante* (Ovid *l.c.* 'uixque tenet lacrimas, quia nil lacrimabile cernit'): one letter misplaced gives *aclrimante* which is barely distinguishable from *admirante*; but the MS reading may have come from *admirere* four lines above.

Very few of Dr Postgate's alterations are without diplomatical probability, like *sontes* for *longas* at III vii 60, where the best correction seems to be Francius' CAS⟨TAS⟩. On conjectures merely suggested in the notes it would not be fair to dwell; so I will only say that the proposal *ille* for *iste* at I ix 32 recognises a difficulty which all other editors have overlooked; that *strinxerat* for *triuerat* in IV vii 10 may well be right; and that the conjectures at I v 7, II i 10, vii 18, xxviii 22 and III xvi 16 are injudicious.

Two changes of punctuation deserve praise: one at III xix 21 where Dr Postgate appears to have discovered what has escaped previous editors, that *uenundata* is neut. plur. and not fem. sing.; and another at IV i 18–20 where a strong stop is placed after *sacro* and a light one after *equo*. Two on the other hand are detrimental. The first is at II xxii 17 sq. 'unicuique dedit uitium natura creato: | mi fortuna aliquid semper amare dedit', *i.e.* 'to every man at his birth has nature assigned some frailty, and the frailty she has assigned to me is to be always in love': in this connexion *fortuna* is just the same as *natura*: Sen. nat. quaest. v 18 8 'nimis delicate *fortuna* nos tractat; nimis dura *dedit nobis corpora, felicem ualetudinem.*' Dr Postgate punctuates 'natura; creato | mi fortuna' cet., which means (or else the change is aimless) 'to every man has nature assigned some frailty, but my frailty of being always in love was assigned to me after my birth by fortune, not by nature.' What is the drift of this fanciful distinction, to which Propertius makes no further allusion? It has nothing to do with the theme of the poem; nay it even snaps the thread of argument: 'you ask *why* I am always in love: love knows no *why*: why do fanatics gash themselves with knives?' – here come our verses, and if they set up a distinction between the origin of Propertius' *uitium* and the origin of others folks' *uitia* they are incoherent. The second change of stops to which I referred is at III xi 34 sqq. where Dr Postgate punctuates thus: 'totiens nostro Memphi cruenta malo, | tres ubi Pompeio detraxit harena triumphos | una; Philippeo' cet. What then is the normal number of shores required to rob a man of three triumphs? and how many places would you have expected Pompey to die in? Dr Postgate in praef. p. vi cites IV vi 68 'una decem uicit missa sagitta rates' to justify the antithesis of *tres* and *una*. There is nothing absurd in the antithesis of *tres* and *una*. The numerals do indeed create the antithesis, but its absurdity resides not in them but in the substantives, which are the names of things between which no antithesis is conceivable. And even if you removed the antithesis by removing *tres*, *una harena* would still remain intrinsically absurd, because a man cannot be assassinated on two shores nor be 'robbed of his triumphs' piecemeal.

At II xxxiv 29 'aut quid *Crethei* tibi prosunt carmina plectri' the letters of the MSS are defended with the remark '*Cretheis* Homeri mater'. The objection to this is that Homer is named at 45, neither alone nor in company with others already named (in which case the repetition might be intentional), but in company with Antimachus || who has not been mentioned before.

I come now to the most important feature of this recension, its transpositions. Since Lachmann in 1816 undid at once the good and evil deeds of Scaliger, the duty of transposition has been much neglected by editors of Propertius; and Dr Postgate's is the first text of the century (Gruppe and Carutti do not count) to employ this method of emendation as freely as another. On the proper limits of transposition in a book like this there may well be two opinions. As a Corpus Poetarum is a work of reference and chiefly meant for the general reader, there is some disadvantage in admitting even the most certain trajections; and in Dr Postgate's pages I fear the general reader will be led a weary dance after sundry verses in such poems as III vii or IV i. On the other hand transpositions are hard to judge of unless they are set before the eye; and a large page presenting more than 200 lines at once affords too good an opportunity to miss. I should not therefore say that there was here too much transposition if the new arrangements, however violent, were anything like certain: but many of them are not; and in some places Dr Postgate has tried to do what cannot be done. It is idle, for instance, to pretend that any transposition of IV v 21–62 can come so near certainty as to earn a place in a text. Here is a mere string of precepts: you might almost as well profess to rearrange the Sententiae of Publilius or the Proverbs of Solomon. One or two points are certain, *e.g.* Propertius never put 45 sq. where the MSS put them; and there is no harm in suggesting a better sequence, but it should stay in the notes. Dr Postgate's rearrangement is moreover ill-judged in some of its details, as in the collocation of 41 sqq. after 58. The poems iv i and xi also, where the task is less hopeless, undergo several transpositions which are neither necessary nor salutary.

The most salutary of the new transpositions is that by which iii xix 15 sq. are placed before 21 so that the passage runs 'crimen et illa fuit patria succensa senecta | arboris in frondes condita Myrrha nouae, | tuque, o Minoa uenundata Scylla figura | tondens purpurea regna paterna coma': thus without the change of a word the second distich acquires a construction and a strengthened sense, and the two examples of unfilial passion are brought into telling contrast. In ii iv, where Mr Birt placed 15 sq. after 8, Dr Postgate further puts 9 sq. (ill punctuated however) to stand after 14 to which they clearly belong: the two couplets had exchanged their stations. Again in iii iv he seems to be certainly right in removing 19 sq. from their present position and probably right in placing them before 11. In i xv he brackets 29–32 as alien from their context: this is the simplest way to connect 33 sq., as they must be connected, with 25 sq. ii x 7 sq. he likewise marks as out of place, which they plainly are. He may too be right in ejecting from iii vii the four verses 21–4 about Argynnus. His rearrangement of iv iv 1–14 is probable in the main, but is accompanied with needless alteration and does not remove all the roughness of the passage, which appears to be mutilated.

Some of Dr Postgate's transpositions are only slight variations on the transpositions of others, now for the better, now for the worse. In iv vii, where Schrader had brought 35–8 into contact with 73–6 by placing them after 76, Dr Postgate places them before 73, which improves the sequence of thought. Again in iii vii, where it had been proposed to put 43–66 and 17–18 between 10 and 11, Dr Postgate more aptly puts them between 8 and 9. But in the same elegy, where Scaliger proposed the arrangement 9–16, 67–70, 25, Dr Postgate spoils it by the more complicated transposition 9–12, 67–70, 13–16, 25. Scaliger's sense is 'Aquilo and Neptune, why did you shipwreck Paetus? Nereids, you should have saved him from drowning: restore his body to the land.' That is the natural order; but Dr Postgate reproaches the Nereids for not saving Paetus before he reproaches Aquilo and Neptune for wrecking him; and makes the command 'reddite corpus humo' include Aquilo, to whom it does not apply; and in order to do this transposes more verses than need transposing. Take again iii xi 47 sqq. '47–68 ita ordinauimus, 51–58 (Housm.), 47–48, 67–68, 59–60 (Pass.), 49–50, 65–66, 61–64.' Dr Postgate's predecessors had restored coherency to the passage at the expense of only five transpositions, 51–8, 65–8, 59–60, 47–50, 61–4: he has modified this arrangement by separating the two distichs 47–8 and 65–6 from the verses which follow them in the MSS. As to 65–6, the place which Dr Postgate finds for them is a good place, though I think the best place is between 60 and 47: the only objection is that they will do very well where they are. But his transposition of 47–8 distinctly injures the sense. Without that ‖ dislocation the passage runs thus: 'did Rome fear a woman's threat of war? what has become of the spoils of Hannibal? what avails it to have banished Tarquin if we must bear a woman's rule?' What Dr Postgate has done is to transpose the mentions of Hannibal and Tarquin, and make Propertius name Tarquin's expulsion in connexion with invasion and Hannibal's overthrow in connexion with tyranny.

IV vii begins 'There are such things as ghosts': 3–5 'Cynthia namque meo uisa est incumbere fulcro, | murmur ad extremae nuper humata uiae, | cum mihi somnus ab exequiis penderet amarus.' Dr Postgate, praef. p. v, like others before him very justly objects to such a vague and useless designation of place as 'extremae uiae', and proposes to transport hither 81–2, so that we get 'uiae, | pomosis Anio qua spumifer incubat aruis | et numquam Herculeo numine pallet ebur'. I for my part do not think that 81–2 can be spared from their context, since the 'hic' of 83 appears to presuppose some more definite indication of locality than is supplied by the 'pelle hederam tumulo' of 79; but that point I do not press. The main point is that the transposition removes only one of the difficulties in verse 4 and leaves two: *murmur uiae*, which Dr Postgate wishes to understand as *murmur fluminis*, and *humata ad murmur* 'buried near a noise'. I have now little doubt that Propertius wrote 'murmur ad extremae nuper humata *tubae*' 'newly buried to the drone of the funeral trumpet': so he has *extremo rogo*, *extremo puluere*, *extremi funeris*; and there were two easy ways from *tuuae* to *uiae*.

I have said already that it would be unfair to dwell on mere suggestions in the notes, so I will make no remark on the proposed transportation of II i 37 sq.

There are one or two changes of orthography: thus this is probably the first edition of Propertius to give the spelling *Suebus* at III iii 45. The effect of this however is rather spoilt by the occurrence of *Philetaeus* only seven lines below and again at IV vi 3.

Hitherto I have spoken only of Dr Postgate's own proposals; but after all the chief feature of the edition is the industry and judgment with which he has used the studies of his predecessors. The vulgate text is here improved and even transformed not only by many corrections published since 1880 but by many dating from the eighteenth or seventeenth century, neglected or expelled by Lachmann and only in part restored by Baehrens. Often too Dr Postgate gives back to earlier critics emendations which till now have been wrongly assigned. He is however himself in error in saying at III ix 9–19 'interpunximus', for the punctuation in question was the vulgate down to 1829. At IV iv 13–14 and once or twice elsewhere he omits to mention the first author of a transposition which he adopts.

The MSS employed are Baehrens' with the addition of Holkhamicus 333 and,

from IV xi 17 to 76, Parisinus 8233 and Vrbinas 641. Dr Postgate has injudi-
ciously complicated his apparatus criticus with two new signs, Δ for DV and Φ
for AF or FL. The value of such signs is that they save space, their drawback is
that they task the memory. When O is used for AFDV the saving of space is
considerable and the good outweighs the bad. But when Δ is used for DV the
space saved is too little to excuse an additional emblem; and Φ will be still more
of a nuisance to the general reader, since it means one thing from I i 1 to II i 63
and another from II xxi 3 to the end.

It is interesting to see the difference between this recension and the Select
Elegies of 1881, and to note how much which was then explained is now emended. That the change is for the better I cannot doubt: true, many alterations are
to my thinking unsuccessful, and import a good deal which is wrong and a great
deal which is doubtful; but the general result is a text which I should call not
only nearer but much nearer to the truth than any which has gone before it.

34

CICERO *PRO MILONE* c. 33 §90*

An ille praetor, ille uero consul, si modo haec templa atque ipsa moenia stare
eo uiuo tam diu et consulatum eius expectare potuissent, ille denique uiuus
mali nihil fecisset, qui mortuus, uno ex suis satellitibus [Sex. Clodio] duce,
curiam incenderit?

This is now the vulgate, since Madvig in 1831 expelled the gloss *Sex. Clodio*.
Mr A. C. Clark however proposes further to expel *duce* and then to write *cui
mortuo unus* instead of *qui mortuus uno*: another editor adopts the proposal, and
I see in the March number of this *Review*, p. 119, that Mr S. G. Owen approves
it.

Between *qui mortuus uno* and *cui mortuo unus*, so far as authority goes, there is
nothing to choose. The MSS split their votes: *qui mortuo unus* H, *cui mortuus uno*
E, *cum mortuus uno* T. The exchange of *qui* and *cui* is quite common; quite
common too is metathesis of inflexion, not only in this simple form, Stat. silu.
III 1 18 *angusto bis seni, angusti bis seno*, Aesch. supp. 373 [[369]] ἀστοῖς...
τῶνδε, ἀστῶν...τοῖσδε, but also in stranger fashions, Ovid am. II 5 27 *Phoebo
...Dianam, Phoebum...Dianae*, Eur. Hipp. 331 αἰσχρῶν ἐσθλά, ἐσθλῶν αἰσχρά.
The choice of reading therefore will depend on other considerations.

cui mortuo unus requires the expulsion of *duce*. Mr Clark says 'I conceive *Sex.
Clodio duce* to have been a marginal note, founded upon Ascon. 34 [[29 Clark]]
populus *duce Sex. Clodio* scriba corpus...intulit, and ib. 55 [[49 Clark]] *Sex.
Clodius, quo auctore* corpus...illatum fuit.' There is nothing impossible about
this; but the supposed adscript is at any rate of a much less common type than
the gloss assumed by Madvig: here then the vulgate has the advantage.

But a much heavier objection to *cui mortuo unus...incenderit* is its rhetorical
inferiority. If Cicero throws away his chance of this impressive figure, the dead
man firing the senate-house, he is not the workman I take him for. Nay, for the
sake of his argument, he cannot afford to throw it away; 'would Publius living
have done no evil when Publius dead burnt down the senate-house by the hand
of Sextus?' has at least a superficial air of plausibility; but 'would Publius living
have done no evil when Sextus burnt down the senate-house in honour of
Publius dead?' gratuitously prompts the retort that you cannot fairly argue
from what Sextus did to what Publius would have done.

* [[CR 10 (1896), 192–3]]

But then on the other hand Mr Clark most justly impugns the sense of *uno ex suis satellitibus duce*: 'if we ask, whom the *satelles* led, the answer can only be, the ghost of Clodius'. When Publius fires the senate-house by the hand of Sextus, Sextus is not *dux*, he is *minister*; and *ministro* accordingly I suspect we should have found, had not the context suggested to Cicero a more vigorous and striking synonym: 'qui mortuus, uno ex suis satellitibus *face*, curiam incenderit'. In Phil. II 19 48 Antony's relation to this same P. Clodius is hit off by this same metaphor: Antony is 'eius omnium incendiorum fax', the match with which he kindled all his conflagrations. The error in the MSS may have begun with the absorption of *f* in the preceding *s*: this often happens, and here in E and T the same cause has stolen away the *S* of *Sex* and left only *ex*.

Since I am writing about Cicero and quoting the second Philippic, I may as well assign to its author the emendation, now thirty years old, of a ridiculous corruption still current in some texts of that speech. In 34 87 are these words: 'iam iam minime miror te otium perturbare; non modo urbem odisse sed etiam lucem; cum perditissimis latronibus non solum de die sed etiam in diem uiuere': these are the dire effects of a guilty conscience. *in diem uiuere* is a well-known phrase and means 'to live for the day alone', 'to take no thought for the morrow', as the Gospel bids us; *de die uiuere* is not a well-known phrase but is supposed to mean 'to live on what the day brings in'. Antony therefore (so intolerable is his remorse for having offered the crown to Caesar) not only lives on what the day brings in, but even takes no thought for ‖ the morrow, in the company of the most abandoned ruffians: the ruffians, I presume, assist him in these brutish excesses. This nonsense was emended, twenty years before C. F. W. Mueller or Hauschild, by Badham; but for fear the editors of Cicero should get wind of the emendation he stowed it away, where no one would think of looking for it, in the index to a recension of Plato's Euthydemus and Laches, and for further security muffled it up in a joke. On the last page of the book, under the promising heading 'ὑγιεινόν et εἰπεῖν οἷον confusa', is this note:

'In Cic. Phil. II 34 absurde legitur: *non solum de die, sed etiam in diem uiuere*. Quam lectionem miror tamdiu τῶν κριτικῶν πονηρίᾳ bixisse.'

That is to say, Cicero wrote 'non solum de die sed etiam in diem *bibere*'.

35

OVID'S *HEROIDES* [I]*

All Ovid's works, except the amatory poems, are now equipped with a decent apparatus criticus. The apparatus to the amatory poems is no more decent than themselves: the three chief MSS containing them were collated by Keil in 1851: his collations were lent to three editors in succession, Merkel Riese and Ehwald, and remain unpublished to this day; for let no one fancy that what stands on pp. xiv–xvi and xx–xxii of Merkel's preface is anything but a string of excerpts. But Korn in the ex Ponto, Korn and Mr Riese in the metamorphoses, Mr Riese and Merkel in the fasti, Mr Ellis in the Ibis, Mr Owen in the tristia, Mr Kunz in the medicamina, Mr Sedlmayer in the heroides, Mr de Vries in the Sappho, have furnished full and exact collations of the principal MSS. Nothing is now lacking but an editor. But Nicolaus Heinsius is dead and buried; and Ovid, in spite of all this new material, is perhaps in a worse condition than he was two hundred years ago.

Merkel and his followers accomplish this result, not merely by depraving the text with a number of bad readings drawn from good MSS, but by two other methods, both efficacious: they expel the emendations of Heinsius, and they insert their own. With few exceptions, of which Mr Palmer is much the most conspicuous, Ovid's modern editors have been unfortunately distinguished by the very least Ovidian qualities in the world: an instinctive distaste for simplicity and a warm affection for the hispid. To read, for instance, the latest German and English texts of the tristia, you would sometimes fancy that the editors had mistaken the meaning of ex Pont. IV 13 19 'Getico scripsi sermone libellum' and supposed the tristia to be the 'libellus' in question. Merkel, whom his adherents call sospitator Ouidii and other such names, and who really did make some good emendations among many bad, is well described by Madvig: 'in textu recensendo iudicii contortioris et ad artificiosa et obscura inclinantis, non ita raro certissimarum emendationum ab aliis factarum contemptor, nouarum inuentor subabsurdarum et prope incredibilium'. Mr Riese is saved by common sense and a comparative purity of taste from the most grotesque excesses of the two Teubner editors, but he is fully their accomplice in their worst offence. It is not that they afford so little illumination themselves: it is that they stand between us and the light. In the 17th and 18th centuries Ovid was as lucky as he is unlucky now.

* [*CR* 11 (1897), 102–6]

He was intently studied and brilliantly emended by the two greatest of all critics of Latin poetry. The discoveries of those critics are uncongenial to our modern editors, who treat them accordingly. They steadfastly ignore the work of Bentley, and they diligently undo the work of Heinsius.

The heroides have been less unfortunate than any other portion of Ovid's works. They have been edited by Mr Palmer, who, if his judgment is not equal to his genius, has at any rate emended Ovid with more success than any man of this century but Madvig. The MSS have been examined and classified with care and discretion by Mr Sedlmayer in his prolegomena critica 1878. They form three families, the first represented by P (Parisinus 8242 saec. XI), beyond comparison the most important MS, the second by G (Guelferbytanus extran. 260 saec. XII), the third less distinctly by a number of MSS among which E (fragmentum Etonense saec. XI) is the oldest but not the best.

I 13–22

In te fingebam uiolentos Troas ituros,
  nomine in Hectoreo pallida semper eram.
siue quis Antilochum narrabat ab Hectore uictum   15
  Antilochus nostri causa timoris erat,
siue Menoetiaden falsis cecidisse sub armis
  flebam successu posse carere dolos.
sanguine Tlepolemus Lyciam tepefecerat hastam,
  Tlepolemi leto cura nouata mea est.   20
denique, quisquis erat castris iugulatus Achiuis,
  frigidius glacie pectus amantis erat.

15. The words 'Antilochum ab Hectore uictum' could not in any context represent what happens at Iliad O 583–91, where there is no combat at all, but Antilochus sees Hector coming and instantly runs off into safety. Least of all can that be the reference here, where Penelope is making the most of her fears and *vanquished* must be held to imply *killed*: see the following verses and especially the summary in 21 '*denique* quisquis erat... || *iugulatus*'. But Antilochus was not killed by Hector. Say it were possible for Ovid to forget not only the Aethiopis but also the express statement of Homer in Od. δ 187 sq. that Antilochus was killed by Memnon: what Ovid could neither forget himself nor hope that his readers would forget is that Antilochus in the Iliad survives Hector and is nowhere so brimful of life as after Hector's death, in Ψ 287–613. The so-called Hyginus indeed in fab. 113 'quem quis occidit' has the words 'Hector Protesilaum, idem Antilochum'. But if that statement is uncorrupt it doubtless comes from this very passage of Ovid, for Ovid is one of Hyginus' authorities. Since however only six lines above in fab. 112 'qui cum quo dimicarunt' he writes 'Antilochus cum Memnone: Antilochus occiditur', and since you expect at least

to find Patroclus among Hector's slain, Moriz Schmidt is probably right in assuming some such lacuna as this: 'Hector Protesilaum, idem *Patroclum. Memnon* Antilochum'.

But what seems to me an even worse and less credible fault than this contradiction of a notorious story is the penury and resourcelessness of *Hectore* and *nomine Hectoreo* in two consecutive lines. Therefore, instead of such bold expedients as changing Antilochus twice over into Amphimachus or Anchialus, I should write

> siue quis Antilochum narrabat ab *hoste reuictum.*

Thus the three examples taken will refer to the three chief champions of Troy: Memnon, Hector, Sarpedon.

uictum is so common and *reuictum* so rare that the false division (compare trist. I 9 33 where the best MS has *turnere lata* for *Turne relata*) is nothing to wonder at: then, under the influence of *Hectoreo* above, *hostere* passed, probably through the transposition *hestore*, into *hectore*. This particular form of error I illustrated in Journ. Phil. vol. XVIII pp. 31 sq. [[this edition pp. 158–9]]: here are more examples: Ovid her. IV 45 *uersare, seruare,* ars ii 729 *seruandus, uersandus,* (I should add Verg. buc. X 68 *seruemus, uersemus*), met. V 246 *detrectas, detractes,* ex Pont. II 10 43 *absim* (read *apsim*), *ipsam,* Plaut. rud. 545 *ballena, bellana,* Sen. Thy. 416 *dantem, tandem,* Herc. Oet. 496 *facilis* in species, faciles inspicies, Stat. Theb. II 311 *descisse, discesse,* copa 34 *prisca, crispa,* Cic. ad Att. IV 5 2 *facerem, feceram.* A close parallel to this corruption of *hostere* by transposition to *hestore* and thence by external influence to *hectore* occurs in her. VIII 69 where Ovid wrote *distinet* but our MSS give *destinat:* the mistake began with the spelling *distenet,* which is not very uncommon in MSS as old as P; then came the transposition *destinet,* and then the grammatical correction *destinat:* at Hor. epist. I 2 5 the MSS exhibit a similar sequence in full, *distinet* the true reading, *distenet, destinet,* and finally *detinet* to make sense.

The verb 'reuinco' is used once again by Ovid fast. VI 432 'iudicio forma reuicta tua est', once by Horace carm. IV 4 24, thrice by Lucretius I 593, IV 488, V 409. In prose it generally means 'refuto' or 'conuinco', and so it does at Lucr. IV 488; at Lucr. V 409 and in Horace it may mean 'uicissim uinco', but need not; at Lucr. I 593 and in Ovid it seems to mean simply 'uinco'.

II 105–18

105 Iamque tibi excidimus; nullam, puto, Phyllida nosti.
   ei mihi, si, quae sim Phyllis et unde, rogas.
  quae tibi, Demophoon, longis erroribus acto
    Threicios portus hospitiumque dedi,
  cuius opes auxere meae, cui diues egenti
11C   munera multa dedi, multa datura fui,

> quae tibi subieci latissima regna Lycurgi
>   nomine femineo uix satis apta regi,
> qua patet umbrosum Rhodope glacialis ad Haemum
>   et sacer admissas exigit Hebrus aquas,
> cui mea uirginitas auibus libata sinistris   115
>   castaque fallaci zona recincta manu.
> pronuba Tisiphone thalamis ululauit in illis
>   et cecinit maestum deuia carmen auis.

Phyllis professes to fear that Demophoon has forgotten her very existence, and proceeds therefore to remind him who she is, – that Phyllis who did him so much kindness, 107 'quae tibi', 111 'quae tibi'. But into the midst of these relatives relating to Phyllis there intrudes the preposterous distich 109 sq., with 'cuius' and 'cui' relating not to Phyllis but to Demophoon; and then after 'quae' for Phyllis in 111 you slip back again to 'cui' for Demophoon in 115: for all the world as if she were explaining to Demophoon who Demophoon was. As for 109 sq., the only way to fit that couplet || for the post it occupies is to write with brutal violence 'cuius opes auxere *tuas, quae* diues egenti' cet. If Ovid put it where it stands he must have written *tuas* and *quae*; but if Ovid had written *tuas* and *quae* the scribes would not have written *meae* and *cui*; therefore Ovid did not put it where it stands. Accordingly Suringar placed 109 sq. after 114: but there they dangle miserably, as 115 sq. already do, from the distant 'tibi' of 111; and they are the merest repetition of what has been said more vigorously above. Madvig, who makes the same transposition, corrects the former vice but does not much disguise the latter by putting a full stop at the end of 114, and writing interrogatively 'cuius opes auxere meae? cui . . . datura fui?' I propose therefore to make one slight alteration more. Transpose the distich with Suringar, put a full stop after 114 with Madvig, and proceed with the fresh sentence thus:

> cuius opes auxere meae, cui diues egenti   109
>   munera multa dedi, multa datura fui,
> *huic* mea uirginitas auibus libata sinistris   115
>   castaque fallaci zona recincta manu.
> pronuba Tisiphone cet.

Down to 114 she enumerates her benefits to Demophoon: then she goes on 'the man for whom I did all this and was ready to do more repaid me only by betrayal': 109 sq. sum up, for the purpose of this contrast, what has already been said at length. *cui* in 115 may come from the loss of the initial and the rearrangement of the letters *uic*.

v 81–8

Non ego miror opes, nec me tua regia tangit,
　　nec de tot Priami dicar ut una nurus;
non tamen ut Priamus nymphae socer esse recuset,
　　aut Hecubae fuerim dissimulanda nurus.
85　dignaque sum et cupio fieri matrona potentis:
　　sunt mihi, quas possint sceptra decere, manus.
nec me, faginea quod tecum fronde iacebam,
　　despice: purpureo sum magis apta toro.

85. Cupio fieri matrona potentis! With these dignified and persuasive words does Oenone expect to win back her lover. She *wants to marry a person of importance*; Paris is the only such person who happens to be handy; surely then he will not say no. And just five lines above she has declared 'non ego miror opes, nec me tua regia tangit'!

Faber proposed 'dignaque sum *regis* fieri matrona potentis', which effectually mends the sense; and there ought to be no doubt that this indecent *et cupio* is a mere stopgap for some lost word which invested 'potentis' with a clearer meaning. But there is no reason to be seen why *regis* should fall out; and Ovid more likely wrote

dignaque sum fieri *rerum* matrona potentis:

rerum perishing between *ieri* to the left of it and *m* to the right. 'rerum potentis' = 'summo imperio praediti', Lucr. II 50 and III 1027 'reges rerumque potentes'.

VI 25–40

25　'Aesonides' dixi 'quid agit meus?' ille pudore
　　haesit in opposita lumina fixus humo.
protinus exilui tunicisque a pectore ruptis
　　'uiuit an' exclamo 'me quoque fata uocant?'
'uiuit' ait. timidum quod amat: iurare coegi.
30　uix mihi teste deo credita uita tua est.
ut rediit animus, tua facta requirere coepi.
　　narrat aenipedes Martis arasse boues,
uipereos dentes in humum pro semine iactos
　　et subito natos arma tulisse uiros,
35　terrigenas populos ciuili marte peremptos
　　inplesse aetatis fata diurna suae.
[deuictus serpens. iterum, si uiuat Iason,
　　quaerimus. alternant spesque timorque fidem.]
singula dum narrat, studio cursuque loquendi
40　detegit ingenio uulnera nostra suo.

I print this passage as I believe it ought to stand. In 29 the admirable reading of E and a few other MSS, *timidum quod amat*, has already been adopted by Mr Shuckburgh, who compares I 12 'res est solliciti plena timoris amor'. This part of the epistle is ‖ torn out of P: the rest of the MSS have *timidum quod ait* or *timidumque mihi* or the like. Some editors accept Heinsius' conjecture 'uiuit, ait *timidus*: *timidum* iurare coegi'; but if Heinsius had known of the reading of E he would not have made that conjecture. At 31 Merkel Riese Sedlmayer and Ehwald give *utque animus rediit,* because it is in G: Mr Palmer reads as above with a few MSS, because he is a competent critic. At XIII 29 occur the very same variants, the metrical interpolation *utque animus rediit* in G, the Ovidian *ut rediit animus* in other MSS; but P, which is absent here, is there present, and of course supports the latter. Round goes the weathercock: Merkel and his retinue adopt in that place the true reading which they reject in this and which they would reject again in that if P were absent. They apparently edit ep. VI before they have read ep. XIII, and do not edit ep. XIII until they have forgotten ep. VI.

Merkel Palmer and Ehwald obelise 31–8 as spurious. I know not which to wonder at more: those who think that 37 sq. are Ovid's, or those who think that 31–6 are not Ovid's. 37 sq. are a shameful interpolation, ungrammatical in language, inept in sense, and destructive of coherency; for all they do is to prevent 'singula dum narrat' from following as it ought on the narration, and to make it follow on an interruption of the narration. But as for 31–6, it is really too bad that Ovid should be robbed of these splendid verses because 'they follow too closely after the similar account vs. 10–14'. The repetition is one of his most triumphant feats. In 10–14 he has related the labours of Iason, and you think you never read a more sterling piece of rhetorical description:

> isse sacros Martis sub iuga panda boues,
> seminibus iactis segetes adolesse uirorum
> inque necem dextra non eguisse tua,
> peruigilem spolium pecudis seruasse draconem,
> rapta tamen forti uellera fulua manu.

Now, to show you how easy it is to him, he relates them over again in new language, and does it even more brilliantly than before: there is no better written couplet in all his works than 35 sq. He stops before he comes to the dragon and the fleece, partly for variety, partly that 'singula dum narrat' may come in the more naturally. The diligent interpolator misses an equivalent to 13 sq. and inserts his precious 'serpens'.

VI 107–8

Illa sibi Tanai Scythiaeque paludibus udae
quaerat et a patria Phasidis usque uirum.

Medea might seek a husband *a Phaside* or *a patria sua*, but not *a patria Phasidis*, for there is no such place. Aethiopia is *patria Nili*: the Nile, 'qui patriam tantae tam bene celat aquae' (am. III 6 40), rises there and flows thence into Egypt. Greece is *patria Alphei*, because Alpheus runs under sea to Sicily; but it is not *patria Eurotae*. *patria Tiberis* can stand for Etruria or for Vmbria, whichever the Tiber takes its rise in, but for Italy it cannot stand; and *patria Phasidis* is the name for nothing on earth. *patria* is *pria*, which is *ripa* with one letter out of place.

Now will it be believed that this necessary and certain emendation was made long before me by Richard Bentley; that it was published three-quarters of a century ago; and that not one editor of Ovid has accepted it, and only one has even mentioned it? Bentley's emendations are the most important contribution to the criticism of Ovid which has been made since Heinsius. Since they were published in the Oxford edition of 1825–6, many MSS of Ovid have been collated with the utmost diligence; but no collation of any MS since 1826, or indeed since 1661, has helped so much towards purifying the text as Bentley's emendations might have helped. Haupt again and again called attention to their value; but who was Haupt, that an editor of Ovid should listen to him? It is hard to write without bitterness of the loss of time inflicted on an intelligent student by editors who cannot even be trusted to hand down the discoveries which their betters have made. You are reading v 121 in a vulgar text:

dixerat: in cursu famulae rapuere furentem.

dixerat is flatly contradicted by *in cursu rapuere*: you think for a long or a short time, you remember am. I 8 109 or fast. v 245, and you write '*uox erat* in cursu: famulae' cet. And this correction was made by Heinsius and approved by Bentley! and not an editor mentions it except Mr || Sedlmayer, who mentions all Bentley's conjectures, not because he thinks they deserve it, but because the Oxford edition is scarce. There would be no end, if I drew up a list of the places in Ovid where I have been put to the trouble of making Bentley's and especially Heinsius' conjectures over again and wasting hours which might have been profitably employed; but I must quote from the heroides one place more, where the correction is necessary and important and absolutely disregarded: VIII 33 sq. 'at pater Aeacio promiserat, inscius acti: | plus *patre, quo* prior est ordine, *pollet* auus' Bentley, for *quoque* (or *quoque qui*)...*posset* (or *possit*): the editors retain the text, with its meaningless *quoque* and its foolish subjunctive, all except Mr Palmer who introduces a conjecture of his own which is rather impossible than improbable.

Sometimes it is the MS reading that one has to recover by guessing. In xv (Sappho) 129 sq. all the editors print this nonsense:

> oscula cognosco, quae tu committere linguae
> aptaque consueras accipere, apta dare.

One immediately corrects 'committere (= coniungere) *lingua*', and compares am. II 5 23 sq. 'inproba tum uero iungentes oscula uidi, | illa mihi *lingua nexa* fuisse liquet'. And *lingua* is the reading of the best MS!

36

OVID'S *HEROIDES* [II]*

VII 23–6

Vror, ut inducto ceratae sulpure taedae,
ut pia fumosis addita tura rogis.
Aeneas oculis semper uigilantis inhaeret,
Aenean animo noxque diesque refert.

24 and 25 are found neither in P nor in G nor in more than a few of the other MSS.

The archetype itself contained many interpolated verses, which appear accordingly in P and G and all the rest. But some of the later MSS proffer new interpolations, from which P and G and many of the others are free. I here enquire whether, in spite of this fact, any of the later MSS preserve genuine verses which have been omitted by P and G.

Some of the inserted lines betray their spuriousness plainly in language or metre, as v 26 'est in qua nostri littera scripta memor' and IV 132ᵃ sq. 'Saturnus periit, perierunt et sua regna: | sub Ioue nunc mundus; iura Iouis sequere': such as these I leave alone. Nor shall I here discuss the couplets with which many MSS have filled up real or imaginary gaps at the opening of certain epistles. But I shall examine five places in the body of the poems where later MSS offer verses which are missing from the oldest.

First VIII (Hermione) 19 sqq.

sit socer exemplo nuptae repetitor ademptae,
nupta foret Paridi mater, ut ante fuit.

So P and G and most MSS. In hopes of making sense, Merkel and others have altered *sit* to *si,* but have made no sense: the meaning is imagined to be 'if your father-in-law had set about reclaiming his bride in your fashion (*exemplo* for *tuo exemplo*!), my mother would have remained the bride of Paris': 'neque oratio constat (neque enim post *si* omitti *esset* aut *fuisset* potest) neque sententia ulla est' says Madvig. Mr Riese has another plan: '*sis* (socer exemplo *est*) nuptae repetitor ademptae: | nupta foret, Priami mater ut ante fuit?' The reader cannot construe this pentameter, so I must explain that Mr Riese intends it to signify 'ought your bride to be what my mother formerly was to Paris?' Now turn

* [[CR 11 (1897), 200–4]]

from these editors to a critic: Madvig adu. crit. 1 p. 46 'Ouidius scripserat: *sit socer exemplo nuptae repetitor ademptae* (sequere exemplum soceri tui); deinde excidit pentameter et hexameter ab *si* incipiens condicionemque continens (si, ut tu, lente raptam coniugem tulisset), cuius apodosis est in u. 22 *nupta foret Paridi mater, ut ante fuit.*' Well, a few late MSS give:

> sit socer exemplo nuptae repetitor ademptae,
>   *cui pia militiae causa puella fuit.*
> *si pater ignauus uacua stertisset in aula,*
>   nupta foret Paridi mater, ut ante fuit. . .

and these verses, in one form or another, are accepted by Heinsius and the old editors in general. The lines fill the gap which Madvig detects; they fill it with the sense which he requires; and they exhibit the homoearchon (*sit* 19, *si* 21) which explains their disappearance from the other MSS. But Burmann pointed out that *stertisset* (this is clearly the original reading: some MSS have the blunder *stetisset*, and others *sedisset* or *plorasset* as attempts to correct that blunder) is a false form for *stertuisset*. It is not indeed in itself suspicious; but Persius has *destertuit*, and it is strange that Probus and Priscian, who quote that for *stertui*, should ignore *sterti* if *stertisset* stood in Ovid's heroides. To be sure, you might conjecture *iacuisset* and assume that the first half of the verb was absorbed by *uacua* and then restored amiss; but it is still perhaps a trifle clumsy that *socer* in 19 should mean '*your* father-in-law' and *pater* in 21 '*my* father'; and if with one MS you read *socer* in 21, that is worse, because *mater* in 22 ought then to mean '*your* mother'. Therefore, I hesitate to say that these two verses, though they make good a real defect, are genuine.

Next I take the best authenticated instance. XIII (Laodamia) 73 sqq.

> pugnet et aduersos tendat Menelaus in hostis:
>   hostibus e mediis nupta petenda uiro est.
> causa tua est dispar.‖

Laodamia says that Menelaus has a reason for risking his life but Protesilaus has none. Not a word is wanting, and no one could suspect an error. But almost all the MSS, except the three oldest, P, G and V (frag. Vindobonense saec. XII), present the passage thus:

> pugnet et aduersos tendat Menelaus in hostis,
>   *ut rapiat Paridi quam Paris ante sibi;*
> *irruat et, causa quem uicit, uincat et armis:*
>   hostibus e mediis nupta petenda uiro est.

Heinsius thought these verses Ovid's, and in themselves they are quite Ovidian. Moreover there is no visible reason why an interpolator should insert them. But in this context they are alien and disturbing. The hexameter 75 with its irrelevant antithesis 'causa quem uicit, uincat et armis' serves merely to distract attention from Laodamia's argument. The pentameter 74 serves just the same purpose as 76, and therefore must be spurious if 76 is genuine. But it may be genuine if 76 is spurious; and surely 74 is much the better and more Ovidian pentameter of the two. I strongly suspect then that what Ovid wrote is this:

> pugnet et aduersos tendat Menelaus in hostis,
>   ut rapiat Paridi quam Paris ante sibi.
> causa tua est dispar.

And this is actually the reading of two Gotha MSS saec. XIII and XV. The variants will then be explained as follows. The true pentameter *ut rapiat...* was early lost and its place supplied by *hostibus e...*: this stage appears in P G V. Later the true pentameter was written in the margin; but then, in the copy from which most of our MSS descend, it was inserted, not instead of the false pentameter, but beside it, and an hexameter was manufactured to stand between them.

     Come now to VII (Dido) 97 sqq.

> exige, laese pudor, poenas, uiolate Sychaei,
>   ad quas, me miseram, plena pudoris eo.

For *Sychaei* some MSS have *Sychaeu* or *Sychaeo* or *Sychaee*. This distich is compact of vice: *pudoris* is impossible beside *pudor*, so Heinsius suggests *ruboris*; the style having been thus improved, what is to be the construction and the sense? if you read '*umbraeque* Sychaei' with Merkel or '*taedaeque* S.' with Mr Birt, those are violent changes; if you read with some old editors 'uiolate Sychaee, | ad *quem*', that is a violent change and a harsh asyndeton into the bargain. Now see how a very few late MSS relieve the passage of all its faults:

> exige, laese pudor, poenas, uiolata*que lecti*
>   *iura nec ad cineres fama retenta meos,*
> *uosque, mei manes, animaeque cinisque* Sychaei,
>   ad quas, me miseram, plena pudoris eo.

I do not understand how anyone can doubt that this interpolator, if interpolator he is, has hit precisely on the seat of corruption: the scribe's eye glanced from a *que* in 97 to a *que* in 99 and he wrote

> exige, laese pudor, poenas, uiolataque Sychaei,

which was then reduced to metre by the conjecture *uiolate* in agreement with 'pudor'. The sense too is just what Ovid must have given. *cinisque* in 99 cannot be right, and Bentley proposes *umbraeque* which might be lost after *animaeque*: for the expression compare met. VIII 488 'fraterni manes animaeque recentes', Verg. Aen. V 80 sq. 'recepti | nequiquam cineres animaeque umbraeque paternae', Sil. XIII 395 'manis animasque suorum'. If the lines are an interpolation, its ingenuity is amazing; but before we call them probably genuine let us take one instance more.

II (Phyllis) 17 sqq.

> saepe deos supplex, ut tu, scelerate, ualeres,
> ipsa mihi dixi 'si ualet ille, uenit'.

This, as may be seen, is neither sense nor grammar. One MS, the old but very corrupt and interpolated Etonensis, saves the grammar and leaves the sense forlorn with the obvious and trumpery conjecture *diis* for *deos*; and one editor, Mr Palmer, proposes *deo* in emulation. Mr Palmer I believe is a student not only of Ovid but of Dickens; so I suppose that is the reason why he makes Phyllis talk like Mr F's Aunt. Now in the first Aldine edition (an. 1502) is given the following supplement: ||

> saepe deos supplex, ut tu, scelerate, ualeres,
> *sum prece turicremis deuenerata focis;*
> *saepe, uidens uentos caelo pelagoque fauentes,*
> ipsa mihi dixi 'si ualet ille, uenit'.

Burmann also found the lines in two MSS: of MSS now known only one, Giessensis bibl. acad. 66 (saec. XIV), presents them, with the reading *cum prece turmoniis sum uenerata sacris*. Here is a deliverance indeed. The pentameter 'ipsa mihi' cet. is now no longer a maundering irrelevancy but apt and beautiful; the homoearchon *saepe* in 17 and 19 shows at a glance how the two lines were lost; and the diction, as Mr Sedlmayer points out prol. crit. p. 52, is thoroughly Augustan: the rare *turicremus* occurs in Ovid himself at ars III 393 'turicremas …aras', and the rarer *deueneror* in Tib. I 5 14 'somnia ter sancta deueneranda mola'. I heartily agree then with almost every editor old and new that the lines are Ovid's; and I wish the lesson taught by this passage to be remembered in dealing both with the passage last considered and with the passage from which I started and to which after this long circuit I now return, VII 23–6.

To begin with, 24 and 25 appear in the same cod. Giessensis which has preserved II 18 and 19; but they appear also in seven other MSS of Mr Sedlmayer's, including the respectable Francofurtanus which is our chief authority for the epistula Sapphus. Necessary to the sense they are not; but that may be thought to tell in their favour, because there was nothing to prompt an interpolation. And if they are genuine there is a plain reason why they should fall out: *uror* and *ut, Aeneas* and *Aenean*. And further, it is surely much more Ovidian to give such different thoughts as the contents of 23 and 26 a distich apiece, than to crowd them in a single couplet. For all these reasons put together I think that 24 and 25 are genuine.

But still to admit them will entail one trifling change. In the distich 'Aeneas oculis semper uigilantis inhaeret, | Aenean animo noxque diesque refert' you cannot have day in both verses and night in the pentameter alone. Therefore I should emend the passage thus:

> uror, ut inducto ceratae sulpure taedae,
> ut pia fumosis addita tura rogis.
> Aeneas oculis semper uigilantis inhaeret,
> Aenean animo noxque *quiesque* refert.

There is perhaps some trace of this in P, which has not *diesque* but simply *dies*: that may mean that when 24 and 25 had been lost and the mention of day became necessary in 26, someone wrote *dies* in the margin, and P substituted this not for *quies*, like the other MSS, but for *quiesque*.

VII 73–8

> Da breue saeuitiae spatium pelagique tuaeque:
> grande morae pretium tuta futura uia est.
> 75   nec mihi tu curae: puero parcatur Iulo.
> te satis est titulum mortis habere meae.
> quid puer Ascanius, quid di meruere penates?
> ignibus ereptos obruet unda deos?

The old vulgate of 75 was the 'nec mihi tu *parcas*' of many MSS, which gives a fair sense, though 'tu' is superfluous and worse: Heinsius introduced from a few MSS the much more elegant 'nec mihi *parcatur*'. He was acquainted with the 'nec mihi tu curae' of P and G, but of course he never dreamt of printing such nonsense. The modern editors all accept it, and evidently have no inkling that there is anything wrong. Yet what could be more preposterous? How can Dido pretend that she does not care for Aeneas? what in the world is she writing this epistle for? what does she mean by saying 22 'unde tibi, quae te sic amet, uxor erit?', 29 sq. 'non tamen Aenean, quamuis male cogitat, odi, | sed queror infidum questaque peius amo', 61 sq. 'perdita ne perdam, timeo, noceamue nocenti, | neu bibat aequoreas naufragus hostis aquas', 170 [168] 'dum tua sit Dido, quidlibet esse feret', 180 sqq. [178–81] 'tempora parua peto, | dum freta mitescunt et amor... | si minus, est animus nobis effundere uitam'? But I am almost ashamed to speak about a point so obvious.

Dido has been plying Aeneas with reasons against sailing: the weather is stormy; the sea is dangerous at the best of times; dangerous especially to oath-breakers; he can have a safer voyage if he will but wait. Now she goes on '*Even if you care nothing for these considerations*, at least have pity on your son.'

> *haec minus ut cures*, puero parcatur Iulo.

hec min' ut cures for *nec mihi tu cure*. I have altered all four words; but the four alterations together are only a trifle: *haec* and *nec* are much exchanged, *minus* and *mihi* at Plaut. truc. 900 and elsewhere, *ut* and *tu* just four lines back at 71, where Madvig restores *ut tum* for *tutum*, and many a time again. To write *nos* or *me* for *nec* is less easy: to write *nil*, which the scribes would spell *nihil*, for *mihi* is equally easy but has less of an Ovidian flow.

VII 81–6

Omnia mentiris; nec enim tua fallere lingua
    incipit a nobis primaque plector ego.
si quaeras ubi sit formosi mater Iuli,
    occidit a duro sola relicta uiro.
haec mihi narraras: at me mouere! merentem   85
    ure: minor culpa poena futura mea est.

This reading of 86 (*ure* P, *inde* G, *illa* al.) and punctuation of the couplet have been rightly adopted by Madvig and the latest editors from Burmann. In 85 the above reading is that of the MSS with no considerable variation except that E and many others have *nouere* for the *mouere* of P and G. The required sense is well stated by Madvig: 'manifestum est intellectumque ab aliis, Dido se incusare, quod non admonita ipsius Aeneae de se narratione fraudem cauerit, poenamque non recusare.' The words are apparently supposed, by those who retain them, to signify: 'you told me this story: *it melted my heart!* torture me, for I deserve it: my punishment will be less than my fault.' But that 'me mouere' should mean anything of the sort is a flat impossibility. 'mouere' in itself is a word of neutral sense and means simply 'to produce an effect upon'. Here, where its subject is a tale of betrayal, its sense, if it ceases to be neutral, can only be 'to produce *its* effect (its natural effect) upon': that is, 'to render mistrustful'. Therefore, if *mouere* is retained, *at* must be altered, with Burmann and a few MSS, to *nec* (I would not suggest *haut*): 'you told me this story, yet it was wasted upon me', – therefore she deserves to suffer for her blindness.

Madvig on the other hand obtains equally good sense by writing '*di* me *monuere*' 'it was a warning from heaven'. I accept *monuere*, but I write with a slighter change

    haec mihi narraras: ſat me monuere: merentem ure cet.

'you told me this story: it gave me fair warning'. The cause of the corruption is obvious. The form *sat* already occurs once in the heroides at XII 75, and I shall have to introduce it once again.

VII 191–6

Anna soror, soror Anna, meae male conscia culpae,
    iam dabis in cineres ultima dona meos.
nec consumpta rogis inscribar Elissa Sychaei;
    hoc tamen in tumuli marmore carmen erit:
'praebuit Aeneas et causam mortis et ensem.   195
    ipsa sua Dido concidit usa manu.'

The *tamen* of 194 has either an absurd meaning or none at all. *sed* would be sense: that would mean 'my epitaph shall not link my name with Sychaeus, but, on the contrary, with Aeneas'. *tamen* means 'my epitaph shall not link my name with Sychaeus, but, in spite of that, it shall link it with Aeneas': which is ridiculous. Bentley, as you would expect, paid attention to this, and rendered *tamen* correct by changing the *nec* of 193 to *et*: that is, 'my epitaph shall link my name with Sychaeus, but, in spite of that, with Aeneas too'.

But the whole tenour of the epistle is surely in favour of *nec*; so I would rather alter *tamen* itself:

hoc *tantum* in tumuli marmore carmen erit.

tantum and *tamen* are eternally confused, and no wonder, when the abbreviation *t̄m* means *tamen* in one MS and *tantum* in another. I think this *tantum* 'merely' is supported by fast. III 547 sqq. where this epitaph of Dido is repeated word for word, with the introduction, also borrowed hence, 'tumulique in marmore carmen | hoc *breue*, quod moriens ipsa reliquit, erat'.

VIII 43-50

Ille licet patriis sine fine superbiat actis,
 et tu quae referas facta parentis habes.
Tantalides omnis ipsumque regebat Achillem:
 hic pars militiae, dux erat ille ducum. ||
tu quoque habes proauum Pelopem Pelopisque parentem;
 si medios numeres, a Ioue quintus eris.
nec uirtute cares. arma inuidiosa tulisti,
 sed tu quid faceres? induit illa pater.

45

50

45. Instead of *regebat*, P has *petebat*, which I suspect to be, as it sometimes is, a corruption of *tenebat* 'commanded', possibly through *tepebat*. *regebat* may then be either a correction of *petebat*, or an explanation of *tenebat*, or a corruption of it, possibly through *tegebat*.

50. The required sense of 'tu quid faceres?' is not 'how could *you* help it?' but simply 'how could you help it?' so the pronoun only cumbers the ground. The required sense of 'induit illa pater' is 'your father put those arms upon you', but it cannot have the required sense: it signifies 'your father put those arms upon himself': 'induo arma' without a dative means 'induo arma mihi', not 'alteri'. Repair the defect by discarding the superfluity:

sed *tibi* (quid faceres?) induit illa pater.

See ars I 197 'induit arma tibi genitor patriaeque tuusque'.

VIII 55–60

Increpat Aeacides laudemque in crimina uertit,   55
    et tamen aspectus sustinet ille meos.
rumpor et ora mihi pariter cum mente tumescunt
    pectoraque inclusis ignibus usta dolent.
Hermione coram quisquam obiecit Oresti,
    nec mihi sunt uires nec ferus ensis adest?   60

59 is thus written by the first hand of P; the first hand of G omits the verse; the second hands of both, which are entirely worthless, amend the metre with *quisquamne*. But *obiecit* remains doubly vicious: it is perfect when it ought to be present; and it lacks an accusative, though no example is quoted of the absolute use of the verb. Therefore, if there were reason to think *quisquamne* the true reading, I should remove these two vices by altering *obiecit* to *obtrectat*.

But the *ne* has no authority, and other MSS give *quisquam haec* and *si quisquam* and *si quicquam* and *quicquamne*: it is quite evident that the line was metrically deficient in the archetype, as it is in P, and has been variously but unskilfully mended. To get rid of all its faults, not in metre only but in sense and grammar too, I propose

      Hermione coram quicquam obiecit ⟨alter⟩ Orestae?

alt-er would easily vanish between *ecit* and *or*. *obiĕcit* = *obicit*.

37

OVID'S *HEROIDES* [III]*

IX 7–10

Hoc uelit Eurystheus, uelit hoc germana Tonantis
laetaque sit uitae labe nouerca tuae;
at non ille uenis, cui nox, si creditur, una
non tanti, ut tantus conciperere, fuit.

uenis in 9, which has no tolerable sense, is given by P and G and the overwhelming majority of other MSS. Three or four have *uelit*, which Heinsius and all modern editors adopt. βροτοῖσιν οὐδέν ἐστ' ἀπώμοτον, but it is improbable almost to the last degree that any scribe would alter *uelit* into *uenis* here, with *ille* standing close by to protect the 3rd pers., and two other *uelit*'s hovering like guardian angels overhead.

The sentence 'cui nox una non tanti fuit, ut tantus conciperere' is the purest nonsense, and editors who deliberately retain it are merely professing their ignorance of what the Latin phrase 'non tanti fuit' means. 'Nam, si priore significatione uti uelis, quid hoc est, noluisse Iouem unam noctem accipere ea condicione, ut tantus fieret Hercules? sin altera, non minus absurdum erit, noluisse Iouem unam noctem subire, ut Hercules tantus efficeretur. praeterea utraque ratione Iuppiter dicitur noluisse Herculem magnum fieri, cum sententia poetae sit, uoluisse' Madvig opusc. II 194. Therefore some write with a few MSS 'non *tanta*'; but the change by a copyist of *tanta* to *tanti* in this context is as nearly impossible as the change of one letter can ever be; and *tanta* after all will only mean 'tam longa', while it appears to me that the sense demands 'sat longa'. So Bentley seems to have thought, for he adopted from a few other MSS the conjecture 'non *satis*': I do not know that this is more violent than *tanta*, but violent it certainly is. Here then in a couple of verses are a couple of very unlikely alterations: we must try another road.

An expedient which may at first sight look attractive is this: to keep the pentameter unaltered and import into the hexameter some noun meaning *spatii* or *ambitus* to agree with *tanti* as a genitive of quality: 'cui nox una non tanti ambitus fuit, ut tantus conciperere'. To write *orbis* for *uenis* would be rough and unsatisfactory: a more plausible change would be to expel *ille uenis* as a stopgap

* [[CR 11 (1897), 238–42]]

for a lost word and write 'at non, ⟨ circuitus ⟩ cui' cet., supposing *circuitus* to have fallen out because of *cui*. But this incurs the same objection as *tanta*, that the sense will require not *tanti* or 'tam longi' but 'sat longi'; and I only make the suggestion in order to deter anyone else from making it.

There is another way which I think much better. Alter *uenis* ($u = b$ and $n = u$) into *breuis*, and *non tanti* into a dative participle with the meaning of *laboranti*:

> at non ille, *breuis* cui nox, si creditur, una
> *luctanti*, ut tantus conciperere, fuit.

If the initial *l* succumbed to one of the many perils of the margin, the neighbourhood of *tantus* would naturally detach -*tanti* and cause it to be taken for a separate word; and the change of the remnant *uc* into *nō* would be almost as easy as the similar change of the abbreviations *ñc* and *u'o* which so often turns *nunc* and *uero* into *non*. *luctanti* is specially appropriate as being a uox amatoria, Prop. II 1 13 and 15 5.

IX 43–6

> Mater abest queriturque deo placuisse potenti,
> nec pater Amphitryon nec puer Hyllus adest.
> arbiter Eurystheus irae Iunonis iniquae
> sentitur nobis iraque longa deae.

The words 'arbiter irae' are doubtless capable of meaning what the editors take them to mean, the dispenser of the wrath of Juno. But I am astonished that either Ovid or any respectable versifier should be supposed capable of writing 'arbiter irae Iunonis iraque longa deae'. And further there is both a general and a particular reason for expecting 'arbiter' to mean something quite different. When the wife of Hercules uses such words as 'arbiter Eurystheus sentitur nobis', the reference, but for the presence of 'irae', would naturally be to Eurystheus' lordship over ‖ the seed of Jove, and 'arbiter' would signify 'arbiter domus nostrae'. And Ovid, though I do not find that the editors mention it, is here copying the language of Virgil Aen. VIII 291 sqq. 'ut duros mille labores | *rege sub Eurystheo fatis Iunonis iniquae* | pertulerit'. I believe then that 'arbiter' in Ovid has the same sense as 'rege' in Virgil, and that 'irae', which prevents 'arbiter' from having that sense, has usurped the place of an ablative explaining how Eurystheus came by his sovereignty. That ablative was not *fatis*, which is much too vague and Virgilian for Ovid, and would not have been lost: several words are possible, but the following seems the most apt and likely:

> arbiter Eurystheus ⟨astu⟩ Iunonis iniquae
> sentitur nobis iraque longa deae.

In eurysthe-*us-as-tu-iu*-nonis the cause of the omission is plain: then *irae* was supplied from below. The reference of course is to Juno's famous trick narrated in Hom. Il. T 95–125: see 96 sq. καὶ τὸν | Ἥρη θῆλυς ἐοῦσα δολοφροσύνης ἀπάτησε, 106 τὸν δὲ δολοφρονέουσα προσηύδα πότνια Ἥρη, 112 Ζεὺς δ' οὔ τι δολοφροσύνην ἐνόησε. It may be worth mentioning that Ovid in his account of the retarded birth of Hercules at met. IX 285 sqq. has 'Iunoni iniquae' 296 and 'iniqua Iunone' 308 sq. Perhaps *furto* is almost equally probable.

IX 131–4

Forsitan et pulsa Aetolide Deianira
　　nomine deposito paelicis uxor erit,
Eurytidosque Ioles et insanii Alcidae
　　turpia famosus foedera iunget Hymen.

133 *et insanii* P, *atque insani* G and most MSS. This latter is an undisguised interpolation in aid of metre and accidence; and *insani* is at once so inept and so disgusting that there is no need to consider it. Bentley suggested *atque Inachii* or *atque Aonii*; but these are based on the falsified text of G. A much more probable conjecture would be *et Sidonii* (= Thebani), if this were not discountenanced by 101 sq. 'haec tu Sidonio (= Tyrio) potes insignitus amictu | dicere? non cultu lingua retenta silet?' and if you did not expect a patronymic to match 'Eurytidos'. I think however that *Sidonii* after all may have something to do with the present state of the text. If the MS reading were once upon a time *et ionii*, then *sidonii* would be a natural conjecture to restore the sense and metre, and the correction *ionii*, by the confusion of *d* with *a*, might easily engender *insanii*. But *et ionii* would stand for *et et-ionii*, that is

Eurytidosque Ioles et *Ech*ionii Alcidae.

For a similar loss see trist. I 10 13 *uastis et* for *uasti secet*. Hercules was sixth in descent from Echion: Hipponome the mother of Amphitryon was the daughter of Menoeceus the grandson of Pentheus.

IX 153–8

　　Heu deuota domus! solio sedet Agrios alto;
　　Oenea desertum nuda senecta premit;
155　　exulat ignotis Tydeus germanus in oris;
　　alter fatali uiuus in igne fuit;
　　exegit ferrum sua per praecordia mater:
　　impia quid dubitas Deianira mori?

156. 'Latet mendum in hoc uersu . . . an *fatali uiuus in igne perit*?' Heinsius; and Bentley too adopts *perit*: Francius with more external probability proposes *cinis*, which hardly gives a just meaning. *fuit* however is quite intolerable: write

alter fatali uiuus in igne *situs*.

If you suppose the last letter to have been lost, the remnant *situ* hardly differs from *fuit* in appearance: the difference between *fuit* and *situs* in point of diction is more considerable.

X 29–32

Inde ego, nam uentis quoque sum crudelibus usa,
uidi praecipiti carbasa tenta noto.
aut uidi aut tamquam quae me uidisse putarem
frigidior glacie semianimisque fui.

In 31 *putarem* is given by P, by V (frag. Vindob. saec. XII), and by other MSS; *putaui* by G and others. *tamquam* is given by G, *fuerant* by V and others: some have *etiam*, but those appear also to have *cum* instead of *quae* and to be interpolated; and I only mention them because the second hand of P is among them, and proves, by writing *etiam*, that *etiam* was not in P. ‖ What was in P is doubtful: Merkel says that it seems to have the same as G, *aut tamquam*, under an erasure; but the later editors Messrs Sedlmayer and Palmer represent it as giving *a///uam*, and Mr Sedlmayer adds that after *a* the remains of *ut* are discernible; and the dimensions of the gap as depicted by him and Mr Palmer will not hold more than one or at most two letters beside those two.

About the required meaning of 31 sq. the editors seem to be quite unanimous. Some of them fancy that the words possess it already, others know that they do not and try to confer it upon them by conjectures and fail, others try again and succeed; but the same meaning, that given for instance by Madvig's 'aut uidi aut *tantum quia* me uidisse *putaui* | frigidior glacie semianimisque fui', is the meaning sought or found by all. Very well then: throw all their explanations and all their emendations into the fire: they are vitiated through and through by an utter misconception of what Ovid is saying. It most unluckily happens that there are two passages which have a strong verbal likeness to this: XVIII (Leander) 31 sq. 'lumina quin etiam summa uigilantia turre | *aut uidet aut* acies nostra *uidere putat*' and Verg. Aen. VI 454 '*aut uidet aut uidisse putat* per nubila lunam': critics have been led astray by these delusive parallels and have fancied that because Ovid here uses or seems to use a similar vocabulary he is conveying a similar thought. But firstly, though it would be just and beautiful to make Ariadne say (like Catullus in 64 55 'necdum etiam sese quae uisit uisere credit') that at her first glimpse of the flying sail she did not know whether it were real or imaginary, I cannot conceive anything much more silly and aimless than to make her say (as the editors do here) that at the time of writing this letter to Theseus she still does not know whether she really saw or only fancied that she saw the sail. And secondly, she proceeds to contradict this notion flatly. When you come to 43 sqq. you read '*iamque oculis ereptus eras. tum denique* fleui: | torpuerant molles *ante* dolore genae. | quid potius facerent quam me mea lumina flerent, |

postquam desierant uela uidere tua?': so she did see the sail, and she knows that she saw it.

As to the meaning and the form of the sentence I feel no doubt at all, but the erasure of P and the divergency of the other MSS make the wording uncertain. It seems clear however that emendation must be based on the *tamquam* of G which is supported against the other MSS by the *uam* of P. Therefore I conjecture

> *ut* uidi, *haut dignam* quae me uidisse putarem,
> frigidior glacie semianimisque fui.

ut is Bentley's and J. F. Heusinger's: both *ut* and *haut* are eternally confused with *aut.* 'quae' is acc. plur. neut.: the meaning is 'when I saw such a sight as methought I did not deserve to see'. Compare II 61 'speraui melius, *quia me meruisse putaui'*, v 7 sq. 'leniter, ex merito quidquid patiare, ferendum est: | *quae uenit indigno poena, dolenda uenit.'*

The corruption would begin with the easy change of *gn* to *qu, dignam* to *di quam*: indeed [*di q*]*uam* itself, for aught I know, may be under the ///*uam* of P; or perhaps in P *dignam* was corrupted to [*di*]*uam* by that frequent loss of *g* beside *n* which at XXI 216 [214] has transformed *digna* to *bina*. I have also thought of 'ut uidi, *indignam* quae' cet., *indi* being absorbed by *uidi* and leaving only *gnam* or *quam* for the scribes to spin into metre. The *etiam* of certain MSS, as I have said, appears to be interpolated and assuredly was not in P; so let no one conjecture *meritam*. The *fuerant* of V is also very suspicious and discountenanced by P; so I would not suggest *uerum*, i.e. *aequum* 'fair'.

But if you like to assume that another word in the verse is corrupt it will be possible to follow the *aut tamquam* of G very closely indeed:

> *ut* uidi, *haut umquam* quae me *me*ruisse putarem,

or perhaps *hautquaquam* (Verg. georg. IV 455 'hautquaquam ob meritum', where by the way one MS has *aut quamquam* as again at Aen. XII 45). The loss of *me-* after *me* and the expansion of *-ruisse* to *uidisse* are corruptions of which I shall elsewhere give several examples but here only one: VI 55 where Mr Palmer emends 'urbe uirum *iuui'*: *iu* was absorbed by *ui* or *m*, and *ui* was expanded to *uidi* which stands in the MSS. Then for the sense and language compare II 61 already cited 'speraui melius quia *me meruisse putaui'*.

x 67–75

> Non ego te, Crete centum digesta per urbes,
>   aspiciam, puero cognita terra Ioui, ||
> *ut* pater et tellus iusto regnata parenti
> 70   prodita sunt facto, nomina cara, meo.
> cum tibi, ne uictor tecto morerere recuruo,
>   quae regerent passus, pro duce fila dedi,

> *tum* mihi dicebas 'per ego ipsa pericula iuro
>   te fore, dum nostrum uiuet uterque, meam'.
>   uiuimus, et non sum, Theseu, tua.   75

Thus should this passage be written and punctuated. The full stop at the end of 70 instead of the usual comma, and the *tum* (from a few MSS) in 73 instead of the usual *cum*, are due to Bentley: these alterations are made in order that the important point contained in 75 may be introduced in a workmanlike and not in a bungling manner. What I have done is to put a comma at the end of 68 instead of the usual full stop, and to write *ut* (= ex quo tempore) in 69 instead of *at*. *at* has no meaning in this place and was altered by Heinsius and Bentley with some MSS to *nam*: the modern editors (except that Mr Ehwald proposes *a*) retain it, because one conjunction is much the same as another.

x 83–6

> Iam iam uenturos aut hac aut suspicor illac,
>   qui lanient auido uiscera dente, lupos.
> forsitan et fuluos tellus alat ista leones.   85
>   quis scit an et saeuas tigridas insula habet?

85 *alat* P, *alit* G et plerique. 86 *et saeuas*] *et haec* P, *haec saeuas* G et alii, *hec etiam* V. *tigridas* G et alii, *tigrides* (*trigides*) P, V, alii. *habet*] *habent* P, sed corr.

I do not think that I can emend verse 86, but I think that I can remove one obstacle to its emendation. The conjectures hitherto proposed either retain 'quis scit an...habet' and are solecistic, or alter it and are violent. The best attempt yet made to correct the grammar is Wakker's, who transposes *habet* with the *alat* of 85. But a much easier transposition will achieve the desired result. Suppose the couplet once stood thus:

> quis sc*it an et* fuluos tellus alat ista leones?
> fors*itan et* saeuas tigridas insula habet.

It will be seen that *itanet* occurs in the first verse immediately above *itanet* in the second. I suggest then that the scribe at that point wandered from the hexameter into the pentameter and wrote

> quis scit an et | saeuas tigridas insula habet...

then saw what he had done, and added the lacking members

> forsitan et | fuluos tellus alat ista leones...

and then appended marks of transposition. But the next scribe, finding a pentameter before an hexameter, concluded that he was to transpose these; and accordingly produced our present text.

I only profess to have mended the grammar: there is much more to mend. *saeuas* is very uncertain, and the elision *insula habet* is not to be defended by

resistere equos penned at Tomi and taken straight from Propertius. I make no
further proposal of my own, but I will say that the best among the various
conjectures, now that it will no longer be solecistic, seems to me to be Gronovius' *saeuam tigrida Naxos habet.*

X 145–6

Has tibi plangendo lugubria pectora lassas
infelix tendo trans freta longa manus.

These two lines and the two which follow them are properly expelled by Bentley
as spurious; but still one need not be too proud to emend them. *longa* in the
pentameter is omitted by P, which probably means that the original ran

infelix tendo trans freta *lata* manus.

The scribe glanced from *ta* to *ta*: at II 122 'aequora lata' a similar error has
caused *lata* to be lost and supplanted by *nota* in G. 'freta lata' is found at met.
XI 749: 'freta longa' is much commoner, her. VII 46, XIV 103, XVI 22, am.
II 11 5, met. VII 67, VIII 142, fast. III 868, V 660, and therefore likely to occur
to a corrector.

XI 121–8

Tu tamen, o frustra miserae sperate sorori, ||
    sparsa, precor, nati collige membra tui,
et refer ad matrem socioque inpone sepulchro,
    urnaque nos habeat quamlibet arta duos.
125   uiue memor nostri lacrimasque in uulnera funde
    neue reformida corpus amantis amans.
tu, rogo, dilectae nimium mandata sororis
    perfer: mandatis persequar ipsa patris.

In the last distich the words *tu . . . perfer* can only be explained as addressed to
a servant who is to carry Canace's letter to Macareus: 'do you *convey*' etc.:
perfer means nothing else. But this is out of the question, and Hor. serm. I 10 92
and Prop. III 23 23 sq. are no parallels at all: such an address cannot form a part
of Canace's epistle. Nor indeed is *tu* intelligible without a vocative, when *tu* in
121 means Macareus. Then further, the words *mandatis persequar* are neither
sense nor Latin: in G and many other MSS they are altered into *mandatis
perfruar*, which is grammatical but laughable: a few MSS try another road and
write *mandatum persequar*, which is better but very bad: the singular *mandatum*
after the plural *mandata* is most incompetent writing, and the corruption into -*is*
of the acc. termination -*um* by the side of a transitive verb is nothing less than
inexplicable. Heinsius accordingly judged the couplet spurious; but he despaired
too soon.

To begin with, the first sentence is excellently emended in one MS, quoted by Heinsius himself, which alters *perfer* to *perfice*. The words are then addressed, as they should be, to Macareus, and make perfect sense: for the corruption compare XIII 122 where *refecta* has been changed to *referre*, and Livy XLV 28 10 there adduced by Madvig where *refici* has been changed to *referri*. I propose to complete the emendation thus:

> tu, rogo, dilectae nimium mandata sororis
> *perfice*: mandatis *opsequar* ipsa patris.

Some accident obliterated *o*, and *psequar* was mistaken for *psequar*.

38

OVID'S *HEROIDES* [IV]*

XII 62–6

Mane erat, et thalamo cara recepta soror
disiectamque comas aduersaque in ora iacentem
inuenit et lacrimis omnia plena meis.
65   orat opem Minyis: alter petit, alter habebit:
Aesonio iuueni, quod rogat illa, damus.

In 65 G and the old editors have *petit altera et altera habebit* which is un-Ovidian in metre and makes nothing fit to be called sense ('my sister asks and my sister shall have'). It is altered by some to *at altera habebat* ('my sister asks the boon but it was mine to give'), by others to *at alter habebit* ('but another, i.e. Iason, will have it'): these changes mend nothing but the metre.

All this while the reading of P is *alter petit alter habebit*. This was commended long ago by Salmasius at Iul. Capit. Maximin. 1 'barbaro etiam patre et matre genitus, quorum *alter* e Gothis, *alter* ex Alanis genitus esse perhibetur', and more lately by Mr Birt in the Goettingische gelehrte Anzeigen for 1882 p. 854 who says 'bei der sentenziösen Form der Rede musste hier für *altera petit* nothwendig *alter petit* eintreten'; and it is printed by the three last editors Messrs Sedlmayer Ehwald and Palmer. The grammar is no doubt correct enough, but the sense is every whit as foolish as before. When you have said that A asks help for B you never add that the asker is one person and the recipient will be another: that is said already, and more than that. Reverse the order, say 'alter petit, alter habebit: soror orat opem Minyis', and you will get something like sense: then you will be saying first that one person makes a request for another, and you will be saying secondly who those two persons are. But the verse as it stands is in the full sense of the term preposterous.

Ovid wrote   orat opem Minyis. alter petit, ⟨ impetrat ⟩ alter:
                    Aesonio iuueni, quod rogat illa, damus.

'My sister asks my aid for the Minyae. The boon is begged by one but extorted by another: it is to Iason that I yield the request preferred by Chalciope.' What moved Medea was not her sister's prayers but her own passion for Iason: this is stated first in the vaguest terms, then explained with particularity in the penta-

* [CR 11 (1897), 286–90]

                                                    [286

meter. The scribe glanced from *petit* to *-petrat* and left the verse defective, so *habebit* was tacked on at the end. A parallel will be found in line 84 of this epistle: Ovid wrote 'sed mihi tam faciles *unde meosque deos?*' which stands in P; but G and other MSS have this wealth of variants, *arbitrer unde deos, unde putabo deos, unde deosque putem, unde deos habeam, esse putabo deos, auguror esse deos*: all springing from an archetypal 'sed mihi tam faciles *unde deos*' with *meosque* missing.

XII 89–92

> Haec animum – et quota pars haec sunt? – mouere puellae
> simplicis, et dextrae dextera iuncta meae.
> uidi etiam lacrimas: an pars est fraudis in illis?
> sic cito sum uerbis capta puella tuis.

It is no use to quote II 51 'credidimus ‖ lacrimis: an et hae simulare docentur?' 'I trusted your tears: are tears also taught to feign?' where the interrogation and the present tense are as appropriate as they are inappropriate here. Here 'pars fraudis' means 'a share in your cajolery of me', and 'illis' therefore means '*your* tears': but it is absurd for Medea to ask whether Iason's tears helped to cajole her: she knows that they did, and she must here be affirming that they did. *an* is therefore altered to *a* by Mr Lucian Mueller, whom Mr Ehwald follows, and to *ac* by Mr Riese. But still we are not out of the wood: *est* should be *fuit*: the tears and the cajolery are both of them past and gone. This second error, though not the former, is abolished by Heinsius' proposal 'an pars *sua* fraudis': he compares met. XIII 350 sq. 'desine Tydiden uultuque et murmure nobis ‖ ostentare meum: *pars est sua laudis in illo*'. If you like to combine this conjecture with one of the others and write, say, '*a*, pars *sua* fraudis in illis', the verse will yield a proper meaning.

But the following is as near to the MSS, nearer to the parallel in met. XIII, and more pointed in sense:

> uidi etiam lacrimas: pars est *sua laudis* in illis,
> *si* cito sum uerbis capta puella tuis.

si is Bentley's and should in any case be accepted. With *laudis* instead of *fraudis* the tense of *est* becomes correct: the glory still endures. Compare II 65 sq. '*sum decepta tuis* et amans et *femina uerbis*: ‖ di faciant *laudis* summa sit ista tuae' and X 130 'non ego sum *titulis* subripienda tuis'. I suppose that *ua* fell out before *la* and left *slaudis*, which was corrupted to *fraudis* by the simultaneous confusion of *s* with *f* and of *l* with *r*, just as, for instance, *fulgebat* was corrupted to *surgebat* at fast. II 500: then *an* is possibly the missing *ua* but more probably a metrical supplement. The conjectures '*a*, pars est *laudis* in illis' and '*a*, pars *et* fraudis in illis' I should think less likely.

XIV 53–66

Saeuus, Hypermestra, pater est tibi: iussa parentis
    effice: germanis sit comes iste suis. –
55   femina sum et uirgo, natura mitis et annis:
    non faciunt molles ad fera tela manus. –
quin age dumque iacet fortis imitare sorores:
    credibile est caesos omnibus esse uiros. –
si manus haec aliquam posset committere caedem
60   morte foret dominae sanguinulenta suae. –
hanc meruere necem patruelia regna tenendo

    .   .   .   .   .   .

finge uiros meruisse mori: quid fecimus ipsae?
    quo mihi commisso non licet esse piae?
65   quid mihi cum ferro? quo bellica tela puellae?
    aptior est digitis lana colusque meis.

This is Hypermestra's soliloquy on her marriage night, as repeated by herself. She argues alternately for and against the murder of her bridegroom: 53 sq. *for*, 55 sq. *against*, 57 sq. *for*, 59 sq. *against*, 61 sq. . . ., 63 sqq. *against*: it is pretty clear, both from the contents (patruelia regna tenendo) and from the place of that distich in the series, that 61 sq. must be *for*. Therefore I have adopted the *hanc* of V and some other MSS: P reads *aut*, G apparently *i*, without meaning; other MSS *haud* or *an* or *non* or *quid*, perverting the sense; Mr Riese proposes *at* which may be right.

The pentameter which I leave blank is erased in P, and the second hand, which is good for nothing else, informs us what the erased words were not, by presenting in a mutilated form the ridiculous and unmetrical verse which we call 62 and which appears in most MSS as *quae tamen externis danda forent generis*. G also has this verse, but between 61 and 62 it exhibits the verse which we call 114, *cum sene nos inopi turba uagamur inops*. V, which in this place omits the four lines between 60 and 65, presents them after 118, and what it there presents is 61, 114, 63, 64, and not 62 at all.

Now come to the neighbourhood of 114:

111   bella pater patruusque gerunt; regnoque domoque
112   pellimur; eiectos ultimus orbis habet.
113   *ille ferox solio solus sceptroque potitur:*
114   *cum sene nos inopi turba uagamur inops.*
115   de fratrum populo pars exiguissima restas:
116   quique dati leto, quaeque dedere, fleo. ||

The couplet 113–14 is not in P and is not in V: the pentameter is tautological after 111 sq., and the hexameter is stamped as non-Ovidian by the scansion *potītur*.

Now can anyone doubt what lies under the erasure in P between 61 and 63?
The verse 114. P ignored 62 and ignored 113, just as V ignores them; and it
placed 114 where V places it, after 61. In the source from which most of the
other MSS descend, 114 was wrongly placed between 112 and 115, just fifty
lines or two pages away, and then the hexameter 113 was fabricated to make it at
home in its wrong place, and the pentameter 62 to fill up its right one; and both
the fabrications bewray themselves by their metrical vices. In the source of G,
though 114 still stood in its right place, 62 was imported from the other family
and set beside it, and 114 was repeated in its wrong place with 113 by a similar
importation. The original reading of P, 114 after 61, and 62 and 113 nowhere, is
exactly preserved (without V's misplacement of 61–4 after 118) by the Gothanus
primus, saec. XIII, which I mentioned in my note on VII 23 sqq. as giving the
right lines in the right order at XIII 73 sqq.

Now I am not the first to perceive that 114 stood in P between 61 and 63: that
has already been recognised by Mr Lucian Mueller d. r. m.[2] p. 27 and Mr Sedlmayer prolegg. p. 54. But they both think that P was here in error, and I believe
I am the first to say what when once said is obvious, that between 61 and 63 is
the right place for 114. The sense is perfect. Hypermestra nerves herself to
strike with the reflexion

> hanc meruere necem patruelia regna tenendo;
> cum sene nos inopi turba uagamur inops. –

'They have earned this doom by usurping our kingdom; we are exiled and
beggared.' Then she renders answer to herself 'Grant that they have deserved
to die: have we deserved to be murderesses?'

XIV 79–82

> Mane erat, et Danaus generos ex caede iacentis
> dinumerat. summae criminis unus abes.
> fert male cognatae iacturam mortis in uno
> et queritur facti sanguinis esse parum.

82. '*facti* sanguinis' is doubtless defensible: Livy XXXV 51 3 'nondum aut
indicto bello aut ita commisso ut strictos gladios aut *sanguinem* usquam *factum*
audissent': the *fusi* of G is therefore neither necessary nor even desirable, far less
the *factum* of other MSS. But I confess that after '*cognatae* iacturam mortis'
I expect something weightier than merely '*facti* sanguinis parum'; and I conjecture *sacri*. That means blood whose shedding is an abomination: Sen. Phoen.
277 sq. of the sceptre of the house of Laius 'nemo sine *sacro* feret | illud *cruore*',
Thy. 94 sq. 'ne *sacra* manus | uiolate *caede*', Hor. epod. 7 19 sq. 'Remi | *sacer*
nepotibus *cruor*', Lucan III 314 sq. 'tractentur *uolnera* nulla | *sacra* manu', X 334
'mens inbuta semel *sacra* iam *caede*': III 124 sq. 'nullasque feres, nisi *sanguine*

sacro | sparsas, raptor, opes' is not quite parallel. The change is very easy, so like is *s* to *f* and *r* to *t*; and at fast. v 670 the two best MSS have *facta* for *sacra*.

XIV 101–8

Per mare, per terras cognataque flumina curris:
     dat mare, dant amnes, dat tibi terra uiam.
quae tibi causa fugae? quid, Io, freta longa pererras?
     non poteris uultus effugere ipsa tuos.
105   Inachi, quo properas? eadem sequerisque fugisque:
     tu tibi dux comiti, tu comes ipsa duci.
per septem Nilus portas emissus in aequor
     exuit insana paelicis ora boue.

At 103 Egnatius long ago enquired whether *Io* here has its first syllable short 'as in the Ibis' or whether it is the interjection *io*. *Io* with its first syllable short is a false quantity: at Ibis 622 *Io* is not ᾿Ιώ but ῎Ιων 'the Ionian'. *io* the interjection is metrical; but anything more exquisitely absurd than that impassioned exclamation in this purely formal apostrophe to a long-departed ancestress I cannot well imagine. Here then is one difficulty recognised: there remain three which seem to receive no attention at all. Has anyone ever asked himself what 'freta longa pererras' means? It describes very well the wanderings of Ulysses, but we are talking about Io: in what human tongue does 'freta longa pererrare' signify to swim the Bosporus? Again: Io is trying to ‖ escape by flight from her own changed form, which clings to her still: am I the only person in the world who finds it comical that one in this situation should be described as 'sibi *dux*'? And again: does nobody else perceive that the hexameter 105 cannot coexist with 103, but must stand at the beginning of the apostrophe or stand nowhere at all?

The two verses 103 and 106 are interpolations prompted by the fact that 104 and 105 have by mischance been placed in inverted order, the pentameter before the hexameter. I have already pointed out a similar interpolation at 62 and 113; and at IX 82 Merkel detected another: 81 and 83 are interpolations prompted by the corruption of 82 from an hexameter into a pentameter. Our passage originally ran thus:

101   per mare, per terras cognataque flumina curris:
102   dat mare, dant amnes, dat tibi terra uiam.
105   Inachi, quo properas? eadem sequerisque fugisque:
104   non poteris uultus effugere ipsa tuos.
107   per septem Nilus cet.

For the contrast of *fugis* and *effugere* compare Lucr. III 1068 sq. 'hoc se quisque modo *fugit*...quem...*effugere* haud potis est.'

XV 39–44

Si nisi quae facie poterit te digna uideri
  nulla futura tua est, nulla futura tua est.   40
at, mea cum legeres, etiam formosa uidebar;
  unam iurabas usque decere loqui.
cantabam, memini (meminerunt omnia amantes):
  oscula cantanti tu mihi rapta dabas.

41. The vice in this line was first detected by Wakker. Reading Sappho's poems could not alter Phaon's opinion about Sappho's looks. What altered that opinion was to see and hear Sappho herself reading her poems aloud: this is plain from the pentameter and from the next distich. Wakker therefore corrected *legeres* to *legerem* and so restored the sense but ruined the metre. There is no such verse in Ovid; the two examples in Propertius are very soon emended; the one example in Tibullus is hard to emend, but his MSS are almost the worst in the world; Manil. I 794 sq. 'censu Tullius oris | emeritus caelum et Claudi *magna* propago' is to be corrected *haud indigna* or *nec* Claudi *indigna*; IV 661 'obruit, et Libyam *Italas* infudit in urbes' has already been corrected *Latias*. Here one MS has *tibi iam* for *etiam*, and this Mr de Vries proposes to accept. But write

at, mea cum *legerem, sat iam* formosa uidebar.

legerēsatiam for *legeresetiam*. Of the form *sat* I spoke at VII 85: the present passage is imitated from Prop. II 18 29 sq. 'mihi per te poteris *formosa uideri*: | mi *formosa sat es,* si modo saepe uenis'.

XV 139–40

Illuc mentis inops, ut quam furialis Enyo
  abstulit, in collo crine iacente feror.

Enyo is given by the best MS: the variants *Eritho* and *Erictho* and *Erinnis* and the like are merely corruptions of this *Enyo* or *Enuo*: see Mart. spect. 24 3 *Ethiuo, Ethriuo,* VI 32 I *Eripo,* Petron. 120, 62 *Erinis,* Lucan I 687 *Erynis,* Sil. x 202 *Erinis,* all blunders for the same name. Here the editors read *Erichtho* and suppose it to be the name of a witch because there is a witch of that name in the sixth book of Lucan. Mr de Vries has an excursus on the passage and is inclined to accept *Enyo*; but since it cannot here mean the goddess of war he diffidently proposes to take it as equivalent to *Erinys*. Mr Palmer reads *Enyo*, in what sense I do not know.

It means Bellona: not of course the Italian goddess of war, but the Cappadocian goddess of hysterics whom the Romans brought home from the Mithradatic campaigns and the frenzy of whose votaries is described at length in Tibull. I 6 45 and more briefly in dozens of other places. Ovid requires a Greek name for Sappho to call her by, and takes the 'Ενυώ which was the recognised equivalent of the other Bellona. The question whether Sappho had ever heard of this divinity was not likely to trouble either him or his readers, who had been accustomed from their childhood to see the Bellonarii misconducting themselves in the streets of Rome. ||

XV 197–8

Non mihi respondent ueteres in carmina uires,
plectra dolore tacent, muta dolore lyra est.

Ovid never wrote such a pentameter as this; and if you say that the writer of this epistle was not Ovid, he never wrote such a pentameter either. Verse 40 cited above is a piece of false taste, but its perpetrator had his eyes open and gloried in his deed: this is a piece of sheer incompetence. Read and punctuate as follows:

plectra dolore *iacent* muta, dolore *lyra*.

est is omitted by one MS: it was not unnaturally added by scribes who did not see the construction. I think it less likely that the poet wrote *lyrae* and the scribes took it for *lyra ē. iacent* is in the ed. Ven. 1558: the change is nothing and the improvement is something, so I adopt it. But '*tacent* muta' is defensible: see Petron. 126 ⟦18⟧ 'fabula muta taces', Ovid met. IV 433, VII 184, Tibull. IV 1 129 ⟦III 7 129⟧ 'muta silentia', Prop. IV 3 53 'omnia surda tacent'.

XV 201–2

Lesbides, infamem quae me fecistis amatae,
desinite ad citharas turba uenire meas.

This is not Latin, any more than Prop. I 19 13 'illic formosae ueniant chorus heroinae': *turba* cannot be thus employed without an epithet. Bentley knew this right well, and accordingly conjectured 'ad *citharae uerba* uenire *meae*'. But all that wants doing is to strike away one letter:

desinite ad citharas turba uenire *mea*.

For the arrangement of words in the verse compare, if it is worth while, x 46 'postquam desierant uela uidere tua'. The phrase *turba mea* or *tua* or *sua* is frequent: am. I 1 6 'Pieridum uates, non *tua turba* sumus', ars III 811 sq. '*mea turba*, puellae | inscribant spoliis, Naso magister erat', trist. I 5 34 'cetera Fortunae, non *mea turba* fuit', Prop. III 3 31 'Veneris dominae uolucres, *mea turba*, columbae', Aetna 580 'sacer in bellum numerus, *sua turba* regenti', Sil. XI 395 'uerum agite, o *mea turba*, precor', Stat. silu. I 1 95 sq. '*tua turba* relicto | labetur caelo', I 2 69 sq. 'duro nec enim ex adamante creati | sed *tua turba* sumus', Theb. X 297 '*sua* quemque cruento | limite *turba* subit'. In her. X 126 'cum steteris *turbae* celsus in ore *tuae*' the text is not quite certain. I have not quoted fast. III 251, where *mea turba* is only a blundering conjecture of Merkel's; but I will quote, for it is almost as apposite, the true reading of that passage, which was discovered long ago by Heinsius and which no modern editor but Mr G. A. Davies has had the wit to adopt, 'mater amat nuptas: *matris* me *turba* frequentat'.

39

OVID'S *HEROIDES* [V]*

XVI 35–40

40
    Te peto, quam pepigit lecto Venus aurea nostro:
        te prius optaui quam mihi nota fores.
    ante tuos animo uidi quam lumine uultus:
        prima fuit uultus nuntia fama tui.
    nec tamen est mirum si, sicut oporteat, arcu
40
        missilibus telis eminus ictus amo.

Verse 38 is so given by P and G and most MSS: V (saec. XII) has 'prima *mihi* uultus'. The sense is poor, and the repetition of 'uultus', first plural, then singular, is poorer. ‖ To all intents and purposes the verse has already been emended by Mr Palmer: 'prima *mihi uulnus* nuntia fama *tulit*': see the metaphor of the next distich. But in writing *mihi* Mr Palmer abandons better MSS for a worse, and in writing *tulit* he abandons all MSS: I would sooner follow them where they agree and desert them where they differ:

prima *tulit uulnus* nuntia fama tui.

'tui' depends on 'nuntia'. I suppose the archetype had

prima *tui* uultus nuntia fama tui,

and *fuit* and *mihi* are alternative corrections of this manifest error.

From 38 to 145 all good ancient MSS fail us and leave us to the mercies of the 15th century. Accordingly the very next verse is corrupt. *oporteat* is not even grammar; the *oportuit actum* or *oportet ab arcu* of Heinsius has no sufficient sense; Bentley rightly expels the couplet and proposes *Apollinis* for *oporteat*, but I think the original form of the interpolation can be recovered with less ado:

nec tamen est mirum si, *sic cum polleat arcus,*
    missilibus telis eminus ictus amo.

Helen's beauty is a bow which discharges the arrows of love: no marvel the arrows fly so far when the bow is so potent. *sic cum* is corrupted to *sic ut* in Livy XXXVIII 21 12 and I daresay elsewhere.

* [CR 11 (1897), 425–31]

XVI 83–4

Dulce Venus risit 'nec te, Pari, munera tangant
utraque suspensi plena timoris' ait.

It is possible that *nec* should be altered to *neu*; but Bentley alters it to *ne*, which
is quite wrong: the asyndeton 'risit, ait' is not to be endured. Loers explains
correctly that *nec* is *et non* and that the conjunction belongs to 'ait' and the
negative to 'tangant': Venus risit et ait 'non te munera tangant'. He gives two
Ovidian examples of this license, Madvig Lat. gramm. §458 obs. 2 adds a third,
and Haupt opusc. III p. 512 a fourth: it is a natural sequel to Ovid's favourite
practice of appending to the first word of a quotation a *que* which belongs to
the verb of speaking, as at met. III 644 obstipui 'capiat' que 'aliquis modera-
mina' dixi. I will here give all the instances which I have noted down, marking
the true construction by a grotesque employment of inverted commas.

her. XVI 83 sq.

dulce Venus risit 'ne' c 'te, Pari, munera tangant
utraque suspensi plena timoris' ait.

XXI 221 sq.

si me nunc uideas, uisam prius esse negabis
'arte ne' c 'est' dices 'ista petenda mea'.

met. V 414

agnouitque deam 'ne' c 'longius ibitis' inquit.

IX 131 sq.

excipit hunc Nessus, 'ne' que enim 'moriemur inulti'
secum ait.

i.e. etenim ait 'non moriemur inulti'.

X 568–70

instantem turbam uiolenta procorum
condicione fugat 'ne' c 'sum potiunda nisi' inquit
'uicta prius cursu'.

XI 134–7

Bacchus peccasse fatentem
restituit pactique fide data munera soluit
'ne' ue 'male optato maneas circumlitus auro,
uade' ait 'ad magnis uicinum Sardibus amnem'.

XI 263

tum demum ingemuit 'ne' que ait 'sine numine uincis'.

fast. IV 597 sq.

> Iuppiter hanc lenit factumque excusat amore
> 'ne' c 'gener est nobis ille pudendus' ait.

In her. XII 202 Ovid takes one step further, and not content with breaking up *neque* into ‖ *et* 'non' and *neue* into *et* 'ne' he breaks up *quam* into *et* '*hanc*':

> aureus ille aries uillo spectabilis alto
> dos mea, qu 'am' dicam si tibi 'redde' neges.

i.e. aries est dos mea, et, si dicam tibi 'hanc redde', neges.

XVI 121–3

> Et soror, effusis ut erat, Cassandra, capillis,
> cum uellent nostrae iam dare uela rates,
> 'quo ruis?' exclamat.

122 'illud *nostrae* friget hoc loco' says Heinsius. One of the very few MSS which contain these verses omits it. It seems pretty clear then that *uento* or *uentis* has been absorbed by *uellent*.

XVII 51–2

> Et genus et proauos et regia nomina iactas.
> clara satis domus haec nobilitate sua est.

'*et* genus' is in most MSS; a few have *quod* or *quid*; but what one expects is a particle indicating that Helen, having just demolished one of Paris' arguments, is now passing to another. Well, P has *ea*: that is *ed*, the remains of *sed*.

XVIII 65–6

> Tu, dea, mortalem caelo delapsa petebas:
> uera loqui liceat, quam sequor ipse, dea est.

The words are right; but here as so often elsewhere the sense is spoilt by the punctuation of editors with their inveterate habit of mistaking nominatives for vocatives. Write

> tu dea mortalem caelo delapsa petebas.

XVIII 119–22

> Si qua fides uero est, ueniens huc esse natator,
> 120   cum redeo, uideor naufragus esse mihi.
> hoc quoque si credis, ad te uia prona uidetur,
> a te cum redeo, cliuus inertis aquae.

'If you believe me when I tell the truth,' says Leander, 'I assure you that in coming hither I seem to myself to be a swimmer, in returning, to be a shipwrecked man.' That one who is swimming seems to himself to be a swimmer is so very credible a statement that the preface 'si qua fides uero est' looks a trifle superfluous. But Leander apparently seems to himself to be a swimmer only when he is swimming 'huc', whatever that may mean: when he is swimming in the other direction he seems to himself to be not a swimmer but – a shipwrecked man. Then are swimmers never shipwrecked? are the shipwrecked never swimmers? why, Hero herself at XIX 185 sq. remarks 'quod cupis, hoc nautae metuunt, Leandre, *natare*: | *exitus hic fractis puppibus esse solet*'! Of course they say that *natator* means one who swims for his own pleasure; but that is a pure fiction. And pray what is *huc*? to make sense it must mean 'to Sestos', yet how can it, when Leander is penning this letter at Abydos? And what diction is *cum redeo* 120, *a te cum redeo* 122! And what prosody is *credis ad*!

The author of this epistle simply wrote

> si qua fides uero est, ad te uia prona uidetur,
> a te cum redeo, cliuus inertis aquae.

An interpolator added

> hoc quoque si credis, ueniens huc esse natator,
> cum redeo, uideor naufragus esse mihi;

and the two couplets have exchanged their first hemistichs.

XVIII 187–94

> Aestus adhuc tamen est. quid, cum mihi laeserit aequor
>   Plias et Arctophylax Oleniumque pecus?
> aut ego non noui quam sim temerarius, aut me
>   in freta non cautus tum quoque mittet amor.   190
> neue putes id me, quod abest, promittere tempus,
>   pignora polliciti non tibi tarda dabo. ||
> sit tumidum paucis etiam nunc noctibus aequor,
>   ire per inuitas experiemur aquas.

191 'promittere id tempus' signifies nothing. Punctuate

> neue putes id me, quod abest, promittere, tempus,

that is 'ne putes me eam rem promittere, quia tempus abest'.

Out of the immense number of Ovid's hyperbata I have selected ten of the most astounding in Journ. Phil. vol. XVIII p. 7 [this edition p. 140]; but here I will confine myself to the heroides. Let me premise that there are always two methods, and never more than two, of punctuating an hyperbaton correctly. The second way in which this couplet may be correctly punctuated is to omit all the commas, 'neue putes id me quod abest promittere tempus | pignora' cet. Any third method will be incorrect; and therefore some third method is usually adopted.

Hyperbata recognised by the editors or at any rate correctly represented by their punctuation will be found at XVI 122 [[124]], 132 [[134]], XX 63 sq. (here Mr Ehwald is wrong, but it may be merely a misprint), and XXI 121.

Examples where most editors are wrong but some critics have recognised and expressed the true construction are the following.

III 19   si progressa forem, caperer ne nocte, timebam.

Thus Merkel Riese Sedlmayer and Palmer; so absurdly that Heinsius preferred to write *forte* for *nocte*. But Madvig, followed by Mr Ehwald, has restored the correct punctuation:

si progressa forem, caperer ne, nocte, timebam:

that is 'timebam ne, si nocte progressa forem, caperer'.

VII 143 sq.   Pergama uix tanto tibi erant repetenda labore,
                     Hectore si uiuo, quanta fuere, forent.

So Riese and Sedlmayer, without sense.

Hectore si uiuo quanta fuere, forent.

So Merkel and Palmer, without construction. The meaning is 'si tanta forent, quanta Hectore uiuo fuere': therefore the punctuation must be either that of Heinsius and Ehwald

Hectore si uiuo quanta fuere forent,

or else

Hectore, si, uiuo quanta fuere, forent.

X 110   illic qui silices, Thesea, uincat, habes.

So the five modern editors. But the construction, as everyone must know, is 'illic habes Thesea, qui silices uincat'; so you must either write 'illic, qui' with Burmann or leave out all the commas with Heinsius.

Now I come to examples like XVIII 191 where hyperbaton is hitherto unrecognised or at any rate unexpressed.

III 55 sq.   scilicet ut, quamuis ueniam dotata, repellas
                    et mecum fugias, quae tibi dantur, opes.

So Heinsius Riese Sedlmayer and Ehwald, with a wrong sense.

> et mecum fugias quae tibi dantur, opes.

So Merkel and Palmer, even worse. The construction is 'et opes, quae mecum dantur, fugias': therefore the punctuation must be either

> et, mecum, fugias, quae tibi dantur, opes,

or else

> et mecum fugias quae tibi dantur opes.

    XV 103 sq.　　nil de te mecum est, nisi tantum iniuria; nec tu,
> admoneat quod te, munus amantis habes.

The reading *tu . . . te* for *te . . . tu* is the excellent and generally accepted correction of Burmann; and it is clear from his note that he quite understood the construction of the sentence: 'nec tu munus habes, quod te amantis admoneat'. But how to express this by punctuation he did not know; and he and all the editors print the passage thus, as if 'amantis' belonged to 'munus'. It should either be

> nec tu,
> admoneat quod te, munus, amantis, habes, ‖

or else all the commas between 'nec' and 'habes' should disappear.

    XX 93 sq.　　hoc quoque, cum ius sit, sit scriptum iniuria nostrum:
> quod de me solo nempe queraris, habes.

So the editors. But of course 'nempe' belongs to the principal verb, not to the relative clause: write

> quod de me solo, nempe, queraris, habes,

or else omit the comma after 'queraris'.

    Here I should like to add that the punctuation of ars II 676 ascribed to me in the new Corpus Poetarum is the property of Heinsius and is not strictly correct. It should be

> adde quod est illis operum prudentia maior,
> solus, et, artifices qui facit, usus adest;

for the construction is 'et usus adest, qui solus artifices facit'.

XIX 175–80

> Vt semel intrauit Colchos Pagasaeus Iason,　　　　　175
>   impositam celeri Phasida puppe tulit.
> ut semel Idaeus Lacedaemona uenit adulter,
>   cum praeda rediit protinus ille sua.
> tu, quam saepe petis quod amas, tam saepe relinquis,
>   et, quotiens graue fit puppibus ire, natas.　　　　180

'You swim, whenever it becomes troublesome to sail.' What in the world is supposed to be the meaning of this? Does Leander sail in fair weather and swim only in foul? Quite the reverse: he swims in fair weather and only in foul does he begin to think about sailing, XVIII 11. But suppose it were so: what have such words to do with the context?

Nemo omnibus horis sapit, not even Nicolaus Heinsius: it was he who adopted the *fit* of P and G and A: his father read *sit* with V, and so did Bentley. But our modern editors, who take little notice of Heinsius when he is scattering pearls and diamonds, are quite willing to make amends by following him where he is wrong, and they all print this *fit*: it is in P, P is the best MS, scientific criticism consists in adhering to the best MS: if it gives sense, be thankful; if none, never mind.

The meaning of the true text,

> et, quotiens graue *sit* puppibus ire, natas,

is this: 'tot facis natationes, quot uelificationes facere graue sit': 'quotiens' belongs not to 'sit' but to 'puppibus ire'. Leander swims to and fro with such frequency that even to *sail* with the same frequency would be a toil and a trouble. He is therefore much unlike to Paris and Iason.

XX 13–16

> Nunc quoque idem timeo, sed idem tamen acrius illud:
>   adsumpsit uires auctaque flamma mora est.
> quique fuit numquam paruus nunc tempore longo
>   et spe, quam dederas tu mihi, creuit amor.

idem timeo stultifies the whole passage: the required sense is unmistakable, *idem cupio*; and *cupio* Bentley conjectures. But write

> nunc quoque ⟨auemus⟩ idem, sed idem tamen acrius illud.

a is merely *q* without a tail: hence the two letters are pretty often confounded, and you find for instance *eadem* interchanged with *equidem* (*eqdem*). Therefore *auem'* is easily mistaken for *quem* and easily lost after *-que*.

XX 175–80

175 Hoc faciente subis tam saeua pericula uitae;
        atque utinam pro te, qui mouet illa, cadat.
    quem si reppuleris nec, quem dea damnat, amaris,
        et tu continuo, certe ego saluus ero.
    siste metum, uirgo: stabili potiere salute,
180   fac modo polliciti conscia templa colas.

On the chaos of 177–9 the first ray of light has been thrown by Mr Ehwald, who has recognised that the apodosis to 'si reppuleris nec amaris' is in 179 and that

178 is ‖ parenthetical. I will neglect for a moment the contents of 178 and will give the gist of the passage to clear the way for their discussion: 'it is the suit of my rival which endangers your life: heaven send that he may perish instead. If you will reject him, and refuse to favour one on whom Diana frowns, then – fear no more, maiden – then will sound health be yours, do you but revere the temple which heard your vow.'

Now *certe*, to begin with, is unmetrical. The elision of a long syllable in the latter half of a pentameter occurs nowhere else in either Ovid or his imitators; and even the 'non ut ames oro, *uerum ut* amare sinas' of xv 96 is easily amended by Heinsius to *me sed*, which fell out after *mesoro*. Secondly, *certe* perverts the sense: 'and you will be well forthwith, *at any rate* I shall' (even if you are not). If Cydippe is not well, neither can Acontius be, for 'iuncta salus nostra est', says he at 233 sq., 'miserere meique tuique: | quid dubitas unam ferre duobus opem?' Thirdly, the MSS vary: P does not contain these verses, G omits *tu* and adds it at the end of the line, cod. Bernensis 478 (saec. XIII) has *tunc* (*tc̄*) instead of it. I would write

(continuo per te ⟨tunc⟩ ego saluus ero)

'straightway, thanks to you, my welfare will be secured': see 233 sq. already cited and also 186 'teque simul serua meque datamque fidem'. *tc̄* fell out after *te* and was inserted before *continuo* with *et* to eke out the verse. *per te* is corrupted to *certe* at Prop. II 18 29 and Sen. Herc. Oet. 1799. The parenthesis, anticipating as it does the contents of the next line, is not at all to be admired; but it is no worse than III 30 'uenerunt ad te Telamone et Amyntore nati | ...Laertaque satus, per quos comitata redirem | (auxerunt blandas grandia dona preces) | uiginti fuluos operoso ex aere lebetas' cet.

XX 197–8
Non agitur de me: cura maiore laboro:
anxia sunt uitae pectora nostra tuae.

Neither P nor G contains these lines, and the oldest MS which does contain them, A (saec. XI–XII), has *uita...tua*; and the ablative is received into the text by Messrs Riese and Sedlmayer, though I do not know what they suppose it to mean. I conjecture

anxia sunt causa pectora nostra tua.

For this confusion compare Cic. pro Clu. 59 164 'habetis, iudices, quae in totam *causam* de moribus A. Cluentii...accusatores collegerunt', where one family of MSS has *uitam*, and Ovid her. VI 54 'milite tam forti *causa* tuenda fuit', which is Merkel's correction for *uita*.

XXI 55–8

Dic mihi nunc, solitoque tibi ne decipe more:
quid facies odio, sic ubi amore noces?
si laedis quod amas, hostem sapienter amabis.
me precor, ut serues, perdere uelle uelis.

58 'locus manifeste corruptus' says Heinsius; and I have never seen any real defence of *uelle uelis*. Burmann absurdly quotes am. III 11 50 'me quoque uelle uelis' where the subject of 'uelle' is 'me'. A much more learned and able attempt is Markland's in his *Remarks on the Epistles of Brutus*, pp. 85–9: he quotes from Cicero and Livy six examples of *nolite uelle*, and Ruhnken adds one of *noli uelle* from Nepos. But these are all imperatives: now the verb 'nolo' in the imperative loses its proper force and merely prohibits. Markland himself thinks that *nolite uelle* will not justify *nolite nolle*: neither, I think, will it justify *nolis uelle*, still less *uelis uelle*. The nearest parallels I know of are met. X 132 '*uelle* mori *statuit*' and Catull. 93 1 'nil nimium *studeo*, Caesar, tibi *uelle* placere'; and these are inadequate. I believe therefore that Heinsius is right in requiring a vocative instead of *uelle*. He proposes *dure*;[1] but Acontius does not mean to injure Cydippe, he injures her without meaning it; so it is not only easier but apter to write

me precor, ut serues, perdere, *laeue*, uelis.

laeuus is a blunderer, a man who when he shoots at a pigeon invariably kills a crow: the best way for him to make Cydippe well will be to wish her ill. Probably in the sequence *leueuelis* one *eu* was omitted, then added overhead, then inserted wrongly, *ueleuelis*. ||

XXI 205–6

Si mihi lingua foret, tu nostra iustius ira,
qui mihi tendebas retia, dignus eras.

Cydippe has been telling Acontius how coldly and rudely she treats his rival: then come these lines, 'locus corruptus', as Heinsius says: 'si mihi lingua foret' is a truly amazing irrelevancy; and besides, she has a tongue. Gronovius proposed 'si *me digna forem*', and van Lennep 'si *mens aequa* foret': the latter is just the sense required but the words are these:

mens nisi iniqua foret, tu nostra cet.

m̄snisi is much like *mihisi*, and *iniqua* is almost the same as *lingua*.

---

[1] Mr Marindin suggests *dire*, which gives a fitting sense. Either word would readily fall out after -*dere*, but I do not know if *uelle* would readily occur to the scribe for a stopgap.

XXI 237–8

Vnde tibi fauor hic? nisi quod noua forte reperta est
quae capiat magnos littera lecta deos.

Cydippe is not saying that such a 'littera' has really been invented: she mentions the notion as barely conceivable; so 'quod reperta est' is wrong. Two of our scanty authorities give *nisi forte noua reperta est*. Write

nisi ⟨si⟩ noua forte reperta est cet.

Compare IV 111 '*nisi si* manifesta negamus' Heinsius, *nisi* P, *nisi nos* the other MSS; Mart. II 8 7 '*quasi si* manifesta negemus' Heinsius, *quae si* some MSS, *quasi nos* others.

VI 139–40

Lemniadum facinus culpo, non miror, Iason.
quamlibet iratis ipse dat arma dolor.

iratis is not in P, which has nothing between *quamlibet* and *ipse*: it is added by the second hand and occurs also in a few other MSS. G and most MSS have *quamlibet* (or *quaelibet* or *quodlibet*) *ad facinus*, which is unmetrical and evidently interpolated from the hexameter. *iratis* gives almost the reverse of the sense required, but for that very reason is probably a relic of the truth and no interpolation. Bentley and J. F. Heusinger proposed *infirmis*, comparing am. I 7 66 '*quamlibet infirmas* adiuuat ira manus'; and this is accepted by Sedlmayer Ehwald and Palmer. Then, when *ipse* has been altered with Madvig to *iste* or *ille*, the sense is altogether satisfactory.

But there is another word which has as good a sense, as good a parallel, and more likeness to *iratis*:

quamlibet *ignauis* iste dat arma dolor.

See Cato monostich. 23 (P.L.M. Baehr. III p. 237) quoted by Heinsius: '*quamlibet ignauum* facit indignatio fortem.'